THE
Good Skiing
Guide 1997

THE
Good Skiing
Guide 1997

The 500 best ski and snowboard resorts
around the world

Edited by Peter Hardy

and Felice Eyston

in association with the
Ski Club of Great Britain

CONSUMERS' ASSOCIATION

Which? Books are commissioned by
Consumers' Association and published by
Which? Ltd, 2 Marylebone Road, London NW1 4DF

Distributed by The Penguin Group:
Penguin Books Ltd, 27 Wrights Lane, London W8 5TZ

First edition of *The Good Skiing Guide*: 1985
This edition August 1996

The Guide has been prepared with the help of the Ski Club of
Great Britain, which is gratefully acknowledged. But the views expressed
herein are those of the Editors, and not necessarily those of the Club.

Editors	Peter Hardy and Felice Eyston
Sub-editor	Caroline Ellerby
Researcher	Zoë Punshon
Contributors	Minty Clinch, Graham Duffill, Nicky Holford, Elisabeth Hussey, Lloyd Rogers, Doug Sager, Patrick Thorne, Arnie Wilson; and the late Lucy Dicker
Design	Editorial Design Partnership
Cover design	Paul Saunders
Cover photo	John Pakington for Skishoot
Maps	Holmes Linnette

British Library Cataloguing-in-Publication Data:
A catalogue record for this book is available from the British Library

ISBN 0 85202 616 1

For a full list of Which? books, please write to
Which? Books, Castlemead, Gascoyne Way, Hertford X, SG14 1LH

Typeset by	Editorial Design Partnership, London
Printed & bound in Great Britain by	Butler & Tanner, Frome

Contents

Which ski resort?

Reference

E-mail address
You can now send your resort reports by e-mail to:
guidereports@which.co.uk

Introduction

The ski season in Europe last year began with what tour operators fear most of all — the poorest early snow cover for a decade across most of the Alps — and ended in similar straits. On the other side of the Atlantic, after a slow start, bumper snowfalls broke all records in Colorado and Utah, and California was not far behind. However, overall it was a drearily average season, which in its final weeks left everyone in Europe, from lift companies to tour operators, hoteliers and shopkeepers, counting the days until the annual lift closure.

It is both surprising and pleasing, therefore, to be able to report that the ski industry — in Britain at least — is in better shape than at any stage since the start of recession in the late 1980s. The number of people who take an annual winter-sports holiday is no longer falling. Indeed, there are strong indications to suggest that it has actually risen for the first time since the 1980s. The reasons for this can be attributed not so much to any concealed upswing in the economy as to a change in the pattern of winter holidays that has rejuvenated interest in skiing, coupled with the firm establishment of snowboarding as a refreshing and integral component.

Fresh horizons

The majority of British skiers are remarkably conservative, confining themselves to less than a dozen resorts, with many of them returning to the same destination year after year. High prices, thanks to the weakness of sterling, together with an understandable feeling that they are no longer always getting value for the considerable amount of money involved, have forced many of those skiers to expand their horizons beyond their habitual week in Austria, Switzerland or France. What some of them discovered last season were the fresh slopes of Italy and Canada, the twin success stories of the year. Favourable exchange rates, relatively low domestic prices and excellent snow conditions combined to make them the most prized of all ski holiday destinations. How long they continue to remain so is open to question.

The Italian dream

Italy offers delightful skiing in a relaxed and friendly atmosphere. For the past two seasons it has been blessed by bountiful snow. Last winter, from Christmas onwards, you needed either considerable luck or influential friends to find a package holiday to any of the main resorts. In the spring, British tour operators were falling over themselves to secure beds in Italy for the 1996–7 season. Package holiday prices for 1996–7 have increased by 3 to 5 per cent, but even so remain highly attractive. However, a fortissimo note of caution should be sounded regarding how long the Italian jamboree can last. It was economic uncertainty that led to the collapse of Italy's international ski industry in the 1970s, and similar circumstances exist today. At the time of writing, Italy's new left-wing coalition has expressed its clear intent of returning the lira to the Exchange Rate Mechanism. The implementation of this may not be so easily achieved. However, if the lira is returned, Italy could lose overnight a substantial part of its attraction as an inexpensive ski destination. On the same note, two successive seasons of excellent snow cover should not be seen as the norm: a series of disastrous winters in the 1980s forced the larger Italian resorts to invest in extensive snowmaking equipment, but man-made pistes are no substitute for the real thing.

However, Italy has earned its position on the podium. Industry research carried out for Crystal Holidays suggests it is now in third position with a UK market share of 18.2 per cent, behind France (27.9 per cent) and Austria (21.6 per cent). Whether or not these figures are accurate, they do produce a sensible indication of the increase in Italy's popularity. In the 1980s Italy's share had dropped to about 6 per cent.

Canadian concern

Canada has emerged as the other most-talked-about destination, again fuelled by prices so low that even with flight included holidays can favourably compare (at the top end of the range) with the Alps. The number of British visitors has doubled, but the Canadian government, naturally excited by the speed of the development of its winter-sports market, quotes ludicrously optimistic statistics. In reality, Canada probably does not attract more than three per cent of British skiers. At present it still has only two resorts, Whistler and Banff/Lake Louise, which can truly be classed as international (although others are being developed). Both offer superb skiing and value for money, but their major disadvantage is the climate: Whistler's coastal position and low base-altitude means that much of the substantial precipitation that it receives each winter falls as rain in the village. Both resorts lack the number of sunshine days to be found in the more clement US resorts, and the temperatures at altitude tend to lie uncomfortably low by European standards for most of the season.

There are also disconcerting signs that a combination of greed and a slow strengthening of the dollar threatens the Canadian success story. Tour operators contracting accommodation for this season found themselves faced with dramatic price jumps from hoteliers (particularly in Whistler) of up to 30 per cent. As one major operator put it: 'I wouldn't say they are actually strangling the golden goose, but some hoteliers are standing on its feet — with ski boots on.'

Against this background, it seems curious that companies as experienced as Airtours and First Choice hope to fill twice-weekly charter flights into Calgary from London via Manchester this winter. Clearly, Canada still has to prove itself as a serious ski destination, which attracts repeat business. It is to be hoped that it will do just that.

The United States, no longer as inexpensive as it was for British visitors, still offers value for money and continues to attract the greater share of business to North America (combined with Canada, about 8 per cent of the market). The number of catered chalets has risen sharply and this holiday format is unquestionably the most economical way of exploring so far afield.

European blues

If all is well on the far side of the Atlantic the same cannot be said nearer to home. Low temperatures in the Alps before Christmas allowed resorts to farm artificial snow and just enough came out of the sky to avert disaster over the main holiday period. However, promised falls in early January amounted to little or nothing, and by the middle of the month whole regions of Switzerland and France were foundering. The first World Cup downhill of the season on the OK course in Val d'Isère was reduced to a Super G for safety reasons, and the Lauberhorn in Wengen was cancelled. A moderate storm saved the Tyrol and Salzburgerland, but it was not until mid-February that the season swung into top gear with substantial falls everywhere.

At times there appeared to be more snow in Britain than anywhere else, although in January good skiing could be found elsewhere in Europe (if you knew where to go) and throughout North America. Unusually, nearly all the early-season snow came from the Mediterranean, providing favourable conditions in the southern French Alps and Italy, while Andorra and both the French and Spanish Pyrenees experienced their best season ever.

An expensive pastime

The bare, inescapable fact is that skiing in the main Alpine countries is now such an expensive holiday that there is a real danger of travel firms and resorts pricing themselves out of the bidding as North America provides a better-value as well as what the mass of readers of this guide describe as a more enjoyable holiday overall.

It is a continuing misconception that Austria and Switzerland are much more expensive destinations than France — they are all expensive. Price differences in recent years between the main Alpine countries have been greatly eroded. Last season we found on-the-ground prices to be marginally lower in Austria, while Switzerland has not suffered from inflated domestic prices in the same way as France. Indeed, it would be foolish to write off Austria: for British skiers, it is still the second most popular destination and if its resorts continue to peg prices to the extent they have over the past two seasons, then Austria will surely regain some of the ground it has lost.

Survival of the fittest

In general the ski boom is long gone and there may never be another. For those destinations throughout the Alps that reaped glorious harvests in the past, often with contemptuous disregard for customer satisfaction, the law of the jungle now applies in earnest: only the fittest will survive long into the twenty-first century. In Austria alone we came across two

resorts where a total of six large hotels had closed their doors in the past
year; one had actually gone into liquidation in February at the height of
the season. Resorts which have for years relied on a majority of German
visitors have suddenly found themselves with an unacceptable number of
empty beds, while Germany (like other European countries) faces its
own economic problems.

In Switzerland, even major ski destinations struggled to attain 85 per
cent hotel capacity in high season, and in January and March figures
there, and some in Austria had sunk as low as an uneconomical 25 per
cent. Of course, the fittest resorts are usually the best-known internationally and the ones that attract the majority of British skiers. Any such
list must include Val d'Isère, the Trois Vallées, St Anton, Kitzbühel,
Obergurgl, Zermatt, Verbier, Breckenridge and Vail.

Getting it right

A number of other villages merit special attention. Lech's continuing policy of limiting the number of skiers on the mountain to 14,000 deserves
particular praise and it is disappointing that other overcrowded resorts
of comparable size have not seen fit to follow its example. We skied there
on the busiest weekend of the year and never waited for more than five
minutes for a lift. One satisfactory consequence for the village has been
a significant increase in the number of skiers who return again and
again, secure in the knowledge that whatever week they choose, overcrowding will not be a problem.

Zell am See, previously criticised in the Guide for traffic problems
and overcrowding, has been transformed this season with the opening of
a 10-km tunnel designed to take heavy through-traffic beneath the town.
For years the resort has been blighted by one of the busiest trunk roads
in Austria passing through its centre. Similarly, mountain access has
been greatly improved.

Mayrhofen, the home of lift queues, is looking for a more positive
label after the opening of a new jumbo gondola to replace the old
Penkenbahn. It has increased uphill capacity from a frustrating 600 to a
possible 2,000 skiers per hour. In May, work finally started in Kitzbühel
on the replacement gondola for the antique Hahnenkamm cable car,
which should have been consigned to a museum at least a decade ago
and has actually acted as a deterrent to tourism. The new £13-million,
six-person gondola should be open well before Christmas 1996, if work
goes according to plan.

Best small resort of the year

Gressoney, in the Italian Val d'Aosta, and Vaujany in the French
Dauphiné share our nomination for the Best Small Resort of the Year.
Gressoney, largely unknown to British skiers until tour operator Crystal
contracted beds there in 1994–5, has the Italian price advantage combined with an attractive small village, and a surprisingly large amount of
intermediate skiing in exceptionally scenic surroundings. Nearby Alagna
also provides good off-piste skiing. Vaujany, a charming satellite of Alpe

d'Huez, shares the larger resort's 82 lifts and 220km of linked skiing, but none of its shortcomings. It is an unspoilt farming community of traditional wood-and-stone dwellings tucked away in an adjoining valley. Thanks to compensation for France's largest hydro-electric scheme further down the valley, Vaujany was able to link itself to the main ski area with what is still one of the largest cable cars in the world. The village also offers what we consider to be some of the best childcare facilities in the Alps.

Changing market

No one could have foreseen that it would take a strong schilling to cure what was once termed 'the Scandinavian problem'. An unwelcome atmosphere was created by the drunken behaviour of young Swedish skiers who regularly converged on the Alps with the central aim of seeing how much alcohol they could consume (at prices a fifth of those at home). Hoteliers complained and St Anton even introduced shorter bar opening-hours in an unsuccessful attempt to curb these excesses. Now those same hoteliers would go down on bended knee for the return of Swedish youths, fondly remembering the money they spent on steaks and Schnapps.

The Dutch have largely supplanted the British in their traditional Austrian and Swiss skiing grounds, while those British who can still afford it concentrate on the half-dozen best known resorts in the French Alps. Rationalisation in a troubled market means that the overall total of resorts offered by British tour operators has been dramatically reduced over the past five years, effectively limiting the choice for skiers unless they are enterprising enough to make their own arrangements. Undeterred, we have continued to expand the number of resorts covered in *The Good Skiing Guide* and hope that, in particular, this will help those prepared to tailor-make holidays to the myriad ski destinations which offer excellent skiing, but are no longer served by a long list of travel companies. This year we have included for the first time a chapter on skiing in Australasia, South America and Japan.

Snowboarding

Only a sporting Luddite can continue to maintain that snowboarding is a passing fad that has already peaked. Not only is snowboarding here to stay, but it has also established itself as an essential and exciting component of the winter sports industry and one on which its future in part depends. Even Park City, Utah, which had tried to hold back the flood waters by steadfastly refusing to accept snowboarders on its slopes, has finally relented this season. The day when the number of snowboarders equals or even exceeds the number of skiers on the mountain may be a long way off, but it would be foolish to ignore the possibility. For the present, the cult of snowboarding is almost entirely youth-orientated, and resorts maintain that while an increasing number of lift passes are sold to riders, the overall 'spend' of an average snowboarder on accommodation, restaurants, shopping and après-ski is insignificant in comparison with that of a skier. That may be so, but it is more than ten years since the sport was introduced in Europe and there is now a growing percentage of older snowboarders with established careers who are consequently more affluent.

Safety helmets

In the past we have campaigned in the Guide for safety helmets for children. Last season saw adults in the United States wearing helmets for the first time for recreational skiing and we hope this is the start of a trend that will spread across the Atlantic. Ten years ago the average cyclist would have scoffed at the idea of wearing a helmet on the busy roads of London, yet now he or she would not set off without one. It is to be hoped that skiing will follow a similar pattern. It seems nothing short of crazy that anyone should pursue a sport where speeds can easily exceed 30mph without some form of protection for the head.

Policing the mountain

It is a sad indictment of the times in which we live, but the presence of police patrols on the piste to combat uncontrolled speeders, drunks and theft is slowly becoming the norm. Aspen led the way a couple of years ago and others have followed. Courmayeur is the latest resort to recruit six uniformed policemen, two of whom are on duty at any one time. They ski all day at leisure, stopping for the occasional refreshment at the mountain restaurant of their choice — nice work if you can get it. Their arrest record is almost non-existent, but, nevertheless, the number of reported ski thefts in Courmayeur fell in the first season from 37 to just one.

Green slopes

We applaud the strong conservation policy of a growing number of resorts in both the Alps and North America. It is vital that the mountain environment is protected for future generations to enjoy. However, a bin marked 'lift passes for recycling' on Lauterbrunnen railway station was maybe carrying the green dream a run too far.

Your help

Each year our dedicated team of researchers visit as many resorts as possible. Ski areas are constantly evolving and the standards of service provided, both on and off the mountain, rarely remain static anywhere for long. However, in the course of a season it is not possible for us to inspect every resort. Therefore, to keep abreast of changes we rely heavily upon your assistance in sending us reports on your holiday destinations. Do please continue to tell us of your skiing experiences — the good and the bad. These contributions are invaluable. Readers who supply the most comprehensive reports will receive free copies of the next edition of the Guide. The e-mail address established last year has proved popular with reporters. Further information on this and details of how you can help can be found on page 587.

Choosing your resort

When to go skiing is almost as important a factor to consider as where to go, but both are just part of the equation that makes a successful skiing holiday. Companions, accommodation and travel arrangements are also crucial factors. You do, of course, also need snow and sunshine; too little of each results in disappointment. The level of occupancy of the resort is also a major consideration: too many skiers means overcrowded lifts and pistes.

Most European ski resorts open in mid-December but will not necessarily run their entire lift system until the weekend before Christmas. American ski resorts traditionally open for Thanksgiving, which falls on the third Thursday of November.

At the start of the season, it is essential to choose a resort with a high top-station where at least some skiing is guaranteed. 'Safe' resorts in Europe include Val d'Isère/Tignes, Val Thorens, Les Deux Alpes, Saas-Fee, Zermatt and Obergurgl.

Prices and crowds peak over Christmas and New Year, with the second week the busier of the two, and the one to be avoided if you mind queuing. Again, it is important to go for altitude. Pretty Christmas-card resorts such as Alpbach, Kitzbühel, Megève, Mürren and Grindelwald do not look quite so festive in a surrounding of green fields. North American resorts are equally crowded, but much more snow-sure.

The low season begins in the second week of January. This is often the best time to visit the big-name resorts like Verbier, Chamonix, Zermatt and Kitzbühel. The North American and European slopes should be at their best in February. Unfortunately, peak conditions are invariably coupled with peak crowds and coincide with school holidays. March and April bring longer, sunnier days and provide some of the best skiing of the winter. It is sensible to bear in mind that by the end of March, during an average winter the best snow will be above 1800m.

April can offer the best skiing of all. Last season was the first in ten years without major falls in the Alps, although cover was adequate and there was plenty of warm sunshine. As the cover transforms into spring snow, the off-piste opportunities can be exceptional.

The French school holidays are now staggered by geographical zones to avoid the gross overcrowding which used to be a feature of the main French resorts. Nevertheless, it is worth choosing alternative dates, if you can, to the Paris, Lyon and Grenoble holidays. Visitors to the French Pyrenees and Andorra should note the holiday dates for Toulouse.

French school holiday dates to avoid in 1996–7 are: 21 Dec–6 Jan (all regions), 19 Feb–5 March (Grenoble, Lyon, Toulouse), 5–19 Feb (Paris), 12–28 April (Grenoble, Lyon, Toulouse), 5–21 April (Paris).

After deciding when to go, you then have to decide where you want to take your holiday. This depends on your individual preference and requirements. The choice is influenced by your budget and your skiing ability.

Complete beginners face the hardest task of all, not helped by the inundation of advice from well-meaning friends. A course of lessons on a dry ski-slope will save some of the time wasted getting to grips with the basics during the first few days of the holiday; do not be put off by how difficult it all seems – a real slope is much easier than an artificial one.

Modern equipment and teaching methods mean the novice outgrows the nursery slopes within a couple of days. You therefore need to choose a resort with plenty of easy runs for the next stage of progress; large resorts with extensive ski areas, and consequently expensive lift passes, are generally not suitable. It is also advisable to take a budget holiday instead of spending a fortune, in case you do not like it.

Intermediates, who make up the vast majority of skiers, can find plenty of runs suited to their ability in most resorts. Advanced skiers will need to choose a resort with a large and varied ski area, which has plenty of black (difficult) slopes and off-piste opportunities. In this Guide we have endeavoured to indicate the resorts, ski areas and runs of major interest to each standard.

The final choice of resort should be dependent on the type of holiday you want, and the importance of the ski area versus the village and off-slope activities. We feel that most intermediates (and therefore most skiers) choose the country first and the resort second.

Where you stay within a chosen resort is largely dictated by how much you wish to spend. In Austria, Italy and Switzerland most accommodation is in hotels. France leads the field in self-catering apartments, but the American condominium is an altogether more luxurious affair. The chalet is a uniquely British and increasingly popular concept, of Swiss origin, but now found in most alpine resorts and in North America. You can take over the entire chalet as a group, or join a chalet party as an individual or a couple. The standard is now generally high, with more and more operators offering a 'luxury' service with 'gourmet' cuisine.

The all-inclusive staffed chalet formula is ideal for families, particularly those with young children. A growing number of operators employ their own qualified nannies to look after pre-ski age children and babies, and will often collect older children from ski school while their parents are still on the slopes. The standard and type of nanny service varies.

Evening entertainment traditionally centres around bars of varying degrees of rowdiness or sophistication. As a rule of thumb, Austria has the liveliest nightlife and the warmest atmosphere, Italy follows, with Switzerland just behind, while France takes the rear. Late-night revellers should seek out the major resorts like St Anton, Kitzbühel, Verbier, Zermatt and Cortina d'Ampezzo. Après-ski in North America is low profile in comparison.

Whichever way you look at it, skiing is an expensive holiday — and is becoming more so. Eastern Europe and Andorra are by far the cheapest destinations. Of the main alpine countries, Italy currently provides the best value because of relative currency rates. North America, and particularly Canada, is becoming increasingly competitive.

Using the Guide

The tables on the following pages record our verdicts on the advantages and disadvantages of the European and North American resorts covered in detail in the Guide. Resorts are listed in alphabetical order by country to aid comparisons: research shows that most readers choose the country first, followed by a resort. Having made an initial selection from the tables, we advise you to compare the appropriate sections in the chapters of your choice. For most aspects of a resort we use a simple measure of good or bad (a tick or a cross); where it is satisfactory we have left a blank.

Most headings are self-explanatory, but a few need further clarification. **Snow probability** is based on the likelihood of skiing being possible in or around the resort, especially at the beginning of the season. Some resorts receive a tick not because of a high altitude, but because of their own micro-climate. **Tree-level** skiing denotes those resorts that offer sheltered skiing on bad-weather days, with the subsequent improvement in visibility.

Ugly mountain scenery does not exist, so we have only used the affirmative tick for particularly **beautiful scenery**, such as in the Dolomites. **Resort charm** applies to villages that either have beautiful architecture, like Kitzbühel, or are rich in atmosphere like Alpbach or Jackson Hole. Aesthetically unpleasing resorts and busy towns with particularly heavy traffic receive a cross.

Big vertical drop applies to resorts that have a difference of at least 1500m in Europe and 1000m in North America from the top to the bottom of the ski area. In assessing how good or bad a resort is for **tough runs**, we have concentrated on whether a resort as a whole is likely to appeal to skiers who relish a challenge. **Après-ski** receives a tick not only for a lively nightlife, but also for a large choice of restaurants, as in Aspen. **Family skiing** refers to a family with a mixture of ages. **Children's facilities** refers to whether or not a resort has ski and non-ski kindergarten as well as babysitting facilities. Resorts rated highly for easy **resort access** are those that present no local difficulties for drivers or are close to an airport.

The key on the right shows the types of lifts and grading of runs on the colour piste-maps.

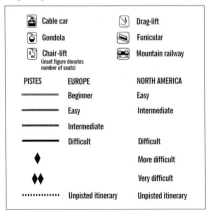

Cable car		Drag-lift	
Gondola		Funicular	
Chair-lift (inset figure denotes number of seats)		Mountain railway	

PISTES	EUROPE	NORTH AMERICA
	Beginner	Easy
	Easy	Intermediate
	Intermediate	
	Difficult	Difficult
◆		More difficult
◆◆		Very difficult
⋯⋯	Unpisted itinerary	Unpisted itinerary

	Large ski area	Tough runs	Intermediate skiing	Easy runs	Nursery slopes	Off-piste/ski touring	Summer skiing	Cross-country	Snowboarding	Lift queues
AUSTRIA										
Alpbach	✗	✗	✓						✗	✓
Badgastein	✓	✓	✓					✓		
Innsbruck			✓	✓			✓	✓	✓	✗
Ischgl	✓	✗	✓	✓		✓			✓	
Kitzbühel	✓	✗	✓	✓				✓		
Lech/Zürs	✓		✓	✓		✓			✓	✓
Mayrhofen		✗	✓	✓	✓	✓				
Niederau	✗	✗		✓	✓					
Obergurgl	✗	✗		✓	✓	✓	✓			
Obertauern			✓	✓	✓	✓		✓		
Saalbach-Hinterglemm	✓		✓	✓	✓				✓	✗
Schladming	✓	✗	✓	✓	✓		✓	✓	✓	
Sölden			✓	✓			✓			
Söll and the Ski-Welt	✓		✓	✓					✓	
St Anton	✓	✓		✗		✓				
Zell am See/Kaprun		✗		✓		✗	✓	✓	✓	✗

	Long runs	Tree-level skiing	Big vertical drop	Skiing convenience	Snow probability	Non-skiing	Mountain restaurants	Beautiful scenery	Resort charm	Compact village	Traffic	Resort access	Late holidays	Low prices	Après-ski	Family skiing	Children's facilities
				✗					✔		✔	✔	✗		✗	✔	
		✔		✗						✗	✗	✔			✔		✗
				✔	✔				✔			✔			✔		
				✔	✗	✗	✔		✔					✗	✔		
				✗	✗	✔			✔		✗	✔	✗		✔	✔	
	✔			✔	✔		✔		✔			✗		✗	✔	✔	
				✗					✔						✔	✔	✔
	✗	✔									✗	✔			✔		
	✗			✔	✔	✗			✔	✔		✔	✗		✔	✔	
				✔	✔	✗			✗	✗		✔			✗	✔	✔
						✔			✗	✔	✔	✗	✗			✔	✔
		✔		✗	✗	✔		✔			✔	✗			✔		
				✔					✗	✗	✗	✔			✔		✗
		✔			✗	✗		✔	✗			✔			✗	✗	
	✔				✔	✗				✗					✔	✗	
				✗	✔	✔		✔	✔			✔	✔		✔	✔	

	Large ski area	Tough runs	Intermediate skiing	Easy runs	Nursery slopes	Off-piste/ski touring	Summer skiing	Cross-country	Snowboarding	Lift queues
FRANCE										
Alpe d'Huez	✔	✔	✔	✔	✔	✔	✔		✔	✔
Les Arcs	✔		✔			✔			✔	
Avoriaz	✔	✔	✔	✔	✔				✔	
Barèges/La Mongie	✔	✗	✔	✔						
Chamonix	✔	✔		✗		✔			✔	✗
Châtel	✔		✔	✔						
La Clusaz		✗	✔	✔				✔		
Courchevel	✔	✔	✔	✔	✔	✔				
Les Deux Alpes			✔	✔	✔	✔	✔		✔	
Flaine	✔		✔	✔	✔	✔			✔	
Megève	✔	✗	✔	✔	✔			✔		
Les Menuires	✔	✔	✔	✔		✔				
Méribel	✔	✔	✔	✔	✔	✔		✔		
Montgenèvre	✔	✗	✔	✔		✔				
Morzine	✔		✔	✔				✔	✔	✔
La Plagne	✔	✗	✔	✔	✔	✔	✔	✔		
Risoul 1850	✔	✗	✔	✔					✔	✔

Long runs	Tree-level skiing	Big vertical drop	Skiing convenience	Snow probability	Non-skiing	Mountain restaurants	Beautiful scenery	Resort charm	Compact village	Traffic	Resort access	Late holidays	Low prices	Après-ski	Family skiing	Children's facilities
✓	✗	✓		✓		✓	✓	✗				✓		✗	✓	✓
✓		✓	✓	✓	✗	✗		✗		✓		✓		✗	✓	✓
✓			✓		✗				✓	✓					✓	✓
				✗	✗				✓		✓	✗	✓			
✓		✓	✗	✓	✓	✗	✓			✗	✓	✓		✓	✗	✗
			✗	✗		✓		✗	✗	✓	✗		✗			
			✗	✗		✓			✗	✗	✓	✗			✓	✓
✓	✓	✓	✓	✓	✗	✓					✓	✗		✓	✓	✓
	✗	✓	✗	✓	✗	✗	✓	✗	✗	✗		✓		✓	✓	✓
			✓	✓	✗			✗		✓	✓			✗	✓	✓
	✓			✗	✓	✓		✓	✗	✗	✓	✗		✓	✓	✓
✓	✗	✓		✗				✗	✗	✗			✓	✗	✓	✓
✓									✗	✗				✗	✓	✓
	✓	✓		✗	✗				✗	✓				✗		
		✗	✗						✗	✓	✗				✓	✓
✓		✓	✓	✓	✗					✓	✓	✓		✗	✓	✓
	✓		✓	✓	✗	✗			✓	✓	✗	✓	✓	✗	✓	✓

	Large ski area	Tough runs	Intermediate skiing	Easy runs	Nursery slopes	Off-piste/ski touring	Summer skiing	Cross-country	Snowboarding	Lift queues
La Rosière	✔	✘	✔	✔	✔	✔				✔
Serre Chevalier/Briançon	✔		✔	✔		✔		✔	✔	✔
Tignes	✔	✔	✔			✔	✔		✔	✔
Val d'Isère	✔	✔	✔	✘	✘	✔	✔		✔	✔
Valmorel		✘	✔	✔	✔					
Val Thorens	✔	✔	✔			✔	✔			
ITALY										
Bormio	✘	✘	✔			✔				
Canazei	✔		✔							
Cervinia	✔	✘	✔	✔	✔	✘	✔			✘
Cortina d'Ampezzo	✔		✔	✔	✔	✔		✔		✘
Courmayeur		✘	✔		✘	✔	✔	✔		
Madonna di Campiglio		✘	✔	✔	✔	✘		✔	✔	✔
Monte Rosa		✘	✔			✔				✔
Passo Tonale			✔	✔	✔					✔
Livigno		✘		✔	✔					
Sauze d'Oulx	✔		✔	✔		✔				✘
Selva Gardena	✔		✔	✔	✔	✔		✔		

Long runs	Tree-level skiing	Big vertical drop	Skiing convenience	Snow probability	Non-skiing	Mountain restaurants	Beautiful scenery	Resort charm	Compact village	Traffic	Resort access	Late holidays	Low prices	Après-ski	Family skiing	Children's facilities
				✗	✗			✓	✗			✗	✓	✗	✓	✓
	✓			✗				✗	✗	✗	✗	✓			✓	✓
✓	✗	✓	✓	✓	✗	✗		✗			✓			✗	✓	
✓	✗	✓		✓	✗	✗		✗			✓			✓		✗
			✓	✗				✓		✓	✓		✓		✓	✓
	✗		✓	✓	✗					✓	✓			✗		✓
✓		✓	✓					✓			✗	✓	✓			✗
✓				✗	✓	✓	✓		✗	✗		✗	✓	✓	✓	
✓	✗	✓		✓	✗		✓	✗	✗	✗	✓	✓	✓		✓	
✓	✓		✗		✓	✓	✓	✓		✗		✗		✓		✓
	✓	✓	✗		✓	✓	✓	✓	✗		✓		✓	✓		
						✓	✓		✗				✗			
					✗			✓						✗		
				✓				✗		✗			✓			
			✓	✓	✗	✗				✗	✗	✓	✓		✗	✗
	✓		✗		✗	✗		✗			✓		✓	✓		✓
✓				✗	✓	✓	✓			✗	✗		✗		✓	✓

	Large ski area	Tough runs	Intermediate skiing	Easy runs	Nursery slopes	Off-piste/ski touring	Summer skiing	Cross-country	Snowboarding	Lift queues
Sestriere	✔		✔	✔		✔				✗
La Thuile	✔	✗	✔	✔	✔	✔				✔
SWITZERLAND										
Crans Montana			✔	✔	✔	✔	✔	✔	✔	
Davos	✔		✔		✗	✔		✔	✔	
Gstaad	✔	✗		✔			✔	✔	✔	✔
The Jungfrau	✔	✗	✔	✔		✔				
Klosters	✔	✔	✔		✗	✔		✔	✔	
Saas-Fee	✗		✔		✔	✔	✔		✔	
St Moritz	✔		✔	✔	✗	✔	✔	✔	✔	✗
Verbier	✔	✔	✔	✗		✔	✔		✔	✗
Zermatt	✔	✔	✔	✗	✗	✔	✔			
NORTH AMERICA										
Aspen	✔	✔	✔	✔	✔	✔		✔		
Banff/Lake Louise		✗	✔	✔						
Jackson Hole			✔		✗	✔	✔			✗
Lake Tahoe	✔	✔	✔	✔		✔		✔		
Mammoth Mountain	✔	✔	✔	✔	✔	✔			✔	✗

Long runs	Tree-level skiing	Big vertical drop	Skiing convenience	Snow probability	Non-skiing	Mountain restaurants	Beautiful scenery	Resort charm	Compact village	Traffic	Resort access	Late holidays	Low prices	Après-ski	Family skiing	Children's facilities
✔				✔	✗	✗		✗								
	✔		✔		✗	✗		✗	✔	✔			✔	✗		✗
✔	✔	✔		✔			✔	✗	✗	✗	✔		✗		✔	✔
✔	✔	✔	✗	✗	✔	✔		✗	✗	✗			✗	✗	✗	
			✗	✗	✔		✔			✗	✔		✗			
✔			✗	✗	✔		✔			✔		✗			✔	✔
✔	✔	✔	✗	✗		✔	✔			✗		✗	✗	✗	✗	
	✗	✗	✔	✔			✔	✔		✔	✗	✔	✗		✔	✔
✔		✔	✗	✔	✔	✔	✔		✗		✗	✔	✗	✔		
✔		✔	✔				✔			✗	✔	✔	✗	✔	✔	✔
✔	✔	✔	✗	✔	✔	✔	✔	✔	✗	✔	✗	✔	✗	✔		✗
	✔		✗	✔	✔	✔		✔					✗	✔	✔	✔
		✗	✔				✔	✗					✔	✔	✔	✔
✔	✔	✔		✗	✔	✗	✔	✔			✗	✗	✔	✔		✔
	✔				✗		✔	✗						✔	✔	✔
				✔	✔	✗		✗	✗		✗		✔		✗	✔

	Large ski area	Tough runs	Intermediate skiing	Easy runs	Nursery slopes	Off-piste/ski touring	Summer skiing	Cross-country	Snowboarding	Lift queues
Park City			✔	✔	✔				✔	
Ski the Summit	✔	✔	✔	✔	✔	✔				
Snowbird		✔	✔	✗	✗	✔				✔
Steamboat	✗	✗	✔	✔	✔				✔	✔
Vail/Beaver Creek	✔		✔	✔	✔	✔		✔	✔	
Whistler/Blackcomb	✔	✔	✔	✔	✔	✔	✔		✔	✗
THE BEST OF EUROPE										
Andorra	✗	✗	✔	✔	✔					✗
Eastern Europe	✗	✗		✔	✔	✗				✗
Norway	✗	✗	✔	✔	✔			✔		✔
Scotland	✗	✗		✔	✔			✔		✗
Spain			✔	✔						

Long runs	Tree-level skiing	Big vertical drop	Skiing convenience	Snow probability	Non-skiing	Mountain restaurants	Beautiful scenery	Resort charm	Compact village	Traffic	Resort access	Late holidays	Low prices	Après-ski	Family skiing	Children's facilities
	✓		✗		✓						✓			✓	✓	✓
	✓		✓	✓							✓	✓		✓	✓	✓
			✓	✓	✗	✗	✓	✗			✓	✓		✗		✓
	✓			✓	✓			✗			✓				✓	
	✓		✓	✓	✗	✗		✓	✓		✓	✓	✗	✓	✓	✓
✓	✓	✓	✓	✓			✓		✓		✓	✓	✓		✓	✓
			✓		✗	✗		✗			✗	✓	✓	✓	✓	✓
✗						✗		✗			✗	✓		✓		
✗	✓			✓							✓	✗			✓	✓
✗			✗		✓	✗		✗			✓			✓		
			✓	✗		✗		✗			✓	✓			✓	✓

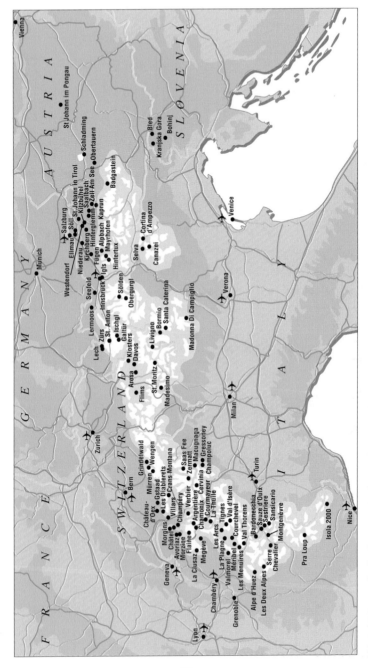

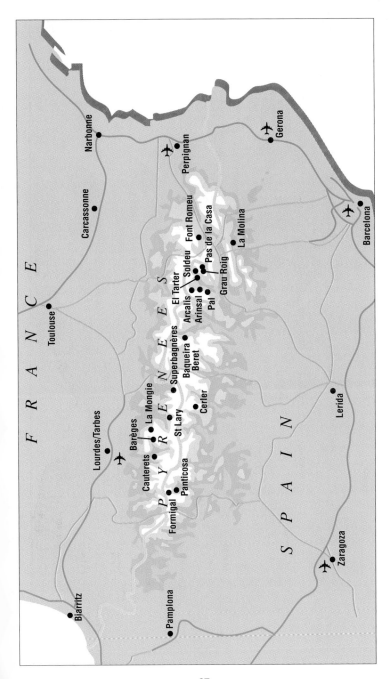

FRANCE

SPAIN

PYRENEES

Narbonne

Carcassonne

Perpignan

Gerona

Barcelona

Toulouse

Font Romeu

Pas de la Casa

La Molina

Soldeu

Grau Roig

El Tarter

Arcalis

Arinsal

Pal

Superbagnères

Baqueira

Beret

Cerler

Lerida

La Mongie

St Lary

Barèges

Lourdes/Tarbes

Cauterets

Panticosa

Formigal

Biarritz

Pamplona

Zaragoza

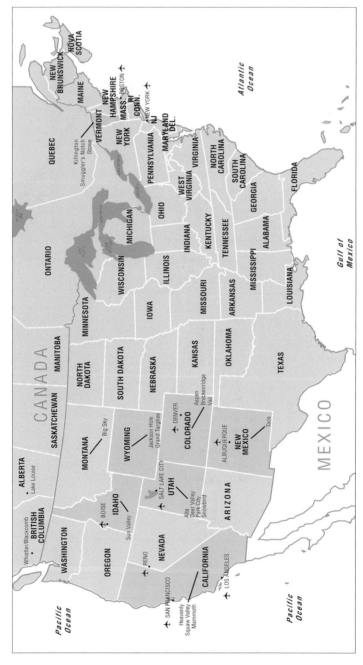

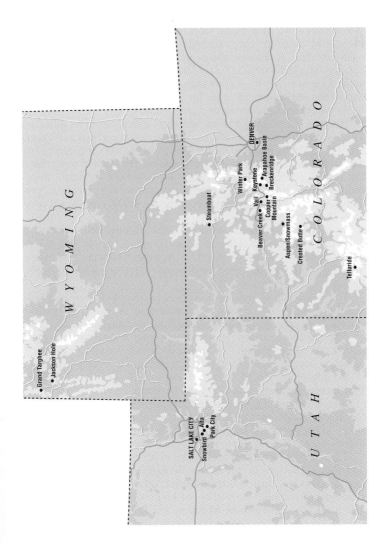

Austria

Austria has suffered in recent years from a decline in tourism brought about by cruel currency exchange rates against the Deutschmark-related schilling. Its ills were also a result of the complacency of the many hoteliers who had it so good for too long. They arrogantly found change, in the form of rivalry from other skiing countries, unacceptable. It took the demise of German affluence for them to come to their senses and rejoin the international forum on a competitive basis.

However, no country has learned more quickly from its mistakes. The blinkered 'valley mentality' too often encountered just a few years ago is firmly in the past, and the importance of Austria's acceptance into the EU has been realised at every social level. The flood of trade that it lost first to France and later to Italy has now been stemmed. Prices remain stable, and for the first time in a decade we can confidently predict an increase of five per cent in business for British mainstream operators to Austria this winter.

To most holiday-makers, mountain village atmosphere is almost as important as the quality of the skiing, and *Gemütlichkeit* is what Austria has in abundance. With few exceptions, Austrian resorts are alpine farming villages that have absorbed the demands of tourism while still maintaining their traditional way of life.

The upgrading of Innsbruck Airport to accept charter as well as scheduled flights has greatly eased access to the popular Tyrolean resorts. Most other resorts are reached from Salzburg or Zurich.

The fact that the average resort altitude is much lower than in France does not necessarily mean that Austria receives less snow. However, to be sure of adequate cover for early or late skiing, it is prudent to pick one of the higher or glacial resorts; these include Obergurgl, Sölden, Obertauern, Kaprun, Ischgl, Zürs and St Anton.

Austria's skiing in general lacks both challenge and variety. While the low and gentle pastures of the Tyrol are scenically beautiful and ideally suited to beginners and lower intermediates, more advanced skiers will quickly tire of this benign terrain in any but the best of powder conditions.

Today's skier demands more than his or her predecessor of the 1950s and 1960s. This may in part explain the defections to the greater challenges of France. Austria does, however, offer a number of linked or semi-linked complexes covered by one lift pass. These include Ski-Welt and Saalbach-Hinterglemm. St Anton and Lech/Zürs are the exceptions. They stand alone as Austria's only ski area that offers truly world-class slopes for advanced skiers.

Skiers will find the standard of accommodation to be higher than anywhere else in Europe. You can still find the occasional Tirolerabend, complete with musical wood-chopping, but the emphasis is now on lively bars and discos.

Alpbach

ALTITUDE 1000m (3,280ft)

Alpbach is a secluded and strikingly attractive village, far removed from the overt commercial influences of mainstream Tyrol and all the better for it. It dates from around 1150 and in the Middle Ages was an important copper- and silver-mining community. Summer and winter tourism started as far back as the 1930s, but unlike its brasher rivals Alpbach has managed to reach the closing years of the century with its rural Austrian charm intact. The Böglerhof and the Jakober hotels date from the sixteenth century and act as the cornerstones of a village which has unsurprisingly been voted Most Beautiful Village in a country full of beautiful villages. The Alpbach Valley still has 120 working farms and is the home of traditional Austrian painted furniture. If your Tyrolean holiday is incomplete without zither, harp, and accordion music produced by rugged mountain lads in stout leather breeches, then you will not be disappointed.

■ GOOD POINTS

Attractive village, alpine charm, lack of queues, ideal for non-skiers, long vertical drop

■ BAD POINTS

Lack of challenging slopes, poor access to slopes, limited number of pistes, unexciting nightlife

Alpbach's long association with Britain begins at the quaint parish church that is mysteriously dedicated to St Oswald, a former king of Northumbria. More recently, the association can be attributed to the temporal enthusiasm of a Major Billy Patterson who arrived in Alpbach on leave from Germany in the 1950s and never left.

In 1968 his wife, still a resident today, founded the Alpbach Visitors Ski Club, which acts as a private booking agency for around 1,500 guests a year and contributes strongly to the fact that as many as 23 per cent of Alpbach's skiers are British.

The ski area is limited in size but offers a long vertical drop and a variety of terrain. It is best suited to beginners and less adventurous intermediates. However, the pitch, length and possible variations of the main runs allow an advanced skier to enjoy a week here in the right conditions. There is also considerable scope for off-piste and no one could fail to appreciate the beauty of the setting. The inconvenience of having to take a free ski bus from the village to the main mountain and back again each day is a drawback, particularly for families with small children confined to the village-centre nursery slopes. However, a number of reporters have commented on the efficiency of the service and one said: 'Never have I done less walking in a ski resort. A car is useful for day trips to other resorts such as **Mayrhofen**, **Söll** or **Kitzbühel** for variety, but parking in the village can be a problem'.

Overall, Alpbach deserves its long-established reputation as a pretty family resort, ideal for a Christmas holiday, although snow in the village can by no means be guaranteed. Like other Austrian destinations it has been hard-hit by recession, and the number of visitors, British included, is falling. Its sleepy way of life, still largely locked into the 1960s, with the emphasis on tradition, has been its greatest asset in the past, but if it is to survive as a ski resort into the twenty-first century the village fathers will have to face up to the reality of modern marketing.

On the mountain
top 2025m (6,643ft) bottom 830m (2,722ft)

Apart from the nursery slopes next to the village and the Böglerlift, with its south-facing blue (easy) run, all of Alpbach's skiing is on the slopes of the Wiedersberger Horn, a five-minute bus ride from the village. One reporter comments: 'It is a great resort if you don't mind doing the same run over and over again'. Mountain access from Alpbach is on the two-stage, six-seater Achenwirt gondola across the wooded north-facing slopes to Hornboden at 1850m. Queuing is not a problem here, although the number of skiers increases at weekends.

Alpbach has a large vertical drop compared to other Austrian resorts of a similar village altitude, and there are a number of long runs. Although it has always had the reputation of being a beginners' resort, all but a couple of the runs on the mountain are marked red (intermediate), and only one, the Familienabfahrt, is blue. Mountain access is also possible by chair-lift from **Inneralpbach** along the valley. Here the lifts join up with the skiing above Hornboden, and a long, easy red run takes you from Gmahkopf back down to Inneralpbach. The top lift here, Hornlift 2000, opens up some higher altitude and more challenging intermediate skiing. Plans to build a new lift to access the open snowfields below the 2228-m Standkopf have progressed as far as a dotted line on the piste-map but no further. Instead, priority is being given to increased snowmaking on the lower, rocky meadows beneath the first stage of the gondola.

Beginners

Complete novices need not stray from the village. Easy nursery runs are served by two drag-lifts in the centre beside the Böglerhof. Once the basics have been assimilated, or if there are poor snow conditions at this low altitude, skiers progress to the Familienabfahrt on the Hornboden, via the gondola. This is a long path from Gmahkopf to Kriegalm, which reporters claim is often icy. The views around Hornboden are superb, and the terrain open and gentle, with several short drag-lifts also suitable for lower intermediates.

Intermediates

With the exception of a couple of moderately challenging black (difficult) runs, the whole mountain is given over to intermediate skiing. The small number of pistes (ten) marked on the local lift map does not do full justice

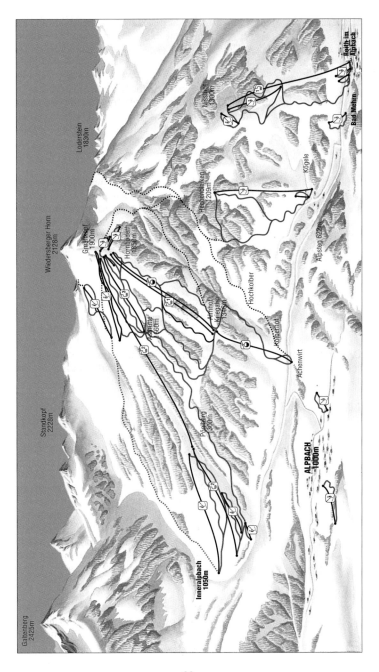

to the actual size of the groomed area; the pistes are extremely wide and an equivalent US resort would manage to triple the number and give them more interesting names. The standard of piste preparation is very high.

Advanced
From Hornboden, a couple of wide pistes run back down to the Kriegalm mid-station, including an FIS racecourse, which is one of the two black runs on the mountain; the other is Brandegg. From here a red run carries on down to the bottom, creating a good, fast course of over 1000m vertical, which is used by British racing clubs for their competitions.

Off-piste
Alpbach is ideal for 'lazy powder skiers'. According to one reporter you can lie in bed after a night of new snow until 10.30am and still cut fresh tracks. The long, red itinerary route from Gmahkopf down to Inneralpbach is not pisted, though it is usually well skied and conditions are not generally difficult. There is some fairly challenging off-piste to be found around the Wiedersbergerhorn, and the ski school runs special tours for this on Saturdays.

Ski schools and guiding
Alpbach Ski School has 60 instructors and a sound reputation. It has 30 years' experience of teaching British skiers and consequently only employs instructors with fluent English. One reporter commented: 'the standard of instruction was about the best I have had anywhere'. Another described it as 'friendly and traditional, absolutely not *avant garde*. In fact, the school mirrors the resort'. Guided powder tours can be arranged through the ski school.

Snowboarding
Despite the fact that last season Alpbach played host to the snowboarding Continental Open, the village authorities take a sadly blinkered view of the board. This is not so surprising when you consider their traditional cultural values stand in direct opposition to the new sport and its exponents; in short, as one reader put it: 'shredders don't pluck with zithers'. Both the Alpbach and Innertal ski schools offer snowboarding courses on

■ **WHAT'S NEW**

Snowmaking on the lower slopes beneath the gondola

demand, but the overall attitude is best summed up by Sepp Margreiter, head of the Alpbach school for the past 12 years, who takes the view that 'snowboarding is unnatural and physically harmful'.

Cross-country
The narrow end of the Alpbachtal, closed to traffic in winter, offers a scenic 17-km loipe, which begins at Inneralpbach. The Alpbach Ski School teaches langlauf and offers a tour every Thursday for experienced cross-country skiers.

Mountain restaurants

The Hornboden is situated 50m vertical beneath the top stage of the gondola, which is fine for skiers but an inconvenience for the many non-skiers who have to walk down a steep stretch of piste to reach it. The lower section is self-service with a pleasant sun terrace. The first floor is given over to a restaurant offering typical Tyrolean food of a reasonably high standard. The Gmahstuben is recommended by one reporter for its good, but expensive food. The Gasthof Wiedersbergerhorn at Inneralpbach is said to be one of the best lunch spots in the region.

Off the mountain

Alpbach is a small, sunny village set on a steep hillside. The compact centre is dominated by a pretty green-and-white church surrounded by old wooden chalets and the buttressed walls of the two medieval inns. A 1953 building regulation ensured that all construction is in traditional Tyrolean style, with the obvious seasonal exception of the ubiquitous Siglu bar at the foot of the nursery slopes. The seventeenth-century farmhouse, Unterberg, at Inneralpbach is a museum of the history of the area. Shopping is limited to just two sports shops, two boutiques and three souvenir shops.

Accommodation

Most of Alpbach's accommodation is in hotels and guest houses, ranging from basic bed-and-breakfasts to the very comfortable. Two of the luxury hotels, both with swimming-pools, are the Alphof and the Alpbacherhof. The village takes considerable pride in the fact that many of its hotels have remained in the same families for centuries, which ensures a high standard of service for guests. Certainly this appears to be borne out at the four-star Böglerhof, which last season became part of the Romantik hotel group. The new management's first move was to axe its Schneeloch disco, thereby robbing Alpbach of much of its limited nightlife. The Blatter is centrally placed, and several reporters found the food and service to be excellent. The Alphof is for the heartier skier as it is a 15-minute uphill walk from the village. Its restaurant is warmly recommended. Less expensive hotels include the Post, Haus Angelika, Haus Elisabeth, Haus Erna and Haus Max. The keenest skiers may find the Galtenberg and the Gasthof Achenwirt well positioned for the gondola, and Inneralpbach, 4km along the valley, is another option for finding a convenient and quiet place to stay.

■ OTHER SPORTS

Swimming, sleigh rides, parapente, tobogganing, indoor tennis at Kramsach (12km away)

Eating in and out

The restaurants do not offer much variety, although the recommended ones include the Gasthof Jakober, Alpbacher Taverne, the Reblaus for pizzas and the Gasthof Wiedersbergerhorn. The most luxurious is the

Skiing facts: **Alpbach**

TOURIST OFFICE
Postfach 31, A-6236 Alpbach
Tel 43 5336 5211
Fax 43 5336 5012

THE RESORT
By road Calais 1080km
By rail Brixlegg 10km
By air Innsbruck 1 hr, Munich 2 hrs
Visitor beds 2,400
Transport free ski bus between village and
gondola runs every 20 mins

THE SKIING
Linked or nearby resorts Reith (n)
Longest run Kafner, 3km (red)
Number of lifts 21
Total of trails/pistes 45km
(22% easy, 56% intermediate,
22% difficult)
Nursery slopes 7 lifts (5 at Alpbach, others
at Inneralpbach and Reith)
Summer skiing none
Snowmaking 20km covered

LIFT PASSES
Area pass (covers Alpbach and Reith)
ÖS1,350 for 6 days
Day pass ÖS310
Beginners no free lifts
Pensioners reduction for 65 yrs and over
Credit cards accepted no

SKI SCHOOLS
Adults Alpbach Ski School and Innertal Ski
School, 10am-midday and 1.30-3.30pm,
ÖS1,300 for 6 days
Private lessons Alpbach Ski School
ÖS1,900, Innertal Ski School ÖS1,800,
both per day
Snowboarding both ski schools, by
appointment, prices and times on request
Cross-country both ski schools, ÖS1,100
for 6 half-days
Other courses ski-touring, off-piste,
monoski
Guiding companies through ski schools

CHILDREN
Lift pass (covers Alpbach and Reith),
6-14 yrs, ÖS820 for 6 days, free for 5 yrs
and under if accompanied by a parent
Ski kindergarten Alpbach Ski School,
ÖS1,900 and Innertal Ski School ÖS1,760,
both for 6 days including lunch
Ski school Alpbach Ski School ÖS1,300 and
Innertal Ski School ÖS1,250, both for 6
days (4 hrs per day)
Non-ski kindergarten 3-5 yrs, Mon-Fri
9.15am-4pm and Sat 9.15am-midday,
ÖS900, extra ÖS70 per day for lunch

FOOD AND DRINK PRICES
Coffee ÖS25, glass of wine ÖS18, small
beer ÖS25, dish of the day ÖS130

restaurant in the Hotel Böglerhof. Rossmoos and Zottahof, both up the
mountain, are popular in the evening. There are two Spar supermarkets
in Alpbach and one in Inneralpbach, which all sell self-catering basics.

Après-ski
If drinking and dancing until dawn are an integral component of your ski
holiday, stay away. The tourist board explanation is that most skiers are
so tired in the evening that they go to bed early, but with such a limited
ski area it is difficult to understand why this should be so. Outside the
main holiday weeks the resort is dead by 11pm, except at weekends

when an influx of visitors gives it much needed cheer. The Siglu, beside the nursery slopes and the bus stop for the gondola, attracts a busy crowd in the late afternoon. There is a long toboggan run at Reith, 7km away.

The Jakober Bar is an early-evening rendezvous point. The Hornbeisl bar next to the lifts in Inneralpbach is recommended. The Waschkuch'l is a good place for a quiet drink, and Birdies Pub in the village centre for a noisier one. The sad demise of the Schneeloch in the basement of the Böglerhof leaves just the Weinstadl as the token disco, 'open late, but absolutely empty', as one frustrated night owl commented. One reporter recommends the horse-drawn sleigh rides up to a 300-year-old inn at the head of the valley.

Childcare

Alpbach has a kindergarten that takes children from three years old. It is also possible to find baby-minders for younger children through the tourist board. The ski school kindergarten takes children all day from four years of age.

Linked or nearby resorts

There is more skiing at **Reith**, 7km down the valley from Alpbach, which includes mainly red runs and some beginners' skiing served by several more nursery slope lifts.

Badgastein

ALTITUDE 1100m (3,608ft)

The Gasteinertal is one of Austria's best-kept secrets; a long, closed valley flanked by the Hohe Tauern mountains, which offer a higher class of skiing than the lowland pastures of the Tyrol. Importantly, the valley is a major spa area. All industry is banned within a 40-km radius and even after weeks of high atmospheric pressure, the air remains free of pollutants.

■ **GOOD POINTS**

Large intermediate ski area, tough runs, tree-line skiing, variety of après-ski, thermal baths, easy rail access, reasonable prices

■ **BAD POINTS**

Lack of skiing convenience, awkward for families with small children, heavy traffic

Five million gallons of hot water bubble up from 17 natural springs around the main and grand resort of Badgastein. Health and skiing are inextricably linked here, and at the end of the day a thermal bath is the greatest of cures for tired limbs. It is conveniently piped into all the main hotels, but the public indoor and outdoor pools at the Felsenbad by the *Bahnhof* (station) are a popular resort rendezvous. Here you can wallow in the waters and, through a haze of steam, watch skiers in action just a few yards away.

One million gallons of this surprisingly sulphur-free water are also piped down the road to **Bad Hofgastein**, a spacious and comfortable spa in a more benign setting on the valley floor, which is particularly popular with families.

Dorfgastein, at the entrance to the Gasteinertal, is a sleepy and unspoilt Austrian village with its own attractive ski area, which extends over the 2027-m Kreuzkogel to the resort of **Grossarl** in a neighbouring valley.

Sportgastein, at the head of the valley, is a separate, high ski area based around an abandoned gold-mining village. In the Middle Ages the area was responsible for ten per cent of the world's gold and silver output. It has no accommodation but is easily reached by ski bus from either of the main resorts.

Badgastein itself is best described as Vienna-on-ice, a collection of grand hotels mostly painted in the imperial yellow of the Schönbrunn Palace and dramatically stacked up a steep hillside around a waterfall, which plunges into the River Ache.

The resort's elegant casino harks back to the days when this was one of the greatest watering resorts of Europe. Schubert and Johann Strauss both composed here. Schopenhauer and Thomas Mann were regular visitors and the guest list never failed to produce at least a couple of

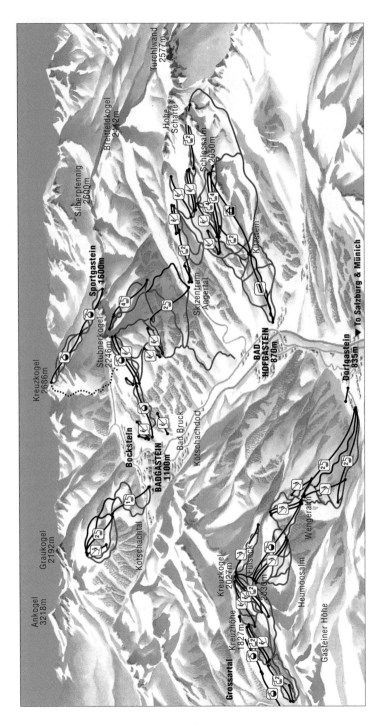

Turchlwand 2577m

Hohe Scharte

Schlossalm 2050m

Kreuzkogel 2686m

Breitfeldkogel 2442m

Silberpfennig 2600m

Sportgastein 1600m

Stubnerkogel 2246m

Skizentrum Angertal

Kreuzstein

Ankogel 3218m

Graukogel 2192m

Bockstein

BADGASTEIN 1100m

Bad Bruck

Kötschachdorf

Kötschachtal

BAD HOFGASTEIN 870m

Dorfgastein 835m

▶ **To Salzburg & München**

Kreuzkogel 2027m

Fulseck

2030m

Heumoosalm

Wengeralm

Gasteiner Höhe

Grossartal

Kreuzhöhe 1827m

39

crowned heads of state.

A close inspection of the resort today, however, reveals the shutters permanently down on the Grand Hotel de l'Europe and a couple of other original hotels. The gold has long since been exhausted and the year-round spa business is not what it was. Winter sports, however, have given the region an injection of new life. The 250km of bus- and mountain-linked skiing is a treat for anyone who believes most Austrian skiing to be too tame.

On the mountain
top 2686m (8,810ft) bottom 850m (2,788ft)

If you are accustomed to clicking into your bindings outside your hotel door and skiing home at the end of the day, then Badgastein is not for you. It was built on a steep hillside as a spa, not a ski resort, and a considerable amount of walking is unavoidable.

The main Stubnerkogel ski area is situated on the western side of the valley and is reached by modern two-stage gondola from the top of the town near the railway station. In theory, the ski and boot store beside it avoids the pain of having to lug equipment up tough gradients from the town centre, but you may not end up here again at the end of the day.

The east-facing runs back down to Badgastein provide good, tough skiing, with a mixture of open ground above halfway, and woods below which are mostly graded red (intermediate), but can be difficult when conditions are poor. A blue (easy) run winds down the mountain and is usually crowded and often icy. The wide top-half of the slope gives plenty of opportunity for off-piste variations.

Stubnerkogel is the starting point for a series of lifts and runs which take you along the side of the valley and down to Bad Hofgastein. There are three other separate areas, all with differing attractions. The Graukogel runs above Badgastein on the far side of the valley are few in number, but long and satisfying descents for good skiers. The friendly skiing shared by Dorfgastein and Grossarl is a confidence-building but at times challenging small area for beginners and intermediates.

Sportgastein, at the head of the valley, is an icy place to find yourself when the weather closes in. However, on a fine day the piste skiing is varied enough to be interesting and the off-piste can be quite exceptional. If snow conditions are poor elsewhere in the valley, Sportgastein can become crowded. However, the bottleneck has been dramatically alleviated in recent years since the old chair was upgraded to the Goldbergbahn gondola.

Regular ski buses link the separate resorts and ski areas but distances are great and to explore the area to its full a car is more of a necessity than a useful asset.

Beginners

The area has five nursery slopes served by drag-lifts but overall cannot be recommended as ideal for beginners or even second-week skiers. From

Badgastein, the main novice slopes are an inconvenient ten minutes away at Angertal. Most blue runs are a pinkish-red in comparison with similar sized Austrian resorts and the whole Gasteinertal is better geared towards more accomplished skiers.

Intermediates

The entire valley is best suited to confident intermediates looking for a combination of mileage and challenge. Graukogel has superb tree-level skiing and is the place where the locals go on a snowy day. Confident skiers will be interested in the long run around the back of the mountain, which is reached either from Höhe Scharte at 2300m or from Kleine Scharte at 2050m. In good snow conditions it is possible to ski 1450m vertical over eight kilometres, all the way to the bottom of the railway. Skiing is possible with only a minimum of snow cover, as most of it takes place on pastureland with few rocks and stones.

Advanced

The north-facing runs down into the Angertal provide some of the best skiing in the region. From Jungeralm a long, undulating black (difficult) run drops directly through the woods.

Off-piste

Untracked opportunities abound above the Schlossalm next to Höhe Scharte. Both the north and south faces of Sportgastein can provide excellent, long powder runs after a snowfall.

Ski schools and guiding

We have good reports of both the Skischule Pflaum and the Skischule Luigi in Badgastein. The size of classes seems to vary between 4 and 12 pupils. The standard of English is high ('the instructor even understood our jokes'). The Bad Hofgastein Ski and Racing School, run by Fritz Zettinig, has a fine reputation. We have no reports on the two alternatives — Robert's Ski School and the Ski School Schlossalm. Ski School Holleisn in Dorfgastein is described as 'small and friendly with useful instruction by helpful locals'. Local high-mountain guide Hans Zlöbl takes groups and individuals off-piste.

Snowboarding

Badgastein and Dorfgastein both have man-made half-pipes, but the most highly recommended is the natural half-pipe at Sportgastein. Both Badgastein's ski schools offer snowboarding tuition.

Cross-country

Both Badgastein ski schools have a langlauf section, as does the Bad Hofgastein Ski and Racing School. Gerhard Gassner runs his Gasteiner Wander-Und Langlaufschule. Nearly 90km of prepared loipe are scattered around the valley. Routes are shown in detail in the Gasteinertal Loipenbuch, obtainable free of charge from the tourist offices.

Mountain restaurants

The area is plentifully served with pleasant huts on the slopes as well as self-service cafeterias at the lift stations. Prices appear to be no higher than in the valley, and there they are low by Austrian standards, which is surprising in a resort of this standing. Reporters particularly recommend the Wengeralm above Dorfgastein for its 'very good, traditional fried potato pancakes'. The top of the Stubnerkogel has both waiter- and self-service sections and is recommended for local venison dishes. The Schlossalm has a warm cosy atmosphere and is famed for its thick *Gulaschsuppe*. The Hamburger Skiheim above Bad Hofgastein has a barbecue and ice-bar. The Panorama at Kreuzkogel has a children's slide between floors. Toni's Almgasthaus at the top of Graukogel serves garlic soup in bowls hollowed out of loaves of bread. Sportgastein's restaurants are at the gondola halfway station and at the base; both are operated by the same family to an extremely high standard.

Off the mountain

The main road and railway bypass the town centre, which is more simply negotiated by the steep footpaths and stairways than by car. The focus of the resort is the casino, the *Wasserfall* and a modern conference centre beside it. The old hotels are flanked by smart little boutiques and expensive jewellers. The resort's upper level, a steep but short climb away, is a rather ordinary collection of the less fashionable spa hotels and newer establishments, which attract skiers in winter because of their more convenient location.

Badgastein has an annoyingly complicated one-way system; traffic is heavy and parking can be difficult. The bus service between the resorts is efficient but 'hideously overcrowded' during high season and confusing, with both city and ski bus lines to different destinations: 'Bus-stops within the resort are not always marked and timetables can be hard to find.' Taxis are plentiful and fares negotiable.

Accommodation

Most of the accommodation is in hotels of which there are quite literally hundreds in the valley, many of them with piped thermal water. The actual position of your accommodation in Badgastein is crucial because of the steep layout of the resort. The modern Elizabethpark beside the *Wasserfall* is said to be 'comfortable but a bit characterless and a long walk from the snow'. Villa Solitude, a magnificent townhouse next to the casino, has been lovingly restored as a designer hotel with six suites furnished as they were in the 1840s.

Among the hotels at the top of the resort within easy walking distance of the Stubnerkogel lifts is the Bärenhof, which is among the most comfortable and expensive. Much more charming and in a quieter position is the simple Fischerwirt. Hotel Mozart, named not after the maestro but his mother, is recommended as comfortable and spacious, and 'well-positioned for the skiing and the nightlife'. We have encouraging reports of the Hotel Lindenhof and the Wildbad. The Salzburgerhof is owned by a Swedish company and readers warmly recommend it for 'exceptional attention to detail'. At the foot of the Graukogel lift is the Schillerhof, recommended for its 'splendid views,

> ■ **OTHER SPORTS**
>
> Skating, curling, indoor tennis, squash, swimming, sleigh rides, tobogganing, rifle shooting, parapente, snow-shoeing

clean and comfortable rooms'. The Grüner Baum, built in 1831 by Archduke Johann as a hunting lodge, is 5km out of town in a beautiful rural setting and has a reputation as one of the great hotels of Austria.

Eating in and out

The choice of restaurants is mainly limited to the hotels, but the Bahnhof restaurant is particularly recommended as good value for money. The Mozart on Mozartplatz is praised for its fondues. The Restaurant am Wasserfall is 'inexpensive and cheerful', as is the Felsenbad. The China-restaurant on Kaiser-Franz-Josef-Strasse 'makes a pleasant change from Wienerschnitzel'. The Villa Hiss offers 'outstanding gourmet fare at a price', and the Hotel Rader in Böckstein provides 'a great evening out for those who care about their food'. Villa Solitude Brasserie has the best food in town along with the Grüner Baum; both are owned by the Blumschein family.

Après-ski

The Felsenbad, opposite the *Bahnhof*, has thermal indoor and outdoor pools as well as a bar, and attracts the crowds as they come off the slopes. Sensibly the Austrians see nothing unhealthy in the marriage of beer and Bad and a promotional video shows spa patients happily imbibing. No visitor should miss the chance to improve their health by taking a train ride to the Healing Galleries 2km inside the mountain near Dorfgastein. The combination of a 90°C ambient temperature, relative humidity and low dosages of rare Radon gas is said to cure respiratory and muscular ailments.

The Gatz Music Club is the hotspot at tea-time and again much later in the evening. Its only late-night rival is the Visage near the *Wasserfall*. Eden's Pub is said to be usually crowded 'not least because a giant moose head takes up most of the room'. For night owls the Blockhäusl Club near Mozartplatz begins to liven up after 1am. The Salzburgerhof Hotel bar has live music ('everything from UB40 to Glenn Miller'). The casino is worth a visit. The Manfreda and Kir Royal bars are ever popular. Other late bars to check out include the Belmondo, Filou, Gasteiner Stamperl, Hexn-Häusl, Weinfassl, Pub am Wasserfall and the Zirbenstube. The bar at the British-owned Hotel Tannenburg is open to non-residents and has the cheapest drinks in town.

Childcare

Like all resorts with a disparate ski area of this nature it is difficult to recommend Badgastein for children. All the villages have ski kindergarten
taking three-year-olds and upwards, but finding someone to care for
younger ones is more difficult. Hotel Grüner Baum in Badgastein does
run a crèche but only for residents. The nursery slopes are ten minutes
from the centre.

Linked or nearby resorts

Bad Hofgastein
top 2686m (8,810ft) bottom 870m (2,854ft)

Bad Hofgastein has neither the inconveniently steep and dark setting,
nor the faded grandeur of its neighbour. It is smaller, but is still a sizeable resort with 18 hotels spread along the broadest part of the valley.
The Kitzstein funicular is a long walk or a bus-ride away. It is a good
base for the valley's walks and cross-country trails, and busy skating and
curling rinks complete the winter scene. There is an outdoor, naturally
heated swimming-pool as well as a modern sports centre with tennis and
squash. Reporters complain that the funicular holds 100 while the cable
car above it has a capacity of only 40; this leads to annoying 30-minute
queues at peak times. Wise skiers take the chair from the top of the train.

The resort has a strong conservation policy and anyone who deliberately skis through sapling plantations is liable to forfeit his or her lift pass.
The kindergarten takes children from three years old. Thermal baths
here are said to be a must, as are the evening sleigh rides.

Accommodation is mainly in hotels. The Gasthof zum Boten is
described as an 'excellent old post house with big, clean comfortable
rooms'. The Kaiser Franz and the more expensive Hotel Norica both
receive good reports, as do the Hotel Moser and the Salzburgerhof. The
most convenient hotels are the more recently built ones lining the road
from the centre to the river. The Tennis Treff opposite the funicular
attracts the main crowd as they come off the slopes with its 'good atmosphere, occasional live music and reasonably priced drinks'. Later on the
action moves to Francky's Kneipe along with Sonia's Pub. The one disco
is not usually busy. The bowling alley is recommended as 'great fun for
a rowdy night out — the best excursion I've ever been on.'

TOURIST OFFICE
Tel 43 6432 71100
Fax 43 6432 711031

Dorfgastein
top 2686m (8,810ft) bottom 835m (2,739ft)

Dorfgastein is the first of the settlements you come to on entering the
Gasteinertal. Too many visitors to the area drive through without stopping. What they miss is a delightful little village with a charming main

Skiing facts: **Badgastein**

TOURIST OFFICE
Haus Austria, Kaiser-Franz-Josef-Strasse 27, A-5640 Badgastein, Salzburgerland
Tel 43 6434 25310
Fax 43 6434 253137

THE RESORT
By road Calais 1200km
By rail station in resort
By air Salzburg 1½ hrs
Visitor beds 7,300
Transport free ski bus with lift pass

THE SKIING
Linked or nearby resorts Bad Hofgastein (l), Dorfgastein (n), Sportgastein (n), Grossarl (n)
Longest run Angertal, 11km (red/blue)
Number of lifts 53
Total of trails/pistes 250km (30% easy, 30% intermediate, 40% difficult)
Nursery slopes 5 lifts and trails
Summer skiing none
Snowmaking 40km covered, 150km in area

LIFT PASSES
Area pass Gastein Super Ski (covers all Gastein resorts), ÖS1,620-1,910 for 6 days

Day pass ÖS340-400
Beginners points tickets
Pensioners 10% reduction for women 60 yrs and over and men 65 yrs and over
Credit cards accepted yes

SKI SCHOOLS
Adults Pflaum and Luigi, ÖS1,690 for 6 days
Private lessons ÖS450 per hr
Snowboarding ÖS1,400 for 3 days
Cross-country private lessons ÖS450 per hr, or 3 days (2 hrs per day) with Paul Lederer, ÖS600. Loipe 90km in area
Other courses off-piste
Guiding companies Hans Zlöbl

CHILDREN
Lift pass 7-15 yrs, ÖS1,150 for 6 days, free for 6 yrs and under
Ski kindergarten 3-5 yrs, ÖS2,600 for 6 days including lunch and some skiing
Ski school Pflaum and Luigi, 3 yrs and over, ÖS2,600 for 6 days including lunch
Non-ski kindergarten 3-5 yrs, ÖS2,280 for 6 days including lunch

FOOD AND DRINK PRICES
Coffee ÖS28, glass of wine ÖS36, small beer ÖS24, dish of the day ÖS90

---

street lined with arcades. It remains untouched by the slightly depressing health-conscious image of its bigger sisters. Horses and carts clatter along the narrow street past the old church. There are several well-kept, friendly and comfortable hotels in the centre. The Steindlwirt and Kirchenwirt are two of the larger ones. The skiing begins at least a five-minute walk from the village. The Gasthof Schihäusl stands at the foot of the slopes. Evenings are said to be livelier than you might expect in a village of this size.

TOURIST OFFICE
Tel 43 6433 277
Fax 43 6463 737

Innsbruck

ALTITUDE 575m (1,886ft)

RESORTS COVERED Axamer Lizum, Fulpmes, Igls, Neustift, Seefeld

The third most important city in Austria is not only a minor ski resort in its own right, but is strategically placed to give easy access to some of the best skiing in the Tyrol and even the Arlberg. It has twice hosted the Winter Olympics and has the advantage of having its own international airport dramatically enclosed by towering mountain-ranges on either side of the Inn Valley. Its geographical situation used to enforce serious restrictions concerning the size of aircraft landing there, and weather conditions also imposed limitations. However, the installation of state-of-the-art air traffic control technology means the airport can now accept charter flights as well as regular scheduled services. The transfer time to most resorts has been cut by half, but a serious question mark is raised over whether, for reasons of profitability, any airline is prepared to continue to fly in here regularly from Britain.

■ GOOD POINTS

Attractive town, short airport transfer, variety of skiing in area, summer skiing on Stubai Glacier, many activities for non-skiers, snowboarding facilities at Axamer Lizum

■ BAD POINTS

Small separate ski areas, weekend lift queues

A variety of good local skiing with attractive lift-ticket arrangements is to be found within short commuting distance of this beautiful and historic city. The most important resorts are also accessible for the day by bus or car. Innsbruck stands at the crossroads of western Austria and is well served by a network of motorways fanning out towards the Arlberg, through the Inn Valley towards the German border, as well as up towards the Brenner Pass and Italy beyond.

The Ötztal and the snow-sure skiing of Obergurgl and Sölden can be reached in under 90 minutes. The journey to Kitzbühel and the Ski-Welt takes an hour. To add to the incentive of staying in the city, a single ski-pass, the Innsbruck Gletscherskipass, covers the six main local areas including **Igls**, **Axamer Lizum** and the **Stubai Glacier**; it gives access to a total of 52 lifts serving 112km of piste.

The two permutations of the more expensive Innsbruck Superskipass also allow you to ski **Kitzbühel** and/or the **Arlberg** for a day as well, thus providing 200 lifts and 500km of piste for your money. Bus travel is included in the price, and anyone staying for more than three days is entitled to a Club Innsbruck discount card, giving a reduction on the passes. Free, efficient ski buses depart from the Landestheater and the Hauptbahnhof each morning, as well as from some of the hotels, and bring skiers back at the end of the day.

Pleisen 2236m

Hoadl 2343m

To Kühtai

Gschwandtkopf 1500m

Seefeld 1200m

Härmelekopf 2050m

Axamer Lizum

Seefelder Spitze 2220m

Axams

Seefelder Joch 2100m

KALKKÖGEL

Nockspitze 2406m

Birgitzköpfl 2096m

Götzens

Solstein

Stubaier Wildspitze 3340m

Pfarrmeskopf 1800m

Mutterer Alm 1610m

Haflekar 2334m

Schaufelspitze 3333m

Schlick

Seegrube 1905m

Mutters

Stubaier Gletscher

Neustift 1000m

Hungerburg

Häbicht

Fulpmes

Schönberg

Patsch

INNSBRUCK 575m

Serles

Neustift 1000m

IGLS 893m

To Brenner Pass & Italy

Heiligwasser

Lans

Aldrans

Patscherkofel 2247m

Sistrans

Rinn

Bar in Tirol

Tulfes

To Vienna, Munich & Salzburg

Glungezer 2677m

Hatsmarter 1613m

2059m

47

Compared to what one might call a conventional ski resort, the cost of staying in the city is considerably lower. The choice of restaurants is wide, and nightlife is both lively and varied. One reporter comments that 'not many places can include *Die Fledermaus* at the opera as après-ski on New Year's Eve'.

The city's best hotel is the Europa, which is attractively wood-panelled and contains the well-respected Europastüberl restaurant. The Grauer Bär is a family hotel with a good atmosphere.

Innsbruck's 'own' skiing is to be found just outside the city across the River Inn, in the Seegrube-Nordkette area above **Hungerburg** on the south-facing slopes of the Hafelekar. The black (difficult) Karrine and the red (intermediate) Langes Tal runs are both challenging. The Glungezer area above Tulfes on the other side of the valley consists of two blue (easy) runs and two reds on the slopes beneath the 2677-m Glungezer.

Axamer Lizum
top 2343m (7,687ft) bottom 874m (2,867ft)

This is a somewhat characterless ski station of four hotels and a huge car park set in the heart of the most appealing all-round ski area at 1553m, beneath the peaks of the Hoadl and Pleisen mountains. Weekend lift-queues, as in all the Innsbruck ski areas, can be a problem, but the ten lifts lead to extensive and varied pistes. The 6.5-km Axamer, graded black, but red by most resorts' standards, takes you all the way down to the quiet village of **Axams** at 874m.

Across the narrow valley, a long chair serves either the black Riesenslalom Herren run back to Axamer Lizum or gives access to the sunny and easy pistes above **Mutters**, the sixth and smallest of Innsbruck's own ski areas. Expectations of an improved link to form a ski circus here have not yet been met, and now seem likely to have evaporated in the light of the growing environmentalist lobby in the Tyrol.

TOURIST OFFICE
Tel 43 5234 8178
Fax 43 5234 7158

Fulpmes
top 2200m (7,218ft) bottom 937m (3,074ft)

Slightly further away, yet easily reached by post bus, the Stubaital offers some of the best skiing in the area. **Mieders**, **Telfes**, **Fulpmes** and **Neustift** all share a lift pass. Above Fulpmes, but not directly accessible from it, there is good skiing in a sheltered bowl now branded as Schlick 2000 Skizentrum. Lifts include a four-seater chair going up to 2200m. Some of the runs are tough and unpisted, but the majority are easy and confidence-building and ideal for lower intermediates. The small, sunny nursery area receives favourable reports, and Innsbruck can be reached by a scenic train/tram ride.

The Hotel Stubaierhof and the Hotel Alte Post are both recommended. Restaurants include the Leonardo Da Vinci ('very popular and good value') and the Gasthaus Hofer, which serves 'simple, plain Austrian farmhouse fare'. The Café Corso, the Ossi-Keller, Platzwirt and Dorfalm discos make it a lively place by night.

TOURIST OFFICE
Tel 43 5225 2235/2892
Fax 43 5225 3843

Igls
top 2247m (7,372ft) bottom 893m (2,930ft)

Igls, 5km up towards the Europabrücke and the Italian border, has the best skiing in the immediate area and is a fine example of a traditional Tyrolean village. The skiing is served by a cable car, a chair-lift and four T-bars, and consists of four runs cut through the trees. The red Olympic downhill presents a challenge on the front face of the mountain. It was here that Franz Klammer threw caution to the wind in 1972 and hurled himself down the mountain to win the greatest Winter Olympics gold of all time. The blue Familienabfahrt follows a less direct route. There are off-piste opportunities from the top of the Gipfel lift. New snowmaking on the Patscherkofel should improve conditions this season.

There are four mountain restaurants, most of them criticised for their high prices, although the one at the top of the cable car receives considerable praise.

The resort manages to support two ski schools, Igls 2000 and Schigls; instructors at both speak good English. The two nursery slopes are covered by snow-cannon and are a five-minute walk from the village centre. A non-ski kindergarten operates from 9am to 5pm. The children's ski school operates between 10am and 4pm, with lunch in the kindergarten.

The village is small and uncommercialised. It has sedate hotels and coffee houses, excellent walks for non-skiers, and the Olympic bob-run, which is open to the public and, according to one reporter, is 'totally brilliant'. The Sporthotel Igls is a smart hotel with a sports and fitness centre and is recommended for its cuisine. The Schlosshotel also rates five stars and is warmly praised. Kurzentrum Parkhotel offers a variety of health-cure treatments. The Astoria and the Batzenhausl are both traditional, family-run establishments. There are two supermarkets for self-caterers.

Après-ski is not the strongest point of Igls, but the bars at the Bon Alpina and the Astoria are the livelier spots. The Sporthotel disco is open until late.

TOURIST OFFICE
Tel 43 512 377101
Fax 43 512 378965

Neustift
top 3200m (10,499ft) bottom 1000m (3,281ft)

The centre of the broad and lush Stubaital, and its main community, Neustift is a large, spread-out village, which has seen great expansion in recent years. Nevertheless, it remains very much at heart the traditional Tyrolean village, centred around one of the more magnificent and ornately decorated churches in this corner of Austria.

Recommended hotels include the Tirolerhof ('excellent food and a warm welcome') and the budget-priced and quaint Hotel Angelika in the centre of town. Nightlife is noisy in the Romanastuben with 'Austrian music, but a great, fun atmosphere'. The Sumpflöchl in the Hotel Stubaierhof is also popular. Neustift has its own gentle ski area on wooded north-facing slopes, but it is also the hotel base for the more important skiing on the Stubai Glacier, 20 minutes away at the end of the valley. A free ski bus operates regularly.

The skiing here is open most of the year, and it is one of the most extensive summer ski areas in Europe. The old four-seater gondola from the base-station at Mutterbergalm has been supplemented by a six-person gondola running in parallel to the first stage at Fernau. From here you can either continue by gondola or chair-lift to a network of drags, which take you up to the top of the ski area. When snow is short elsewhere, the slopes can become unbelievably crowded and, out of season, German bank holidays are to be avoided. The glacial ski area is also extremely well-equipped and efficiently run. The ski shop at the top-station is highly recommended for repairs as most of its customers outside the winter months are international racing teams.

Keen skiers will stay in the Alpensporthotel Mutterberg, a comfortable establishment right at the base of the lifts. It has its own swimming-pool, disco and bowling alley, which is just as well as it is particularly isolated. Separate ski schools operate in both Neustift and on the glacier, and each has a kindergarten. The Stubai Superskipass covers a small area at Milders and all the assorted lifts in the valley.

TOURIST OFFICE
Tel 43 5226 2228
Fax 43 5226 2529

Seefeld
top 2100m (6,890ft) 1200m (3,937ft)

Seefeld is a tiny version of Salzburg, Innsbruck, Kitzbühel and the other beautiful towns of Austria, with its frescoed houses and medieval architecture. Everything about the village shouts style and sophistication: the seven luxury hotels, a casino, an extensive health centre, horse-drawn sleighs and a pedestrianised village centre, complete with exclusive jewellery shops, sports shops and boutiques.

Seefeld's main winter activity is cross-country skiing. However, there are also three small, pisted ski-areas for those who want to try their hand at alpine skiing in beautiful surroundings: Geigenbühel is the nursery slope area, Gschwandtkopf is a low peak next to the cross-country loipe which is used mainly by the ski school, and Rosshütte is a more extensive area with steeper runs and a long, satisfying off-piste trail. All three areas are reached from the village centre by the free bus-service.

Rosshütte is the main eating-place in the area of the same name. It has a large sun-terrace filled with a throng of skiers and non-skiers at lunch-time. The restaurant on the Gschwandtkopf mountain is recommended, as is the Café Christina, which is waiter-service only. The Sportalm restaurant is conveniently situated next to the Olympia Sport and Congress Centre and at the base of the Gschwandtkopf.

Seefeld boasts some unusual and exotic hotels including the five-star Klosterbräu, a former sixteenth-century monastery with indoor and outdoor swimming-pools and a Roman sauna with steam grotto. The Creativhotel Viktoria's rooms are individually decorated to reflect different periods and places from Tibet to New York. On a more reasonable price scale the family-run Hotel Bergland is in a quiet location on the edge of the pedestrian zone. Another four-star is the Best Western Karwendelhof, which is conveniently placed across the road from the railway station, adjoining the casino and on the edge of the pedestrian zone. The Kaltschmidt has 'palatial apartments' and is 'very handy for the nursery slope with a nice pool on the fourth floor'. The luxury Gartenhotel Tümmlerhof is set in its own park and offers all-day childcare as well as a children's playground. The resort kindergarten is based in the Olympia Sport and Congress Centre.

Gourmets can try the Alte Stube in the Hotel Karwendelhof, and the many alternative eating-places include Beim Jörg, the Diana Stüberl and the Seefelderstuben. A handful of Italian restaurants are available for those who do not appreciate Austrian food, including Emilia Romagna, Da Pino's, Pizzeria Angelo and Pizzeria Don Camillo.

Café Nanni and Café Moccamühle are popular after-skiing places for a drink or snack. The Big Ben bar is as English as its name suggests, with an old red telephone box; the Brittania Inn is another popular English pub. Monroe's disco-bar attracts the late-night crowd, as do the Miramare and the popular Postbar in the Hotel Post. The Kanne in the Hotel Klosterbräu, the centre of the village's social life, has live music at night as well as tea-dancing. Reporters also recommend the Lammkeller in Hotel Lamm. The bar Fledermaus has live jazz in the evenings. The casino is worth a visit, but men are obliged to wear a jacket and tie.

Non-skiing activities include riding down the bobsleigh run on an innertube. The Olympia Sport and Congress Centre houses a 'saunarium' which includes a rock sauna, steam sauna and grotto. Its indoor-outdoor swimming-pool has a whirlpool and a waterslide.

Snowboarding

Axamer Lizum is one of the top snowboarding resorts in Austria and is particularly popular with freestyle riders. The resort is busy at weekends because of its proximity to Innsbruck. The snowboard park is well-maintained, with a half-pipe, and there are plenty of competent local riders for company. Alpine riders are also well catered for, with a high proportion of wide open pistes to the relatively small size of resort.

Cross-country

Seefeld is a year-round resort, and in winter cross-country skiing is its *raison d'être*. Cross-country started here as a recreational sport in 1964 when Seefeld hosted the Winter Olympics Nordic events. The resort then went on to host the events in the 1976 Winter Olympics and in the 1985 Nordic World Championships.

The excellent facilities include a team of specialist cross-country instructors at the Nordic Ski School in the Olympia Sport and Congress Centre. The 200km of loipe are mechanically prepared here, and a special cross-country trail map is available from the tourist office.

TOURIST OFFICE
Tel 43 5212 2313
Fax 43 5212 3355

Ischgl

ALTITUDE 1400m (4,592ft)

Ischgl was formerly the exclusive domaine of wealthy German skiers who regarded it as the most important winter destination in Austria. In recent years it has steadily raised its profile and lives up to its reputation as one of Austria's most snowsure and upmarket resorts. Geographically, it is a near neighbour of awesome St Anton, yet it has somehow managed to remain largely unknown internationally.

A major criticism in the past has been the high-season lift queues to which the joint Austro–Swiss ski area was prone, but these have greatly been resolved by the introduction last season of the largest double-decker cable car in the world.

If Hannes Schneider, founder of the Arlberg Ski School, had been born in the remote and beautiful Paznaun Valley instead of Stuben in the St Anton ski area, history might have smiled more favourably on this delightful resort. As it was, Ernest Hemingway was about the only celebrity to root for Ischgl. He dropped in one afternoon in 1925 and became so entranced with the region that he stayed for the season.

An increasing number of skiers are now discovering that Ischgl provides the near-perfect mix of skiing and snow reliability together with alpine charm; it has an extensive ski area and some of the liveliest nightlife in Austria. The skiing is linked with duty-free **Samnaun** in Switzerland. As well as bargain shopping, the Swiss side of the mountain has the better restaurants and some of the best skiing in the area. The new cable car makes it an attractive, alternative base from which to explore the skiing.

> ### ■ GOOD POINTS
> Reliable snow cover, variety of easy runs, large ski area, beautiful scenery, alpine charm, ski-touring possibilities, lively nightlife
>
> ### ■ BAD POINTS
> Few challenging runs, high prices, lack of mountain restaurants (on Austrian side)

On the mountain
top 2864m (9,394ft) bottom 1377m (4,517ft)

The skiing consists of mainly open slopes above Ischgl; long descents through woods to the village and a series of high, rocky bowls above with plenty of open, easy pistes. A long mountain crest, which forms the Austro–Swiss border, is reached by lift and is easily accessible on skis in a number of places, opening up a less extensive but delightful area on the Swiss side above Samnaun. The slopes on the Ischgl side face north-west and west, while on the Samnaun side they look mainly south and east.

Mountain access from Ischgl is from both ends of the village: two gondolas take you up to Idalp, a broad and sunny, open plateau with a ski school, restaurants, hotel and nursery slopes. A third gondola ascends to Pardatschgrat, 300m higher, with runs back down to Ischgl or an easy connection with the rest of the lift system via Idalp.

In the past, Ischgl has suffered from terrible queues, which came about largely because the Austrian side of the frontier ridge had almost twice the uphill capacity of the Swiss side. On the first sunny day of each week Ischgl-based skiers took a day trip to Samnaun with disastrous queuing consequences when they tried to return home.

The problem has been alleviated by the introduction of the 180-person double-decker cable car from Ravaisch, 3km from Samnaun to Alptrida Sattel. The quad-chair from Alptrida to Idjoch helps the flow of skiers, but a direct lift from Alptrida Sattel to Greitspitz on the border ridge is the ultimate solution. However, this wearily remains as a dotted 'projekt' line on the piste-map.

Grandiose plans for a new Silvrettabahn access gondola from Ischgl, together with an underground tunnel with an airport-style people-mover, have been put back for at least another season.

Beginners

A short tow at the northern end of the village can be used by novices if snow conditions permit. Otherwise, beginners head up to the plateau at Idalp where there is an extensive variety of blue (easy) runs. Number 8 is usually busy with ski school classes, but it is a place to find your ski legs. After gaining a little confidence, skiers should be able to tackle the long run down from Inneres Viderjoch on the border ridge. However, readers point out that most blues here have the occasionally vicious red (intermediate) patch and you should explore with caution. It seems a pity that there is no blue run back to the village. Beginners have no sensible choice but to return by gondola.

Intermediates

Many of the red runs are long enough to test most intermediates to the full. A long and enclosed chair-lift, which provides necessary protection against the weather in mid-winter, takes you from Gampen Alp up to Palinkopf. It is relatively little-used and number 40 is a scenically beautiful descent for accomplished skiers; on the other side of the ridge number 80 takes you all the way down to Samnaun. Number 20, from the top of the Palinkopfbahn, is an interesting and challenging run, which leads on into blue 24 and takes you to the Höllkar Parallellifte.

Advanced

Ischgl's skiing contains few really difficult runs. The pistes down to Ischgl from Pardatschgrat are among the best for accomplished skiers, some of them giving an uninterrupted and demanding 1200m vertical across open slopes and on down through swathes cut through the trees. These runs are graded intermediate or difficult. Black (difficult) run

55

number 4 down to the mid-station seems more worthy of a red classification. In the late afternoon these runs become crowded with skiers who
cannot always handle the terrain, making it hazardous for themselves
and for those skiers who can. Elsewhere in the resort, piste-grading
seems mixed.

Off-piste

The off-piste and more exacting touring possibilities in the region are
extensive and, importantly, because Ischgl does not have the fashionable
cachet of St Anton, it does not immediately become 'skied out' after a
proper snowfall. Piz Val Gronda at the top of the Fimbatal has been ear-
marked as a potential projection of the lift system, with long runs down
the back past the Heidelberger Hütte as well as down the front face to
link into number 40. However, for the moment, powder enthusiasts
must hoof it to the top on skins for their own private descents.

Ski schools and guiding

The Silvretta Ski School has retained a solid reputation over many years
but, according to some reports, the lack of competition can lead to complacency. One reporter encountered an English-speaking instructor who
insisted on conducting the class only in German. Another spoke of
'chaos and time loss' as the classes were organised at the beginning of
the week. In fact, most instructors speak good English. The number of
pupils in a class ranges from 10 to 12.

Off-piste tours can be arranged through the ski school in what is
exceptional ski-touring terrain, particularly late in the season. Stefan
Wolf is the local guiding company.

Snowboarding

Both Ischgl and Samnaun have their own permanent half-pipes for
snowboarders. The village was the venue for the 1991 European
Snowboard Championships and has taken the sport seriously ever since.

Cross-country

A panoramic loipe leads up the Silvretta to Galtür where it joins a more
challenging high-altitude circuit. In all there are 28km of prepared tracks
of varying degrees of difficulty.

Mountain restaurants

The Paznauer Taja is recommended for its 'truly wonderful panoramic
views' and it sometimes has a live band on the terrace. Nearby Bodenalp
('hard to reach, but worth it') is an attractive alternative, as is the pleasant hut at the bottom of the Höllenkar. The restaurant at the foot of the
nursery slope in Alptrida is reportedly good, provided you avoid peak
hours. All reporters found a noticeably higher standard of cuisine on the
Swiss side ('try the *Rösti*'). The absence of duty is not noticeable in
restaurant prices, which are in Swiss francs, although Austrian schillings
are accepted everywhere.

Off the mountain

Ischgl is an old village, which has developed in a harmonious way with a high standard of new buildings and accommodation, and a high price level to go with it. What the 50 working farmers lose on EC cheese prices they recoup in winter lets. More recent building is said to be less, rather than more, environmentally conscious in conception and some hotels are in danger of losing their traditional character with the addition of charmless modern extensions. The centre positively bustles with activity and excitement in the early evening. The remainder of the village sprawls along the valley in the shadow of the steep,

> ### ■ OTHER SPORTS
> Parapente, skating, indoor tennis, indoor climbing, swimming, sleigh-rides, tobogganing at Kappl

wooded mountainside, which makes up the ski slopes. Parts of the village are hilly, with several staircases and steep paths that can become dangerously icy.

A free ski-bus service links Ischgl, **Kappl** and **Galtür** infrequently during the day and not in the evening. There are interesting walks for non-skiers, both in the valley and up the mountain to the restaurants at Bodenalp. The Silvretta Sports Centre has a swimming-pool and a bowling alley. The farming museum at Mathon on the bus route to Galtür is also worth a visit.

Accommodation

Much of the accommodation is centred around the lift departure points at either end of the village. Although Ischgl has grown in recent years, it takes only a few minutes to walk from one end to the other and therefore location is not a priority in choosing where to stay. The Goldener Adler, near the Silvretta gondola, is described as 'a fine example of a proper Austrian hostelry in the old style'. The Post is centrally positioned. The Antony, on a hillside opposite the village, is 'very pleasant, with spacious rooms and excellent food'. Pension Paznaunhof is said to be 'very clean with a good breakfast in a pleasant atmosphere'.

The Albona is situated far enough from the centre to be quiet, but still convenient for the gondola. It is recommended for its 'outstanding food'. One guest complained that the British were housed in the basement, while Germans had rooms on the upper floors ('handy for the sauna, but lacking in views'). Hotel Verwall has 'comfortable family rooms, friendly staff, and a predominance of German guests'. Hotel Elizabeth is said to be 'excellent, with fine food and service, a swimming-pool and sauna'. Hotel Solaria, which has come under considerable criticism in the past for the attitude problem of the staff, has reportedly improved. Some of the outlying gasthofs operate a courtesy mini-bus service.

Eating in and out

Most of the restaurants are in the hotels and one reporter comments on the 'sameness' of both menus and prices. The best eating places are tucked away from the main street. The Trofana Alm bar-restaurant has a warm atmosphere and 'delicious pizza cooked on a wood-burning stove, with an interesting salad table'. The Goldener Adler is recommended for mouth-watering fresh trout and other gourmet food in its wonderful traditional setting. Niki's Stadl in the Piz Buin Hotel and the restaurant at the Hotel Tyrol are also worthy of note. The Sports Centre is suggested for good-value food and 'the lack of atmosphere was compensated for by the lack of cigarette smoke'. Popular fondue expeditions to the Heidelberger Hütte by snowcat or horse-drawn sleigh are organised most evenings.

Après-ski

Ischgl becomes extremely lively when the lifts are closed for the night. Action starts at the outdoor bar of the Hotel Elizabeth. One reporter claimed the village square was virtually taken over from 4pm to 6pm by Scandinavians. 'The Trofana Alm is the place to go if you are up to it. Dancing on the tables, loud music and much alcohol flowing — but no loutish behaviour.' Later on the Tenne is popular. Nicki's Stadl and the Kitzloch are recommended for 'real early evening Austrian après-ski'. Tea-dancing, that ancient Austrian courtship ritual from which no doubt the Manhattan singles bar was derived, is alive and flourishing in Ischgl. There is also plenty of traditional entertainment of the yodel-and-schühplatte variety, complete with log-chopping.

For a quieter coffee and cakes, reporters recommend the Konditorei Salner and the Dorfcafé. Thommy's Bar is suggested for those who want a quiet drink. The Madlein Wunderbar has a reputation for being the hot spot in town with live action including strip shows ('come and meet 300 of the Tyrol's prettiest girls'), which one reader found 'pretty offensive'. Another commented on the '60s and '70s evening: 'Whatever Austrians were listening to in these two decades, it never reached England, thank God'.

Childcare

The main nursery slopes are a 20-minute cable car ride up the mountain, but there is also a nursery drag-lift near the village. Three hotels have crèches as well as the Gästekindergarten at Idalp, which takes potty-trained children and, although inconveniently situated up the mountain, is warmly recommended by reporters. One reporter commented: 'Don't be put off by the primitive nursery conditions, the staff are charming and make up for the lack of amenities'.

Linked or nearby resorts

Galtür
top 2300m (7,546ft) bottom 1585m (5,200ft)
This pleasant little Austrian village is only a few minutes' drive from Ischgl but offers an altogether more relaxing, crowd-free environment coupled with limited but interesting skiing. It has a total capacity of 3,500 visitor beds and it is certainly not tiny. It enjoys a sunnier position

than Ischgl at the widening head of the valley. The lifts are a bus ride away at **Wirl**. Buses are reliable and frequent but only run during peak hours; the more energetic can pole their way home at the end of the day.

Avalanche slopes on both sides of the village mean that it can be completely isolated for short periods after a major storm. The main access to the slopes is by a covered chair and the skiing is concentrated on a series of interesting red and black runs down a wide, undulating bowl. The skiing immediately above Wirl is of a more intermediate nature with a couple of long blues giving nearly 600m vertical, and an assortment of easy reds. Lift queues are non-existent and one reporter describes the skiing as 'the perfect example of how skiing should be everywhere: no queues, well organised, pretty and reasonably varied for a small resort'.

The two mountain restaurants are said to be adequate, with the one near the main chair-lift offering the best food and prices. The ski school is recommended for 'friendly and competent teaching'. The kindergarten takes children aged three years and over, and we have glowing reports of the standard of child instruction.

The nightlife is much quieter than in Ischgl, but there are a number of cheerful bars, some with live music and tea-dancing, including the popular La Tschuetta. The Hotel Rössle is recommended for its comfortable rooms and 'the best restaurant in the village'. The Hotel Post and the Fluchthorn are centrally located, and the Ballunspitze is slightly further out but an equally sound choice. The family-run Alpenrose is 'quiet, very welcoming, and offers excellent food'. We have good reports of the Alp Aren apartments ('luxurious with colour television, coffee machine, and dishwasher'). The hotels at Wirl are isolated, but have their own excellent facilities. The Almhof is said to serve good-value lunches and has a swimming-pool. The Wirlerhof is a convenient place to stay with children.

Other activities here include skating and curling, a floodlit tobogganing run and the smart sports centre, which has a swimming-pool, squash, tennis and bowling.

TOURIST OFFICE
Tel 43 5443 521
Fax 43 5443 52176

Samnaun
top 2864m (9,394ft) bottom 1840m (6,035ft)

Samnaun is one of those anomalous communities in high, cul-de-sac corners of the Alps, which has stayed alive thanks to its duty-free status coupled with its existence as a ski resort. This Swiss village is not exactly booming; it is little more than a large cluster of shops, hotels and supermarkets selling electrical goods, cigarettes and alcohol. Petrol is very cheap, but ski equipment and perfume are not such great bargains. The shops thoughtfully sell backpacks.

The new double-decker cable car now makes Samnaun an attractive base for the ski area. The lift starts from **Raveisch**, a three-minute free bus ride from the village, and you have to walk to the edge of Samnaun

Skiing facts: **Ischgl**

TOURIST OFFICE
Postfach 24, A-6561 Ischgl, Tyrol
Tel 43 5444 5266-0
Fax 43 5444 5636

THE RESORT
By road Calais 1017km
By rail Landeck 30km, frequent buses from station
By air Innsbruck 1½ hrs
Visitor beds 8,000
Transport free bus service (with guest card) links Ischgl, Kappl and Galtür

THE SKIING
Linked or nearby resorts Samnaun (l), Galtür (n), Kappl (n)
Longest run Idjoch–Ischgl, 7km (red)
Number of lifts 41
Total of trails/pistes 200km (27% easy, 63% intermediate, 10% difficult)
Nursery slopes 3 lifts
Summer skiing none
Snowmaking 40 hectares covered

LIFT PASSES
Area pass Silvretta Ski Pass (covers Ischgl, Samnaun, Galtür, Kappl and See) ÖS2,390 for 6 days, VIP pass ÖS1,850 for 6 days

Day pass OS380 (Ischgl/Samnaun)
Beginners books of tickets
Pensioners ÖS1,350 for 60 yrs and over
Credit cards accepted no

SKI SCHOOLS
Adults Silvretta Ski School, 9am-midday and 1.30-3.30pm, ÖS1,380-1,450 for 6 days
Private lessons ÖS2,000 per day
Snowboarding ÖS1,200 for 3 half-days
Cross-country as regular ski school. Loipe 28km
Other courses telemark
Guiding companies Stefan Wolf

CHILDREN
Lift pass ÖS1,145 for 6 days
Ski kindergarten 3-5 yrs, ÖS580 per day including lunch, or ÖS1,930 for 6 days
Ski school 4 yrs and over, ÖS1,780-1,930 for 6 days including lunch
Non-ski kindergarten Children's Room at the Idalp, 4 yrs and under, 10am-4pm, ÖS170 per day, extra ÖS75 per day for lunch

FOOD AND DRINK PRICES
Coffee ÖS25, glass of wine ÖS15-18, small beer ÖS25, dish of the day ÖS70

---

to catch it; readers say this is no real inconvenience. The four-star Hotel Montana is enthusiastically recommended ('the find of a lifetime'). The village has a 10-km cross-country track plus a ski school, which specialises in organising ski-tours and has a kindergarten at Alptrida. Access by car is from the Inn Valley south of Landeck, not far from **Serfaus** and **Nauders**.

TOURIST OFFICE
Tel 41 81 8685858
Fax 41 81 8685652

Kitzbühel

ALTITUDE 760m (2,494ft)

At last, Kitzbühel has heeded the cries of its critics over the past two decades and invested in a new £13-million lift, which in a single stroke this season restores the resort to its position as one of the greatest ski towns in Europe. Kitzbühel is a walled medieval settlement of heavily buttressed buildings painted with delicate frescoes, which survives the relentless battering of a nine-month tourist season with measured aplomb. Only in April and May, and again in November when the snow has either just gone or is about to arrive, is Kitzbühel devoid of visitors.

In winter it is the one destination in the Tyrol really suitable for skiers and non-skiers alike. This contributes strongly to its international status as one of the smartest European resorts. At the heart of its world popularity is

■ GOOD POINTS

Large ski area, beautiful architecture, alpine charm, lively après-ski, wide range of activities for non-skiers, short airport transfer, extensive cross-country skiing

■ BAD POINTS

Lack of tough runs, poor snow record, heavy traffic outside pedestrian centre, lack of skiing convenience

the Hahnenkamm, the toughest downhill on the World Cup calendar. With the understandable exception of the Second World War and the occasional failure of nature to provide snow, this competition has been held here annually since 1931. In fact, the Hahnenkamm is not the race, but the name of the steepest of Kitzbühel's two separate mountains. Locals, and the visitors who each January check into a range of sumptuous four-star hotels to watch their gossamer-skinned gladiators risk all on this alpine coliseum, call it the Streif. Racers, who negotiate its tortuous twists and mighty jumps at speeds of up to 85mph, say that every survivor is a winner. However, the aura surrounding this annual event gives an entirely erroneous impression that Kitzbühel's skiing is for experts only.

When not prepared for racing, most of the Streif course is given over to the pleasant red (intermediate) *Familienabfahrt* piste, which meanders down through the trees and rolling summer pastureland to the nursery slopes on the edge of town. The notorious Mausfalle, the nastiest and most technical section, is roped strictly out-of-bounds and the recreational skier not present on race day might well wonder what the fuss is all about.

Kitzbühel's early wealth came from its key position on the trade route between Bavaria and Italy, as well as its success as a copper- and silver-mining centre in the sixteenth century, but its winter popularity has centred around skiing for over 100 years. In January 1893, local lad Franz

Reisch obtained a pair of skis by mail order from Norway, thereby introducing the sport to the Tyrol and at the same time changing the face of retail shopping.

On the mountain
top 2000m (6,562ft) bottom 760m (2,493ft)

The main skiing is divided between two mountains: the Kitzbüheler Horn and the more challenging Hahnenkamm. For an international resort of its standing, the Kitzbühel lift system has long been a disgrace. The Hahnenkamm cable car was built in 1928 and continued to function until the end of last season with the kind of obscene queues its manufacturers simply could not have imagined 68 years ago. Two-hour morning waits were not uncommon and the introduction of a tedious timed-ticket system barely papered over the problem. All that has now changed. A new six-person gondola will be in operation by the start of the 1996–7 season, increasing uphill capacity from 400 to 2,000 skiers per hour. The old mountain station will become a museum as the new gondola docks in a restaurant complex slightly higher up the mountain.

The new lift has been installed against a background of considerable opposition from a lobby of locals who feel the old lift was a part of the fabric of Kitzbühel. It argued that the gondola would merely replace early-morning queues with overcrowded pistes. The compromise is a lift of more limited capacity than the situation demanded, but at peak times skiers still have the option of taking a ski bus to the hamlet of **Klausen**, which is 3km away on the road to **Kirchberg**. From here the Fleckalm gondola takes them swiftly into the lift system.

■ **WHAT'S NEW**

Opening of Hahnenkamm gondola for 1996-7 season

Alternatively, you can plod across the nursery slopes to the two-stage Streifalm chair, which deposits you at a slightly higher point than the cable car. From here an interesting network of mainly red and blue (easy) cruising runs spreads out down three faces of the mountain and surrounding 'peaklets' over undulating terrain to form the largest and most challenging of Kitzbühel's two main ski areas.

Lift connections are not all they should be, and a couple of notorious bottlenecks can result in annoying queues during high-season weeks. However, even though the area is confined, the variety of runs and scenery gives you a pleasant impression that you are going somewhere rather than skiing the same slopes over and over again.

Kitzbühel's second ski area is the Kitzbüheler Horn to the east of town, across the main road and the railway tracks. It towers above the resort, a distorted but beautiful pyramid of rock and ice. A cable car takes you up to 2000m, the highest point in the area, where the views from the top of the rocky Wilde Kaiser peaks are spectacular. The skiing is pleasant and gentle, but experienced skiers will quickly find the Horn a disappointment, with pistes much easier than they are graded. Only

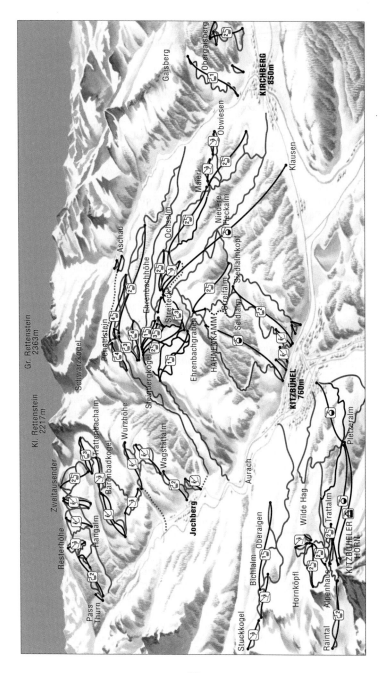

when conditions are bad do the runs become more difficult; towards the bottom of the mountain this is often because they mostly face south-west.

Aurach, a ten-minute ski bus ride away from Kitzbühel, is a third separate region served by a single-chair and a couple of drag-lifts, which provide access to three gentle blue runs and a marginally steeper reddish alternative. These are hardly skied and, if there has been a fresh snowfall, they are worthy of a morning's skiing.

The £13 million splashed out on the new Hahnenkammbahn is money well spent, but Kitzbühel's insuperable problem is its lack of altitude. Outside the middle winter weeks you must be prepared to accept slushy conditions as the norm — at least at lower levels — and be grateful if they are otherwise. However, snowmaking was successfully introduced on the Streif four years ago, and the network of snow-cannon is being slowly extended.

Beginners

Kitzbühel has four good nursery slopes near the town and plenty of easy skiing for second-weekers. The blue Pengelstein run from the top of the chair of the same name all the way down to Kirchberg is one of the best in the resort.

Over on the Kitzbüheler Horn, the long Hagstein blue run (number 3 on the piste-map) is a gentle but interesting cruise all the way from top to bottom. However, nervous skiers should beware of the Pletzerwald variation through the trees, which turns into a choice between an awkward red and the steep black (difficult) Horn Standard.

Intermediates

Kitzbühel is essentially a resort for cruisers. Pengelstein-Süd is a long, flowing red that starts at the top of the Pengelstein double-chair and is the gateway into the Ski Safari (see below). It brings you down to the hamlet of Trampelpfad. The Hochsaukaser red at Pengelstein is a wide, fast piste with wonderful lips and rolls — one side is usually left unprepared and becomes a challenging mogul field.

The celebrated Ski Safari, marked by elephant signposts, is an enjoyable pisted itinerary that takes you from the Hahnenkamm up the Kitzbühel Valley to **Jochberg** and **Pass Thurn**. Anyone with a couple of weeks of ski experience can manage the outing, which consists of a series of blue and gentle red runs linked by lifts along the east-facing slopes of the valley. The wooded skiing on the Wurzhöhe above Jochberg is always uncrowded and it is worth spending some time here before moving on up the valley.

Pass Thurn is an isolated ski area in its own right at the southern end of the valley, overlooking the town of Mittersill, which is the home of Blizzard skis. Wrap up well in mid-winter as it can be extremely cold. However, the broad band of runs accessed by a sole double-chair from the roadside holds the best snow in the region. The downside is that the Safari is no circuit — it can only be fully skied in one direction. To return to Kitzbühel you have to queue for a bus for the 19-km road journey from Pass Thurn. You can ski back to Jochberg, which is only 9km from home, but you may wait much longer for a bus here because most seats have already been filled by skiers joining at the Pass.

Advanced
The best of the steep skiing is reached via a network of lifts in the Ehrenbach sector of the Hahnenkamm. Try the Sedlboden and Ochsenboden. The black variation of Oxalm-Nord is part of the otherwise long intermediate run down to Kirchberg. Rettenstein at Pass Thurn is a short, sharp black, which ends up at the bottom of the Zweitausender double-chair.

Off-piste
Those who are new to off-piste skiing can find plenty of easy powder skiing close to the pistes in the Hahnenkamm area after a fresh snowfall. Pass Thurn is particularly recommended. Bichlalm is another enjoyable area for powder skiing. Kitzbühel has a specialist off-piste ski school called Ski Alpin-Kir.

Ski schools and guiding
Kitzbühel has four separate ski schools including the famous Rote Teufel (Red Devils). All have a generally good reputation and the resulting competition between them is healthy indeed. However, we have had mixed reports of the Red Devils, which it seems must look to the opposition. One reporter in a class of 13 notes that 'the instructor was a gloomy soul, older than usual, and his English was pretty basic'. There are a number of complaints regarding oversized classes and instruction that amounted to little more than guiding, with no individual tuition.

Snowboarding
There is a special half-pipe for snowboarders on the Kitzbüheler Horn and all the ski schools offer lessons. Boards can be rented from Heinz Snowboard Center at the Horn and from Snow Fun Center at the Hahnenkamm.

Cross-country
Both the Red Devils and Total schools have langlauf instructors who organise lessons for all standards on Kitzbühel's four loipe, which total 30km. There are a further 120km of prepared tracks in Kirchberg, **Aschau**, **Reith**, **St Johann**, Pass Thurn and around Mittersill. All are easily accessible by free ski bus.

Mountain restaurants
The Alpenrose at the top of the Kitzbüheler Horn is noted for its *Germknödel* (rounded sweet dumplings). The Hagstein, also on the Horn, is 'small, reasonably priced and overflowing with charm'. The Ochsalm on the Hahnenkamm is renowned for its *Apfelstrudel*.

Trattenbergalm between Jochberg and Pass Thurn has some of the best simple food in the region. Panorama-Alm above Pass Thurn has a glass-walled bar outside to keep out the wind, and a roaring log fire and cheerful service within.

The Pengelstein restaurant has been expensively extended, but still tends to be crowded. One reporter recommends the Ehrenbach at the bottom of the Steinbergkogel summit chair for its food and because 'it is always empty'. The Brandseit ('cheap and uncrowded') is situated near the bottom of the Fleckalm gondola.

Off the mountain

The town centre is mercifully traffic-free, but the one-way ring road is usually heavily congested. Reporters consistently remark on improvements to the free ski bus service, which ferries skiers to and from the Hahnenkamm and the easier slopes of the Kitzbüheler Horn. However, the buses to surrounding villages are seriously oversubscribed at peak times. For skiing convenience Kitzbühel gets a heavy minus mark, but the overwhelmingly elegant architectural beauty of the pedestrian Vorderstadt,

■ OTHER SPORTS

Curling, skating, indoor tennis and squash, swimming, hot-air ballooning, parapente, hang-gliding, shooting range

with its backdrop of snowy mountains, makes up for all its detractions. Serious shoppers will, however, be disappointed. Apart from Louis Vuitton, the local Sportalm fashion outlet, and a scattering of ski shops and boutiques, Kitzbühel lacks the designer retailers you might expect in what is one of the most upmarket resorts in Austria.

Accommodation

For both comfort and service the Goldener Greif and the Jägerwirt head an impressive list of 16 four-star hotels. The Maria Theresia has undergone considerable refurbishment as well as improving the standard of its restaurant. The converted hunting lodge of Schloss Lebensberg, on the outskirts, offers a hedonistic level of pampering. This includes a swimming-pool, solarium, massage and Turkish bath as well as free baby-sitting on weekdays. The Tiefenbrunner has a loyal following. The formerly gloomy Hotel zur Tenne in the town centre has been dramatically refurbished and is now an upmarket establishment.

The Weisses Rössl, once the town's prominent coaching inn, is a picture of faded splendour, slightly ragged around the edges but still enormously popular. The more reasonably priced three-star Haselsberger and the Montana, near the Hahnenkamm lift, are recommended. Regular visitors praise the family-run Mühlberghof, on the edge of town. Schloss Münichau, in the village of Reith on the far side of the Schwarzsee, is a 500-year-old castle, which is said to be 'delightfully quiet, with reasonable prices and superb food'. It can be reached by ski bus, but you really need a car to stay here.

Eating in and out

Austrian alpine food wins few gastronomic prizes, but you can eat better and with more variety in Kitzbühel than in most resorts. The Tennerhof is acknowledged as the best restaurant in town, and this is where you will find the wealthier locals. The Goldener Greif is renowned for its *Salzburgerknockerl*, a kind of hot meringue soufflé. The chef in the Hotel zur Tenne in the Vorderstadt specialises in a variety of unusual ways of cooking fresh trout. The Huberbräu Stüberl serves excellent *Wienerschnitzel* in an intimate atmosphere. Landgasthof Oberaigen at the Bichlalm mid-station offers 'an enjoyable evening out, with wholesome cooking and a mountain ambience'. Chinarestaurant Peking in the Kirchplatz rings the culinary changes. The existence of a McDonald's seems a shame in such beautiful surroundings, but its presence is muted.

Après-ski

Life after skiing revolves almost entirely around the pedestrian-only streets in the centre. Praxmair is the original coffee house and brasserie where you will find more locals than tourists. The Goldener Gams, also in the Vorderstadt, is a modest restaurant and bar with live music and a sophisticated Tyrolean atmosphere that attracts all ages. 'S Lichtl, in the same road, is a bar with a warm atmosphere. Big Ben and The Londoner are noisy pubs, which act as a magnet for every young Brit in town.

Seppi's Pub is where Austria meets London's Old Kent Road. One reporter recommends La Fonda, opposite the casino, for a quiet drink. Biwak, in Bichlstrasse, is a small and trendy drinking spot. The Happy Horse, at the back of the Hotel Postkutsch, a five-minute walk from the centre, is a cheap and cheerful disco-bar that closes at midnight. The late-night crowd move on to the Royal Dancing and K and K discos, both in the Hinterstadt. The Aquarena health centre is free to those with a ski pass.

Childcare

Five lifts make up the extensive nursery area on the golf course at the foot of the Hahnenkamm. There is a ski kindergarten in the resort, which has been joined recently by a non-ski kindergarten run by Anita Halder. The end-of-season Easter Bunny Package, promoted by the tourist board, is extremely good value: children up to 15 years are offered free lift pass, ski or board rental, lessons and accommodation in a room shared with parents.

Linked or nearby resorts

Kirchberg
top 2000m (6,562ft) bottom 850m (2,788ft)

Once upon a time Kirchberg was the no-frills dormitory village that gave you a back door into Kitzbühel's skiing at knockdown prices, but without its medieval charm. This once poor relation, only a couple of kilo-

Skiing facts: **Kitzbühel**

TOURIST OFFICE
A-6370 Kitzbühel, Tyrol
Tel 43 5356 21550
Fax 43 5356 2307

THE RESORT
By road Calais 1130km
By rail station in resort
By air Salzburg 1½ hrs, Munich 2½ hrs, Innsbruck 2 hrs
Visitor beds 7,300
Transport free ski bus

THE SKIING
Linked or nearby resorts Kirchberg (l), Jochberg (l), Pass Thurn (l), St Johann in Tyrol (n), Aurach (n)
Longest run Pengelstein Süd, 6.8km (red)
Number of lifts 28 in Kitzbühel, 64 in linked area
Total of trails/pistes 60km in Kitzbühel, 160km in linked area (39% easy, 46% intermediate, 15% difficult)
Nursery slopes 5 lifts in Kitzbühel, 7 in linked area
Summer skiing none
Snowmaking 10.5km covered in Kitzbühel, 12.5km covered in linked area

LIFT PASSES
Area pass (covers Kitzbühel, Kirchberg, Jochberg, Pass Thurn and includes ski bus, swimming-pool and reduction for sauna) ÖS1,890 for 6 days
Day pass ÖS390
Beginners points cards
Pensioners 20% reduction for women 60 yrs and over and men 65 yrs and over
Credit cards accepted no

SKI SCHOOLS
Adults Red Devils and Total ÖS1,400 for 6 days, Kitzbüheler Horn ÖS1,350 for 5 days, Hahnenkamm ÖS1,500 for 5 days, all 9am-4pm
Private lessons Red Devils and Total, ÖS2,100 per day, Kitzbüheler Horn prices on demand, Hahnenkamm ÖS1,900 per day
Snowboarding Red Devils, ÖS2,100 for 6 days, prices of other ski schools on demand
Cross-country Red Devils, ÖS1,500 for 6 days. Loipe 30km in Kitzbühel, 120km in area
Other courses telemark
Guiding companies Ski Alpin-Kir and through ski schools

CHILDREN
Lift pass ÖS945 for 6 days
Ski kindergarten Total, ÖS1,400 for 6 days, Hahnenkamm ÖS1,800 for 6 days, Kitzbüheler Horn ÖS1,650 for 5 days. All 3-14 yrs and extra ÖS80 per day for lunch, times as adults
Ski school all ski schools, 3-14 yrs, 9am-4pm, ÖS1,400 for 6 days, extra ÖS80 per day for lunch
Non-ski kindergarten Anita Halder, ÖS80 per hour or ÖS400 per day, including meals

FOOD AND DRINK PRICES
Coffee ÖS23, glass of wine ÖS30, small beer ÖS30, dish of the day ÖS95

metres around the shoulder of the Hahnenkamm at the head of the Brixental, still gives alternative access to Kitzbühel's main ski area, but its personal circumstances have changed and it now boasts an astonishing 25 three- and four-star hotels.

Kirchberg has its own small beginner and intermediate lifts on the Gaisberg, as well as access to the Hahnenkamm by a two-stage chair and the Klausen gondola. It has a kindergarten and two ski schools. The town's layout is not designed for skiing convenience; distances are considerable and the ski bus service is seriously oversubscribed. Choose your accommodation with care in relation to both price and where you want to ski.

The Tiroler Adler Schlössl, run by the Egger family, is neither particularly convenient nor cheap, but is one of the best in town. The less expensive Landhaus Brauns looks not just towards the West but also to Austria's newer ski market — owner Gabriele Schmolz and her staff speak Polish, Russian and Czech. The nightlife is just as busy as in Kitzbühel, but less sophisticated. Charley's Club and Le Moustache are among the main centres of activity.

TOURIST OFFICE
Tel 43 5357 2309
Fax 43 5357 3732

Lech/Zürs

ALTITUDE Lech 1450m (4,756ft), Zürs 1720m (5,642ft)

In its efforts to produce the smoothest and safest of ski areas, **Lech** hit upon the idea seven years ago of paying shepherds to graze their flocks on the highest runs during the off-season months. The sheep would trim and manure the grass, thereby making a secure snow base with a reduced risk of avalanche. Unfortunately, the sheep huddled in only one area and, to the detriment of Lech's substantial summer trade, ate all the wild flowers while the shepherds smiled all the way to the village banks. Nevertheless, the failed experiment shows just how seriously Lech looks after its skiers.

In 1906 in the tiny hamlet of **Zürs**, no more than a cluster of huts and an inn at the top of the Flexenpass around the shoulder of the Valluga from **St Anton**, the first ski school in Austria was started. In 1937 Zürs went on to have the country's first T-bar, although today the ski area is proudly T-bar-free.

■ GOOD POINTS

Alpine charm, beautiful scenery, long runs, plenty of intermediate skiing, efficient lift system, varied off-piste skiing for all standards, good artificial snow cover, high standard of hotels, lack of queues, facilities for families

■ BAD POINTS

Difficult road and rail access, lack of mountain restaurants, high prices

Zürs is still little more than a collection of buildings astride the pass, albeit the huts have been replaced by four- and five-star hotels and a small assortment of marginally less exotic establishments. Lech, situated beside the river of the same name in what in winter is a closed valley, has grown into the larger and more cosmopolitan resort of the two. It is the text-book example of a charming Austrian village: a farming community centred around its onion-domed church. And despite major expansion over 35 years into a wholesale dependency on tourism, Lech has still managed to retain its rural character.

Lech continues to be no stranger to the international stage. In 1964 Egon Zimmerman, then a hotel chef, became Olympic downhill champion. In 1992 Patrick Ortlieb, born and raised in **Oberlech**, won the Olympic downhill gold, and in 1996 became downhill World Champion. This satellite, once the summer home of herdsmen and shepherds, is on the open pastureland above Lech, and is reached by cable car from the village. The collection of chalets and hotels here are ideally placed for the skiing and provide a safe and car-free centre for families with small children. The construction of a network of underground tunnels beneath the top cable-car station and the hotels means that visitors do not have to lug suitcases across the piste.

Zug, 3km through the woods from Lech up a pretty valley, also offers

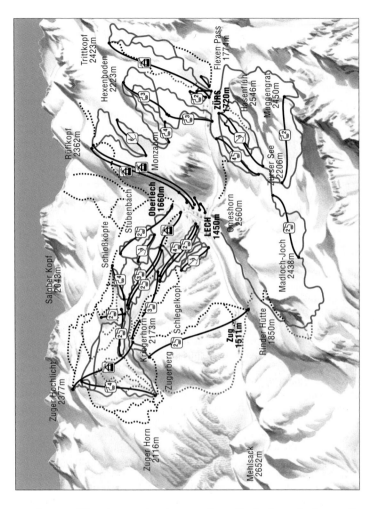

rural tranquillity. An evening journey from Lech through the starlit woods by horse-drawn sleigh is delightful and romantic. Zug is fully integrated into the lift system linking Lech with Zürs.

The resorts share a varied and extensive ski area, although advanced skiers might be more interested in the off-piste and ski-touring opportunities that abound. St Anton (40 minutes' drive away), with its larger choice of expert piste terrain, is included in the same Arlberg Ski Pass, but annoyingly the bus service is not. Reporters complain that if you only plan to ski Lech and Zürs the lift pass is extremely expensive.

Lech and Zürs lie close to the major road- and rail-link between Austria and Switzerland, but the journey is an awkward one. The

Flexenpass can be blocked for hours or, on rare occasions, days, after a major storm. Parking in both villages is restricted and ruthlessly policed.

On the mountain
top 2450m (8,036ft) bottom 1445m (4,741ft)

The Lech/Zürs circuit of 110km of prepared pistes, spread over three mountains and served by 34 lifts, provides mainly intermediate skiing of the highest quality. The circuit can be skied only in a clockwise direction, which results in crowds of people all heading for the same lifts at the same time, and used to mean high-season queues. However, the steady upgrading of the lifts has alleviated the problem; most of the chair-lifts have been speeded up and have 'moving carpets' (conveyor belts) which enable skiers to progress on to the lift more quickly.

■ **WHAT'S NEW**

Beginner lift ticket
Expansion of luggage tunnels under Oberlech

Both resorts also limit the number of skiers on the mountain at any one time and priority is given to hotel guests. Once 14,000 tickets have been sold, the tills are closed and motorway signs warn approaching day visitors to ski elsewhere. Consequently, when we skied it on what happened to be the busiest Sunday of the year we never had to wait for more than ten minutes at any lift in Lech, and the waiting times in Zürs were even shorter.

Mountain access to the circus is via the twin Rüfikopf cable cars, which scale an impressive wall from the centre of Lech, too steep to be skied directly (except in springtime, by experts) but with long, difficult and spectacular unprepared runs off the shoulder; these are often closed after a heavy snowfall. These lead down in either direction through the woods to the road by Zürs, or back to Lech via a scenic itinerary through the Wöstertäli. Alternatively, you can enjoy the lengthy and benignly beautiful pistes towards Zürs.

Lech's main skiing area, on the other side of the valley, is contrastingly open and mostly gentle, although the slopes immediately above the village are of a more challenging gradient. Mountain access on this side is by an assortment of four lifts, including a detachable quad-chair, from different points in or near the village. Above Oberlech, lifts and pistes are spread in a wide, fragmented basin below the peaks of the Kriegerhorn and the Zuger Hochlicht. The two are linked by a cable car with spectacular views.

Beginners

First-timers can get by with the new beginner's ticket and should not buy the expensive Arlberg ski pass until advised to do so by their instructor. Lech has excellent nursery slopes behind the church as well as at Oberlech. Beginners should quickly progress to a whole range of blue (easy) runs on the Oberlech side of the valley. One of the attractions of the resort for second-week skiers is that they should be able to negotiate the blue Rüfikopf run from the top of the cable car, which in turn links into the Familienabfahrt to bring them all the way to Zürs with an ego-boosting sense of achievement.

Intermediates

Confident skiers head up the Rüfikopf cable car for the choice of red (intermediate) pistes down the Hexenboden and Trittkopf. Follow the local lift map with care: appropriately coloured circles indicate pisted runs, while 'ski routes' are marked by diamonds. It is easy to think that a red diamond with a thin black border is a hard intermediate run. In fact, it is an extreme itinerary that is neither patrolled nor pisted, although some are so well skied that they turn into piste.

From Zürs you can take either the scenic Zürsertäli or choose more direct routes down to the Zürsersee and on via the Madloch towards Lech.

Advanced

Zürs has the steeper skiing of the two main resorts, including a couple of short, sharp black (difficult) pistes, notably the Hexenboden Direkte. Langerzug and Tannegg are two challenging runs down the shoulder of the Rüfikopf, and Südhang is another recommended piste. The ski-routes marked on the lift map offer considerable challenge, with number 33 from Zürs to Lech a particularly satisfying one.

Off-piste

When fresh snow falls, both Lech and Zürs are a delight. Experts can try the various descents of the 2173-m Kriegerhorn and the Zuger Hochlicht beyond it. The long run down from the top to the village of Zug via the narrow Zuger Tobel can be spectacular in the right snow conditions. Langerzug and Tannegg around the shoulder of the Rüfikopf are dramatic in the extreme. For environmental reasons, it is strictly forbidden to ski off-piste through the trees — anyone caught doing so risks having their lift pass confiscated. Ski-touring and heli-skiing are popular, and some ski school instructors we spoke to spent most of their time taking private clients heli-skiing.

Ski schools and guiding

The Austrian Ski School in Lech, Oberlech and Zürs has a particularly fine reputation and we have received no adverse reports. At the ski-school meeting area you will notice the instructors' names nailed to the class boards; the reason is that the same instructors teach the same level year after year. This means that classes do not suffer from a change of instructor mid-week or even daily, as is the case in some other resorts. The instructors speak good English, because of the international clientèle. However, one reporter said that because of a majority of German guests the instructors have to be reminded to translate. Eighty per cent of the instructors in Zürs and over fifty in Lech are booked for private rather than group lessons each day — an indication of the spending power of the clientèle.

Snowboarding

Lech has created a fun-park, which is 300m long and 100m wide. It contains obstacles such as funboxes (humps), gaps (jumps) and a quarter-pipe. Zug has a natural half-pipe when snow conditions allow. All the ski schools offer snowboarding tuition.

Cross-country

In Lech, the langlauf track starts at the skating rink and goes through Zug towards Älpele for 15km. There are shorter practice loipe from Lech to **Oberstubenbach** (1km) and at **Stubenbach** (1km).

Mountain restaurants

The choice of mountain restaurants is extremely limited, surprisingly so in an area that attracts so many discerning lunchers. This is because the hotels on the slopes in Oberlech and Zürs all serve lunch, so there is no need for other restaurants. Hotel Burg in Oberlech is consistently praised but needs to be booked in advance at weekends and during high season. The Mohnenfluh is criticised for its 'excruciatingly slow service'. The Rüfikopf restaurant (not to be confused with the burger bar) is also acclaimed ('serves mainly vegetarian food of a very high standard and is rarely crowded'). The Seekopf at Zürs is recommended. The Palmenalpe above Zug is one of the better self-service eating places of its type, provided you avoid peak hours. The Sonnenburg is another reasonable self-service.

Off the mountain

Every skiing nation has at least one ultra-smart resort, which lures the 'beautiful people' to its manicured slopes and the pampered luxury of its hotels. Austria has Lech, with Princess Diana a regular visitor along with the Dutch, Jordanian and Spanish royal families. Zürs is annually patronised by Princess Caroline of Monaco. 'Lech and Zürs', says one reporter, 'are best suited to skiers who regard cost as secondary'.

Lech was first inhabited by Swiss immigrants in the fourteenth century, and this corner still looks more towards Switzerland, its nearest neighbour, than to the main part of Austria. The modern expansion of the resort has been unobtrusive, but despite the presence of luxury hotels and designer boutiques, Lech still has a real village feel to it.

Regular, but not frequent, post buses connect Lech, Zug, Zürs, Stuben and St Anton, as well as the railhead at **Langen**. Reporters complain of overcrowding, and public transport comes to a halt in the early evening. Taxis are expensive, but there is now a late-night service called 'James' which will collect you or take you home (wherever you are staying in Lech, Zürs or Zug), as long as it is before 4am, for a set fee of ÖS40 per person. A car is only useful if you want to ski St Anton, as weekend traffic jams are hideous and parking is difficult. There is capacity for 300 cars in an underground car park beneath the church at a cost of ÖS100 for 24 hours, further open-air parking at the Stubenbach end of the village, and hotels have their own private spaces.

Non-skiers have a rather greater choice of facilities here than in most other Austrian resorts, but it can be weather-dependent. The toboggan run and the curling rink are both liable to close in warm weather or heavy snow. Non-skiers can buy return tickets on the Rüfikopf and Oberlech cable cars to join skiing friends for lunch.

Zürs stands in an isolated position above the tree-line astride the Flexenpass and lacks much of the charm of Lech, although resort-level snow is guaranteed for most of the season. It is little more than a collection of extremely smart hotels. While it may completely lack the showy gaudiness of St Moritz or Gstaad, the degree of opulence of its clientèle is often even greater — Zürs just wears it more discreetly.

Accommodation

Accommodation is mostly in comfortable and expensive hotels, plus some apartments and the occasional tour-operator chalet. The village is fairly compact, and location is not particularly important (although we recommend that families with small children stay in Oberlech). The smartest hotel, indeed one of the most celebrated five-stars in Austria, is the ornately frescoed Gasthof Post. It has only 40 rooms and you need to book a year in advance. The Arlberg, Gotthard, Krone and the Almhof Schneider are all warmly recommended by regulars. The Tannbergerhof is popular with British people and is the centre of Lech's social life.

Hotel Elizabeth is said to be 'very comfortable, with a swimming-pool that is little used'. There are numerous less formal hotels and plenty of *Fremdenzimmer* (bed-and-breakfasts) but nowhere is cheap.

In high season, rooms of any kind can be extremely hard to find. It is worth noting that even the smartest hotels do not generally accept credit cards.

■ **OTHER SPORTS**

Skating, curling, swimming, helicopter rides, indoor tennis and squash, tobogganing, sleigh rides, winter walks, paragliding

Oberlech has several comfortable hotels near the cable-car station and chalets spread widely around the hillside. The main reason for staying here is to avoid ski-school crowds on the Schlegelkopf lifts out of Lech itself, and to holiday in a car-free environment. The Sporthotel Petersboden is known for its piste-side Red Umbrella bar, and Hotel Montana is owned by Patrick Ortlieb's family. The underground tunnels linking the main hotels with the cable-car station are being extended.

Zürs has three five-star hotels, one of which is the Zürserhof. This establishment comes strongly recommended for its excellent facilities, including indoor tennis, a swimming-pool and an in-house kindergarten. Its restaurant is also highly praised. The Arkona Clubhotel Alpenrose is an all-inclusive club that caters for a mainly German clientèle. The four-star Arlberghaus receives glowing reports from readers and has a curling-rink on its roof. Zug's original inn, the Rote Wand, is now a luxury four-star hotel.

Eating in and out

Good restaurants abound, as you might expect in resorts of this calibre, but most are in hotels and none is cheap. In Lech, the Brunnenhof is strongly recommended, together with Bistro s'Caserole, Rudi's Stamperl and the Dorf Stüberl. For a special evening, Hotel Gasthof Post and the Almhof Schneider are good bets. Pizzeria Charly is consistently popular with reporters for 'sound Italian fare served with a smile, not as schilling-snatching as others'. The Käsknöpfle's food is described as 'a bit too Austrian, but the restaurant is good fun and friendly'. In Oberlech, the Ilga Kellerstübli and the Goldener Berg are famous for fondues. In Zürs, the Chesa Verde is an award-winning restaurant, while in Zug the Klösterle is highly recommended.

Après-ski

The average age of the clientèle in Lech and Zürs is higher than that of many other alpine resorts. Wherever you look you will see bronzed and fit 60-year-olds of both sexes wearing the latest in designer ski suits, as well as more youthful 30-somethings who will aspire to look like this in the autumn of their lives. Consequently, après-skiers at these resorts prefer to put their hair up, rather than let it down.

The ice-bar outside the Tannbergerhof in Lech is where, weather permitting, the evening begins in earnest as the slopes close. Guests filter inside to join in the tea-dancing, which swings into action as night falls. The hotel also hosts a disco with a good atmosphere later on in the evening. The Sidestep Bar in the Hotel Krone attracts a rival crowd of over-25s for dancing, and the Klausur Bar in Hotel Almhof Schneider is popular. After 5pm the Rüfikopf cable car transforms into a 'flying bar' for a minimum of ten guests who pay ÖS170 each; a glass of champagne is included. Sleigh rides to Zug for dinner are a treat, and you can take the cable car up to Oberlech and toboggan down afterwards (the cable car closes at 1am). The s'Pfefferkorndl bar in Lech is where skiers flock during the early evening.

Die Vernissage in Zürs is recommended, and the Zürserl in the Hotel Edelweiss is the biggest disco in town. The Rote Wand and the Sennkessel in Zug are both lively discos.

Childcare

The area lends itself well to family skiing, particularly at Oberlech, site of the main nursery slopes. A number of hotels run their own crèches, and we have good reports of the ski kindergarten, which has a mainly English-speaking staff and a sympathetic attitude. Children five years of age and under ski for ÖS100 for the whole season. The ski school takes children all day and supervises lunch (parents must remember to provide lunch money each day). However, there is no non-ski kindergarten, so privately hired baby-sitters are the only alternative.

The kindergarten in Zürs takes children from three years old and provides ski instruction for children from four years of age and upwards.

Skiing facts: **Lech/Zürs**

TOURIST OFFICE
A-6764 Lech, A-6764 Zürs, Arlberg
Tel Lech: 43 5583 21610
Zürs: 43 5583 2245
Fax Lech: 43 5583 3155
Zürs: 43 5583 2982

THE RESORT
By road Calais 1100km
By rail Langen 17km, frequent buses daily
By air Innsbruck 2 hrs, Zurich 2½ hrs
Visitor beds 6,800
Transport buses to resorts in linked area
not included in lift pass

THE SKIING
Linked or nearby resorts Zürs (l), St Anton
(n), Stuben (n), St Christoph (n), Zug (l)
Longest run Madloch – Lech, 5.2km (red)
Number of lifts 86 in linked area
Total of trails/pistes 110km in Lech
(40% easy, 40% intermediate,
20% difficult), 260km in linked area
(30% easy, 40% intermediate,
30% difficult)
Nursery slopes 4 lifts
Summer skiing none
Snowmaking 60 hectares covered

LIFT PASSES
Area pass Arlberg Ski Pass (covers Lech,
Oberlech, Zürs, Rauz, St Christoph, St
Anton, Stuben, Sonnenkopf-Klösterle)
ÖS2,060 for 6 days
Day pass ÖS455 (Arlberg)
Beginners points tickets

Pensioners Senior ticket for women
60 yrs and over, and men 65 yrs and over,
ÖS1,750 for 6 days. Snowman ticket for
seniors 80 yrs and over, ÖS100 for season
Credit cards accepted no

SKI SCHOOLS
Adults Lech and Oberlech, 9am-midday
and 1.30-5pm, ÖS1,600 for 6 days
Private lessons Lech and Oberlech,
ÖS2,140 per day
Snowboarding Lech and Oberlech ski
schools, times and prices as ski lessons
Cross-country private lessons only.
Loipe 17km
Other courses telemark, slalom,
race training
Guiding companies through Lech and
Oberlech ski schools

CHILDREN
Lift pass (covers resort and linked area)
6-15 yrs, ÖS1,240 for 6 days. Snowman
ticket for 5 yrs and under,
ÖS100 for season
Ski kindergarten Oberlech, 3½ yrs and
over, 9am-4pm, ÖS1,420 for 6 days, extra
ÖS80 per day for lunch
Ski school Lech, 12 yrs and under,
10am-3pm, ÖS1,500 for 6 days
Non-ski kindergarten not available,
babysitting service through tourist office

FOOD AND DRINK PRICES
Coffee ÖS30, glass of wine ÖS50, small
beer ÖS30, dish of the day ÖS150-250

Mayrhofen

ALTITUDE 630m (2,066ft)

Mayrhofen is a resort transformed. For years it has struggled to justify its reputation as one of the best ski learning centres in the Tyrol and its place in the top five most popular destinations in Austria. However, last season the new Penkenbahn 15-person gondola finally replaced the old cable car, which had been at the root of all Mayrhofen's problems.

For decades the resort had suffered from completely unacceptable queues during the main weeks of the year, creating a misery that led one experienced reporter to comment: 'I would frankly rather be at home in Stoke'. Overnight the frustrating waits of up to 90 minutes for the antique 50-person cable car in both directions (you cannot ski down), which had been a grim, dark feature of the resort, simply disappeared. The new lift from the centre of town has increased uphill capacity from a dismal 600 to 2,000 people per hour. 'I couldn't believe it was the same resort', said one reader. Another reporter commented: 'You no longer dread the end of the day and the crush to come down'.

Nevertheless, given that the skiing is neither convenient for beginners nor challenging enough for experts, Mayrhofen's popularity would still be an unsolved mystery unless you appreciate that mass-market tour companies operate two seasons here per year; it is a busy centre for lakes-and-mountains folk in the summer months and year-round preferential hotel rates for the tourist trade are the key.

Mayrhofen's setting in the heart of the Zillertal is certainly a beautiful one: a long and steeply wooded offshoot of the Inn Valley. Its hotels are numerous, clean and comfortable. Away from the slopes there is much to do, and the nightlife in Dutch- and British-dominated bars and discos is both raucous and energetic. The ski schools have the finest reputations for coping with beginners who do not speak German. The Zillertal Superskipass covers all lifts, buses and trains in the valley.

■ GOOD POINTS
Reputable ski school, improved lift system, lively après-ski, short airport transfer, beautiful scenery, sunny slopes, varied skiing, extensive family facilities, snow-sure glacier at Hintertux

■ BAD POINTS
Little challenging skiing, lack of skiing convenience

On the mountain
top 2250m (5,355ft) bottom 630m (2,066ft)

The skiing takes place on both sides of the valley. The main area is the Penken, which can also be reached by gondola from the village of

Schwendau (a bus-ride away to the north) and from **Finkenberg**, an inconvenient journey of equal length further up the Zillertal.

The secondary area is the Ahorn, reached by ancient cable car from a car park one kilometre from most of the accommodation. For all these lifts there is a free bus service, which is often overcrowded, although the new lift has eased the pressure on the number of skiers who want to return in the afternoon from the Horbergstal gondola at Schwendau.

The 2095-m Penkenjoch provides Mayrhofen's main skiing. The new gondola climbs over unskiable, wooded mountainside to the sunny Penken balcony just above the tree-line. Two awkwardly linked chair-lifts take you on up to the top of this rounded mountain, which naturally lends itself to varied bowl-skiing.

Beginners
The gentle slopes of the Ahorn at 2000m make an excellent beginner and lower-intermediate area surrounded by outstanding views down the Zillertal. Wide, confidence-building pistes are served by five short drag-lifts and a chair. An intermediate trail goes down through the woods to the Wiesenhof restaurant and it is possible to ski on down from here to the bottom of the Ahornbahn on the banks of the Ziller.

Intermediates
Most skiers head for the Penken. The main skiing area consists of a rel-atively narrow band of open and lightly wooded skiing on the north and south sides of the Penkenjoch. The runs are short, generally more red (intermediate) than blue (easy), with the gentlest ones back along the ridge towards Penken. Accomplished intermediates can explore the wider range of skiing, which can be reached by bus, elsewhere in the Zillertal.

Advanced
From the bottom of the Penken chairs it is possible to ski all the way down to the Horbergbahn gondola station via an ungraded route through the trees, which is steep and awkward in places; in good snow conditions this is one of the best runs in the resort for accomplished skiers.

Off-piste
From just below the Horberg gondola top-station, a double-chair climbs up to 2250m on the sunny Gerent side of the Horberg Valley. The unpisted run down beneath the lift is long and steep with pitches of around 27 degrees, which can become heavily mogulled.

Ski schools and guiding
Mayrhofen has earned a strong reputation over many years as one of the foremost ski tuition centres in the Alps. Generations of British beginners have mastered the basics here on the gentle nursery slopes of the Ahorn and Finken before moving on to other resorts that offer more of a chal-

lenge. Mayrhofen has four ski schools which promotes a healthy level of competition. The standard of all is said to be high, but encouragingly we still have particularly warm reports of the original Uli Spiess school, which seems to thrive under the challenge. Large classes in all the schools remain a high-season drawback.

Snowboarding

A snowboard park with assorted jumps is situated off the Tappenalm chair-lift and there is a half-pipe beneath the Penken lift. Snowboard Institut near the Penken gondola station is the only dedicated snowboard shop and few of the sports shops offer soft boots for hire. All the ski schools teach snowboarding.

Cross-country

Langlaufers have a choice of nine loipe totalling a respectable 20km. The longest is the Hollenzen, which starts opposite the petrol station and connects with another track by the Gasthof Zillertal. A free plan of the trails is available from the tourist office.

Mountain restaurants

Vroni's Skialm at Penkenjoch receives the most favourable reports out of a cluster of eating-places all offering much the same standard of Austrian fare. The Almstüberl by the mid-station of the Finkenberg gondola is recommended for its *Gulaschsuppe* and homemade bread. Hilde's Schitenne, a third of the way down the Tappenalm chair on Piste 8, is praised for its cosy atmosphere. The Ahorn now has three restaurants as well as the Weisenhof on the way down.

Off the mountain

Mayrhofen is a large, traditional village of chalet-style buildings with ornate frescoes. Despite the village's huge expansion into a major tourist centre, it still manages to retain its charm. It is a lively place, full of young people, and this 'fun resort' atmosphere is an enduring reason for skiers to return in successive seasons. The valley road bypasses the main part of the town and, although traffic can be heavy around the outskirts and parking is a problem, congestion in the streets is not a major drawback. Action centres on the long, wide main street, between the market-place near the station and the Penken gondola, which is busy and bustling by day and night. There is no public transport in the evening.

The resort has a modern swimming-pool with aquaslide, whirlpool and a separate children's area, as well as a sauna and solarium. There are plenty of attractive excursions to **Innsbruck** and Salzburg.

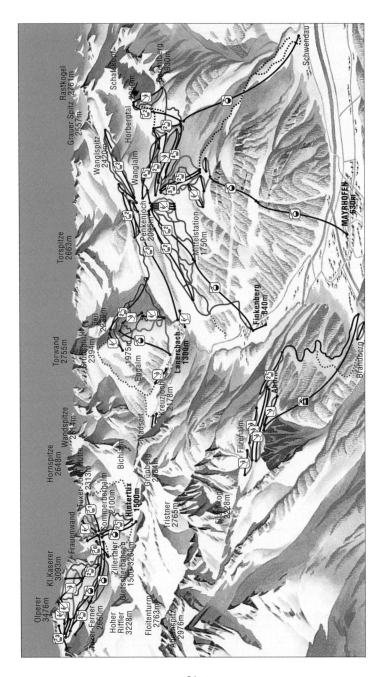

Accommodation

Most accommodation is in traditional hotels, gasthofs and small pensions with the usual high standards of service and cleanliness, if not necessarily of haute cuisine. We have favourable reports of the Hotel Neuhaus and the Landhaus annexe opposite it ('everything you expect of a fine Austrian hotel'). Hotel Strass has lively après-ski. The more expensive Sporthotel has its own squash courts. One reporter praised the Strass Chalets, family-run guesthouses at various locations throughout the village, as 'the best value I have ever found in Austria'. Hotel Pramstraller is also strongly recommended, 'although rather inconveniently situated a long walk from either lift'.

Eating in and out

Alt Ginzling, on the outskirts, is famed for its fresh trout. The 400-year-old Wirtshaus zum Griena, an old beamed farmhouse, is recommended for its traditional Austrian food and 'marvellous atmosphere'. The Neuhaus and the Alpenhotel Kramerwirt restaurants are recommended for good four-course dinners, and Die Gute Stube is a gourmet restaurant. Pizzerias include Mamma Mia, Pizzeria Manni, Pizza und Strudl, and the pizzeria at the Hotel Rose. Other recommended eating places are the Edelweiss, Mount Everest and The Sporthotel. The restaurant in Hotel Strolz caters for special diets.

Après-ski

Evening entertainment is lively by any standard, with the full range on offer from tobogganing and sleigh rides to Tyrolean evenings of thigh-slapping and yodelling, through to late-night discos. The two most popular après-ski venues are the Ice Bar next to the Penkenbahn and the Schlüssel Alm ('full of Germans, and blasts a musical combination of oompah and manic disco'). The garishly painted Rundum in Scheulingstrasse is a quieter café which serves 'gorgeous hot chocolate'. Mo's Bar has a New Orleans theme, and the Movie Bar is recommended by reporters. Arena in the Sporthotel has techno music and attracts snowboarders; the Trodelkeller is also popular. Gerry's Rock Café is a small, smoky bar with a loyal following. The Scotland Yard pub still draws a mainly British clientèle.

Childcare

Mayrhofen claims to have the best facilities for children in Austria and goes a long way towards justifying this assertion. Wuppy's Kinderland caters for children from three months to seven years of age. You can rent prams, baby-slings and cots. Ski-age children have a choice of four ski kindergarten with all-day care.

Linked or nearby resorts

The Zillertal Superskipass covers the entire valley and opens up the possibility of an enormous range of skiing. South of Mayrhofen the Zillertal splits into three smaller valleys, one of which leads on into the Tuxertal along a narrow, steeply wooded passage between the mountains, at the end of which is the **Tuxer Glacier**, Austria's steepest year-round skiing. Just above Mayrhofen, the compact little village of **Finkenberg**, home of former Olympic downhill champion Leonard Stock, shares Mayrhofen's main Penken ski area. Further on, **Vorderlanersbach** and **Lanersbach** have their own ski areas, which are tentatively planned to link into the system. For keen skiers who are happily prepared to put up with little or no après-ski, these resorts have the

■ **OTHER SPORTS**

Parapente, swimming, skating, curling, indoor tennis, squash, tobogganing, sleigh rides, winter walks

advantage of easy access to the snow-sure skiing on the glacier. A regular but oversubscribed bus service operates from Mayrhofen to **Hintertux**.

To the north of Mayrhofen, back towards the River Inn and along the banks of the Ziller that flows into it, lies an assortment of small resorts with their own ski areas. **Zell am Ziller** (not to be confused with Zell am See in Salzburgerland) is the most important of these, followed by **Kaltenbach** and **Fügenberg**. All can easily be reached by bus.

The Tuxer Glacier
top 3250m (10,663ft) bottom 1500m (4,920ft)

This provides Austria's steepest year-round skiing and for that reason is much favoured by national team downhill trainers. There is no village of Tux as such; the community is made up of Lanersbach, **Juns**, **Madseit** and Hintertux. Lanersbach has 20km of interesting open skiing on the 2300-m Eggalm slopes of the Beilspitz, as well as a further 13km of generally easier skiing on the sunny Lämmerbichl plateau. A free shuttle bus runs every 30 minutes to and from Vorderlanersbach to the bottom of the Tuxer Glacier.

The glacier is a cold and forbidding place on a harsh winter's day, but snow cover is guaranteed when much of the rest of the Tyrol is green. A rather tired gondola and parallel double-chair start a kilometre beyond the small village of Hintertux. They climb over steep, wooded slopes to the summer pastureland of Sommerbergalm, a sunny platform with restaurants beneath the Tuxerjoch and an easy, east-facing ski area served by two drag-lifts and a quad-chair. The main glacier area is separated from here by a narrow gorge.

The second stage of the gondola or a state-of-the-art 24-person 'glacier bus' gondola take you up to the Tuxerfernerhaus restaurant at 2660m, which is the bottom of the summer ski area. Two more slow and bitterly cold chairs take you on up to just below the top of the aptly named Gefrorene Wand (frozen wall). The broad, open slopes here are served by T-bars and a central chair-lift, and a triple-chair, off the back gives access to sunny skiing at the top of the Schlegeisgletscher.

While the runs on both sides are generally easy, the glaciers are considerably steeper than most. On the western side, in particular on the

Skiing facts: **Mayrhofen**

TOURIST OFFICE
Postfach 21, A-6290 Mayrhofen, Zillertal
Tel 43 5285 2305
Fax 43 5285 411633

THE RESORT
By road Calais 1000km
By rail station in resort
By air Innsbruck 1 hr, Munich 2 hrs
Visitor beds 8,033
Transport free bus service around Zillertal
included in lift pass

THE SKIING
Linked or nearby resorts Finkenberg (l),
Fügen (n), Gerlos (n), Hintertux (n),
Kramsach (n), Lanersbach (n), Ramsau (n),
Schwendau (n), Kaltenbach (n),
Vorderlanersbach (n), Zell am Ziller (n)
Longest run Ahorn-Abfahrt, 4.5km (black)
Number of lifts 30 in Mayrhofen, 154 in the
Zillertal
Total of trails/pistes 91km in Mayrhofen
(23% easy, 61% intermediate,
16% difficult), 463km in the Zillertal
Nursery slopes 3 runs and lifts
Summer skiing 18km of runs and 7 lifts on
Hintertux Glacier
Snowmaking 12km covered in Mayrhofen

LIFT PASSES
Area pass Zillertal (covers whole Zillertal
Valley) ÖS1,965 including glacier, or
ÖS1,600 not including glacier, both for
6 days

Day pass ÖS340
Beginners no free lifts
Pensioners no reduction
Credit cards accepted no

SKI SCHOOLS
Adults Uli Spiess, Manfred Gager, Max
Rahm, Peter Habeler, ÖS1,450 for 6 days
(4 hrs per day)
Private lessons all ski schools,
ÖS470 per hr
Snowboarding all ski schools, ÖS350 for
2 hrs, private lessons ÖS470 per hr
Cross-country all ski schools,
ÖS840 per day. Loipe 20km
Other courses ski-touring
Guiding companies Peter Habeler

CHILDREN
Lift pass Zillertal, ÖS1,180 including
glacier, or ÖS960 not including glacier,
both for 6 days
Ski kindergarten 4 yrs and over,
9am-3pm, ÖS730 per day including
lunch
Ski school all ski schools, 4-14 yrs, ÖS600
per day (4 hrs) not including lunch
Non-ski kindergarten Wuppy's Kinderland,
3 mths-7 yrs, 8am-6pm, ÖS320 per day or
ÖS1,500 for 5 days, extra ÖS50 per day for
lunch

FOOD AND DRINK PRICES
Coffee ÖS23, glass of wine ÖS20,
small beer ÖS27, dish of the day ÖS130

long runs down both above and below glacier level, there are more
demanding stretches than you might expect. A new six-seater chair
returns you to Sommerbergalm from which point you can either take a
tricky ungraded route, which is steep and narrow in places, or a red
down the western flank of the mountain through the trees. A more
attractive alternative for experienced skiers is to take the Tuxerjoch
chair-lift and then traverse an unnervingly steep slope to reach what is a

delightful run down the bowl of the Schwarze Pfanne. It is all off-piste, but is an extremely popular and by no means difficult run.

TOURIST OFFICE
Tel 43 5287 6060
Fax 43 5287 624

Zell am Ziller
top 2559m (8,396ft) bottom 600m (1,968ft)

Zell is a large and not particularly remarkable village downstream from Mayrhofen, and has long been a popular summer resort. It has gained considerable popularity in winter, due more to the desire of tour operators to maintain favourable two-season contracts with hoteliers than to any particular merit as a ski centre. Neither the main Kreuzjoch ski area, which opened in 1978, nor the minor Gerlosstein/Sonnalm are conveniently situated and both have to be reached by ski bus. The old Kreuzjoch gondola has been replaced with eight-person cars, which take you all the way up to Rosenalm. From here a choice of lifts fan out across a sunny bowl up to Kreuzjoch at the top of the ski area. The runs down are a mixture of blues and flattering reds. The Sportbahn Karspitz double-chair from Wiesenalm serves a more challenging black run, which takes you back to Wiesenalm.

The Gerlosstein area, 5km from the centre, is accessed via a cable car. Runs down are a mixture of mainly undemanding reds and easy blues. One mostly north-facing red offers a pleasant cruise of 1000m vertical all the way to the base-station. This area can also be reached from the village of **Ramsau** via a chair, which takes you up to Sonnalm halfway down this road. A double-chair from Sonnalm takes you on up to Arbiskogel.

TOURIST OFFICE
Tel 43 5282 2281
Fax 43 5282 228180

Niederau

ALTITUDE 830m (2,722ft)

Niederau is the capital of a small group of Tyrolean resorts south of the Inn Valley between **Alpbach** and **Söll**, collectively known and marketed as the Wildschönau. Despite this savage-sounding name the skiing here is extremely gentle and ideal for the mainly beginner and early-intermediate visitors, many of whom return year after year before finally moving on to larger ski areas that offer a greater challenge. The resort has easy nursery slopes where, as one reporter put it, 'you are not constantly bombarded by experienced skiers swishing past to the lifts at the end of a long run, and skiers of different standards can easily meet for lunch'. Prices are five per cent lower than in other resorts in the region and you will find a considerable proportion of skiers are British. The skiing is such that if it was not for this latter consideration the Wildschönau would not feature in this book on its merits alone.

On the mountain
top 1900m (6,232ft) bottom 830m (2,722ft)

The skiing immediately above Niederau is in two small linked areas, reached by the Lanerköpfl lift and by an eight-person gondola, which has replaced the old Markbachjoch chair and improved mountain access. The network of mainly blue (easy) and red (intermediate) runs provides few challenges but is well laid out and the views are spectacular.

Oberau and neighbouring **Roggenboden** are a short bus ride away along the valley floor and are served by eight short drag-lifts offering nothing more than nursery slopes. The one exception is the red run down from the Riedlberg lift.

Auffach, further along the valley, has a gondola rising from a busy car park to the south of the village, and offers more, although not necessarily more interesting, skiing including one long red run from Schatzberg at 1903m, which provides over 1000m vertical.

Beginners
Essentially, this is a resort for beginners. Easy nursery slopes situated sensibly away from the bustle of the main mountain runs provide ideal novice terrain. When snow conditions in the valley are poor, novices start

on the easy pistes at the top of the Markbachjoch, which are now less of an effort to reach via the gondola.

Intermediates

The two runs down from the top of the Lanerköpfl lift are both long reds, and the more westerly one is given the status of 'ski-route', which means that while it is not groomed it should still be checked periodically by the ski-patrol. Both runs are sound intermediate trails cut between the trees and offer no surprises but plenty of confidence-building terrain. The short run above them from the summit of Lanerköpfl is graded black (difficult), but is not discernably steeper. Intermediates will also enjoy the longer but no more difficult descents from the summit of the Schatzberg above Auffach.

Advanced

This is not a place for skiers searching for a challenge. A couple of ski-routes, including one directly beneath the Niederau gondola, are graded black but are by no means difficult in average snow conditions.

Off-piste

Given good powder conditions and the services of a local guide it is always possible to find interesting terrain, even in an area that concentrates on beginners, and the Wildschönau is no exception. The Auffach gondola gives access to some long off-piste variations down to the valley, which are not marked on the lift map.

Ski schools and guiding

Good instruction from both the Skischule Wildschönau and the Skischule Aktiv is what has given Niederau its reputation as an ideal resort for beginners, and we continue to receive enthusiastic reports. As one correspondent says: 'The care taken in bringing on the starters was excellent, but really ambitious up-and-coming intermediates would not choose Niederau as it lacks the ability to stretch this level of skier'. Another reporter commented: 'All of the instructors that I met were particularly likeable'. English is widely spoken, and a number of the instructors are native English-speakers.

Snowboarding

A snowboarding piste with a half-pipe has been set aside at Auffach.

Cross-country

Thirty-eight kilometres of prepared tracks, which are suitable for all standards, line the valley between Niederau and Auffach. There is a practice circuit at Oberau, as well as a testing loipe from Auffach to Mühltal.

Mountain restaurants

Overcrowding is a problem in the limited choice of mountain eating-places. Most reporters choose to eat in the easily accessible restaurants at the bottom of the lifts in Niederau. However, we have good reports of the 'elderly establishment' above the Hotelhanglift. The restaurant at the Auffach gondola mid-station is said to be 'reasonably priced, not crowded, and clean'.

Off the mountain

The village, which sprawls away from the foot of the two main ski areas, has modern hotels and gasthofs built in traditional style, as well as a village square. However, it somehow seems to lack the real heart of so many similar resorts in this part of Austria. While it is not particularly charming, the skiing is certainly convenient to the point of being door-to-door from some hotels.

Non-skiers who are not content to potter along gentle paths between the villages will find activities in the Wildschönau extremely limited. A few local craft shops and the usual sports outfitters are the extent of the shopping.

Accommodation

The most convenient hotels are the four-star Austria and the Alpenland, situated at the base of the nursery slopes and close to the double-chair that provides the main mountain access. The Hotel Staffler is nearby and is 'basic but efficiently run', but a couple of reporters complain that 'the dining-room doubles as the main sitting area, so if you dislike eating in a smoky atmosphere, avoid it'. Pension Jägerrast is said to have larger-than-usual bedrooms, and separate dining- and living-rooms. The Hotel Vicky is one of the focal points of the nightlife.

■ **OTHER SPORTS**

Parapente, skating, curling, swimming, tobogganing, sleigh rides, night-skiing

The four-star Sonnschein, a few minutes' walk from the centre, is said to shine above the others ('excellent, quiet, elegant service, and tasty food'); it has an indoor swimming-pool, a children's playroom, and vegetarians are catered for. The friendly Pension Diane is run by an Englishwoman and her Austrian husband. The Jägerhof has four-star apartments for those who prefer to self-cater.

Eating in and out

As is usual in Austria, the restaurants are mainly in the hotels, and these can vary from more formal dining-rooms serving typical Austrian dishes to those specialising in pizzas and pasta. Hotel Austria has an à la carte restaurant, the hotels Wastlhof and Harfenwirt are among the best value, and the pizzas in the Café Lois are said to be substantial.

Après-ski

Niederau's skiers are a faithful lot who return annually to the resort because, apart from knowing every inch of every run, they are also on first-name terms with every village barman. The resort offers a lively

Skiing facts: **Niederau**

TOURIST OFFICE
A-6311 Niederau, Wildschönau
Tel 43 5339 8255
Fax 43 5339 2433

THE RESORT
By road Calais 1114km
By rail Wörgl 10km
By air Innsbruck 1½ hrs, Salzburg 2 hrs
Visitor beds 8,290
Transport ski bus to Oberau and Auffach,
free with lift pass

THE SKIING
Linked or nearby resorts Oberau (n),
Auffach (n), Mühltal (n), Roggenboden (n),
Thierbach (n)
Longest run Schatzberg, 7.5km (red)
Number of lifts 30 in area
Total of trails/pistes 42km (6% beginner,
56% easy, 32% intermediate, 6% difficult)
Nursery slopes 3 lifts in Niederau,
2 in Oberau
Summer skiing none
Snowmaking none

LIFT PASSES
Area pass Wildschönau (covers Niederau,
Oberau, Auffach) ÖS1,475 for 6 days
Day pass ÖS310
Beginners points tickets
Pensioners 60 yrs and over, as children
Credit cards accepted yes

SKI SCHOOLS
Adults Wildschönau, 10am-midday and
2-4pm, Aktiv, 10am-midday and 1-3pm,
both ÖS1,280 for 6 days
Private lessons both ski schools,
ÖS400 per hr
Snowboarding both ski schools,
ÖS900 for 3 half-days, ÖS1,100 for
4 half-days
Cross-country both ski schools,
ÖS1,050 for 6 half-days. Loipe 38km
in the valley
Other courses ski-touring
Guiding companies Wildschönau Ski
School or Bernd Opperer mountain guiding

CHILDREN
Lift pass 6-15 yrs, ÖS885 for 6 days,
free for 5 yrs and under if accompanied by
an adult
Ski kindergarten Wildschönau,
9.30am-4.30pm, ÖS800 for 6 days, not
including lunch
Ski school Wildschönau and Aktiv, 4 yrs
and over, times as adults, ÖS1,240 for
6 days
Non-ski kindergarten Wildschönau, 2-6
yrs, 9.30am-4.30pm, ÖS800 for 6 days,
not including lunch

FOOD AND DRINK PRICES
Coffee ÖS24-26, glass of wine ÖS20-22,
small beer ÖS23, dish of the day ÖS65-140

choice of entertainment after the lifts close for the day, and swimming is available at some of the hotels, including the Austria and the Sonnschein, and the Hotel Sportklause has a bowling alley. The Vicky is popular with British visitors and has live music two nights a week ('go early if you want a seat').

The Dorfstuben Café and the Cave Bar beneath the Staffler are for late-night drinkers. The latter also has a disco, as does Gasthof Schneeberger. The Alm Pub is a more traditional nightspot. Sleigh rides are popular, and Oberau has floodlit skiing.

Childcare
The children's ski school has a formidable reputation and takes children from four years old for the entire day. Younger non-skiers, from two years old, are cared for in the Gästekindergarten. The nursery slopes are gentle and convenient. There are more extensive baby slopes at Oberau.

Linked or nearby resorts
Oberau
top 1150m (3,773ft) bottom 935m (3,067ft)
Oberau is an attractive and friendly little village with its own nursery slopes but no access to Niederau's more extensive skiing. A free ski bus runs every 15 to 20 minutes to and from Niederau. Oberau is strictly for beginners and has its own ski school. Hotel Tirolerhof, in the centre by the beginners' lift and the ski school, is said to be extremely comfortable with live entertainment most evenings. The hotel's Sno'Blau Bar is the centre of the somewhat limited nightlife. The attractive Gasthof Kellerwirt, which was once a monastery, has a popular restaurant, a busy bar, and organises harp-music evenings.

TOURIST OFFICE
Tel 43 5339 8255/22
Fax 43 5339 2433

Auffach
top 1903m (6,243ft) bottom 870m (2,854ft)
Auffach has developed relatively little as a resort. It consists of a gathering of chalets around the church as well as a line of hotels and gasthofs along the road beyond the gondola station. Hotel Bernauerhof, the Weissbacher and Gasthof Platzl are all recommended. The Schönangeralm restaurant is also praised for its 'great local venison and cheerful staff'. The Avalanche Pub is the main après-ski gathering point.

TOURIST OFFICE
Tel as Oberau
Fax as Oberau

Obergurgl

ALTITUDE 1930m (6,330ft)

Obergurgl has a reputation as the most snow-sure family resort in Austria, a high-altitude village close to the Italian border at the head of the remote and beautiful Ötztal. Its wealth of four-star hotels (18 at the last count) attract an upmarket, but by no means aloof clientèle predominantly from Germany but traditionally bolstered by British families. The old village, centred around the old church and the original hotel, the Edelweiss und Gurgl, manages to maintain its character despite the lashings of luxurious, modern accommodation that has sprung up around it. Development has remained largely in the hands of three families who have neither sought nor needed outside investment and, sensibly, have largely limited the number of beds in proportion to the capacity of the lift system.

Obergurgl's position discourages day-trippers and keeps its beautifully unspoilt terrain exclusive for its paying guests. It is almost as if there is a sign on the final approach road saying: 'keep out (unless you can afford it) — exclusive family ski area'. It is interesting to note that the resort is devoid of coach parking facilities.

The resort is hugely popular, particularly at Christmas and Easter, with the same families returning annually for virtually guaranteed snow conditions. Guests confess to being bowled over by the natural, unspoilt beauty of the resort, which exerts an unfailing loyalty. As one reader put it: 'I almost didn't want to send in this report in case too many others discover this lovely resort.'

It therefore comes as a surprise to discover that the size of the ski area and the challenge offered by it are limited to the point of inadequacy in comparison to other European resorts of such formidable reputation.

Hochgurgl, just a few kilometres away by regular free ski bus, is seen, at least by Obergurgl, as part of the same resort. In reality it is an entirely separate destination with a different character and a different clientèle, but the same lift pass. While Obergurgl draws families like a moth to a searchlight, Hochgurgl has a more serious ski image perhaps because there is little else to do here. Only limited **Vent** and mass-market Sölden are within easy reach for a day out. Lift passes are not compatible and most Obergurgl visitors are more than content to remain secure in their elegant eyrie at the head of the valley.

Obergurgl made its mark on the European map of skiing on 27 May 1931 when a Swiss aviation pioneer, Professor Auguste Piccard, force-landed his hot-air balloon on the Gurgler-Ferner Glacier. What he had just achieved was the world altitude record of 16203m, and what he was about to achieve was world recognition for one of Austria's most exclusive ski resorts. Local mountain guide Hans Falkner spotted the balloon landing in the last light of the day. The following morning he carried out a triumphant rescue of the explorers, leading them between the crevasses to Obergurgl and glory for the village and all concerned.

On the mountain
top 3080m (10,104ft) bottom 1793m (5,881ft)

The slopes of both Obergurgl and Hochgurgl occupy a north-west-facing area at the southern end of the Ötztal on the Italian border. Most of the skiing is above the tree-line and runs are intermediate. Not all of the handful of black (difficult) runs justify their gradings, and expert skiers, unless they are interested in ski-touring (for which the area is outstanding), will tire of the limited pistes within hours. However, there is plenty to keep less adventurous skiers and families occupied in what are truly magnificent surroundings.

The skiing takes place over three small areas naturally divided by the contours of the terrain. Hochgurgl offers the greatest vertical drop off the glacier and adds the variety of a wide, wooded hillside down to Untergurgl, which is little more than a roadside lift station and car park. Obergurgl's two sectors, linked in one direction only, generally comprise more interesting terrain with the steeper runs at the top and some good off-piste alternatives. Access to the Festkogl area is via a modern gondola on the outskirts of Obergurgl, while Gaisberg is reached by a chair-lift, which rises lazily over gentle slopes from the village centre.

Beginners

Complete novices start on nursery slopes near the cross-country track and set well away from the village. While Obergurgl has easy skiing in both its main sectors, Hochgurgl has a far more comprehensive selection of blue (easy) pistes. The top of the long glacier is served by two chairs, one a high-speed covered quad-chair, which affords some protection against the often severe elements at this altitude. Even on a sunny day in February extremely low temperatures can be the price you pay for high-quality snow.

Intermediates

The Festkogl gondola rises steeply to a sunny plateau with a restaurant and a couple of drag-lifts. The area of mainly red (but not difficult) intermediate skiing is served by a modern quad-chair, which takes you up to the highest point of the skiing at 3035m. Less confident skiers will enjoy the blue run down from the gondola station to the bottom of the Rosskar double-chair.

While Hochgurgl's skiing is generally less challenging, the Schermer-Spitz chair with conveyor-belt entry gives access to a wide and easy red piste, the start of nearly 1500m vertical all the way down to Untergurgl. A two-stage, covered quad-chair takes you up to the summit of the Wurmkogl, which offers an exciting descent for strong intermediates.

The drag-lift on the southern side of the ski area, with a short, steep second section to it, serves an interestingly long and varied red run with moguls. One reporter describes the bottom half as 'much more difficult than any other red run in the resort'.

Advanced

The pistes offer little serious challenge or scope. In the Gaisberg sector a long, antique single-chair goes up to the Hohe Mut at 2670m. The first part of the only official run down is a ski-route, which in turn becomes a black piste, but the 1.8-km descent is not difficult when snow cover is deep, and you cannot but suspect that the grading is designed to reduce traffic and avoid bottlenecks at the outdated lift.

Accomplished skiers will enjoy the black itinerary down the Ferwalltal from the top of the Festkogl gondola. However, the run is prone to avalanche danger, and great care should be taken. In Hochgurgl a black variation off the red run is served by the Vorderer Wurmkogllift and dips into the scenic Königstal, ending up at the same place.

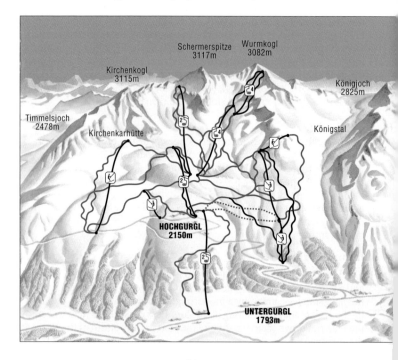

Off-piste

The head of the Ötztal, with its 21 glaciers, is one of the great ski-touring centres of Europe. More limited opportunities also exist for those who prefer to take their powder by lift than on skins.

An off-piste run off the back of the Hohe Mut takes you down through what in good powder conditions is a glorious descent, and ends up near the Schönwieshütte.

Ski schools and guiding

Obergurgl is one of the homes of the Austrian Instructors' Ski School and it is therefore not surprising that the standard of teaching and organisation here is among the highest in Austria. We have generally favourable reports of the Austrian Ski School in Obergurgl. However, some reporters have complained that classes, in theory restricted to 12 pupils, can have as many as 15 during high season, and division into language groups is not always well organised.

In contrast the Austrian Ski School in Hochgurgl comes in for considerable criticism. Gripes include lack of English-speaking instructors, poor group selection and 'almost non-existent tuition skills'.

Snowboarding

There is a snowboard park with a quarter-pipe in the Festkogl ski area.

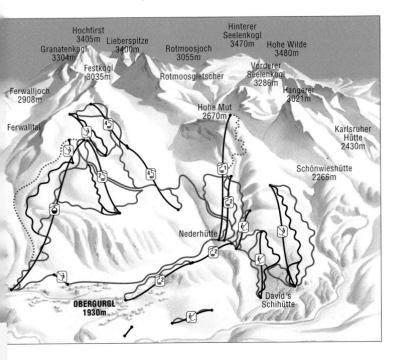

Mountain restaurants

The Hohe Mut Hütte, at the top of the single-chair at Gaisberg, provides magnificent views of the Ötztal and the Dolomites. You can make the return journey by chair, but the alternative post-prandial prospect of the black ski-route down acts as a deterrent and means that the old wooden chalet is the least crowded restaurant in the area. On fine days there is an ice-bar and barbecue on the terrace. The Schönwieshütte, a 15-minute walk from the Sattellift piste, is a touring refuge which serves simple meals ('best *Gulaschsuppe* and *Kaiserschmarren* ever'). David's Schihütte at the bottom of the Steinmannlift is recommended particularly for its *Tirolergröstl*. The Festkogl mountain restaurant is described by a number of reporters as 'indifferent'. The Nederhütte is warmly recommended for 'good food and an excellent atmosphere'.

In Hochgurgl, the Wurmkogl by the top of the Wurmkogl quad-chair is the best of the three altitude restaurants. Reporters warn that restaurants in Hochgurgl itself are nearly all attached to the smart hotels and considerably more expensive. Toni's Almhütte is a rustic wooden hut attached to the Sporthotel Olymp and is highly praised. The sun-terrace of the Hotel Riml has 'the best views on the mountain'.

Off the mountain

Building in Obergurgl has reached capacity within the avalanche-safe area, and despite the large number of luxury hotels, it remains a small village set on the lower level around the church and a handful of shops, and on the upper area around an open-air ice rink. At the heart of it all is the Edelweiss und Gurgl Hotel, once the local inn and now the focal four-star around which much of village life rotates. A regular free bus service operates from the centre to Untergurgl and to Hochgurgl. Post buses run to Sölden and beyond. Cars are banned from the village between 11pm and 6am, and parking is not easy. The handful of shops is strictly limited to sports and souvenirs.

Accommodation

Most of the accommodation is in smart hotels and, to a lesser extent, in gasthofs and pensions. It is also possible to rent attractive and spacious apartments by contacting the resort direct. Hotel Crystal is a monster of a building, completely out of keeping with resort character, but extremely comfortable inside. The Deutschmann has nothing to do with the predominant nationality of its guests, but is the name of an old Obergurgl family which owns it. The second group of hotels is clustered around the ice rink on high ground above the centre. The Bergwelt ('art deco furniture and a great pool') and the Austria are both warmly recommended. Hotel Gotthard is also highly praised and 'the welcome matched the luxurious surroundings'. In the centre, the Edelweiss and Gurgl is well thought of, although its bedrooms are not as large nor as well equipped as in the new four-stars. The Jenewein is also commended for its friendly service and 'quite exceptional demi-pension food'. Hotel

Skiing facts: **Obergurgl**

TOURIST OFFICE
A-6456 Obergurgl, Ötztal
Tel 43 5256 258
Fax 43 5256 353

THE RESORT
By road Calais 1200km
By rail Ötztal 54km, buses from station
By air Innsbruck 1½ hrs
Visitor beds 3,900
Transport free ski bus between Obergurgl and Untergurgl

THE SKIING
Linked or nearby resorts Hochgurgl (n), Sölden (n), Untergurgl (n), Vent (n)
Longest run Wurmkogl-Untergurgl, 8.5km (black/blue/red)
Number of lifts 22
Total of trails/pistes 110km (32% easy, 50% intermediate, 18% difficult)
Nursery slopes 4 runs and lifts
Summer skiing none
Snowmaking 9.4km covered

LIFT PASSES
Area pass Gurgl (covers Obergurgl, Untergurgl, Hochgurgl) ÖS2,090 for 6 days
Day pass ÖS420
Beginners coupons ÖS140
Pensioners 60 yrs and over, as children
Credit cards accepted no

SKI SCHOOLS
Adults Obergurgl ÖS1,420 for 6 days,
Hochgurgl ÖS1,970 for 6 days,
Hochgurgl/Untergurgl ÖS1,490 for 5 days,
all 10am-midday and 2-4pm
Private lessons Obergurgl ÖS1,400 and Hochgurgl/Untergurgl ÖS1,350 per 2-hr lesson
Snowboarding Obergurgl, ÖS900 for 3 half-days or ÖS1,700 for 6 half-days, private lessons through Obergurgl and Hochgurgl/Untergurgl ski schools
Cross-country Obergurgl, ÖS300 per half-day, private lessons through ski schools. Loipe 12km
Other courses snow-shoeing, telemark, monoski
Guiding companies through Obergurgl Ski School

CHILDREN
Lift pass 6-14 yrs, ÖS1,280 for 6 days, free for 5 yrs and under if accompanied by an adult
Ski kindergarten as ski school
Ski school Obergurgl, 5-14 yrs, ÖS1,520 for 6 days. Hochgurgl/Untergurgl, 3 yrs and over, ÖS1,490 for 5 days, times as adults
Non-ski kindergarten Obergurgl Ski School, 3 yrs and over, 9.30am-12.30pm and 1.30-4.30pm, ÖS1,420 for 6 days, extra ÖS180 per day for lunch

FOOD AND DRINK PRICES
Coffee ÖS24-26, glass of wine ÖS20-22, small beer ÖS23, dish of the day ÖS65-120

Alpina is described as 'outstanding, with wonderful hospitality from the owners'. Hotel Gamper is 'excellent and conveniently situated'.

Eating in and out
Dining is largely confined to the main hotels, most of which have separate à la carte restaurants. Pizzeria Romantika in the Hotel Madeleine provides some respite from the ubiquitous rounds of Wienerschnitzel.

The Edelweiss has a comfortable candlelit stübli, which offers 'relaxed elegance'. The Bergwelt is recommended for its nouvelle cuisine. Pizzeria Belmonte in Haus Gurgl has 'the best pizzas in town'. Restaurant Pic-Nic is also praised. One reporter speaks warmly of fondue evenings organised at the Nederhütte. One small supermarket looks after the needs of self-caterers.

Après-ski

Obergurgl is surprisingly active in the evenings. The Nederhütte at the top of the Gaisberg lift becomes crowded as the lifts close for the day. Tea-dancing and copious measures of glühwein prepare you for the gentle run down to the village. The outdoor bar of the Edelweiss at the foot of the Gaisberg lift continues to attract customers until darkness falls. The Joslkeller has a cosy atmosphere and good music, which gets louder with dancing as the evening progresses. You find the occasional person in ski suit and ski boots still here in the early hours. The Krump'n'Stadl is noisy, with yodelling on alternate nights. Hexenkuch'l has live music along with Toni's Almhütte in Sporthotel Olymp in Hochgurgl. The Edelweiss' cellar disco is said by most reporters to be the best in town.

Childcare

The Gästekindergarten takes non-skiing children aged between three and five years old. A number of hotels operate their own crèches, usually free of charge, and the minimum age accepted varies from hotel to hotel. These include the Alpina, Austria, Bellevue, Bergwelt, Crystal, Hochfirst, Hochgurgl, and Mühle. Obergurgl Ski School takes children from five years old and Hochgurgl accepts children as young as three for lessons.

Linked or nearby resorts

Hochgurgl
top 3080m (10,104ft) bottom 2150m (7,052ft)

Hochgurgl is little more than a collection of modern hotels perched by the side of the road leading up to the Timmelsjoch Pass, which is closed in winter. It has a loyal following among reporters who admit they return here 'to ski, and only to ski'. We have had good reports of the Hotel Riml and the less expensive Hotel Ideal ('it is, as the name implies!'). The three-star Alpenhotel Laurin is highly recommended for its excellent food ('superb farmers' buffet').

TOURIST OFFICE
Tel as Obergurgl
Fax as Obergurgl

Obertauern

ALTITUDE 1740m (5,707ft)

If there is snow in Austria, then you will find it in Obertauern. What is Austria's best, or indeed only, shot at a purpose-built resort lies on a high pass in the Niedere Tauern mountains, 90km south of Salzburg. When other resorts are struggling to cope with a lack of cover during lean winters, Obertauern is usually rolling in metres of snow. It was for this reason that 70 years ago a group of local enthusiasts built a stone refuge at the highest point of the pass. In the 1930s this developed into a handful of huts, which in turn evolved into what today is one of Austria's top five tourist centres, with a predominance of German and Dutch visitors.

Thanks to a motorway tunnel, the Tauern Pass (once an important Roman trade route at the only point in the range where the altitude falls below 2000m) is now a quiet backwater. The impressive peaks of the Niedere Tauern surround the road around the resort, allowing the construction of lifts from a central point to fan out into a natural ski circus. It is possible to ski the arena in either direction and, unlike most Austrian ski resorts, it is also possible to ski to and from the doorsteps of nearly all the accommodation.

■ GOOD POINTS
Excellent snow record, reliable resort-level snow, superb piste-grooming, skiing convenience, extensive nursery slopes, interesting off-piste skiing, variety of easy runs

■ BAD POINTS
Late-season queues, lack of non-skiing activities, quiet après-ski, spread-out village

Although the village is far higher than most Austrian resorts, the skiing only rises a further 573m and pistes extend 100m below village altitude. The area is not particularly extensive, but provides an interesting variety of gradient and terrain.

A car is not necessary for getting about the village, but it is an advantage for making use of some of the other skiing in the area. **Schladming** and a host of other resorts are included in the Top-Tauern Skischeck lift pass. Obertauern's favourable micro-climate has one disadvantage: when other resorts are suffering from lack of snow its easy accessibility means a large daily influx of coaches and cars, particularly at weekends. Serious queues are reported late in the season, when the cows are out on the lower pistes of the Tyrol.

On the mountain
top 2313m (7,587ft) bottom 1640m (5,379ft)
The circus can be skied in both directions, but the skiing is concentrated on the north side of the resort, spread around a broad, undulating and

mainly treeless bowl ringed by rocky peaks. Four main lifts rise from around the bowl to points near the rim. Two of them ascend to approximately 2000m from almost the same point at Hochalm (1940m); the Seekareckbahn quad chair-lift takes you up over a steep east-facing slope, and the Panorama triple-chair over a more varied south-facing one.

The Hundskogel chair serves a slightly longer slope offering a choice of routes down, with a moderately steep piste away from the lift on the north side as well as off-piste routes more directly down on the south side. A little further down the pass the Schaidberg double chair-lift serves the steepest run on the north side of the resort. It also gives access to a short drag, which is gentle enough to be used as a high-altitude beginner slope. There is an easy run back to the village from here.

A clockwise circuit of this northern part of the area need not involve any of the higher, more difficult runs. However, the pistes of most interest to timid skiers are the easy, open runs across the middle of the bowl, served by drag-lifts including the long Zentral lift from just below the village.

On the south side of the resort the mountains rise more dramatically, keeping the village in shade for much of the day in mid-winter. The major lift is the Zehnerkar cable car, climbing over 500m from the western extremity of the village and giving access to a long, moderately testing run branching to various points along the pass. One reporter comments that the cable car continues to be a major bottleneck ('long queues for most of the day').

The local lift map fails to show either piste names or numbers, but the signposting of the clockwise and anticlockwise circuits is generally sufficient. Thanks to the fact that no less than seven different lift companies share the ski area, the quality of grooming brought about by competition between them is unsurpassed anywhere in Austria. There is substantial artificial snowmaking.

Beginners

The nursery slopes are excellent, with a short, gentle drag-lift in the heart of the village, just north of the main road, and another longer one on the lower slopes at the east end. Another runs parallel to and just south of the road, although it is out of the sun for much of the day in mid-winter. The high Gamskarlift, at the top of the steep Schaidberg chair, also provides gentle skiing.

Intermediates

The entire circuit is geared towards intermediates with some truly excellent long, but not over-demanding, descents from the lip of the bowl. Some of the best are accessed from the Panorama Sesselbahn and Hundskogel lifts. The top of the Plattenkarbahn quad-chair is the starting point for a challenging run of over 400m vertical.

Advanced

There is enough to keep advanced skiers happy here for a week, although the more adventurous will want to explore the other resorts in

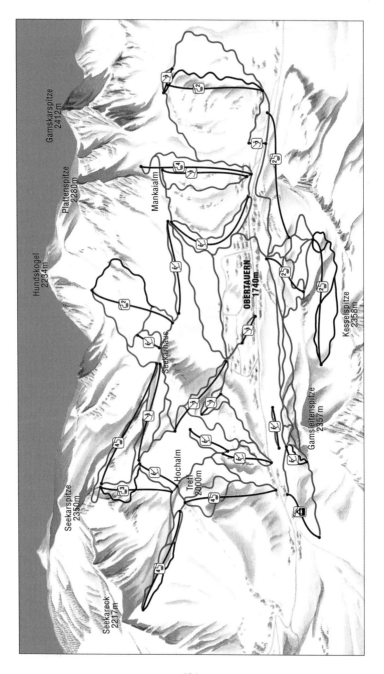

the region. Pistes can become heavily mogulled around the edge of the bowl and a couple of runs are positively steep. The upper Gamsleiten 2 chair serves a seriously steep, unprepared run from the high point of the system. When snow is in short supply, this rocky slope may lack adequate cover despite its north-east orientation.

Off-piste
In powder conditions the off-piste skiing is spectacular, with long runs both above and below the tree-line. To find the best and safest runs you need the services of a local guide.

Ski schools and guiding
Obertauern now has five ski schools including the Krallinger Obertauern-Süd, which has a higher than average number of female instructors and is much favoured by tour operators. The others are Schischule Koch Obertauern-Nord, CSA (known as Skischule Willi Grillitsch), Schischule Top, and Schischule Frau Holle. We have favourable reports of most of them, and as one reporter suggests, 'choose the one most convenient for your hotel'.

Snowboarding
Christian and Werner Schmidt run their dedicated Snowwave Snowboardschule from the Hotel Solaria. The ski schools also give snowboarding lessons.

Cross-country
Langlauf opportunities abound here with four loipe, including the testing 10-km Gnadenalmloipe, 4km towards **Radstadt**, and at Obertauern Langlauf School. There is also a delightful loipe starting at **Untertauern**.

Mountain restaurants
Because of the ski-in ski-out nature of Obertauern, it is quite easy to ski back to the village for lunch. Nevertheless, the supply of mountain restaurants is more than adequate. The Seekarhaus at Kringsalm is a cosy spot with enjoyable food, but it can become crowded. Similarly, the Sonnhof is swarming with people at peak times and has a 'busy and chaotic self-service system that entails a scrum and a long wait'. The Schaidberg Liftstube has an extensive menu. The Achenrainhütte at Gamsleiten is 'pleasant but small'.

The open-air grill at the top of the Grünwaldkopbahn serves four kinds of sausage with tarragon mustard and 'a wonderful garlicky dish in a frying-pan that you could smell half-way down the red run at the back of the restaurant'.

Off the mountain
The resort itself is no classic beauty. If you are expecting a chocolate-box Austrian village with onion-domed church, frescoes and ornately fret-

Skiing facts: **Obertauern**

TOURIST OFFICE
A-5562 Obertauern, Salzburgerland
Tel 43 6456 252
Fax 43 6456 515

THE RESORT
By road Calais 1222km
By rail Radstadt 20km
By air Salzburg $1\frac{1}{2}$ hrs
Visitor beds 6,200
Transport no bus system

THE SKIING
Linked or nearby resorts Schladming (n)
Longest run Seekarspitz-Bahn, 1.5km (red)
Number of lifts 26
Total of trails/pistes 120 km (20% easy,
60% intermediate, 20% difficult)
Nursery slopes 6 runs
Summer skiing none
Snowmaking 45 hectares covered

LIFT PASSES
Area pass ÖS1,675 for 6 days
Day pass ÖS365
Beginners points tickets
Pensioners no reduction
Credit cards accepted no

SKI SCHOOLS
Adults Krallinger ÖS1,400 for 4-6 days,

Frau Holle ÖS1,460 for 6 days, Koch
ÖS1,500 for 6 days, CSA ÖS1,630 for 6
days, Top ÖS1,450 for 4-6 days
Private lessons all ski schools,
ÖS450 per hr
Snowboarding Snowwave, ÖS960 for 3
days (8 hrs), Frau Holle, ÖS1,210 for 3 days
($2\frac{1}{2}$ hrs per day
Cross-country all ski schools, times and
prices as regular ski lessons.
Loipe 17km
Other courses off-piste
Guiding companies through
ski schools

CHILDREN
Lift pass 15 yrs and under, ÖS1,055 for 6
days
Ski kindergarten all ski schools, 3 yrs and
over, 10am-12.30pm and 2-3.30pm,
ÖS1,450 for 6 days, extra ÖS120 per day
for lunch
Ski school all ski schools, 4-15 yrs, 10am-
12.30pm and 2-3.30pm, ÖS1,400-1,580
for 6 days
Non-ski kindergarten Hotel Alpina, up to
2 yrs, ÖS550 per day including lunch

FOOD AND DRINK PRICES
Coffee ÖS25, glass of wine ÖS40, small
beer ÖS30, dish of the day ÖS110

worked balconies, you will be disappointed. Under its usual blanket of snow, the long straggle of roadside hotels and bars looks more like a Wild West town. It is by no means devoid of charm, but its growth in recent years has not always been absorbed with grace ('expanding rapidly from an isolated village at the top of a remote pass to a large and less attractive holiday town'). The range of non-skiing activities is limited, although the building of a sports centre has gone some way towards rectifying this.

Three large car and coach parks at either end of the resort absorb most of the weekend traffic. It takes around 20 minutes to walk from one end to the other. The main cluster of buildings, which constitutes the centre, is around the village nursery slope and the tourist office.

Accommodation

Nearly all the accommodation is in hotels and guesthouses, few of them cheap. Location is not particularly critical unless you have small children (choose a hotel within easy walking distance of one of the kindergarten). Hotel Krallinger, across the road from the Gamsleiten chair and close to the Kurven lift, is recommended as a good ski-in ski-out base with satellite television in the rooms. Haus Kärntnerland is said to be 'clean, comfortable and friendly, with exceptional food'.

The four-star Hotel Rigele is praised for its food. The Alpenrose apartments in the village centre are said to be 'cosy and well-appointed'. The lavish Sporthotel Marietta remains a favourite with reporters. Hotel Enzian is also mentioned for its excellent skiing location. Petersbühel Sporthotel is 'owner-run and it shows with the best rooms we have seen in years — clean as a whistle'. Pensions Sailer and Gästehaus Weinberger are also praised.

Eating in and out

Most of the restaurants are in hotels. The Stüberl restaurant in the Hotel Regina is reported to be extremely good value ('quiet, candlelit, and serves enormous portions'). The Lurzeralm requires reservations and serves 'well-presented, good food, although the service is slightly on the sniffy side'. The Latsch'n'Stüberl has friendly service and well-prepared food. Café Samson is recommended along with the Lurzeralm and Da Giorgio's. Two supermarkets have the basics for self-caterers.

Après-ski

This is centred on the main hotel bars, of which more than 15 offer music and dancing. The Edelweisshütte is the place to go at the end of the skiing day, along with the Gamsmilch Bar. Later on, the action moves to La Bar and Premillos, next to the Hotel Steiner. The Gasthof Taverne reportedly has the most liveliest disco later in the evening. Hotel Enzian's bar and the Red Bull pub are both popular.

Childcare

Non-skiing children can be left all day in the Hotel Alpina crèche and all the ski schools run ski kindergartens with lunch provided on request.

Saalbach-Hinterglemm

ALTITUDE 1000m (3,280ft)

Saalbach-Hinterglemm is the collective marketing name of two once separate villages in the pretty Glemmtal near **Zell am See**. The narrow valley, with uniform 2000m peaks on either side, lends itself to a natural ski circus, which can be skied as happily in one direction as in the other.

It was justly chosen to host the 1991 Alpine World Championships, and it provides some of the best intermediate and advanced skiing in Austria, second only to that of the Arlberg.

The two villages, a ten-minute drive apart, have grown so much over the years that they now stretch along the valley, almost meeting. Those looking for two cheap and cosy little Austrian villages will be disappointed; both are expensive, even by Austrian standards. Saalbach is larger and brasher, while Hinterglemm is marginally more fam-

ily-orientated. A third village, **Leogang**, provides a back door into the ski area and is a quieter, more attractive alternative.

On the mountain
top 2096m (6,877ft) bottom 1000m (3,280ft)

Both sides of the valley are lined with a network of 60 lifts, which is also linked to neighbouring Leogang. Much of the system has been upgraded to provide an easy traffic flow around the 200-km circuit of prepared pistes; this can be skied in either direction, although the anticlockwise route is longer. The resort was previously criticised for its annoying sur- feit of T-bars; however, many of these have now been superannuated.

From the bottom of Saalbach, the Schattberg-Ost cable car gives direct and easy access, in good snow conditions, to the southern half of the circuit. The 100-person lift is prone to serious queues when the sunny side of the valley opposite has scarce snow cover. A triple-chair at the top end of the village is the starting point for the northern half of the ski area.

From Vorderglemm, which is a ski-bus ride down the valley towards Zell am See, the two-stage Schönleitenbahn gondola takes you up to Wildenkarkogel and into the Leogang ski area. You can also find your way here from Saalbach via a cluster-gondola, which feeds a network of gentle south-facing runs.

Beginners

Both villages have their own nursery slopes, and the north side of the valley is dotted with seven T-bars serving an unusual variety of beginner terrain. When you feel capable of graduating to the main circus, start on the gentler southern side, which offers a vast area of blue (easy) runs. When snow conditions are not all they could be, take either gondola to the 1984-m Zwölfer; the long *Familienabfahrt* back to the valley usually holds the snow well. From Schattberg-Ost the 7-km Jausernabfahrt is a gentle cruise down to Vorderglemm, from where you can take the Wildenkarkogel gondola up the other side of the valley for the easiest of cruises back to Saalbach.

Intermediates

Anyone who can ski parallel will enjoy the full circuit, although it is possible to shorten the outing by cutting across the valley at four separate points. Timid skiers will have a field day here as most of the southern side of the valley is devoted to an easy blue playground. Challenging exceptions to this are the Schönleiten Talstation from beneath the Brundlkopf, the thigh-tingling women's downhill from Kohlmaiskopf and a few shorter red (intermediate) runs above Hinterglemm. The Leogang sector has some usually uncrowded terrain that is well worth exploring at weekends when the main slopes are at their busiest.

Advanced

Schattberg-Ost, Schattberg-West and Zwölferkogel north-facing slopes make up the more challenging skiing. The north face of the Zwölfer is a classic, harsh black (difficult) run, which can be heavily mogulled down its entire 3km. The home run from Schattberg-Ost can be extremely icy and desperately crowded. A far more interesting route begins with the Westgipfel triple-chair to Schattberg-West, from where you can take a run down the steep black to the bottom and, after another chair ride, follow the challenging, unpisted itinerary down to Bergstadl.

Off-piste

The north side of the valley offers some exceptional powder runs, but a local guide is necessary to discover which slopes are safe, and when.

Ski schools and guiding

Since deregulation permitted the establishment of alternative ski schools in Austria, no less than nine now compete for the resort's big business. Schischule Wolf ('wonderful off-piste guide') based in Hinterglemm, attracts a disproportionate number of Anglo-Saxon guests. The smaller Mitterlengau is praised for 'excellent instruction, with clear and precise analysis of bad habits and practical help in correcting them'.

Snowboarding

Saalbach has devoted 13km of slopes for riders of all levels and is recognised as a major resort for snowboarders. Off-piste opportunities are

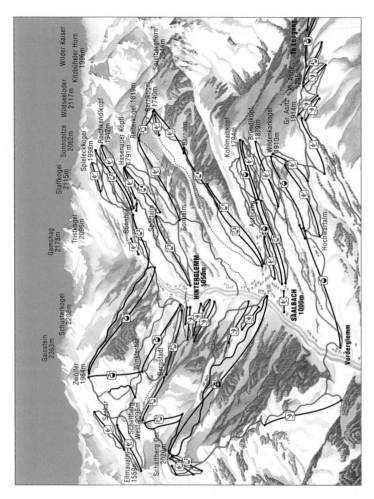

exceptional, with good riding down to the main valley road, which is served by a regular, free shuttle-bus. The snowboard park includes two half-pipes and a boardercross course. All nine ski schools give lessons.

Cross-country
The picturesque Glemmtal offers considerable langlauf opportunities. Saalbach itself has an 8km loipe and Hinterglemm has another of 10km. A further 40km of prepared track are based around Leogang.

Mountain restaurants
Saalbach-Hinterglemm has a wide selection of mountain eating-establishments. As one reporter put it: 'there are almost as many restaurants

and delightful huts as there are runs. The Pfefferalm above Hinterglemm is the most picturesque old farmhouse we have ever encountered. Don't be startled by the huge rabbits jumping about in the snow outside; you haven't had too much to drink — they live here.' The Goatssalm is equally rustic and is recommended for its glühwein. The good-value Rosswaldhütte is an attractive chalet where the friendly staff wear traditional costumes. The rather twee Wildenkarkogel Hütte at the top of the Vorderglemm gondola is also accessible for non-skiers.

The Stockalm self-service at the Leogang gondola mid-station is complimented on its high standard of service. Barnalm is a small, attractive restaurant at the top of the triple-chair at Bernkogel, which serves very good-value lunches; dishes include the Austrian speciality *Kaiserschmarren* (pancakes with stewed plums and sugar). The Panorama Alm on the Kohlmais is much praised and its *Lederhosen*-clad owner, Alex, is prone to dispensing free Schnapps. At the foot of Zwölferkogel the Gondelstube is 'not the usual self-service nightmare, but well-decorated with a wide choice of snacks'.

Off the mountain

The steep and thankfully pedestrianised main street of Saalbach, with its smart hotels and high-priced fashion boutiques, gives one the distinct feeling of having strayed on to the set of a Hollywood studio preparing to shoot some twenty-first-century sequel to *The Sound of Music*. The alpine charm is authentic, but positively Disneyesque in depth. Old it may appear, but most of the village dates from the 1980s. Hinterglemm is little more than a collection of stolid Austrian hotels, which act as an alternative base at the far end of the ski system.

The atmosphere is lively and friendly. Both villages used to suffer from a surfeit of drunken Scandinavians; however, like the Brits (who once claimed this delightful valley for their own), the Scandinavians have dwindled in number due to rotten exchange rates. Their mainly Dutch replacements party almost as loudly, but with more charm.

Accommodation

Alpen Hotel Hechenberg is a 'very comfortable and welcoming' four-star. The Karlshof is praised for its buffet breakfast. Hotel Hasenauer in Hinterglemm is convenient for the lifts, but one reporter comments: 'Rooms, water and staff were all rather too cool for comfort'. Hotel Glemmtalerhof is described as 'pleasant enough, but German-orientated, and we could well have done without the Mexican evening'. Haus Wolf is said to be 'clean and very friendly'. The Hotel Ingonda in Saalbach is among the most luxurious. The fact that there are more than 30 four-star and nearly as many three-star hotels here indicates the wealth of the clientèle, and shops and restaurants reflect this in their high prices. However, the resort also has some more reasonably priced establishments; Hotel Sonnblick at Hinterglemm has 'excellent food and a friendly bar — it is difficult to see the need to pay more for one of the posher hotels'.

Eating in and out

Bäckstättstall is the most exclusive restaurant in town. The Hotel Bauer is said to be 'good value, with a much more varied menu than you expect in Austria'. Hotel Hasenauer in Hinterglemm is 'cheaper than anywhere else'. The Bärenbachhof is 'not as expensive and better than most'. The Hubertushof in Hinterglemm has 'great pizza and the locals come here, so it must be reasonably priced'. Two reporters spoke warmly of the Gollinger Hof's 'dumplings of every possible variety'.

Après-ski

The endearing feature of Saalbach is the immutable jolly Austrian formula. True, the folk dancers now save their thigh-slapping and yodels for the more appreciative lakes-and-mountains clientèle in the summer, but the waitresses still wear their *Dirndl* dresses and genuine smiles of welcome as they pocket your money in the same bulging leather wallets.

Après-ski starts with a drink at the Bäckstättstall Umbrella Bar with 'a disco/band and striking views over Saalbach; they also do a potent glüh-wein to add some challenge to the very short run down to the street'. The

■ **OTHER SPORTS**

Indoor tennis, swimming, skating, curling, hang-gliding, sleigh rides, tobogganing, ice hockey, squash, parapente

Schirmbar is also recommended. Hinterhagalm has a huge copper pot of glühwein on the bar, and it is on draft at Bauer's Schialm. The Siglu in Hinterglemm has low prices and is wall-to-wall with Dutch after the slopes close. The snow-bar of the Glemmtalerhof is always crowded. Lumpi's Bla Bla in Hinterglemm has a good atmosphere. The Pfeiffenmuseum Café in the Glemmtalerhof houses a quite enormous collection of pipes and smoking paraphernalia. Later on, the villages' 15 discos come to life: King's is popular with teenagers. The Londoner is the hot-spot for all age groups in Hinterglemm.

Childcare

Schischule Wolf operates a ski kindergarten every day except Sunday for children from four years old. Lunch is provided on request. Hotels including Partners, Gartenhotel Theresia, Lengauerhof and Egger care for non-skiing children from two-and-a-half years of age.

Linked or nearby resorts

Leogang
top 2096m (6,875ft) bottom 800m (2,625ft)

Leogang is a spread-out farming community, which claims, with some justification, the title of the longest village in Europe. A smart, modern gondola takes skiers up to Sitzhütte at 1758m. A short run down there is a quad-chair, and three subsequent T-bars, which bring you into the Glemmtal and the ski circus. Accommodation is in a mixture of hotels

Skiing facts: **Saalbach-Hinterglemm**

TOURIST OFFICE
A-5753, Saalbach, Salzburgerland
Tel 43 6541 72720
Fax 43 6541 7900

THE RESORT
By road Calais 1193km
By rail Zell am See 19km
By air Salzburg 1½ hrs
Visitor beds 17,130
Transport free ski bus with lift pass

THE SKIING
Linked or nearby resorts Badgastein (n),
Bad Hofgastein (n), Grossarl (n), Kaprun
(n), Leogang (l), Zell am See (n)
Longest run Jausernabfahrt, 7km (blue)
Number of lifts 60
Total of trails/pistes 200km (45% easy,
47% intermediate, 8% difficult)
Nursery slopes 9 lifts
Summer skiing none
Snowmaking 65 hectares covered

LIFT PASSES
Area pass (covers Saalbach-Hinterglemm
and Leogang) ÖS1,600-1,940
Day pass ÖS380-400
Beginners points tickets
Pensioners reductions for women 60 yrs
and over, men 65 yrs and over
Credit cards accepted yes

SKI SCHOOLS
Adults Fritzenwallner, Fürstauer,
Heugenhauser, Hinterholzer,
Zink, Gensbichler, Lechner,
Mitterlengau and Wolf ski schools, all
10am-midday and 2-4pm, ÖS1,550
for 6 days
Private lessons ÖS550 per hr
Snowboarding as regular ski lessons
Cross-country as regular ski lessons.
Loipe 58km in linked area
Other courses telemark, ski-touring,
race training
Guiding companies through ski schools

CHILDREN
Lift pass 6-10 yrs ÖS850, 11-15 yrs
ÖS985-1,160, both for 6 days, free for
5 yrs and under
Ski kindergarten Schischule Wolf, 4 yrs
and over, 10am-4pm, ÖS1,550 for 6 days
including lunch
Ski school as ski kindergarten
Non-ski kindergarten Gartenhotel
Theresia, Hotel Lengauerhof, Hotel Egger,
all 3 yrs and over, and Hotel Partners, 2½
yrs and over, all 10am-4pm, ÖS500
per day including lunch

FOOD AND DRINK PRICES
Coffee ÖS25, glass of wine ÖS25-28,
small beer ÖS25-27, dish of the day ÖS130

and chalets. We have excellent reports of the Chalet Thurnhaus, an eight-minute walk from the gondola. Readers recommend both the Skischule Gerhard Altenberger and Skischule Franz Deisenberger. The five cross-country loipes total more than 40km, and snow-rafting is also available. The kindergarten in Hotel Krallerhof takes children from two years old.

TOURIST OFFICE
Tel 43 6583 234
Fax 43 6583 7302

Schladming

ALTITUDE 745m (2,444ft)

Schladming is one of the most popular ski destinations for Austrians, and yet remarkably few British skiers know of its existence. Indeed, 50 per cent of all visitors to the Tauern Alps are Austrians. In a country where the majority of the population likes to ski and has a huge choice of where to go, this must in itself say rather a lot. Schladming is a small medieval market town in the province of Styria, a one-hour drive from Salzburg airport and with good rail connections. The resort claimed international fame when it hosted the World Championships in 1982.

Schladming acts as the hub of a 152-km ski area served by 85 lifts. Each year more snow falls on the Niedere Tauern mountain range than anywhere else in Austria. In mixed winters such as 1995–6, when other resorts were struggling to cope with green fields in late January, the villages in this corner of Austria were rolling in snow. A mighty 80 per cent of the runs immediately around Schladming are covered by snow-cannon, making it possible to ski down from as early as November.

■ **GOOD POINTS**

Large ski area, lively après-ski, extensive nursery slopes, tree-level skiing, excellent cross-country, short airport transfer, summer skiing on Dachstein Glacier, variety of mountain restaurants

■ **BAD POINTS**

Lack of tough runs, poor skiing convenience

This all sounds pretty impressive until you appreciate that the skiing takes place in 18 areas on half-a-dozen mountains served, albeit, by an efficient ski-bus service. But only two, Planai and Hochwurzen, are linked by lift.

However, we are pleased to say that at last, after a decade of discussion with the environmentally conscious state government, all this is about to change. Six new high-speed chairs will link Schladming with the picturesque village of **Haus-in-Ennstal** to the east, and the slopes of Hochwurzen and Reiteralm at the western end of this pretty valley. Most of the work is to be completed in time for the expected influx of visitors for the Nordic World Championships at nearby **Ramsau** in 1999.

The skiing also includes the snow-sure but limited alpine pistes of the **Dachstein Glacier**.

On the mountain
top 2015m (6,609ft) bottom 750m (2,460ft)
Schladming lies in the centre of a long and beautiful valley, with the main slopes that are covered by the Skiparadies lift pass spread disparately

across the mountains on the southern side. Planai at 1894m and Hochwurzen at 1850m are the mountains closest to Schladming and are linked by a two-stage chair-lift at valley level, a long walk or a short bus-ride from the town. Easier access to Planai is via a two-stage gondola from the edge of Schladming, a comfortable walk from the centre. The Kessleralm mid-station of the gondola can also be reached by car. Hochwurzen offers several long red (intermediate) runs — and a tobog-gan run — served by two steep drags, a jumbo gondola and a double-chair.

The next mountain, Hauser Kaibling (2115m) towers over the pretty village of Haus-in-Ennstal. A long walk east of the village takes you to a huge car park where a gondola pro-vides the main mountain access.

■ **WHAT'S NEW**

Fageralm ski area included in lift pass
Definite plans to link main ski areas

Motorists can drive up to Knappl on the eastern side of the mountain and avoid queues by working their way into the system via two drag-lifts. The Krummholzhütte summit can also be reached directly from the western end of Haus via a small and inefficient cable car.

Still further along the valley the Galsterbergalm at 1976m offers a few mainly gentle slopes reached by cable car from the village of **Pruggern**. This in turn gives access to a couple of T-bars for some open skiing above the tree-line.

At the western end of the valley, the slopes of the Reiteralm at 1860m provide a variety of red (intermediate) and blue (easy) tree-lined runs down to the villages of **Pichl** and **Gleiming** on the banks of the River Enns. Access is either by gondola from the edge of Gleiming or by dou-ble-chair from an isolated riverside lift station across the valley from Pichl. The small, separate Fageralm ski area is now also included in the local lift pass.

Most of these slopes are north-facing and gentle. Indeed, such is the lack of variety in the terrain that it is often difficult to tell one run from another. At higher altitudes, there is some skiing above the tree-line on the west- and east-facing flanks of Planai and Hauser Kaibling. An effi-cient network of snow-cannon covers the main runs.

On the other side of the valley from Schladming, the commune of **Ramsau Ort** at 1200m has no less than 19 lifts scattered around the hills on either side of the village. All are short beginner and easy slopes. Turlwand, outside Ramsau, is the starting point for the cable car up to the Dachstein Glacier; it has limited year-round skiing that is too gentle to be of much more than scenic interest for alpine skiers, and is served by a chair-and three drag-lifts.

Beginners

The area is as inconvenient for beginners as it is for everyone else. At this altitude the functioning of the 25 listed nursery slopes is heavily depen-dent on the weather. The gentle **Rohrmoos** meadows on the lower slopes of Hochwurzen provide the best arena for first turns when snow

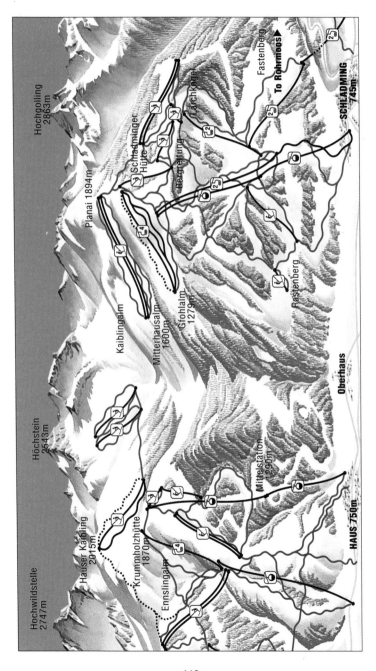

cover permits, with plenty of easy alternatives on the higher slopes of the main mountains.

Intermediates

Despite the lack of variety, there is enough red and blue cruising terrain to keep any skier busy for a week. The World Cup racecourses on both Planai and Hauser Kaibling should please fast intermediates and the long downhill course on Hochwurzen is thigh-burning. The usually uncrowded Reiteralm also gives plenty of opportunity for high-speed cruising. Less confident skiers will enjoy the two short drag-lifts that serve a remote area of gentle skiing at Kaiblingalm, which has no crowds but benefits from good snow and a friendly restaurant.

Advanced

This is not a place for advanced piste-skiers who will quickly tire of the limited terrain. However, Schladming is an attractive base from which to explore a huge range of skiing including **Obertauern** and the **St Johann im Pongau** ski circus. For an extra £7 to £15 — depending on high or low season — you can buy the six-day Top-Tauern Skischeck lift pass, which gives access to 270 lifts serving 660km of prepared runs in this corner of Austria. All the resorts covered on the pass are less than an hour's drive from Schladming.

Off-piste

Skiing outside the marked pistes is discouraged on the main mountains, except on the ski-routes. In good snow conditions the north face of Hauser Kaibling offers great scope, and the runs through the trees from Bergstallalm on Planai are recommended. There are plenty of opportunities for ski-touring in the region. In fresh snow conditions, a guide from the Alpinschule Schladming-Rohrmoos will help you find untracked powder.

Ski schools and guiding

The Weltmeister Keinprecht Kahr Ski School, owned by the veteran Austrian team-trainer Charly Kahr, has an outstanding reputation and counts Arnold Schwarzenegger among its annual pupils. The Franz Tritscher Ski School is also recommended ('good English, good teaching, good fun'). We have no reports of the Brandner or Ski Total schools in Haus-in-Ennstal.

Snowboarding

Snowboarding has been a commercial success in Schladming, not least because it is the home of former European champion Gerfried Schuller, who runs his own school here, as well as the Blue Tomato snowboard shop. He also operates Kids On Board, Europe's first children's snowboard school, which takes 'Jungen Shreddern' from five years of age. The school also organises various camps for riders throughout the season. Group and private lessons are offered by the local ski schools.

Cross-country
The Schladming area has some of the best cross-country skiing in Austria, with 250km of loipe against a dramatically scenic backdrop and plenty of small huts to call in at for refreshments.

Mountain restaurants
'Never', said one reporter, 'have I been to a resort with so many mountain restaurants. Food and service vary, but at their best they are excellent'. The Krümmelholze at Haus receives particular recommendation. On Planai the Mitterhausalm and Schladmingerhütte are praised, along with Onkel Willy's Hütte ('buzzing with atmosphere, and serves great ham and eggs in an individual frying pan') for live music and a sunny terrace. The Eiskarhütte on Reiteralm, the Seiterhütte and Hochwurzenhütte on Hochwurzen, are all recommended.

Off the mountain
Schladming is essentially an ordinary Austrian town that derives much of its income from outside skiing. Not much happens here. Indeed, during its entire 674-year history — unless you count a little bloodshed in the sixteenth century, the birth of Arnold Schwarzenegger, and the staging of the 1982 Ski World Championships— you would be hard pushed to find any single event of international significance. Day-to-day life in this attractive provincial town with its onion-domed church and magnificent eighteenth-century town square, the Hauptplatz, continues at a rhythm that is not solely dictated by tourism. The resort also has the smallest brewery and the largest lift pass in Austria.

> ■ **OTHER SPORTS**
> Curling, skating, hot-air ballooning, sleigh rides, parapente, bowling, indoor tennis and squash, swimming, tobogganing

These factors make Schladming an utterly charming and unspoilt base from which to explore huge tracts of intermediate skiing entirely unknown to the majority of British skiers. As well as wooden chalets with painted shutters, there are sober, old stone buildings, including the remains of the town walls, which date back to 1629. The town is compact — most of its shops and a good many of its hotels, restaurants and bars concentrated around the broad Hauptplatz. Anyone looking for Lederhosen-und-oompah gemütlichkeit will discover that it still thrives here.

Accommodation
Most guests stay in hotels and guesthouses around the Enns Valley. Without a car, location is crucial and many reporters found themselves staying too far from the town centre or the lifts — or both. The Sporthotel Royer receives rave reviews, as do the Neue Post and the Alte Post ('small bedroom, but good food with Strauss, Mozart and Haydn in the background'), which are both in the main square. Haus Stangl, a simple bed-and-breakfast place, is also recommended.

Eating in and out

The restaurants are mainly in the hotels. We have good reports of the Rôtisserie Royer Grill in the Sporthotel Royer and of the Restaurant Bachler, described as having 'friendly staff and good food at not ridiculous prices'. The Alte Post is recommended for 'excellent trout and other dishes in a pretentious but friendly atmosphere. Its *postreindl* (pork fillet with creamed mushrooms and *gnocchi*) is not to be missed.' The Neue Post has two recommended à la carte restaurants, the Jägerstüberl and the Poststüberl. Le Jardin is a warmly commended French restaurant. The Gasthof Kirchenwirt is 'unmatched for quality of food, price, atmosphere and service'. Charly Kahr's Restaurant is also praised.

Après-ski

Après-ski starts early at Onkel Willy's Hütte on Planai before filtering down to the Siglu in the Hauptplatz. Later on the action moves to The Pub, La Porta, the Hanglbar and — still later — to the Sonderbar disco. The Schwalbenbraü brewery is worth a visit, although the deliberately cloudy beer it produces is not to everyone's taste and may explain why it is the smallest brewery in Austria. The Planaistub'n, also known as Charly's Treff, draws large crowds. Café-Konditorei Langland and Niedal are both praised. One reporter favoured Ferry's Pub in the Steirergasse, another the Hanglbar; the bowling alley behind the latter is said to offer a good night out. The Beisl bar is 'intimate and lively with good music'. La Porta is 'small, crowded, with a great atmosphere'. The toboggan run from the top to the bottom of Hochwurzen down the hairpin road can only be used at night (when the road is closed) and is claimed to be the longest in Austria.

Childcare

Few resorts receive such resounding reviews for both their non-ski and ski kindergartens. 'Outstanding facilities for very young children', commented one reader, 'there were 40 small children in the ski kindergarten and the facilities were brilliant; this is definitely the area to bring small children to be looked after well and to learn to ski,' said another.

Linked or nearby resorts

Rohrmoos
top 1850m (6,070ft) bottom 870m (2,854ft)

This diffuse satellite has easy skiing to and from many of its hotel doorsteps. Among the choice of good-value hotels and guesthouses is the Austria, well-placed at the point where the lower, gentle slopes of Rohrmoos meet the steeper slopes of Hochwurzen. The smarter Schwaigerhof has an excellent position on the edge of the pistes and is one of the few places with a swimming-pool. Après-ski is informal and centres around the hotel bars. The café at the Tannerhof is a tea-time favourite. Barbara's and the Alm Bar are busy later on.

Skiing facts: **Schladming**

TOURIST OFFICE
Postfach 1, A-8970 Schladming, Styria
Tel 43 3687 22268
Fax 43 3687 24138

THE RESORT
By road Calais 1235km
By rail station in resort
By air Salzburg 1hr, Munich $2\frac{1}{2}$ hrs
Visitor beds 3,500
Transport free ski bus with lift pass

THE SKIING
Linked or nearby resorts Haus (n),
Obertauern (n), Rohrmoos (n),
Ramsau/Dachstein (n), St Johann im
Pongau (n)
Longest run Hochwurzen, 7.7km (red/blue)
Number of lifts 85
Total of trails/pistes 152km (28% easy,
61% intermediate, 11% difficult)
Nursery slopes 25 lifts in area
Summer skiing nearest on Dachstein
Glacier
Snowmaking 100km covered

LIFT PASSES
Area pass (covers Dachstein-Tauern
region) ÖS1,695-1,825 for 6 days
Day pass ÖS345-365
Beginners reductions available
Pensioners reductions for women 60 yrs
and over and men 65 yrs and over

Credit cards accepted yes

SKI SCHOOLS
Adults WM-Skischule Planai, Skischule
Tritscher and Hopl Skischule, ÖS1,300 for 6
days, times on application
Private lessons both ski schools, ÖS450
per hr
Snowboarding Dachstein Tauern
Snowboardschule and Snowboardschule
Tritscher, ÖS1,700 for 5 half-days. Gertfried
Schuller, details on request
Cross-country all ski schools, ÖS760 for 3
half-days. Loipe 250km in area
Other courses off-piste, race training,
moguls
Guiding companies Alpinschule
Schladming-Rohrmoos

CHILDREN
Lift pass 16 yrs and under ÖS885
Ski kindergarten Tritscher, Planai and
Hopl, 4 yrs and over, 9am-5pm, ÖS1,800
for 5 days including lunch
Ski school all ski schools, 4 yrs and over,
ÖS1,800 for 5 days including lunch
Non-ski kindergarten Gastekindergarten,
2 yrs and over, 7am-4pm, ÖS1,100 for 5
days including lunch

FOOD AND DRINK PRICES
Coffee ÖS23, glass of wine ÖS25-30, small
beer ÖS25, dish of the day ÖS130

TOURIST OFFICE
Tel 43 3687 61147
Fax 43 3687 6114718

Haus-in-Ennstal
top 2015m (6,611ft) bottom 750m (2,460ft)

Haus is a quiet village with its farming origins still in evidence, although it has a considerable amount of holiday accommodation in guesthouses and apartments. There are a couple of shops and cafés, one of which has jazz nights. The upmarket Hauser Kaibling has a swimming-pool and is recommended for its cuisine. Gasthof Kirchenwirt is a traditional hotel in the village centre, the Gasthof Reiter is a fine old chalet, which is much cheaper than most, and the Gurtl is a quiet family-run hotel, well-situated for the cable car. There is a gentle nursery slope between the village and the gondola station.

TOURIST OFFICE
Tel 43 3686 2234
Fax 43 3686 22344

Sölden

ALTITUDE 1380m (4,526ft)

The high-altitude, and therefore snow-sure resort of Sölden has long been a popular destination with mass-market tour operators who are also attracted by the great number of available tourist beds in this spread-out village near the end of the isolated Ötz Valley. Two developed glaciers —. the Rettenbach and the Tiefenbach — which are separate from the main ski area, are useful when snow conditions on the main mountain are poor, and secure Sölden's popularity as a ski destination.

The vertical drop is substantial by Austrian standards and, at least in high season, the après-ski entertainment is lively to the point of being raucous. The off-piste and touring opportunities are extensive, but the piste-skiing itself is limited and lacks variety, although not to the extent of that at **Obergurgl**, its more upmarket neighbour. The lift system has been systematically upgraded; most of the bottlenecks that choked the resort during peak-season weeks have disappeared and overcrowding is no longer a problem.

> ■ **GOOD POINTS**
> Late-season holidays, glacier skiing, modern lift system, lively après-ski
>
> ■ **BAD POINTS**
> Lack of skiing variety, heavy traffic, few facilities for small children, spread-out village

Like Verbier, Sölden has a partisan following, and any mention of its basic drawbacks produces a torrent of protest. Intermediates seeking more challenge from the nightlife than the mountain will particularly enjoy this resort; they are augmented by weekend crowds from Innsbruck, which is a 90-minute drive away.

Hochsölden is a collection of hotels set on a shelf with dramatic views of the Ötztal, 700m up the mountainside, which gives easy access to the slopes on the more mundane and busier side of the mountain.

On the mountain
top 3058m (10,030ft) bottom 1377m (4,517ft)

Sölden's ski area is in two sections linked by chairs up both walls of the narrow Rettenbachtal, which provides the toll road up to the two glaciers. Both sectors are reached by gondolas at either end of the village, which are in turn linked by a ski bus that runs efficiently every nine minutes. The skiing is extensive, with a drop of nearly 1700m vertical — half above and half below the tree-line — which offers less variety than the piste-map suggests.

The main mountain access is via the Gaislachkogl 24-person gondola at the far end of the resort. The principal run down through the trees from the mid-station can be icy and overcrowded, especially at the end of the day, and should be skied with caution.

The top stage of the gondola rises steeply over 850m to the craggy peak of the Gaislachkogl at 3058m. The Hochsölden ski area can be reached via a flat traverse from the gondola mid-station or via a continuation of the red (intermediate) run from Gaislachkogl, which starts at the top of the Stabele double-chair at the bottom of the Rettenbachtal.

Alternative mountain access to Hochsölden is via a 20-minute chair-lift from the other end of Sölden or a gondola up to Giggijoch. Above this gondola is a wide, open expanse of gentle mountainside served by a variety of lifts. This part of the mountain used to be prone to the worst congestion, but new lifts, including a quad-chair to the top of the Hainbachjoch, have greatly relieved the pressure, at least for good skiers who will enjoy the small mogul-field at the top and the overgraded black (difficult) run down.

The Rettenbach and Tiefenbach glaciers are reached by toll road and separated by a tunnel through the mountain. A total of ten lifts serve a selection of mainly blue runs.

Beginners

The best nursery slopes and easy beginner runs are found above the gondola at Giggijoch. A short button-lift, which has been installed adjacent to the Hainbachkar lift, is a welcome addition. Novices do not have to buy area lift-passes as first-week skiers can use points tickets on the nursery lifts. Wobbly second-weekers will find themselves largely confined to the same area, apart from tackling the stiff blue down to Hochsölden.

Intermediates

Sölden offers mainly red runs, most of which are too challenging for the struggling learner. As one reporter put it: 'All the pistes in Sölden should be considered red; blue or black grades really only describe the degree of difficulty of what is actually a red run'.

Open slopes around the Gaislachkoglbahn mid-station provide easy intermediate skiing served by a couple of chair-lifts, one of which gives access to a long red run down to Gaislachalm at 1982m, where the sunny terraces of the restaurants prove popular lunching places. A long path takes you back on to the lower pistes of Sölden at **Innerwald**.

Advanced

The front face directly beneath and to the south of the Gaislachkogl gondola top-station is an exciting expert descent. Great care should be taken; though it can look like a piste at the top due to the many who choose to ski it, there are no markers and considerable expertise is

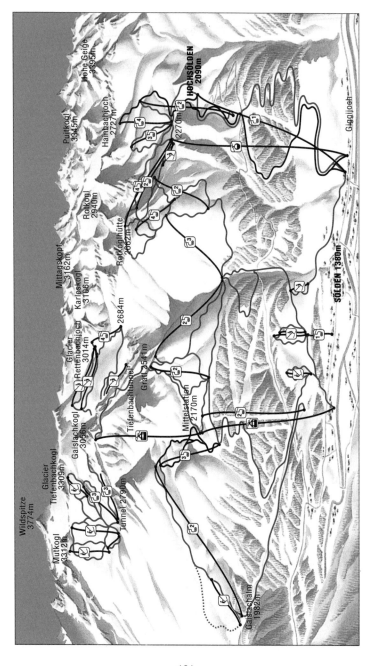

required in hard-packed or icy conditions. The top is deceptively easy, but after a few hundred metres the bowl divides into two. The southern couloir (to the right as you descend) is the wider and therefore easier of the two. It is not dauntingly steep — 33 degrees at its worst — but the length is such that any fall would be serious.

Off-piste

There are considerable off-piste opportunities from the top of the Stabele double-chair and, given reasonable snow conditions, on the sunny slopes accessed by the Langegg 1 chair and the Silberbrünnl chair on the other side of the valley. Return in both cases is along paths at the edge of the road to the chair-lifts.

Ski schools and guiding

Sölden benefits from competition between its three ski schools: the Sölden/Hochsölden, Total Vacancia and Ötztal 2000. We have favourable reports of the Sölden/Hochsölden ('our middle-aged instructor spoke fluent English, he was very sound on technique with lots of useful feedback; as a result our skiing improved tremendously in just four half-day lessons'). One reporter who used Total Vacancia, said she was 'very impressed with their attitude'.

Snowboarding

All the ski schools offer snowboard lessons. The Giggijoch area has a snowboard park with a 100m by 17m half-pipe.

Cross-country

There are two loipes totalling 8km in Sölden, and further langlauf trails at **Zwieselstein** and **Vent**, both of which can be reached by post bus.

Mountain restaurants

The ski area has a larger than usual choice of mountain restaurants, with two new ones at the middle and top stages of the Gaislachkogl gondola. The Gampe Alm, Eugen's Obstlerhütte and Löple Alm are all authentic huts with plenty of atmosphere. The Giggijoch is a large modern complex with a sun terrace ('lots of choice, but it should be avoided during peak hours'). The Rotkoglhütte has 'sound Austrian fare' and is 'not overcrowded or overpriced'. Both the Gaislachalm and the Silbertal at Gaislachalm have sun terraces, a wide variety of food, and live accordion music.

Off the mountain

The resort stretches over 2km on either side of the road and river along the valley floor. It is an unmemorable collection of hotels, restaurants and bars that lack charm. Nevertheless, it would be uncharitable to dismiss the whole as unattractive. Most visitors come here by car and traffic is a real hazard throughout the day. Once in the resort a car is neither necessary nor desirable, except for visits to Vent, the glaciers and the

Gurgls, and parking is extremely difficult. Ski buses run regularly around the resort and the post bus service in the valley is efficient. Hochsölden is served by morning and afternoon buses, but there is no service after dark and taxis are expensive.

Accommodation

Location is moderately important here; better skiers should base themselves in the southern end of town within easy reach of the Gaislachkogl gondola, while less experienced visitors will need to access Giggijoch from the other. As one reporter put it: 'A hotel near one of the two main lift stations is a must'. The Hotel Regina, right by the Gaislachkoglbahn, is strongly recommended ('good sized rooms, friendly staff, ample portions of good food'). Gästehaus Sonneheim, in the same area, is praised for being 'extremely cheap and reasonably sited - we shall come here again'.

Eating in and out

Most of the restaurants are in the hotels and serve traditional Austrian food. Dominic is said to be the best eating place in the village ('friendly, beautifully furnished and decorated,

> ### ■ OTHER SPORTS
> Parapente, skating, curling, indoor tennis and badminton, indoor rifle shooting, swimming, tobogganing

with excellent and well-presented food — try the filettopf'). The Kupferpfanne in the Hotel Tirolerhof is famed for its venison and steaks. The à la carte restaurants in the Alpina, Stefan and Hubertus hotels are also recommended. Hotel Tyrol and Hotel Alpenland are cheaper alternatives. La Tavola is said to be excellent value. Hotel Sonne has a Stüberl with a cosy atmosphere.

Self-caterers are warned that here, as elsewhere in Austria, all supermarkets and grocery stores are closed on Sundays, which makes for a hungry start to the week for those who do not come prepared.

Après-ski

Once the lifts close Sölden swings into life. Café Philip at Innerwald, reached via an often rocky run down, has a lively atmosphere and is a focal gathering point for young people. The single-chair down from here runs until 6pm for those whose legs are wobbly from the skiing or otherwise. The Hinterer, Dominic and Café Heiner near the Giggijoch gondola are always crowded. The Park Hotel and the Nanu Bar are recommended for a quieter drink. Later in the evening, Jakob's Weinfassl attracts a thirty-something clientèle in 'beautiful décor and surroundings'. The Piano Bar in the Hotel Central is a sophisticated disco with free entry but double-price drinks.

Childcare

Apart from private babysitting, Sölden has no special facilities for small non-skiing children. The Sölden/Hochsölden Ski School runs a ski kindergarten with a play area, for skiers aged three years old and above.

Skiing facts: **Sölden**

TOURIST OFFICE
Postfach 80, A-6450 Sölden, Tyrol
Tel 43 5254 22120
Fax 43 5254 3131

THE RESORT
By road Calais 1000km
By rail Ötztal-Bahnhof 35km, Innsbruck 88km
By air Innsbruck $1\frac{1}{2}$ hrs
Visitor beds 9,662
Transport free ski bus runs through village every 9 mins

THE SKIING
Linked or nearby resorts Hochsölden (n), Untergurgl (n), Hochgurgl (n), Obergurgl (n), Vent (n), Zwieselstein (n)
Longest run Gaislachkogl, 10km (red)
Number of lifts 22 in Sölden (excluding glacier), 33 in Ötztal Arena
Total of trails/pistes 101km (42% easy, 43% intermediate, 15% difficult)
Nursery slopes 3 lifts and trails
Summer skiing 10 lifts on Rettenbach and Tiefenbach glaciers
Snowmaking 50 hectares covered

LIFT PASSES
Area pass (including glacier) ÖS2,020 for 6 days
Day pass ÖS440
Beginners points tickets
Pensioners reductions for women 60 yrs and over and men 65 yrs and over
Credit cards accepted no

SKI SCHOOLS
Adults Sölden/Hochsölden, ÖS1,600 for 6 days (4 hrs per day). Total Vacancia,
ÖS1,050 for 6 days ($2\frac{1}{2}$ hrs per day).
Ötztal 2000, ÖS2,400 for 6 days ($4\frac{1}{2}$ hrs per day)
Private lessons Sölden/Hochsölden, ÖS1,400 per 2-hr lesson, Total Vacancia, ÖS1,400 per $2\frac{1}{2}$-hr lesson, Ötztal 2000, ÖS1,400-2,200 per 2-hr lesson
Snowboarding Sölden/Hochsölden ÖS1,990 for 6 days, Total Vacancia ÖS1,320 for 6 days ($2\frac{1}{2}$ hrs per day), Ötztal 2000 ÖS2,400 for 6 days ($4\frac{1}{2}$ hrs per day).
Private lessons: Sölden/Hochsölden ÖS1,600 for 2 hrs, Total Vacancia ÖS1,400 for $2\frac{1}{2}$ hrs, Ötztal 2000 ÖS1,400 for 2 hrs
Cross-country Sölden/Hochsölden ÖS1,600 for 4 hrs, Total Vacancia ÖS1,240 for $2\frac{1}{2}$ hrs, Ötztal 2000 ÖS2,400 for $4\frac{1}{2}$ hrs.
Private lessons also available. Loipe 8km near Sölden and 5km at Zwieselstein
Other courses telemark, monoski
Guiding companies through ski schools

CHILDREN
Lift pass 6-14 yrs, ÖS1,150 for 6 days, free for 5 yrs and under
Ski kindergarten Sölden/Hochsölden, 3 yrs and over, 9.30am-4pm, ÖS1,610 for 6 days including lunch
Ski school Total Vacancia, 4 yrs and over, 9.30am-midday and 1-3.30pm, ÖS1,500 for 6 days, extra ÖS110 per day for lunch.
Ötztal 2000, 4 yrs and over, 10am-midday and 1-3pm, ÖS2,300 for 6 days, extra ÖS70 per day for lunch
Non-ski kindergarten not available, private babysitting on request

FOOD AND DRINK PRICES
Coffee ÖS25, glass of wine ÖS35, small beer ÖS30, dish of the day ÖS95-250

Söll and the Ski-Welt

ALTITUDE 703m (2,306ft)

Söll has an unfair and unfounded reputation as the lager-lout capital of skiing, a resort better known for its uninhibited partying than the challenge of its pistes. In fact, this rather unmemorable village is positively staid in comparison with many other destinations in Austria, with its skiing offering much more than its après-ski. It lies at the heart of a vast ski circus, made up of a total of 11 resorts, with 90 lifts and 250km of skiing (almost all of which is interlinked) on one lift pass. It is best suited to intermediates but the area, which is unendearingly known as Ski-Welt, has enough on- and off-piste skiing to keep the most adventurous skier happy for a week.

Söll attracts the budget end of the market (if 'budget' skiers can possibly afford to ski in Austria at present), and is considerably more attractive to singles and groups than it is to families. However, anyone looking for a wild time here will be disappointed. The resort seems mournfully quiet in comparison with the flesh-pots of **Kitzbühel** a few kilometres down the road. You have to wonder whether, in the lurid minds of sensational tabloid news editors, Söll sometimes becomes confused with Sölden or even with Soldeu. Both the latter, elsewhere in Austria and in Andorra, are considerably more prone to the 'ere-we-go, 'ere-we-go school of skier who is no more prominent in Söll than anywhere else.

The resort aims itself, with not inconsiderable success, at a clientèle mainly in their twenties to early thirties. According to reporters, it is not ideal for those in search of 'a quiet drink after a long day's skiing'. The one popular disco may thump away through the night, and the main three bars are full until the early hours, but the majority of their clients are Dutch rather than British. There is a wide variety of other sports for non-skiers, but the shops are disappointing and the village is deserted during skiing hours.

■ **GOOD POINTS**

Large linked ski area, attractive scenery, efficient lift system, short airport transfer, tree-line skiing, extensive cross-country trails

■ **BAD POINTS**

Limited après-ski, unreliable bus service, few facilities for families, lack of activities for non-skiers, low altitude

On the mountain
top 1829m (5,999ft) bottom 622m (2,040ft)

The skiing is some of the most underrated in the whole of the Alps. Kilometre upon kilometre of varied piste will take an average intermediate from one typically Tyrolean village to another, with the chance to stop en route at a number of pleasant little mountain restaurants, many of them with panoramic views over the valley.

The whole Ski-Welt area ranges from 622m at **Hopfgarten** to 1829m. Söll's skiing takes place on north-facing slopes on the far side of the main road, a testing walk from the village or free ski-bus ride away. The distance is an annoying inconvenience that makes Söll unsuitable as a base for families with small children. A car is useful and means you can join the Ski-Welt system from other nearby resorts.

Mountain access is by the fast and efficient Hochsöll gondola. At the top is Salvenmoos, the hub of Söll's ski area from where a cluster of lifts fan out. A single chair takes you up to Hohe Salve at 1829m, the highest point of the system.

Access to **Westendorf** from Söll is via the covered bubble-chair from the mid-station (thereby avoiding Hohe Salve), a choice of excellent runs down to **Brixen** (via Hoch Brixen), and finally a bus-ride to the Westendorf gondola station. Apart from having to make the short bus connection to Westendorf or another to the much smaller area of **Kelchsau**, the rest of the huge circus can be reached on skis.

The lift system is, on the whole, fairly modern by Austrian standards. The Ski-Welt lift companies insist that their policy is only to build new and larger lifts when they are quite sure about the safety of allowing extra skiers in that part of the ski area. More realistically, it is the local government's 'green' policy that forbids further expansion.

The lack of piste hazard-warning signs is an on-going complaint, especially at those times when snow cover is insufficient, with reporters continually coming across bare pistes: 'I lost count of the number of runs I came down, only to find that halfway down I had to negotiate mud for about 200 metres'.

Beginners

The nursery slopes are in the open fields between the village and the bottom of the mountain. The low altitude means snow here is uncertain and in the event of poor cover, beginners are taken up to Salvenmoos. A scenic blue (easy) run leads back down to the base-station of the gondola when snow conditions permit. For much of the winter it is wiser to download.

Intermediates

Ski-Welt was designed for intermediates; it is an interlocking network of runs spread over low but varied mountains from **Going** at one end to Westendorf and Kelchsau at the other. This is excellent cruising terrain, both above and below the tree-line, with plenty of steep and usually undergraded pitches to keep the adrenalin flowing.

Advanced

Advanced skiers should try the challenging black (difficult) run at **Scheffau**, which is marked with a skull-and-crossbones sign at the starting point. Westendorf has a black mogul field from the top of the Alpenrose chair and a run to **Santenbach** and **Kandler**.

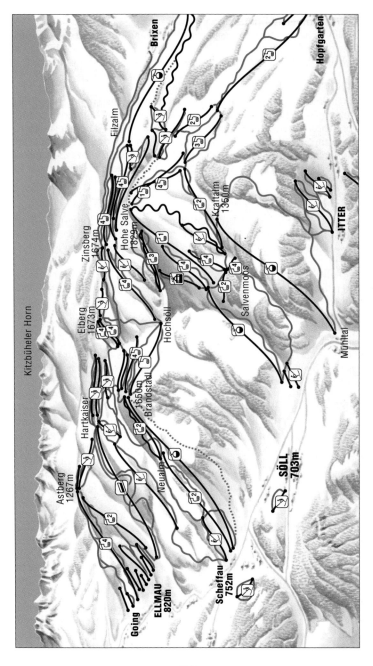

Many of the red (intermediate) runs in the area are steep enough to qualify as blacks elsewhere, including the Abfahrt in **Ellmau** and the runs down from the four-seater chair in Söll. From Hohe Salve, Grundried is a challenging black mogul-slope, back down to the Salvenmoos area.

Off-piste
Satisfying off-piste skiing can be found under the single-chair from Hohe Salve. The small bowl here usually holds its snow in good conditions for longer than any of the neighbouring pistes. The unpisted run down through the trees at Kasbichl, between Rigi and Salvenmoos at Hopfgarten, can also be challenging. Innere Keat above Söll has a number of off-piste opportunities, including an itinerary route to **Brixen im Thale**.

Ski schools and guiding
The two ski schools are Söll-Hochsöll and Austria Söll. Reports for both are of friendly instructors. However, 'too many classes in the first few days of the week were crowded on to the limited nursery area'.

Snowboarding
There is a half-pipe on the Salvenmoos slope and a Fun Park, complete with jumps and a landing area, on the Stöckl piste. Both of Söll's regular ski schools offer group lessons.

Cross-country
This is a major langlauf centre with prepared trails all the way along the valley. Söll itself has the easy 12-km Sonnseitloipe as well as the intermediate, 9-km Schattseitloipe.

Mountain restaurants
In the Söll area, mountain restaurant queues of up to half an hour are not uncommon during busy weeks. However, most of the eating-places are reported to be comfortable, reasonably priced and serve a wide variety of food. The Rigi restaurant at the top of the Kasbichl chair above Hopfgarten has a wonderful view of the valley and some of the neighbouring resorts ('you can smell the barbecued chicken from a mountain away — it is not to be missed').

Similarly, you can soak up the sunshine and the awesome panorama of the Wilder Kaiser from the Gipfel self-service restaurant above Hopfgarten. Owner Georg Arger, a former professional ski champion, uses the restaurant walls as a showcase for his cups and medals. All grades of skier can meet up here as it is easily reached by the gondola and chair-lift from Söll. Kraftalm, at the top of the **Itter** gondola, is one of the area's original restaurants and remains the most popular stop-off point at the end of the skiing day. Fitzalm, in Brixen, is an attractive old hut run by an elderly farmer whose specialities are home-made bread and home-cooked food. Jochstube, at the top of Zinzberg in Scheffau, is another old hut with a large open fireplace and several tiny rooms.

Off the mountain

Söll has a small, traffic-free centre based around the church and original village inn. The local council is particularly keen on entering competitions and has won all kinds of prizes, not least one for being the best 'pedestrian and bicycle village in Austria'. It even won the European 'Village Improvement Project' award but, for all that, it is no great charmer. Hotels, chalets and guesthouses fan out from the middle of town in an untidy sprawl. The proximity of a major trunk road makes Söll ideal for easy transfers to Innsbruck and Munich, but otherwise cuts an unpleasant swathe across the pastures. Although there is a lack of the typical Tyrolean atmosphere found in nearby resorts such as Kitzbühel, the local inhabitants have a sensible cosmopolitan attitude towards tourism.

Accommodation

The main hotel in the pedestrian zone is the Postwirt; a comfortable modern annexe has been added to the old, traditionally furnished hotel. We have favourable reports of both the Greil and the Austria, also in the town centre. The Hotel Tyrol is recommended with 'rooms not exactly large, but comfortable and clean'. Another reporter comments: 'Meals were excellent and well worth the cost'. Hotel Maria at the northern end of the resort is 'fairly basic, but offers friendly and helpful personal service and

> **■ OTHER SPORTS**
>
> Skating, curling, sleigh rides, tobogganing, swimming, rifle range, squash, hang-gliding, parapente, winter walks

superb food'. Sporthotel Modlinger is commended for its 'excellent, polite and quick service, but the portions of food were on the small side'. Hotel Teresa is said to be 'small, but with delicious food and a friendly atmosphere'. The Alpenschlössl is a luxury four-star hotel.

Eating in and out

The majority of Söll's skiers tend to eat at their hotels on a half-board basis. The choice of restaurants is limited, but the cost of eating out is by no means as prohibitive as in some resorts. The Schindlhaus and the Greil are renowned for their Austrian nouvelle cuisine, and the Postwirt restaurant is also recommended. At the cheaper end of the scale, the Venezia Pizzeria and the Christophorus offer value for money. The Hotel Tenne is reported as 'basic, but good value', while the Dorfstube offers traditional Austrian cooking. The hotels Postwirt and Gänsleit serve vegetarian meals on request. The Elbow Bar Pizzeria is 'excellent'. The three supermarkets are 'cheap, spotlessly clean and well-stocked with all you could need'.

Après-ski

The upstairs bar of the Hotel Austria is said to have 'excellent '60s and '70s evenings, which invariably end up as a hugely enjoyable sing-song; do not expect a seat after 8pm'. For a quiet evening in more traditional Tyrolean surroundings, the Dorfstube is recommended. The après-ski starts at 4pm with the focus on the village's three main bars. Whisky

Mühle, housed inside a giant beer-barrel in the pedestrian zone, has over the years established itself as a Söll landmark; it was beginning to fall apart from years of manic misuse, but has finally been refurbished. Pub Austria and the Elbow Room are said to be 'more civilised'. The Christophorus has live music.

Childcare

The Mini Club situated next to the gondola base-station takes children from three to five years old, either all day or mornings-only, six days a week. The emphasis is on play, with a chance to take first steps on skis within the safe confines of the club. The ski schools take children from five years old, but the distance from the village to the gondola makes this an inconvenient resort for families with young children.

Linked or nearby resorts

Ellmau
top 1829m (5,999ft) bottom 820m (2,690ft)

Ellmau's once compact centre has expanded in recent years and now straggles the whole 400m up to the ski area. It has more shops, bars and general après-ski facilities than the other Ski-Welt resorts and is a livelier place to stay than Söll. Where you stay is no longer of any real importance as the maximum walk to the centre or the lifts is ten minutes. There is a nursery-slope T-bar in the village centre, and five other nursery-slope lifts in the main ski area. The resort supports three ski schools.

Mountain eating-places include the self-service Bergrestaurant Hartkaiser ('over-busy at peak times, but great *Gulaschsuppe*'). The Alte Post is one of the more comfortable hotels. Après-ski venues include Café Widauer, the Helden bar, Café Breit, Café Kaiserman, Café Monica, and the Memory Pub. Recommended restaurants include Pizzeria Sojer, Renate's Bistro, and Café Restaurant Hermann. Late-night revellers gather at the Rendezvous, Ellmauer Tenne, and the Helden discos.

TOURIST OFFICE
Tel 43 5358 2301
Fax 43 5358 3443

Going
top 1829m (5,999ft) bottom 800m (2,624ft)

A quainter place than most of the others in the Ski-Welt, Going is a village of attractive, old, wooden chalets at the far end of the valley towards St Johann in Tirol. The north-facing slopes, although they start at a low 800m, hold their snow longer than some of the neighbouring resorts.

TOURIST OFFICE
Tel 43 5358 2438
Fax 43 5358 3501

Hopfgarten
top 1829m (5,999ft) bottom 622m (2,040ft)

The mainly south-facing and sunny slopes here do not hold their snow well, and if you are planning to use the resort as a base it is advisable to go during the first half of the season. The village, which is placed between Westendorf and Itter, has an ancient appearance, with its steep, cobbled streets and compact centre. For no known reason, it attracts a disproportionate number of South Africans, Australians and New Zealanders. This gives the village an unexpected international air. Café Mayer and the Old English Pub are popular, and the restaurant Brixental is recommended.

TOURIST OFFICE
Tel 43 5335 2322
Fax 43 5335 2630

Scheffau
top 1829m (5,999ft) bottom 750m (2,460ft)

Scheffau is not as well placed for skiing as some of its neighbours. The actual village is a short bus-ride away from the slopes on the far side of the main road. However, the rustic solitude of the village, with hotels dotted around the pastures and a pretty green-and-white church, more than makes up for this inconvenience. Reporters speak warmly of it: 'Small, quiet and friendly, and an ideal access point for the Ski-Welt'. The free bus to and from the slopes runs regularly. The slopes are reached by gondola or chair-lift, and the runs back down to the base-station are open and wide. The chair-lifts at Eiberg are fast and usually uncrowded. The only queues are for the gondola in the morning and the Brandstadl chair at lunchtime and in the evening.

Scheffau is known for holding its snow better than any of the other Ski-Welt villages, and access into Ellmau and Söll's skiing, on either side of Scheffau, is straightforward. Hotel Alpin serves 'four-course dinners and plenty of it' and has a swimming-pool. Gasthof Weberbauer, in the village centre, is recommended for its 'excellent bedrooms and bathrooms and excellent evening meal'. Pub Royal, the main nightspot, is a friendly place with live music, the Kaiseralm disco is expensive, and Conny's Corner attracts mainly locals.

TOURIST OFFICE
Tel 43 5358 8137
Fax 43 5358 8539

Westendorf
top 1892m (6,207ft) bottom 800m (2,624ft)

Westendorf is next in line along the valley from Brixen and joins into the whole ski area by a free bus link. An efficient six-person gondola starts in the village, and beside it is an immense beginners' ski area, well covered by snow-cannon, at the foot of the principal slopes. The main runs are generally more demanding than elsewhere in the region. One reporter comments: 'They were steeper, icier and more difficult than we expected'. Much, of course, depends on snow conditions. The only lift queues of more than a few minutes seem to be for the nursery-slope drag, an indication of the immense popularity of this resort for beginners. The tourist office claims that more British visitors have learned to ski here than anywhere else in the Alps. Recommended mountain eating-places include Alpenrose and Breckhornhaus. The Talkaiser at the top of the gondola is said to lack charm.

Westendorf is one of the most compact and attractive of all the Ski-Welt villages and has a genuine Tyrolean atmosphere coupled with a liveliness lacking in resorts such as Scheffau and Going. The general standard of accommodation appears to be high, with the most expensive hotels also the most conveniently placed. Hotel Jakobwirt is recommended for its 'friendly staff, good food, good facilities and central location'. The Schermerhof apartments are described as suitable for families.

The après-ski has plenty of variety and is very lively. The Cow Shed at the bottom of the gondola is recommended, and Café Angerer is a popular meeting place. Skiers dine early here with restaurants filling up by 7pm; reservations are recommended. Chez Yves is rated for pizza and steaks, the Schermer for fresh farm produce and local venison, and Pizzeria Toscana is also recommended. The Bichlingerhof and the Jakobwirt restaurant are more expensive. Gerry's Inn attracts the young disco crowd.

Westendorf has all the makings of a good family resort. It is traffic-free, the slopes are a five-minute walk from the centre of the village (a free bus is available), and both ski schools (Ski School Westendorf and Ski School Top) have non-ski and ski kindergartens catering for children from two years old. We have mixed reports of Ski School Westendorf, which is the larger of the two. One reporter complains that 'the sole playing point consisted of a mountain of ice made from previously piled-up snow. No sledges, toys or other such useful items were available'. Reporters said that Ski School Top appears to offer a more personal service for adults and children alike.

TOURIST OFFICE
Tel 43 5334 6230
Fax 43 5334 2390

The remaining Ski-Welt resorts are **Brixen im Thale** at 800m (the bus connection point for Westendorf), **Itter** at 730m between Söll and Hopfgarten, and **Kelchsau**, a small, unconnected farming village between Hopfgarten and the Wildschönau area.

Skiing facts: **Söll**

TOURIST OFFICE
Postfach 21, A-6306 Söll, Tyrol
Tel 43 5333 5216
Fax 43 5333 6180

THE RESORT
By road Calais 1114km
By rail Kufstein 12km, St Johann 17km,
Wörgl 12km (2 hrs from Munich and 1½ hrs
from Salzburg)
By air Innsbruck 45 mins, Salzburg 1½ hrs
Visitor beds 4,100
Transport free bus between village and
ski area

THE SKIING
Linked or nearby resorts Brixen im Thale
(l), Ellmau (l), Going (l), Hopfgarten (l), Itter
(l), Kelchsau (n), Kirchberg (n), Kitzbühel
(n), Scheffau (l), Westendorf (n)
Longest run Hohe Salve–Kraftalm–Söll,
7.5km (red)
Number of lifts 12 in Söll, 90 in Ski-Welt
Total of trails/pistes 250km in Ski-Welt
(43% easy, 49% intermediate, 8% difficult)
Nursery slopes 3 lifts and runs
Summer skiing none
Snowmaking 125 hectares covered

LIFT PASSES
Area pass Ski-Welt (covers all lifts in area)
ÖS1,660 for 6 days
Day pass Söll ÖS330, Ski-Welt ÖS350
Beginners points tickets
Pensioners no reduction
Credit cards accepted no

SKI SCHOOLS
Adults Söll-Hochsöll, ÖS1,290 for 5 days.
Austria Söll, ÖS1,300 for 6 days, both
9.30am-4.15pm
Private lessons both ski schools,
ÖS460 per hr
Snowboarding both ski schools,
ÖS400 per day
Cross-country both ski schools,
ÖS400 per day, private instruction on
request. Loipe 30km
Other courses telemark, race training,
moguls
Guiding companies through ski schools

CHILDREN
Lift pass 7-16 yrs, ÖS940 for 6 days,
free for 6 yrs and under if accompanied by
an adult
Ski kindergarten Söll-Hochsöll, 3-5 yrs,
9.30am-4.30pm, ÖS300 per day including
lunch and snack
Ski school Söll-Hochsöll, 5-14 yrs,
9.30am-4.15pm, ÖS1,250 for 5 days
(extra ÖS100 per day for lunch).
Austria Söll, 5-14 yrs, ÖS1,250 for
6 days (4 hrs per day) including
lunch
Non-ski kindergarten Mini Club, 3-5 yrs,
9.30am-4.30pm, ÖS300 per day including
lunch and snack

FOOD AND DRINK PRICES
Coffee ÖS22-25, glass of wine ÖS18-27,
small beer ÖS22-25, dish of the day
ÖS90-140

St Anton

ALTITUDE 1304m (4,278ft)

St Anton is to skiing what St Andrews is to golf. The Arlberg region, of which St Anton is the capital, is the birthplace of the modern technique and in part responsible for the way we ski today. The neighbouring hamlet of **St Christoph** is the seat of the Bundessportheim, Austria's Ski Academy and the highest teaching body in the land.

For those who love skiing and its accompanying traditions, St Anton is the best resort in Austria. When it comes to variety and degree of difficulty, its slopes are world-class and on a par with those in Val d'Isère, Verbier and Chamonix.

■ **GOOD POINTS**

Expert ski terrain, extensive off-piste, large ski area, ski-touring opportunities, efficient lift system, lively après-ski

■ **BAD POINTS**

Limited for beginners, not ideal for families, few activities for non-skiers, crowded pistes

Skiing came to the Arlberg in the late nineteenth century – a pastor in Lech visited his parishioners on skis as early as 1895. In 1921 Hannes Schneider opened the Arlberg Ski School, which proved to be the father of all ski schools, a role model that set a precedent for subsequent advances worldwide. Generations of Europeans grew up with the distinctive Arlberg technique — skis clamped together, shoulders facing down the hill — a contrived yet elegant style that dominated the sport until the French, with Jean-Claude Killy their greatest exponent, declared technical war in the 1960s.

Piste preparation, courtesy of two men and a roller, was pioneered in the resort in 1949. Today 38 snow-cannon, 22 drivers and 16 snowcats work for up to nine hours a night to ensure good coverage, even on the lower slopes near the town.

The price of such fame is the presence of ski bums — notably Scandinavians drawn by the challenge of the resort's radical slopes. For years St Anton has suffered from extremes of raucous drunken behaviour, which begins before the lifts close for the day and escalates through the evening and early hours of the morning. Steps to curb these excesses have included closing the bars and nightclubs at 2am instead of 3am, but this had little effect. However, painful currency exchange rates have done much to solve the problem by keeping large numbers of the troublemakers at home — even ski bums have to pay for drinks. Closing times have now been restored to the later hour.

St Anton lies barely within the Tyrol on the border of the Vorarlberg, Austria's most westerly province. Austria's main east–west railway runs straight through the middle of town, and in March you can even travel to

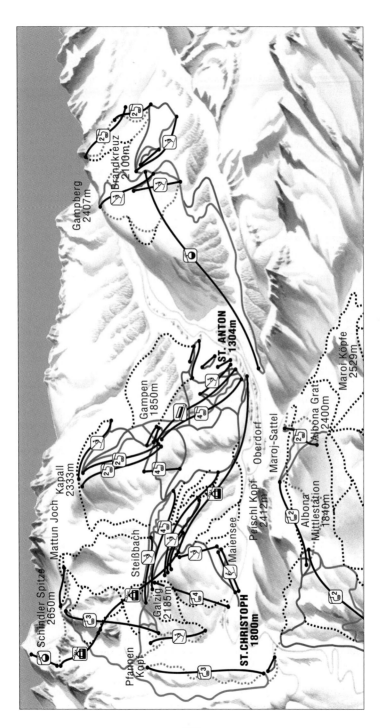

Schindler Spitze 2650m
Mattun Joch
Kapall 2333m
Gampen 1850m
Brandkreuz 2100m
Gampberg 2407m
ST. ANTON 1304m
Maroi Köpfe 2529m
Albona Grat 2400m
Maroi-Sattel
Oberdorf
Peischl Kopf 2412m
Maiensee
Steißbach
Galzig 2185m
Pfannen Kopf
ST. CHRISTOPH 1800m
Albona Mittelstation 1846m

the snow aboard the Orient Express, which stops here at the start of its nine-month season.

On the mountain
top 2811m (9,222ft) bottom 1304m (4,278ft)

The Arlberg Ski Pass covers the linked area of St Anton, St Christoph and **Stuben**, as well as adjoining **Lech** and **Zürs**. It provides excellent value for skiers based in St Anton, but is wildly expensive for those who base themselves in the much smaller separate region, the Princess of Wales being among them.

St Anton's skiing takes place on both sides of the valley, but the most challenging area is on the northern slopes dominated by the 2811-m Valluga.

A gradual upgrading of the lift system has done much to improve mountain access, and the high-speed quad chair to Gampen takes the morning strain off the Kandahar funicular and the Galzig cable car. They all take you to the skiing so you simply choose the shortest queue.

As you rise up to mid-mountain level, the ski area splits into two, separated by a valley. Gampen at 1850m has a restaurant and children's ski enclosure. It is a sunny plateau with two chair-lifts rising to the higher slopes of Kapall at 2326m. Galzig is the focal point of the serious skiing in St Anton.

From Galzig you can ski down to St Christoph at 1800m, a small hamlet crowned by the Hotel Arlberg-Hospiz. Above Galzig lie the more sublime challenges of the Valluga and the Schindlergrat at 2605m.

The Valluga is reached by a second and oversubscribed cable car from Galzig, which is operated with a confusing and unsatisfactory numbered-ticket system; you take a ticket and ask the lift attendant to translate it into a time so that you know when to return.

The alternative is to ski down into the valley behind Galzig and take the quad chair-lift up to the Schindlergrat. The skiing from here is some of the best in St Anton.

The Rendl at 2100m is a separate ski area on the other side of the St Anton valley and is reached by the Rendlbahn gondola, a short ski bus ride from town. It offers interesting and often uncrowded skiing and catches so much sun its local nickname is Rendl Beach.

Beginners

St Anton is not a beginner's ski resort, and anyone less than a confident intermediate would be well advised to avoid it. The few blue (easy) slopes that exist would nearly all be classified as intermediate elsewhere. Even the crowded main run back into the village is seen as a challenging red (intermediate) by most skiers. There are three learner T-bars spread between **Nasserein** and the funicular railway. The Gampen has a children's ski area and the gentle Gampenlift T-bar. St Christoph has its own Maiensee beginner lift. Those with a little experience may also find some of the runs on the Rendl negotiable.

Intermediates

Confident intermediates head for Galzig. The sunny slopes below are served by the Ostbahn high-speed quad, and the main runs are sufficiently self-contained to encourage confidence but vary dramatically in degree of difficulty. A delightful and easy blue run takes you down into St Christoph. Timid skiers should note that St Anton has dispensed with black (difficult) runs in favour of unpisted ski-routes, in what some critics see as a negation of responsibility. These appear on the map as either plain red or black-bordered diamonds. For red read black, for black-border read double-black.

Advanced

Depending on the snow conditions, almost all of St Anton's skiing can be considered advanced. From the Vallugagrat, three of St Anton's finest long runs lead back to the broad, flat valley of the Steissbachtal, a corridor between the Valluga runs and those on the adjoining Kapall.

The toughest of the three is the Schindlerkar, a wide 30-degree mogul marathon that seems to go on forever. Strong skiers can repeat it continually by riding the Schindlergratbahn high-speed quad, but its south-facing aspect makes it vulnerable to early-morning ice and late-afternoon slush. The Mattun is a series of mogulled bowls linked by traverses, less steep in pitch but more intriguing because of the variety of its challenges. The third much easier option, the long dog-leg via the Ulmerhütte, opens up the Valluga to confident intermediates. It is also the starting point for the run to the high, cold outpost of Stuben.

Off-piste

The off-piste possibilities are limitless, and a guide can find fresh powder a week after the last fall. An experienced skier wanting to truly enjoy St Anton should view the services of a local guide, along with accommodation and food, as part of the basic cost of the holiday. In some resorts guides can effectively do little more than find a bit of untracked snow beside a piste, but in St Anton they can open up whole hidden valleys.

The patio-sized top of the Valluga is accessed by a six-person cable car confined to sightseers or skiers accompanied by a qualified guide. From the top, it is possible to ski down the Pazieltal into Zürs and Lech. The valley itself is not difficult to ski, but the first few metres of the north face of the Valluga are terrifying, with a cliff ready to take away anyone who falls.

The Malfon Valley over the back of the Rendl is a wide, enjoyable off-piste run which, when there is sufficient snow, ends on a road at the base of the lift. Above Stuben, a 20-minute walk up the Maroi Kopfe gives entry to the Maroital Valley.

St Anton's mainly south-facing slopes have a good snow record but also harbour an extremely high avalanche risk.

Ski schools and guiding

The Arlberg Ski School has 180 instructors, half of whom teach ski-school classes at any one time while the other half are hired out as private guides. The rival St Anton school, run by Franz Klimmer, has 30 instructors. Competition between the two is fierce, which helps to maintain standards with class sizes usually restricted to ten. We have excellent reports of both: 'the patient instructor spoke good English because he was English' (St Anton) and 'excellent instruction in private lesson' (Arlberg). Alpine Faszination is a recommended off-piste guiding service.

Snowboarding
Snowboarders were once few in this traditional alpine ski resort. Today, the off-piste appeals to increasing numbers of riders, although relatively few are attracted to the main runs. The Rendl has a snowboard fun-park with obstacle courses and a 100-m World Cup standard half-pipe.

Cross-country
There are 40km of loipe in the area. These include scenic tracks along the banks of the Rosanna river to Flirsch and back to St Anton.

Mountain restaurants
According to reporters, most restaurants in the area offer reasonable fare at high-altitude prices. The Albonagrat is highly rated ('superb, great atmosphere, cheap food'). The bleak self-service at Galzig has panoramic views over the slopes and inevitably gets overcrowded, but it does have an adjoining waiter-service restaurant. Stopp's at St Christoph is popular. The Sennehütte and s'Grabli are both recommended. The Taps, below Kapall, is also praised. The terrace of the Arlberg-Hospiz is also popular with 'attentive service from traditionally dressed waiters; Prince Edward has eaten here, but prices are not outrageous.' Hotel Post in Stuben and the Maiensee Stube in St Christoph are both praised.

Off the mountain
St Anton's setting is hardly seductive — a meandering valley along the main railway line between Zurich and Vienna. There is not much that is distinguished about the architecture, which is a blend of old and new that owes little to planning and a lot to those who recognised an opportunity and seized it before the current strict zoning regulations came into force. A fierce policy of no outside ownership, no holiday homes, and no expansion in the number of guest beds has saved it from otherwise inevitable blight.

The opening of St Anton to the outside world began in 1884 when the railway tunnel under the Arlberg Pass was completed. What had been little more than a hamlet grew steadily into a village, with its narrow main street running parallel to the tracks. In the days before the road tunnel under the Arlberg Pass and the St Anton bypass were opened in 1977, the street was a traffic nightmare. Today, it is a relatively peaceful pedestrian zone lined with shops, cafés and traditional hotels.

The rest of the town straggles along the road in both directions, towards Mooserkreuz at the top of the resort to the west, and towards the satellite villages of Nasserein and St Jakob to the east. British clients without their own transport should note that British tour operators have a price-led love affair with grim, low-budget Nasserein, frequently featured in the St Anton section in brochures. Access to the ski area was greatly improved by the opening of the Mulden chair-lift but, as the shuttle bus does not run in the evening, the nightlife is limited.

Accommodation

The area has two five-star hotels: the historic and expensive Arlberg-Hospiz at St Christoph and the modern St Antoner Hof near the bypass. The four-star options are headed by the Post ('accommodation excellent, but staff snotty'), the Alte Post and the Schwarzer Adler ('comfortable and convenient'), all much richer in tradition and much closer to the lifts. With a strong British tradition and presence here it comes as no surprise that St Anton has an abundance of chalets.

One reporter strongly recommends Haus Lina for its 'fabulous breakfasts, en-suite bathrooms, Austrian décor and few Brits'. Hotel Arlberg is praised for 'excellent food and rooms and

> **■ OTHER SPORTS**
>
> Curling, swimming, indoor tennis and squash, sleigh rides, paragliding, tobogganing, bowling, skating

friendly, helpful, English-speaking staff'. The Goldenes Kreuz is a family-run three-star hotel described as 'clean, friendly, and very good value'.

Eating in and out

With the exception of the restaurants in the Arlberg-Hospiz and the Hospiz-Alm, dining out is not a strong feature of St Anton. Elsewhere the emphasis is on substantial rather than sophisticated fare. The restaurants in the Post and the Alte Post are better than their more contemporary rivals. Café Sailer serves reasonably priced cuisine. Fondue is also popular, especially at the family-run Montjola. The Brunnenhof in St Jakob has 'some of the best food in the region'. The old inn in the forest at Ferwall specialises in local game and is best reached by a brisk 45-minute sleigh-ride along one of the most beautiful valleys in the Alps. The Ski Museum functions in the evening as a restaurant.

Après-ski

St Anton's undeniably vibrant après-ski starts to warm up from lunchtime in the Sennehütte before sliding down to the Mooserwirt and the Krazy Kangaruh, just above the final descent to the resort. The Mooserwirt ('absolutely rocking') has at last ousted its Australian-inspired rival as the number-one spot, but both bars remain packed to bursting point long after the lifts close. Most guests, after dancing in their ski boots and consuming copious amounts of drink, still manage to negotiate, on skis in the dark, the final 800m home past a battery of active snow-cannon.

Down in the resort the action continues until sundown on the terrace of the Hotel Alte Post before switching to the refurbished Postkeller or to the Underground, which has good live music. The St Antoner Hof Bar is recommended for 'a quiet, sophisticated drink'. Late-evening entertainment is centred on the ever-crowded Postkeller. The Piccadilly in the same building is also busy. Bobo's Mexican bar and the Hazienda ('shamelessly modern') are both recommended. Platz'l Après is a cocktail bar with live music and comfortable sofas.

Childcare

St Anton is not recommended for children. It can, for reasons explained above, be noisy at night and has limited easy skiing. The main children's area, with cut-out figures to ski through, is on the Gampen. It is accessible either by chair-lift or more conveniently by the funicular railway. There are nursery slopes at the base of the mountain, but the valley is so deep at this point that the sun does not penetrate to its base for much of the day during winter. The kindergarten takes youngsters from two years of age, and children from five years of age (or four by arrangement) are welcome at the ski school.

Linked or nearby resorts

Stuben
top 2811m (9,222ft) bottom 1407m (4,616ft)

The village was named after the warm parlour (Stube) of a solitary house on the Arlberg Pass, where pilgrims used to shelter 200 years ago. Only 32 houses have been added since then and Stuben has a mere 104 residents and 650 guest beds. The Post Inn, now a four-star hotel, was where mail-coach drivers changed horses for the steep journey up the pass. With its small collection of hotels and restaurants, Stuben is seen by some as an ideal way to enjoy the Arlberg without any of the bustle of the major resorts.

TOURIST OFFICE
Tel 43 5582 761
Fax 43 5582 7626

St Christoph top 2811m (9,222ft) bottom 1800m (5,906ft)

Further up the Arlberg Pass, St Christoph was the last resort for pilgrims making their way between the mountains. In 1386 a shepherd called Heinrich Findelkind von Kempten built a hospice on the pass with his own savings and manned it in the winter with two servants. The Brotherhood of St Christoph (a charitable foundation of locals inspired by von Kempten) still exists, but the hospice burned down in 1957. The five-star Arlberg-Hospiz hotel was built on the site. St Christoph has five other hotels, the Bundessportheim Ski Academy, and very little else.

Skiing facts: **St Anton**

TOURIST OFFICE
A-6580 St Anton, Arlberg
Tel 43 5446 22690
Fax 43 5446 2532

THE RESORT
By road Calais 1092km
By rail station in resort
By air Innsbruck 75 mins, Zurich 3-4 hrs, Munich 3-4 hrs
Visitor beds 8,000
Transport free ski bus

THE SKIING
Linked or nearby resorts St Christoph (l), Lech (n), Pettneu (n), Stuben (l), Zürs (n), Klösterle (n)
Longest run 8km, from the top of the Vallugagrat via the Ulmerhütte and Steissbachtal to the resort (black/blue)
Number of lifts 42 (86 on the Arlberg Ski Pass, including Lech and Zürs)
Total of trails/pistes 260km of prepared pistes (30% easy, 40% intermediate, 30% difficult)
Nursery slopes 8 lifts
Summer skiing none
Snowmaking 18km covered

LIFT PASSES
Area pass Arlberg Ski Pass (covers St Anton, St Christoph, Stuben, Lech, Zürs, Klösterle) ÖS2,190 for 6 days
Day pass ÖS455
Beginners no free lifts, ÖS345 per day

(valid only for beginner lifts)
Pensioners reduction for women 60 yrs and over and men 65 yrs and over
Credit cards accepted no

SKI SCHOOLS
Adults Arlberg ÖS1,490, St Anton ÖS1,350, both for 6 days (4 hrs per day)
Private lessons Arlberg ÖS1,410 and St Anton ÖS1,300, both per 2-hr lesson
Snowboarding Arlberg ÖS1,250, St Anton ÖS1,000, both for 3 half-days
Cross-country Arlberg and St Anton, as regular ski school prices. Loipe 40km
Other courses telemark, off-piste, heli-skiing, ski-touring
Guiding companies Alpine Faszination, or through ski schools

CHILDREN
Lift pass Arlberg Ski Pass, 6-15 yrs, ÖS1,310 for 6 days, 5 yrs and under, ÖS100 for season
Ski kindergarten Arlberg, 4 yrs and over, ÖS2,470 for 6 days (4 hrs per day) including lunch
Ski school Arlberg, 5-14 yrs, 9am-4.30pm, prices as adults
Non-ski kindergarten Jugendcenter, $2\frac{1}{2}$ yrs and over, 8.30am-4pm, ÖS1,080 for 6 days including lunch

FOOD AND DRINK PRICES
Coffee ÖS24, glass of wine ÖS21, small beer ÖS25, dish of the day ÖS80

TOURIST OFFICE
Tel as St Anton
Fax as St Anton

Zell am See

ALTITUDE 750m (2,460ft)

Zell am See is an attractive little medieval town in an idyllic lakeside setting just an hour from Salzburg. Its summer trade, which centres on water sports, is even larger than its winter trade, and the resort's huge international popularity rests on its hard-to-beat location at the foot of the 2000-m Schmittenhöhe. The mountain provides an ample amount of easy intermediate skiing and the towering presence of the Kitzsteinhorn above neighbouring **Kaprun** means that snow is guaranteed. Kaprun has the best developed glacier in Austria, with year-round skiing on the upper slopes. In times of poor snow cover the glacier becomes a daily point of pilgrimage for thousands of tourists from other resorts in Salzburgerland, and overcrowding can be unacceptable.

Kaprun and Zell am See have joined forces and market themselves under the unoriginal name of Europa Sport Region. The shared ski pass provides a total of 130km of skiing and access to 58 lifts.

In the past we have severely criticised Zell for skiing inconvenience, lift queues and heavy traffic. The town used to be dangerously bisected by a traffic-clogged trunk road, which, pollution apart, made reaching the slopes a hazardous business. Happily this is no longer so. A 10-km tunnel, which opened before the start of the 1996–7 skiing season, now takes all the through-traffic underground from **Schüttdorf** to the northern end of the lake, thereby restoring Zell to the peaceful backwater it used to be.

Mountain facilities have also improved, although Zell prides itself on its 'green' image and has vowed to replace old lifts but not to build any entirely new ones. The focus on uphill transport to the Schmittenhöhe has switched from the slow and overcrowded Schmittenhöhebahn at Schmittental to Schüttdorf; the Areitbahn gondola from here is being extended by two further stages so that the summit of the mountain can be reached in just 20 minutes. No longer will skiers from Schüttdorf have to ski down from the top of the first stage to the Hirschkogelbahn chair where the simultaneous arrival by gondola of skiers from Zell am See creates the worst bottleneck on the mountain.

Plans to upgrade the old double-chair to a detachable quad have so far been vetoed by the Mittelstation landowner.

Großvenediger
3674m

Sonnkogel
1850m

Maurerkogel
2074m

Schmittenhöhe
2000m

Sonnalm
1400m

Sonnalm-Pfiff

Sonnblick
3083m

Areitbahn 3

Sonnenalm-Pfiff

Mittelstation
1320m

ZELL AM SEE
758m

Hirschkogel
1720m

Areitbahn 2

Areitalm
1411m

Areitbahn 1

Kitzsteinhorn Glacier
3203m

Hochelser
3206m

Gletscherbahn
(Gipfelbahn)
3029m

Glocknerblick
1675m

Krefelder Hütte

Salzburger
Hütte

Maiskogelalmhütte

KAPRUN
770m

Schüttdorf

On the mountain
top 1965m (6,445ft) bottom 750m (2,460ft)

The Schmittenhöhe looks like a germknödl, the sweet, round dumpling to be found in the nine mountain restaurants which are on it. Its gentle slopes provide long, red (intermediate) runs both back down to the village itself and along the southern flank to the satellite of Schüttdorf. Steeper slopes drop down from a bowl and provide the most challenging skiing in the area.

Until the tunnel opened, the main mountain access was on the 'wrong' side of the busy trunk road, where the Zeller Bergbahn gondola rises to the mid-station at 1320m.

From Schmittental, 2km from the centre of Zell, the old Schmittenhöhe cable car rises sedately to the summit, or a second cable car takes you into the Sonnalm area on the sunny, south-facing side of the bowl, which is served by two more chairs and a drag-lift. Many skiers prefer to take the free bus and start the day on the Areitbahn gondola at Schüttdorf.

A small area of blue (easy) and red runs behind the summit is served by a chair- and a couple of drag-lifts. None of the skiing could be classified as difficult in good snow conditions, although a steepish pitch down the black (difficult) run below Sonnalm can present problems when it is worn and icy.

The Ebernberglift, above the road between Zell and Schüttdorf, is mainly used for slalom practice. The run down is short and fairly steep, offering panoramic views of the town. There is artificial snow on the black runs down into the pit of the bowl (without snow these can become dangerously icy) as well as on the nursery slopes.

Thumersbach, on the other side of the lake, has a chair-lift and three short drags that provide a couple of gentle, uncrowded runs back down the wooded slopes with wonderful views of Zell am See.

The pretty village of Kaprun, a five-minute journey on the ski bus, also has its own larger ski area comprising mainly blue runs. However, the best of its skiing is on the Kitzsteinhorn Glacier, 20 minutes from Zell. A choice of gondola, followed by quad-chair, or the original underground funicular, takes you up to the Alpincenter at 2450m, where lifts take you on up to the top of Kaprun's ski area at 3029m.

The Alpincenter includes a modest hotel, restaurants and a first-class ski shop. The glacier offers good, but exposed, blue and red runs, most of which are open nearly all year round (August skiing is usually limited to a couple of T-bars). A cable car takes you to the Aussichtsrestaurant at the top and gives access to the only difficult run: a short, steep mogul field. There is also a year-round cross-country circuit below the ridge at the top of the bowl. In winter, a long red takes you down to the mid-station of the funicular and ends in a push along the plastic floor of a long tunnel.

The construction of a gondola up to the glacier has done much to reduce queuing, but when snow cover is poor in this part of Austria the extensive car parks fill up with coaches at first light.

Beginners
At present, the ski school meets at the bottom of the Schmittenhöhebahn, although no doubt this will change as the lift's importance is downgraded. The main novice slopes are on the top of the mountain and you will need to take the lift down again at the end of the day. There are also nursery slopes at the bottom of the cable car and at Schüttdorf.

Intermediates
Intermediates will enjoy all the skiing here, which presents few real challenges. South of Schmittenhöhe, a succession of gentle, broad and sunny pistes descends along the ridge and on down to Schüttdorf. A right fork takes you to Areitalm, arrival point for the first stage of the Schüttdorf gondola; the cruising piste down to the bottom does not keep its snow in warm weather. The left fork brings you down to the Zell am See mid-station. The Sonnalm area also provides plenty of easy cruising.

Advanced
The two black runs that branch off over the southern lip of the bowl provide the best advanced terrain. These soon steepen into testing, but not intimidating, long runs with the occasional pitch of almost 30 degrees. The other two runs to the base-stations are less severe, but get more sun.

Off-piste
Zell's strong environmental policy means that off-piste skiing is severely restricted to the point of almost being forbidden. After a fresh fall, a number of tree-level runs look particularly enticing, but protection of saplings is a priority and you risk confiscation of your lift pass.

Ski schools and guiding
Ski schools in the valley seem to vary in quality and we have mixed reports of the eight schools in the region. None of them have priority in the lift lines, so it is not worth taking lessons just to jump the queues. The Wallner Prenner in Zell am See is the most recommended with 'excellent instructors, all of whom speak good English'. The Zell am See/Schmittenhöhe has a number of Australian teachers and also receives considerable praise. The Kitzsteinhorn Ski School operates year-round and has a high standard of instruction, particularly for advanced skiers.

Snowboarding
Zell am See is committed to the development of snowboarding and has a boardercross park, where competitions are held regularly; four riders race simultaneously down a challenging course, and the two fastest go through to the next round. Kaprun also has a half-pipe, which is in operation (snow permitting) all year round. Snowboarders should note that what little off-piste is available on the Schmittenhöhe is not available for them: snowboarding is forbidden outside the marked runs.

Cross-country

The cross-country skiing here is extensive, with 75km of loipe giving a choice of blue, red and black trails, which run from **Saalfelden** via the lake at Zell am See to either Kaprun or to **Bruck** at the foot of the Grossglockner mountain. The route incorporates several restaurants and part of the loipe is floodlit at night.

Mountain restaurants

Zell am See has a wide choice of mountain eating places and prices are reasonable, although there are crowds during busy weeks. The black run down from Sonnalm has a pleasant hut for those who can get to it. The Sonnenalm-Pfiff is praised for its 'delicious hot chocolate'. Schmiedhofalm has amazing views from its sunny terrace. The mid-station restaurant serves 'huge and excellent *Kaiserschmarren*' (chopped pancake with stewed plums). Glocknerhaus, on the way down to Schüttdorf, is also popular. Hans' Schnapps Bar on the summit has a live rock band twice a week, and attracts dancing in ski boots, even on the bar.

Off the mountain

Zell am See, at the gateway to Austria's highest mountain, the Grossglockner, is an established town first settled by a monastic order in the eighth century. Its medieval guest houses and shops cluster around a tenth-century tower, which houses an uninspiring museum of local history. In recent years the town has done much to smarten up its image. The town centre has been pedestrianised and it has an upmarket look to it, resembling a mini-Kitzbühel.

■ **OTHER SPORTS**

Parapente, hang-gliding, luge-ing, hot-air ballooning, sleigh rides, skating, curling, indoor tennis and squash, swimming, shooting range, climbing wall, tobogganing, snow rafting, ice-hockey

The range of shops is wide, as you would expect in a market town of this size. Buses run every 15 minutes to the lifts and regularly to Kaprun and the Kitzsteinhorn. Reporters complain that they tend to become very crowded, and if snow conditions confine skiing to the Kitzsteinhorn then a car is more of a necessity than a luxury. There is a regular bus service to Thumersbach, but you can also walk across the lake in mid-winter. If you don't want to ski you can always skate or take a sleigh ride around the lake.

Accommodation

Three large hotels have unfortunately shut their doors, including the once popular Neue Post. The luxurious Grand Hotel, jutting out over the lake, narrowly missed a similar fate, but was bought and relaunched by the five-star Salzburgerhof, the smartest hotel in town. Four-stars include the Alpin, Fischerwirt and the Alpenblick. Hotel Bellevue is a recommended three-star. Hotel St Georg is one of the best hotels in town, with its smart, pine-panelled rooms and views of the lake. The Tirolerhof is highly recommended ('friendly staff with good English, and the four-course meals were excellent with individual attention to a vegetarian in our party'). Hotel Berner is set above the town, has a heated outdoor swimming-pool and is popular with reporters ('decorated in a rather grand style, but the owners and staff are friendly'). One reporter stayed in Thumersbach: 'The apartment was comfortable, but taxis were necessary to enjoy the nightlife'.

Pension Daxer, at the top end of the village and close to the cable car stations, is said to be convenient for the skiing and not for the après-ski, but is otherwise 'small, friendly and highly recommended'. Also well positioned for the lifts is the Schwebebahn. The three-star Traube in the pedestrian zone is small and comfortable. The expensive Hotel Salzburgerhof is also praised. For those who stay in hotels with television sets in the bedrooms, fixed weather cameras on both the Kitzsteinhorn and the Schmittenhöhe allow you to check the weather on top before you get out of bed in the morning. There is a good range of comfortable apartments of all sizes in the Zell am See area, including Hagleitner, Sulzer and Skiner. A comprehensive list is available from the tourist office.

> ■ **WHAT'S NEW**
>
> Road tunnel beneath town
> Extension of Areitbahn gondola

Eating in and out

The Alpenkönig, Steinerwirt and Chataprunium are considered the best value for money along with the Kupferkessel and the Saustall. Hotel St Georg has a pleasant restaurant with good quality food. The Ampere, Landhotel Erlhof and the Salzburgerhof are also recommended for their high standards of cuisine. The Pizza House is said to be great value. Several reporters praise Zum Hirschen for its cosy atmosphere and tasty food; the *Wienerschnitzel* is particularly recommended. Others include a Chinese, Italian and even a Greek restaurant. The Baum-Bar in Kaprun has a very un-Austrian-style restaurant in a large, modern conservatory with stripped pine floor.

Après-ski

Zell am See is lively by any standards. Once the lifts have closed for the day the first stop could be the Kellerbar of the Hotel Schwebebahn near the lifts, Café Feinschmeck with its vast choice of pastries, or the Mösshammer in the main square, which also has good coffee and cakes. Tea-dancing still exists in Zell and a number of reporters have enjoyed watching major-league ice-hockey matches. Away from the traditional Austrian entertainment there are bars and discos to suit all pockets. Crazy Daisy is a focal point for Anglo-Saxon visitors, but said by one reporter to be 'very expensive and unpleasantly crowded'. Another commented that the local Austrian bar game, which involves driving nails into logs, enlivened many an evening.

The Kellerbar of the Hotel zum Hirschen is lively and the main bar of the Tirolerhof is a relaxing place to have a drink, and at the same time

Skiing facts: **Zell am See**

TOURIST OFFICE
Kurverwaltung, Brucker Bundesstrasse,
A-5700 Zell am See, Salzburgerland
Tel 43 6542 2600
Fax 43 6542 2032

THE RESORT
By road Calais 1296km
By rail station in resort
By air Salzburg 1½ hrs
Visitor beds 14,380
Transport free ski bus with lift pass

THE SKIING
Linked or nearby resorts Kaprun (l),
Saalbach-Hinterglemm (n)
Longest run Schüttdorfabfahrt, 6.5km
(blue)
Number of lifts 28 in Zell am See, 58 in
Europa Sport Region
Total of trails/pistes 80km in Zell am See
(38% easy, 50% intermediate, 12%
difficult), 130km in Europa Sport Region
Nursery slopes 5 lifts
Summer skiing 15 lifts on Kitzsteinhorn
Glacier (open all year)
Snowmaking 30km covered

LIFT PASSES
Area pass Europa Sport Region
(covers Zell am See, Kaprun), ÖS1,930 for
6 days
Day pass Zell am See only or Kitzsteinhorn
only, ÖS400
Beginners special price of ÖS10-20 per
ride for lower drag-lifts
Pensioners 10% reduction for women 60
yrs and over and men 65 yrs and over
Credit cards accepted no

SKI SCHOOLS
Adults Wallner Prenner (9.30am-4pm),
Schmittenhöhe (9.30am-4pm), Areitbahn
(10am-6pm), all ÖS1,500 for 6 days.
Thumersbach, ÖS850 for 6 half-days
Private lessons Wallner Prenner,
Schmittenhöhe and Areitbahn
ÖS500 per hr, Thumersbach ÖS400 per hr
Snowboarding Wallner Prenner,
Schmittenhöhe and Areitbahn
ÖS1,050 for 3 half-days.
Private lessons ÖS550 per hr
Cross-country Markus Werth/Schüttdorf,
ÖS900 for 5 days, private lessons ÖS370
per hr. Harald Nicka/Schüttdorf, ÖS870
for 5 days, private lessons ÖS400 per hr.
Loipe 75km
Other courses telemark, monoski
Guiding companies Ludwig Kranabeller,
Helmut Göllner, Mont Alpin

CHILDREN
Lift pass 6-15 yrs, ÖS1,170 for 6 days,
free for 5 yrs and under if skiing
with parents
Ski kindergarten all ski schools, times as
adults, ÖS1,650 for 6 days
Ski school as ski kindergarten
Non-ski kindergarten Areitbahn, 3 yrs
and over, 9am-4.30pm, ÖS1,650 for 6 days.
Feriendorf Hagleitner, 12 mths and over,
10am-4pm, ÖS1,200 for 5 days. Ursula
Zink, 2 yrs and over, 9.30am-3.30pm,
ÖS1,500 for 6 days

FOOD AND DRINK PRICES
Coffee ÖS25-27, glass of wine ÖS40-42,
small beer ÖS21-23, dish of the day
ÖS112-120

hear yourself think. The Wunderbar, a glass conservatory on the roof of the Grand Hotel, has views of the lake and mountains. Sugar Shake and the Schnelle Bier are popular. Late-night action switches to the Viva nightclub, which swings on until dawn, Evergreens for the over 25s, and the Diele Bar, which attracts a young crowd until 2am. The Baum-Bar in Kaprun is much frequented.

Childcare

The children's facilities are generally more than adequate, with a kindergarten taking children from 12 months old. Ski lessons are given from the age of three. One parent described it as better than the adult ski school he attended: 'We have no complaints about the standard of tuition or care of the children'. The Feriendorf Hagleitner runs its own crèche.

Linked or nearby resorts

Kaprun
top 3029m (9,938ft) bottom 770m (2,526ft)

Kaprun is a delightful, typical Austrian holiday village, a few kilometres back into the mountains from the lakeside. It has seen considerable expansion in recent years and has developed into a year-round ski resort. Despite new hotel and apartment developments, Kaprun has managed to retain its essential village atmosphere based around the church and stream. It has a handful of sports and gift shops, the odd tea-room, and has made a serious attempt at providing a nightlife for its visitors, who range from lakes-and-mountains walkers to winter-holiday skiers and the professionals, who use the glacier as their workbench during the summer months.

The Baum-Bar, on the edge of town, is worthy of special mention as the liveliest nightclub in the valley. The more culturally minded will enjoy a visit to the castle ruins on the outskirts.

The four-star Orgler has comfortable accommodation and one of the best restaurants. The Barbarahof and the Sportkristall are both recommended. The Sonnblick and the Kaprunserhof cater for families. We have favourable reports of the Pension Salzburgerhof ('pleasant, spacious bedrooms'), and Hotel Toni has excellent food and friendly staff, and has recently added a self- catering annexe.

TOURIST OFFICE
Tel 43 6547 8643
Fax 43 6547 8192

Round-up

RESORTS COVERED Bad Kleinkirchheim, Lermoos,
Maria Alm, St Johann im Pongau, St Johann-in-Tirol, Waidring

Bad Kleinkirchheim
top 2000m (6,560ft) bottom 1080m (3,543ft)

Bad Kleinkirchheim — or BKK as it is usually known — is the home resort of Austrian super-hero Franz Klammer and, as one reporter put it: 'What is good enough for Franz is good enough for me'. These days the greatest of all downhill champions spends more time in Colorado than in Carinthia, but the old spa town and thriving summer resort continues to develop its skiing in his absence. The ski area is linked to the neighbouring village of **St Oswald** and together the two provide 85km of mainly intermediate pistes served by 34 lifts. BKK is quite spread out and has a wide choice of hotels, but après-ski is limited. There are a few bars, one disco and some value-for-money restaurants. The excellent spa facilities include indoor and outdoor thermal pools.

The ski area is low, with the top lifts only reaching 2000m; snow conditions are consequently unreliable both early and late in the season. The World Cup downhill course was designed by Klammer himself and includes a sequence of jumps, which even when prepared as a recreational run require considerable concentration. Most runs are wide and gentle, and queues are reported during high season. The lift pass also covers the neighbouring resorts of St Oswald and **Falkert**.

The BKK-St Oswald Ski School gives group and private tuition in skiing, snowboarding and cross-country, the latter on its 42km of loipe. Three- to six-year-olds can attend the kindergarten for full- or half-days where a mixture of games and skiing is offered.

TOURIST OFFICE
Tel 43 4240 8212
Fax 43 4240 8537

Lermoos
top 2200m (7,216ft) bottom 1004m (3,293ft)

Lermoos and nearby **Ehrwald**, at the foot of the impressive Zugspitze, are typical Tyrolean working villages. The two are linked by bus and lift, and are in an attractive area to the north-west of **Innsbruck** near the German border. Both villages are unspoilt and have plenty of bars and reasonably priced restaurants.

The skiing is divided into four small separate sections all covered by one lift pass. Beginners can try the nursery slopes at the Lermoos base and graduate to a longer gentle run by taking the gondola up Ehrwalder

Alm. Intermediates will find wide pistes and easy red (intermediate) runs in the Zugspitze Bowl, which lead over the border into Germany. Advanced skiers will find the area limited; there is one black (difficult) run on the Grubigstein above Lermoos. However, in good snow conditions you can ski down from the Zugspitze Glacier. This is an excellent area for cross-country with more than 100km of prepared tracks.

TOURIST OFFICE
Tel 43 5673 2401
Fax 43 5673 2694

Maria Alm
top 2000m (6,560ft) bottom 800m (2,624ft)
Maria Alm is a compact and largely unspoilt village in the Hochkönig-Skischaukel area, close to Zell am See. It is dominated by a church boasting the second highest spire in Salzburgerland. Maria Alm has twice won awards as the most beautiful village in this part of Austria. Many of its hotels are small with good-value menus and cosy bars.

The lift pass covers Maria Alm as well as the linked skiing of **Saalfelden**, **Hinterthal**, **Hintermoos**, **Dienten** and **Mühlbach**. The pistes are well-groomed and ideal for intermediates who enjoy tree-lined runs that challenge rather than terrify. The expert will find the skiing here limited, but there is adequate variety to satisfy anyone else for a week. The main criticism we have of the area is the age and poor quality of the lifts.

TOURIST OFFICE
Tel 43 6584 7816
Fax 43 6584 7600

St Johann im Pongau
top 2188m (7,177ft) bottom 650m (2,132ft)
The four valleys of St Johann, **Wagrain**, **Flachau** and **Zauchensee** lie only 45 minutes from Salzburg and provide an intermediate playground offering some impressive statistics: a dozen resorts with 320km of linked (albeit not always on the mountain) skiing, served by 120 lifts all covered by one ski pass. St Johann itself (not to be confused with St Johann-in-Tirol) is a cathedral town that was all but devastated by a disastrous fire in 1852; consequently, it lacks the medieval charm of Austria's other county towns and larger resorts.

The ski area, which is known as the Sportwelt Amadé, has one of the best-value lift passes in Austria. It is popular with almost every nationality apart from the British; this is partly because few British tour operators come here as they cannot contract enough hotel beds to make the area's inclusion in the brochures a commercial viability. Attractive Wagrain is the heart of the region, from where it is easy to access both ends. Flachau is an almost equally attractive alternative. St Johann has its own small, separate ski area, and the link into the Sportwelt Amadé is via the hamlet of **Alpendorf**, which is a 4-km ski-bus ride away. The pistes in the area are well-catered with eating-places, from small huts to larger self-services.

Each of the resorts has at least one ski school and St Johann has three: Skischule St Johann, Toni's and Red-White-Red. We have good reports of all three as well as those in Flachau. St Johann has a fun park with special facilities for snowboarders. Vitamin B and Board Unlimited are two specialist boarding schools in Alpendorf. Langlaufers are well-served by 160km of trails along the valleys.

Accommodation in St Johann includes the luxurious Sporthotel Alpenland, three-star Hotel Brückenwirt-Tennerhof, and Gasthof-Pension Taxenbacher. Après-ski is strictly limited to a few lively bars. The inconvenient bus journey to Alpendorf means that St Johann is not ideal for families.

The small village of Wagrain has fortunately been able to develop away from the minor road from St Johann to Flachau and **Radstadt**. Hotel Grafenwirt is discreetly upmarket, Hotel Enzian and the Wagrainerhof are both recommended. There is a ski kindergarten that takes children from three years old.

Neighbouring Flachau has undergone considerable expansion in recent years. The main accommodation is in large chalet-style hotels and inns, as well as apartment blocks. Beginners learn to ski on a gentle piste in the village. There is a non-ski kindergarten and the Griessenkar Ski School takes children from three years old. Hotel Reslwirt is central and medium-priced, along with Gasthof Salzburgerhof. There are two four-star hotels — Hotel Vierjahreszeiten and the luxurious Hotel Tauernhof.

The attractive market town of **Altenmarkt** is a centre for the local sportswear and ski equipment industries where Atomic skis and Steffner sweaters, among others, are manufactured. A modest ski area is linked to neighbouring Radstadt, but the main skiing is a bus-ride away at Zauchensee (or Flachau). British-run Fun Ski is based in Zauchensee and offers specialist skiing courses. The kindergarten cares for children from three years old. The cross-country opportunities, as in the rest of the area, are extensive. The village has 22 hotels, including six of a luxury standard.

Filzmoos is another small village in the Sportwelt Amadé, which dates back to Edwardian times when it was a popular holiday spot for the wealthy Viennese. Today, it has a ski area of 17 lifts, shared with neighbouring **Neuberg**. The **Dachstein Glacier** is only 18km away, and the main ski circus is reached by bus via Flachau.

The kindergarten takes children from three years old and has English-speaking staff. The choice of accommodation in 25 hotels and a selection of apartments is large in relation to the size of the village, which is known as the hot-air ballooning capital of Austria.

TOURIST OFFICE
Tel 43 6412 6036
Fax 43 6412 603674

St Johann-in-Tirol
top 1700m (5,576ft) bottom 680m (2,230ft)

St Johann-in-Tirol is a large, busy town with a small ski area. Its expansion from a pretty Tyrolean village to a sprawling light-industrial centre, has done little for its charm. Nevertheless, the centre, with its ornately frescoed buildings and fine old coaching inns, remains largely unspoilt and the heavy traffic is confined to the outskirts.

St Johann, not to be confused with St Johann im Pongau, offers a pleasant setting for a lively and quite varied winter holiday at prices that are reasonable by Austrian standards. Queues are generally not a problem, either at village level or up the mountain, but are increased by weekend visitors from Innsbruck and Munich when conditions are good. However, the northward orientation of the slopes and efficient grooming generally keeps the slopes in fine condition.

St Johann is particularly geared towards beginners, with six nursery-slope lifts scattered between the town and the hamlet of **Eichenhof**, which is served by ski bus. The rolling lower pastures are ideal novice terrain, with a choice of blue runs higher up to which beginners can progress after a few days. Practically all the skiing on the top half of the mountain is graded red. The area is limited in size and lacks any real challenge. Another major drawback is the distance across town to the lifts.

The choice of 18 mountain restaurants is way above average for a resort of this size. Practically every piste has a welcoming hut at the top, bottom or part-way down. The cross-country skiing is extensive and covers 75km of prepared tracks from St Johann to **Oberndorf**, **Going**, **Kirchdorf**, **Erpfendorf** and **Waidring**.

The central feature of St Johann is the three-star Hotel Gasthof Post, which dates from 1225 and is beautifully frescoed. Hotel Park, near the gondola, is recommended and we have good reports of Hotel Fischer. Hotel Goldener Löwe is strongly endorsed for families. St Johann's après-ski is vibrant and is mainly aimed at a young crowd.

Fieberbrunn
top 1870m (6,135ft) bottom 800m (2,625ft)

Ten kilometres up the road from St Johann-in-Tirol is the sprawling village of Fieberbrunn. Its small but attractive ski area is north-facing and is known as a 'schneewinkel', or snowpocket. The main skiing is at tree-level, with several long and easy runs and some varied off-piste including treks over to **Kitzbühel**. St Jacob im Haus is another small ski area on the opposite side of the valley.

TOURIST OFFICE
Tel 43 5354 6304
Fax 43 5354 2606

Waidring
top 1860m (6,102ft) bottom 780m (2,558ft)

This unspoilt village is less than 20km from St Johann-in-Tirol and is situated in the same snowpocket as **Fieberbrunn**. The resort is known for its family skiing, with convenient nursery slopes in the village centre. The rest of the skiing is at **Steinplatte**, 4km from the village, and is suited to beginners and intermediates. There are five mountain restaurants on the slopes. The best hotel is the Waidringerhof, which has a swimming-pool and a pleasant dining-room. The central Hotel Tiroler Adler is also recommended. The nightlife in Waidring is relaxed and informal, with the Schniedermann Bar and the Alte Schmiede both popular venues.

TOURIST OFFICE
Tel 43 5353 5242
Fax 43 5353 52424

France

More British skiers holiday in France than in any other country. The Savoie, Haute Savoie and Dauphiné mountains offer more challenge than their counterparts in Austria, as well as a better chance of early- and late-season snow cover. The Pyrenees offer less demanding but nevertheless attractive skiing and considerably lower prices. Myriad resorts have been developed at enormous expense over the past 30 years and are far better equipped than their equivalents in either Switzerland or Italy.

France offers the largest and most sophisticated lift systems in the world. The size of some is truly staggering; Méribel has 16 gondolas, and the Trois Vallées has 200 lifts linking 600km of piste.

However, the popularity of the sport among the French has sharply declined, and the cost of running a ski resort has risen. Consider that a jumbo gondola costs more to build than a Boeing 737; Alpe d'Huez's bill for piste-grooming last season was £4 million, and snowmaking cost £18,500 a day.

Unlike their alpine neighbours, the majority of French resorts are purpose-built *stations de ski*, which provide ski-in ski-out convenience but often at a high cost to their ambience. However, the French have learned their lesson from the original architectural follies of the 1960s, such as Tignes, Flaine and the earlier villages of La Plagne. Valmorel, Risoul and other more recent developments have been constructed with more consideration for their natural mountain environment.

In all the resorts there is more accommodation in apartments than in hotels, and the earlier concrete *résidences* were constructed with rooms that are far too small for the demands of today's tourist.

Many readers complain that French resorts lack the atmosphere of their Austrian cousins. Certainly, the welcome can be muted to the point of rudeness, although competition for custom and the growth of international business has done much to improve matters.

French telephone area codes change on 18 October 1996. The numbers given here are the new ones

With a few notable exceptions like Chamonix and Les Deux Alpes, après-ski struggles to survive in the country in which the phrase originated. In the main purpose-built resorts, visitors find themselves forced to prop up the neighbourhood bar or make their own entertainment in their apartments. Discos are often grossly overpriced, underfrequented and play unrecognisable 'euromusak'.

However, none of these shortcomings seriously detracts from what the French Alps have to offer. The inescapable reason why more British now ski here than anywhere else is because, taking every factor into consideration, the skiing is the best in Europe.

Alpe d'Huez

ALTITUDE 1860m (6,100ft)

Alpe d'Huez is best known internationally for annually staging what is recognised as the toughest endurance test in sport, and one which has nothing whatsoever to do with skiing: on what is unerringly the hottest day of July the riders of the Tour de France push their hearts, legs and machines through 1130 vertical metres and 22 tortuous hairpin bends from the valley town of **Bourg-en-Oisans** to this hotch-potch of a ski resort in the Dauphiné.

Winter visitors who make the same ascent at the end of the 90-minute journey by coach from either Grenoble or Lyon airports are mercifully allowed to make it in greater comfort. They are left only to imagine the pain of the gladiators and to marvel at the graffiti skills of fanatical Tour supporters who decorate the road surface permanently with the names of their heroes.

But the sights of skiers are set considerably higher — at the 3330-m summit of Pic Blanc that dominates Les Grandes-Rousses, the fifth largest ski area in France and one of increasing importance to the British market. Alpe d'Huez, its capital and the hub of 220km of linked skiing served by 82 lifts, is not a purpose-built resort, but so great are the additions to the original village that it has all the convenience of one. The lower satellites of **Auris**, **Oz**, **Vaujany** and **Villard-Reculas** have emerged as resorts in their own right and, to some extent, are in danger of eclipsing their grizzled old master.

In 1936, Jean Pomagalski, a young engineer of Polish extraction, watched members of the French national ski team in training as they plodded again and again up towards the Plat de Marmottes for a brief downhill run. He decided that the team might improve more rapidly with the aid of a little uphill transport. With an ancient tractor engine and a rope borrowed from a farmer he promptly invented the poma drag-lift.

Alpe d'Huez was chosen as one of the venues for the Killy Winter Olympics in 1968. The village authorities in their enthusiasm plumbed new depths in Olympian disorganisation by building a sunny south-facing bobsleigh run. For a while the village fathers toyed with the notion of cultivating the 'exclusif' tag, which is attached to Megève and Courchevel 1850; in the end, the need to pay for what is one of the most modern lift systems in the world pointed them in the direction of the mass-market.

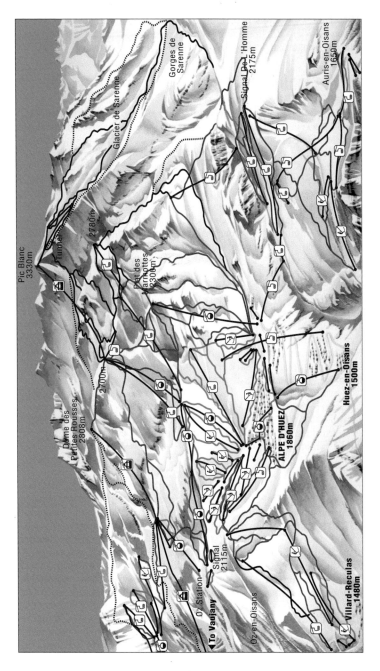

The clientèle remains predominantly French, but with the number of domestic skiers still in decline, Alpe d'Huez is working hard at an international image that is not solely confined to that hot, hard day in July.

On the mountain
top 3330m (10,922ft) bottom 1100m (3,608ft)

Alpe d'Huez is a genuine all-round ski resort with excellent nursery slopes, good intermediate runs, long black (difficult) trails and extremely serious off-piste opportunities. Mountain access is multiple; two main modern gondolas feed traffic out of the village into the Pic Blanc sector, and there are alternatives at peak times. Such is the efficiency of the lift system, capable of shifting 90,000 people per hour, that Alpe d'Huez claims to have dispensed with the lift queue. With the exception of the older cable car up to the highest point of the ski area this is largely true. However, a number of readers say that high-season queues for both the first and second stages of the DMC gondola can develop into a scrum. Feeding a larger number of skiers more efficiently into any system has an obvious down side, and the pistes immediately above the village (Les Chamois, Le Signal and Le Lac Blanc) are prone to overcrowding.

First glances can be deceptive, and none more so than here. The skiing as seen from Les Bergers lift station looks disarmingly mild: an open mountainside served by an array of gondolas, chair- and drag-lifts. However, skiers who have cut their teeth on the gentle pastures of the Tyrol will be shocked by the hidden severity of the skiing. Much of the Pic Blanc is concealed from sight by the lie of the land. From its 3330-m summit it is possible to ski over 2000m vertical in good snow conditions down to well below Alpe d'Huez.

The area divides naturally into four main sectors: Pic Blanc, Signal de l'Homme/Auris, Signal/Villard-Reculas, and Oz/Vaujany. The central part of the skiing takes place immediately north-east of the resort on sunny slopes and is reached by the impressively efficient two stages of the 25-person DMC gondola.

Beginners

The first stage of the DMC gondola serves an enormous area of green (beginner) runs close to the resort. The green Rif Nel piste is the gentlest of the long pistes from the base of the gondola back down to Les Bergers.

All the satellites have nursery slopes, some of them more novice-friendly than others. Vaujany's ski area starts from Montfrais, a sunny balcony above the resort, which is reached by gondola. A series of short drag-lifts give access to green and blue (easy) runs, which are ideal debutant terrain. The nearby village of **Oz-en-Oisans** has reasonable beginner skiing, snow permitting.

Intermediates

From the mid-station of the DMC gondola, the Lièvre Blanc chair gives access to a lot of challenging skiing. It serves its own red (intermediate) piste but also leads to the satisfyingly secluded red Balme, which takes you all the way down to Alpe d'Huez.

From the top of the DMC gondola try the long red Les Rousses (110 on the local piste-map). Take the usually mogulled and crowded first 100m slowly so as not to miss the path that cuts north-west beneath the cableway into the Vaujany sector. From here you can ski all the way down to Oz or to Vaujany.

Signal is the second mountain of Alpe d'Huez, a rounded, snow-covered peak adjacent to the resort itself. This is reached by a four-seater chair or a choice of drag-lifts and provides some of the most varied intermediate runs in the area, which are easily accessible from the heart of the village. Behind Signal, longer runs drop down the open west-facing slopes above the satellite of Villard-Reculas.

■ **WHAT'S NEW**

Pistes down to L'Enversin d'Oz, creating longest vertical drop in the Alps

Advanced

The 1995–6 season saw the opening of a new piste that takes you all the way down to the hamlet of **L'Enversin d'Oz**, linked to Vaujany by a cluster gondola. From the summit of Pic Blanc this represents a mighty vertical of 2330m, claimed to be the longest in the Alps (with lifts to take you back up again).

The top of the Clocher de Mâcle chair-lift is the starting point for some interesting black runs. These include the beautiful Combe Charbonière past Europe's highest disused coal mine and from there either down into the Sarenne Gorge or back to the resort. The short run down from Clocher de Mâcle to Lac Blanc is steep, but the snow is usually good.

From the top of Pic Blanc two black pistes, the Sarenne and the Château Noir, take you all the way down into the Sarenne Gorge and are claimed, at 16km, to be the longest black runs in the Alps. However, it should be pointed out that they accrue most of their length from the run-out along the bottom of the gorge. Only some pitches of the Sarenne are really difficult, but the run is long and tiring. Both pistes are narrow in places and can produce awkward bottlenecks.

The front face of Pic Blanc is accessed via a tunnel through the rock, 200m below the summit, with an awkward path at the end of it. The steep and usually icy Tunnel mogul field that awaits you can be extremely daunting when no snow has fallen for some weeks.

Off-piste

Opportunities for *ski sauvage* from the top of Pic Blanc are superb. Variations include the Grand Sablat, the Combe du Loup and a long and tricky descent via the Couloir de Fiole. A 20-minute climb from the cable car station takes you to the top of La Pyramide, the off-piste starting point for more than 2000m of vertical, bringing you down through a range of gulleys and open snowfields all the way to Vaujany or Oz. The top can be very icy, and ropes may be needed to negotiate the steeper couloirs in packed snow conditions.

The off-piste variation from the ridge separating Oz from Alpe d'Huez is a gloriously steep powder field, which filters into the tree-studded gorge at the bottom. It is prone to avalanche and should only be attempted in the morning. There are seven itineraries in the area, all of which are marked on the piste-map.

Ski schools and guiding

The French Ski School (ESF) has 300 instructors based in Alpe d'Huez, Auris, Oz and Vaujany. Reports of the ESF are improving, with more English-speaking instructors than in the past. One reporter remarks that although the initial impression of the ski school in Alpe d'Huez was one of 'total chaos, with hundreds of instructors and students jostling together', the instructors were 'excellent, always cheerful and friendly with excellent English'. The International Ski School (ESI) offers English-speaking classes restricted to eight.

BASI (British Association of Ski Instructors) instructor Stuart Adamson runs International Masterclass courses in Alpe d'Huez for English-speaking clients. Force 10 Adventure is another independent ski school set up by a British instructor in the resort: Steve Scott runs both group and individual courses for all standards, and one reporter claimed he received 'the best instruction ever'.

Snowboarding

Planète Surf is the major snowboarding school here. The ESI holds *nouvelle glisses* courses, which include snowboarding as one of the options, and the ESF offers snowboard tuition. As in all major French resorts, the sport has really taken off. Fun Evasion is said to be the best shop for hiring boards.

Cross-country

The area has around 50km of prepared trails. The main area is situated near Alpette and has the advantage of easy access to Chalet du Lac Besson, the best restaurant on the mountain. There is also a challenging loipe above the Sarenne Gorge on the right of the piste-map.

Mountain restaurants

The Poutran in Oz offers quality and good-value food. Auberge de l'Alpette, a stone hut below the top of the Alpette gondola on the Oz piste, offers simple farmhouse fare and home-made cheeses at reasonable prices. Les Airelles is a delightful restaurant built into the rock at the top of Les Airelles nursery drag above Vaujany. It has a rustic atmosphere with roaring log fire and classical music. La Cabane du Poutat, above Alpe d'Huez, has the rare distinction for a mountain restaurant of being awarded a knife-and-fork in the Michelin Guide. Le Chardon Bleu at La Villette below Mont Frais is 'a wonderfully unexpected gastronomic surprise in the prettiest of farming hamlets'.

La Bergerie, on the red run down to Villard-Reculas, is an alpine museum which doubles as a restaurant; the setting, complete with open fire and cow bells, is particularly attractive. The Chalet du Lac Besson, on the cross-country trail between the DMC gondola and Alpette, has a sunny terrace and specialises in grilled meat.

Le Tetras in Auris serves fine pizzas and has a varied wine list. The Auberge Forêt de Maronne below Auris can usually only be reached in mid-winter via a choice of long blue or black runs through scenic alpine meadows; the reward is veal served in a creamy *mélange* of three types of local wild mushrooms, picked and preserved by the patron, but beware of the return drag-lift — it is as steep and difficult as the black run it serves. Combe Haute in the Sarenne Gorge has a welcoming atmosphere and is renowned for its salads.

Off the mountain

Alpe d'Huez first opened as a resort in 1931 with a handful of tourist beds. At the time of the 1968 Olympics it was little more than a one-street alpine village dominated by a futuristic modern church. The massive, apparently uncontrolled building surge that followed saw the resort spread out in all directions in a profusion of architectural styles. 'One of the worst blots on the landscape anywhere, but fortunately you only have to lift your eyes to the superb surroundings', said one reporter.

Traffic remains a problem, although it must be pointed out that as there is no through-road from the resort to anywhere else, it is more a question of over-crowded parking than busy main roads. A bucket lift acts as the primary people-mover. A shuttle bus takes skiers up to the slopes from the lower reaches of what is a steep resort for pedestrians, but several reporters say there was no sign of a bus during their entire stay. Shops are limited to a few boutiques and tacky T-shirt and souvenir establishments.

> **■ OTHER SPORTS**
>
> Ice-driving, snow-mobiling, snow-shoeing, aeroclub, parapente, hang-gliding, swimming, helicopter rides, skating, curling, ice-climbing, indoor tennis, climbing wall

Alpe d'Huez is one of the few resorts that can be reached directly by aircraft as it has its own altiport. Les Deux Alpes is a few minutes away by helicopter or 45 minutes by road.

Accommodation

The higher up the hill you are, the easier it is to get to and from the skiing. The hardcore of one four-star (The Royal Ours Blanc) and eight three-star hotels is supported by numerous family establishments.

Le Petit Prince is a small, family-run hotel that guests find relaxing but a little quiet ('an excellent standard of service'). The Christina is friendly and charming and one of the few attractive chalet-style buildings at the top of the resort. The Chamois d'Or is considered the best hotel with a highly regarded restaurant. L'Ourson is a family-run hotel. The best apartments include those in the Rocher Soleil, which has its own outdoor heated swimming-pool and optional catering (our studio was very clean but rather small'). Maeva's Les Bergers apartments are recommended by our reporters.

Eating in and out

Dining is an important business in Alpe d'Huez, a legacy from its more exclusive days. There are over 50 restaurants in the resort itself. Au Petit Creux ('intimate atmosphere and wonderful, but avoid weekends') is one of the best restaurants here. Le Chamois d'Or, Le Lyonnais and L'Outa all vie with each other as the best centres for haute cuisine in town. Le Colporteur is a new restaurant with a growing reputation. La Pomme de Pin is praised for its 'enormous helpings — a meal like this would have cost quite a lot more in the Home Counties'. La Cordée, Génépi, La Crémaillère and Caribou all offer mountain specialities. Pizza Origan is 'friendly and serves a good range of pizzas and pasta'. La Taverne has mainly pizza and crêpes. The restaurant in Vaujany's Hotel Rissiou is open to non-residents and has excellent cuisine and wines.

Supermarkets in Alpe d'Huez are adequate, and reporters recommend Les Bergers in the Centre Commercial as convenient and well stocked. Serious food shoppers can drive down to the Rallye supermarket in Bourg d'Oisans.

Après-ski

Charley's Bar, with pool and table football, is popular. The Cactus Bar has a live band most nights and reasonably priced beer. Le Petit Bar has live Blues every night. The Lincoln Pub and the Avalanche Bar are 'lacking in atmosphere' with 'music and loud holidaymakers'. Le Sporting, which overlooks the skating rink, is 'a pleasant piano bar with an interesting and reasonably priced menu'. Le Chalet has a smarter image. The Underground is 'noisy, crowded, and packed with Scandinavians'. Etoile des Neiges is a typical French café. Alpe d'Huez has four discos.

Childcare

The ESF Club des Oursons takes children from four years of age at Grandes-Rousses and at Bergers. Both have playgrounds and their own drag-lifts. The ESI runs Club des Mickeys et des Papotines, which starts at three years, and the Club des Marmottes is for 4- to 13-year-olds. The Club des Eterlous, next to the Club Med building, takes children from 6 months to 14 years of age. The crèche in Vaujany is one of the best equipped we have come across in the Alps and, if you have small children, almost a reason in itself for choosing the resort. It takes children from three months up to three years. There is also a crèche in Oz.

Linked or nearby resorts

Auris-en-Oisans
top 3330m (10,922ft) bottom 1600m (5,249ft)

Auris consists mainly of apartment blocks and is somewhat isolated from the bulk of the skiing in Les Grandes-Rousses, but well positioned for outings to **Les Deux Alpes**, **Briançon/Serre Chevalier** and **La Grave**. The Beau Site hotel attracts predominantly French guests. Down the hillside in the old village are the more traditional Auberge de la Forêt de Maronne with its fine cuisine, and Hotel Les Emeranches, as well as chalets and *gîtes* to rent.

TOURIST OFFICE
Tel 33 4 76 80 13 52
Fax 33 4 76 80 20 16

Oz Station
top 3330m (10,922ft) bottom 1350m (4,429ft)

This small, purpose-built village lies above the old village of Oz-en-Oisans. It is reached by a fast all-weather road from the valley in only 20 minutes and thereby provides an excellent back door into the lift system. The resort consists of some large apartment blocks built of stone and wood in pleasing harmony with the environment. Two gondolas branch upwards in different directions, one to L'Alpette above Vaujany and the other in two stages to the mid-station of the DMC gondola above Alpe d'Huez. The resort's shopping and nightlife are limited.

TOURIST OFFICE
Tel 33 4 76 80 78 01
Fax 33 4 76 80 78 04

Vaujany
top 3330m (10,922ft) bottom 1250m (4,101ft)

Vaujany is a sleepy farming community which, but for a quirk of fate, would have slowly crumbled into agronomic oblivion: compensation in the 1980s for a valley hydro-electric scheme made the village rich beyond its residents' wildest dreams. Oz benefited to a lesser extent from the scheme, and the two villages plunged their millions into the winter sports industry. This explains why, in the case of Vaujany, an apparently impoverished mountain village manages to own a state-of-the-art 160-person cable car, which still ranks among the top half-dozen in the world. No one has yet to see a queue here, but who is complaining? Considerable, but considered, development is taking place, and a number of new chalets and apartments have been built, as well as an excellent crèche. However, the community retains its rural atmosphere.

There are four simple hotels in the village centre. L'Etendard, closest to the lift station, is the après-ski hub. The Rissiou is under British management in winter and produces a much higher standard of food and accommodation than you might expect in a village of this size. Le Chardon Bleu restaurant in the neighbouring hamlet of **La Villette** offers a high standard of cuisine. Nightlife is centred around a few bars, the Hotel Rissiou, and Le Sabot nightclub. Vaujany has a fine, outdoor, artificial skating rink.

TOURIST OFFICE
Tel 33 4 76 80 79 40
Fax 33 4 76 80 79 52

Skiing facts: **Alpe d'Huez**

TOURIST OFFICE
BP 28, F-38750 Alpe d'Huez, Dauphiné
Tel 33 4 76 80 35 41
Fax 33 4 76 80 69 54

THE RESORT
By road Calais 934km
By rail Grenoble 62km
By air Lyon 2 hrs, Grenoble $1\frac{1}{2}$ hrs
Visitor beds 32,000
Transport free ski bus

THE SKIING
Linked or nearby resorts Auris (l),
Oz-en-Oisans (l), Vaujany (l),
Villard-Reculas (l), Les Deux Alpes (n),
La Grave (n)
Longest run Sarenne, 16km (black)
Number of lifts 82
Total of trails/pistes 220km (36%
beginner, 28% easy, 25% intermediate,
11% difficult)
Nursery slopes 8 including extensive
nursery runs immediately above Alpe d'Huez
Summer skiing Sarenne Glacier (July
and August only)
Snowmaking 100 hectares covered by 385
snow-cannon

LIFT PASSES
Area pass (covers whole Grandes Rousses
area) 960FF for 6 days, includes entry to
sports centre
Day pass 200FF weekdays,
160-175FF weekends
Beginners 2 free lifts at Alpe d'Huez and
Visalp Initiation Pass, 1380FF for
6 morning lessons
Pensioners free 70 yrs and over
Credit cards accepted yes

SKI SCHOOLS
Adults ESF, 890FF for 6 days, $5\frac{1}{2}$ hrs per

day. ESI, 9.30am-midday, 672FF for 6
mornings, or 3-5pm, 505FF for 6 afternoons, International Masterclass and Force
10, details on request
Private lessons ESF and ESI, 180FF per hr
Snowboarding Planète Surf, 800FF for 6
days, private lessons 160FF per hr. ESI,
private lessons 160FF per hr
Cross-country ESF, 850FF for 6 days, 5 hrs
per day. Loipe 50km
Other courses monoski, moguls, freestyle,
slalom, off-piste, competition, couloir
skiing, Stuart Adamson's Ski Academy
Guiding companies La Compagnie de
l'Oisans

CHILDREN
Lift pass 13 yrs and under 672FF, 18 yrs
and under 864FF, free for 5 yrs and under
Visalp Initiation Pass, 1,300FF for 6 days
including 6 morning lessons
Ski kindergarten ESF Club des Oursons at
Bergers and at Grandes-Rousses,
4 yrs and over, 9.45am-12.45pm and
2.30pm-5pm, 60FF per hr. ESI Club des
Mickeys et des Papotines, 3 yrs and over,
9.30am-midday, 580FF for 6 mornings,
or 3-5pm, 505FF for 6 afternoons.
Les Eterlous, 2-14 yrs, 9am-5.45pm,
1,290FF for 6 days
Ski school ESF, 4-13 yrs, 700FF for 6 days
($5\frac{1}{2}$ hrs per day). ESI Club des Marmottes,
4-13 yrs, 9.30am-midday, 580FF for 6
mornings, or 3-5pm, 460FF for 6 afternoons
Non-ski kindergarten Les Eterlous, 6 mths
and over, 9am-5.45pm, 1,290FF for 6 days,
including lunch. Crèche Vaujany, 3 mths-3
yrs, 9am-5pm, 650FF for 6 days including
lunch

FOOD AND DRINK PRICES
Coffee 10FF, glass of wine 6-15FF, small
beer 12-20FF, dish of the day 40-60FF

Villard-Reculas
top 3330m (10,922ft) bottom 1500m (4,921ft)

This rustic old village is linked into the ski area by chair- and drag-lift. Much has been done in recent years to renovate the village; a number of apartments are additions to the single hotel and the converted cowsheds and barns. Sustenance is provided by one small supermarket and a couple of small bars and restaurants including the popular Bergerie. A blue piste from the bottom of the Petit Prince runs to the village, offering an alternative route to the steeper runs. The road to Allemont on the valley floor is wide and easily accessible in winter, but the one-track road to Huez is normally closed during the season.

TOURIST OFFICE
Tel 33 4 76 80 45 69

Les Arcs

ALTITUDE 1600-2000m (5,248-6,560ft)

More than any other third-generation French resort, Les Arcs epito-
mises a high-altitude, modern, snow-sure *station de ski* (an arena
specifically built for skiing). Critics of purpose-built, French-resort
architecture generally concede that Les Arcs is not unpleasing and is certainly innovative, both off and on the slopes. With its proven graduated
ski-length teaching method (ski évolutif) and particularly good nursery
slopes, those interested in learning quickly and enjoying the process will
find this resort a pleasant and even exciting ski college.

Les Arcs comprises three separate, predominantly self-catering
resorts (1600, 1800 and 2000), which share 200km of skiing and 79
lifts.

On the mountain
top 3226m (10,581ft) bottom 850m (2,788ft)

With so much variety, skiers are unlikely to find their enthusiasm flag-
ging, no matter what their ability. Strong skiers have a wealth of choice,
from unusually long runs that start way above the tree-line and progress
down through the woods, to traditional villages like **Le Pré** and
Villaroger, and the extensive off-piste
opportunities. Intermediates can
cruise forever, and beginners are especially well catered for. The greatest
concentration of lifts, slopes and therefore skiers is above **Arc 1800**, where
sunny and gentle slopes attract intermediates and families. The skiing
above **Arc 1600** is steeper and more
wooded, with some rewarding off-
piste opportunities.

■ **GOOD POINTS**

Large ski area, modern lift system,
excellent facilities for children, skiing
convenience, extensive off-piste,
beautiful scenery

■ **BAD POINTS**

Lack of alpine charm, few activities
for non-skiers, limited après-ski

Another claim to fame of Les Arcs
is its Olympic speed-skiing track on the lower face of the Aiguille Rouge,
which can be tested by members of the public. With typical Les Arcs
panache, the course has been used to establish records for motorbikes
and even mountain bikes.

Lift queues are not generally a problem, although there are a few
exceptions. At Carreley 20 and Chantel 21 reporters came across 'huge
queues until 10am and again at the end of the day'. Some reporters
encountered mid-afternoon crowds for the Villandry 74 lift. The piste
map is said to be 'accurate and well marked; it was easy to find our way
around even in poor visibility'.

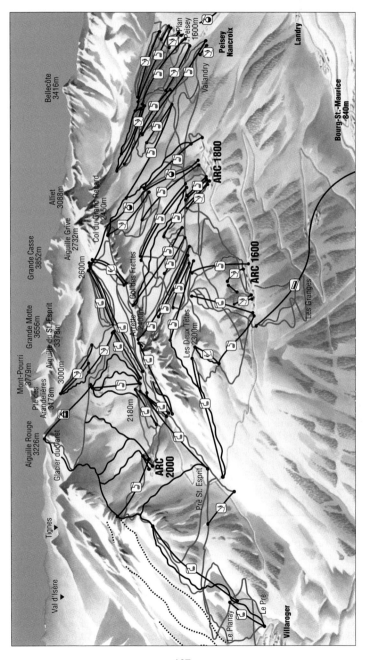

Beginners

Les Arcs is the home of ski évolutif, where absolute beginners start with very short skis of one metre and change to a slightly longer pair each day. This concept produces a fast learning curve, enabling most beginners to manage embryonic parallel turns by the end of the week, when they can choose from 24 green (beginner) runs. Each of the three villages has nursery slopes close by, with the most extensive just above Arc 1800 around the altiport and Le Chantel area, and in the bowl above Arc 2000. Above Arc 1600, strong beginners and timid intermediates can enjoy the long blue (easy) run from Les Deux Têtes.

Intermediates

As a rule, the bigger the ski area the more scope there is for intermediates, and Les Arcs is certainly no exception. Of the resort's 112 runs, 70 are divided equally between blue and red (intermediate) trails, and many of the reds are not difficult. The slopes above Arc 1800 are packed with relatively easy intermediate slopes. The classic black (difficult) bump-run down Comborcières to **Pré-St-Esprit** is a good test for strong intermediates. There are cruising runs between the Grand Col, Aiguille Grive and Arpette.

> ■ **WHAT'S NEW**
>
> Four-seater chair-lift from Col de la Chal

There is much classic intermediate terrain above **Peisey-Nancroix** and **Vallandry**. The Aigle and L'Ours reds are recommended by reporters as 'nice, not too testing runs down through the trees'. Malgovert, down to Arc 1600, is described as 'quite narrow — it felt like an off-piste run but without the worry, and hazards were marked; it leads down to the wonderfully wide and flattering Mont Blanc blue run'.

Advanced

A classic run is the 7-km descent from the top of the Aiguille Rouge all the way down to Le Pré and Villaroger. Of the total 18 black runs, the Piste de l'Ours from Arpette is one of the most exciting. Varet is a long, steep piste from the top of the Aiguille Rouge, which is a real challenge, especially in deep snow. The Robert Blanc, named after the man who helped found Les Arcs, is an excellent run off the north face. Drosets, down to St Esprit, is another testing run from the Aiguille Rouge. The Dou de l'Homme chair accesses several long black trails.

Off-piste

There are so many off-piste opportunities in Les Arcs that it really does pay, both in terms of safety and finding the best terrain, to hire a guide. In fresh snow conditions the most exhilarating and steepest powder skiing is below the Aiguille Rouge. There is good, steep bowl-skiing beneath the Crête de l'Homme, accessed by a traverse to the right as you exit the Aiguille Rouge cable car. Other good off-piste is behind the Aiguille Grive and the Aiguille Rousse at the south-western edge of Arc 1800's ski area. Exciting off-piste descents start from the Grand Col to

Villaroger, with the route continuing behind the Aiguille Rouge, and from the Aiguille Grive down to Peisey-Nancroix. The Comborcières slopes offer a number of challenging opportunities.

Serious off-piste experts can try a cluster of couloirs over the back of the Aiguille Rouge on the East Face, but special permission has to be given by the Vanoise Park authorities, who charge for access to these slopes.

Ski schools and guiding

Les Arcs has the French Ski School (ESF) in all three villages, while the International Ski School (ESI)/Arc Aventures, Virages and Henalu are all based in Arc 1800.

Snowboarding

Les Arcs, with its innovative *nouvelles glisses* concept of trying anything that slides on snow, now accepts that the love-affair it once had with the mono-board is over and that the snowboard, or 'surf' as they prefer to call it, has dethroned it. The ESF and ESI both run snowboard courses. The Tip Top snowboard school also runs special courses for children.

Cross-country

Although Les Arcs itself has only a small amount of cross-country skiing (15km shared by all three satellites), there is another 25km between Arc 1800 and Peisey-Nancroix, plus a further 14km at Nancroix itself.

Mountain restaurants

Mountain eating-places are not a particular strength of Les Arcs ('we were not too impressed and the selection was limited'), but there are some attractive, rustic-style establishments. The restaurants on the rather bleak terrace at the base of Arc 2000 (Le Red Rock and Le St Jacques) seem cheerful when the sun is shining. There are two popular lunch spots at Pré-St-Esprit below Arc 2000. Of these, the rustic Bélliou la Fumée is the smaller and more attractive, with better food and wait-service. L'Arpette, above Arc 1800, is a busy mainstream restaurant. La Crèche, at the top of the Transarc gondola, is a self-service restaurant that also has a dining-room with table service.

There are good reports of the cosy Solliet restaurant on the way down to Villaroger, and in nearby Le Pré, the Aiguille Rouge and La Ferme attract lunchtime skiers when the long run down is open. In nearby **Le Planay**, Chez Léa provides wholesome food in an old farmhouse.

Off the mountain

There is little to do off the slopes ('I wouldn't like to be a non-skier stuck here'). Of the three distinct villages that make up Les Arcs, Arc 1600 is the lowest. Arc 1800 has three sub-sections of its own: Charvet, Villards and Charmettoger, and is the heart of the resort with most of the accommodation, shops, après-ski, and wonderful views across to Mont Blanc.

The highest and bleakest village is Arc 2000 (opened in 1979), which sits in its own secluded bowl at the foot of Les Arcs' main mountain, the Aiguille Rouge (3226m), and is close to some of the best skiing. One reporter dubs it 'a totally characterless garage in the sky'. All three villages are served by a road from **Bourg-St-Maurice**; however, the Arc en Ciel ('rainbow') funicular takes just seven minutes to reach Arc 1600. Although Les Arcs is largely car-free and the resorts are linked by bus, a car is useful to reach the other resorts available on the same lift pass.

Accommodation

About two-thirds of the skiers visiting Les Arcs stay in apartments, and of these, the majority find themselves in Arc 1800. Les Arcs has now sold off virtually all its accommodation to outside property companies; the lion's share to Maeva and others to Pierre et Vacances. Few chalets are available.

The best of the hotels include the Mercure at Charmettoger in Arc 1800. The Golf is the largest and most central, and its Arc 1800 stablemate, Latitudes, is also a three-star. The Cachette at Arc 1600, renowned for its all-day crèche and tasty food, has been completely renovated. Also at 1600, the old Winston Hotel has been modernised and renamed L'Explorer's. The Trois Arcs, also in 1600, is a small and friendly hotel now owned by the resort. At Arc 2000, the two-star Aiguille Rouge remains popular. The Mélèzes, formerly the Eldorador, has been elevated to three stars. There is a Club Med and a Club Aquarius at Arc 2000.

■ OTHER SPORTS

Ice-driving, snowmobiling, snow-shoeing, aeroclub, parapente, hang-gliding, swimming in Bourg-St-Maurice, skating

Les Lauziers apartments in 1800 are convenient for the slopes but have their drawbacks ('a functional building with strange sloping floors; we didn't like the cramped and spartan interiors').

Eating in and out

Self-catering rules in Les Arcs, but no one wants to cook every night of the week. The best choice of restaurants is at Arc 1800; L'Equipe is the biggest but not necessarily the best ('excellent for a posh meal, with Savoyard dishes and a fixed-price menu'). Last winter, visitors spoke highly of the fondues, raclette and pierrade at Le Choucas. Casa Mia specialises in Italian food ('basically a pasta and pizza place, décor rustic — after a fashion — and the service was friendly and informal'). L'Onglet and Le Coq Hardy are also recommended. For value-for-money family fare the Laurus is worth visiting. At Arc 2000 Le Red Rock is popular and informal with live music, and Le St Jacques is more intimate with higher prices. Les Chabottes at Pont Baudin near Peisey-Nancroix serves 'excellent local specialities at prices lower than at Les Arcs'.

Self-caterers will find a wider selection and lower prices in Bourg-St-Maurice, with its two hypermarkets on the outskirts of town. In 1800 there are 'some fine bakeries, an expensive butcher and a small supermarket with limited fresh supplies'.

Visitors considering an outing to the traditional restaurants in

Skiing facts: **Les Arcs**

TOURIST OFFICE
F-73706 Arc 1800, Savoie
Tel 33 4 79 07 12 57
Fax 33 4 79 07 45 96

LONDON AGENT
Erna Low Consultants, 9 Reece Mews,
London SW7 7HE
Tel 0171-584 2841
Fax 0171-589 9531

THE RESORT
By road Calais 937km
By rail Bourg-St-Maurice 15km, buses and
direct funicular to Arc 1600
By air Lyon 2½ hrs, Chambery 2 hrs,
Geneva 2½ hrs
Visitor beds 31,807
Transport free shuttle bus between Arc
1600, 1800 and 2000. Also bus to
Bourg-St-Maurice (48FF)

THE SKIING
Linked or nearby resorts
Bourg-St-Maurice (l), Peisey-Nancroix (l),
La Plagne (n), Le Pré (l),
Vallandry (l)
Longest run Aiguille Rouge, 7km (black)
Number of lifts 79
Total of trails/pistes 200km
(22% beginner, 31% easy,
31% intermediate, 16% difficult)
Nursery slopes 11 runs
Summer skiing none
Snowmaking 20 hectares covered

LIFT PASSES
Area pass (covers Les Arcs, Villaroger,
Peisey and Vallandry and includes skiing in
La Plagne and 1 day in La Rosière/Trois
Vallées/Tignes and Val d'Isère),
960FF for 6 days
Day pass 208FF

Beginners 3 free lifts
Pensioners no reduction
Credit cards accepted yes

SKI SCHOOLS
Adults ESF, 800FF for 6 days, ESI/Arc
Aventures 890FF for 6 days, Virages 895FF
for 6 days, Henalu in 1800, details
on request
Private lessons ESF and ESI 180FF per hr,
Virages 185FF per hr
Snowboarding Tip Top, 660FF for 3 days (3
hrs per day), ESF, 620FF for 6 days (2 hrs
per day), ESI/Arc Aventures, 580FF for 5
days (2½ hrs per day),
Virages, prices on request
Cross-country ESF, 600FF for 6 days
(3 hrs per day). Loipe 15km in Arc 1800,
1600 and 2000
Other courses monoski
Guiding companies ESF or ESI/Arc
Aventures

CHILDREN
Lift pass 7 yrs and over, 960FF for 6 days,
free for 6 yrs and under
Ski kindergarten ESF Pommes du Pin
Club, 3 yrs and over, 8.45am-5.45pm,
780FF for 6 days. Arc 1600, 3-7 yrs
1,790FF, 7-12 yrs 2,050FF for 6 days, both
including lunch
Ski school ESF and ESI/Arc Aventures, 3-7
yrs, 780FF for 6 days, Virages 880FF for 6
days, details on request
Non-ski kindergarten Arc 1600, 3 mths-3
yrs, 1,350FF for 6 days. Arc 1800, 1-3 yrs,
775FF for 6 days, 4-6 yrs, 850FF for 6 days.
Arc 2000, 3 yrs and over, 770-850FF for 6
days. All 8.30am-5pm

FOOD AND DRINK PRICES
Coffee 7FF, glass of wine 10FF, small beer
15FF, dish of the day 60FF

outlying villages between Les Arcs and Bourg-St-Maurice can try the Bois de Lune at **Montvenix**. Booking is recommended, and the restaurant will collect you and take you back. Chez Mimi at Vallandry, L'Ancolie at Nancroix and Chez Léa at Le Planay are other options.

Après-ski

When the lifts close in Arc 1800, skiers and instructors tend to divide themselves between two bars at Le Charvet (Le Gabotte and Le Thuria). At nearby Les Villards, much of the action is at the Pub Russel and the Saloon Bar, which features live music. At 2000 the Red Rock is the 'in' place for a vin chaud. The Hotel du Golf has live jazz and Le Fairway disco in the basement. All three resorts have discos, including the Arcelle in 1600 and Rock Hill in Le Charvet, while snowboarders prefer the Carré Blanc in Les Villards. The music at KL 92 in Arc 2000 is said to be sufficiently 'sympa' to allow conversation.

Childcare

Les Arcs has a 'three-kids' grading (the highest) of the 'Label Kid' stamp of approval from the Ministry of Tourism, denoting that the resort offers children a safe environment with plenty of entertainment, toys and equipment. Toddlers aged 12 months and over are welcome in the day nurseries at Bourg-St-Maurice, Arc 1600 and Arc 1800. The nursery at Arc 2000 accepts children for skiing and non-skiing activities. Babies from three months old are welcome at crèches in Bourg (Garderie Pomme d'Api) and at the Hotel de la Cachette in Arc 1600. The ESF organises courses for children aged three years and over in the Pommes de Pin Club. Older children can enrol in Ski Nature courses to explore the mountain environment and study animal tracks in the snow.

Linked or nearby resorts

Peisey-Nancroix-Vallandry
top 3226m (10,581ft) bottom 1350-1600m (4,428-5,248ft)

Skiers in Les Arcs tend to regard this cluster of villages at the south-western end of the ski area as a useful tree-level bolt hole in bad weather. French families, who have been coming here since the Second World War, prefer to think of it as a peaceful, undemanding ski area that is occasionally invaded by Johnny-Come-Latelys from Les Arcs. The area offers a more rural setting and a cheaper accommodation base for the region. Peisey is a traditional farming community and Nancroix is the starting point for 39km of cross-country trails. The small ski resorts of Plan Peisey and Vallandry are linked by gondola to Peisey in the valley below. Three lifts serve the nusery slope area.

TOURIST OFFICE
Tel 33 4 79 07 94 28
Fax 33 4 79 07 95 34

Barèges/La Mongie

ALTITUDE 1250-1800m (4,092-5,904ft)

Skiers who have tired of the characterless and overcrowded ski circuses of the French Alps with their ever-rising prices should look westwards towards the Pyrenees for a quiet and unspoilt alternative. Here you will find that elusive combination of a timeless French country village with reasonable prices, a short transfer time from an international airport and, to cap it all, the varied runs of a large ski area.

Barèges fills all these requirements. Another major attraction of the resort (indeed also of the rest of the French Pyrenees) are the people, who seem to be genuinely friendly and welcoming — a rare occurrence in some of the more popular resorts in the Alps. The locals have managed to retain their traditional way of life and at the same time to adapt to the needs of tourism without the compulsion to milk their visitors dry.

■ GOOD POINTS

Large intermediate ski area, short airport transfer, sunny slopes, low prices, variety of easy skiing, small and unspoilt village of Barèges

■ BAD POINTS

Weekend lift queues, limited tough runs, lack of resort-level snow, unsuitable for late-season holidays, few activities for non-skiers, bleak village of La Mongie

At first sight, Barèges is a down-at-heel, grey spa town near the head of a narrow valley. However, it has a friendly atmosphere, largely due to its small size, and is not at all claustrophobic. Prices are low by French standards, but there is little to do after skiing except soak up the sulphur waters of the thermal spa.

Barèges was one of the original ski resorts of the Pyrenees. The village also comes into the spotlight in July when it becomes part of the Tour du France route. Its lift system follows the course of the road, which (in summer only) leads over the Col du Tourmalet to the more modern resort of **La Mongie**.

Although hardly the Trois Vallées, the area offers a variety of terrain and skiing for all standards, and while the mountains may not be as awe-inspiring as the Alps, the views are pleasant, in particular from the ridge beside the Col du Tourmalet.

La Mongie is the larger, higher, but considerably less charming of the two resorts. It offers no more facilities than Barèges and is set in the blander half of the ski area. It is, however, a better base for complete beginners or nervous second-weekers. There are easy slopes immediately around the resort that keep their snow relatively well. The lifts linking the two resorts are sometimes closed because of bad weather.

On the mountain
top 2350m (7,708ft) bottom 1250m (4,100ft)

Snowfall in the Pyrenees is a subject that always causes disagreement. There is little to support the belief that the mountains receive less precipitation in winter than the Alps; the trouble is that it does not always fall as snow. Because the mountains are further west and closer to the warm Atlantic, the winter is shorter, but the advantage is the high number of sunny days. For the last two seasons conditions have been excellent. Indeed, during 1995–6, snow cover in the Pyrenees was consistently the best in Europe.

Barèges and La Mongie form the largest ski area in the Pyrenees, sharing 100km of wide, mainly easy to intermediate pistes served by 53 lifts. The area's upper slopes are open and sunny, while the lower ones above Barèges offer sheltered tree-level skiing. The slopes are reached from Barèges by either of two mountain access lifts. The track of the old Ayré funicular was recently rebuilt and climbs steeply from the village centre through the woods to serve red (intermediate) and black (difficult) runs down to a clearing at Lienz. This is some of the best skiing in the area when conditions are favourable.

La Laquette gondola is the alternative access lift from the resort and provides the direct route towards La Mongie, as well as the way up to the ski-school meeting place. At Tournaboup, from the top of the lift, an

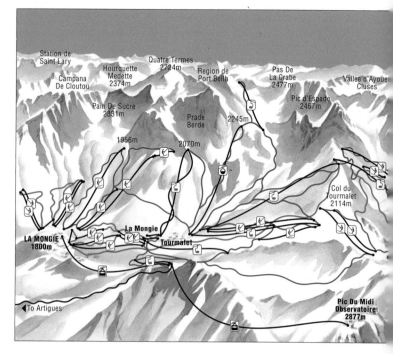

easy link-run leads on to **Super Barèges**, which is little more than a restaurant. A development to the north of Super Barèges, below the Lac d'Oncet, has in recent years added to the size of the whole ski area.

Queues can be a serious problem at weekends, especially on Sundays; as Barèges cannot cope with many cars, the lifts from the top of the village and from Tournaboup are crowded, and the Col du Tourmalet can be a bottleneck in both directions.

Beginners

Barèges itself has no nursery slope; the main one is at the top of La Laquette gondola. La Mongie is the better place for first-timers; a large area of nursery slopes around the resort keeps its snow relatively well but suffers from being a popular thoroughfare. Tournaboup, just outside Barèges, has a small nursery slope and there is also a baby lift at **La Mongie-Tourmalet**. At Barèges, second- and third-week skiers can make their way across to Lienz from the mid-station of the Ayré funicular. Of the two runs from there down to the resort, the green (beginner) run is a path that begins with an uphill section.

Intermediates

A variety of short intermediate pistes covers the sides of the hill at the top of La Laquette gondola to Lienz on one side and to Tournaboup on the

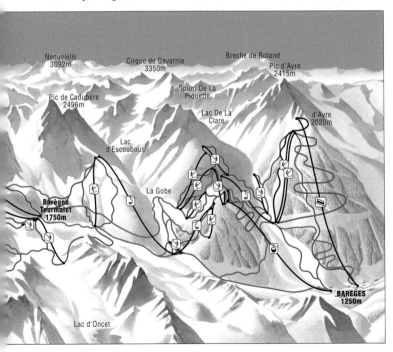

other. Above La Mongie the runs are mainly wide and easy. A gondola is the main lift on the north-facing side, serving a long and shaded blue (easy) gully. The slopes beneath the Sud chair-lift are not particularly gentle, and the blue run contains a narrow section. On this sunny side of the mountain, the most interesting trails are reached from the top of the Coume Lounque drag and chair, where there are a couple of reds. One trail follows a valley down to La Mongie, the other leads down to Super Barèges; part of the run is steep enough to be graded black and can be icy in the morning.

Advanced

Ayré at 2020m has some of the area's steepest skiing, and there is no easy way down from the top of the funicular. There are some fairly sheer, west-facing slopes below the Col du Tourmalet, including a selection of short mogul fields. The rocky slopes bordering La Mongie and the road are steep and although there are lifts, the terrain does not give much scope for pistes. The most challenging run around La Mongie is the black under the Prade Berde chair-lift.

Off-piste

The itinerary round to the Lac d'Oncet is a good place for spring snow even in mid-winter. At Tournaboup there is a long chair-lift over a wide and fairly steep, west-facing mountainside, which is left unpisted although it is much skied in good conditions.

At the top of the Coume de Pouteilh gondola above La Mongie, the 4 Termes chair-lift has added to the overall length of the run and gives access to an off-piste itinerary down the Aygues Cluses Valley, ending at Tournaboup.

Ski schools and guiding

French Pyrenean resorts have made considerable efforts to improve the standard of their ski schools in recent years, and the number of fluent English-speaking instructors has risen. Ecoloski in Barèges offers, among other classes, tuition in off-piste skiing, moguls and telemark. However, we have disappointing reports of this school: 'I was in much too difficult a group, and when I asked to change groups I was told to "have courage"'. The French Ski School (ESF) also operates in Barèges. Henri Nogué is a high-mountain guide who organises off-piste courses and ski-touring in the area. There are ski schools at both La Mongie and La Mongie-Tourmalet.

Snowboarding

Both the ESF and Ecoloski offer snowboarding lessons, but there are no special facilities on the mountain.

Mountain restaurants

The mountain eating-places are inexpensive in comparison with prices in the Alps, but are few and far between. Chez Louisette is popular, Auberge

La Couquelle is a small and friendly place with the highlight 'a delicious warm goat's cheese salad with honey dressing'. There is a restaurant at the Col du Tourmalet, and Le Yeti in La Mongie is recommended.

Off the mountain

Barèges is little more than a single street climbing steeply beside a river, enclosed by tree-lined mountainside. There is no natural site for a village and none would have appeared had it not been for the sulphur springs that became famous in the seventeenth century. Avalanche barriers allowed the construction of permanent dwellings, which stand today as a grey and unmemorable (except for the spa itself) mixture of renovated and grand old buildings at the top of the narrow village. Parking space is restricted, and the ski bus cannot cope when runs to the village are closed and too many skiers have ended up at Tournaboup.

■ **OTHER SPORTS**

Winter walks, snowmobiling, 4-wheel motorbiking circuit, swimming, tobogganing, ice climbing, snow-shoeing, parapente, aqua-gym

La Mongie is divided into two parts. The lower village is the main one, a bleak and charmless place with a crescent of restaurants, shops and hotels, with a car park in the middle. The upper village of La Mongie-Tourmalet is a long and jagged complex with a single hotel, a restaurant and apartments. The two sections are linked by a day-time bucket lift.

The access road up to La Mongie from Bagnères-de-Bigorre is extremely busy at weekends and can be closed when the resort is full.

Accommodation

Those in search of luxury will be disappointed as Barèges has nothing more superior than simple two-star hotels. The family-run Richelieu is a friendly place just below the funicular station. L'Igloo is run by a former ski champion and is close to La Laquette gondola. Some reporters found the Hotel Central unfriendly. The one-star Poste and Modern hotels both offer basic but clean bedrooms. The British-run Les Sorbiers is a popular, small hotel, which 'provides simple, attractively furnished, clean accommodation. The bedrooms were warm but the public areas rather chilly. The vegetarian options were superb'. Shops are confined to a good chemist and the most simplistic of ski-hire and souvenir shops. There is a single supermarket for self-caterers.

La Mongie has a three-star hotel, Le Pourteilh, plus three two-stars and two other smaller hotels. La Mongie-Tourmalet has just one three-star hotel, the Lamandia.

Eating in and out

La Rozeli is for fondues and pizzas, and the Toscane is a pizzeria-take-away. Le Pichounet serves a delicious *fondue au chocolat noir*. La Couquelle, with its welcoming fireplace, is close to Tournaboup and is open in the evenings as well as at lunchtime. The main event of the week is an evening at Chez Louisette, organised by the ski school, which culminates in a torch-light descent. You can also reach the restaurant by snowmobile, snowcat, or on foot. The staple diet of the region appears to be *Magret de Canard* and *Confit de Canard*, not to mention *foie gras*; as one reporter put it: 'I never want to see or taste another duck as long as I live'.

Après-ski

After-skiing entertainment centres on a few bars, a handful of restaurants and two discos. The liveliest places are Pub l'Oncet, L'Isba and the Café Richelieu. The discos open at 11pm and do not fill up until 1am; Le Club Jonathan is the most popular. Many visitors come to Barèges for the spa, which dates from the seventeenth century. Today, the treatments take place in an austere building at the top of the high street. Facilities include whirlpools, saunas, thermal baths and showers, an aqua-gym and aqua massage, all of which use the special healing waters — great for relaxing after a hard day on the slopes. La Mongie has a few restaurants and bars.

Childcare

The ESF and Ecoloski both have a ski kindergarten for children from four to eight years old. The two non-ski kindergartens take children from two to six years old and lunch can be provided. There is also a kindergarten at La Mongie.

TOURIST OFFICES
Tel Barèges: 33 5 62 92 68 19/La Mongie: 33 5 62 91 94 15
Fax Barèges: 33 5 62 92 66 60/La Mongie: 33 5 62 95 33 13

Linked or nearby resorts

Cauterets
top 2350m (7,710ft) bottom 1000m (3,280ft)

This attractive thermal resort became a ski station in 1962 and today it has more than 22,000 visitor beds in a large selection of hotels. The nearest airport is Lourdes, 40km away. The skiing is in the open and often very exposed Cirque du Lys bowl, accessed by a two-stage cable car, which also brings skiers back to the resort at the end of the day. The terrain is best suited to beginners and intermediates. There are 20 runs, including one black, with the rest equally divided between reds, blues and greens. The 29km of pistes are served by 13 lifts. There is another small but developing ski area nearby at **Pont d'Espagne**, renowned for its cross-country trails.

The ski school offers instruction in freestyle, snowboarding, parapente and off-piste, as well as ordinary group and private lessons. Les Marmottes non-ski kindergarten takes children from 3 months to 6 years old. Children from 4 to 10 years old are taught in the ski school.

The extensive choice of accommodation includes *gîtes*, chalets and hotels, some of them dating from the Belle Epoque. Hotel Bordeaux is recommended as a comfortable three-star with a good restaurant. The Hotel Club Aladin has a fitness centre, with a swimming-pool, squash courts and sauna among its facilities. The Astérides is the other three-star, and Etche-Ona is a two-star near the scenic Pont d'Espagne. The Royalty pub is popular, as is the St Trop video bar. Other resort facilities include a theatre, cinema, casino, two discos, a large indoor skating rink and the thermal spa.

TOURIST OFFICE
Tel 33 5 62 92 50 27
Fax 33 5 62 92 59 12

Font-Romeu
top 2204m (7,229ft) bottom 1800m (5,906ft)
The resort, 19km from Perpignan and 200km from Toulouse, is set on a sunny plateau known for its mild climate, making it unreliable for snow at the beginning and end of the season. The skiing is 4km from the village, and is linked by a bus service. The 52km of piste and 32 lifts suit beginners to intermediates as well as families. Weekend queues are a problem as the resort is popular with both French and Spanish skiers. Fifty per cent of the total skiing terrain is covered by snow-cannon.

There are two-dozen hotels and pensions, over a dozen youth hostels and various self-catering apartments. Après-ski activities include a wide choice of restaurants, a casino, cinemas, three discos and ten bars. Cross-country skiing is very important here, with two specialist schools, Pyrénées Ski Nordique and ANCEF. There is also a snowboarding park.

TOURIST OFFICE
Tel 33 5 68 30 68 30
Fax 33 5 68 30 29 70

St-Lary
top 2450m (8,038ft) bottom 830m (2,722ft)
St-Lary-Soulan, 80km from Lourdes, is a typically Pyrenean village of stone-built houses and one main, rather narrow street. The skiing is suitable for beginners to intermediates and it begins a four-minute walk from the village centre at the cable car to **St-Lary Pla d'Adret** (1680m), itself a small, dull modern ski station with some accommodation. From here a bus runs to two other small centres, **St-Lary La Cabane** and **St Lary Espiaube**. The ski area is served by a chain of 32 lifts, including a new quad chair, but is mainly treeless and lacks variety. It has a snow-board park in the Vallon du Portet sector. There are six nursery slopes and three ski schools. Two mountain guiding companies arrange ski-tours, which are popular here.

Grand Hotel Mir is recommended, as well as the Mercure Cristal

Parc and Hotel La Terrasse Fleurie. The Andrédéna is in a quiet position. At Espiaube, Hotel La Sapinière provides reasonable accommodation at the bottom of the pistes.

TOURIST OFFICE
Tel 33 5 62 39 50 81
Fax 33 5 62 39 50 06

Superbagnères
top 2260m (7,415ft) bottom 1800m (5,904ft)

Luchon is a thermal spa town with shops and three nightclubs, Superbagnères is the quieter ski station 17km away by road and a few minutes by cable car. Spain is just half-an-hour from Luchon, and Toulouse (France) is the nearest airport. Superbagnères is one of the highest resorts in the Pyrenees, with ten drag-lifts, six chairs and one cable car serving the area's 24 pistes. There are two mountain restaurants, Céciré and La Hount, and two nursery slopes. There is an ESF ski school, which also runs a comprehensive ski kindergarten, with its own slope and ski lift, and cares for non-skiing children from two years of age.

Most of the accommodation at Superbagnères is in apartments and the remainder in the two hotels, the Isard and the Aneto. Club Med has a base in the resort. There are two restaurants, two cafeterias and a supermarket. Activities outside skiing are a disco, swimming, indoor tennis, parapente and a thermal spa centre. Luchon has more than 30 hotels including a three-star, the Corneille, and over a dozen restaurants ranging from pizzerias to those serving local cuisine.

TOURIST OFFICE
Tel 33 5 61 79 21 21
Fax 33 5 61 79 11 23

Chamonix

From a skier's point of view, Chamonix is not so much a resort as a chain of unconnected areas set along both sides of the valley dominated by Mont Blanc. On stormy days, of which there are many, it is a brooding place, menaced by razor-sharp peaks and tumbling walls of ice. On sunny days, it is glitteringly beautiful and deceptively tranquil. Its focus is the town of Chamonix, a core of hotels and villas built around the turn of the century and subsequently hemmed in by the neo-brutalist architecture of post-war tourism. Less than half of the winter visitors are skiers.

The name Chamonix first appeared in 1091 in connection with the foundation of the monastery of St-Michel-de-la-Cluse. The arrival of the monks marked the start of farming in the valley, a dour form of subsistence agriculture practised by people known for their resistance to outside authority,

■ **GOOD POINTS**

Unsurpassed scenery, large vertical drop, extensive off-piste skiing, outstanding mountain guides, short airport transfer, wide choice of non-skiing activities, cosmopolitan atmosphere, vibrant nightlife

■ **BAD POINTS**

Poorly linked ski areas, unsuitable for families and mixed-ability groups, unpredictable weather patterns, decrepit lift system, heavy traffic

especially when it came to paying taxes. Such rugged individualism stood them in good stead when Chamonix's peaks became a magnet for climbers from all over the world: locals formed the Compagnie des Guides, the oldest and best mountain guiding service in the world.

As in many other parts of the Alps, the pioneering climbers were British. The celebrated Middle Eastern explorer, Richard Pococke, and his 24-year-old companion, William Windham, arrived in the Chamonix Valley from Geneva in 1741. Their party of 13 had expected to encounter 'savages' along the way and was consequently armed to the teeth. To further confuse the peasants they actually encountered along what is now the Autoroute Blanche, Pococke was dressed as an Arab, for reasons best known to himself.

Forty-five years later, the locally born doctor Michel-Gabriel Paccard and his reclusive partner, Jacques Balmat, conquered Mont Blanc; this was the most famous of many first ascents that have made Chamonix pre-eminent in climbing lore.

Over the past 30 years Chamonix has acquired a comparable status among skiers due to the first descents made by radical extremists like Jean-Marc Boivin and Patrick Vallençant, who now lie buried in the local churchyard. Today, the ski extreme torch is carried by Pierre Tardivel, the one-time Chamonix bank clerk whose descents include Everest.

On the mountain
top 3842m (12,605ft) bottom 1035m (3,396ft)

The Chamonix Valley caters for all levels of skier, but not in the same place, which makes it difficult for mixed-ability groups to ski on the same mountain. There are six main base-stations, most of which are a bus ride from the town centre. The closest is the celebrated Aiguille du Midi cable car, which takes skiers up on to the shoulder of Mont Blanc for the descent down the Vallée Blanche. Le Brévent and La Flégère provide the bulk of the intermediate skiing and this season they have finally been linked by jumbo gondola. The toughest and easiest skiing lies further up the valley at **Argentière** and **Le Tour** respectively, while **Les Houches**, on the other side of town, has extensive slopes; a number are below the tree-line, which makes them popular when visibility is poor.

For many years, the area has relied on reputation rather than regeneration to bring in the clients, a policy that has resulted in antiquated lift systems, a lack of snowmaking equipment and general inertia. Chamonix's legions of enthusiasts — most of them ski fanatics — love it unreservedly, but the authorities now believe that the time is ripe for investment if the resort is to hold its position into the twenty-first century.

Les Houches has led the way with the installation of two high-speed quads and the promise of more to come. Sixty-seven snow-cannon covering 7km of piste have also been added. A new gondola linking Les Houches to **St-Gervais** is scheduled to open for Christmas 1997, making Les Houches part of a 350-km linked ski circus.

A jumbo gondola linking Le Brévent to La Flégère should be in operation for the start of the 1996–7 season, and will open up a whole range of new runs. Underground parking for 400 cars is under construction at the foot of Le Brévent. At the Grands Montets, a new gondola replaces the ancient Bochard chair-lift and will take 3,000 skiers per hour to the summit of Bochard. The adjacent Herse chair will also be replaced with a high-speed quad when funds permit. In 1997 work begins on a link over the Tête de Balme to combine Le Tour with **Vallorcine** and the Swiss resort of **Finhaut**.

Beginners

Learn to ski in Chamonix if you must, but do not necessarily expect to like it. The town has small training areas for absolute beginners at Les Planards and Le Savoy, but once the basics are in place the best practice slopes are at Le Tour, the most far-flung of the valley's outposts. As it is tree-free, the light is often hostile, but on a clear day the comfortable gondola access to Charamillon and the wide, empty slopes that fan out across the Col de Balme above it are very user-friendly. The protected area for bad-weather is the small network of blue (easy) runs at the top of Prarion in Les Houches.

Intermediates

Chamonix may be short of motorway networks, but there is more than adequate compensation in the diversity of the pistes on offer. Skiers with

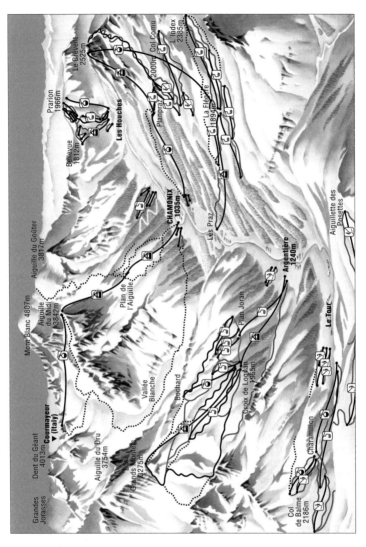

the skills to tackle a red (intermediate) run with confidence can spend a week in the valley without going to the same place twice. The most convenient starting point is Le Brévent where the six-seater gondola to Planpraz gives access to a choice of inviting blue runs down to the Col Cornu chair. This in turn opens up several moderately challenging reds, the longest of which goes to the bottom of the La Charlanon drag-lift. Planpraz is also the launch point for the dramatic cable car ride up to Le Brévent itself, a 2525-m crag with unsurpassed views of Mont Blanc.

La Flégère is reached from the suburb of **Les Praz**, a ten-minute bus-ride from the town centre. The terrain is similar to Le Brévent, with long red and blue runs from the top of L'Index to the mid-station and a black descent back to base. The link with Le Brévent creates a viable ski area.

No visit to Chamonix is complete without a ride up the two-stage Aiguille du Midi cable car, the highest in Europe. This is the departure point for the 20-km glacier run down the Vallée Blanche, a gentle cruise through some of the most grandiose mountain scenery in the world. As it can readily be tackled by low intermediates, it provides thousands of skiers with their first unforgettable taste of high-mountain off-piste adventure. The trickiest part comes early in the day in the shape of the infamous steps cut into the spine of the ridge between the cable-car station and the skiing start point.

Experienced mountaineers ignore both the safety rope and the vertical drop-offs on either side, trotting down effortlessly as if they were in Chamonix's main street; but first-timers, burdened with skis on their backs, can freeze with the horror of it all. Some guides rope their clients together, a precaution that can increase the feeling of danger if several people slip at once — the reality is that everyone gets down safely in the end. The golden rule at this resort is to ski the Vallée Blanche when the sun shines and Les Houches when the weather closes in. By comparison with its neighbours, Les Houches is low, which severely restricts skiing when there is not enough snow. Access is via the Bellevue cable car or the Prarion gondola, both of which connect with the extensive network of red and blue runs on the Col de Voza.

Advanced

When enthusiasts talk of Chamonix, they really mean the Grands Montets at Argentière. This is a truly magnificent mountain for experts, steep, complex and dramatic with seemingly unlimited possibilities. It is accessed either by the 80-person cable car to Lognan or the high-speed quad chair to Plan Joran, both of which terminate at the Argentière base-station. When the cognoscenti arrive at Lognan, they join the rush — and almost inevitably the queue — for the Grands Montets cable car.

The huge popularity of this lift is undiminished either by the supplement payable on top of the Mont Blanc lift pass or the 200 slippery metal steps leading from the top-station to the start of the skiing. This reveals itself to be a bumpy defile that divides into two black runs, Les Pylones under the cable car and the awkwardly cambered Point de Vue, which, as its name suggests, provides stunning views of the glacier as it tracks down its edge. The Bochard lift, now a new gondola, opens up another huge section of the mountain, including the tough 4.5-km Chamois descent to the Le Lavancher chair.

Off-piste

On a powder morning, the rush for the Grands Montets is fierce and fearsome, but the area is so enormous that skiing it out in a hurry is beyond even the powers of Europe's most dedicated first-track pack.

Although there are plenty of open snow fields, bowls and gullies between the marked pistes, maximising the experience means hiring a guide to safely negotiate the glacier; a web of crevasses and seracs changes position from season to season.

Although the more macho of the temporary residents claim to know the mountain well enough to ski it alone, the truth is that to go without a qualified guide is to court death. From a skiing point of view, the most challenging descent is the Pas de Chèvre, a run from the top of Bochard via one of several extreme couloirs down the Mer de Glace to the bottom of the Vallée Blanche. Another classic is the Envers route down the Vallée Blanche, reached from the top of the Aiguille du Midi cable car, but far removed from the regular run in terms of degree of difficulty.

> ■ **WHAT'S NEW**
>
> Gondola link between Le Brévent and La Flégère
> Parking for 400 cars at Le Brévent
> Gondola replaces Bochard chair-lift
> 7km of snowmaking at Les Houches
> New restaurant complex at Lognan

Ski schools and guiding

The Chamonix branch of the French Ski School (ESF) and the Compagnie des Guides share an office in the downtown area, but the less traditional Ski Sensation takes a wilder approach to the learning curve, said to be popular with British clients. The Association of Independent Guides is one of several alternative guiding services, but British adventurers are advised to contact fluent English-speakers like Roland Stieger directly (see Skiing by Numbers). The ESF also has an office in Argentière, while Les Houches is served both by the ESF and the International Ski School (ESI).

Snowboarding

Most of Chamonix's snowboarders are powder surfers who shred the Grands Montets in hot competition with regular skiers. The tiny minority who prefer to practise tricks can be found at the surf park at Charamillon, the mid-station at Le Tour, and the half-pipe near the Kandahar chair in Les Houches.

Cross-country

From Chamonix up to Argentière there are 43km of loipe, nearly half of which are graded easy.

Mountain restaurants

The Chamonix Valley is not recommended for skiers who like to lunch on the mountain seriously. Le Brévent and La Flégère have crowded self-service cafeterias, while Le Tour's Hotel Olympique is acclaimed for its sunseeker's terrace, but less so for its food, which is dismissed as 'so-so' and service, 'the worst in the valley'. Those who ski the Vallée Blanche have little choice but to eat at the spectacularly sited Requin refuge, now under new ownership and recommended for its fruit tarts. Ironically, the best restaurants are on the Grands Montets, the place where skiers are least likely to stop for lunch.

Lognan has an entirely new restaurant complex. It is necessary to book in advance for La Chavanne, a tin hut under the Bochard lift station that is decidedly more promising inside than out. The spacious Plan Joran has an extensive self-service area, with decent, reasonably priced hot and cold food, and a small wait-service restaurant offering more sophisticated fare.

Off the mountain

Chamonix took shape before cars took over, and its current concerns are mostly with traffic management. Most visitors to the valley rightly consider a car to be essential, the alternative being a local bus service that links the base-stations with moderate efficiency but little comfort, especially at peak hours.

The original village square is fully pedestrianised and the main street is closed to traffic during daylight hours. This allows for the free flow of shoppers at the cost of considerable congestion on the outskirts, especially in the ever-expanding new township of **Chamonix Sud**. The problem has not been improved as much as was hoped by the addition of a 300-space car park at St-Michel. The shopping facilities are so comprehensive here that one reporter comments: 'almost a range of shops that one would expect to find in any British town'.

A subsidiary worry is the proposed second tunnel under Mont Blanc, a scheme rigorously opposed by the majority of Chamonix's 10,000 permanent inhabitants on the grounds of massive pollution. As it is favoured by Brussels on the grounds that the existing tunnel will become a bottleneck when the four-lane access roads on the Italian and French sides are completed, most residents fear the worst.

Accommodation

Chamonix offers the full spectrum from dormitory-style youth hostels to four-star hotels, plus a wide choice of chalets and apartments. The seven privately owned Les Autannes apartments, in a former old stone-built hotel near La Tour, are some of the best appointed accommodation here.

The most luxurious hotels are the Albert 1er and Auberge du Bois Prin, owned by brothers Denis and Pierre Carrier. In the three-star category, the Sapinière recalls the heyday of the British Empire, both in its furnishings and its clientèle. The Richemond also trades on the faded glories of yesteryear, but from a more central location. The Alpina is a central, quality three-star hotel.

Eating in and out

No one denies that the Michelin-rated Albert 1er has the best food in Chamonix, but prices have risen to such a level that even the rich hesitate to go there except on special occasions. The Auberge du Bois follows it closely in both quality and price, and the food at the Hotel Eden in Les Praz is also recommended.

In a more accessible bracket, the once reliable National and Atmosphere restaurants have suffered from changes of ownership. La Bergerie serves Savoyard specialities, while the Bistro de la Gare is known for its cheap daily special. Le Sarpe in **Les Bois** is praised for quality combined with good value. L'Impossible, the ancient barn in Chamonix Sud converted by Sylvain Saudain, is a winner for atmosphere. Other recommendations include La Cantina for Mexican cuisine and Le Cafeteria, which is said to provide 'very reasonably priced, wholesome food'. Self-caterers are well served by specialist food shops and supermarkets.

> ### ■ OTHER SPORTS
> Indoor tennis and squash, ice-driving, snow-shoeing, hang-gliding, parapente, curling, skating, swimming

Après-ski

The ski-mad early evening trade may concentrate on the fashionable video bars of Le Choucas and Driver, but there is no shortage of alternative entertainment. There is floodlit skiing at Les Bossons and a bowling alley and billiard school in Chamonix Sud.

After dinner the action focuses on Arbat, which has the best live music in town. Wild Wallabies, inspired by St Anton's Krazy Kangaruh, is another top choice, while real late-nighters end up at the Blue Night, which stays open till 5am.

The Bumble Bee and the Mill Street Bar in Chamonix are both recommended, as is The Office Bar in Argentière. Jekyll and Hyde and The Ice Rock Café in Chamonix Sud are both popular; the latter is a large basement bar incorporating half a truck and various motor-bikes, and is packed until the early hours.

Childcare

The ESF in Chamonix and Argentière have classes for children aged between 4 and 12 years of age. Alternatively the Panda-Club in Argentière provides care for children aged three months to three years, seven days a week. For three- and four-year-olds, Panda-Ski offers daily sessions in the Jardin des Neiges near the Lognan lift station. In addition, a municipal crèche provides entertainment for children aged 18 months to 6 years of age.

Linked or nearby resorts

Argentière
top 3842m (12,605ft) bottom 1240m (4,067ft)

In winter, Argentière's main street becomes Ski Bum Alley, with a large proportion of its rooms let out cheaply for the season. After dark, the bars hum with macho talk of the day's derring-do. The Office Bar, now relocated in larger premises, is the favoured British watering hole. The

Skiing facts: **Chamonix**

TOURIST OFFICE
85 Place du Triangle de L'Amitié, F-74400
Chamonix Mont Blanc, Haute Savoie
Tel 33 4 50 53 00 24
Fax 33 4 50 53 58 90

THE RESORT
By road Calais 900km
By rail station in resort
By air Geneva 1½ hrs
Visitor beds 56,000
Transport free bus service from Le Tour to
Les Houches included in lift pass

THE SKIING
Linked or nearby resorts Argentière (n),
Courmayeur (n), Les Houches (n), Megève
(n), St-Gervais (n)
Longest run Les Grands Montets, 8km
(black/red)
Total of trails/pistes 140km (52% easy,
36% intermediate, 12% difficult)
Nursery slopes 17 beginner runs
Summer skiing none
Snowmaking 80 snow-cannon

LIFT PASSES
Area pass Mont Blanc Skipass (covers 13
resorts in Mont Blanc region), 920FF for 6
days
Day pass 80FF, or 178FF for Grands
Montets
Beginners no free lifts
Pensioners 20% reduction for 60 yrs
and over

Credit cards accepted yes

SKI SCHOOLS
Adults ESF, 740FF for 6 days, Ski
Sensation, details on request
Private lessons ESF, beginners only,
190FF per hr
Snowboarding ESF, 660FF for 3 after-
noons, private lessons, 500FF for 2 hrs
Cross-country ESF, prices as regular ski
lessons. Loipe 43km around Chamonix and
Argentière
Other courses heli-skiing
Guiding companies Compagnie des Guides
de Chamonix, Association Internationale
des Guides, Stages Vallençant, Mont Blanc
Ski Tours, Sensations International

CHILDREN
Lift pass Mont Blanc Skipass, 12 yrs and
under, 640FF for 6 days
Ski kindergarten ESF, 4-12 yrs, 1,250FF
for 6 days including lunch. Panda Club, 3-
12 yrs, 1,425FF for 6 days including lunch
Ski school ESF, 4-6 yrs, 620FF for 6 days,
6-12 yrs, 610FF for 6 days
Non-ski kindergarten Halte-Garderie, 18
mths-6 yrs, (Mon-Fri) 8am-6.15pm, 220FF
per day, extra 19FF per day for lunch. Panda
Club, 3 mths-3 yrs, 1,400FF for 6 days
including lunch

FOOD AND DRINK
Coffee 6-10FF, glass of wine 10FF, small
beer 15-20FF, dish of the day 45-55FF

Rusticana is more cosmopolitan, while the Savoie dares to remain resolutely French. The Dahu Hotel, a prominent landmark on the congested road from Chamonix to Martigny, is recommended both for comfort and food.

TOURIST OFFICE
as Chamonix

La Clusaz

ALTITUDE 1100m (3,608ft)

La Clusaz is a large, spread-out resort off the Autoroute Blanche on the way to Chamonix, less than two hours' drive from Geneva Airport. Consequently, it is extremely attractive to skiers from Britain and Holland who have bought apartments here and visit for weekends. It is also popular with Geneva-based skiers and, when snow conditions are fine, weekend crowds can be a problem. La Clusaz has none of the exclusive cachet of **Megève**, its sophisticated neighbour; the atmosphere is no-frills provincial French in what has been a ski and summer resort since 1898. Municipal records show that La Clusaz received a substantial 4,000 tourists in 1908.

The layout of the resort is annoyingly inconvenient and to avoid long walks in ski boots it is advisable to choose your accommodation with care.

■ **GOOD POINTS**

Variety of skiing for beginners, easy road access, short airport transfer, excellent for children, wide choice of mountain restaurants, facilities for non-skiers

■ **BAD POINTS**

Unreliable snow cover, heavy traffic, lack of skiing convenience, few tough runs, unsuitable for late holidays, weekend crowds

However, the real drawback is its lack of altitude. The village itself is only 1100m, which is extremely low by Haute Savoie standards, and the ski area, with its 56 lifts, only goes up to 2600m. This means there is usually little or no snow at resort level for much of the winter, and the danger is always that some precipitation will fall as rain over most of the ski area. The resort's proximity to Geneva means that it is prone to overcrowding at weekends, although serious city skiers tend to head down the Autoroute Blanche to the more diverse attractions of the Chamonix Valley.

Reblochon, one of the greatest cheeses of France, comes from here. During the madness of the French Revolution, La Clusaz attained fame similar to that of Gretna Green; marriages were declared legal if the happy couple walked three times around the designated tree of liberty in the village square. Divorce was as easily accommodated — in reverse.

More recently, La Clusaz has become famous for its Flying Kilometre (speed skiing) course on the top half of the Vraille run in the Balme sector, where a number of world records were set in the 1980s. It has now fallen into disuse because it is simply not steep enough to match the records being set in Les Arcs.

The 40 lifts of nearby **Le Grand-Bornand** are included in the regional lift pass, as is the connecting ski bus. A car is useful for access to the different sectors of the inconveniently arranged ski area, or for excursions further afield into the Chamonix Valley.

On the mountain
top 2600m (8,528ft) bottom 1100m (3,608ft)

La Clusaz has five ski areas spread around the sides of a number of neighbouring valleys facing north, east and west. Mountain access to Beauregard and L'Aiguille is via lifts from the resort centre. The other three (Balme, L'Etale and Croix-Fry/Merdassier) are reached from various points along the valleys via a satisfactory ski-bus network. Despite roads and rivers all five are linked by lift or piste, although some of these connections are long green (beginner) pistes that involve a plod; another is a trans-valley cable-car shuttle.

Beauregard, served by a single cable car from the bottom of the resort, is a 1690-m flat-topped wooded mountain, with easy skiing in attractive pastoral surroundings at the top.

L'Etale is an enjoyable area of short, gentle runs through the trees, spread over a knoll between the cols of La Croix-Fry and Merdassier. It is mainly served by a single cable car, which takes you up to the top at 2200m. Skiing is limited to the north-west-facing flank of the mountain, which is open and fairly steep on the upper half, with a network of drag-lifts serving the gentler and more spacious slopes at the bottom. These provide access to an easy run across to the Merdassier sector, which offers considerable variety.

There are steeper and more open runs on the other side of Merdassier, as well as a gentle run across to L'Etale, which provides the return link. Apart from the attraction of the extra skiing, the area is well supplied with restaurants beside the two cols.

L'Aiguille is the largest of the sectors and is directly accessible from the village by efficient chair- and drag-lifts. The Crêt du Merle mid-station has a small nursery slope, ski school assembly area and restaurants. None of the runs down from here offers any degree of difficulty. From the next stage the Crêt du Loup is a long, west-facing run to the valley, which offers more than 600m vertical.

The north-west-facing slopes of the Massif de Balme provide the highest and most challenging pistes, with enjoyable long runs down the Combe de la Balme and the Combe de la Torchère, providing over 1200m vertical with plenty of scope for off-piste variations. Two long, flat green runs lead back to the resort; the lower one requires a lot of poling.

Beginners
There are small but good nursery slopes close to the village centre and at the bottom of each sector, but snow cover may not be satisfactory at this low altitude. The best novice slopes are at Crêt du Merle in the Aiguille sector and on the top of Beauregard. Two long blue (easy) and green runs take a line around both shoulders of Beauregard back to the resort.

Intermediates
All the areas offer plenty of scope for confident parallel skiers, although the longer runs in the Balme area are the most enjoyable. Moderate red (intermediate) runs descend from both top-stations here, and a long blue

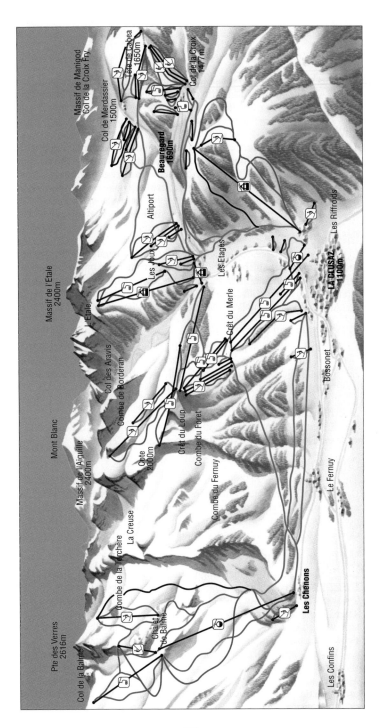

Pte des Verres 2616m

Col de la Balme

Mont Blanc

Massif de l'Aiguille 2400m

Massif de l'Etale 2400m

Massif de Manigod
Col de la Croix Fry

Tête de l'abea

Col de la Croix 1477m

Col de Merdassier 1500m

Col des Aravis

Combe de Borderan

Col de la Balme

La Creuse

Combe de la Torchère

Chalet de Balme

Cote 2000m

Crêt du Loup

Combe du Foret

Combe du Fernuy

Beauregard 1690m

Altiport

L'Etale

Les Juzs

Les Etages

Crêt du Merle

Les Chênons

Le Fernuy

Les Confins

Les Riffrods

Les Riffrods

LA CLUSAZ 1100m

Bossonet

winds its way down more sedately from the top of the Bergerie chair. Try also L'Aiguille run from the top of the drag-lift of the same name and Tétras from the top of L'Etale.

Advanced

The pistes of La Clusaz are of limited appeal to truly advanced skiers. La Noire, one the resort's three black (difficult) pistes, follows the fall-line down the front face of Beauregard. The run starts gently but becomes steeper, with a couple of awkward pitches. Le Vraille, down the Combe de la Torchère in the Balme sector, may no longer be steep enough for speed-skiing records, but the gradient is sufficient to test anyone's skills.

Off-piste

In deep snow the area beneath the Crêt du Loup chair-lifts in the Aiguille sector, as well as in the bowl above them, provide good opportunities for off-piste skiing. Itineraries include the Combe de Borderan and the Combe du Fernuy; both are long, steep gullies in the wall of the Chaîne des Aravis. Ski-touring is available with the Ski Académie ski school.

Ski schools and guiding

La Clusaz has three ski schools: the French Ski School (ESF), Aravis Evasion and Ski Académie. We have reports of oversubscribed classes run by the ESF ('our instructor just could not remember 15 names'). We have no reports of either of the other schools.

Snowboarding

The ESF and Ski Académie both teach snowboarding. La Clusaz has a snowpark (a specially prepared snowboarding piste).

Cross-country

The resort's 70km of loipe includes a scenic route around Lac des Confins, which reportedly holds the snow well and is served by a regular bus service. The area on top of Beauregard is well laid out and sign-posted, but it is busy and there is more chance of conflict with downhill skiers. Cross-country touring is available through the ESF.

Mountain restaurants

La Clusaz has a surprisingly high number of recommended mountain eating-places. The disadvantage is that some of the better ones are on the lower pistes and are not always accessible because of scant snow cover. They are mainly attractively old-fashioned and inexpensive in comparison with those in other French ski areas, especially at La Croix-Fry/Merdassier.

Le Vieux Ferme at Merdassier is lavishly praised by reporters ('outstanding cuisine in a wonderful setting'). Chez Arthur at the Crêt du Merle is praised for its welcoming atmosphere ('tasty food at reasonable prices — the perfect place for a rainy afternoon'). Le Bercail on the Crêt du Merle piste is an old Savoie farmhouse with a log fire. Balme does not offer such a high standard, with both restaurants at the top and bottom of the gondola 'disappointing and expensive'.

Off the mountain

The resort has considerable charm, not least because it functions as a year-round farming community, and its economy is not solely dependent on the seasonal influx of skiers. While the village centre, with its limited choice of shops but wider range of restaurants, remains relatively compact, buildings have burst out of the natural setting along the steep sides of the wooded valleys that surround it. The village, nevertheless, remains attractive, and as one reporter enthuses: 'The scenery is as impressive from the town as it is from the slopes'. The newer suburbs are complicated by a series of road junctions and roundabouts. It is a confusing place to find your way around, and traffic can be a serious problem during the late afternoon and at weekends. Parking is difficult, and the village is well policed, although there is an underground car park.

The heart of the village is pleasantly traditional, built around a large church, with a stylish modern shopping precinct beside it and a fast-flowing stream below. The shops are few in number but varied, and you can still find the ordinary French café of the lowland villages, not normally so apparent in a ski resort. The spread-out nature of the skiing makes La

■ OTHER SPORTS

Parapente, snow-shoeing, ice-fishing, hang-gliding, tobogganing, skating, swimming, winter walks, ice-biking

Clusaz dependent on an efficient bus service, which it has by and large, although reporters complain of long waits on some routes. The hourly service to Col de Merdassier seems hopelessly inadequate, and the heavy traffic does not contribute to its smooth operation.

Its identity as a real village, rather than just a *station de ski*, makes La Clusaz a reasonable choice for non-skiers. Activities here include swimming and skating, along with snow-shoe excursions.

Accommodation

Accommodation is divided between tour-operator chalets and a number of hotels of markedly varying quality. We have exceptionally glowing reports of the three-star Hotel Beauregard, close to L'Aiguille lifts ('extremely well-fitted, modern pine interior, the food is excellent and it really deserves a four-star rating'). Another reporter commented: 'It is rare and delightful to find a hotel of this quality at a price you can afford'.

It is important to find out where the lifts are in relation to where you are staying and to discover whether there is a bus-stop nearby. The skiing convenience here is one of the lowest we have found among French resorts, and any visit here involves considerable clomping about in ski boots. In the centre of the resort are lots of simple, reasonably priced hotels. The Alpenroc is strongly recommended ('excellent rooms with satellite television, splendid and varied food with a local accent'). Hotel

Skiing facts: **La Clusaz**

TOURIST OFFICE
F-74220 La Clusaz, Haute Savoie
Tel 33 4 50 32 65 00
Fax 33 4 50 32 65 01

THE RESORT
By road Calais 820km
By rail Annecy 32km, frequent bus service
to the resort
By air Geneva 1 hr 50 mins
Visitor beds 19,500
Transport free ski bus

THE SKIING
Linked or nearby resorts Le Grand-
Bornand (n)
Longest run La Motte, 4km (green)
Number of lifts 56
Total of trails/pistes 132km (34% easy,
37% intermediate,
29% difficult)
Nursery slopes 10 lifts
Summer skiing none
Snowmaking 13 hectares covered

LIFT PASSES
Area pass Aravis (covers La Clusaz and Le
Grand-Bornand), 740FF for 6 days. La
Clusaz (covers Croix-Fry/Merdassier),
700FF for 6 days
Day pass La Clusaz 140FF
Beginners points tickets
Pensioners no reduction
Credit cards accepted yes

SKI SCHOOLS
Adults ESF, 730FF for 6 days (4 hrs per
day), Aravis Evasion, 440FF for 6 half-days,
Ski Académie, 340FF for 4 days (2 hrs per
day)
Private lessons ESF 175FF, Aravis Evasion
170FF, Ski Académie 175FF, all per hr
Snowboarding ESF, 440FF for 4 days (3
hrs per day), Ski Académie, 590FF for 5
days (3 hrs per day)
Cross-country ESF, 656FF per day ($4\frac{1}{2}$
hrs), 150FF per hr, Centre Ecole Ski de
Fond, 610FF per day ($4\frac{1}{2}$ hrs), 125FF per
hr. Loipe 70km around Beauregard and in
Les Confins Valley
Other courses telemark, race training,
moguls, monoski, slalom, off-piste, Skwal
Guiding companies through ESF

CHILDREN
Lift pass 5-15 yrs 530FF for 6 days, free for
4 yrs and under
Ski kindergarten Le Club des Champions,
$3\frac{1}{2}$-6 yrs, 8.30am-6pm, 630FF for 6 days,
extra 59FF per day for lunch
Ski school as ski kindergarten
Non-ski kindergarten Club des Mouflets, 8
mths-$4\frac{1}{2}$ yrs, 8.30am-6pm, 630FF for 6
days, extra 59FF per day for lunch

FOOD AND DRINK PRICES
Coffee 5-10FF, glass of wine 12FF,
small beer 20-30FF,
dish of the day 40-70FF

Nouvel is also praised, and the chalet-style Hotel Christiania and Hotel
Floralp receive favourable reports. We have good reports of the
Résidence du Centre apartments, which are close to the church and ide-
ally situated 100m from the Praz chair-lift to L'Aiguille.

Eating in and out
La Clusaz has a much wider choice of restaurants than you would expect
in a resort of this size. Le Foly is a particularly attractive and expensive

log-cabin in the Confins Valley. Le Symphonie in the Hotel Beauregard offers 'excellent cuisine with a cheerful service in a warm atmosphere'. Le Coin du Feu is recommended for its 'delicious *crêpe sucré*'. The Cremaillère specialises in fondue and raclette. One reporter raved about the chilli and burgers at the Tex-Mex Café. Other popular choices are the La Taverne, La Chaumière and L'Outa.

Après-ski

Most of the muted action centres around a few bars. Le Pressoir is the 'in' place for snowboarders, the Tex-Mex Café is always busy, and the Angelus is suitable for a quiet drink. Resort workers meet in the Lion d'Or. L'Ecluse is said to be the best of the discos, with a glass dance-floor over the river, while Le Club 18 attracts the locals and an older clientèle. The nightlife is quiet during the week, some would say too quiet, but can become extremely lively during weekends.

Childcare

Le Clusaz has a '3 Kids' rating as one of the best-equipped French resorts for children. The Club des Mouflets crèche takes youngsters from eight-months-old up to four-and-a-half-years of age. The Club des Champions ski kindergarten gives lessons for three-and-a-half- to five-year-olds. The tourist office has a mothers-and-babies room.

Les Deux Alpes

ALTITUDE 1650m (5,412ft)

When Monsieur Rudolphe Tessa built a tiny hunting lodge at the Alpe de Mont de Lans in 1934 and opened it in the winter, he sowed some of the early seeds of this international ski resort. Shortly afterwards he announced that he would buy any car capable of climbing the mule track to his premises. Several manufacturers attempted this challenge, but a Peugeot with a special mountain axle accomplished it best; 'However,' the archives inform us, 'it was necessary to carry the car on the bends'.

One Easter just before the outbreak of the Second World War, a Heath-Robinson-style rope-tow was opened with great ceremony, but fell down 15 minutes later. It was not until the late 1950s that a new gondola and one of France's first ski passes — costing 2.50FF per day — paved the way for Les Deux Alpes to develop into a proper ski area. Today, this efficient and only partly purpose-built resort between Grenoble and **Briançon** has 63 lifts, which distribute a potential 61,000 skiers an hour to every point on the mountain. It is a large ski factory, but with fresh air and impressive scenery. Both village and ski area are long and narrow, and there is less skiing terrain than one would imagine for such a high vertical drop. However, the skiing links with **La Grave**, one of the most dramatic off-piste ski areas in Europe.

Venosc, an attractive village in the valley below Les Deux Alpes, is well worth a visit, with its cobbled streets and three 'extremely pleasant, atmospheric and inexpensive' restaurants. It is also a good place to stay if you prefer the rustic charms of a 'real' village, yet still want to be able to ski. The village can be reached either by gondola or a 40-minute walk (90-minute walk back up again); you cannot ski back to the resort.

On the mountain
top 3600m (11,808ft) bottom 1600m (5,249ft)

The chamois hunters and old shepherds who once roamed what are now the ski slopes would scarcely recognise their traditional haunts today. Indeed, it is easy for skiers to be confused by such a multitude of lifts and 200km of piste within a relatively confined area. Apart from a smaller, uncrowded sector to the west of the village, between Pied Moutet at

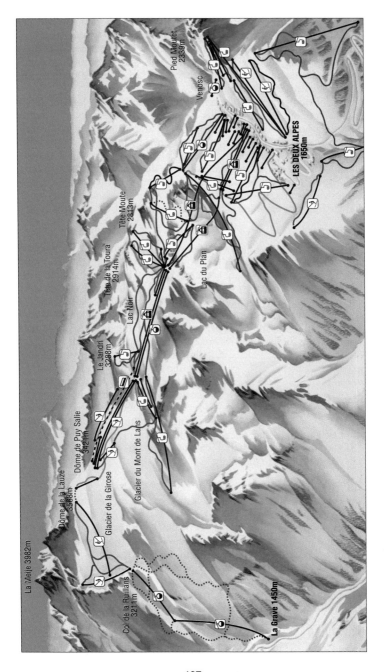

2100m and the Alpe du Mont de Lans, the bulk of the skiing is between the village and La Toura (2600m) to the east. Reporters criticise the 'sameness' of the pistes: 'A huge array of blue (easy) and green (beginner) runs, all of which are rather dull', and 'it seems to be something of a damning indictment that a resort which claims 200km of piste, has so few runs of any real interest'.

Of the numerous lifts, the principal bulk carrier is the Jandri Express jumbo gondola, which deposits skiers on the glacier in 20 minutes. Above La Toura the terrain narrows down to something of a bottleneck, where it can sometimes be difficult to thread your way through skiers and pylons, until the Col de Jandri at 3200m. Here it widens again to include some good intermediate cruising down towards Roche Mantel before reaching the broader glacier plateau. This sector offers easy slopes and even a sub-glacial funicular for novice skiers who find wind-blown drag-lifts daunting. There is also some skiing below the village.

Beginners

Those who learn to ski at Les Deux Alpes will be surprised at how easy and convenient it is when they move on to another resort. The most extensive nursery slopes are at the top of the ski area on the Glacier du Mont de Lans, while the lower slopes just above the village are too steep for beginners; this combination is the reverse of what most resorts have to offer. However, the excitement of being able to ski high on the mountain with magnificent views of the Oisans mountain range more than compensates for having to download to the resort by lift at the end of the day. There are 22 green runs, including nursery slopes beside the village. The runs back to the village are not suitable for novices or timid skiers; one reporter comments: 'It is not worth taking the green track at the north end of the village more than once per holiday — it was icy, ill-defined in poor visibility, and very crowded. It is a lot safer and more pleasurable to take the gondolas back to the village'.

> ■ **WHAT'S NEW**
>
> Additional quad-chair at Signal
> European Ski School ski kindergarten

Intermediates

Intermediates can enjoy themselves at Les Deux Alpes on most of the upper slopes, although less experienced skiers may find themselves somewhat overwhelmed by the steep homeward-bound runs, which can become crowded at the end of the day. One way to escape from the mainstream skiing is to try the runs through the trees, which are a rarity in Les Deux Alpes. There is an enjoyable piste down to the village of **Bons** at 1300m, while Mont de Lans can be reached from both ski areas. Les Gours, the new run down to La Voute quad-chair, has converted a celebrated off-piste itinerary into an easy red (intermediate) run.

Advanced

Advanced skiers inevitably gravitate towards the Tête Moute area, which provides some of the steepest terrain on the mountain. They will be tempted to go straight from the Alpe de Venosc end of the village by gondola to Le Diable at 2400m, which can also be reached by a more roundabout route via the Télésiège du Thuit. From Le Diable, the Grand Diable chair reaches the Tête Moute itself where there are steep, north-facing runs to Lac du Plan and onwards towards the Thuit chair. Le Diable run offers a challenging and often mogulled 1200-m descent to the village. There are seven other black (difficult) runs.

Off-piste
Les Deux Alpes has enclosed bowl-skiing, which is ideal for those trying off-piste for the first time, and for seasoned deep-snow skiers there are a number of easily accessible but not so easily skiable couloirs. However, on its doorstep is La Grave, one of the most exciting off-piste ski areas in the Alps. There is an 'over-the-top' link from Les Deux Alpes via the Glacier du Mont de Lans, which involves a 20-minute walk.

Ski schools and guiding
There are two rival ski schools: the main French Ski School (ESF) at Les Deux Alpes and the International Ski School (ESI) at **St-Christophe**. Both offer group and private lessons. Special courses include snow-boarding and telemark. The British-run European Ski School offers English-speaking classes of up to four pupils: 'I cannot speak highly enough of the teachers, who explained everything fully and taught with a high degree of understanding and patience'. Two of their instructors are British and the others speak English fluently. Courses are for two hours each day and include video analysis and computerised ski simulators, and all classes have lift-queue priority.

Snowboarding
Each October, snowboarding takes pride of place here as an aperitif to the ski season. It is the venue for the World Snowboard Meeting and Grand Prix des Deux Alpes, which claims to be 'the highest and biggest exhibition of snowboarding on the planet'. The events are held on the glacier and include slalom, giant slalom and half-pipe competitions. Stage Nano Pourtier, Stage Snowboard Luc Pelisson, Yellow Cab Surfing and the European Ski School all offer snowboarding courses.

Cross-country
Two trails lead through the woods on the approach road to the resort. There is also plenty of scenic skiing to be found in the Vénéon Valley, reached by the gondola down to Venosc. Really experienced langlaufers will enjoy high-altitude trails on the Mont de Lans Glacier. The loipe is easy, but a guide is essential because of the crevassed terrain.

Mountain restaurants
Les Deux Alpes does not receive many bouquets for its six mountain restaurants, and if it were not so inconvenient more skiers might con-

sider lunching in town. 'Uninviting' and 'overpriced' are among comments expressed by reporters. The Panoramic is reportedly 'friendly but
a bit crowded at peak hours'. The highest restaurant, Les Glaciers, is, as
its name suggests, on the glacier. Chalet de La Toura over the back is 'a
useful find in an area otherwise bereft of gastronomic comforts'. The
other mountain restaurants are La Patache at les Crêtes, and La Troika.
La Meije has a 'friendly, efficient service of local specialities at very reasonable prices'. La Petite Marmite is also recommended.

Off the mountain

Les Deux Alpes is a narrow, rather higgledy-piggledy and bustling small
town that has developed from the two separate farming communities of
Mont de Lans and Alpe de Venosc. Although the town itself is not attractive, it is by no means the worst example of modern French architecture.
The resort links with the quaint old hamlet of Venosc with its cobbled
streets via a six-person gondola. More than 25 per cent of non-French
visitors here are British.

Accommodation

Most of the accommodation is in apartments, with the remainder in the
resort's 40 hotels and pensions. At the top end of the market there are
three four-star establishments, of which the Bérangère is particularly
praised. There are nine three-star hotels and 21 two-stars. The Edelweiss
is warmly recommended for its 'wonderful gourmet dinners, with local
produce properly cooked and well pre-
sented; the staff were patient and helpful and the bedrooms large, with
furnishings OK, if a little spartan'. The
Brunerie is described as 'welcoming'.

Ten rental agencies deal with apartments and there is 'a range of supermarkets, plus a good spread of
boulangerie, boucherie and pâtisserie shops'.

> **■ OTHER SPORTS**
>
> Parapente, bungee-jumping,
> swimming, skating, curling, helicopter
> rides, ice-climbing, indoor tennis
> and squash

Eating in and out

The 45 restaurants range from pizzerias such as L'Apri and pasta houses
like La Spaghetteria, to more sophisticated establishments including
Restaurant de la Bérangère, which has a Michelin star. Gourmets will also
enjoy the Chalet Mounier. La Patate is for raclette and fondue, Les
Crêpes à Gogo is singled out for its ambience, and the Paellou Brasserade
Grill is also well spoken of. Meilleurs Voeux (serving crêpes and pizzas)
has 'a fabulous log fire and a bar made from old Scotch Whisky cases'.

Après-ski

Les Deux Alpes teems with après-ski opportunities: Mike's Bar, near the
Jandri lift, Smokey Joe's and Le Windsor are all popular haunts. The
Rodeo, at the Venosc end of town, has a bizarre mechanical bull, which

Skiing facts: **Les Deux Alpes**

TOURIST OFFICE
BP 7, F-38860 Les Deux Alpes, Dauphiné
Tel 33 4 76 79 22 00
Fax 33 4 76 79 01 38

THE RESORT
By road Calais 953km
By rail Grenoble 70km
By air Grenoble 1½ hrs, Lyon 2 hrs
Visitor beds 30,000
Transport free ski bus

THE SKIING
Linked or nearby resorts La Grave (l),
Alpe d'Huez (n), Serre Chevalier/Briançon
(n), St-Christophe-en-Oisans (l), Venosc (l)
Longest run Les Gours, 5km (blue)
Number of lifts 63
Total of trails/pistes 200km (62% easy,
28% intermediate, 10% difficult)
Nursery slopes 2 free lifts and 2 runs
Summer skiing mid-June – Sept, 16 lifts
covering 200 hectares of skiable glacial
terrain
Snowmaking 14 hectares covered

LIFT PASSES
Area pass 892FF for 6 days (includes 1 free
day in Alpe d'Huez, Serre Chevalier, Puy-St-
Vincent or the Milky Way)
Day pass 178FF
Beginners 3 free lifts
Pensioners reduction for 60 yrs and over
Credit cards accepted yes

SKI SCHOOLS
Adults ESF, 700FF for 6 mornings (9.15am-
12.15pm), 590FF for 6 afternoons (2.30-
5pm). ESI, 9.30am-midday and 2.30-5pm,
620FF for 6 days, European Ski School,
650FF for 5 days (2 hrs per day)
Private lessons ESF 175FF per hr, ESI
185FF per hr
Snowboarding ESF, 1,290FF for 6 days, ESI
960FF for 6 days, Yellow Cab Surfing,
1,590FF for 6 days, Stages Nano Pourtier,
1,300FF for 6 days, Stages Snowboard Luc
Pelisson, 1,290FF for 6 days, European Ski
School, as regular ski lessons
Cross-country ESF, 9.15am-12.15pm,
700FF for 6 mornings. ESI, 130FF for one
afternoon. Loipe 20km
Other courses ski-touring, monoski,
telemark, slalom
Guiding companies Aventures Verticales,
ESF Bureau des Guides

CHILDREN
Lift pass 7-13 yrs, 668FF for 6 days,
4-6 yrs 80FF per day, free for under 4 yrs
Ski kindergarten ESF, 4-6 yrs, 585FF for 6
mornings, ESI, 490FF for 6 days (am or pm)
Ski school ESF, 6-12 yrs, 930FF for 6 days.
ESI, 6-12 yrs, 900FF for 6 days, European
Ski School, 5-8 yrs, 650FF for 5 days (2 hrs
per day)
Non-ski kindergarten La Crèche du Clos
des Fonds, 6 mths-2 yrs, 170FF per day
including lunch. Le Bonhomme de Neige,
2-6 yrs, 900FF for 6 days including lunch

FOOD AND DRINK PRICES
Coffee 5-10FF, glass of wine 6-10FF, small
beer 12-16FF, dish of the day 40-70FF

inevitably attracts the wilder element of après-skiers. The Asterix Bar, in the hotel of the same name, is 'not very pretty, but has a friendly service'. Le Pressoir and Le Tonic are described as 'useful watering-holes'. The four discos are La Casa, Le Club 92, L'Avalanche and L'Opéra.

Childcare

Children under four can use the ski lifts, swimming-pool and skating rink free of charge. Among the bridges, tunnels and animal characters at the Espace Loisirs playground there is a trampoline, a small slalom course, toboggan run, ski-biking, inner-tubing and an inflatable bob run, with organised races most days. Qualified staff welcome children from six months to two years old at a slope-side crèche, and the Snowman's Kindergarten (Le Bonhomme de Neige) caters for two- to six-year-olds.

The ESF operates a kindergarten slope in the centre of town close to the Jandri Express, and the ESI has its own kindergarten. Both ski schools offer half- or full-day courses for children over four years of age who wish to ski, snowboard or mono-ski. Yellow Cab Surfing has created a snow garden, Papoose Valley, and runs snowboarding courses for children over four years old.

We have mixed reports of the ESF children's ski school: 'The French instructors spoke adequate English and even in the worst of the weather they took the wee souls out for at least part of the three-hour lesson. When they got cold, wet and fed up they returned to the ESF chalet to dry out and watch videos'. However, another reporter says: 'Frankly, we were not impressed with the ESF ski kindergarten. On the first day we found our four-year-old son alone in the kindergarten hut, crying'.

Linked or nearby resorts

La Grave
top 3550m (11,647ft) bottom 1450m (4,757ft)

This ancient, rugged village straggling along the road up to the Col du Lauteret has in the past earned its reputation as a climbing centre rather than as a ski resort. It crouches in the shadow of the 3983-m La Meije, which in 1876 was one of the last great European peaks to be conquered. Its reputation is founded on the fact that it has just one short piste and two lifts. This may sound insignificant until you realise that one of those lifts takes you up over 2000m vertical. The steep, unpisted routes down provide some of the most challenging advanced skiing in Europe. The glacial area is heavily crevassed, the couloirs are steep, and skiers are strongly advised to use the services of a local guide at all times. La Grave has only a couple of simple hotels and little to offer anyone who does not climb or ski.

TOURIST OFFICE
Tel 33 4 76 79 90 05
Fax 33 4 76 79 91 65

Flaine

ALTITUDE 1600m (5,248ft)

Flaine is a wholly functional resort within easy reach of Geneva via the Autoroute Blanche. It has a surprisingly large international following of skiers, a fair proportion of whom are British. Visitors come here for the skiing, not for the ambience which, as one reporter put it, 'simply doesn't exist'.

Apart from purists who see Flaine as an interesting example of the Bauhaus school of design, most visitors view it as an architectural disaster area created in the 1960s at the same time as Les Menuires, Chamrousse and some of the other French resorts of its generation.

The liberal use of grey, unfinished concrete is depressing enough even when the resort is cloaked under a blanket of fresh snow. In the springtime, when the white disappears and the rains come, it defies description. However, one reporter commented that 'compared with the area of east London where I work, Flaine is quite pretty'.

■ **GOOD POINTS**

Large ski area, excellent family facilities, skiing convenience, short airport transfer, car-free resort, wide range of easy and intermediate runs, reliable resort-level snow, lack of queues, variety of off-piste skiing

■ **BAD POINTS**

Unattractive architecture, lack of alpine charm, limited après-ski

Unfortunately, the compact convenience of the original concept no longer exists for much of the village due to expansion; the original aim was to provide doorstep-skiing at affordable prices, though with no regard for appearance and little for the other qualities that give the older (and more recently, the more modern) resorts their broader appeal.

Despite all this Flaine's good points outnumber the bad, making the whole a not entirely unattractive proposition. It benefits from having excellent nursery slopes, few queues and from being car-free. Add to these ingredients a short transfer from Geneva Airport, and the resulting popularity with families is easy to understand. Flaine used to be considered value for money, but recently reporters have found 'prices incredibly high even before the appalling exchange rate'.

Flaine's bowl-skiing connects with the three lower and more traditional resorts of **Samoëns**, **Morillon** and **Les Carroz**, and a piste also takes you down the Combe de Gers to the charming village of **Sixt**. These areas greatly add to Flaine's skiing and replace some of its vital missing ingredients: sheltered tree-level skiing, long runs and atmospheric mountain eating-places. Unfortunately, the lift links can sometimes close down for several days at a time in bad weather or poor snow cover, severely limiting the skiing to the Flaine bowl alone.

On the mountain
top 2480m (8,134ft) bottom 690m (2,263ft)

Flaine is the core of the large ski area of Le Grand Massif, which comprises around 260km of linked skiing served by 80 lifts. It divides naturally into separate segments. Flaine's own skiing is ranged around the
north-facing part of its home bowl, with lifts soaring to nearly 2500m
around the rim. Most of the skiing is open and unsheltered above the
tree-line. The main mountain access from the village centre is a huge
gondola up to Grandes Platières, a high, wide plateau with panoramic
views. A large number of runs go from here down to the resort; most are
graded red (intermediate) or blue (easy).

In general, the skiing in the enclosed Flaine bowl is somewhat limited
and its real attraction lies in its link with the remainder of Le Grand
Massif area; this is via the Grand Vans chair-lift, which, because of its
exposed top-station, is usually the first to close in bad weather.

The Tête du Pré des Saix is the central point of the whole Grand
Massif system. From here, north-facing runs drop down steep mogul
slopes towards Samoëns. Halfway down, the descent is broken by the
lifts which go up to **Samoëns 1600**. Next is an 800-m drop down to
Vercland on the outskirts of Samoëns itself; the steeper black (difficult)
option goes through the trees, but does not hold snow well. On the other
side of the valley the parallel easier pistes towards Morillon are long and
gentle trails in the tree-line, passing a couple of restaurants. There is an
efficient gondola from Morillon village to Morillon Grand Massif.

The runs to Les Carroz are short, but offer a wide variety of trails,
including more difficult sections at the top of the red runs and some
good off-piste. The blue run to the village is often crowded and bare of
snow. We have received complaints that L'Airon chair-lift, which provides the best link to Flaine, is often closed; without it a long traverse or
a 180-m uphill walk are necessary. Access to the slopes is via Le Kédeuse
gondola, which is reported to have a long queue in the mornings.

Sixt, along the road from Samoëns, has its own small ski area and a
cross-country track linking with Samoëns and Morillon. Sixt is directly
linked into the Grand Massif via a piste down the Combe de Gers. This
begins with the Styx black run, served by its own drag-lift, and continues
with a 6-km blue run. One reporter complains that narrow, plunging
pitches alternate with uphill sections 'where we encountered cross-country skiers coming towards us'. A bus connects skiers with Samoëns.

Beginners
Flaine has good novice slopes in the middle of the village. For improvers
there are some wide, snaking blues on the bowl's west-facing slopes.
Crystal and Serpentine are long, sweeping runs that beginners will be
able to tackle by the end of their first week.

Intermediates
The whole area is essentially designed for intermediates. Day-long
forays into the far corners of the Grand Massif are well within the

capabilities of most skiers with a few weeks' experience. However, it is important to allow plenty of time for the return journey. The Tourmaline blue from Les Grands Vans down to Le Forêt is usually well-groomed and is one of the classic runs of the resort.

Advanced

The more difficult skiing sections of the Flaine bowl are in the middle, and are graded black under the gondola and red to each side. The black Diamant Noir is an enjoyable mogul slope. Unlike some other large linked areas, there are plenty of steep runs and a good variety of terrain, making Flaine a suitable destination for advanced skiers.

Off-piste

Flaine and Le Grand Massif area offer outstanding off-piste possibilities. The proximity to Mont Blanc creates a unique micro-climate and the area has a much better snow record than its altitude might suggest. The rocky terrain means that powder hunts can easily end on a cliff and the services of a guide who really knows the region are essential.

Ski schools and guiding

Flaine has two ski schools. We have mixed reports of the French Ski School (ESF): 'Large classes, but our instructor was extremely helpful', and 'we found our instructor typically volatile and he twice committed the cardinal sin of skiing on without waiting for all the class to catch up'. We continue to receive disastrous criticism of the International Ski School (ESI): 'Little or no teaching — little more than 2 pieces of advice in 12 hours of tuition might be described as frugal'. Another reporter comments: 'Never, in 30 years of skiing, have I seen such disorganisation. Our children hardly ever had the same teacher from morning to afternoon, let alone from day to day'.

Snowboarding

The resort has its own snowboard park in the main Flaine bowl. Lessons can be taken with the ESI.

Cross-country

Flaine has a 700-m beginners' loipe on the Cascade Plateau as well as 4km at L'Arbaron, close to a handy mountain restaurant, and a further 4km through the woods to Vernant. Additional extensive loipes can be found in the valley between Samoëns and Sixt, and at Les Carroz.

Mountain restaurants

Those in the immediate Flaine vicinity are limited, especially in the Aujon area, but there is a wide choice further afield. Close to the resort the Blanchot is recommended and Chalet Bissac is 'busy, but has quick hot food'. Bar L'Eloge, by the Flaine gondola, has a simple choice of food and friendly service. La Combe, in the Morillon area, has 'terrific ambience'. The Oréade, at the top of La Kédeuse gondola, is recommended for its food and large, sunny terrace. The restaurant on the Chariande piste at Samoëns has reasonable prices and an excellent view from the terrace. Le Pativerdans at Vercland, near the foot of the gondola, is reported to be good value, and has English hosts who have become part of the local community. The Chalet Les Molliets is said to be cheaper than most, and the bar at the Tête du Pré des Saix sells 'the biggest and hottest hot chocolate in the resort'.

Off the mountain

The first view down into Flaine is a surprising one; it sits ostentatiously in an isolated bowl where you would not expect to find any habitation at all. The grey concrete of what some would call an ugly, at best inoffensive, purpose-built village matches the grey rock formation. Reporters' opinions of Flaine vary from 'no soul' and 'a ski ghetto, which does not give one the feeling of being in France', to 'a pleasant atmosphere because it is so compact'. In counterpoint to this grey image, Flaine has developed a reputation as a centre for fine art. Sculptures by Picasso, Dubuffet and Vasarely are dotted around the village and other works are housed in the resort's arts centre.

Two enclosed people-mover lifts operate day and night between the higher and lower villages. The Hameau area is served by a free bus, which runs from the chalets to the nursery slopes every 15 minutes during the day, but is apparently not reliable at night.

Accommodation

The heart of the resort is Flaine Forum where the main shops and restaurants and the ski school meeting-place are based. The Hotel Totem, with Picasso's statue of the same name standing outside, is the main pisteside hotel. Reporters' views range alarmingly from 'expensive with clinical, modern décor', and 'still living on its old reputation' to 'a truly grand establishment'. The food is praised by most. The Cascade, situated above the Forum, was according to one family 'a bit of a disappointment; the rooms were very compact and the whole place decidedly chilly. This is the first time we had to wear thick jerseys and fleecy jackets for meals. Some petty rules like a refusal to serve boiled eggs to some guests who arrived a few minutes late for breakfast did not encourage a good atmosphere'.

Les Lindars, once Flaine's most famous, family-oriented hotel, is now a Club Aquarius. It is still accepting tour-operator bookings this season, but the jolly eight-to-a-table Club formula is not necessarily to the taste of its original British clientèle: 'The food is much improved in quantity and quality, but a French Butlins was not what we thought we were booking'. Another reporter commented: 'The hotel's previous reputation as being ideal for families and small children is no longer justified. The long queues in the dining-room mean that food is often cold, and newly introduced evening entertainment creates so much noise that getting children to sleep is difficult'. The three-star Hotel Le Flaine has now reopened and the basic two-star Aujon has a loyal following.

Flaine Fôret, on a shelf above Flaine Forum, has mainly self-catering accommodation and its own shops and bars. Most of the rental apartments in the resort are now owned by property giant Pierre et Vacances and some much-needed refurbishment has taken place. The apartments are small, even by French standards ('thank goodness we had booked an apartment for eight for the six of us').

The Hameau de Flaine, on the mountain at 1800m, is a later development of attractive Scandinavian-style chalets inconveniently situated for the ski area. It has its own sports shop, a bar, restaurant and supermarket.

■ **OTHER SPORTS**

Parapente, snow-shoeing, hang-gliding, snowmobiling, ice-driving, climbing wall, swimming

Eating in and out

Chez La Jeanne is 'small and friendly with excellent pizzas and good house wine'. La Perdrix Noire in Flaine Fôret is voted best restaurant by a number of reporters. La Pizzeria in the Forum is 'excellent and reasonably priced', and La Trattoria has a 'pleasant, almost Italian atmosphere and good wine'. There are well-stocked supermarkets on both Forum and Fôret levels.

Après-ski

People do not come to Flaine for the nightlife and many tend to opt for quiet evenings in, especially those with small children. The Diamant Noir bar attracts the locals, and the Cîmes Rock Café in Flaine Forum has live music. The White Grouse Pub, that little piece of Scotland that is forever France, has raised its standards and fought its way back to being one of the principal meeting places. The Bodega is the main disco.

Childcare

Flaine has a long-established reputation as one of the best resorts in the Alps for families with young children. Certainly it is car-free and safe, with a large central playground and pleasant nursery slopes, and it has a short airport transfer. However, much of its reputation has been based on the crèche and kindergarten run by Hotel Les Lindars, which accepted young children whether or not they were staying in the hotel. Child facilities are now said to be disorganised and are only available for club guests.

The Green Mouse Club (Souris Verte) at the ESI hopes to reduce its lower age limit from four to two years to fill the gap left by Les Lindars. Children aged six months to four years old can still be cared for at the resort's Petits Loups kindergarten, but you need to book at least two months in advance. The Green Mouse Club is recommended by several reporters, with staff speaking reasonable English and 'happy to accommodate children's wishes to ski or not'. The carers were also praised for 'playing with the children, rather than sticking them in front of the video'. The ESF Rabbit Club is a parallel service for three- to twelve-

Skiing facts: **Flaine**

TOURIST OFFICE
F-74300 Flaine, Haute Savoie
Tel 33 4 50 90 80 01
Fax 33 4 50 90 86 26

LONDON AGENT
Erna Low Consultants, 9 Reece Mews,
London SW7 7HE
Tel 0171-584 2841
Fax 0171-589 9531

THE RESORT
By road Calais 890km
By rail Cluses 25km, frequent bus service
to resort
By air Geneva 1½ hrs
Visitor beds 6,500
Transport free ski bus between Flaine and
Hameau de Flaine

THE SKIING
Linked or nearby resorts Les Carroz (l),
Morillon (l), Samoëns (l), Sixt (n)
Longest run Cascade, 14km (blue)
Number of lifts 31 in Flaine, 80 in Le Grand
Massif
Total of trails/pistes 150km in Flaine
(35% easy, 50% intermediate, 15% diffi-
cult), 260km in Le Grand Massif
Nursery slopes 2 slopes and 3 free lifts
Summer skiing none
Snowmaking 3km covered

LIFT PASSES
Area pass Grand Massif (covers Flaine, Les
Carroz, Morillon, Samoëns and Sixt), 820FF
for 6 days

Day pass Flaine 150FF, Grand Massif
175FF
Beginners 4 free lifts in area and special
beginner pass at 80FF per day for adults,
65FF per day for children
Pensioners 60 yrs and over, as children
Credit cards accepted yes

SKI SCHOOLS
Adults ESF 440FF and ESI 460FF, both for 6
days (2 hrs per day)
Private lessons ESF 185FF per hr, ESI
170FF per hr
Snowboarding ESI, 695FF for 6 days (3 hrs
per day)
Cross-country ESI and ESF, prices and
times on application. Two tracks of 4km at
L'Arbaron and a 700m beginners' circuit
Other courses off-piste
Guiding companies through ski schools

CHILDREN
Lift pass 5-16 yrs, 580FF for 6 days (Le
Grand Massif), free for 4 yrs and under
Ski kindergarten ESF Rabbit Club, 3-12
yrs, 9am-5pm, 1,200FF for 6 days including
lunch. ESI Green Mouse Club, 4-12 yrs,
9am-5pm, 1,100FF for 6 days including
lunch
Ski school as ski kindergarten
Non-ski kindergarten Garderie des Petits
Loups, 6 mths-4 yrs, 9am-5pm, 160FF per
day, not including lunch

FOOD AND DRINK PRICES
Coffee 9FF, glass of wine 7.50-14FF, small
beer 13-18FF, dish of the day 50-70FF

year-olds but more oriented towards French children. Both the ESF Rabbit Club and the Green Mouse collect children from their accommodation each morning and return them at the end of the day.

Linked or nearby resorts

Les Carroz
top 2480m (8,134ft) bottom 1140m (3,739ft)

Les Carroz is large and, in the view of most correspondents, more pleasing to the eye than Flaine. However, its drawback is a low altitude. The resort spreads across a broad, sunny slope on the road to Flaine and attracts many families and weekend visitors who use it as an access point for this substantial ski area.

The gondola and chair-lift are a steep walk from the centre of the village, but within easy reach of some attractive, simple old hotels including Les Airelles and the Croix de Savoie. The well-located Hotel des Belles Pistes, run by an English couple, is said to be decorated 'Cotswolds-style with little local character, but the chef is French and very good'. The Front de Neige is reported to cope well with the needs of small children.

Most of the self-catering accommodation is much less conveniently placed. The bus is not included in the lift pass and there are only three services per day to Flaine; late-night taxis are hard to find.

TOURIST OFFICE
Tel 33 4 50 90 00 04
Fax 33 4 50 90 07 00

Samoëns
top 2480m (8,134ft) bottom 720m (2,362ft)

The beautiful old town of Samoëns in the Giffre Valley has been a ski resort since 1912 and is the only one in France to be listed as a historical monument. It was once a thriving stone-cutting centre and twice a week the tourist office organises guided tours around the town's architectural sites. In the town centre is a botanical alpine garden with over 4,000 species of mountain plants from around the world. Traditional-style bars and restaurants abound in what is a resort largely undiscovered by other nationalities, in particular the British. The Neige et Roc and Les Sept Monts hotels are recommended, together with Les Drugères. One reporter speaks highly of Le Pierrot Gourmet restaurant.

Samoëns has its own ski school, a crèche for children from six months old, and a ski kindergarten for children aged three to six years old. It also has 72km of loipe and a cross-country ski school.

TOURIST OFFICE
Tel 33 4 50 34 40 28
Fax 33 4 50 34 95 82

Megève

ALTITUDE 1100m (3,608ft)

In 1916, while holidaying in Switzerland, Baroness Maurice de Rothschild decided to find a resort in her home country to rival St Moritz. She took advice from her Norwegian ski instructor and went to visit the tiny village of Megève. So impressed was she that five years later she returned to build the Palace Hotel Mont d'Arbois, which helped transform Megève into an international resort.

Later on in its history, Megève boasted that at the height of the season it was home to more crowned heads of state than any other ski resort in Europe. The Aga Khan and a host of celebrities, including Rita Hayworth, Roger Vadim and Brigitte Bardot, installed themselves for the winter. During the boom years of the 1960s a visit to Megève, staying for at least one week in the Mont Blanc with its Jean Cocteau murals, was as mandatory as St Tropez in August for anyone with international social aspirations. Then its reputation faded. The stars migrated to brighter galaxies, more certain snow and better skiing. Courchevel 1850 took on its mantle.

■ **GOOD POINTS**

Long and easy runs, wide range of activities for non-skiers, large choice of restaurants, ideal for family skiing, lively après-ski, short airport transfer, tree-line skiing, attractive village centre

■ **BAD POINTS**

Lack of difficult skiing, low altitude, unreliable resort-level snow, heavy traffic outside pedestrian area

However, thanks to the changing face of European skiing, Megève is undergoing a renaissance. The return of family business — 70 per cent of skiers who come here are French — attracts those who are bored with purpose-built resorts and are prepared to forgo skiing convenience for high-quality accommodation, resort atmosphere, après-ski, and a mixture of extensive, yet mainly easy, skiing. The resort still has an upmarket image; its exclusivity is largely due to keeping prices high in the restaurants and nightclubs, thereby keeping the mass-market out.

The village is built around a fine medieval church and carefully restored old buildings. The streets are colourful with designer boutiques and brightly painted sleighs. There are no architectural eye sores and recent additions have been built in a sympathetic chalet style.

On the mountain
top 2350m (7,708ft) bottom 850m (2,788ft)

The skiing takes place on smooth and well-groomed pistes. Two of the three areas, Mont d'Arbois and Rochebrune, are connected at their bases by cable car. Mont d'Arbois is the most extensive and it, in turn, is accessed by separate gondolas from La Princesse outside **Combloux**, **Le Bettex** above **St-Gervais**, and **St-Nicolas-de-Véroce**. The skiing around Mont d'Arbois is mainly gentle, although there are some more challenging runs higher up on Mont Joux.

The Rochebrune area was until recently only reachable by Megève's original cable car, which was built in 1933 and begins on the outskirts of town. The old cable car is still in action, but there is now a less creaky alternative: a swift 12-person gondola, which starts from the town centre. Rochebrune offers arguably the most attractive runs in the area in delightful tree-lined settings, and reporters claim that it is less crowded than Mont d'Arbois.

Megève's third skiing area is Le Jaillet, completely self-contained and reached by gondola only after a lengthy walk or ski-bus ride from the middle of town. Its runs are mainly gentle but do not hold their snow well.

Piste-grading in the area, according to reporters, is not always consistent: some black (difficult) runs are said to be easier than the red (intermediate) trails due to careful grooming, while some blue (easy) runs have difficult sections.

Beginners

The nursery slopes at Mont d'Arbois are easily accessible by cable car or ski bus. The resort also abounds in green (beginner) runs and gentle blues for the next stage of learning. From Mont Joux, long easy runs descend to Les Communailles near Le Bettex, with drag-lifts running back up to the ridge. The runs into Megève itself are mostly wide and easy, including a long green piste. There is a drag-lift for novices among the trees at the top-station of Jaillet, and the runs in this area are both gentle and pleasant, being mainly suited to beginners and early intermediates.

Intermediates

The scope of skiing at Mont d'Arbois has been greatly increased by the chair-lift rising over an open slope of more than 30° in places to the high point of the area at 2350m. A choice of long and fairly gentle red runs takes you down into the attractive little village of St-Nicolas-de-Véroce. The large ski area is well suited to intermediates, although lack of snow makes the season a short one.

Advanced

Megève is not recommended for expert skiers. However, provided you have a car, this is the most pleasant resort in the Mont Blanc area in which to base yourself to enjoy the 13 resorts (including **Chamonix** and **Argentière**) covered by the Mont Blanc lift pass. Mont Joux, the next peak along from Mont d'Arbois, on the ridge which climbs towards Mont Joly, has some of the steeper slopes around the bowl. The pistes on the north-facing La Princesse side of the mountain are wooded and more challenging than most in the area, but the black grading is not altogether justified.

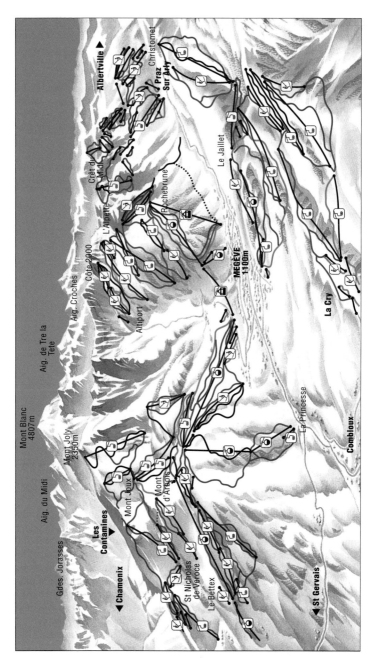

From the top of the gondola at Rochebrune, further lifts take you on up to Alpette, the start of Megève's downhill course. The highest point, Côte 2000, provides some of the toughest skiing in the area.

Off-piste

The area through the trees towards La Princesse provides excellent powder skiing after a fresh snowfall, as does Côte 2000. The off-piste is far less skied than in most of the other Mont Blanc resorts and is therefore likely to remain untracked for longer. You can also ski from the top of Mont Joly, after a 20-minute uphill walk, over to the resort of **Les Contamines**.

Ski schools and guiding

Megève's ski schools have fine reputations, particularly for beginners who progress speedily from the nursery areas to the long and flattering easy and intermediate slopes. The resort has its own guiding company, Bureau des Guides de Megève, which is warmly recommended. It employs 16 mountain guides who take skiers off-piste and organise ski-tours in the area.

Snowboarding

Both the French (ESF) and International (ESI) Ski Schools offer group courses for all standards of snowboarder. The ESF also runs special snowboarding classes for children.

Cross-country

Langlaufers have a choice of four circuits totalling 75km, including a long, tricky but wonderfully scenic track from the Mont d'Arbois cable car to Bettex and St-Nicolas-de-Véroce; another links with the resort of **Praz-sur-Arly**. Unusual activities for cross-country enthusiasts include one-day guided outings off-piste between Val d'Arly and Beaufortain, plus night cross-country racing through the village streets.

Mountain restaurants

Megève certainly has no shortage of lunch venues, adding to its gourmet attraction. The ski area is home to around 30 mountain establishments, most of which are marked on a special walker/cross-country skier lift map. Reporters do, however, note that mountain eating is expensive. Particularly recommended is a trip to the Alpette restaurant. Its position on the piste high above the Rochebrune cable car and gondola station would normally restrict its customers to skiers, but the restaurant runs a 45FF snowcat service from the lift station. L'Auberge du Grenand, also in the Rochebrune area towards Praz-sur-Arly, offers typically French cuisine and local specialities. La Côte 2000 restaurant is recommended for 'fresh, well-cooked food'. Lower down at Rochebrune, the self-service La Caboche is good value by local standards.

At Mont d'Arbois, Le Rosay is a 'reasonable self-service with an excellent balcony'. Chalet Idéal Sport, a popular place for the fur-coated at the top of La Princesse gondola, has excellent food and 'not prohibitive' prices. L'Igloo has a terrace with magnificent views of Mont Blanc. Higher up in the same area, La Ferme de Chateluy is warmly recommended. The Jaillet Supérieur has a cosy atmosphere and serves traditional alpine meals.

Off the mountain

Megève has grown to become one of France's largest ski towns, with a mass of suburbs stretching out in all directions. The attractive medieval heart is made up of a traffic-free main square with four streets branching off it, all teeming with an 'abundance of fur coats and matching dogs'. Reporters praise the town as 'a window-shopper's paradise'. This includes jewellers, perfumeries, delicatessen, antique shops, chocolate-makers, children's clothing shops, designer boutiques and popular fashion outlets such as Poivre Blanc, Cacharel and Benetton, as well as the famous Aallard department store.

Traffic is a problem, particularly during the main window-shopping hours from 4 to 7pm; a main road runs through the town, although the actual centre is bypassed. Road-works are planned to improve the flow of traffic and the safety of pedestrians. Ski buses link the mid-town with the lifts, and coaches run to other nearby resorts covered on the Mont Blanc lift pass. Megève is one of the easiest ski resorts to reach; not only is it close to Geneva (70km), but it also has two Motorail termini close by at Sallanches and at St-Gervais.

Accommodation

Megève has more than 50 hotels, as well as luxurious and more utilitarian private chalets. The standard of its five four-stars and some of its 15 three-stars is outstanding. The Parc des Loges has art deco rooms, each with its own fireplace. Chalet du Mont d'Arbois is located some distance from the town near the Mont d'Arbois cable car. The Hotel Mont Blanc, which had until recently fallen into disrepair, has been entirely refurbished and transformed with the lavish use of warm wood and rich plaids into one of the finest hotels in Europe. The style is New England and each of the 43 rooms is individually decorated. At the bottom of La Princesse ski area is the four-star Hotel Princesse de Megève, which has only 14 rooms.

Les Fermes de Marie, a hotel ten minutes' walk from the centre of town, is under the same family ownership as the Mont Blanc and is just as sumptuous. The heart of the hotel is a sixteenth-century cowshed with vaulted ceiling; a collection of farm buildings in the grounds have been converted into luxury suites. It has a fitness and beauty centre with a swimming-pool. Le Fer à Cheval is a centrally placed, chalet-style hotel. We also have good reports of Hotel au Coin du Feu and La Chauminé.

Megève is not for those who count their centimes, but budget-conscious visitors would be wise to stay in one of the self-catering *résidences* such as Gollet or Richmond.

Eating in and out

A reporter comments on the 'extensive quantity and variety of eating places to suit all budgets'. This is certainly true; Megève has more than 80 restaurants and is, along with Courchevel 1850, one of the gourmet dining-centres of the French Alps. However, it also offers a reasonable choice of less exotic places. Le Bar du Chamois is a lively bistro with good local white wines and fondues. At Le Piano à Bretelles you can eat and dance the night away. Good-value restaurants include Les Griottes, which has à la carte specialities, and La Maisonnette.

At the top of the range, the Hotel Mont Blanc's Les Enfants Terribles has 'delicious but expensive food'. The Chalet du Mont d'Arbois used to be the Rothschild family home and is now a high-quality restaurant with an interesting wine cellar. Les Fermes de Marie offers good Savoyard cooking, and Le Fer à Cheval serves a fine dinner but is also recommended for its English breakfast. Le Phnom Penh offers unusual Cambodian food.

Après-ski

This is taken almost more seriously than the skiing, and the choice of venues is enormous, ranging from the simplest of bars to the most exotic of nightspots. Le Prieuré and Cascade are recommended for tea and cakes at 5pm. Le Chamois is a traditional place with a warm atmosphere. The Village Rock Café is popular with teenagers.

Later on, the nightlife is not cheap and largely revolves around Megève's nine nightclubs and piano bars. Club de Jazz Les Cinq Rues is one of the most popular evening venues, set in cosy surroundings complete with open fire; during the season it attracts some of the big international names in jazz. The most popular nightclubs include L'Esquinade, which is also a casino with Sacha Distel and Charles Aznavour among its regulars. Le Rols Club is the place for those who like their evening entertainment on the

■ OTHER SPORTS

Parapente, hang-gliding, skating, curling, indoor tennis, climbing wall, snowmobiling, snow-shoeing, winter walks, dog-sledding, snow polo, ice hockey, light aircraft flights, sleigh rides, swimming, night-skiing

decadent side. The Glamour is half piano bar and half disco. Les Caves de Megève has a young atmosphere. The Pallas and Harri's bar keep going until dawn.

The Palais des Sports contains an Olympic-size skating rink and a vast swimming-pool; you can also learn to curl, rock climb and trampoline. Other non-skiing activities in Megève include dog-sledding on the slopes of Le Jaillet, a ride in a light aircraft from the altiport and a torchlit descent on snow-shoes, after dinner in a mountain restaurant.

Childcare
In keeping with its family values, Megève has some of the most comprehensive childcare facilities of any resort in France, with separate ski
kindergarten conveniently situated at the foot of each ski area. The
Meg'Loisirs kindergarten, is housed in a well-equipped, two-storey
building next to the Palais des Sports. Creative children who want to take
a break from skiing can attend Megève Matériaux, run by Marie-
Christine Ours on the outskirts of town. Here, 6- to 13-year-olds can try
their hands at stencilling, painting on wood and fabric, plaster moulding
and lots more for 85FF per morning.

Linked or nearby resorts
Les Contamines-Montjoie
top 2000m (6,562ft) bottom 1164m (3,818ft)
This unspoilt Savoyard village is near the head of the narrow Montjoie
Valley just over the hill from Megève. It has a keen following despite the
fact that the whole set-up is badly planned; the long village is on one side
of the river and the ski area on the other, and Le Lay base-station is a
long uphill walk from the centre. Prices are, on the whole, below average
for this area of France and the accommodation is modest.

The east-facing bowl, which makes up the ski area, tends to hold its
snow well and offers a good alternative when neighbouring resorts like
Megève have none. We have experienced some excellent and virtually
untouched powder all over the area after a fresh snowfall.

Two efficient gondolas, Auberge du Télé and Le Pontet (reporters
recommend the latter as it is further down the valley and therefore quieter) take skiers up to a plateau at 1470m where the gondola to Le
Signal and the start of the main skiing can become a bottleneck. The parallel chair does not take you as high. There is a small nursery lift at Le
Signal at 1900m, which can often be busy when snow is poor on the village nursery slopes.

There are 44 runs of which half are intermediate; the higher runs
towards Mont Joly are steeper and more testing. A large number of the
runs are spread around a vast, mainly north-east-facing bowl behind Le
Signal. The Col du Joly at 2000m separates the main bowl from a
smaller, but also open, area. The six mountain restaurants include the
rather basic one at Signal, which has views of Mont Blanc, but one
reporter found it 'crowded, even on a quiet day, with no charm', and
another calls it 'the pits'. Ferme La Ruelle is a 'rather rustic establishment, which is worth a visit'. Another of the mountain eating places,
Auberge de Colombaz, is on an off-piste itinerary towards the village.

The village runs along a single street with an old church, old-fashioned hotels and a few shops and cafés. The best location is on the east
side of the river near the gondola. The Chemenaz is the only three-star
hotel, the rest have only one or two stars, and there is a wide variety of
self-catering apartments. The 18 restaurants include half-a-dozen

Skiing facts: **Megève**

TOURIST OFFICE
BP 24, F-74120 Megève, Haute Savoie
Tel 33 4 50 21 27 28
Fax 33 4 50 93 03 09

THE RESORT
By road Calais 890km
By rail Sallanches 12km, regular bus
service to resort
By air Geneva 1½ hrs
Visitor beds 10,000
Transport free ski bus with lift pass (links
centre with access lifts). Coach shuttles run
between the 13 ski resorts in the Mont
Blanc region

THE SKIING
Linked or nearby resorts Chamonix (n),
Combloux (l), Flumet (n), Le Bettex (l),
Les Contamines (n), Les Saisies (n), Nôtre-
Dame-de-Bellecombe (n), Praz-sur-Arly
(n), St-Gervais (l), St-Nicolas-de-Véroce (l)
Longest run Milloz, 3.6km (red)
Number of lifts 81 in Megève, 190 in
Mont Blanc ski area
Total of trails/pistes 300km in Megève
(30% easy, 45% intermediate, 25%
difficult), 700km in Mont Blanc ski area
Nursery slopes 4 runs and 4 lifts
Summer skiing none
Snowmaking 30 hectares covered

LIFT PASSES
Area pass Evasion Mont Blanc (covers
Megève and region) 728-837FF for 6 days
Day pass Megève only 155FF, Evasion
Mont Blanc (covers Megève, St-Gervais,
St-Nicolas-de-Véroce, Combloux) 314FF for
2 days
Beginners single lift tickets available
Pensioners 60 yrs and over as children
Credit cards accepted yes

SKI SCHOOLS
Adults ESF (5 centres), 9.30-11.30am,
470FF for 6 half-days. ESI, 10am-midday,
585FF for 6 half-days
Private lessons ESF 180FF, ESI 200FF,
both per hr
Snowboarding ESF 840FF and ESI
650-780FF, both for 6 half-days (2 hrs
per day)
Cross-country ESF (Mont d'Arbois), times
and prices as regular ski school. Loipe
75km in Megève area
Other courses telemark, monoski,
race training, artistic/acrobatic skiing,
off-piste, heli-skiing, Fat Boys initiation,
competition
Guiding companies Bureau des Guides de
Megève, and through ESI

CHILDREN
Lift pass Evasion Mont Blanc, 12 yrs and
under, 519-669FF for 6 days. Skipass Mont
Blanc, 12 yrs and under, 640FF for 6 days.
Free for 4 yrs and under with pass required
only on cable cars
Ski kindergarten Alpage, 3-6 yrs, 9.15am-
5.15pm, 375FF per day. Princesse, 3-6 yrs,
9am-5pm, 260FF per day. Caboche, 3-10
yrs, 9am-5.30pm, 285FF per day.
(All prices include lunch).
ESI, as regular ski school
Ski school ESF, 5-12 yrs, 9.30-11.30am
and 3-5pm, 720FF for 6 days. ESI, 4-12 yrs,
10am-midday and 3-5pm, 875FF for 6
days. ESI Club 7 (maximum of 7 children),
1-3pm, 780FF for 5 days
Non-ski kindergarten Meg'Loisirs, 1-6 yrs,
8am-6pm, 205FF per day including lunch

FOOD AND DRINK PRICES
Coffee 12FF, glass of wine 10-14FF, small
beer 18-23FF, dish of the day 70FF

crêperies. Two well-stocked supermarkets cater for those staying in apartments. Nightlife is severely limited ('virtually dead after 7pm'), with a skating rink, a cinema, one disco and concerts in the village church being the only form of entertainment. La Galipette Garderie, housed in an attractive wooden chalet, accepts children from twelve months to seven-years old and can combine its service with half-day ski lessons.

TOURIST OFFICE
Tel 33 4 50 47 01 58
Fax 33 4 50 47 09 54

St-Gervais Mont-Blanc
top 2350m (7,708ft) bottom 850m (2,788ft)

As a spa, St-Gervais has attracted tourists since 1806. The town is an informal if busy one ('full of traffic, even during the night'). It is popular with families wanting a cheaper alternative to Megève. A reporter recommends it as an ideal base for visiting other resorts. Nearby **Le Bettex** is a quieter village with a few comfortable hotels and some cross-country skiing

The main ski area of St-Gervais is on the slopes of Mont d'Arbois and is linked with that of Megève. It is accessed by a fast, 20-person gondola from the edge of the resort to Le Bettex at 1400m. The second stage goes up to what is known on this side of the mountain as St-Gervais 1850. This is a popular and often crowded entrance to Megève's ski area. Skiing on the Mont Blanc side of St-Gervais is served by the Tramway, a funicular that climbs slowly to the Col de Voza at 1653m where it links to the skiing above **Les Houches**. The only run back to St-Gervais is off-piste and sometimes unskiable. Hotel-Restaurant Igloo and the Terminus in Le Fayet both have good reputations for their cuisine.

St-Gervais has its own kindergarten, which takes children between six months and six years old, and three nursery-slope lifts. The ESF St-Gervais and ESI at Le Bettex both teach snowboarding, monoskiing, telemark, slalom and off-piste, as well as the usual group classes. There is also a local mountain guiding company.

Hotels here include the Carlina with a swimming-pool, the Val d'Este, L'Adret and the Edelweiss. A reporter recommends the Regina with its simple rooms, reasonable prices and friendly staff. At Le Bettex, the quiet Arbois-Bettex has a heated outdoor swimming-pool, and the Flèche d'Or is also recommended. St-Gervais has a moderate range of restaurants with two of particularly good value: L'Eventail and the Dômes de Miage. Le Four and Le Robinson are all popular eating places serving a variety of local specialities. La Tanière and La Chalette at Le Fayet are traditional. Après-ski is said to be 'extremely limited'. The only disco is La Nuit des Temps, although the Chardon Bleu restaurant in Le Fayet has a dance floor.

TOURIST OFFICE
Tel 33 4 50 78 22 43
Fax 33 4 50 47 76 08

La Plagne

ALTITUDE 1250m (4,100ft)-2100m (6,889ft)

It may be hard to imagine it today, but in 1960 the huge snow bowl above the town of Aime in the Tarentaise Valley was a natural mountain wilderness. Thirty-six years later, it is the heart of the ten-village complex that makes up the resort of La Plagne. Skiing convenience is so superior that it regularly heads the popularity charts in the French domestic market. For this, the world can thank the then Mayor of Aime, Dr Borrione, who noticed that the area was a developer's dream waiting to happen and that the Tarentaise was becoming depopulated at an alarming rate as young people left for the cities. When he formed an association with three neighbouring towns to build Plagne Centre on their common land, his prime purpose was to provide jobs.

Such was his success that the building was still in progress 20 years later. The original architect of that success was the celebrated skier Emile Allais who was employed to design the layout of the slopes.

La Plagne's six high villages lie in this central area at altitudes ranging from 1800m to 2100m. In the order in which they were built, they are **Plagne Centre**, **Aime La Plagne**, **Plagne Villages/Plagne Soleil**, **Bellecôte**, **Belle Plagne** and **Plagne 1800**.

Its four lower villages — **Montchavin**, **Plagne Montalbert**, **Les Coches** and **Champagny-en-Vanoise** — lie on different access roads in far-flung parts of the mountain, but all are connected by lift with the central complex.

Although the farming village of Montchavin was adapted to become a satellite ski resort in the early 1970s, the smell of manure from winter cowsheds still lingers in the air. In 1995, two chair-lifts — the four-seater Dos Rond and the innovative six-seater Pierre Blanches — replaced three ancient drags, revolutionising the village's accessibility. Montchavin has a gondola link to neighbouring Les Coches, a modern ski complex with its own wooded slopes.

Champagny-en-Vanoise, at the base of the south-facing back of the mountain, is a series of hamlets in a quiet valley linked to the ski area by an efficient gondola. Plagne Montalbert and its satellite holiday centre at **Longefoy** have inferior snow conditions on west-facing slopes in the immediate vicinity and its lift connections into the main bowl are less convenient.

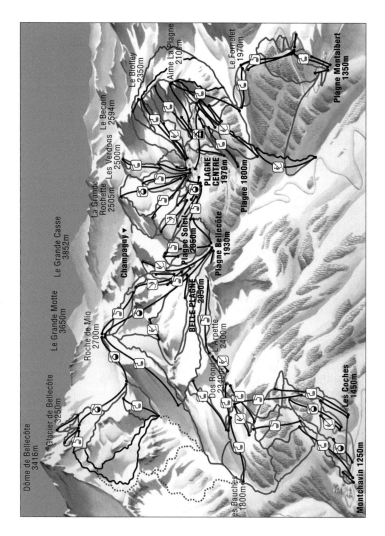

On the mountain

top 3250m (10,660ft) bottom 1250m (4,100ft)

La Plagne represents the ultimate in ski-in ski out convenience. To point your skis in any direction from the nexus in Plagne Centre is to lock into the network of lifts on the shallow gradients of La Grande Rochette, Les Verdons and Le Biolley. The Bellecôte gondola provides the most efficient connection with Roche de Mio, a steeper mountain with more challenging terrain; from here you can take the lift up to the Bellecôte Glacier, the highest point in the resort.

The Montchavin/Les Coches area is connected to the central arena through Arpette, a direct quad-chair ride from Bellecôte. The predominantly wooded Plagne Montalbert-Longefoy pistes lie on the other side of the resort below Aime La Plagne. Access to Champagny-en-Vanoise is via Les Verdons, the midway point on the rim of the main bowl, or Roche de Mio.

With 113 lifts catering for 114,000 skiers per hour, La Plagne has few queues in good weather, but the links to the outlying areas close down rapidly as soon as storms move in, causing congestion in the centre.

Beginners

With the exception of Champagny-en-Vanoise, all parts of the mountain have extensive beginner slopes. Those in the other three low-altitude villages gain in visibility by being below the tree-line, but this is balanced by less reliable snow conditions, especially in spring when the slopes are icy in the morning. Aesthetics aside, there can be no more encouraging place to learn to ski than La Plagne's central area in fine weather. The pistes on either side of the Arpette ridge above Bellecôte offer gradients so gentle that even the most fearful novice should gain in confidence, while the web of blue (easy) runs between Belle Plagne and Plagne Centre make for a natural second-week progression.

■ **WHAT'S NEW**

Les Balcons de Belle Plagne hotel/résidence
Rossa and Barselier drag-lifts above Champagny upgraded to quad- and six-person chairs

Intermediates

As befits a state-of-the-art ski area, La Plagne offers most to those skiers dedicated to racking up kilometres. This can be done most readily on the red (intermediate) runs on the eastern side of the bowl above Aime La Plagne. However, Roche de Mio has more varied terrain, with the run back to Belle Plagne via a long tunnel, particularly recommended. An adventurous alternative is the Crozats piste down to Les Bauches 1800, which has a link back to the main circus via two chair-lifts. The summer ski drag-lifts at the top of the glacier are not usually open in winter, but La Combe and Le Chiaupe runs to the Bellecôte gondola base-station hold no terrors for committed motorway cruisers. Enterprising intermediates will enjoy the exhilarating Mont de la Guerre run from Les Verdons to Champagny-en-Vanoise, but check conditions first as the descent is extremely rocky when snow is sparse. The same applies to the more wooded route from the Roche de Mio, via Les Borseliers.

Advanced

Although glaciers are not generally known for steep skiing, La Plagne's is one of the exceptions. The disadvantage is the 45-minute trek to the top from the centre of the resort, but once in place advanced skiers will find plenty to test them, especially the black (difficult) Bellecôte and Le Rochu runs to the bottom of the Chalet de Bellecôte chair. The other steep area is off Le Biolley ridge above Aime La Plagne. When conditions are good (which often they are not), the Morbleu piste is a compellingly direct drop to Le Fornelet cross-country area; return is via the Coqs chair. On the east-facing side of the ridge, the Emile Allais descent to the bottom of the outlying Charmettes chair at the side of the Olympic bob run is the longest black run in the resort.

Off-piste

If La Plagne is not a favourite among dedicated powder skiers, it is because of lack of ambience rather than lack of opportunity. As with the expert pistes, the best areas are on the fringes of the resort; the long, sweeping descent from the top of the glacier down to Les Bauches is high on most experienced skiers' lists. From here, the choice lies between an easy blue piste to Montchavin, a return to Arpette via the Bauches chair or, more dramatically, an itinerary down to **Peisey-Nancroix** in the adjacent valley.

The other prime off-piste area lies on the western slopes of Le Biolley; it is especially enjoyable towards the end of the season when spring snow is at its best. The back of the Bellecôte Glacier offers the demanding Col du Nant run into the remote valley of **Champagny-le-Haut**, followed by a return to Champagny-en-Vanoise by shuttle bus. The woods above Montchavin and Les Coches provide exciting powder skiing in the trees, but access is often restricted, at least as far as downtown La Plagne is concerned, by the closure of the link through Arpette.

Ski schools and guiding

The French Ski School (ESF) has offices spread throughout the resort. The numbers are so great that the ESF has been able to introduce teenage ski classes for greater peer-group pleasure. They also have guided off-piste courses in La Plagne and the surrounding outposts of the Tarentaise Valley.

Snowboarding

The ESF offers tuition and guided off-piste courses, but the resort has no special facilities for snowboarders. On powder mornings, the wide, open spaces between the network of groomed runs in the central bowl offer exhaustive opportunities for practice.

Cross-country

La Plagne has 79km of marked trails with 35km in Champagny-le-Haut and 12km spread between the high-altitude villages. Montchavin, Les Coches and Plagne Montalbert have 32km. Cross-country touring is available through the ESF.

Mountain restaurants

In an area that is not known for its mountain restaurants, there are two outstanding choices. The Au Bon Vieux Temps, just below Aime La Plagne, is recommended for its sunny terrace, traditional Savoyard dishes and efficient service. The Petit Chaperon Rouge, just above Plagne 1800, has equally good food and wait-service, and on a snowy day is the wiser choice because of its open fires. The Lincoln pub in Plagne Soleil serves generous portions and English beer, while the self-service restaurant at the Roche de Mio scores for its fast food (the chips with everything variety). The restaurant at Les Bauches is a sun-trap with reasonable self-service food. Good value is represented by the Dou au Praz above Plagne Villages and the Crêperie at the top of the Champagny gondola.

Off the mountain

La Plagne's success lies in its diversity; whatever visitors want, they will be sure to find it somewhere. As far as modern architecture is concerned, later is better: Belle Plagne's attractive village centre, with its integrated arcs of apartment buildings, is a fine example of imaginative design, while the low-rise wood-clad complexes at Plagne 1800 and Plagne Villages are inspired by Savoyard tradition. These are a far cry from the monolithic 'battleship' at Aime La Plagne or the square slabs at Plagne Centre. Some British visitors like Bellecôte's semi-circle of high-rise reddish blocks, but Belle Plagne is the firm favourite. Inevitably, the complexities of the area are confusing at first, which may explain why regulars prefer to book the same apartment in the same block from one year to the next, rather than take a chance on unknown territory.

■ **OTHER SPORTS**

Snowmobiling, snow-shoeing, night-skiing, parapente, swimming, skating, bob-rafting, taxi-bob, Olympic bob-sleigh run, squash, hang-gliding, paragliding, climbing wall

All ten villages are self-sufficient, with their own selection of shops, bars and restaurants. The six high villages are connected by bus or covered lifts from 8am to 1am. As its name suggests, Plagne Centre has the lion's share of essential services — banks, a post office, police and doctors — in the environs of its bleak subterranean commercial precinct. Aesthetic it is not, but it scores highly for convenience, as does Bellecôte, which also has banks and a post office.

Accommodation

Two-thirds of La Plagne's 45,000 beds are in the high-altitude villages, and one-third is in the satellites down the valley. Only eight per cent of all accommodation is in hotels, so the vast majority of visitors opt for self-catering apartments. Many are owned by Maeva or Pierre et Vacances; they are studio-style rabbit hutches with bunks in the passage and sofas that convert into beds in the only living area. It is best to remember this when deciding how many apartments your group needs. As with the architecture, newer tends to be better (and more spacious), which gives the edge to Plagne Soleil and 1800.

Les Balcons de Belle Plagne is a new hotel/*résidence*, which opens for

Skiing facts: **La Plagne**

TOURIST OFFICE
Le Chalet, BP 62, 73211, Aime Cedex
Tel 33 4 79 09 79 79
Fax 33 4 79 09 70 10

UK Agent:
Erna Low, 9 Reece Mews, London SW7 3HE
Tel 0171-584 2841
Fax 0171-589 9531

THE RESORT
By road Calais 930km
By rail Aime 18km
By air Lyon or Geneva 3 hrs
Visitor beds 45,000
Transport inter-resort link by télébus, télémetro and télécabine (15FF return). Free ski bus between Plagne 1800, Centre and Bellecôte

THE SKIING
Linked or nearby resorts Les Arcs (n), Peisey (n), Vallandry (n), Trois Vallées (n), Val d'Isère (n), Tignes (n)
Longest run Roche de Mio to Montchavin, 10km (red)
Number of lifts 113
Total of trails/pistes 210km (66% easy, 28% intermediate, 6% difficult)
Nursery slopes 1 lift in each centre
Summer skiing 4 lifts and 2 runs on Bellecôte Glacier open July and August
Snowmaking 3km covered in Montchavin, also at Belle Plagne

LIFT PASSES
Area pass 985FF for 6 days (covers Les Arcs and 1 day in L'Espace Killy or Trois Vallées)
Day pass 213FF
Beginners free lift in each centre
Pensioners 740FF for 60 yrs and over
Credit cards accepted yes

SKI SCHOOLS
Adults ESF in all centres, 900FF for 6 days (6 hrs per day)
Private lessons 180FF per hr
Snowboarding ESF, 1300-1450FF for 6-day Multiglisse course including equipment
Cross-country group and private lessons as regular ski school. Loipe 79km in area
Other courses off-piste, speed skiing, ski-touring, teenager group lessons (including lift pass), freestyle, heli-skiing, monoski, handicapped
Guiding companies through ESF

CHILDREN
Lift pass 7-16 yrs, 740FF for 6 days, free for 6 yrs and under
Ski kindergarten in all 10 villages, times, prices and ages vary, example: ESF Belle Plagne Snow Garden, 3 yrs and over, 1,210FF for 6 days including lunch
Ski school ESF all centres, under 14 yrs, times as adults, 790FF for 6 days
Non-ski kindergarten in all 10 villages, times, prices and ages vary, example: ESF Belle Plagne, 18 mths-3 yrs, 1,110FF for 6 days including lunch

FOOD AND DRINK PRICES
Coffee 6-7FF, glass of wine 10FF, small beer 10-12FF, dish of the day 60FF

the 1996–7 season and should provide much-needed high-quality accommodation. The Chalet/Hotel Les Montagnettes in Belle Plagne represents a welcome wind of change, with comfortable six- to eight-person apartments and up to twelve-person chalets. They can be rented for self-catering or with full hotel services.

Eating in and out

Gourmet dining is guaranteed in La Soupe au Schuss in Aime La Plagne, an expensive restaurant serving specialities from the Périgord region. Alain Cressend's Le Matafan in Belle Plagne stays closer to home, with a range of medium-priced Savoyard dishes including raclette and fondue. Le Loup Garou, a short sleigh ride (or walk) down the path from Plagne Centre to Plagne 1800, serves similar dishes in a festive atmosphere. The Cheyenne Café in Belle Plagne provides a cheap, cheerful and substantial mixture of Tex-Mex and French. All the villages have supermarkets for the self-catering brigades, but there is a shortage of specialist food shops.

Après-ski

By comparison with its Tarentaise neighbours, **Val d'Isère** and **Courchevel**, La Plagne's nightlife is decidedly low profile, with such clubs as there are confined to Plagne Centre and Bellecôte. The current favourites in Plagne Centre are the King Café, which has live music most nights, and Le Must disco. The Jet 73 disco in Bellecôte is also popular. Mat's is a faithful re-creation of a British pub, making it a winner among Brits staying in Belle Plagne. The watering-hole of choice in Bellecôte is the Showtime Café, while the Lincoln is the winner in Plagne Soleil.

The most exhilarating non-skiing activity in La Plagne is the Olympic bob-run, which is open to the public whenever conditions permit. The softer option is the Bob-Raft, a four-man foam-rubber cocoon that hurtles down in gravity-propelled mode in 90 seconds. The Taxi-Bob is the more genuine experience, with two rookies sandwiched between a professional driver and a brakeman for a breathtaking 50-second descent at speeds of up to 105km per hour.

For those with energy to spare after skiing, the Winform fitness centre in Belle Plagne has facilities that include a 10-pin bowling alley and an electric golf clinic. Bellecôte has an ice rink and a swimming-pool.

Childcare

The ESF has learn-to-ski programmes for children aged three to seven in specially designed snow gardens in several of the villages. The Montchavin/Les Coches nursery has a mixed programme of skiing and other learning activities for children aged three and upwards.

La Plagne has ten nurseries for toddlers and upwards; those in Montchavin/Les Coches, Belle Plagne and Plagne Centre accept children as young as nine months old. The Eldorador Hotel has a children's mini club from 9am to 5pm and babysitting by arrangement in the evening.

Portes du Soleil

ALTITUDE Avoriaz 1800m (5,904ft), Châtel 1200m (3,936ft),
Morzine 1000m (3,280ft)

Les Portes du Soleil is one of Europe's three largest ski areas. It straddles the French–Swiss border close to Geneva and is an uneasy marketing consortium of a baker's dozen of ski villages; these range from large, internationally recognised resorts to the tiniest of unspoilt hamlets. The published statistics talk about 650km of piste served by 228 lifts, a well-linked circus covering vast tracts of land bordered by Lac Léman; in reality, Les Portes du Soleil consists of a series of naturally separate ski areas. Most are joined by awkward and often confusing mountain links, while a few like **St-Jean d'Aulps/La Grande Terche** and **Abondance** are entirely independent and include themselves in the association only for promotional reasons.

While it is possible to complete a circuit of the main resorts in one day, this actually involves limited enjoyable skiing and a considerable amount of time spent on lifts and in lift queues. To explore the region fully, you need four weeks, at least two different bases and a car.

Les Portes du Soleil might be considered as one of Europe's greatest overall ski areas were it not for one major fault: it is far too low. With a top height of only 2350m and the villages mostly below 1200m, snow cover is by no means guaranteed at any stage of the season, and the links are liable to rupture at any time. Out of all 13 resorts, only Avoriaz can be recommended as a snow-sure base and, when cover is poor or non-existent elsewhere, the overcrowding here becomes a complete misery. However, keen skiers will want to base themselves at this end of the circuit, where the slopes are the most challenging.

Signposting has been vastly improved, as has the overall Portes du Soleil piste-map, which indicates the links from area to area, as well as rather over-optimistic figures for the suggested times they take. Skiers who want to explore more than the main circuit still, infuriatingly, have to obtain separate piste-maps on arrival in each resort. Seven hundred slope-markers should tell you where you are, the difficulty of the run and where it is taking you. Not all reporters agree about the success of the system, and one said: 'I can hardly be rude enough about the piste information'.

■ GOOD POINTS

Large ski area, suitable for all standards of skier, extensive cross-country loipe, good childcare facilities, car-free resort of Avoriaz, short airport transfer, excellent for snowboarders (particularly Avoriaz)

■ BAD POINTS

Low altitude (except Avoriaz), few activities for non-skiers, lack of skiing convenience (Morzine)

When the snow is good there are few better playgrounds in Europe for intermediate skiers who enjoy fast cruising and want to feel that they are actually going somewhere each day. Skiers are advised to carry passports as well as two sets of currency; both countries accept both types of franc, but not always at an advantageous rate. Customs controls do exist, with border patrols on the snow, and in the countryside where smuggling is a centuries-old profession, we have heard tales of rucksacked skiers being chased by excise men.

Les Portes du Soleil takes its name from a 2000-m col, which separates the French Haute Savoie from the Swiss Valais above the small Swiss resort of **Les Crosets**. Much credit is due to Jean Vuarnet (founder of Avoriaz) in establishing the largely successful *entente cordiale* between two 'tribal' groups of mountain folk on both sides of the border.

On the mountain
top 2350m (7,708ft) bottom 1100m (3,608ft)

The skiing around **Avoriaz** itself can be divided into four main areas. Above the village is an extension of the main nursery slopes (Le Plateau), with a variety of drag-lifts serving a series of confidence-building green (beginner) runs, which link with the series of lifts coming up from Morzine. In the opposite direction are pistes down to Les Marmottes, from where lifts branch off towards Châtel; these runs are by no means always easy and are often crowded. From Les Marmottes a satisfyingly easy red (intermediate) run goes on down a beautiful gorge to Ardent, from where you can take a jumbo gondola back up. This also provides a useful access point into the best skiing for those staying in **Châtel**, **Torgon** and the other lower resorts at this end of the system.

At the bottom of Avoriaz you are faced with three choices. Directly to the south is the main Arare sector, which from Avoriaz looks steeper than it really is; the skiing here is mainly above the tree-line. Such is the volume of traffic that the separate marked runs amalgamate to form a whole pisted face to the mountain. The runs are mainly easy, with a few more difficult pitches towards the bottom. This sector is much frequented by the ski school, and parts are often closed for slalom practice so it does become seriously congested. A long chair-lift from the same area at the bottom of the village takes you up to Hauts Forts, which offers the most challenging skiing in Avoriaz.

Several routes take you down all or part of the way to **Les Prodains**, 650m below Avoriaz and a full 1300m vertical from Hauts Forts. The often heavily mogulled pistes here narrow considerably as you descend into the trees, and are prone to ice. The blacks are genuinely black (difficult), and the main red run from the Arare sector has an extremely difficult pitch, which causes major problems for otherwise confident intermediates. The lower runs are usually busy in the late afternoon and extremely popular when visibility is poor above the tree-line.

The third direction is by chair- and drag-lift to the north-west-facing

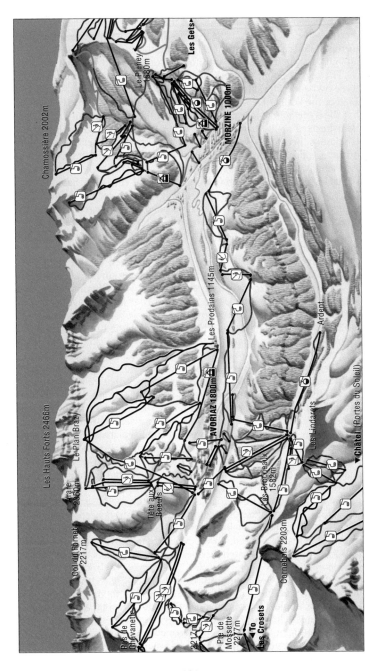

bowl between Pas de Chavanette and the Col du Fornet. This is another area of wide, open intermediate skiing above the tree-line. More adventurous skiers can return from Chavanette through the next valley; after an initial mogul field a pleasant run leads down to Les Marmottes.

The border point, where Avoriaz meets the big, open pastures of the three Swiss resorts, starts with the Chavanette (also known as the Swiss Wall or the Wall of Death); it is the most notorious black run in Europe, but the hype is considerably greater than the degree of difficulty. The faint-hearted or the plain sensible can take the chair down during icy conditions. Below the Wall, acres of open snowfield are served by the lifts on either side of the Chavanette chair-lift, connecting with the slopes of Planachaux above **Champéry** and with the adjacent bowl of Les Crosets. Planachaux is reached from Champéry by cable car or by chair-lift from Grand-Paradis. The run down at the valley end is a delightful one, winding its way gently through sleepy hamlets and across the river against the dramatic backdrop of the Dents du Midi; snow disappears early in the season here. Annoyingly irregular and crowded buses connect Grand-Paradis with Champéry.

Les Crosets sits above the tree-line surrounded by abundant wide pistes, some of them north-facing but most of them sunny. There are lifts up to the French border. The connection with **Champoussin** and **Morgins** is via the Pointe de l'Au, and a series of linked drags serve easy to intermediate pistes. The mountainside above Champoussin is wide but has little variety of terrain; the addition of a quad-chair from above Champoussin to the ridge has greatly improved the skiing. The pistes here are ideal for intermediates who need to build up their confidence.

Morgins has little skiing on the approach side from Champoussin, but it includes an excellent north-facing intermediate run, cut through the woods above the village. Those who wish to continue skiing the circuit must walk across the village or take a short bus ride to the nursery slopes and the lifts for Super-Châtel and France. In strong contrast to the sometimes bleak ski-fields of Avoriaz and Planachaux, the pistes here wind through the trees and are connected by a series of short drag-lifts.

The Morclan chair from **Super-Châtel** up to 1970m serves the most challenging slope, a moderately difficult mogul field. The black piste down to the village presents no real problems provided snow cover is reasonable. The top of this chair is the departure point for Torgon, one of the further extremities of Les Portes du Soleil, back across the border in Switzerland. The remainder of the skiing around Super-Châtel is mostly blue (easy) and red, on wide areas both above and below the lift station. The valley runs catch the afternoon sun and can be tricky in poor snow conditions.

Les Portes du Soleil circuit breaks down at Châtel and, whichever way you are travelling, the link cannot be made on skis. If going in a clockwise direction, a green traverse from the Linga lift delivers you to Châtel's nursery slopes, leaving you with a walk across the village to the jumbo gondola for Super-Châtel. If travelling anti-clockwise, a bus ride takes you from Châtel to the 10-person gondola up to Linga; this is the

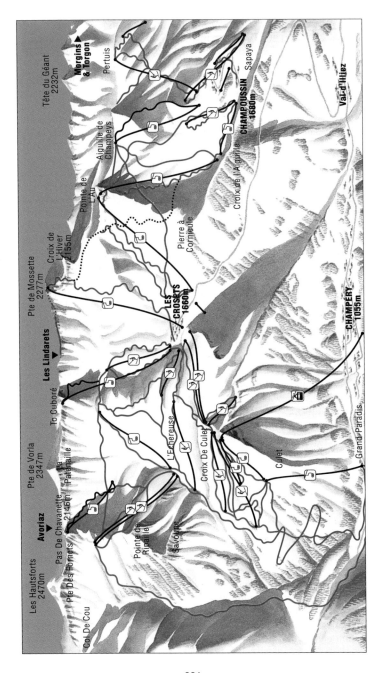

first of a long chain of lifts and pistes towards Avoriaz and to the chair from Pré-la-Joux. The skiing in this sector offers more variety than other major legs of the circuit and includes a long, challenging black beside the Linga gondola for clockwise skiers or those with time to play en route.

The fairly steep slope above the gondola, served by chair-lift, has a blue traverse cut into it, as well as the red and black routes shown on the local piste-map. The run down by the Combes chair-lift towards Avoriaz is a satisfying red. The Cornebois chair, which goes up from the same point, has good intermediate pistes of its own and also connects with the top of the Chaux des Rosées chair-lift from Plaine Dranse; the runs below this chair are seriously challenging. One more lift and one easy run bring you down to Les Marmottes for the return to Avoriaz.

A cable car from the satellite of Les Prodains connects **Morzine** with Avoriaz, and on the other side of Morzine, a gondola and a cable car climb steeply to Le Pleney (1500m), which is more of a sunny ridge than a peak. From the lifts you look down on the less enticing sections of the direct black run down from Le Pleney, which is fairly steep and often scraped to an icy glaze by too many skiers. Easy skiing can be found on the north-west side of the mountain, including a long blue down to the resort. An attractive area on the eastern side provides a series of mainly red runs, complicated only by a number of piste crossroads.

From Les Fys at the eastern end of this area, a quad-chair gives access to Plateau de Nyon. The Fys chair climbs back to the top of the ridge (Belvédère), where easy link-runs go down both wooded flanks of the ridge; south-westward runs take you to **Les Gets**, south-eastward pistes to the junction of Le Grand Pré, where a chair and a drag-lift link with **Nyon**, and the long Charniaz chair climbs gently up to the Tête des Crêts. This lift is the usual access route to Les Gets ski area and the runs beneath it: a red, which is mostly a schuss, followed by a green along the road are the only ways back to Morzine.

The Plateau de Nyon can be reached by cable car from just outside Morzine. Its appeal is mainly for good skiers: the Pointe and Chamossière chairs reach the high points of the system and serve its most challenging summits — shadowy north-facing ridges beneath the sharp peaks, which tower over Morzine's ski area and keep the early sun off much of it. The wide bowl below the Chamossière lift offers plenty of off-piste opportunities. Behind Chamossière there is a pleasant red run, which offers interesting off-piste alternatives before following a road through the woods to Le Grand Pré. From the Plateau de Nyon you can either ski down to the bottom of the cable car or the whole 11.5km directly back to Morzine via a flimsy-looking, but well-protected, bridge over a gaping river gorge.

The Tête des Crêts is near the top of the north-facing half of Les Gets ski area. This is gentle, with long runs over lightly wooded slopes to the resort. These pistes pass through **Les Chavannes**, a cluster of restaurants and hotel buildings with a nursery-slope area, walking trails and cross-country loipe that link up with Le Pleney. It is accessible by road as well as by lift from Les Gets. Only one of Les Chavannes' drags climbs to Tête

233

des Crêts, for access not only to Morzine but also to a broad, upper bowl. The direct blue run to Les Gets from here is not obvious; the piste down La Turche drag to the edge of the village is an equally gentle alternative.

The south-facing skiing of Les Gets is on Mont Chéry and is reached by a six-seater gondola; its base-station is a short walk across the road from the Chavannes lifts and runs. Good snow on the lower red and black runs is a rarity for much of the winter. The top half of the mountain has easier, open skiing with magnificent views to the south of the Mont Blanc massif. The fairly steep, open slope behind Mont Chéry has good black and red runs to the Col de l'Encrenaz.

Most queuing problems in Les Portes du Soleil are in the Avoriaz sector; this is more because of the great volume of skiers here than due to any major deficiencies of the lift system in this quarter.

Beginners
Given acceptable snow conditions, it does not really matter which end of the circus you choose. Châtel and Morgins both have good ski schools, easy nursery slopes and plenty of tree-level skiing to which novices can graduate after a few days. Morzine, and in particular the runs around Super-Morzine, are ideally suited to learners.

Intermediates
The whole of Les Portes du Soleil is ideal cruising territory. Less confident skiers will prefer the long, sweeping runs at the Châtel end of the circuit. Stronger skiers will look towards the greater challenges of Champéry and Avoriaz. Les Gets is also an ideal base from which to explore some of the best intermediate skiing. Little resorts like St Jean d'Aulps/La Grande Terche, Abondance and **La Chapelle d'Abondance** can also provide excellent skiing when the region is crowded.

Advanced
Ideally, advanced skiers should base themselves at the Avoriaz end of the circuit, although Champéry is a delightful alternative with easy access to the Avoriaz area. The Swiss Wall is the most notorious run in the area; a sign at the top warns that it is only to be attempted by experts, and certainly the initial angle of descent is such that you cannot see what lies ahead. But the wall itself is wide and after the first 50m it flattens out considerably, although it still maintains an average gradient of 34 degrees. Like all black runs, the degree of difficulty depends on snow conditions; it is normally heavily mogulled within hours of a major dump of snow. Great care should be taken, not least because of the volume of less competent skiers who attempt it. This run certainly has to be skied, but there are plenty of other equally challenging pistes in the region, including the World Cup run from Le Plan Brazy above Avoriaz.

Off-piste
Again, the best powder runs are to be found above Avoriaz on both sides of the Swiss border. After a fresh snow fall various itineraries parallel to

the Swiss Wall can be far more exhilarating than the actual run itself. The area is prone to considerable avalanche danger, and the services of a qualified guide are essential.

Ski schools and guiding

Views on the French Ski School (ESF) in Avoriaz and Morzine range from 'miserable' to 'superb'. Regardless of the questionable attitude of instructors, the standard of teaching, particularly for beginners, seems high at both. Châtel also has a solid reputation, and we have positive reports of the Swiss Ski School (ESS) in Champéry and in Morgins. However, the establishment that has received rave reviews is the British Alpine Ski School in Morzine and Avoriaz. This enterprise, set up by a couple of BASI instructors (who have passed the tough *équivalence* exam that allows them to teach legally in France), is described by one reporter as 'everything the ESF is not – small classes and good technical advice in one's mother tongue. Highly recommended and deserves a gold medal'.

Snowboarding

Avoriaz was the first resort in Europe to realise the importance of the new sport in the early stages of its development, and was also the first to build a half-pipe. It is now recognised as the world's snowboard capital. The resort has special areas set aside for snowboarders in the Arare area, which include a snowboard park, half-pipe and a slalom run. A special reduced-price restricted-area pass gives access to these facilities. The whole Arare area offers great freeriding terrain, and the detachable chair provides fast access. La Bleue du Lac piste is particularly recommended for freestylers. For alpine riders, the Arare piste is hard to beat for high-speed carving. Off-piste opportunities for riders include the Cretes, Le Fornet and La Suisse.

The British Snowboard School in Avoriaz run by Dave Peek operates under legal French licence and is strongly recommended. Street Trash is the only snowboard specialist, with two shops serving the needs of freestylers and freeriders; instruction is also available through them.

Morzine shares the glory of Avoriaz as the home of snowboarding, and the percentage of riders found at this end of the circuit is higher than in any other ski area in Europe. The run down to Morzine is superb in plentiful snow.

Cross-country

There are trails scattered throughout area, ranging from 22km at La Chapelle d'Abondance, which are some of the best loipe in the region, to 20km at Morgins. Morzine has five separate areas, which total 97km, including one around the scenic Lac de Montriond.

Mountain restaurants

Les Portes du Soleil has a mixed bag of restaurants ranging from over-crowded self-service to wonderful old huts off the beaten track. Prices are generally high on both sides of the border, and all our reporters agree that there are simply not enough restaurants. Coquoz at Planachaux has a circular open-fire and offers wonderful local Swiss specialities. **Les Lindarets**, the hamlet just north of Avoriaz, has the best concentration of eating places with competitive prices. La Cremaillère is considered to be outstanding ('delicious *chanterelle* omelettes and wild myrtilles tart'), and Les Marmottes and the Pomme de Pin are also recommended.

Les Prodains, at the bottom of the Vuarnet run from Avoriaz, is much praised, not least for its reasonable prices. The restaurants at Plaine Dranse are singled out as 'inexpensive and good'. Two restaurants at the top of Le Pleney are said to be always busy, 'but the wait is worth it'. The one at the top of the Super Morzine gondola receives compliments for its 'good food and prices and spectacular view'. Les Raverettes at Les Gets is a handy stop before skiing back to Morzine. There is a good eating-place halfway down the blue piste from Le Pleney to Morzine. The Perdrix Blanche at Pré-la-Joux is recommended for its warm atmosphere and good-value food. Chez Gaby in Champoussin is highly praised ('we were ecstatic about the tomato fondue, but get here early or you won't find a free table'). Le Corbeau above Morgins is said to be 'a rustic, family-run affair with thoroughly reasonable prices'.

Off the mountain

Avoriaz is mainly a collection of apartment blocks perched on the edge of a cliff far above Morzine and built in what for the 1960s was a truly futuristic style. Unfortunately, many of the older blocks are showing their age, and no amount of face-lifts can improve the lack of space in their interiors. The resort is reached from the valley either by a narrow, winding road or by cable car from Les Prodains. You are strongly advised to leave your car 'downstairs', or indeed to leave it at home. One reporter comments: 'there are too many cars already in Morzine, so don't spoil the environment even further by bringing one'. Certainly it has no useful application in car-free Avoriaz, and the charges in either car park are iniquitous. It is apparently legal to leave your car on the roadside on the outskirts of the resort, but you run the risk of it being buried or damaged by a snowplough.

Transport to your apartment block or hotel is via expensive horse-drawn sleigh, piste machine or on foot. Between snowfalls, the amount of horse manure combined with dog-dirt deposited on the resort 'roads' does little to improve the ambience. When not on skis, moving around is made easier by public lifts within the apartment blocks to different levels of this steep resort. The busiest part is the middle section, around the foot of the nursery slopes; there are lots of bars and restaurants linking the slopes, and shops for ski gear, fashion and food. The best supermarket is, by consensus, the Codec near the tourist office.

Châtel is still a farming village, but caring for livestock and tilling the fields takes a poor second place to the more lucrative business of tourism. Unfortunately, precious little planning has gone into the development of the village, which is a huge, ungainly straggle of buildings up towards the Morgins Pass and Switzerland, as well as down the hillside and along the valley towards the Linga lift and the connection with Avoriaz. One reporter describes it as 'an excellent resort for a couple not too worried about après-ski, but who want to ski gently in breathtaking scenery'.

The valley lift departures are linked by free ski buses; these are crowded in the afternoon and have to fight their way through a village centre that is often choked with traffic. The disparate nature of the resort makes a car an advantage for reaching the out-of-town lift stations and for travel to the other unlinked resorts on the circuit.

Morzine is a market town and long-established resort with a Gallic atmosphere at the foot of the road up to Avoriaz. It has all the appeal of an old-style chalet resort set in charming, wooded surroundings. Its biggest fault is its lack of altitude (1000m), which means that resort-level snow is scarce.

The town covers a large area on both sides of a river gorge and is on several levels. It has a serious traffic problem, but a high footbridge over the river makes getting around less torturous for pedestrians than for motorists. The main congested shopping street climbs from the old village centre beside the river to more open ground at the foot of Le Pleney, where the resort has developed, with hotels and shops around the tourist office.

> ### ■ OTHER SPORTS
>
> **Avoriaz**: parapente, hang-gliding, sleigh rides, snow-mobiling, skating, swimming, squash
> **Châtel**: parapente, snow-shoeing, skating
> **Morzine**: hang-gliding, parapente, dog-sledding, snow-shoeing, ski-jumping, ice-hockey, skating, curling, climbing wall, swimming

Such is the diffuse nature of the resort that the free buses are an essential form of transport. Horse-drawn taxis are an alternative means of getting around, although one reporter said he felt guilty when the horse ran out of steam on the steep hills. Being a real town, the range of shops is far above the standard of most ski resorts. Morzine has a large sports centre with an indoor ice rink.

Accommodation

The accommodation in Avoriaz is nearly all in apartment blocks, which vary in quality according to their age. Alpage 1 apartments are said to be 'clean, but fairly cramped', La Falaise units are similarly well-scrubbed but 'seriously short of storage space and maybe a bit cramped', and La Thuya apartments are 'rather dilapidated'. In general, it seems prudent to halve the number of advertised bed spaces. Hotel des Hauts Forts is recommended as 'surprisingly cheap'. Location within the resort is of no importance for skiing purposes, although some of the village streets, which are also pistes, may prove difficult for novices.

Châtel has a wide choice of hotels, most of them chalet-style and simple. Location is important and it is well worth checking out the distance from a main lift before booking. The Améthyste is said to be 'excellent and cheap', the Résidence Yeti is recommended, and Hotel Fleur de Neige is praised for the quality of its food — 'more like a restaurant with rooms than a hotel'. The Flèche d'Or apartments are described as being 'clean and comfortable, provided you halve the recommended occupancy figure'. Hotel Les Rhododendrons is 'perfectly located and typically French'.

Morzine has a plentiful supply of hotels in each price bracket; most are chalet-style and none is luxurious. In the central area, Les Airelles is one of the more comfortable, while Hotel Concorde is family-run and has a relaxed atmosphere. We continue to receive rave reports of the Hotel Dahu ('excellent and friendly, with lovely rooms — the children loved the pool'). In the Hotel Sporting 'staff could not do enough for us, even buying our 15-month-old son a new high-chair'.

Eating in and out
Avoriaz has a choice of around 30 restaurants, most of which are rather overpriced as you would expect in a *station de ski* of this type. Les Intrets is a favourite with three reporters for its raclette, fondue and pierrade. Le Petit Vatel serves rustic fare including fresh trout, frogs' legs and snails. The Bistro opposite the Children's Village is 'good, but expensive'. Les Fontaines Blanches is 'reasonably priced, with a wide range of excellent food, a good French atmosphere and occasional live music'. US One serves Tex-Mex, and Le Savoyard has plenty of local flavour.

In Châtel, La Bonne Menagère is popular, as is the Vieux-Four ('slow service but food is good, basic French'). The Fleur de Neige has some of the best cuisine. Le Kitchen, out of town, is recommended for raclette and has 'a great atmosphere created by its English owner'.

In Morzine, Le Dahu is again recommended for its 'mouth-watering dinners, night after night'. The Neige Roc at Les Prodains and Le Tremplin are also rated highly by reporters. L'Etale serves regional specialities in a 'wonderful, authentic mountain atmosphere'. In Les Gets, the Tyrol is recommended for '*châteaubriand* cooked on an open fire'.

Après-ski
The Place in Avoriaz has live, non-French music and an 'excellent atmosphere'. Le Choucas is recommended by reporters; it has live music and is usually not too crowded. Le Tavaillon is described by one reporter who spent five weeks here as 'the nerve centre of Avoriaz'. The nightclubs are said to be generally overpriced and empty, except on strip-tease nights, when audience participation is invited. The discos Le Festival and Le Roc Club both have entrance fees, and the Midnight Express has a free 'bucking bronco'.

Châtel has a bowling alley and an ice rink, but otherwise the after-slopes entertainment is mainly limited to a handful of bars, including the popular L'Isba, which has a lively atmosphere and shows ski videos. One reporter claimed: 'There was nothing to do and nowhere to go after 2.30am'. The Slalom bar is British-owned. Morzine abounds with civilised tea-rooms and bars. Inside the Wallington complex are a bowling alley, pool hall, bar and disco. Le Pacha is another popular disco, which becomes extremely lively later on.

Childcare

The Children's Village in Avoriaz has a justified reputation as one of the better childcare establishments in France. Children from three years old are taught in the centre of the village, using methods developed by celebrated French ski champion Annie Famose. Younger non-skiing children are looked after in Les P'tits Loups day nursery, of which we have good reports.

Châtel has the Village des Marmottons for children as young as 14 months, with a mixture of games and skiing for the older ones. The ESF operates classes for five-year-olds and upwards.

The Morzine crèche takes infants of two months to four years old, with one-hour ski lessons for children of three years and over. One reporter was dissatisfied with the service: 'The instructor did not speak English, the location was awkward, and the attitude was unsympathetic to slow starters'.

Linked or nearby resorts

Abondance
top 1800m (5,906ft) bottom 930m (3,050ft)

This tiny, historic village lies 7km from La Chapelle and is not linked into the main Portes du Soleil system. It has its own small ski area on the slopes beneath the Col de l'Ecuelle, served by a gondola and a series of drags.

TOURIST OFFICE
Tel 33 4 50 73 02 90
Fax 33 4 50 73 04 76

Champéry
top 2350m (7,708ft) bottom 1053m (3,455ft)

This traditional Swiss village is set in dramatic surroundings at the foot of the Dents du Midi. The one-way main street is lined with attractive wooden chalets, most of the hotels, shops and restaurants. However, the focus of development has moved down the hill to the valley road that skirts the village, where the 125-person cable car up to Planachaux is based. The lift is served by a free mini-bus that circles the village. The four-star Hotel Suisse is 'very Swiss with a formal dining-room and old-fashioned bedrooms'. The centrally located Hotel de Champéry is comfortable.

Champéry has one of the best restaurants in the area: the Grand-Paradis is 2km outside the village at the foot of the slopes. It has an atmospheric, wood-panelled interior with an open fire. Le Vieux Chalet is 'reasonably priced by Swiss standards' and Restaurant de la Paix is popular. Grill Le Mazot in the Hotel Champéry has the best and most expensive steaks in town. The village is not known for its nightlife. Le Pub bar and restaurant and the Farinet Bar are recommended.

Champéry has a gentle nursery slope with a simple rope-tow right in the middle of the village; snow permitting, this provides an ideal beginners' area for small children. The ESS Mini Club takes children up the mountain for the whole day.

TOURIST OFFICE
Tel 41 25 79 11 41
Fax 41 25 79 18 47

Les Crosets
top 2350m (7,708ft) bottom 1660m (5,445ft)

Les Crosets is a tiny ski station in the heart of the open slopes on the Swiss side of Les Portes du Soleil. It has some modern chalets, a couple of hotels and a handful of restaurants. The hamlet is fairly functional and, apart from a visit to the Sundance Saloon disco, has no obvious appeal to anyone but serious skiers who want an early night. The main uphill transport from here is a detachable quad-chair. The Hotel Télécabine is simple, British-run and serves excellent food.

TOURIST OFFICE
Tel 41 25 77 20 77
Fax 41 25 77 37 73

Champoussin
top 2350m (7,708ft) bottom 1580m (5,182ft)

Champoussin represents more of an attempt to create a mini resort than Les Crosets does. Its new, rustic-style buildings are almost all apartments, but most of our reporters stay in the main hotel, the Alpage Ambassador, which receives mixed reports. It has a sauna, a swimming-pool and a disco. The Alpage Ambassador apartments are highly recommended. The hotel runs its own kindergarten and mini-club, and parapente school. Après-ski, which is limited to the hotel and Le Poussin bar/restaurant, is 'almost non-existent'.

The resort is dominated by Dutch visitors. The small ski school does not receive impressive ratings. Two of our reporters have violently opposing views on the resort. One writes 'great for family holidays, but singles and extreme skiers should look elsewhere'. The other says: 'Champoussin is so small and remote that just looking at it could give you cabin fever'.

TOURIST OFFICE
as Les Crosets

La Chapelle d'Abondance
top 1700m (5,577ft) bottom 1010m (3,313ft)

This small resort lies 6km down the valley from Châtel. It is an old farming community, straddling both sides of the road, without any defined centre. On one side, two long chairs take you up to Crêt Béni at 1650m, from where a series of drags serve a choice of mainly easy runs through the pine forest. On the other side of the road a recently built gondola and a chair-lift link into Torgon, Châtel and the main Portes du Soleil system. Hotels Les Cornettes du Bis and the Alti Mille both have swimming-pools and fitness centres. The Cornettes restaurant provides one of the best gastronomic experiences in the Abondance Valley.

TOURIST OFFICE
Tel 33 4 50 73 51 41
Fax 33 4 50 73 56 04

Les Gets
top 2350m (7,708ft) bottom 1175m (3,854ft)

Les Gets is situated on a low mountain-pass 6km from Morzine, with lifts and pistes on both sides and good nursery slopes on the edge of the village and higher up at Les Chavannes (1490m), which is reached by road or gondola. This attractive village, an old farming community that has expanded almost out of recognition, has a large and under-used floodlit piste. Parts of the ski area and many of the restaurants within it are accessible on foot. There is a bus service to Morzine for access to Avoriaz but it starts late in the morning and is infrequent.

Les Gets has three ski schools, and we have favourable reports of them all. Ski Plus has 'excellent private tuition in English', and there is a choice of kindergarten; Ski Espace ('lots of fun, they don't take the skiing too seriously') receives better comments than the ESF. The non-ski Bébé Club takes children from three months to two years old.

Much of the accommodation is in tour-operator chalets. Hotel L'Ours Blanc is 'comfortable, with good service, and we would go back there again'. Hotel Regina is well placed on the quieter part of the village, and the Labrador and the Alissandre are both said to offer a high standard of service. Le Meridien, La Cachette and the Clé des Champs chalets are recommended, along with Le Soleil and La Bouillandire apartments. Restaurants include Le Tyrol for pizzas and Le Gallichou for 'excellent cider and crêpes'.

Most of the nightlife centres around hotel bars, but there are also three discos. The English-run Pring's and the piano bar in the Hotel Régina are popular. There is an open-air skating rink in the centre, a motor-tricycle circuit, a mechanical museum and two cinemas.

TOURIST OFFICE
Tel 33 4 50 75 80 80
Fax 33 4 50 79 76 90

Skiing facts: **Avoriaz**

TOURIST OFFICE
Place Central, F-74110 Avoriaz, Haute Savoie
Tel 33 4 50 74 02 11
Fax 33 4 50 74 18 25

THE RESORT
By road Calais 889km
By rail Thonon les Bains 43km, Cluses 40km
By air Geneva 2 hrs
Visitor beds 16,000
Transport traffic-free resort

THE SKIING
Linked or nearby resorts Abondance (n), Champoussin (l), Champéry (l), La Chapelle d'Abondance (l), Châtel (l), Les Crosets (l), Les Gets (l), Montriond (l), Morgins (l), Morzine (l), Saint Jean d'Aulps/La Grande Terche (n), Torgon (l)
Longest run Crozats, 4km (black)
Number of lifts 42 in Avoriaz, 228 in Portes du Soleil
Total of trails/pistes Avoriaz 150km (8% beginner, 55% easy, 27% intermediate, 10% difficult), 650km in Portes du Soleil
Nursery slopes 7 lifts
Summer skiing none
Snowmaking 18 mobile snow-cannon

LIFT PASSES
Area pass Portes du Soleil (covers 13 resorts), 885FF for 6 days
Day pass Avoriaz 150FF, Portes du Soleil 195FF

Beginners 391FF for 4 days
Pensioners reductions for 60 yrs and over
Credit cards accepted yes

SKI SCHOOLS
Adults ESF, 790FF for 6 days,
Ecole de Glisse, 500FF for 5 days (2 hrs per day), British Alpine Ski School, details on request
Private lessons ESF and Ecole de Glisse, both 165FF per hr
Snowboarding ESF, 1,150FF for 6 days, Ecole de Glisse, 500FF for 6 half-days (2 hrs per day), British Snowboard School, details on request
Cross-country ESF 78FF for 2 hrs (morning), or 120FF for 3 hrs (afternoon). Loipe 45km at Super Morzine
Other courses telemark
Guiding companies through ski schools

CHILDREN
Lift pass 5-16 yrs, Avoriaz 111FF per day, Portes du Soleil 584FF for 6 days, free for 4 yrs and under
Ski kindergarten as ski school
Ski school Village des Enfants, 3-16 yrs, 1,095FF for 6 days including lunch
Non-ski kindergarten 3 mths-5 yrs: Halte Garderie, 9am-5.30pm, 205FF per day; Les P'tits Loups, 9am-6pm, 1,025FF for 6 days including lunch

FOOD AND DRINK PRICES
Coffee 6FF, glass of wine 12FF, small beer 18FF, dish of the day 65FF

Montriond
top 2350m (7,708ft) bottom 950m (3,116ft)

Montriond is little more than a suburb of Morzine, with no discernable centre and a number of simple, reasonably priced hotels. A bus links it to the resort's gondola, which provides direct access into the main lift system.

TOURIST OFFICE
Tel 33 4 50 79 12 81
Fax 33 4 50 79 04 06

Morgins
top 2350m (7,708ft) bottom 1350m (4,428ft)

Morgins is situated a few kilometres from Châtel, just over the pass of the same name, and is the border post with Switzerland. It is a spacious, residential resort spread across its broad valley, but it is not the ideal base for keen skiers because, quite simply, the best of Les Portes du Soleil's skiing is elsewhere. A car is useful for visiting other resorts in the region, but traffic is a problem at the beginning and end of the day due to day-trippers from other parts of Les Portes du Soleil.

Most of the accommodation is in chalets and apartments. We have received poor reports of the once popular Hostellerie Bellevue, which is described as 'rather tatty' with 'dinners uninspiring at best'. The resort is relaxed but short of any real character. It has a crèche, of which we have extremely positive reports. The large nursery slope in the centre of the village is prone to overcrowding.

Après-ski is limited to a natural skating rink, indoor tennis courts and a few bars. The Hotel Bellevue's disco provides some measure of lively late-night entertainment in season, and its swimming-pool is open to the public.

Several reporters have enjoyed the thermal baths at **Val d'Illiez**. The three cross-country loipe total 15km, and there is a long, marked but unprepared route to Champoussin. The village has three supermarkets as well as a butcher's shop and a bakery.

TOURIST OFFICE
Tel 41 25 77 23 61
Fax 41 25 77 37 08

St Jean d'Aulps/La Grande Terche
top 1800m (5,906ft) bottom 900m (2,952ft)

St Jean is the village, and La Grande Terche is the name given to a tiny development of apartments at the foot of the lifts, which are a 15-minute drive from Morzine. The skiing is not as yet fully linked into the system but it is surprisingly good and well worth a visit if you are staying elsewhere in the area. It has a combined ski area with **Bellevaux**.

Skiing facts: **Châtel**

TOURIST OFFICE
F-74390 Châtel, Haute Savoie
Tel 33 4 50 73 22 44
Fax 33 4 50 73 22 87

THE RESORT
By road Calais 900km
By rail Thonon les Bains 45 mins, regular
bus service to resort
By air Geneva 2 hrs
Visitor beds 18,000
Transport free bus between village and
Pré-la-Joux lift, and around resort

THE SKIING
Linked or nearby resorts Abondance (n),
Avoriaz (l), Champéry-Planachaux (l),
Champoussin (l), La Chapelle d'Abondance
(l), Les Crosets (l), Les Gets (l), Montriond
(l), Morgins (l), Morzine (l), Saint Jean
d'Aulps/La Grande Terche (n), Torgon (l)
Longest run Linga, 1km (red/black)
Number of lifts 40 in Châtel, 228 in Portes
du Soleil
Total of trails/pistes 82km in Châtel (22%
beginner, 27% easy, 39% intermediate,
12% difficult), 650km in Portes du Soleil
Nursery slopes 13 runs
Summer skiing none
Snowmaking 10 mobile snow-cannon

LIFT PASSES
Area pass Portes du Soleil (covers 13
resorts), 885FF for 6 days. Châtel only
660FF for 6 days
Day pass Châtel 150FF, Portes du Soleil
195FF
Beginners no free lifts
Pensioners 60 yrs and over, Châtel 491FF

for 6 days, Portes du Soleil 584FF for 6 days
Credit cards accepted yes

SKI SCHOOLS
Adults ESF, 510FF for 6 days (2 hrs per
day), ESI, 9am-midday, 610FF for 6 days,
Stages Henri Gonon, 600FF for 5 days (3 hrs
per day) with video
Private lessons ESF 168FF per hr, ESI
175FF per hr, Stages Henri Gonon, prices on
request
Snowboarding ESF, 2.30-5pm, 740FF for 6
days. ESI, 2-5pm, 550FF for 5 afternoons
Cross-country ESF, 9.30am-midday,
510FF for 6 days. Loipe 24km (largest loipe
5km at Super-Châtel)
Other courses telemark, monoski, slalom,
moguls, Skwal
Guiding companies through ski schools

CHILDREN
Lift pass Châtel, 5-16 yrs, 491FF for 6
days, Portes du Soleil 584FF for 6 days, free
for 4 yrs and over
Ski kindergarten Le Village des
Marmottons, 14 mths-10 yrs, 9.30am-4pm,
1,020FF for 6 days including lunch
Ski school ESF, 5-14 yrs, 390-460FF for 6
days (2 hrs per day). ESI, 8 yrs and over,
610FF for 6 afternoons or ESI Juniors Club,
9am-5pm, 1,490FF for 5 days including
lunch
Non-ski kindergarten Le Village des
Marmottons, 14 mths-3 yrs, 8.30am-
5.30pm, 670FF for 6 days including lunch

FOOD AND DRINK PRICES
Coffee 6FF, glass of wine 12FF, small beer
15FF, dish of the day 65FF

Skiing facts: **Morzine**

TOURIST OFFICE
BP 23, F-74110 Morzine, Haute Savoie
Tel 33 4 50 74 72 72
Fax 33 4 50 79 03 48

THE RESORT
By road Calais 880km
By rail Cluses or Thonon les Bains 30km
By air Geneva 1½ hrs
Visitor beds 16,000
Transport free bus service runs throughout
Morzine and to Avoriaz (Les Prodains)

THE SKIING
Linked or nearby resorts Abondance (n),
Avoriaz (I), Champéry-Planachaux (I),
Champoussin (I), La Chapelle d'Abondance
(I), Châtel (I), Les Crosets (I), Les Gets (I),
Montriond (I), Morgins (I), Saint Jean
d'Aulps/La Grande Terche (n), Torgon (I)
Longest run Piste Chamossière, 11km
(red)
Number of lifts 66 in Morzine, 228 in
Portes du Soleil
Total of trails/pistes 133km in Morzine
(13% beginner, 37% easy, 37% intermedi-
ate, 13% difficult), 650km in Portes du
Soleil
Nursery slopes 2 lifts
Summer skiing none
Snowmaking 85 hectares covered

LIFT PASSES
Area pass Pleney-Nyon/Les Gets, 695FF for
6 days. Portes du Soleil (covers 13 resorts)

885FF for 6 days
Day pass Pleney-Nyon/Les Gets 139FF,
Portes du Soleil 195FF
Beginners special prices for some lifts
Pensioners as children
Credit cards accepted yes

SKI SCHOOLS
Adults ESF, 520FF for 6 half-days, British
Alpine Ski School, details on request
Private lessons ESF, 165FF per hr
Snowboarding ESF private lessons 165FF
per hr, group lessons as regular ski school
Cross-country ESF private lessons 165FF
per hr. Loipe 97km in Vallée de la Manche,
Super-Morzine, Pleney and around Lac de
Montriond
Other courses race training
Guiding companies through ski school

CHILDREN
Lift pass 5-16 yrs, Morzine only 522FF for 6
days, Portes du Soleil 584FF for 6 days, free
for 4 yrs and under
Ski kindergarten ESF, 4-12 yrs, 8.30am-
6pm, 875FF for 6 days (2½ hrs per day).
Leisure Centre OUTA, 8.30am-6pm,
1,275FF for 6 days
Ski school as ski kindergarten
Non-ski kindergarten Halte Garderie, 2
mths-4 yrs, 8.30am-6pm, 865FF for 6 days

FOOD AND DRINK PRICES
Coffee 6FF, glass of wine 12FF, small beer
15FF, dish of the day 65FF

TOURIST OFFICE
Tel 33 4 50 79 65 09
Fax 33 4 50 79 67 95

Torgon
top 2350m (7,708ft) bottom 1100m (3,608ft)

Torgon is perched above the Rhône close to Lac Léman on the outer edge of Les Portes du Soleil. Although it is in Switzerland, it is linked in one direction with La Chapelle and in the other with Châtel, both of which are in France. Access is only possible by road from the French side of the lake; this makes it somewhat isolated. The distinctive and none-too-pleasing A-frame architecture contains comfortable apartments. Last season the resort's two lift companies went into receivership, a fact that emphasises the uneasy relationship between the member resorts of Les Portes du Soleil. However, we are assured that the links will remain in operation. There is little else to do here but ski.

TOURIST OFFICE
Tel 41 25 81 31 31
Fax 41 25 81 46 20

Risoul 1850

ALTITUDE 1850m (6,068ft)

Risoul is a purpose-built family resort, inconveniently located three to five hours' drive from Chambéry, Turin or Lyon, where sunshine and tree-level skiing rival the Colorado Rockies at less than half the price. Risoul, which overlooks the Ecrins National Park, was planned as a ski resort back in the 1930s but the area never actually came into being until 1977. It is sometimes described as the largest ski network in southern France; its 54 lifts and 170km of pistes shared with **Vars** are known as the Domaine de la Forêt Blanche. Risoul is free of weekend overcrowding. The clientèle is both family- and budget-oriented. Eastern European visitors are now arriving by the bus-load, supplanting British skiers among the 30 per cent of skiers who are not French. Although animated, the resort is seldom rowdy.

■ **GOOD POINTS**

Sunny and scenic tree-level skiing, value-for-money, convenient for families, lack of queues, good snow record, late-season skiing

■ **BAD POINTS**

Long resort transfer, limited chalet and hotel accommodation, lack of restaurants on and off the mountain

On the mountain
top 2750m (9,020ft) bottom 1650m (5,412ft)

Risoul is primarily a resort for beginners and intermediates, although there are also off-piste opportunities — skiing through the larch trees in the sunshine at an altitude of 2000m is an experience seldom enjoyed in the main Alps. Lifts fan out from the village base: one leg goes to the snowboard area at L'Homme de Pierre, while a long, tiring drag-lift leads left to Pointe de Razis and the liaison with Vars. From Risoul the skiing looks easy and most of it is, although experts can find some challenging terrain. Risoul offers three slalom race-training areas, a mogul-training course and a speed-skiing piste. Except for the 'back bowl' area, as the Col de la Valbelle sector is known locally, both Risoul and Vars have slopes exposed to an advertised 300 days of sunshine per year. Risoul's lift system still has a predominance of drag-lifts and is in need of upgrading; the only high-speed chair and the only gondola are in Vars. Queues from the Risoul departure point are rarely longer than 15 minutes even during the French school holidays.

Beginners
Vars has the longest and easiest runs of the two resorts. It is possible to ski from Risoul to Vars and back on blue (easy) runs, although the long

drag-lift from Risoul is discouraging. The green (beginner) runs with a children's park and snowmaking at the bottom of Risoul are some of the most attractive in the Alps. The French Ski School (ESF) beginner area has its own bucket-lift.

Intermediates
A number of readers have complained that the resort has arbitrarily changed some of its blue runs to red (intermediate). The official explanation is that these runs can be exactingly narrow for beginners. However, more cynical observers suggest that Risoul wants to upgrade its 'too easy' image. The liaison reds marked 17 and 19 on the piste-map are crowded. More interesting are the ridge-line run from Risoul's high point, Crête de Chabrières, and the return to the village from the liaison on Razis (numbers 21/22), which requires a hike back up from below the car park. Virtually unskied are the long, wide, mogul-free reds into **Vars-Sainte-Marie**.

Advanced
There are only eight black (difficult) runs, which readers say are graded more for their lack of grooming rather than their gradient. This is not a place for advanced piste-bashers.

Off-piste
Risoul has neither glaciers nor couloirs, but it does have a lot of gladed powder skiing in fresh snow conditions. There is a natural half-pipe shared by skiers and boarders in the back bowl by Valbelle. It is possible, given enough snow and the taxi fare home, to ski below the resort to the old village of Risoul. The ungroomed area to the skier's left of the Chardon chair also offers reasonable challenges.

Ski schools and guiding
The ESF claims an average of ten skiers per class, but reporters have spotted groups of 15 and complain that not enough instructors are available during peak holiday periods. One reader complains that British clients are a low priority when the resort is filled with French visitors. The rival International Ski School (ESI) guarantees no more than eight pupils per class, 'even during school holidays'.

Snowboarding
Risoul is on the way to becoming a major snowboarding centre, the best in France according to some riders. *News Cool* is a local weekly snowboarding newsletter, which tells you where to find the best snow and which areas to avoid, as well as announcing details of frequent surf events. The Surfland snowboard park on L'Homme de Pierre was the venue for the world's biggest boardercross competition last season. It has a Renault 16 to jump over, a quarter-pipe and numerous obstacles to 'bonk' (snowboard jargon for bump into and slide off). There is a natural half-pipe in the back bowl area. Gliss Concept is the specialist snowboard shop.

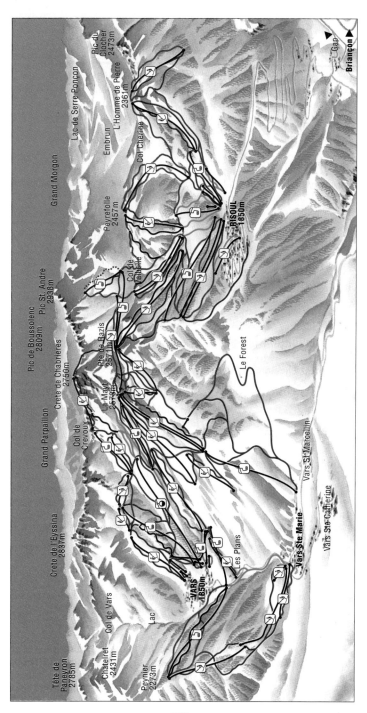

Tête de Paneyron
2785m

Crete de l'Eyssina
2837m

Grand Parpaillon

Col de Vars

Chatelret
2431m

Col de Crevoux

Crete de Chabrieres
2750m

Grand Morgon

Pic de Boussolenc
2809m

Pic St. André
2938m

Pic du Clocher
2473m

L'Homme de Pierre
2361m

Lac de Serre-Poncon

Embrun

Col Chérine

Peyrefolle
2457m

RISOUL
1850m

Col de l'Aiguille

Pte de Razis
2571m

La Mayt
2578m

Le Forest

Peynier
2273m

Lac

Les Plans

VARS
1850m

Vars-Ste-Marie

Vars-St-Marcellin

Vars-Ste-Catherine

Gap

Briançon

Mountain restaurants

If skiing with a sandwich is ever to make a comeback it may be in Risoul, where the eating places are cheap enough but seriously lacking in both cuisine and character. Barjo at the bottom of the Mayt chair on the Vars side offers overnight accommodation and food. Vallon and Valbelle are small spaghetti and steak-frites joints.

Off the mountain

Attractive as the skiing and wood-and-stone apartment complexes are, the small 'downtown' section is ruined by illegally parked cars, a lack of proper pavements and a ghastly profusion of signboards. All except 200 of Risoul's 13,000 guests stay in self-catered apartments. There is no shuttle bus, nor is there shopping of any note. Risoul has a small cinema and a skating rink, but no swimming-pool. The resort features live bands and fireworks during holiday periods, plus night-time snowboard jumping contests.

■ OTHER SPORTS

Snow-shoeing, parapente, snow mobiling, Skwal, ruissiling (hiking with crampons and ice axes on frozen rivers)

Accommodation

The two-star Le Morgan is the only hotel in Risoul 1850, and is right in the centre. The hotels down in the valley in the old village of Risoul are not practical to stay in without a car. There is some chalet accommodation, but most visitors opt for self-catering apartments. Les Mélèzes is functional and Le Bélvèdere is bigger and better. La Forêt Blanche offers both character and comfort, particularly in its split-level apartments.

Eating in and out

'It doesn't really matter where you go to eat', claims a reporter who lives in Risoul. Most of the eateries are unambitious in price as well as menu. Cheap and plentiful are the burgers and frites at Snack Attack, and Au Point Chaud is the place to go for pizzas. Phil Good and Le Cesier Snowboard Café have low prices and frequent special offers. L'Assiette Gourmand is the closest thing to gourmet cuisine.

Après-ski

The Grotte du Yeti is the young person's haunt for happy hour after the lifts close. Safari Club and Morgan's are the only two discos, the former featuring exotic shows with 'Jane and her serpents'. Phil Good has live bands and games but is still quiet enough for a conversation.

Childcare

Les Pitchouns crèche is conveniently located above the tourist office and takes children from six months to six years of age. A packed lunch must be provided if children are to be left all day. Both the ESF and ESI have children's learning areas.

Skiing facts: **Risoul 1850**

TOURIST OFFICE
Risoul 1850, F-05600 Guillestre,
Hautes-Alpes
Tel 33 4 92 46 02 60
Fax 33 4 92 46 01 23

THE RESORT
By road Calais 1024km
By rail Montdauphin 30 mins, bus
connection with Risoul
By air Grenoble 3 hrs, Marseille 3 hrs
Visitor beds 12,700
Transport none

THE SKIING
Linked or nearby resorts Vars (l),
Vars-Sainte-Marie (l)
Longest run Les Marmottes, 2.1km (blue)
Number of lifts 54
Total of trails/pistes 170km (24% easy,
69% intermediate, 7% difficult)
Nursery slopes 6 lifts
Summer skiing none
Snowmaking 29 hectares covered in Risoul
and Vars

LIFT PASSES
Area pass (covers Risoul and Vars) 780FF
for 6 days
Day pass 150FF
Beginners 80FF per day and 1 free lift
Pensioners reduction for 60 yrs and over,

free for 70 yrs and over
Credit cards accepted yes

SKI SCHOOLS
Adults ESF 395FF and ESI 540FF, both for
6 x 2 hrs
Private lessons ESF 160FF per hr, ESI
175FF per hr
Snowboarding ESF 390FF and ESI 540FF,
both for 6 x 2 hrs
Cross-country ESF 85FF for 2 hrs. ESI,
prices on request. Loipe 30km
Other courses monoski, Skwal, telemark,
slalom
Guiding companies through ESF and ESI

CHILDREN
Lift pass 5-11 yrs, 660FF for 6 days, free
for 4 yrs and under
Ski kindergarten ESF Mini-Club, 5-12 yrs,
380FF for 6 x 2 hrs. ESI, 4-12 yrs, 85FF for
2 hrs
Ski school ESF, 3 yrs and over,
395FF for 6 x 2 hrs. ESI, 2-3 yrs,
115FF for 3 hrs
Non-ski kindergarten Les Pitchouns,
6 mths-6 yrs, 8.45am-5.15pm, 600FF for
6 days not including lunch

FOOD AND DRINK PRICES
Coffee 7FF, glass of wine 7FF, small beer
12FF, dish of the day 60FF

Linked or nearby resorts
Vars
top 2750m (9,020ft) bottom 1850m (6,068ft)
Vars is less attractive than Risoul and also less welcoming to the British.
No tour operators currently come here. The old village is linked by drag-lift to the modern station, but you have to hike across town to access Vars' gondola and high-speed chair back to Risoul.

Serre Chevalier/Briançon

ALTITUDE 1200-1500m (3,936-4,920ft)

Serre Chevalier is not one but three separate villages grouped along a valley between the Col du Lautaret and the ancient garrison town of Briançon. Ten other hamlets share the ski area, and Briançon, just five minutes' drive away, has a gondola link.

Of the three main villages, **Villeneuve/Le Bez** (marketed as Serre Chevalier 1400) is the most central and lively, while **Monêtier-Les-Bains** (Serre Chevalier 1500) is both the sleepiest and prettiest. **Chantemerle** (Serre Chevalier 1350) and Villeneuve share most of the visitor accommodation and have the best after-skiing facilities. All three are hamlets, which over the years have been added to with a hotch-potch of newer architecture mainly along the busy Grenoble–Briançon road, which cuts through their centres. **Briançon** is a pleasant town in a beautiful setting, with the added attraction of hill-top fortifications built by Napoleon's engineer, Le Marquis de Vauban. These enclose a maze of delightful streets and alleyways reminiscent of a miniature Carcassone.

A car is a definite plus and helps you to take advantage of the off-slope facilities in both Serre Chevalier and Briançon, and the Grande Galaxie lift pass, which covers five nearby resorts including **Montgenèvre** in the Milky Way area, 15 minutes down the road. The skiing is for all standards, but is particularly well suited to the good intermediate, who will enjoy the 250km of cruising and the well-linked, albeit now rather old-fashioned, lift system.

■ GOOD POINTS

Large ski area, good artificial snow-cover, varied off-piste, tree-level skiing, extensive cross-country trails, good children's facilities, value for money

■ BAD POINTS

Heavy traffic along main highway, strung-out resort, unreliable resort-level snow, long airport transfer

Reporters are unanimous in their praise of the resort and its skiing: 'Serre Chevalier is one of France's best-kept skiing secrets. I loved being here and would unhesitatingly come again and bring all my friends'. Friendly locals are another plus: 'The ski-lift attendants, instructors and bus drivers are noticeably more cheerful than in established international resorts such as Méribel — a very helpful and unspoilt lot'.

On the mountain
top 2800m (9,184ft) bottom 1200m (3,936ft)
The three main mountain access-points are by gondola and cable car from Villeneuve/Le Bez, Chantemerle and Briançon, with most of the lifts and pistes concentrated in the area above Villeneuve and

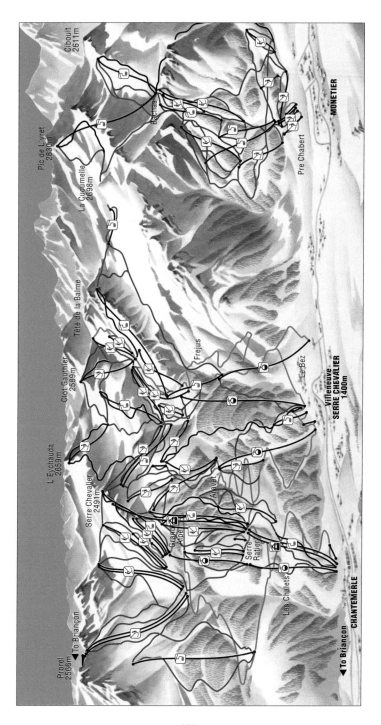

Ciboul 2611m

Barrus

MONETIER

Pre Chabert

Pic de L'yret 2830m

La Cucumelle 2698m

Tête de la Balme

Frejus

Le-Bez

Villeneuve
SERRE CHEVALIER
1400m

Clot Gauthier 2589m

L'Eychauda 2659m

Serre Chevalier 2491m

Aravet

Grand Alpe

Serre Ratier

Les Chalets

Prorel 2566m

▼ To Briançon

▼ To Briançon
CHANTEMERLE

253

Chantemerle. The Monêtier section also has its own lifts starting from the base and is the most appealing in the whole area, although the least accessible. Serre Chevalier's upper slopes are open and rather exposed to the weather, but the lower slopes are well protected by trees. Briançon has a floodlit piste for night-skiing. Snowmaking is extensive on the lower runs, and a good bus system links all the villages. According to reporters 'the piste-marking leaves a lot to be desired'. However, the area is praised for its lack of queues.

Beginners

Novice skiers are well catered for with a choice of ten nursery slopes, and ski schools offering beginner tuition in all the main villages. The Grand Alpe area above Chantemerle has a good but sometimes busy beginner area, and Briançon has a beginner area of its own at the 1625-m gondola mid-station. Both Monêtier and Villeneuve have commendable nursery slopes and beginner lifts at their bases. For those who have mastered the nursery slopes, a long green (beginner) run from Col Méa at the top of the ski area, all the way down to Villeneuve/Le Bez, is the next step.

Intermediates

The area is best suited to intermediate skiers. One reporter notes: 'For an average skier there are few better places'. Monêtier has some enjoyable red (intermediate) pistes through the woods. The Vallon de la Cucumelle above Fréjus is a recommended red run, but it can become icy in spring — 'varied from being wide and treeless at the top to narrow and mogulled in a few places, although nothing a three- to four-week skier could not cope with'. From Bachas at 2180m down to the valley at Monêtier there is a good choice of intermediate runs through the woods. Le Bois is a short but fun red piste through the trees.

Advanced

Overall, Monêtier is the best area of the mountain for advanced skiers, although the high and exposed link with Villeneuve can sometimes be closed, both in harsh weather conditions and at the end of the season when the slopes quickly lose their snow. Isolée is an exciting black (difficult) run, which starts on the ridge from L'Eychauda at 2659m and plunges down towards Echaillon. Tabuc is a long black through the woods with a couple of steep and narrow pitches. The Casse du Boeuf, a sweeping ridge through the trees back to Villeneuve, is 'outstanding' and 'the best black run we have ever skied'.

Off-piste

The Fréjus-Echaillon section above Villeneuve provides some of the best runs for experienced skiers, with short and unprepared trails beneath the mountain crest. The Yret chair gives easy access to some off-piste runs including the testing face under the lift, which has a gradient of 35 degrees at its steepest point and often becomes mogulled. The Serre Chevalier lift map includes a separate map of off-piste itineraries.

Ski schools and guiding

We have generally favourable reports of the French Ski School (ESF) in both Serre Chevalier and Briançon, although a sound knowledge of spoken English is not always high on the list of the instructors' qualities. There are five ski schools in Serre Chevalier and six mountain guiding companies for off-piste skiing. The Buisonnière Ski School is 'excellent, with small groups; the instructor had a sense of humour and the tuition was clear'. Both the ESF and Buisonnière's private lessons are recommended, but we have no reports of the International Ski School (ESI) in Villeneuve/Le Bez and Chantemerle.

Snowboarding

All the ski schools offer snowboarding lessons for all ages. First Tracks, which is run by the ESF, is a specialist ski school in Villeneuve. Its snowboarding camps include half-board accommodation, lift passes and video tuition for beginners through to advanced-level boarders. There is a half-pipe at the bottom of the Yret chair-lift.

Cross-country

Serre Chevalier is a major centre for *ski de fond* with loipe for all standards. Chantemerle has three tracks, and there are four at Villeneuve. Monêtier has the most variety, with five tracks providing a total of 45km of loipe in the area.

Mountain restaurants

The choice of eating places is small for an area of this size and the quality is mixed. La Bachas is recommended, and Jacques A is 'crowded, but the place to go to at 4.40pm every day as it has the best atmosphere'. Neighbouring Le Brianche was also praised by one reporter. L'Echaillon is said to be 'pretty and off the beaten track, with friendly staff', but is also said to be the 'poorest value for money'. Le Grand Alpe serves 'big portions', and Aravet 2000 at the top of the Aravet gondola is criticised as 'mediocre, with bland food and casual service'.

Off the mountain

Monêtier is the furthest resort from Briançon and is the quietest and least-affected by modern architecture. It is a charming rural spa village, which attracts fewer tourists than its neighbours. Next along the valley is Villeneuve, with its oldest section, Le Bez, at the top of the village and closest to the slopes. At the bottom of the village beside the river is an attractive narrow street with bars and restaurants. In the centre and above the main road is Villeneuve itself, a collection of modern apartment buildings including a small shopping centre. Chantemerle is the closest village to Briançon and acts as a base-station for commuters staying elsewhere in the valley. It has a good shopping centre.

The old town of Briançon became a ski resort when the Prorel gondola was built just a few years ago. It is the main commercial centre of the region and the last major town before the Italian border. It does not have the atmosphere of a typical ski resort. However, the advantages of staying in a real town include a large choice of shops and restaurants.

Accommodation

Most of Serre Chevalier's accommodation is in apartments, some 40 hotels throughout the three main villages and more than 20 in Briançon. The Altea, Vauban and Parc hotels are the town's three-stars. The Pension des Ramparts is a small and simple hotel with a loyal following. Le Clos de Chantemerle is a popular two-star with good food. L'Alliey in Monêtier is a charming and central hotel with a fine menu. L'Auberge du Choucas, also in Monêtier, is known for its gastronomic cuisine. The Christiania in Villeneuve is on the main road, so make sure you ask for a room overlooking the river rather than the traffic. The Lièvre Blanc, also in Villeneuve, is a British-owned two-star, which is warmly recommended.

■ **OTHER SPORTS**

Ice-driving, snow-shoeing, aeroclub, parapente, hang-gliding, swimming, helicopter rides, skating, husky rides, winter walks, night-skiing, sleigh rides

Eating in and out

A car is useful for visiting the many restaurants along the valley. Le Petit Duc is a friendly crêperie beside the river in the lower part of Villeneuve/Le Bez. Pastelli in Le Bez has been criticised for its 'unimaginative food'. Le Bidule in Le Bez ('excellent, with a huge choice') has a friendly ambience and specialises in fresh fish and seafood. L'Auberge du Choucas in Monêtier serves fine regional cuisine. L'Aigle Fin in Chantemerle's new commercial centre is recommended. Le Passé Simple in Briançon has a historic Vauban menu with recipes from the seventeenth century. Le Napoleon is praised for its pizzas. The Rallye hypermarket in Briançon is the best place for food shopping.

Après-ski

All three villages are quiet places after dusk, with nightlife mainly confined to the bars, although Le Frog and L'Iceberg discos in Villeneuve are both recommended. Others include Le Serre Che in Chantemerle, La Bàita in Villeneuve/Le Bez and Le Sous Sol in Monêtier. Le Yeti in Chantemerle is lively with 'a real, comfortable, warm bar upstairs'. The old fortified town of Briançon is well worth a visit; as well as its steep cobblestone streets and range of shops and restaurants, the views from the ramparts are breathtaking.

Childcare

Each village has its own crèche and children's ski school. Kids de l'Aventure in Monêtier is a fully-catered course for children aged between 10 and 15 years old, which includes ski tuition and other activities. Le Petit Train, a toy train on road wheels that carts skiers and non-skiers around Villeneuve, is extremely popular with small children.

Skiing facts: **Serre Chevalier**

TOURIST OFFICE
BP 20, F-05240 La Salle Les Alpes,
Hautes-Alpes
Tel 33 4 92 24 71 88
Fax 33 4 92 24 76 18

THE RESORT
By road Calais 1159km
By rail Briançon 6km, regular bus service
to resort
By air Lyon 3 hrs, Turin 2 hrs,
Grenoble 2½ hrs
Visitor beds 30,000
Transport free ski bus with lift pass and
regular bus service between all centres

THE SKIING
Linked or nearby resorts Briançon (l),
Montgenèvre (n), La Grave (n), Les Deux
Alpes (n), Puy-St-Vincent (n)
Longest run L'Yret, 1.3km (red)
Number of lifts 72 in Grand Serre Chevalier
area
Total of trails/pistes 250km in
linked area
Nursery slopes 10 runs
Summer skiing none
Snowmaking 13km covered

LIFT PASSES
Area pass Grand Serre Chevalier
(covers all centres) 835FF for 6 days
including 1 day in each of Les Deux Alpes,
La Grave, Montgenèvre, Puy-St-Vincent
and Alpe d'Huez
Day pass 167FF
Beginners no free lifts
Pensioners 60 yrs and over as children
Credit cards accepted yes

SKI SCHOOLS
Adults ESF (1350, 1400, 1500) and ESI
(1350, 1400), 610-780FF for 6 days
Private lessons 155-165FF per hr
Snowboarding ESF (1350, 1400, 1500)
and ESI (1350, 1400), prices as regular ski
lessons. First Tracks, 2,700-3,400FF for 6
days, including video tuition, lift pass and
half-board accommodation
Cross-country ESF (1350, 1400, 1500)
and ESI (1350, 1400), 160FF for 3 hrs,
licence 130FF per wk. Loipe 45km
Other courses telemark, monoski, Skwal,
race-training
Guiding companies Bureau des Guides du
Serre d'Aigle, Compagnie des Guides de
L'Oisans, Ecole Buissonnière, Montagne et
Ski, Montagne à la Carte, Ecole de
l'Aventure

CHILDREN
Lift pass 6-12 yrs, 550FF for 6 days, free
for 5 yrs and under
Ski kindergarten Kids Club (1500), 9am-
7pm, 1,450FF for 5 days including lunch
Ski school ESF (1350, 1400, 1500) 505FF
for 6 days, ESI (1350, 1400) 780FF for 6
days
Non-ski kindergarten Les Poussins,
8 mths and over, 9am-5pm, 205FF per day
including lunch. Les Schtroumpfs, 6 mths
and over, 9am-5pm, 175FF per day not
including lunch. Halte de Pré Chabert, 18
mths and over, 180FF per day not including
lunch, 1,000FF for 6 full days

FOOD AND DRINK PRICES
Coffee 6FF, glass of wine 18FF, small beer
15FF, dish of the day 35FF

The Trois Vallées

ALTITUDE Méribel 1450-1700m (4,756-5,576ft), Courchevel 1300-1850m
(4,264-6,068ft), Val Thorens 2300m (7,544ft), Les Menuires 1850m (6,068ft)

The French, who rarely venture beyond their own mountains, claim with dubious justification that the Trois Vallées is the largest ski area in the world. While the true winner in this category is almost certainly the Sella Ronda in the Dolomites, the Trois Vallées team is top on the international podium for best all-rounder.

MERIBEL
■ GOOD POINTS

Superb mountain access, large ski area, widest choice of luxury chalets in the Alps, resort-level snow (1700m), extensive nursery slopes, suitable for all standards of skier

■ BAD POINTS

Heavy traffic and limited parking, skiing inconvenience from much of the accommodation, limited nightlife

At one end, above the Bozel Valley, sits chic **Courchevel 1850** with its not-so-chic satellites of 1650, 1550 and Le Praz beneath it. At the other end, the pastoral Belleville Valley is dominated by functional **Val Thorens** and the *bête noire*, **Les Menuires**. In the middle is cosmopolitan **Méribel** with its British bulldog overtones. The skiing is reached by two winding mountain roads from Moûtiers or by an under-used gondola from **Brides-Les-Bains**.

What puts the Trois Vallées ski-lengths ahead of its rivals in the super-circus league is the range and sophistication of the resorts it contains, coupled with the variety of skiing on offer. An ideal topography means that even the links between each valley are serious runs in their own right.

Its critics claim that 90 per cent of the skiing is geared towards intermediates, but then 90 per cent of skiers are intermediate, and it still provides more than adequate scope for those of greater or lesser ability. This substantial chunk of the French Alps is covered by what is considered to be the most efficient overall lift system in any country.

The combination of cable cars, gondolas, detachable chairs and tows is of gargantuan proportions and improves each year. Mammoth, the largest US resort, has 30 lifts; the Trois Valleés has 200, all of them linked by a mighty 600km of prepared slopes and uncounted hectares of off-piste terrain. Méribel alone has an extraordinary 16 gondolas.

Given a single week's holiday, a competent skier will barely scratch the surface. It takes a whole 20-week season based in at least two different resorts to get to serious grips with it. However, the area is not without faults. The mountains are managed by an uneasy alliance of seven separate lift companies, each of which looks after itself extremely well and pays lip service to its agreement with the others. The result is a series of exasperating shortfalls; ski passes are checked on almost every lift, and the unnecessarily complicated ticket struc-

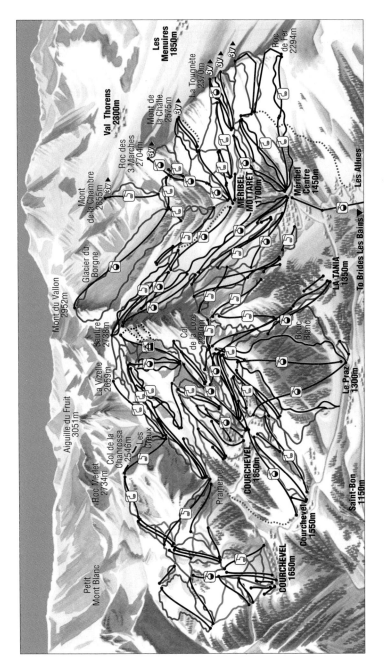

ture does not include half-day area lift tickets.

The French regard the Trois Vallées as their premier destination. At peak holiday times all 115,000 beds will be taken, but even at New Year it passes the acid test of good ski areas: when the whole area is operational you will struggle to find a queue of 15 minutes anywhere on the mountain.

Each resort has its own character as well as its individual ski area, aside from the hundreds of kilometres they share. Méribel has such a strong British chalet-holiday tradition that in some bars French is either the second language or not spoken at all. Courchevel is ultra-chic and international, at least at 1850, where designer ski suits outnumber their chain-store counterparts. Les Menuires could not be a bigger contrast: it is a budget resort where the main evening entertainment for the hard-core of bourgeois French who make up its winter inhabitants comes from watching the rented television set in their rented apartment or walking the dog that accompanies them on holiday. Val Thorens, architecturally slightly more pleasing, is for skiers who want to be as sure of finding snow in early December as in late April. Brides-Les-Bains in the valley below Méribel is connected by a 25-minute gondola ride and provides a budget base and useful back door into the system.

COURCHEVEL
■ GOOD POINTS

Big vertical drop, excellent nursery slopes, suitable for all standards of skier, long cruising runs, tree-level skiing, resort-level snow (1850m), gourmet restaurants, wide choice of luxury accommodation, skiing convenience, large ski area

■ BAD POINTS

Limited activities for non-skiers, high prices in Courchevel 1850

On the mountain
top 3300m (10,825ft) bottom 1300m (4,264ft)

Each resort has its own large ski area, which is covered by a single-valley local pass. Less than confident intermediates are strongly advised to take stock of what is on offer before buying the more expensive Trois Vallées pass. The links between the three valleys are liable to be suspended when snow-cover is insufficient, or in storm conditions. You should also note that the standard Trois Vallées lift map is printed back to front, and Courchevel 1650, which appears to be the most westerly resort in the complex, is in fact the most easterly. What appear to be south-facing slopes are in fact north-facing and consequently hold the snow well.

Les Allues Valley, dominated by Méribel and its higher satellite of **Mottaret**, lies in the middle and provides the ideal jumping-off point for exploring the whole area, but does not necessarily give the easiest access to the most rewarding of the skiing.

Both sides of the open valley are networked with modern lifts for all standards of skier. The western side culminates in a long skiable ridge, which separates it from the beautiful Belleville Valley and the resorts of Val Thorens, Les Menuires and **Saint-Martin-de-Belleville**.

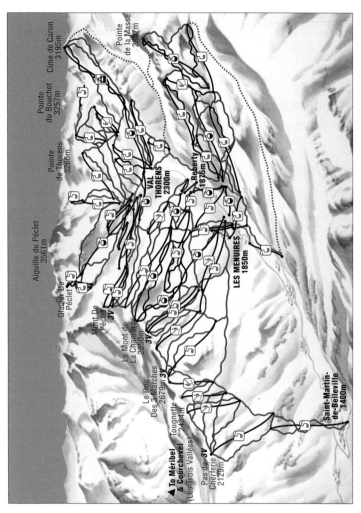

The eastern side rises to the rocky 2738-m summit of Saulire and the Col de la Loze at 2274m. Beyond lies the Bozel Valley and Courchevel — not one but four separate resorts at different altitudes — as well as the modern, purpose-built addition of **La Tania**. At the head of Les Allues Valley lies the 2952-m Mont du Vallon, the most easterly of the horseshoe of 3300-m peaks accessed from Méribel and Val Thorens, which provides some of the most scenic and demanding off-piste in the region.

The ski area has now been extended over the back, beyond Val Thorens and the Cime de Caron into a fourth valley, the Maurienne. The red (intermediate) run down of 660m vertical takes you down to the Chalet Refuge de Plan Bouchet at 2350m, from where a fast chair takes you back up to the Col de Rosaël. Last season a new gondola opened from Orelle (880m) in the Maurienne, which carries skiers up to Plan Bouchet. The small town of **St Michel de Maurienne**, previously known only for the quality of its carved choir stalls, has now become a new tourist gateway into the Trois Vallées. The area is now within a two-hour drive from Turin via the Fréjus Tunnel, and a large increase in the number of Italian skiers can be expected.

VAL THORENS
■ GOOD POINTS

Resort-level snow, long skiing season, large ski area, glacier skiing, ski-in ski-out convenience at its best

■ BAD POINTS

Lack of tree-level skiing, exposed and cold in mid-winter, limited for non-skiers, lack of après-ski, late-season lift queues

LES MENUIRES
■ GOOD POINTS

Suitable for all standards of skier, large ski area, long cruising runs, sunny slopes, off-piste skiing, well-run children's village, budget prices, extensive snowmaking

■ BAD POINTS

Ugly architecture in centre, heavy traffic, limited après-ski, lack of tree-line runs, limited for non-skiers

Beginners

Facilities for beginners are good in all the major resorts of the Trois Vallées, although the sheer volume of visitors here is bound to lead to a level of impersonal instruction, which is not conducive to the early-learning process. The runs surrounding the altiports at both Courchevel and Méribel are excellent beginner areas with enough length to help build confidence. The green (beginner) Truite run connecting Mottaret with Méribel is popular with novice ski classes, but more proficient skiers taking the whole run 'in the tuck' on their way to lunch can be unnerving.

Once the basics have been conquered, the area lends itself to easy exploration. Les Teppes Noires followed by Le Gros Tougne and L'Allée take you from Méribel via the Tougnette gondola down to Les Menuires. It is an ideal chance for second-week skiers to feel they are really going somewhere.

Intermediates

The Trois Vallées constitutes what many skiers rightly regard as the greatest intermediate playground in the world: a seemingly endless network of moderately graded runs that provide challenge to all levels of skier. The Combe de Vallon is a magnificent cruise of 1100 vertical metres from the top of Mont Vallon all the way down to Méribel Mottaret. The Cime de Caron above Val Thorens is more famous for its Combe du Caron black (difficult) descent, but there is also a red (intermediate) variation around the shoulder, as well as the long and scenic Itinéraire du Lou.

The blue (easy) Arondiaz trail from the top of Courchevel 1650 back down to the resort is a great last run of the day, and its north-facing aspect usually guarantees excellent conditions.

Advanced

With a maximum gradient of around 38 degrees, the couloirs of Courchevel are among the most radical black runs marked on any piste-map in the world. Take the 150-person cable car up from the Courchevel side of Saulire and exercise special care on the entry route, which can be dangerously icy. In most conditions, the runs are not as difficult as they look from below.

The Courchevel side of Saulire is the starting point for a magnificent descent of 1400 vertical metres to **Le Praz**. It is more tiring than techni-cally difficult, apart from the black Jockeys piste on the final section, which is shaded for most of the winter and consequently icy.

La Masse above Les Menuires boasts Les Enverses and the usually icy La Dame Blanche.

Off-piste

The guided off-piste opportunities are outstanding, and one of the great charms of the Trois Vallées is that after a major dump the best powder runs are some of the most accessible. The long runs down to Les Menuires from the Méribel ridge are exciting.

The summit of La Masse on the far side of the Belleville Valley is also the starting point for long itineraries towards St-Martin as well into the Vallon du Lou. Roc Merlet above Courchevel 1650 is the jump-off point for a glorious descent around the shoulder into the Avals Valley, which brings you back, after a short walk, to 1650. Mont Vallon and the Col du Fruit offer further excitement.

Ski schools and guiding

Courchevel has Masterclass, its own British ski school, run by Alan Hole and Kenny and Sue Dickson. It is staffed by eight BASI instructors who have all passed the rigorous *équivalence* test, which allows them to work legally as instructors in France. We also have positive reports of Ski Academy at Courchevel 1850, where class size is restricted to seven and instructors are described as 'patient and sympathetic'. Ski Cocktail in Méribel provides a viable alternative to the French Ski School (ESF); instructors are praised for their sympathetic attitude, although the stan-dard of English is not always as high as could be expected of a school set up primarily for the Anglo-Saxon market. The ESF International Section provides the only real competition. Magic in Motion in Méribel maintains a lower profile. Both Val Thorens and Les Menuires have the ESF and International Ski School (ESI).

Snowboarding

Méribel has a half-pipe at the top of the Plattières gondola. In Courchevel 1850 the Gansen slope is especially for boarders. The ESF and several of the independent schools teach snowboarding, but there is a surprising lack of dedicated specialists.

Cross-country

Méribel has some the most delightful terrain for *ski de fond* in the region. There are 33km around the Lac de Tueda and the altiport. The Belleville Valley offers 28km of loipe around Les Menuires and St-Martin.

Mountain restaurants

The majority of mountain restaurants in the Trois Vallées serve bland fast-food at truly shocking prices, and regular visitors tend to head down into the resorts at lunchtime. Pierre Plat at the top of the Saulire gondola wins a special award for overpriced fare and sullen service. Staff refuse to supply tap water for free.

Try Bel-Air at the top of the Courchevel 1650 gondola and La Soucoupe above Courchevel 1850. Chalet de Pierres above Courchevel 1850, with liveried waiters hovering on the edge of the piste, is a gastromic delight, but very expensive. Le Kalico at Courchevel 1850 is recommended. Le Bouc Blanc at the top of La Tania gondola is always welcoming. Pub Le Ski Lodge down in La Tania is said to offer 'the cheapest lunches in the Trois Vallées'. Roc Tania is a new restaurant on the Col de la Loze ridge.

Les Castors, at the foot of the Truite run in Méribel, has great spaghetti cooked in individual copper pans. Roc des Trois Marches offers consistently good value. Plein Soleil at Mottaret is 'perfect for a sunny day lunch'. Les Rhododendrons offers 'a smashing burger and chips'. Les Crêtes, at the top of the Tougnètes gondola, is recommended along with the Chalet de Togniat at the top of the Combes chair-lift above Mottaret.

L'Ours Blanc is the smartest hotel in Les Menuires and serves 'excellent value lunches'. Chez Jacques is an old hut just off the piste above Les Menuires. Jacques doesn't always cook, but when the mood takes him, his are the finest and cheapest *steak frites* on the mountain. Quatres Vents above Les Bruyères has a strong following.

Off the mountain

Méribel alone attracts more British skiers than anywhere in the Alps, except for Val d'Isère, which explains why half the legally bonded British tour operators are offering holidays here this season. Indeed, so many British people holiday or work in the resort during the winter months that any attempt to order a drink or a meal in French can be met with a look of blank incomprehension. It is a smart, expensive resort, which offers more luxury-class chalets and apartments with en-suite bathrooms than any other ski destination.

The resort was founded by an Englishman; dedicated pre-war skier Colonel Peter Lindsay built the first lift here in 1938. Amazingly, the resort has stayed faithful to his original concept of a traditional chalet village; every building has been constructed in local stone and wood in harmony with the mountain setting. Today, it has stretched with little or no long-term planning into a hotch-potch of confusingly named hamlets at different altitudes. Their convenience for skiing, shopping and nightlife varies considerably.

'The Heart of The Trois Vallées' is Méribel's marketing slogan, but because of its diffuse layout, it is devoid of a single heart and its atmosphere is muted accordingly. Méribel Centre (1450m) is now known generally as Méribel and is the commercial core, a one-street village with the tourist office 'square' as its focal point. It has a number of boutiques and souvenir shops beyond the usual sports shops and one main supermarket. The bi-weekly street market provides colour and the occasional clothing bargain.

Méribel Mottaret (1700-1800m), now 23 years old, is a separate satellite further up the valley, which is itself now divided into separate hamlets. The higher altitude of Mottaret ensures good snow cover and is the starting grid for the best motorway skiing. This may explain why Alain Prost built his winter home here, but it has few other obvious temptations.

The different sectors of Méribel are all connected by what is now a regular, free bus-service. Traffic, parking and pollution from petrol fumes remain serious problems, which are not adequately addressed.

Courchevel is not one but four quite separate resorts at different altitudes, linked on-piste but with nothing else in common. Before booking a holiday here it is crucial to ascertain exactly where you will be staying. Courchevel 1850 is the international resort with the jet-set image, and most tour operators are happy for you to think their accommodation is here, even when it is not.

Courchevel 1850 is the most fashionable of all French ski destinations. Like rival Megève, a high proportion of its designer-clad visitors come here to see and to be seen. The only exercise they take is to ferry gastronomic delights from plate to mouth at the resort's clutch of fine restaurants. Unlike Megève, Courchevel 1850 offers seriously challenging skiing, which is some of the best and most accessible in the whole of the Trois Vallées; its high altitude ensures early and late snow-cover. For all that, it is not a particularly charming resort in aspect: a sprawl of chalet-style wooden buildings over four serpentine bends in the road leading to the central lift-station.

A covered mall houses expensive boutiques, and a couple of supermarkets cater for the more mundane needs of self-caterers. The secluded Jardin des Alpins sector is a Millionaire's Row of sumptuous chalets and shockingly expensive hotels tucked discreetly away in the trees; it provides at least an illusion of privacy.

Courchevel 1650 is 200 vertical metres lower down the mountain and the social scale. Many would argue that this is '*le vrai* Courchevel', with its year-round population and atmosphere of the farming community it once was. The intermediate skiing here is both extensive and isolated from the main Trois Vallées thoroughfares; consequently, it is wonderfully uncrowded even at peak times.

Courchevel 1550 is off the beaten track, away from the heart of the skiing. It is little more than a cluster of apartment buildings and a few hotels. It is popular with self-catering French families.

Le Praz (sometimes known as Courchevel 1300) is a farming village at the foot of the lift system, which is becoming an increasingly popular and cheap base for Courchevel's skiing. Snow cover is by no means guaranteed in the hamlet, but two gondolas swiftly take skiers up towards the Col de la Loze or to 1850.

At 2300m **Val Thorens** is the highest ski resort in Europe, while Obergurgl, which has a church, used to claim to be the highest ski parish. After 23 years Val Thorens has established itself as the place for late-season skiing and has also built its own little church to sneak away with both titles.

This is one of the only resorts in Europe where you are virtually guaranteed snow at resort level over both Christmas and Easter. On a sunny day its functional, purpose-built architecture is attractive compared to its neighbour, Les Menuires. You can ski into the centre of the car-free village, and the horseshoe of surrounding peaks is dramatic.

In bad weather, this far above the tree-line, you may be forgiven for thinking you have been stranded amid the mountains of the moon; few places in the Alps are colder, and a white-out is just that.

Poor **Les Menuires** down the valley from Val Thorens at 1850m, has a joke reputation as the ugliest resort in the Alps. Certainly, the original centre of **La Croisette** is a prime example of the alpine architectural vandalism of the 1960s. Minuscule apartments are housed in anonymous box-like buildings clad in unpainted concrete. However, a small fortune was spent cleaning up the place for the 1992 Winter Olympics. No longer do you get the feeling that you might be mugged while wandering around here at night.

The more modern satellites of **Reberty** and **Les Bruyères** are far more appealing, and you can holiday in comfort, hardly ever venturing into La Croisette. Both are on the piste and have their own hotels and restaurants as well as all the shops you might need, apart from a chemist (there is one in La Croisette).

The main skiing here is exceptionally sunny. A bank of snow-cannon installed for the Olympic slalom keep the home run in good condition until late in the season.

Accommodation

Méribel began as a chalet resort and so it remains. In the short summer months the village rings to the sounds of saw and hammer as new luxury establishments sprout in response to demand.

The four-star Grand Coeur was one of the resort's first hotels and remains its finest: 'the food and service are excellent; its understated luxury appeals equally to the Brits and the French'. The lavish Aspen Park is now a Club Med, but other four-star hotels include L'Antarès and Le Chalet. The Marie Blanche is 'small and friendly'. Le Yeti and the Merilys are also recommended.

Mottaret has five hotels including the three-star Les Arolles and La Tarentaise, but most guests stay in apartments. These vary from the compact Pierre et Vacances studios for four to the unashamed indulgence of The Ski Company's Olympie III chalet.

Courchevel 1850 has a host of four-star de luxe hotels (there are no five-stars in France), which pamper their exotically wealthy guests. The Byblos de Neige is the star. Les Airelles is owned and managed by the redoubtable Raymonde Fenestraz, the property princess of Courchevel, and is more discreet. The three-star La Sivolière provides four-star comfort. The reasonably priced Courcheneige is situated on the edge of the piste near the altiport and caters for families. The quality of some of the luxury catered chalets here ranks alongside the smartest hotels. The Forum apartment complex is much praised by reporters ('modern, with a perfect location').

Courchevel 1650 consists mainly of chalets. Le Praz has the comfortable Hotel Les Peupliers ('delightful base from which to ski Courchevel without paying through the nose').

Accommodation in **Val Thorens** is divided between the standard French apartments and mainly unremarkable hotels. The four-star Fitz-Roy is the exception. Readers report that the apartments in the Naska block of the Temples du Soleil complex are 'surprisingly spacious with enormous bathrooms'. Résidence Altineige is said to be 'extremely noisy thanks to the Ski Rock Café next to the reception area'. Hotel Trois Vallées in the centre of Val Thorens is praised as 'comfortable, convenient and friendly'. Le Bel Horizon and Le Sherpa ('best hotel in town, very friendly') are reporters' favourites, along with Le Val Chavière where 'staff are actually pleased to see you'.

Les Menuires is also apartment territory: the older ones in **La Croisette** are cramped and largely to be avoided. Their more modern counterparts in **Les Bruyères** are beginning to show signs of exhaustion. However, reporters praise the Necou apartments at **Reberty 2000** ('a high-quality, well-designed ski-in ski-out complex'). Hotel Les Latitudes in Les Bruyères offers some of the best-value accommodation and five-course dinners in the region ('quite exceptional food, pleasant rooms and ideally situated on the edge of the piste — don't tell anyone else').

Eating in and out

Méribel has a surprisingly limited choice of recommended restaurants for a resort of its size, mainly because such a large proportion of its clientèle eat in their self-catered chalets. La Cava is for fondue, and Le Jardin d'Hiver has fresh seafood. The refurbished La Taverne offers pizzas and Savoyard dishes and has established itself as one of the focal points of Méribel Centre. Chez Kiki specialises in charcoal grills, and the surroundings are appealing. Santa Marina is praised for its 'excellent pizza and pasta'. Bibi Crêperie in the main street is said to be good value. Le Croix Jean-Claude is 'a fine Savoyard restaurant with a pretty dining-room'.

■ OTHER SPORTS

Méribel: skating on Olympic ice rink, snow-shoeing, parapente, hang-gliding, tobogganing, swimming
Courchevel: parapente, tobogganing, flying club, skating, luge, ice-climbing, squash, swimming, snow-shoeing, snowmobiling
Val Thorens: micro-lighting, car-racing on ice, swimming, indoor tennis and squash, golf simulator, volleyball, climbing wall
Les Menuires: parapente, skating, swimming, snowmobiling, hang-gliding, snow-shoeing

In **Mottaret Le Hameau**, Ty Sable is recommended. Hotel Tarentaise, on the edge of the piste, is British-managed and popular with the French for its food. The central Côte Brune restaurant is still a culinary mainstay. Pizzeria du Mottaret is the bar/restaurant with the best atmosphere and reasonable prices. There is a small supermarket at Le Hameau and a larger one in Mottaret.

Courchevel 1850 abounds in fine restaurants. The Chabichou Hotel has two coveted Michelin stars, as does Le Bateau Ivre. The seafood restaurant at Byblos de Neige is a wonder to behold; however, few reporters found themselves in this envious price bracket. On a more mundane scale, Jack's Bar (La Saulire) in the square at 1850 is a resort institution serving modestly priced French food in a welcoming ambience.

Restaurants at **Courchevel 1650** are less Parisian in price. La Poule au Pot is warmly recommended for classic French fare, and Le Yeti for its fresh seafood. Try the Hotel l'Adret at **Courchevel 1550** for a quiet but provincial French lunch or dinner.

Le Praz (Courchevel 1300) is famed for the outrageously expensive but nevertheless compelling Bistrot du Praz and Charley, its *bon viveur* host. A *dégustation* of four different types of *foie gras* is the house speciality. Hotel Les Peupliers, the original village inn, is also worth a visit for lunch or dinner and is more modestly priced.

Val Thorens has a limited choice of restaurants. El Gringo's Café in the Péclet shopping centre is the most popular. Le Galoubet is recommended at lunchtime for its dish of the day. Le Choucas, Le Scapin and La P'tite Ferme are also noted by readers.

Les Menuires is no gastronomic delight, but the half-board food in Hotel Les Latitudes is described as 'much more exciting than we could have hoped for'. Better restaurants include La Bouitte in nearby St-Marcel, and La Mascotte and Chalet Necou in St-Martin-de-Belleville.

Self-caterers heading for the Trois Vallées are strongly advised to stock up at the large hypermarket on the outskirts of Moûtiers before beginning the climb up to the resorts: prices are markedly cheaper at lower altitude.

Après-ski

In **Méribel** much of the nightlife revolves around the bustling French Connection and the Mark Warner Pub. La Taverne, owned by the British financial consortium that also owns Dick's Tea-Bar in Val d'Isère, is a contender for the most popular bar in town. Saint-Pères, once the sole disco, now has serious competition from L'Artichaud, which has live bands and a fun atmosphere and stays open into the early hours.

In **Courchevel 1850** the Albatross bar has 'good value beer and snack meals'. La Grange and La Bergerie are outrageously expensive and crowded nightclubs. The real action is at the Dakota Rock Bar.

At **Courchevel 1650**, Le Signal is the bar-restaurant where the locals meet. Le Phlouc (it means clown in France or pimple in Scotland) is a small, smoky and busy bar. By night Le Green Club has a modest entry fee, a British DJ and the best music in Courchevel at any altitude. Rocky's Bar is also always busy.

Le Praz is not the place for a raucous nightlife. The crêperie has 'the best *vin chaud* in the business'. The Bar Brasserie (it bears no other name) is 'the only place with any life'.

Childcare

All the main resorts are well-served with both ski and non-ski kindergartens. However, it is important to note that the kind of facilities offered may not be conducive to the enjoyment of your holiday as parents. The Gallic approach to childcare may seem harsh by northern European standards, with a serious emphasis on learning to ski without any accompanying element of enjoyment. The number of children who dig in their heels and tearfully refuse to return to these French establishments on day two of their holiday has led most major tour operators to set up their own more sympathetic crèches and even ski classes. If you decide upon this option, choose a tour operator with a flexible nanny service, where staff will pick up your children from ski school at lunchtime and care for them during the afternoon.

The ESF runs children's villages in all the resorts. The best reports came from Les Menuires, where staff at Les Schtroumpfs are praised for their friendliness and dedication in looking after children from three months to two-and-a-half years old in the nursery, and up to seven years in the kindergarten section. The village has a rope-lift for beginners and a longer drag. ESF teachers also take classes out on the mountain, and there are play facilities and a video room for non-skiing children.

The equivalents in Courchevel 1850 and in Courchevel 1650 are criticised as being 'too serious' in their approach. We have good reports of the ESF children's ski school in Méribel: 'although the classes were large, the teachers made the lessons fun. This was the first time my son really enjoyed ski school and wanted to go back each day'. In **Val Thorens**, the ESF has built a new children's village with a non-ski kindergarten for children from three months old and upwards. Stage Etoile is for skiers from five to twelve years old.

Linked or nearby resorts

Two contrastingly different little villages provide alternative bases for skiing the Trois Vallées while avoiding the hustle of the mainstream resorts and their high prices.

St-Martin-de-Belleville
top 3300m (10,825ft) bottom 1400m (4,593ft)

This is the 'capital' of the Belleville Valley, a farming community at pastoral counterpoint to the high-tech world of the ski network above it. Reporters praise it as 'quiet and lived in, unlike the larger towns in the area'.

The old cheese-making village has considerable charm and a couple of fine restaurants. L'Etoile de Neige is a lunchtime favourite with ski guides. Les Airelles, on the main road out of the village, is said to offer 'delicious food'. La Bouitte in neighbouring Saint Marcel is a serious exercise in gastronomy. The Eterlou Bar is where the locals meet.

St-Martin is connected into the system by a slow triple-chair. Loading has been speeded up with the addition of a 'moving carpet' conveyor belt. If staying in Méribel, do not linger too long over lunch; allow a full 45 minutes to reach the ridge of the valley on your way home.

TOURIST OFFICE
Tel 33 4 79 08 93 09
Fax 33 4 79 08 91 71

La Tania
top 3300m (10,825ft) bottom 1350m (4,429ft)

This purpose-built but pleasing village, a couple of kilometres by road from Le Praz, is linked by piste to Courchevel 1850 as well as to Méribel via the Col de la Loze. It was constructed as a dormitory satellite for the thousands of extra visitors expected to attend the Albertville Olympics; in the event they stayed at home and watched it on television.

It is a pleasant and reasonably priced base served by a jumbo gondola and, despite its youth, has developed its own village atmosphere. During a heavy snowfall, the tree-lined slopes above it provide some of the most enjoyable powder skiing in the whole of the Trois Vallées area, yet are always under-used.

Hotel Montana has 'clean and comfortable rooms, good food, but not particularly generous portions for hungry skiers'. The supermarket has a limited stock and is said to be 'unimpressive'. One reporter was also unmoved by the nightlife ('the place is a cemetery after dark').

TOURIST OFFICE
Tel 33 4 79 08 40 40
Fax 33 4 79 08 54 71

Skiing facts: **Méribel**

TOURIST OFFICE
BP1, F-73551 Méribel, Savoie
Tel 33 4 79 08 60 01
Fax 33 4 79 00 59 61

THE RESORT
By road Calais 920km
By rail TGV Moûtiers 18km, regular bus
service to resort
By air Chambéry 2 hrs, Geneva 3 hrs,
Lyon 2½ hrs
Visitor beds 33,000
Transport free ski bus can be included with
lift pass

THE SKIING
Linked or nearby resorts La Tania (l),
Courchevel (l), Val Thorens (l), Les
Menuires (l), St-Martin-de-Belleville (l)
Longest run Campagnol (Mont Vallon),
3.6km (red)
Number of lifts 57 in Méribel, 200 in Trois
Vallées
Total of trails/pistes 105km (58% easy,
28% intermediate, 14% difficult), 600km in
Trois Vallées
Nursery slopes 7 lifts
Summer skiing at Val Thorens
Snowmaking 20km covered

LIFT PASSES
Area pass Trois Vallées 1,035FF, Méribel
Valley 845FF, both for 6 days
Day pass Méribel Valley 176FF, Trois
Vallées 215FF
Beginners 1 free lift at Le Rond Point and 1
in Méribel Mottaret (special beginners' pass
also available)
Pensioners reductions for 60 yrs and over
Credit cards accepted yes

SKI SCHOOLS
Adults ESF 210FF per day, 1,128FF for 6
days. Ski Cocktail, 750FF for 6 mornings.
Magic in Motion, 720FF for 10 hrs
Private lessons 185FF per hour, 1,450FF
per day
Snowboarding beginners (10am-1pm),
intermediates (1.45-4.45pm), 720FF for 5
half-days
Cross-country ESF, prices as regular ski
school. Loipe 33km
Other courses slalom, telemark, moguls,
off-piste
Guiding companies through ski schools

CHILDREN
Lift pass 5-16 yrs, Trois Vallées 776FF,
Méribel Valley 591FF, both for 6 days, free
for under 5 yrs
Ski kindergarten Les P'tits Loups (at
Méribel and Méribel Mottaret), 3-5 yrs,
9.15am-5pm, 840FF for 6 days
Ski school ESF, 4-8 yrs, 1,233FF for 6 days
not including lunch
Non-ski kindergarten Club Saturnin,
18 mths and over, 9am-5pm, 1,227FF
for 6 days including lunch

FOOD AND DRINK PRICES
Coffee 10FF, glass of wine 12-15FF, small
beer 10FF, dish of the day 65-75FF

Skiing facts: **Courchevel**

TOURIST OFFICE
BP37, La Croisette, F-73122 Courchevel,
Savoie
Tel 33 4 79 08 00 29
Fax 33 4 79 08 15 63

THE RESORT
By road Calais 925km
By rail TGV Moûtiers 25km, frequent buses
By air Chambéry 2 hrs, Geneva 3 hrs,
Lyon 2½ hrs
Visitor beds 32,000
Transport free ski bus with lift pass

THE SKIING
Linked or nearby resorts La Tania (I),
Méribel (I), Val Thorens (I), Les Menuires (I),
St-Martin-de-Belleville (I)
Longest run Les Creux, 4.2km (red)
Number of lifts 68 in Courchevel, 200 in
Trois Vallées
Total of trails/pistes 180km in Courchevel
(26% beginner, 27% easy, 36% intermedi-
ate, 11% difficult), 600km in Trois Vallées
Nursery slopes 26 slopes
Summer skiing at Val Thorens
Snowmaking 474 snow-cannon

LIFT PASSES
Area pass Trois Vallées 1,035FF,
Courchevel 845FF, both for 6 days
Day pass Courchevel 176FF, Trois Vallées
215FF
Beginners 12 free lifts
Pensioners 60 yrs and over, Courchevel
591FF and Trois Vallées 776FF, both for 6
days, free for 80 yrs and over
Credit cards accepted yes

SKI SCHOOLS
Adults ESF: (1850) 980FF and (1650)
840FF for 6 days, (1550) 500FF for 6 half-
days. Ski Academy, 650-750FF for 6 days,
Ski Masterclass, details on request
Private lessons (1850) and (1650)
1,450FF, (1550) 1,300FF, Ski Academy
1,500FF, all per day (7 hrs)
Snowboarding ESF 1850, 9.30am-midday
or 2.30-5pm, 1,100FF for 6 days
Cross-country all ski schools, times and
prices on request. Loipe 66km
Other courses slalom, ski-touring,
telemark, monoski, competition
Guiding companies through ski schools

CHILDREN
Lift pass 5-16 yrs, Courchevel 591FF and
Trois Vallées 776FF, both for 6 days, free for
under 5 yrs
Ski kindergarten (1850) ESF Village des
Enfants, 3-12 yrs, 9am-5pm, 1,020FF for
6 days, extra 70FF per day for lunch.
(1650) ESF Vacances des Petits, 3-5 yrs,
prices and times on request, (1550) ESF
Jardin des Neiges, 3-6 yrs,
9.30am-4.30pm, 920FF for 6 days not
including lunch
Ski school (1850) ESF Village des Enfants,
3-12 yrs, 9am-5pm, 1,155FF for 6 days
including lunch. (1650) ESF Vacances des
Petits, 3-5 yrs, 1,100FF for 6 days
including lunch
Non-ski kindergarten (1850) Village des
Enfants, 2 yrs and over, 9am-5pm, 250FF
per day including lunch. (1650) Vacances
des Petits, 2-7 yrs, 9am-5pm, 215FF per
day including lunch

FOOD AND DRINK PRICES
Coffee 10FF, glass of wine 12-15FF,
small beer 10-13FF, dish of the day
70-75FF

Skiing facts: **Val Thorens**

TOURIST OFFICE
F-73440 Val Thorens, Savoie
Tel 33 4 79 00 08 08
Fax 33 4 79 00 00 04

THE RESORT
By road Calais 928km
By rail TGV Moûtiers 34km, frequent buses to resort
By air Chambéry 2 hrs, Geneva 3 hrs, Lyon 2½ hrs
Visitor beds 21,000
Transport free ski bus

THE SKIING
Linked or nearby resorts La Tania (I), Méribel (I), Les Menuires (I), Courchevel (I), St-Martin-de-Belleville (I)
Longest run Boulevard Cumin, 3.6km (blue)
Number of lifts 29 in Val Thorens, 200 in Trois Vallées
Total of trails/pistes 120km in Val Thorens (40% easy, 50% intermediate, 10% difficult), 600km in Trois Vallées
Nursery slopes 2 lifts
Summer skiing 4 lifts and 4 runs on Péclet Glacier
Snowmaking 72 snow-cannon

LIFT PASSES
Area pass Trois Vallées 1,035FF, Val Thorens 770FF, both for 6 days
Day pass Val Thorens 175FF, Trois Vallées 215FF
Beginners 2 free lifts
Pensioners 60 yrs and over, Val Thorens 540FF, Trois Vallées 776FF, both for 6 days.

50% reduction for 65 yrs and over, 70 yrs and over free in Val Thorens and half-price for Trois Vallées, 80 yrs and over ski free in whole Trois Vallées
Credit cards accepted yes

SKI SCHOOLS
Adults ESF, 675FF for 6 half-days. ESI Ski Cool, 600FF for 5 half-days
Private lessons ESF 180FF per hr, ESI Ski Cool 190FF per hr
Snowboarding ESF and ESI Ski Cool, 600FF for 5 days (3 hrs per day)
Cross-country ESF, 140FF per half-day, 605FF for 6 half-days. Loipe 3km
Other courses telemark, moguls, Skwal
Guiding companies through ESF

CHILDREN
Lift pass 5-15 yrs, Val Thorens 540FF, Trois Vallées 776FF, both for 6 days, free for under 5 yrs
Ski kindergarten ESF Miniclub, 5 yrs and over, 9am-5.30pm, 1,350FF for 6 days including lunch. Bambi ski courses, 2½-4 yrs, 1,350FF for 6 days
Ski school ESF, 5-12 yrs, 745FF for 5 days (5½ hrs per day), ESI Ski Cool, 4-12 yrs, 1,100FF for 5 days including lunch. ESF Stage Etoile, 5-12 yrs, 9am-5pm, 1,350FF for 6 days including lunch and 2 hrs play time
Non-ski kindergarten ESF, 3 mths-3 yrs, 1,315FF for 6 days including lunch

FOOD AND DRINK PRICES
Coffee 10FF, glass of wine 10FF, small beer 10FF, dish of the day 65FF

Skiing facts: **Les Menuires**

TOURIST OFFICE
BP22, Les Menuires, F-73440
St-Martin-de-Belleville, Savoie
Tel 33 4 79 00 73 00
Fax 33 4 79 00 75 06

THE RESORT
By road Calais 960km
By rail TGV Moûtiers 28km
By air Geneva 3 hrs, Lyon $2\frac{1}{2}$ hrs,
Chambéry 2 hrs
Visitor beds 22,000
Transport free ski bus around resort

THE SKIING
Linked or nearby resorts Méribel (I),
Courchevel (I), Val Thorens (I), La Tania (I),
St-Martin-de-Belleville (I)
Longest run La Masse, 3.5km (red)
Number of lifts 48 in Les Menuires and
St-Martin, 200 in Trois Vallées
Total of trails/pistes 120km in Les
Menuires, 600km in Trois Vallées
Nursery slopes 6 green and 12 blue runs
Summer skiing in Val Thorens
Snowmaking 70 hectares covered in Les
Menuires and St-Martin

LIFT PASSES
Area pass Les Menuires 850FF, Belleville
Valley 965FF, Trois Vallées 1,035FF,
all for 6 days
Day pass Les Menuires 175FF, Trois

Vallées 215FF
Beginners 6 free lifts and Réseau Redruit
beginners area with 11 lifts (100FF per day)
Pensioners 60 yrs and over as children
Credit cards accepted yes

SKI SCHOOLS
Adults ESF 910FF for 6 days, ESI 860FF for
6 days, both $5\frac{1}{2}$ hrs per day
Private lessons ESF 175FF per hr
Snowboarding prices as regular ski
school
Cross-country ESF, 910FF for 6 days
($5\frac{1}{2}$ hrs per day). Loipe 28km
Guiding companies through ESF and ESI

CHILDREN
Lift pass 5-16 yrs: Les Menuires 635FF,
Belleville Valley 750FF, Trois Vallées 776FF,
all for 6 days, free for under 5 yrs
Ski kindergarten Village des Schtroumpfs,
3 mths-7 yrs, 850FF for 6 days
Ski school ESF 765FF for 6 days. ESI 755FF
for 6 days
Non-ski kindergarten Village des
Schtroumpfs, 3 mths-6 yrs, 9am-5.15pm,
1,252FF for 6 days including lunch. Les
Marmottons, $2\frac{1}{2}$-6 yrs, 1,252FF for 6 days
including lunch

FOOD AND DRINK PRICES
Coffee 7FF, glass of wine 10FF, small beer
13FF, dish of the day 50-60FF

Val d'Isère/Tignes

ALTITUDE Val d'Isère 1850m (6,068ft), Tignes 2100m (6,888ft)

Whenever two or three skiers are gathered together anywhere in the world the conversation will inevitably turn towards Val d'Isère. Early each December — if snow permits — the self-crowned capital of modern European skiing traditionally hosts the first World Cup men's downhill. Between then and the May Bank Holiday more British skiers come to this remote and rather unprepossessing resort at the head of the Tarentaise Valley than anywhere else.

It is a destination for serious enthusiasts, which somehow manages to blend a cocktail of high ski-tech and mass-market tourism with a smooth topping of sophistication. It is a social melting pot, and although it may not attract as many millionaires as Courchevel, those who it does can usually ski like a dream. The ski area is directly linked to neighbouring Tignes and is jointly marketed as L'Espace Killy after its most revered son who swept the board of gold at the 1968 Winter Olympics. The fact that Jean-Claude Killy actually comes from lowland Alsace bothers no one at all.

■ GOOD POINTS

Large ski area, variety of intermediate and expert skiing, extensive off-piste, summer skiing at Tignes, reliable snow record, excellent lift system, extensive facilities for snowboarding, lively après ski (Val d'Isère), skiing convenience (Tignes), tough runs

■ BAD POINTS

Unattractive resort of Tignes, limited skiing for beginners, restricted choice of mountain restaurants, few activities for non-skiers, poor piste maintenance, lack of tree-level runs

The quality of the skiing in the area is so varied and demanding that it has raised a whole genre of international experts who ski here at least twice a year and never anywhere else. A huge vertical drop of 1890m, coupled with 102 lifts including two high-speed underground railways, six gondolas and four cable cars form the hard-core infrastructure. But for the expert the real joy lies in the unlimited off-piste opportunities to be found in this wild region on the edge of the Vanoise National Park. Prices are high, but as one reader puts it: 'You are in one of the prime ski areas of the world; playing golf at Wentworth, shopping at Harrods or dining at the Dorchester aren't cheap either'.

On the mountain
top 3439m (11,279ft) bottom 1550m (5,084ft)

Val d'Isère alone has eight major points of mountain access, which means that queues hardly exist at all, even at peak holiday times. The long valley floor is covered by an efficient ski-bus service known as Le

Train Rouge, and a little experience means you can avoid even the smallest of rush-hour lift lines.

L'Espace Killy divides naturally into six separate ski sectors. On the Val d'Isère side there are Col de l'Iseran/Pissaillas, Solaise and Bellevarde, which are strung in a row along the curving road between the satellites of **Le Fornet** and **La Daille**. The first two sectors are linked by lift at altitude, but Solaise and Bellevarde only at valley level just beside the main resort. Bellevarde links with Tignes via the Tovière ridge.

The skiing at Tignes divides itself into three areas: Tovière, Grande Motte and the glacier, and Palet/Aiguille Percée. Tignes has a state-of-the-art underground railway. Passengers are whisked at high speed up through the rock and permafrost from Val Claret at 2100m to the Panoramic restaurant at 3030m in just six minutes.

An alternative network of lifts takes you from **Tignes-Le-Lac** up towards the dramatic rock formation of L'Aiguille Percée in one direction or towards the greater demands of Val d'Isère's ski area in the other. In the depth of winter there is more skiing in Tignes down to the lower lying hamlets of **Les Boisses** at 1850m and **Les Brevières** at 1550m.

Once up the mountain it is the dispersal of skiers that is so clever. The lie of the terrain encourages you to ski further into the mountain range, rather than immediately returning towards the valley, with the result that you rarely find yourself wanting to ski the same run twice. The choice of where to go and what to ski is enormous.

Piste-grooming has dramatically improved thanks largely to the investment in equipment for the 1992 Olympics. However, the complexity and severity of the terrain makes it hugely prone to avalanches, and after a big dump, visitors are often disappointed to discover that most lifts remain closed for a day. Those in the know take a day out on the protected pistes of **Sainte-Foy**. However, in windy conditions both Val d'Isère and Tignes benefit enormously from their underground railways. The Funival at La Daille gives guaranteed access to the Rocher de Bellevarde and some of the best runs in the resort.

Both Val d'Isère and Tignes are resorts for serious skiers. You do not have to be an expert, but it certainly helps. You do have to be keen, however. If your idea of a skiing holiday is to eat, drink and dance, with just the occasional potter down the slopes between meals, these are not the resorts for you. According to some dubious French statistics, the average skier in Courchevel skis for one hour a day, and his or her counterpart in Val d'Isère and Tignes skis for more than five.

Beginners

Val d'Isère is unfairly denigrated as a resort for beginners. In fact, it has acceptable nursery slopes right in the centre of the village and a wide choice of ski schools. The problem stems from the fact that it is suitable for absolute novices only, and not for wobbly second-weekers. Once you have graduated on to the main mountain, most of the slopes are too steep to give any confidence to lower intermediates.

The nursery slopes are free, but the big problem is where to go next.

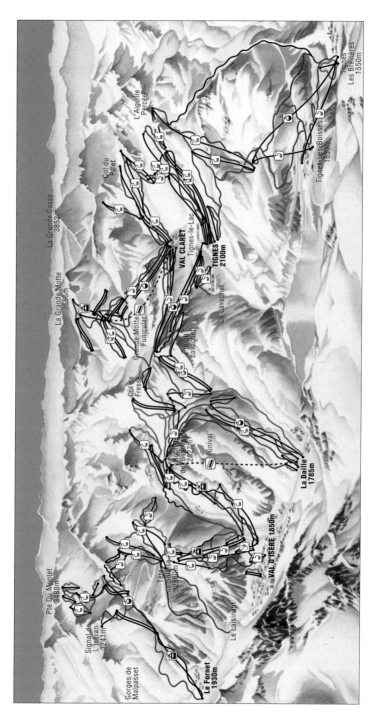

277

Do not trust the piste-map; some of the runs marked green could frighten the daylights out of you. The Col de l'Iseran sector has some gentle runs, but here, as in other parts of the resort, it is too difficult to ski back to the valley. Tignes has a good choice of blue (easy) runs on the glacier, but it is a cold place in which to be falling about.

Intermediates

Piste-grading is not Val's strongest point, and colour coding is on the dark side — some blues would be red (intermediate) runs elsewhere, and you may find the odd red that is positively black (difficult) by Tyrolean standards. The Bellevarde sector provides plenty of variety. The Solaise Bumps down the front face of the 2560-m Tête de Solaise are classic, and the moguls can be the size of 2CVs. The OK run around the shoulder of the Rocher de Bellevarde is the World Cup downhill course; when it is not prepared for racing this trail provides an excellent cruise. Orange, from the same starting point, is also superb.

Advanced

The Face de Bellevarde, reached by the Funival funicular railway, became the men's downhill course for the Albertville Olympics in 1992. It was sculptured by veteran Swiss racer Bernhard Russi at a reputed cost of £2 million (he even changed the route during construction to preserve the habitat of a rare wild flower). In February 1992 Austrian victor Patrick Ortlieb announced rather churlishly from the rostrum that he thought the course was terrible, and it may never be raced again. However, the legacy is a superb black run, which takes you back to Val in rather more than the two minutes it takes the world's top racers.

Sache, a superb long black, starts from the blue Corniche run below L'Aiguille Percée and takes you almost down to **Tignes-Les-Brevières** where it merges with the red Pavot. The run down through the trees from the top of Le Fornet can, at times, be the best in the resort.

Off-piste

The starting points for some of the most challenging itineraries are ill-advisedly marked on the piste-map. Once you begin, you are on your own and it is easy to get lost — or worse. It is imperative to use a local guide.

In fresh powder the Tour Charvet is a particular favourite. The Signal de l'Iseran/Glacier de Pissaillas sector provides some of the most dramatic runs, but the beauty of Val and Tignes is the accessibility of good off-piste throughout the region.

Ski schools and guiding

To get the best out of this extraordinary ski area you need some expert help: the two resorts now have more than a dozen ski and snowboarding schools and 800 instructors at peak times. Back in 1976 the French Ski School (ESF) had the monopoly throughout the country on instruction. Patrick and Jean Zimmer, two young ex-racers from Alsace, took on the

ESF in true David and Goliath fashion — all the way to the French high court — and won the right to open their own ski school in Val d'Isère. Since their precedent, alternative schools have sprung up in almost every resort, but the Zimmer brothers' Top Ski has a cult following. The secret of its success is that it has remained small. Jean and Patrick take groups of six skiers off-piste in the mornings and guarantee to find you the best snow in the resort. They also give instruction on piste technique in the afternoons and arrange ski-tours, heli-skiing, summer skiing and tuition for children aged eight and over.

Other alternative ski schools include Snow Fun, Alpine Experience, and Evolution 2. The ESF operates in both resorts, but Anglo-Saxons tend to favour the alternatives, which are more linguistically and emotionally geared towards the needs of the calibre of skier who wants to get the best out of this extraordinary area.

We have continuing good reports of Snow Fun: 'The instructors were personable, spoke fluent English and made the effort to learn the names of their pupils'. 'We were highly impressed by their organisation and emphasis on group grading', said another reporter. We have encouraging reports of Mountain Masters, which has been criticised in the past. One reporter described a guide from Alpine Experience as 'the best I have every come across anywhere'.

Snowboarding

L'Espace Killy is at the forefront of the snowboarding movement. Hors Limites Surf School runs free introductory lessons, with equipment included, on the nursery slopes on Sunday afternoons. It takes riders from as young as 5 years old. Most of the ski schools offer lessons. Surf Rider Snowboard Club specialises in off-piste snowboarding and heli-surfing in Italy. The specialist school in Tignes is Kebra Surfing.

Mountain restaurants

Good mountain restaurants are both sparse and expensive. It costs about as much to build a new WC up a mountain as it does to install a lift, and L'Espace Killy concentrates on the latter. The better establishments are on the Val side and include Trifollet (with acceptable WCs), which is halfway down to La Daille, and La Folie Douce, at the top of La Daille gondola ('revolting loo, no running water and you have to pay 2FF'). A new addition is La Fruitière, next to the Folie Douce, which is strongly praised. Le Signal, at the top of the Fornet cable car, maintains a consistently high standard. The top of Tovière is the place for a fine *steak frites* and a great view. La Datcha at the foot of the Cugnai chair is criticised: 'The food is expensive, the staff surly and the service poor'.

Wise skiers return to the valley at lunchtime, where restaurants are as busy as they are by night. The family-run Crech'Ouna near the Funival station is the favourite among reporters. Clochetons is also praised for its 'reasonably priced table d'hôte lunch, which is beautifully cooked and served'. The Bouida, by the gondola at Les Brevières, is said to be good value for money.

The small restaurant at the Col du Palet is described as 'very welcoming'. La Savouna, near Palafour above Tignes-Le-Lac, is popular as is La Sache at Les Brevières.

Off the mountain

Apart from its eleventh-century church, precious little remains of the old village of Val d'Isère, which used to be called L'Aval de Tignes and was home to the hunting lodges of the Dukes of Savoie, before becoming a winter sports resort in 1932. Today, it has grown into a hotch-potch of a ski town, which sprawls from the apartment blocks of La Daille at one end to Le Fornet at the other. Until the mid-1980s the centre was an ill-defined area where the petrol stations, concrete *résidences* and the occasional pleasing chalet gave way to a row of shops and bars on either side of the wide and busy main road.

However, a cluster of old-style stone buildings (created for the 1992 Olympics) house the smarter boutiques and restaurants, and provide the pleasant village with a focal point, which it previously lacked. Attempts to limit the traffic, which tends to clog this long, drawn-out resort, have been partially successful. Anyone who does not use the underground car park or the parking lots on the edge of town risks a hefty fine. Le Train Rouge, the frequent and efficient free ski bus service, provides the main form of transport. The town centre has a number of expensive boutiques and delicatessen as well as the usual sports shops.

The old village of Tignes disappeared beneath the waters of the Lac du Chevril when the valley was dammed in 1952. Its replacements, a series of high-rise housing estates, at varying altitudes around the 2000m mark, represent some of the most ghastly excesses of French alpine architecture of the 1960s.

The 'hamlets' of **Val Claret**, Tignes-Le-Lac, **Le Lavachet**, and even the much lower community of **Tignes-Les-Boisses**, would all benefit aesthetically from a compulsory demolition order. Only the valley farming community of Tignes-Les-Brevières should be reprieved. Demolition has never been an option. Instead, serious but unsustained attempts have been made to reclad the worst of the untreated concrete with pine. New buildings are constructed in a far more sympathetic mountain style.

Skiing is a year-round commitment in Tignes. Permanent winter conditions on the Grande Motte Glacier allow racers and dedicated recreational skiers to practice on its wide and open slopes even in July and August. In winter, at least, the ugliness of the resort itself is completely counterbalanced by the glory of the skiing.

Buses between the two resorts are neither frequent nor cheap, and taxis can be extortionate. If you have your own car and want a change of scenery, day trips to **Les Arcs**, **La Plagne**, **La Rosière**, and Sainte-Foy are all possible.

Accommodation

In Val d'Isère a cluster of four-stars heads a choice of 39 hotels. The Blizzard and the Christiania are the most comfortable, while the

Savoyarde and the Tsanteleina have a strong British following.

Most skiers stay in chalets or in self-catering apartments. The Ski Company has a collection of the most sumptuous designer chalets in what has become its own Millionaire's Row up above Club Med. YSE, the largest specialist chalet operator here, runs Mountain Lodges, a seventeenth-century farmhouse divided into two units, which provides a similar hedonistic level of accommodation. Ski Scott Dunn has some of the more luxurious chalets in Résidence Squaw Valley, tucked behind the piste near the church. Maeva and Pierre et Vacances share a *résidence* in La Daille. Both are typically cramped, but the Maeva apartments are said to be the superior of the two.

In Tignes, most accommodation is in self-catering apartments, which vary dramatically in quality in direct relation to their age. The more modern developments are much more spacious and it is important to check carefully before booking. Of the handful of hotels, reporters strongly recommend the two-star Hotel de la Vanoise ('convenient, with an excellent breakfast and five-course dinner, and a fine room with bathroom and large balcony').

Eating in and out
In Val d'Isère the Grand Ourse is always dependable. La Solaise is the smartest in town — the kind of place where two people help you on with your coat — and worthwhile for a treat. Perdrix Blanche is unpretentious and renowned for its fresh seafood. Au Bout de la Rue, run by Jean Zimmer, provides 'wholesome food in a relaxed and welcoming atmosphere'. Chalet du Crêt is the new and 'wonderfully gastronomic' smart restaurant. Hotel fare in French ski resorts is often some of the best. The restaurants in the three-star Savoyarde and Tsanteleina are both excellent for dinner, and Sur Le Toit at the Sofitel can be outstanding.

Bananas is an old favourite among reporters. Try also the Brasserie des Sports and the Belle Etoile next to the swimming-pool. Crêpe Val, close to the post office, is recommended for regional specialities as well as crêpes. Le Pré d'Aval is also popular with reporters both at lunchtime and in the evening. L'Arolay in Le Fornet has 'fine food but disastrous service'.

> ### ■ OTHER SPORTS
> Val d'Isère: parapente, snow-shoeing, ice-driving, dog-sledding, snowmobiling, curling, swimming
> Tignes: ice-diving, bowling, skating, squash, tennis, parapente, hang-gliding, climbing walls, husky sleigh-rides

In Tignes, L'Osteria in Le Lavachet is recommended for raclette and pierrade. The Wobbly Rabbit in Val Claret serves Mexican food and fondues. The Codec supermarket in Val Claret is expensive but has a wide range of goods for self-caterers.

Après-ski
Val d'Isère positively buzzes with a fun-seeking après-ski crowd unparalleled elsewhere in France. 'Have An Affair in Val d'Isère' proclaimed the T-shirt of the 1980s as it gyrated sensually in the strobe-lighting of

Skiing facts: **Val d'Isère**

TOURIST OFFICE
BP 228, F-73155 Val d'Isère, Savoie
Tel 33 4 79 06 06 60
Fax 33 4 79 06 04 56

THE RESORT
By road Calais 960km
By rail Bourg-St-Maurice 30km
By air Geneva or Chambéry 2½ hrs, Lyon 3 hrs
Visitor beds 26,480
Transport free ski bus between La Daille and Le Fornet

THE SKIING
Linked or nearby resorts Tignes (l), Sainte-Foy (n)
Longest run OK, 4.8km (red)
Number of lifts 51 in Val d'Isère, 102 in L'Espace Killy
Total of trails/pistes 300km in L'Espace Killy (59% easy, 33% intermediate, 8% difficult)
Nursery slopes 7 free lifts
Summer skiing at Grande Motte, and limited on Glacier de Pissaillas
Snowmaking 125 snow-cannon in Val d'Isère, 225 in L'Espace Killy

LIFT PASSES
Area pass L'Espace Killy, 960FF for 6 days
Day pass L'Espace Killy 209FF
Beginners 7 free lifts
Pensioners 60 yrs and over 810FF for 6 days, half-price for 70-74 yrs, free for 75 yrs and over
Credit cards accepted yes

SKI SCHOOLS
Adults ESF 1,030FF and Snow Fun 1,020-1,030FF, both for 6 days
Private lessons ESF, 9.30am-5pm, 1,420FF per day
Snowboarding ESF, 550FF for 6 half-days. Off-piste 590FF for 5 days (3 hrs per day). Snow Fun, Surf Rider and Hors Limites, group and private lessons, times and prices on request
Cross-country ESF private lessons, 400FF for 2½ hrs. Loipe 44km in L'Espace Killy
Other courses telemark, ski-touring, off-piste, slalom
Guiding companies Top Ski, Snow Fun, Altimanya, Bureau des Guides, Evolution 2, Heliski Alpine Experiences, Mountain Masters

CHILDREN
Lift pass 6-12 yrs, 675FF for 6 days, free for 5 yrs and under
Ski kindergarten Snow Fun Club Nounours, 3-6 yrs, 9.30pm-5pm, 130FF for 3 hrs. Snow Fun, 5-12 yrs, 9.30am-5pm, 1,100FF for 6 days including lunch. ESF, 4-6 yrs, 9.30am-5pm, 1,100FF for 6 days including lunch
Ski School ESF and Snow Fun, as ski kindergarten
Non-ski kindergarten Garderie Isabelle, 2½-8 yrs, 210FF per day. Petits Poucets, 3-8 yrs, 8.30-5.30pm, 210FF per day

FOOD AND DRINK PRICES
Coffee 8-15FF, glass of wine 10-14FF, small beer 10-14FF, dish of the day 60-70FF

Dick's T-Bar. The T-Bar is still here and it continues to be one of the most celebrated discos in the Alps. Café Face and the Couleur Café are riding high. G Jay's has cheap beer, sausages and beans, chalet girls, and a crush of homesick ex-pat ski bums. Le Pavillon does 'a lovely *vin chaud* in a cafetière'. The Mars Bar in La Daille is 'reasonably cheerful'.

'What après-ski?' said one reporter of Tignes. Certainly it is limited in comparison with that of its smoother, more sophisticated neighbour. Harri's Bar and the predominantly British-frequented Cavern Bar in Le Lavachet have a strong following. The Caves du Lac in Tignes-Le-Lac has a small disco floor. Other discos are the Xyphos in Le Lac and Les Chandelles, Blue Girl, and Graffiti in Val Claret. One reporter summarised it: 'When the lifts close skiers just melt back to their apartments without stopping off for one or two drinks before dinner'.

Childcare
Facilities for small children in Val d'Isère have improved but remain limited. If you want to take your under-eights on holiday, there are better equipped and more convenient resorts; this resort's charm is an adult one. In Tignes, the Petits Lutins takes babies from three months old, and Les Marmottons from two years. The ESF offers ski lessons from four years of age, and the International Ski School (ESI) from five.

Linked or nearby resorts
Sainte-Foy
top 2620m (8,596ft) bottom 1550m (5,084ft)
Sainte-Foy is an unremarkable old hamlet that you drive through on the road up from **Bourg-St-Maurice** to Tignes and Val d'Isère. But just above it and reached by a side road lies the ski resort of the same name. To call it a resort is an exaggeration; the lift ticket office, ski shop and bar provide the main base facilities of this raw and exciting ski area. The locals come to Sainte-Foy to enjoy untracked powder after a fresh fall. When high winds or unstable conditions shut down the main components of L'Espace Killy, this is the place to spend the day.

Three chair-lifts take you up to the Col de l'Aiguille and the starting point for 600 vertical metres of challenging piste. Advanced skiers can ski off the back with a guide, while intermediates will find plenty of satisfying runs on the lower half of the mountain. At the moment Sainte-Foy remains remarkably unspoilt; plans to extend the lift system and to build accommodation may change all this. At present, the only place to stay is the simple but pleasant Hotel Le Monal in the old village.

TOURIST OFFICE
Tel 33 4 79 06 91 70
Fax 33 4 79 06 95 09

Skiing facts: **Tignes**

TOURIST OFFICE
BP 51, F-73321 Tignes, Savoie
Tel 33 4 79 06 15 55
Fax 33 4 79 06 45 44

THE RESORT
By road Calais 960km
By rail Bourg-St-Maurice 25km
By air Geneva or Chambéry 2½ hrs, Lyon
3 hrs
Visitor beds 28,000
Transport free ski bus between Les Boisses
and Val Claret

THE SKIING
Linked or nearby resorts Val d'Isère (l),
Sainte-Foy (n)
Longest run Double M, 1.4km (red)
Number of lifts 49 in Tignes, 102 in
L'Espace Killy
Total of trails/pistes 300km in L'Espace
Killy (62% easy, 29% intermediate, 9%
difficult)
Nursery slopes 3 lifts
Summer skiing 13 pistes and 14 lifts on
Grand Motte Glacier
Snowmaking 100 snow-cannon in Tignes,
225 in L'Espace Killy

LIFT PASSES
Area pass L'Espace Killy, 960FF for 6 days
Day pass L'Espace Killy 209FF
Beginners 3 free lifts
Pensioners 60 yrs and over 810FF for 6
days, half-price for 70-74 yrs, free for 75
yrs and over

Credit cards accepted yes

SKI SCHOOLS
Adults ESF, 900FF for 5 days. Evolution 2
and Ski Action, times and prices on request
Private lessons ESF, 230FF per hr,
1,340FF per day
Snowboarding ESF 590FF for 5 half-days.
Beginners 145FF per half-day. Ski Fun,
Kebra Surfing, Ski Action, Evolution 2, times
and prices on request
Cross-country ESF, 590FF for 5 half-days,
beginners 145FF per half-day. Loipe 44km
in L'Espace Killy
Other courses off-piste, slalom, race
training, moguls, heli-skiing
Guiding companies Bureau des Guides,
Association 9 Valleys, Stage 2000

CHILDREN
Lift pass 6-12 yrs, 675FF for 6 days, free
for 5 yrs and under
Ski kindergarten Les Marmottons,
8.30am-5pm, 2-10 yrs, 1,450FF for 6 days
including lunch
Ski school ESF, 4-10 yrs, 840FF for 5 days
Non-ski kindergarten Les Petits Lutins,
crèche for 3 mths and over, Les Marmottons
day nursery for 3 yrs and over at Tignes-Le-
Lac and Val Claret, both 1,500FF for 6 days
including lunch

FOOD AND DRINK PRICES
Coffee 8-15FF, glass of wine 10-14FF,
small beer 10-14FF, dish of the day 60-
70FF

Valmorel

ALTITUDE 1400m (4,592ft)

Valmorel is an architecturally attractive village with a wide range of skiing mainly below advanced level, situated three hours by road from either Lyon or Geneva. When the resort was planned in 1976 it was targeted at the family market — and it still is.

The resort's pistes are linked to those of **St François-Longchamp** in the neighbouring Maurienne Valley by intermediate pistes in both directions. The resulting network of 50 lifts and 163km of pistes is called Le Grand Domaine. Central Valmorel is often referred to as Bourg-Morel to distinguish it from the satellite residential areas called *hameaux* lying some distance outside the centre. There are a further 20km of cross-country pistes below Valmorel where wild boar have been sighted, even in winter.

■ GOOD POINTS

Enclosed and protected learning areas for adults and children, sympathetic architecture, family atmosphere, central pedestrian area, value-for-money

■ BAD POINTS

Few non-skiing activities, no shuttle bus around residential satellites

Readers have importantly pointed out that the colour-coding of the local lift map flies in the face of all accepted procedure in Europe for reasons that are not at all clear. Green is listed as easy, blue as intermediate, red as difficult, and black as very difficult. The tourist director is unable to shed any light on this, and the most logical explanation is that Valmorel takes a patronising view of its mainly family-oriented clientèle whom it feels would be happier to be told a piste is more demanding than it is.

On the mountain
top 2550m (8,364ft) bottom 1250m (4,100ft)

Valmorel is a planned family resort with exceptional nursery slopes (both for adults and children), which are closed off to passing skiers, and enough testing terrain to keep competent skiers interested for a week. Mountain access is from various satellite hamlets at different altitudes. The Télébourg gondola runs from Bourg-Morel in two stages up to the hamlets of Crève-Coeur and Mottet, but is designed more as a people-carrier than a ski lift.

Queues can build up on the Beaudin chair and on the one lift that links Valmorel with Longchamp and St François, but these rarely exceed 20 minutes. The skiing is mostly as easy as it appears. Le Grand Domaine network is divided into the bowl above Valmorel and a straight up and down system of lifts between Longchamp and St François across the Col de la Madeleine. All three sectors are accessible by blue pistes. It is important to allow enough time to make the journey back to Valmorel at the end of the day, as a taxi ride of two hours is the only alternative. Valmorel has night-skiing with various weekly exhibitions on one of its pistes.

Beginners

Valmorel is one of the best resorts in the Alps for beginners. There is a good, protected nursery area with a rope-tow at the Saperlipopette kindergarten down by the Télébourg tower, as well as a totally enclosed area with toys and a lift up the mountain on Pierrafort. Unusual if not unique in the Alps is a similarly enclosed adult training area, also with its own drag-lift and with hillocks and slalom snowplough runs specially designed to give confidence. Second-week skiers should be able to make the traverse to St François and Longchamp, which have the best easy slopes in the network.

Intermediates

This is a resort where you always feel you are going somewhere, rather than skiing the same runs or similar pistes in the same bowl over and over again. The long runs down into the Celliers Valley and the steeper options off the Col de Gollet provide classic skiing. Bump bashers will want to hit the two reds under the Madeleine chair where the snow keeps cool and crisp. Both runs (numbers 86 and 87) off the Lauzière chair offer steeper options.

Advanced

There are not many black runs, nor are they especially ferocious, though the monster bumps (number 31) under the Gollet chair have been used in championship competitions. The Mottet chair also leads to some testing bumps (number 44) and is the starting point for the longest and most interesting black (number 74), which after a short drag-lift uphill takes you all the way to the valley floor. According to the piste map, Valmorel considers its red runs to be difficult.

Off-piste

The beauty of Valmorel's off-piste is that even during the high-season weeks you can usually find whole stretches of untracked powder long after a snowfall. With its family image, the resort does not normally attract advanced skiers. However, it is also part of the Nine Valleys ski safari, for which a guide is required. Most terrain is rolling rather than steep and narrow. Excellent powder skiing after a storm can be found down the ridge between Mottet and Gollet.

Ski schools and guiding

Classes meet at the French Ski School (ESF) headquarters at the top of the Télébourg people-mover. Lessons are given in English in the afternoons from Sunday to Friday, and in French in the mornings, from Monday to Saturday. The 70 permanent instructors seem dedicated and professional. ESF instructors/guides take private clients off-piste. There

is an independent mountain guides bureau, which has no office but can be contacted by phone.

Snowboarding

There is no independent snowboarding school. The ESF conducts first-day beginner lessons on the enclosed, gentle incline of the children's learning area, which has its own lift. The Surf Machine is the only snowboard specialist shop. French championship events have been held here, and the Papousasia Snowboard Park with permanent pipe and boardercross obstacles is a project for the future.

Mountain restaurants

These are mostly self-service and offer value for money rather than haute cuisine. The Alpage at the top of the Beaudin chair-lift is recommended: 'A basic cafeteria with ample space and inspiring views'. Le Prariond under the Pierrafort was the 'in' place last season thanks to the wacky antics of its owner and the higher-than-average standard of its Savoyard specialities. L'Arbet at the top of the Lanchettes chair has a sunny terrace and good-value spaghetti and chips. Altipiano on Pierrafort is smarter, while the Refuge on Col de la Madeleine is self-service but characterful, with rustic tables and a log fire. Les 2 Mazots has the best *croûte du fromage* and Le Grenier, next to the ski school, is still extremely popular. Le Cheval Noir in Longchamp receives praise for its pizzas and Le Slalom opposite the St François nursery slopes 'serves excellent food and beers from around the world'.

Off the mountain

Valmorel was conceived 20 years ago as a self-professed 'fourth-generation' resort, the disastrous third-generation resorts of Les Arcs and La Plagne being examples of what Valmorel's Dutch owners assiduously tried to avoid. The wood-and-stone cladding of its six residential developments makes Valmorel the least offensive of French planned communities. There is no shuttle bus around the hamlets, and the Télébourg people-mover delivers residents either too high or too low for convenience. Shopping is limited to a single car-free street, which is not without charm and shopkeepers are friendly and helpful. An inordinate number of stray dogs and wailing children create hazards underfoot and discord to the ears.

> ■ OTHER SPORTS
>
> Tobogganing, parapente, snowshoeing, dog-sledding, winter walks

Valmorel is within easy driving distance for a day's skiing at **Courchevel**, **Méribel**, **La Plagne** and **Les Arcs**.

Accommodation

The resort has only three hotels, none of which is in the luxury class. Self-catered apartments, all constructed within the past decade or so, are

Skiing facts: **Valmorel**

TOURIST OFFICE
La Maison de Valmorel, Bourg-Morel,
F-73260 Valmorel, Savoie
Tel 33 4 79 09 85 55
Fax 33 4 79 09 85 29

THE RESORT
By road Calais 910km
By rail Moûtiers 15km, regular bus service
to resort
By air Geneva 3 hrs, Lyon 3 hrs
Visitor beds 8,500
Transport traffic-free village centre,
Télébourg gondola between
village sectors

THE SKIING
Linked or nearby resorts St François-
Longchamp (l)
Longest run La Madeleine, 3.5km (blue)
Number of lifts 50 in Le Grand Domaine
Total of trails/pistes 163km in area (70%
easy, 20% intermediate, 10% difficult)
Nursery slopes 4
Summer skiing none
Snowmaking 30 hectares covered

LIFT PASSES
Area pass Le Grand Domaine (covers
Valmorel and St François-Longchamp),
697-880FF for 6 days. Valmorel 632FF for 6
days
Day pass Valmorel 125-157FF, Le Grand
Domaine 129-163FF

Beginners no free lifts
Pensioners 60 yrs and over, as children
Credit cards accepted yes

SKI SCHOOLS
Adults ESF, 565FF for 6 half-days.
Beginners course 1,075FF for 6 half-days
including lift pass
Private lessons ESF, 248FF for $1\frac{1}{2}$ hrs
Snowboarding 565FF for 6 half-days
Cross-country 565FF for 6 half-days,
private lessons 248FF for $1\frac{1}{2}$ hrs.
Loipe 20km
Other courses monoski, off-piste,
race training
Guiding companies through ESF

CHILDREN
Lift pass Valmorel 559-708FF, Le Grand
Domaine 591-753FF, both for 6 days
Ski kindergarten Saperlipopette, 3-7 yrs,
8.30am-5pm, 724-867FF for 6 days, extra
62-66FF per day for lunch
Ski school ESF, 4-13 yrs, 525FF for 6 half-
days. Beginners courses, 1,025FF for 6
half-days including lift pass.
Non-ski kindergarten Saperlipopette, 6
mths-3 yrs, 724-867FF for 6 days, extra
62-66FF per day for lunch

FOOD AND DRINK PRICES
Coffee 8-10FF, glass of wine 12FF, small
beer 12-13FF, dish of the day
47-60FF

---

generally larger and better designed than their counterparts in other French purpose-built resorts. Most apartments have balconies and provide easy access to the pistes. The two-star Hotel du Bourg, used by most British tour operators, is situated in the main village centre. Its rooms are unadorned boxes, and the beds are as narrow as coffins. The Hotel la Fontaine has bigger, better rooms. Hotel Planchamp, above the main village, is convenient for skiing down from but not handy for evenings out.

Eating in and out

If proof were needed that the French now live off pizza and fast food, then Valmorel is it. There is no gourmet restaurant, but Le Creuset is considered the best in town. Ski-Roc is best for rabbit filet with garlic, and La Galette for its pierrade stone-grilled steaks. Le Perce-Neige is also recommended. Jumbo Lolo serves Tex-Mex, and La Marmite advertises couscous and paella but you should stick with the steak-frites. Chez Albert is best for pizza. Self-caterers have a wide choice of tempting *traiteurs*, and the Superette du Bourg and Etoile des Alpes, right across the main street from each other, have a full range of groceries.

Après-ski

It is not that there isn't any, but it is all rather innocent and uninteresting. Jean's Club under the Télébourg tower is the only disco. Loud Top-20-type music is played in the Perce Neige, Café de la Gare and at La Cordée. The Shaker Bar in the Hotel la Fontaine has comfortable sofas and karaoke evenings. Other entertainment includes evening sleigh rides and night-skiing at Planchamp on Thursdays.

Childcare

The only childminding service is the Saperlipopette nursery. The school has bedrooms and playrooms for infants from six months. Children from 18 months to three years of age have their own enclosed outdoor area. Older children have their own fenced-off ski slope with a rope-tow. Reservations should be made well in advance of leaving Britain, as the school keeps to a strict ratio of five children per nanny. 'Good English, good care, and exceptionally well-organised' was one of a number of positive comments this year on a nursery that has been criticised in the past for its 'unfeeling' attitude.

Round-up

Isola 2000
top 2610m (8,561ft) bottom 1800m (5,904ft)

Isola is a purpose-built resort and the most southerly ski area in France. In reasonable weather conditions it is 90 minutes' drive north from Nice along the dramatic road beside the Tinée ravines. The resort was built by a British property company in the 1960s. Created with families in mind, it has a convenient complex of shops, bars, economically designed apartments and hotels, and a large, sunny nursery area. Isola is not accessible from the north, which in part accounts for why so few tour operators offer it in their brochures. British skiers do, however, make up a big slice of the winter business and many of them own apartments here.

The resort's original building, the ugly and soulless Front de Neige Centre, is right on the slopes. In an attempt to dress it up, the more attractive, wood-clad additions of Le Bristol, Le Hameau and Les Ardets were built behind it. These are less convenient, but contain bigger and better apartments and a luxurious hillside hotel. This has greatly helped the overall look of Isola 2000, dissipating some of its claustrophobic atmosphere.

The ski area is limited, but varied enough for beginners, families with small children and intermediates. There are 46 pistes covered by 24 lifts with 35 hectares of snowmaking. The resorts of **Auron** and **Valberg** are both within easy reach for a day's skiing.

TOURIST OFFICE
Tel 33 4 93 23 15 15
Fax 33 4 93 23 14 25

Pra-Loup
top 2500m (8,200ft) bottom 1600m (5,248ft)

This small resort in the Hautes Alpes has a surprisingly extensive range of beginner and intermediate trails but few advanced. The 160km of piste is shared with neighbouring **La Foux d'Allos**. Named after the wolves that once frequented these pine forests, Pra Loup is a collection of hotels and apartments built in the 1960s, along with some older chalets. Prices at the restaurants and bars are lower than in better-known French resorts, and there is one disco, the Marmotel.

The skiing takes place on two main mountains, accessible by cable car from the top of the village. Intermediates will find open-bowl skiing and good tree-line runs with spectacular scenery. There is extensive off-piste, for which you will need a guide, but only five black (difficult) runs.

TOURIST OFFICE
Tel 33 4 92 84 10 04
Fax 33 4 92 84 02 93

Valloire
top 2600m (8,528ft) bottom 1430m (4,690ft)

Valloire is an attractive, reasonably large village set in an isolated bowl above the Maurienne Valley. It is still very much a traditional French farming community, and the odd whiff of manure mingling with the aroma of freshly baked bread is all part of the morning walk to the lifts. It is a reasonably priced resort, friendly and uncrowded except in peak season. However, the resort's proximity to the Italian border means that it can be busy and very noisy.

The 150km of pisted skiing comprises 89 mainly intermediate runs. The skiing takes place in two areas: La Sétaz and Le Crey du Quart, on adjacent mountains reached by lifts which start a few minutes away from the village centre and rise up to 2500m. The terrain is varied, and some of the runs are as long as 1000 vertical metres. The skiing is not difficult; even the black runs would be red (intermediate) by many other resorts' standards.

Mountain access to La Sétaz is by a six-person gondola from the village up to Thimel, followed by a chair- and drag-lift to the summit. From here the main route down to the village is an enjoyable red run. Served by artificial snow-cannon and groomed to a high standard, the area provides a choice of runs from the wide but sometimes icy red, to the gently meandering blue (easy) runs towards **Les Verneys** or **Valloire**. An alternative is to catch the end of the green (beginner) path of Les Myosotis, which takes you to the centre of the village. You can also fork right below the Thimel quad-chair and follow Les Myosotis all the way down as it curves gently through the trees. Several reporters point out that in sunny weather Les Myosotis quickly becomes worn, rutted and rocky.

Access to Le Crey du Quart ski area is either by the Montissot and Colerieux chair-lifts via Les Myosotis, or directly from Valloire on two long chairs. A gondola is planned for this area in the near future. The skiing at Le Crey du Quart is mainly of the red motorway variety, with gentler slopes going down towards Valloire. **Valmeinier 1500** is a small and traditional village with a satellite at 1800m.

TOURIST OFFICE
Tel 33 4 79 59 03 96
Fax 33 4 79 59 09 66

Italy

Over the past two seasons Italy has developed into the 'hottest' of all ski destinations. The sorry state of sterling is matched only by the lira. Extremely favourable exchange rates have made ski holidays here a more attractive proposition than in any of the other main alpine countries. Not only is the price of a package holiday markedly less expensive, but all the inescapable on-ground extras, from ski rental to mountain lunches, are positively cheap in comparison with France, Austria and Switzerland.

The skiing in the Dolomites is some of the most charming and extensive anywhere, and airport improvements have greatly eased access to the resorts. Courmayeur and Cervinia are the traditional resorts of the Aosta Valley, but rural Gressoney and Champoluc have blossomed more recently. The staging of the Alpine Ski World Championships in Sestriere this winter will focus attention on the delights of the extensive Milky Way area. The country's share of the British market has shot from 5 per cent to more than 20 per cent, a ceiling dictated only by the number of tourist beds that tour operators have managed to maintain.

However, Italy is no newcomer to skiing. Winter tourists first appeared in Cortina d'Ampezzo as long ago as 1902, and the resort hosted the Winter Olympics in 1956. Through the boom years of the 1960s Italy ranked alongside Austria, Switzerland and newly emergent France as an equal alpine partner in ski tourism. Its position was washed away in the meltwater of economic uncertainty which followed the OPEC oil crisis in the 1970s. Travel firms moved their operations to less hazardous parts of the Alps, and the Dolomite resorts lost their share of the international market.

The lean years that followed were marked by a disastrous snow record. But as Italy's economy was restructured, so too were its ski resorts. Multi-million pound lift systems have slowly replaced rickety drags and second-hand chairs. Business booms once again, but cheap holidays here are unlikely to last forever — enjoy them while you can.

First-time visitors will be delighted by the Italian zest for enjoyment both on and off the slopes, and as a nation they have raised the pastime of eating on the mountain to an art form. From long before midday, delicious scents wafting from every wayside hut in resorts like Courmayeur are enough to tempt you in for a lunch that can last way into the afternoon. The Italian penchant for partying extends to the après-ski, which starts early and carries on late into the night.

Although the Italians are well-known for their love of children, the major resorts are mysteriously lacking in childcare facilities. This is possibly due to the fact that Italian families often travel as a whole — complete with granny to look after the *bambini*. Exceptions to the rule include Cortina d'Ampezzo and Courmayeur, which both have kindergartens of exceptionally high standards.

Bormio

ALTITUDE 1225m (4,018ft)

Bormio's history dates from Roman times, when its location at a crossroads in the Valtellina in the mountains of Lombardy made it a natural staging post for trans-Alpine traffic. Attracted by hot springs and spectacular views over what is now the Stelvio National Park, the Romans built a town and thermal bath complex at the foot of the pass. The town prospered during the Middle Ages, and its ancient, cobbled streets date from that time. In subsequent centuries it was sidelined by history, but the post-Second World War tourist boom has restored some of its former vitality. Today its ugly suburbs spread over the broad valley floor, but without impinging on the charm of the pedestrianised centre.

Bormio shares a lift pass, but not a lift link, with the neighbouring village of **Santa Caterina** and with the small Valdidentro ski area above the village of **Oga** on the opposite side of the valley. The lift pass is also valid for **Livigno**, which is an hour's drive away over a pass to the west. **St Moritz**, across the Swiss border in the Engadine, is another option for a day's excursion.

On the mountain
top 3012m (9,879ft) bottom 1225m (4,018ft)
Bormio's first lifts opened in the 1960s, but the resort came of age in 1985 when it hosted the World Alpine Championships. The slopes rise steeply on a single broad mountain served by two base-stations, both within a few minutes' walk of the town centre. The main one is the starting point for the two-stage cable car to the Cima Bianca via **Bormio 2000**, a substantial mid-station with a large family hotel and a small shopping mall. This can also be reached by car in most conditions. The alternative is the six-seater gondola to **Ciuk**, a lower mid-station, which also has accommodation and restaurants.

The top third of the mountain is above the tree-line, with a network of chair-lifts providing a variety of choices. The pistes are now more user-friendly thanks to a grinding machine that reduces stones to sand. Lower down, the skiing is in glades cut from the forest, ensuring good visibility when the weather closes in.

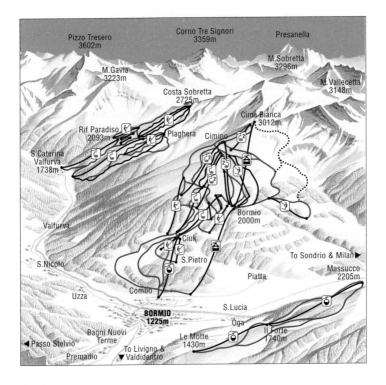

Beginners

The only nursery slopes are at Bormio 2000, a mixed blessing as everyone has to buy a lift pass from day one. On a more positive note, it means
that everyone learns halfway up the mountain, which gives more of a
feeling of what skiing is all about. After a few days of mastering the basic
manoeuvres, beginners will find plenty of easy pistes in the wooded area
down to Ciuk. By the end of the week, many will be skiing the blue (easy)
runs from the top of the cable car.

Intermediates

For the two-week-plus brigade, Bormio's slopes are to die for; there are
no particularly steep sections and lots of high-speed cruising. The 14-km
descent from the Cima Bianca to the town is just one of many exhilarating options. The bottom section of the Bosco Basso piste has been
widened to provide an alternative route back to the gondola station.

Advanced

Strong piste-skiers may be frustrated by the lack of challenge on
Bormio's slopes, as the two short runs that are graded black (difficult)
might well be red in a steeper resort. The Stelvio FIS course, which runs

from just above La Rocca, past Ciuk to the bottom of the gondola, is one of the less demanding and therefore occasional choices for the World Cup circuit.

Off-piste

The powder opportunities off the Cima Bianca more than compensate for the shortage of black bump runs. To the west of the main piste there is a steep, open bowl leading down to some shallow gradient tree-level skiing. Those who plan to go below the right-hand turn-off to Bormio 2000 should check first that the Ornella drag-lift is running. To the east of the pistes, a wider choice of terrain gives access to a more heavily wooded area. A long trail leads back to the Praimont chair. An alternative is to ski down the flattering run to Santa Caterina. Those who are prepared to hire a guide and climb on skins will find magnificent terrain in both winter and summer on the Stelvio Glacier. There is also summer skiing on the glacier but it is not covered by the Bormio lift pass.

Ski schools and guiding

Of the six competing ski schools in Bormio, the Alta Valtellina based near the nursery slopes at Bormio 2000 is highly recommended for its young, friendly English-speaking instructors. The Scuola Sci Bormio receives mixed reports: 'Well organised but tuition was rudimentary, consisting of mainly follow-my-leader with odd comments every now and then'. The more traditional alternatives include the Nazionale and Bormio 2000. The Anzi School is for hotel guests only. The Sertorelli and the Capitani organisations specialise in summer ski-touring, retaining only a skeleton winter staff for valued clients.

Snowboarding

The three main ski schools, Alta Valtellina, Nazionale and Bormio 2000, have group classes when there is sufficient demand. The off-piste opportunities are extensive, but there are no specialist on-mountain facilities for surfers. For those who want to experiment, boards can be rented by the hour or half-day at Bormio 2000.

Mountain restaurants

The favoured stopping-off point for lunch or refreshments is La Rocca, an old-fashioned hut on the main trail from the top of the mountain to Bormio 2000. It has two rooms, each with a wood-burning stove, and friendly service. It also hosts dinner followed by a torchlight descent whenever there is sufficient demand.

The Rhondendri near the top of the Rocca chair is also recommended ('quiet, small and pleasant, with a splendid viewing position at the top of a black mogul run'). The Girasole Hotel and the self-service cafeteria at Bormio 2000 are equally convenient though less traditional alternatives — 'we were pleasantly surprised by the moderate prices', commented one reporter.

Off the mountain

Bormio is the most Italian of resorts, with a strong sense of style in its immaculate shops and restaurants. In the early evening, chattering crowds stroll down the narrow, cobbled streets and fill the bars and cafés on the historic Via Roma, the centre of activity in the old town. The new town, with its modern hotels and high-rise apartment blocks, makes a stark contrast. As one reader summed it up: 'Bormio is much nicer than the brochures suggest. It is upmarket yet cheaper than the UK. It is authentically Italian, ideal for families and couples but not suitable for those looking for a rowdy nightlife'.

> ■ **OTHER SPORTS**
>
> Swimming, squash, parapente, snow-mobiling, helicopter rides, climbing wall, indoor tennis, tobogganing, skating, thermal baths

Bormio's nearest airports are Bergamo and Milan, both officially three-and-a-half hours away, although reporters have experienced transfer times of up to six-and-a-half hours from Bergamo. The drive from Milan includes a dramatically beautiful section along the shore of Lake Como.

Accommodation

The modernised four-star Hotel Posta, on a pedestrianised street in the old town, offers luxurious accommodation, a swimming-pool and fitness centre. The alternative four-star recommendations are the Rezia and the Palace. Those who prefer to be near the lifts should consider one of the modern three-star options: the Derby, the Nevada or the Funivia. In the two-star category, the family-run Dante and the atmospheric Gufo offer exceptional value in central locations. Hotel Aurora is praised by reporters: 'The hotel was very clean and warm, the staff friendly and helpful, and the food excellent. However, few rooms with baths were available'.

As the town of Bormio is only ski-in ski-out when snow conditions are good in January and February, there is an excellent case to be made for staying in the three-star Girasole at Bormio 2000. This is especially true for holidays over the Easter period when the main resort begins to wind down. The hotel is run with a strong emphasis on family entertainment by the hospitable Alfredo Cantoni and his English wife, Elizabeth.

Eating in and out

Although *pizzocheri*, a rather gritty indigenous pasta, is something of an acquired taste, the Valtellina also has an interesting range of specialities including *charcuterie*, mushrooms and locally produced wines. The best places to try them are the Rasiga (a beautifully converted saw mill), the Vecchia Combo, the Taulà, and Al Cambrin. All four restaurants will prepare multi-course gourmet feasts at modest all-inclusive rates, provided they are booked in advance. Bormio also has five pizzerias and a spaghetteria. Self-catering is not the norm in a resort with a wide choice of cheap eating places, but the specialist grocery shops on Via Roma certainly stock all the necessary ingredients for home cooking on a magnificent scale.

Skiing facts: **Bormio**

TOURIST OFFICE
Via Roma 131/B, I-23032 Bormio,
Lombardy
Tel 39 342 903300
Fax 39 342 904696

THE RESORT
By road Calais 1146km
By rail Tirano 39km
By air Milan or Bergamo $3\frac{1}{2}$ hrs
Visitor beds 6,035
Transport free ski bus with lift pass

THE SKIING
Linked or nearby resorts Livigno (n),
Santa Caterina (n), San Colombano (n)
Longest run Pista Stelvio, 14km (red)
Number of lifts 16
Total of trails/pistes 25km in Bormio only
(23% easy, 68% intermediate, 9% difficult)
Nursery slopes 4 on the mountain at Ciuk
and Bormio 2000
Summer skiing 20km on Stelvio Pass
between May and November
Snowmaking 8.5km covered

LIFT PASSES
Area pass (covers Bormio, Livigno, Santa
Caterina, San Colombano) L210,000-
235,000 for 6 days
Day pass (Bormio only) L43,000-46,000
Beginners no free lifts
Pensioners 65 yrs and over as children

Credit cards accepted yes

SKI SCHOOLS
Adults Alta Valtellina, 9-11am or
11am-1pm, L95,000 for 6 x 2-hr lessons.
Nazionale, 10am-12.30pm or 2-4.30pm,
L140,000 for 6 half-days. Also Anzi,
Bormio 2000, Capitani and
Sertorelli ski schools,
details on request
Private lessons L40,000-45,000 per hr
Snowboarding all ski schools, times
and prices on request
Cross-country Scuola Sci Fondo, L82,000-
92,000 for 6 days, private lessons L34,000
per hr. Loipe 12.5km
Other courses off-piste, telemark
Guiding companies Casa delle Guide
Alpine Bormio, Associazione Guide Alpine
Alta Valtellina

CHILDREN
Liftpass 13 yrs and under, L145,000-
160,000 for 6 days
Ski kindergarten none
Ski school Alta Valtellina, 4 yrs and over,
10am-1pm, L180,000-200,000 for 6 days
Non-ski kindergarten none

FOOD AND DRINK PRICES
Coffee L1,400, glass of wine L1,500, small
beer L4,000, dish of the day L10,000-
15,000

Après-ski

The Bagna Vecchi, a few miles out of town, has a natural sauna and
curative hot baths in a cave in the hillside. These are part of a very atmospheric turn-of-the-century spa complex offering a range of treatments
for weary skiers. In town, the natural hot water has been put to good use
in the large public swimming-pool. The Gorky on the Via Roma and the
Vagabond in the church square are currently the most popular pubs,
both after skiing and after dinner. Late nightlife focuses on the King's

Club disco, open until 3am, with the piano bar at the Aurora hotel a less frenetic option.

Childcare
The Alta Valtellina Ski School provides excellent English-language group lessons for children of four years old and over. There is no formal crèche service, but the Girasole arranges local babysitters during the day and in the evening.

Linked or nearby resorts

Santa Caterina
top 3296m (10,814ft) bottom 1737m (5,697ft)
Santa Caterina, or San Cat as it is known, is a quiet, attractive village 30 minutes away by bus up a mountain road that is a dead-end in winter when the Gavia Pass is closed. It usually has better snow than its larger neighbour, Bormio, with which it shares a lift pass. Local skiing is on the north-east-facing slopes of the Sobretta. The higher slopes are fairly steep and graded black; there are also some winding, intermediate trails down between the trees.

The Santa Caterina Ski School receives mixed but generally favourable reviews. There is a 10-km cross-country loipe beyond the resort and skating on a natural rink.

The San Matteo Hotel is recommended for comfort and food. Self-caterers have a choice of two well-stocked supermarkets. Nightlife is limited, with one fairly large disco and a number of cosy bars that remain open until after midnight.

TOURIST OFFICE
Tel/fax 39 342 935598

Cervinia

Cervinia is a potpourri of a resort — concrete mixed in with newer façades of wood and natural stone — set at the dead end of a valley running south to the east–west Aosta Valley. Ugly in the eyes of many, and challenging the skiing abilities of few, Cervinia is one of the most popular resorts in Italy with the British, mainly due to its high altitude and snow reliability. According to one tour operator it was 'almost impossible to get a bed in the resort last season'.

Perched on the Swiss–Italian border on the sunnier and much snowier side of the Matterhorn, Breuil-Cervinia, as the resort is officially known, is a two-and-a-half-hour drive from either Turin or Geneva. The ambience is over-whelmingly Italian, making weekends and school holiday periods chaotic and prone to queues, though cheerful and unaggressive. This is one resort where British skiers are welcomed with open arms, as they make up the largest proportion of foreign visitors.

■ **GOOD POINTS**

Excellent snow record, value for money, alpine scenery, sunny slopes ideal for intermediate cruising, summer glacier skiing, extensive skiing season, long runs

■ **BAD POINTS**

Heavy traffic, inconvenient lift access, lift queues, unattractive village, lack of expert and off-piste terrain ·

Cervinia is more expensive than Italian resorts further from Switzerland and not as chic as Cortina or even Courmayeur. The lift system was futuristic in 1936 when the first cable car to Plan Maison opened; after that it was only updated in parts, with one essential cable car, Furggen, closed without notice of eventual replacement. Today, some 34,000 skiers per hour can be transported to an official count of 120km of pistes on 34 lifts, though not without waiting for some of the most essential links.

Cervinia's skiing is linked to the nearby village of **Valtournenche** (1524m) on the same lift pass, and to **Zermatt** and the glacier, although a hefty daily supplement must be paid to ski in this resort. **Courmayeur** and **Chamonix** are easy day trips, as are the smaller resorts of **Gressoney** and **Champoluc**.

On the mountain
top 3490m (11,447ft) bottom 1524m (4,999ft)

Cervinia is a resort for beginners and intermediates, with excellent slopes for learning and improving technique at all levels. With the highest skiing in Italy, mostly around a sunny west-facing bowl, Cervinia is one of the best mountains in the Alps for early- and late-season skiing on long pistes.

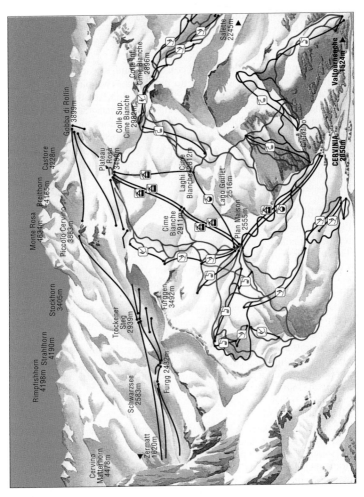

Mountain access is most direct from the queue-prone gondola and cable car, which are an irritating hike uphill from the village. This is often complained about; in fact, it is no more than a five-minute warm-up exercise, which is made easier by stairs on the direct attack, and less steep if the longer, winding road is taken. Access is also possible from drag-lifts to the left of the village in the nursery area, or from the satellite areas of **Cieloalto** and Valtournenche. Naturally, most skiers insist on getting to the top of the mountain at Plateau Rosa, even if they do not plan on paying extra, to go on to Zermatt. To avoid queues, travelling up to Plateau Rosa via the Laghi Cime Bianchi 12-person gondola, which carries 2,400 skiers per hour, is a good idea. Valtournenche at

1524m is a sector of uncrowded runs, but does not provide access to Cervinia's hub.

Beginners

If you learn to ski in this resort you will wonder what all the fuss is about. Beginners tend to spend no more than two days with the ski school on the conveniently accessed nursery slopes at the village edge. Cervinia's excellent snow record means that novices have good conditions on the nursery slopes beside the village, before moving up to the network of green (beginner) and blue (easy) pistes at Plan Maison. There are few resorts where beginners can graduate so quickly and are able to ski runs as high as the top-to-bottom, wide and well-groomed blue piste from Plateau Rosa down to the village, which is a drop of nearly 1500 vertical metres.

Intermediates

Flattery comes into skiing in a big way at the intermediate level. Many red (intermediate) runs in Cervinia would be graded blue in Switzerland. The truly enjoyable Ventina (marked no. 7 on the piste-map) from Plateau Rosa down to Cervinia is one of the most famous runs in the Alps. Most accounts clock it at 8km, although the tourist office describes it as 11km.

Similarly, the run down into Valtournenche, starting over in Zermatt at the Klein Matterhorn, is perhaps not quite the 22km claimed, though taken non-stop, except for the required drag-lift connection, it is enough to turn any advanced skier's legs to noodles. In fact, skiers used to the intimidating steeps in Chamonix or Val d'Isère will find the gradual pitch of Cervinia's pistes both ego-boosting and useful for advancing technical skills.

Advanced

'Ski Cervinia and die!' — only from boredom if you are a truly advanced skier who insists on sticking to the groomed and patrolled pistes. Despite warnings 'Solo per Esperti!' (experts only), the marked black (difficult) runs on Cieloalto and down from Plan Maison will not increase anyone's insurance premium. The one testing black piste, to the skier's right of the confusingly named Cieloalto drag-lift (on the opposite side of the mountain from the Cieloalto sector), was last year taken off the map and is now considered off-piste.

Off-piste

The cliff band and bowl at Furggen are now lost, as there are no plans to replace the cable car that used to run up there. On powder days, especially when wind closes upper lifts, as it tends to do, the trees on the shoulder above Cieloalto are a good off-piste option. More ambitious routes require guides and mountaineering gear. Heli-skiing is available on the Zermatt side of the mountain and, in addition to ski-touring, provides access to a wealth of glacier runs.

Ski schools and guiding

The main Cervino Ski School in Cervinia is more organised than the smaller school in Cieloalto; the younger instructors appear to be more motivated and speak better English. One reporter noted that the teachers at Il Cervino seem to do whatever they feel like, rather than following a strict method, 'the way they do in Austria'. Valtournenche has its own ski school. Mountain guides from the local bureau in Cervinia charge considerably less than their Swiss counterparts but have equal expertise on the border peaks like the Matterhorn (or Il Cervino as it is known in Italy).

Snowboarding

Aside from the ski school there is no independent, dedicated snowboard school. Neither is there a snowboard park or half-pipe. Cervinia's wide, pisted slopes provide good training ground for early intermediate boarders, but the terrain is disappointing for freeriders looking for natural jumps and drop-offs. Angelo Vallet by the Hotel Cristallo is the closest the resort has to a specialised snowboard shop.

Cross-country

A fee is charged for the 6km of prepared trails at village-level in Cervinia and the additional 9km in Valtournenche. All the trails are graded easy to intermediate, and the longest is 4.5km.

Mountain restaurants

The new piste-map now shows where to stop for lunch, but gives no guide to the few restaurants with decent WCs. Cervinia's mountain meals are not cheap by Italian standards, but are still much better value than on the other side of the Matterhorn in Zermatt. Bar Ventina on the eponymous run down from Plateau Rosa, Bar Bontadini on the slope of the same name and Bar Etoile near the Rocce Nere chair-lift are among the best for polenta and fondue. Although not very high up the mountain, Bàita Cretaz da Mario on the nursery slopes receives outstanding reviews for its cuisine, relaxed and attentive service and lovely linen tablecloths. The Igloo, run by English exile Pauline at the top of the Bardoney chair, is praised for its tasty food and large portions.

Off the mountain

Cervinia became the summer headquarters for mountain climbers at the end of the nineteenth century. It was known as Breuil until Mussolini changed the name to capitalise on the Matterhorn. Today Cervinia is functional rather than fashionable. Despite some tarting up, buildings have no authentic mountain charm, nor do the shops have much class — this is the Italy of Fiat rather than Ferrari. The Italian side of the Matterhorn, unlike Zermatt, is not car-free. Attempts to create a pedestrian zone are obviated by anyone who feels like shunting aside the moveable barrier. Parking at weekends is chaotic, since the influx from Milan and Turin insist on parking in the street instead of in the five free and one fee-paying parking areas.

It is regularly reported that Cervinia has no bus system. There is no free ski bus, but a municipal bus makes circuits every 20 minutes as far as Cieloalto until 8pm.

Accommodation

Cervinia has virtually no chalet or self-catering accommodation. Its hotels date from the 'brutal' era of Italian architecture in most instances, and are seldom convenient for the lifts. The four-star Punta Maquignaz is an attractive wood-clad hotel close to the ski school and drag-lifts, and was consequently booked out all season last year. You can ski back to the Petit Palais, much closer to the cable car and about five minutes from the village centre. The Cristallo is the oldest hotel, an ugly arc of white concrete, though nicely decorated inside and with a swimming-pool. The Furggen is a tiring ten-minute walk uphill from town, but is ideal for skiing down to the lifts and is home to Cervinia's best sunset views. Blocks such as downtown Breuil and the utilitarian Astoria (right by the cable car) are the hotels most popular with British skiers.

■ OTHER SPORTS

Parapente, skating, snowmobiling, tobogganing, swimming

Eating in and out

The resort has a wide range of restaurants (around 29 not counting hotels), which are priced rather highly compared to British expectations of Italy, but are mostly good value. Il Capriccio in the centre of Cervinia is rated by locals as having the most elegant décor and the most discriminating cuisine. Le Nicchia is similarly rich for pocket and paunch. La Tana is recommended for wild boar, venison and everything with *porcini* mushrooms. La Maison de Sausure is the place to try the Valdostana specialities typical of the region. It is hard to beat the pizzas at Al Solito Posto, which is the locals' favourite.

Après-ski

Even people who have spent several seasons in Cervinia admit that the nightlife lacks lustre. 'Like the skiing', says one reporter, 'it is all intermediate'. Of the two discos, the Garage is the more trendy while the Chimera is more sedate. There are no piano bars. Yel Matrob cocktail bar is the liveliest, thanks to its animated patron Renzo. Very popular is the Copa Pan Irish bar, which serves Murphy's beer. The scruffy Dragon bar is said to have the cheapest beer in town.

Childcare

The Italians appear to bring their grandmothers or nannies with them as Cervinia still does not have a daycare centre aside from outdoor courses with the ski schools. The tourist office has a list of officially sanctioned babysitters but admits that few speak English.

Skiing facts: **Cervinia**

TOURIST OFFICE
Via Carrel 29, I-11021 Breuil-Cervinia,
Aosta
Tel 39 166 949136
Fax 39 166 949731

THE RESORT
By road Calais 1000km
By rail Châtillon 27km, regular buses
to resort
By air Turin or Geneva $2\frac{1}{2}$ hrs
Visitor beds 5,700
Transport free bus from Camper's Square
to the church

THE SKIING
Linked or nearby resorts Zermatt (I),
Valtournenche (I)
Longest run Ventina, 8km (red)
Number of lifts 73 with Zermatt
Total of trails/pistes 120km in Cervinia
(34% easy, 53% intermediate,
13% difficult). 230km with Zermatt
Nursery slopes 2 lifts
Summer skiing on Plateau Rosa, 8 lifts and
a cable car
Snowmaking 7 hectares covered

LIFT PASSES
Area pass (covers Cervinia and
Valtournenche) L240,000 for 6 days

Day pass L49,000
Beginners points tickets
Pensioners no reduction
Credit cards accepted yes

SKI SCHOOLS
Adults Cervino and Cieloalto ski schools,
10am-1pm, L180,000 for 6 days
Private lessons both ski schools,
L47,000 per hr
Snowboarding Cervino Ski School, 10am-
1pm, L180,000 for 6 days, private lessons
L47,000 per hr
Cross-country Cervino Ski School, details
on request. Loipe 6km on edge of village
Other courses off-piste, telemark,
heli-skiing at Zermatt
Guiding companies Guide del Cervino

CHILDREN
Lift pass 6 yrs and over as adults,
free for 5 yrs and under
Ski kindergarten none
Ski school both ski schools,
5 yrs and over, 10am-1pm, L240,000
for 6 days
Non-ski kindergarten none

FOOD AND DRINK PRICES
Coffee L1,300, glass of wine L1,500, small
beer L2,000, dish of the day L25,000

Cortina d'Ampezzo

ALTITUDE 1224m (4,015ft)

Cortina d'Ampezzo has at long last been allowed to resume its old role as Italy's premier *Gran Turismo* resort. It sits in isolated and stately splendour in the Ampezzo Valley, a two-and-a-half-hour journey from Venice. Unlike its neighbours in the German-speaking Sud Tirol, Cortina is Italian to its voluptuous core and largely devoid of German and Austrian tourists. Some 90 per cent of its visitors are Italian.

■ **GOOD POINTS**

Extensive nursery slopes, variety of restaurants, long intermediate runs, many activities for non-skiers, beautiful scenery, skiing for all standards, extensive cross-country, tree-level skiing, attractive town, lively après-ski

■ **BAD POINTS**

Spread-out ski areas, crowded cable cars, limited for late-season holidays, heavy traffic outside pedestrian area

The resort was extensively developed for the 1956 Winter Olympics, and ranks with St Moritz and Chamonix as one of the world's few all-round winter sports resorts. Cortina's downhill skiing includes some of the best nursery slopes anywhere and long, challenging runs for intermediate to accomplished skiers; all of this takes places amid stunningly beautiful scenery.

Cortina has an upmarket reputation, which can put off those skiers who see Italy as the destination for cheap and cheerful holidays, but it is not an exclusive or overtly expensive resort. There are plenty of pleasant, family-run hotels with reasonable prices, as well as simple, characterful bars.

On the mountain
top 2948m (9,669ft) bottom 1224m (4,015ft)

The skiing is divided between the main Tofana-Socrepes area to the west of town, which is reached via the Freccia nel Cielo (arrow in the sky) cable car, and Staunies-Faloria on the other side of town, which consists of two sectors separated by a minor road. A scattering of smaller ski areas along the Passo Falzarego road still belong to individual farmers. Passo Falzarego, further down the road and 20 minutes in all from the town centre, links with the Sella Ronda ski area.

The disparate nature of the skiing is one of the resort's irritating points, but only detracts slightly from its total enjoyment as it is easy to plan a day in each separate area. According to readers this year, the free ski bus service, which runs between the two cable-car stations (Tofana and Faloria) has improved and is now 'frequent and punctual'. Buses also travel to and from the more distant ski areas.

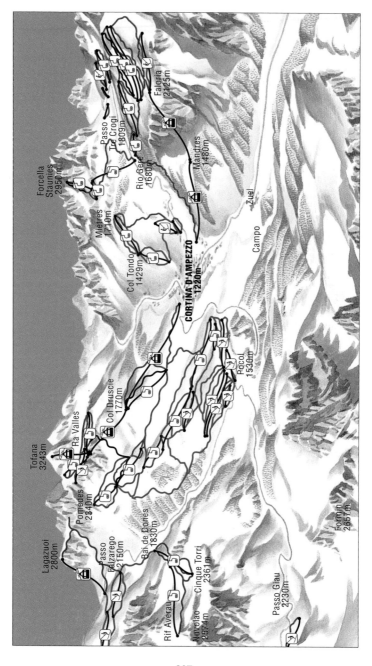

Both Tofana and Faloria can be reached on foot from most of the accommodation if you are prepared for a long slog in ski boots. Morning queues for the Tofana cable car are not a problem due to the late rising-time of the average Cortina skier — the morning rush-hour never starts before 10.30am. However, one reporter commented: 'The waiting at the Tofana and Faloria cable cars was not too bad, but being packed in like sardines was not a great start to the day'. The top section of Tofana is designated for sunbathers and sightseers only.

Beginners

A long serpentine blue (easy) piste takes you down from Tofana's mid-station to link with Socrepes, a delightful, undulating area of blue runs above the road at Pocol, which is served by easy drag-lifts and covered by snow-cannon. Pierosà-Miétres is an equally gentle sector.

Intermediates

The majority of Cortina's skiing is of intermediate standard, with long runs in both the main ski areas. Between the resort and Col Druscié the Tofana cable car travels over gentle, tree-lined terrain and open fields with wide and easy trails, which cross rough roads without much warn-ing for either skiers or drivers. Snow conditions often make these runs testing, which gives them their red (intermediate) and black (difficult) gradings. The second stage of the cable car climbs the sheer, rocky mountainside to Ra Valles, in the middle of a pleasant bowl.

A day trip into the **Sella Ronda** ski area should not be missed for any-one of intermediate standard and upwards. This starts from Passo Falzarego, where a dramatic cable car soars 640 vertical metres up a cliff-face to Lagazuoi, linking into the area via a beautiful 11-km red run past a shimmering turquoise ice-fall and several welcoming huts to **Armentarola** and **San Cassiano** beyond. Reporters recommend taking an early bus from Cortina to Passo Falzarego, skiing down from Lagazuoi to the restaurant at Sare, and from there catching a taxi-bus to Armentarola and skiing over to **Corvara**. However, the whole day is a rush and can be stressful: 'Like Anneka Rice in *Treasure Hunt* on skis'. 'By the skin of our teeth we managed to get the last lift down from **Colfosco** to Corvara at 5pm', warned one reporter, 'from there it was a £40 taxi ride to Cortina'. The Dolomiti Superski lift pass covers both Cortina and the Sella Ronda and is good value.

Advanced

Higher up at Tofana, the Ra Valles sector at 3000m offers the best snow in the resort. Near the bottom of the Tofana bowl, a gap in the rock gives access to an exhilarating black trail, which has a fairly steep south-facing stretch in the middle. The run ends up at the Pomedes chair-lifts, an area which itself offers some excellent runs including a couple of good blacks and the spectacular Canellone downhill racecourse.

From the foot of Monte Cristallo at Faloria, where the great Olympic and World Champion Alberto Tomba can sometimes be seen honing his gate technique, a two-stage chair-lift climbs to Forcella Staunies, one of the best couloirs in the area. The top section of the descent necessitates some testingly sharp turns, as it is both narrow and very steep.

Off-piste

After a fresh snowfall, Forcella Staunies becomes an appealing off-piste area, as do the higher reaches of Tofana. Gruppo Guide Alpine, the resort's ski guiding organisation, arranges day ski-tours.

Ski schools and guiding

The main Scuola Sci Cortina has meeting places at Socrepes, Pocol and Pierosà-Miétres. The standards appear to be mixed, depending mainly on the standard of English spoken by the instructor. One reporter praised his lessons as: 'Well organised, with a friendly, English-speaking instructor who took pains to give everyone in the class individual attention when necessary'. Scuola Sci Azzurra is a smaller alternative.

Snowboarding

There are no special facilities for snowboarding on the mountain, but lessons are available through the Scuola Sci Cortina.

Cross-country

Long and varied cross-country trails include one extended loipe that follows the old railway track to **Dobbiaco**. Another takes you all the way to **Villach** in Austria. The Scuola Italiano Sci Fondo Cortina has 24 instructors and is based at **Fiames**.

Mountain restaurants

Eating is a memorable experience in Cortina, and the choice of restaurants is extensive in the main ski areas. Rifugio Duca d'Aosta is recommended for its wood-panelled walls and heart-warming local dishes. Rifugio Berghaus Pomedes has hand-carved furniture and a varied menu. If you want to continue skiing after lunch it would be wise to avoid the *Kanederli*; consumption of these heavy dumplings of ham, bread, cheese and other kitchen leftovers is not conducive to an afternoon of athleticism on the slopes. Reporters praise El Farel at the foot of Socrepes, and Col Taron in the same area, which serves delicious pasta.

Next stage down the mountain from the Duca d'Aosta is Bàita Pie Tofana, a relaxed eating place with a good sun-terrace and attractive interior. Rifugio Averau at Cinque Torri has stunning views and is voted best restaurant in the ski area by one reporter. Rifugio Lagazuoi is situated a steep but worthwhile walk from the top of the Falzarego cable car.

Expensive places for serious lunching include El Camineto at the bottom of the Olympic piste, just by the Pie Tofana chair-lift. This is the most prestigious of all lunchtime venues, where skiers join their fur-coated friends for exotic fare served in silver-domed dishes by a battalion of white-coated waiters.

Other recommended eating places are the Son Forca and Tondi

restaurants. Rifugio Scotoni on the long run down to Armentarola in the Sella Ronda is highly recommended for mid-morning refreshments, or lunch for late starters.

Off the mountain

Cortina is a large, attractive town, centred around the main shopping street of Corso Italia and the Piazza Venezia with its green-and-white bell tower. The large, frescoed buildings have an air of faded grandeur, and the views of the pink rock faces of Monte Cristallo are some of the most sensational in the Dolomites. More recent architectural additions display a sympathetic Italian alpine style in keeping with the town's dramatic surroundings.

■ OTHER SPORTS

Skating, ice-hockey, curling, parapente, hang-gliding, indoor tennis, swimming, polo on the frozen lake, snow rafting, tobogganing, winter walks, skijoring, sleigh-rides, bobsleigh, dog-sledding, snowmobiling, ski-jumping, snow-shoeing, hang-gliding

The centre is mercifully traffic-free, with cars confined to a busy one-way perimeter road. Parking is a problem in the centre and reporters warn: 'If your hotel provides a private parking space at extra cost, pay up and don't complain'. Drivers should aim to avoid the huge Friday night/Saturday morning exodus, with queues that tail back all the way to the motorway exit.

Accommodation

Hotels range from the large international variety to simple, family-run establishments. There is also a large number of private apartments and chalets. The resort's smartest hotel, the Miramonti Majestic, is 2km out of town. The Cristallo is the other five-star hotel.

The four-stars include the attractive Hotel de la Poste in the heart of Cortina, which is especially noted for its food. Also well-located and comfortable is the Ancora on the Corso Italia, run by the eccentric Flavia Bertozzi. The Parc Victoria is advantageously placed and furnished with antiques collected by the Angeli family, who own the hotel.

The three-star, family-run Aquila is highly recommended. The Italia is a popular two-star with wholesome food and a loyal following. The Menardi is praised for its food and reasonable prices. The Olimpia is one of the cheapest and most central bed-and-breakfasts and is said to be 'comfortable with large rooms and friendly staff'. Its bar is reasonably priced and 'a pleasant place to spend part of the evening'.

Eating in and out

Dining is taken seriously in Cortina. More than 80 restaurants cater for all tastes, from simple pizzas to gourmet dining. El Camineto is popular with skiers at lunchtime and is also open in the evenings. Tivoli on the edge of town has a warm ambience with delicious and often unusual cooking. El Toula is a converted hayloft with a good atmosphere. Il

Skiing facts: **Cortina d'Ampezzo**

TOURIST OFFICE
Piazzetta San Francesco 8, I-32043 Cortina d'Ampezzo, Belluno
Tel 39 436 3231
Fax 39 436 3235

THE RESORT
By road Calais 1200km
By rail Calalzo-Pieve di Cadore 35km
By air Venice 2 hrs
Visitor beds 22,700
Transport free bus connects the town centre with the main lifts

THE SKIING
Linked or nearby resorts Armentarola (I), San Cassiano (I), San Vito di Cadore (n), Kronplatz (n)
Longest run Son Forca-Rio Gere, 9km (black/red)
Number of lifts 53 in area
Total of trails/pistes 140km in area (44% easy, 49% intermediate, 7% difficult)
Nursery slopes 5 runs, 3 lifts
Summer skiing none
Snowmaking 51km covered

LIFT PASSES
Area pass Cortina only L215,000-247,000 for 6 days. Superski Dolomiti (covers 450 lifts), L243,000-279,000 for 6 days
Day pass Cortina L45,000-50,000, Superski Dolomiti L47,000-54,000
Beginners coupons available
Pensioners 20% reduction for over 60s
Credit cards accepted no

SKI SCHOOLS
Adults Scuola Sci Cortina, 9.30am-midday, L255,000 for 6 days. Scuola Sci Azzurra, 9.15am-1pm, L570,000 for 6 days
Private lessons Cortina L56,000 per hr, Azzurra L60,000 per hr
Snowboarding Scuola Sci Cortina, 9.30am-midday, L370,000 for 6 days, or midday-2pm L250,000 for 6 days
Cross-country Scuola Italiana Sci Fondo, private lessons L50,000 per hr. Loipe 58km in the valley north and east of Cortina
Other courses race training, off-piste, telemark, ski-touring
Guiding companies Gruppo Guide Alpine Cortina

CHILDREN
Lift pass 30% reduction for under 14 yrs
Ski kindergarten Scuola Sci Cortina and Scuola Sci Azzurra, 2 yrs and over, times and prices as children's ski school
Ski school Scuola Sci Cortina, 9.30am-midday, L370,000 for 6 days.
Scuola Sci Azzurra Cortina, 15 yrs and under, 9.15am-1pm, L420,000 for 6 days
Non-ski kindergarten Natural...Mente, nursery for 1-3 yrs, recreational and sporting activities 1-14 yrs, both from 7.45am, prices on request

FOOD AND DRINK PRICES
Coffee L1,500, glass of wine L1,500-1,800, small beer L2,800-3,000, dish of the day L10,000

Meloncino on the road to **Passo Falzarego** has the freshest homemade pasta around. The Croda Caffé, Il Ponte and the Cinque Torri are all good for pizzas. Lunch at the Hotel de la Poste is 'brilliant, delicious and expensive'. Leone e Anna specialises in Sardinian cuisine, while El Zoco has grilled meats. For self-caterers or those trying to save money, the Cooperativa department store has 'an outstanding wine selection at reasonable prices.

Après-ski
'In one week you can only scratch the surface of Cortina's après-ski', comments one reporter. At around 5pm the early evening *passeggiata* along the Corso Italia heralds the start of the off-slope festivities. The street becomes alive with fur-clad Italians admiring the elegant shop windows and each other. Cortina's shopping is absorbing and varied and includes antique and jewellery shops, sportswear and designer boutiques, interesting delicatessen and the six-storey Cooperativa department store. As one reporter commented: 'It's the only town we know where the Co-op has marble floors and sells designer clothes'.

After dinner the action starts at the Enoteca Bar and Jerry's Wine Bar, then moves on to the throbbing Hyppo, Area and VIP discos. The entrance fee for the nightclubs does not subsidise the drink prices, as in some comparably smart resorts.

Childcare
Cortina has some of the most extensive nursery slopes we have ever encountered in an area strangely reminiscent of a sloping Kensington Gardens. Non-skiing children are also well catered for at Natural...Mente, a highly flexible operation that picks children up from their parents in the morning and returns them after skiing.

Linked or nearby resorts
Cortina links, in one direction only, into the Sella Ronda circuit at **Lagazuoi** and shares the Superski Dolomiti lift pass. You need to start early in the day in order to achieve any distance on skis. Taxis wait at Armentarola to take skiers back to Lagazuoi, but a bus service from Armentarola brings you back to Falzarego.

Kronplatz
top 2275m (7,464ft) bottom 900m (2,953ft)
This resort on the Italian–Austrian border is covered by the Superski Dolomiti lift pass. It is virtually unknown outside Italy, yet is an easy day trip just 60km from Cortina. Reporters comment on its excellent lifts and good variety of runs.

TOURIST OFFICE
Tel 39 471 979111
Fax 39 474 55/5545

Courmayeur

ALTITUDE 1230m (4,034ft)

Courmayeur is a delightful old village, which established its reputation first as a climbing base for the forbidding, granite peaks of Western Europe's highest massif, and second as a popular nineteenth-century spa for its curative, pungent-smelling waters. Its role as an internationally acclaimed ski resort did not begin to take shape until 11.31am on 14 August 1962. That was the moment when a delighted Italian miner thrust his fist through a hole in the rock-face five kilometres beneath Mont Blanc and swapped a bottle of Asti Spumante for Veuve Clicquot with his French counterpart.

The Mont Blanc Tunnel, then at 11.6km the longest underground road route in the world, ended Courmayeur's international isolation and linked it with Chamonix. Suddenly, Geneva Airport was only a 90-minute drive away.

■ GOOD POINTS
Beautiful scenery, excellent restaurants, alpine charm, easy resort access, varied off-piste skiing, long vertical drop, tree-level skiing, lively après-ski, extensive snowmaking

■ BAD POINTS
Lack of skiing convenience, limited nursery slopes, few tough runs, lift queues at weekends and peak periods

Today it remains an attractive medieval village, with the narrow cobbled streets and alleyways of its pedestrianised centre lined with smart boutiques and welcoming bars. While serious **Chamonix** shivers throughout much of the winter in the northern shadow of the great mountain, bubbly Courmayeur basks in the sunshine.

As a consequence of this, the snow here is normally of secondary quality, although that was by no means the case last season, and low prices made it one of the most fully booked resorts in the whole of Europe. Courmayeur is the favourite resort of the Milanese, a clientèle for whom lunch is frequently a greater priority than skiing, and as a result it proudly boasts some of the finest mountain restaurants in the Alps.

On the mountain
top 3470m (11,381ft) bottom 1370m (4,494ft)

The main mountain access is via a cable car across the river gorge, and the arterial Mont Blanc Tunnel road. This takes you up to Plan Checrouit, a sunny plateau from where, annoyingly, you have to plod a further 75m to the foot of the lifts. At the end of the day there is no direct alternative but to take the cable car back down. It is possible to leave boots and skis in lockers at Plan Checrouit, but the procedure is nevertheless inconvenient. Ancient plans to build a piste to the bottom have never been realised and are now unlikely to be so. The mountain can also be reached by cable car from Val Veny and by a desperately ancient 'egg' gondola from the satellite of **Dolonne**. Queues at the bottom of the Plan Checrouit cable car can be a problem at peak times, but all this fails to detract from the overall appeal of Courmayeur as a ski resort.

Reporters consistently remark on the friendliness of the locals, in startling contrast to the dour Gallic attitude of those on the other side of the tunnel. Extensive investment in snow-cannon has done much to improve skiing on the lower slopes down to Plan Checrouit and, over the mountain, down to Val Veny. However, the skiing is not satisfactory for everyone; the pisted runs are mainly short and lack challenge.

Advanced skiers will be more interested in the separate ski area shared with Chamonix, reached by the three-stage Mont Blanc cable car at **La Palud**, near the village of **Entrèves** on the tunnel side of Courmayeur.

Beginners

Courmayeur's nursery slopes are somewhat hazardous, with those at Plan Checrouit cramped by buildings and crowds of skiers descending from the main pistes. The baby slopes at the top of Val Veny and Dolonne are considerably quieter.

Intermediates

The east-facing Checrouit bowl has many quite short intermediate runs served by a variety of lifts, including a six-seater gondola. The pistes are often crowded, especially at the bottom where they merge. There are some surprisingly steep and narrow passages, even on some of the blue (easy) runs. The wooded, north-facing Val Veny side of the mountain is linked in a couple of places with the Checrouit Bowl; it has longer and more varied pistes with two red (intermediate) runs and a black (difficult) trail following the fall-line through the trees. Queuing for the Plan Checrouit and Mont Blanc areas is much worse at weekends when the crowds arrive from the closest cities of Turin and Milan. Quad-chairs at La Gabba and Zerotta have eased some of the other bottlenecks on the mountain, but the Youla cable car can still be a problem.

> ■ **WHAT'S NEW**
> Quad chair from Plan Checrouit

Advanced

The pistes served by the Gabba chair, at the top of the ski area and to the west of Lago Checrouit, keep their snow well. The off-piste run underneath them is testing. The Youla cable car above Lago Checrouit opens up a deep and sheltered bowl, which serves a single, uncomplicated red run with plenty of space for short off-piste excursions. It is also possible to ski (with a guide) the long itinerary run off the back of Youla down into Val Veny.

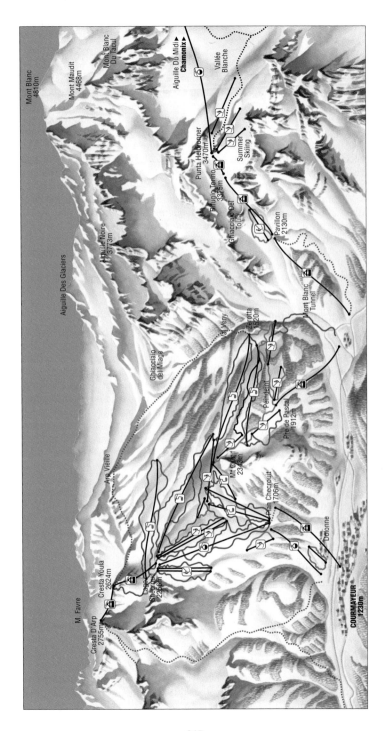

Mont Blanc 4810m

Mont Maudit 4468m

Mont Blanc Du Tacul

Aiguille Du Midi ▶
Chamonix ▶

Vallée Blanche

Aiguille Noire 3773m

Punta Helbronner 3470m

Summer Skiing

Rifugio Torino 3325m

Aiguille Des Glaciers

Ghiacciaio Del Toula

Pavillon 2130m

Mont Blanc Tunnel

Ghiacciaio del Miage

Val Veny

Zerotta 1520m

Peindeint

Pre de Pascal 1912m

Arp Vieille

Mt Chetif 2343m

Plan Checrouit 1706m

Dolonne

M. Favre

Cresta D'Arp 2755m

Cresta Youla 2624m

Chécrouit 2256m

COURMAYEUR 1230m

Off-piste

The top of the two-stage cable car at Cresta d'Arp is the starting point at 2755m for a couple of long and demanding powder runs. One takes you down through 1500m vertical to the satellite village of Dolonne or to the river bank near **Pré-St-Didier**; the other brings you through the beautiful Vallon de Youla to **La Balme**, a few kilometres from **La Thuile**. The second stage of the cable car only runs until 11.30am because of the high risk of avalanche later in the day, and you are strongly advised to use a local guide.

From the nearby hamlet of La Palud, the Mont Blanc cable car rises over 2000m to Punta Helbronner, giving easy access to the Vallée Blanche avoiding the dreaded ice steps. There is an afternoon bus back from Chamonix. Alternatively, you can cruise the 10km back down the Toula Glacier to La Palud; it is steep at the top and involves a clamber along a fixed rope and the hair-raising negotiation of an exposed and awkward staircase. The bottom stage of the cable car from Pavillon has a long, uncomplicated red piste that is rarely skied.

Ski schools and guiding

We continue to receive mixed reports of the Scuola di Sci Monte Bianco, which has the monopoly here. The standard of spoken English has greatly improved in recent years, and the general verdict is that private instructors and guides are excellent value, but that group instructors are often jaded: 'Our instructor gave the impression that he wasn't interested in our skiing at all. He was never enthusiastic or encouraging.' However, the strong presence of Interski, a British tour operator which has been allowed to establish its own private BASI ski school for a mixed clientèle of adults and schoolchildren, has served to raise the standards dramatically.

Snowboarding

Private and group lessons are available at the ski school. The off-piste at Cresta d'Arp makes for some excellent snowboarding, and the less advanced Plan Checrouit has plenty of intermediate runs around the main ski area. Beginners will need to go to the nursery slopes at Val Veny.

Cross-country

Opportunities for cross-country are enormous here, with a major nordic centre at Val Ferret, a five-minute drive away at the foot of the Grandes Jorasses. It offers four loipe totalling 35km, which wind through spectacular scenery. Nordic tours can be arranged in the spring through the ski school.

Mountain restaurants

In our experience there is nowhere you can eat better for less money in a greater variety of mountain restaurants than in Courmayeur. In fact, food in Courmayeur is taken just as seriously as the skiing. By midday on the mountain the scent of cooking wafting from 24 restaurants scattered across the area weakens the resolve of even the most dedicated skier. The prices are actually lower than in the resort itself. The self-service at the top of the Checrouit gondola sets the pace with a heaped bowl of spaghetti for £3, a hamburger for £4.45, and even an entrecôte steak for £5. One reporter comments: 'It is really hard to ski when you could be eating. The atmosphere in the huts scattered around the mountain is an integral part of our annual visit here.'

The Christiania at Plan Checrouit is singled out for special praise ('the freshest seafood I have ever tasted. The owner comes from Elba and obviously pines for home'). The Château Branlant serves full meals with wait-service and 'heavenly desserts'. La Grolla at Peindeint on the Val Veny side is outstanding ('expensive, but worth it and difficult to find — thank goodness').

Other recommendations are the Petit Mont Blanc at Zerotta, and Chiecco and Le Vieux Grenier for pasta. On the Mont Blanc side there are bars at each lift stage. The Rifugio Pavillon at the top of the first stage of the cable car is reportedly excellent and has a sun-terrace. Rifugio Torino, at the next stage, is also said to be good. Rifugio Maison Vielle at L'Aiguille Noir, which has a large wood-burning stove, and Rifugio Monte Bianco, between the Zerotta and Peindeint chairs, both serve pasta, polenta and sausages, and have a long wine list.

Off the mountain

The heart of the old village is a charming maze of cobbled alleys, which are largely traffic-free and lined with attractive fashion boutiques, delicatessens, antiques shops, and even a delightfully good-value toy shop. There are more bars, cafés and restaurants than could ever seem necessary, with a lively clientèle. The atmosphere is, as one reader puts it, 'completely compelling — this is real Italy, garnished with real skiing'. These days the suburbs stretch endlessly outwards, and for anyone interested in observing and therefore contributing to the prolonged après-ski *passeggiata* along Via Roma, it is important to find accommodation within easy walking distance of the pedestrian precinct.

Accommodation

The four-star Gallia Gran Bàita is described as 'wonderfully worthy of its rating, but too far out of town unless you have a car'. Few of the great variety of hotels, apartments and chalets are well situated for the main cable car. Several reporters stress the undesirability of hotels located on the main road used by countless lorries on their way to the Mont Blanc Tunnel (not to be confused with the main street through the village). The comfortable and expensive Hotel Pavillon is well-situated 150m from the cable car and has a swimming-pool and sauna. Hotel Courmayeur is 'friendly, with a roaring log-fire in the sitting area'. The Edelweiss and the two-star Berthod are value for money. The Bouton d'Or is located just off the main square and the Roma is 'simple and cheap'. Mark

Warner's Télécabine in Dolonne has its own crèche and is endorsed by a number of reporters.

Eating in and out

Restaurants are varied, plentiful and lively. A favourite is the Turistica in via Donzelli, which is good value and serves large helpings. Pierre Alexis rates as one of the best restaurants in town ('owner Ino Cosson has an extraordinary wine list to complement great food'). Chalet Proment da Floriano on the cross-country track at Val Ferret combines fine cuisine with an intimate atmosphere. The Coquelicot is recommended for its grills. Le Bistroquet offers 'wonderfully prepared regional dishes'. La Palud is known for its fresh fish.

■ **OTHER SPORTS**

Parapente, skating, ski-jumping, hang-gliding, indoor tennis, dog-sledding, climbing wall

Courmayeur also has plenty of pizzerias, including Mont Frety with its regional dishes, and La Terrazza. La Maison de Filippo at Entrèves is an exercise in unparalleled gluttony; it offers a fixed-price menu of at least 30 courses. Self-caterers are advised to shop at the Desparu supermarket on the Via Regionale directly above the cable-car station, as there are no supermarkets in town and the few market shops are pricey.

Après-ski

After-skiing entertainment begins with early evening cocktails in Steve's Privé or the American Bar, and evolves into a hanging-out situation, with certain times for certain bars, and often more than one in a night or a return visit after dinner. The Bar Roma, with its comfortable sofas and armchairs, fills up early and is especially recommended if you are tired after skiing. The American Bar has cocktails while Ziggi's is more beer-oriented. Cadran Solaire is where the sophisticated Milanese go. The Abat-Jour and Le Clochard are the discos. The swimming-pool is 5km away at Pré-St-Didier, and the floodlit skating rink in Courmayeur is open every evening until midnight, complete with disco music.

Childcare

The Kinderheim up at Plan Checrouit has excellent facilities and looks after children from six months old. Staff pick up children from the bottom of the cable car in the village if parents want a day-off from the mountain. The Scuola di Sci Monte Bianco has private and group lessons for children, with lunch included.

Skiing facts: **Courmayeur**

TOURIST OFFICE
Piazzale Monte Bianco, I-11013
Courmayeur, Aosta
Tel 39 165 842060
Fax 39 165 842072

THE RESORT
By road Calais 921km
By rail Pré-St-Didier 5km, regular buses from station
By air Geneva 2 hrs, Turin 3 hrs
Visitor beds 20,722
Transport ski bus, not included in lift pass

THE SKIING
Linked or nearby resorts Cervinia (n), Champoluc (n), Chamonix (l), Gressoney-la-Trinité (n), Pila (n), La Thuile (n)
Longest run Internazionale, 7km (red)
Number of lifts 32
Total of trails/pistes 100km (44% easy, 52% intermediate, 4% difficult)
Nursery slopes 1 at Dolonne, 1 at Plan Checrouit, 1 at Maison Vieille
Summer skiing none
Snowmaking 14km covered

LIFT PASSES
Area pass (Courmayeur Mont Blanc) L212,000-245,000 for 6 days
Day pass L46,000 (Courmayeur only)
Beginners 3 free lifts
Pensioners no reduction

Credit cards accepted yes

SKI SCHOOLS
Adults Scuola di Sci Monte Bianco, 10am-4pm, L180,000 for 6 days
Private lessons L49,000 per hr
Snowboarding through ski school, details on request
Cross-country through ski school. Nordic centre and 35-km loipe at Val Ferret
Other courses monoski, off-piste, slalom, ski-touring, heli-skiing
Guiding companies Società delle Guide di Courmayeur

CHILDREN
Lift pass L212,000-245,000 for 6 days, free for children under 1.1m accompanied by parent
Ski kindergarten Kinderheim and Scuola di Sci Monte Bianco, 9am-4pm, both L370,000 for 6 days including lunch
Ski school Scuola di Sci Monte Bianco, 10am-1pm, L180,000 for 6 days
Non-ski kindergarten Kinderheim, 6 mths and over, 9am-4pm, L260,000 for 6 days

FOOD AND DRINK PRICES
Coffee L1,500-1,800, glass of wine L2,000-4,000, small beer L4,000-6,000, dish of the day L25,000-30,000

Livigno

ALTITUDE 1820m (5,970ft)

Livigno is high, open and duty-free, which makes it user-friendly for skiers and revellers alike. Thanks to fiscal privileges dating back to 1600, it can lay claim to the title of cheapest of all alpine resorts. The special status of this remote Walser farming community was confirmed in 1805 when Napoleon, then the ruler of the Kingdom of Italy, granted 'customs benefits' that were validated by the Austro–Hungarian Empire in 1818, and by the European Community in 1960.

Livigno's main problem has always been access. The community developed near but not on the Roman Road from Milan to Innsbruck, a route that crossed the neighbouring Passo di San Giacomo, one of the lowest in the Alps. As frontiers moved back and forth, the Spol Valley became a distant border outpost of Switzerland, Italy and the Austro–Hungarian Empire in turn. Today, it has slow road links with **Bormio** to the east, **St Moritz** to the west and **Davos**, via the one-way Munt La Schera tunnel, to the north. This means that visitors have a choice between Milan and Zurich airports, each approximately a five-hour drive from the resort, or Begamo, which is four hours.

Livigno has an efficient, free bus-service linking the four hamlets of **Santa Maria**, **San Antonio**, **San Rocco** and **Trepalle**, which stretch over 12km and make up the resort. A car allows for day trips to Bormio and **Santa Caterina** (both on the area lift pass) and to St Moritz and Davos across the Swiss border.

On the mountain
top 2798m (9,180ft) bottom 1816m (5,958ft)

International visitors began skiing in Livigno in 1964 when the Munt La Schera tunnel opened the resort up to northern Europe. In those days there was one lift; today there are 28, serving 100km of predominantly gentle slopes on both sides of the valley. The core of the skiing is the ski-in ski-out south-east-facing Carosello, which catches the morning sun. The two-stage Carosello 3000 gondola provides rapid access from the town to the highest point.

The Carosello links in with two supplementary areas, one served by

the Federia drag-lift on the back side of the mountain where the snow is better protected from the sun, and the other on Costaccia, where the recently opened high-speed Vetta quad along the ridge has widened options considerably. Plans to replace or augment the Tagliede Valandrea chair with another quad will result in further improvement.

The skiing is generally steeper on the west-facing side of the valley, where the setting sun attracts skiers late into the afternoon. The gondola station for Mottolino is at Teola, a long walk or a short bus-ride from the town centre. There are notoriously chilly chair-lift connections with Monte della Neve, the departure point for the best skiing in the resort, and Trepalle, a windswept outpost on the road to Bormio.

In recent years, Livigno has become the self-appointed telemark capital of the Alps, thanks to La Skieda International Festival, which takes place in the spring. In 1996 the week-long programme of tuition, races and social events attracted enthusiasts from 14 countries. Expectations are even higher for the third Skieda, a week-long event due to commence on 5 April 1997.

Beginners
Livigno is justly proud of a lift system that provides blanket coverage of sun-soaked, resort-level nursery slopes within a stone's throw of the main street. The runs straggle along the flank of the mountain on the Carosello side, leaving beginners with no excuses for not practising when classes are over. The best graduation slopes for progressive novices are from Monte della Neve and Mottolino to Trepalle.

Intermediates
The heart of the skiing is Carosello and the linked area of Bruschetta, which offer the widest choice of long descents. The toughest intermediate options in a generally flattering environment are on the slopes above Val Federia. On the other side of the valley, the rolling red (intermediate) runs from Mottolino, Monte Sponda and Monte della Neve back to Teola are rewarding, but those to Trepalle are rather short.

Advanced
The creators of the piste-map have taken pains to include some statutory black (difficult) runs, but the grading is strictly complimentary. This is not a resort for experts. Livigno's two main mogul fields are at the extremes of the resort, below Costaccia and on the descent from Carosello. A longer and much better black run winds down from Monte della Neve to the bottom of the Monte Sponda chair.

Off-piste
As very few visitors to Livigno have any intention of skiing off-piste, extensive possibilities exist for those prepared to hire a guide and go exploring. The most accessible options are from Carosello 3000 and the ridge above Costaccio to Val Federia, or from Monte della Neve down the Vallaccia to Trepalle — but be prepared for long walk-outs.

Ski schools and guiding

Livigno has four ski schools. As far as British clients are concerned, Sci Livigno Italy is the major player. However, minority interests are better served by the Azzura and Inverno-Estate schools which offer telemark, touring and mountaineering in addition to regular tuition. There is also a specialist nordic ski school.

Snowboarding

Although Livigno has no special arrangements for snowboarding, its gentle open slopes make it ideal for safe learning. All four local ski schools offer group and private lessons. The chalet-style Sport Adventure shop is a centre for board culture.

Cross-country

The broad valley floor alongside the River Spol provides easy nordic terrain. The marked 30-km Sgambeda touring trail loops across the resort from Val Fedaria to Tresenda, but lacks any great sense of adventure as it runs parallel to the main road. Alternatively, there are options at the Spol race track.

Mountain restaurants

The main self-service restaurants at the top of the Mottolino and Carosello gondolas offer consistency at competitive prices, while La Costaccia is known for its outdoor barbecue. More atmospheric mountain lunches can be found in the Teas, the mountain huts once used by herdsmen working the summer pastures.

The Tea Borch, below Carosello, and the Tea del Plan, below Costaccia, specialise in *pizzocheri*, the brown local pasta that is traditionally prepared with cabbage and cheese. Mottolino's Passo d'Eira has a range of typical dishes while the Fior di Bosco concentrates on local cheese and salami.

Off the mountain

Although many of the individual buildings are very attractive, Livigno's lack of town planning makes it unsympathetic overall. Its high, bleak location has earned it the nickname 'Piccolo Tibet' (little Tibet), a description that is particularly apt in bad weather. A pedestrianised zone has been achieved by blocking off the centre section of the main road through San Antonio. It provides a rather tacky focus, crammed full of hotels, restaurants and noisy bars. Santa Maria, a neighbourhood in which the original stone and wooden houses cluster round the church, is more distinguished architecturally, but its charm is diluted by heavy traffic in its narrow streets.

> **■ OTHER SPORTS**
>
> Ice-driving, horse riding, snow mobiling, skating, snow-shoeing, parapente, tobogganing, sleigh rides, swimming

Skiing facts: **Livigno**

TOURIST OFFICE
Via dala Gesa 65, I-23030 Livigno, Sondrio
Tel 39 342 996379
Fax 39 342 996884

THE RESORT
By road Calais 1,107km
By rail Tirano 2½ hrs
By air Milan or Zurich 5 hrs,
Bergamo 4 hrs
Visitor beds 8,179
Transport free ski bus around resort

THE SKIING
Linked or nearby resorts Bormio (n), St
Moritz (n) Valdisotto (n), Valdidentro (n),
Santa Caterina (n)
Longest run Femminite, 4.8km (red)
Number of lifts 28 in Livigno, 34 in linked
area
Total of trails/pistes 100km (44% easy,
45% intermediate, 11% difficult)
Nursery slopes 12 lifts and 5km of runs
Summer skiing at Stelvio Pass/Diavolezza
Snowmaking 15km covered in Livigno

LIFT PASSES
Area pass (covers Bormio, Santa Caterina,
Valdidentro, Valdisotto and 1 day in St
Moritz) L240,000 for 6 days
Day pass L48,000 (Livigno only)

Beginners no free lifts
Pensioners 65 yrs and over, as children
Credit cards accepted yes

SKI SCHOOLS
Adults Scuola Italiana Sci Livigno
Inverno-Estate, Sci Azzurra Livigno,
Sci-Livigno Italy, Sci Livigno Soc Coop, all
L115,000 for 6 days (2 hrs per day)
Private lessons all ski schools, details on
request
Snowboarding all ski schools, L190,000
for 6 days (2 hrs per day)
Cross-country Scuola Italiana Sci
Fondo Livigno, L110,000 for 6 days,
private lessons available.
Loipe 50km
Other courses monoski, telemark
Guiding companies Lodovico Cusini

CHILDREN
Lift pass L160,000 for 6 days
Ski kindergarten none
Ski school all ski schools, 4 yrs and over,
L115,000 for 6 days (2 hrs per day)
Non-ski kindergarten none

FOOD AND DRINK PRICES
Coffee L1,300-1,500, glass of wine L1,500-
2,000, small beer L3,000-3,500, dish of the
day L12,000-15,000

Livigno's *raison d'être* is shopping, with stores dedicated to cheap alcohol, clothing and consumer durables. Anyone who is not perceived as Italian is addressed in German by over-eager assistants.

Accommodation
The two four-star hotels, the Golf Parc and the Intermonti, are in Teola on the hillside overlooking the town — a suitable place to stay for the Mottolino lifts but not for the nightlife. In the pedestrian zone, the three-star Hotel Bivio has a swimming-pool and a terrace. Also convenient for both nursery slopes and après-ski are the Alpina, the Helvetia, the Victoria, the Sonne and the Alpenrose. In Santa Maria, Damiano

Bormolini, ex-Italian freestyle champion and fourth-generation hotelier, offers two quiet and expertly run family hotels, the Livigno and the St Michael ('nothing was too much trouble').

Eating in and out

With 97 hotels, most of them with restaurants, and a pizzeria on every corner, Livigno is not short of choice, but the emphasis is on quality local fare rather than haute cuisine. The Pesce d'Oro daringly advertises 'fresh fish every week' but still enjoys a sound reputation. So, too, do La Mirage, La Stua, La Pioda and Il Passatore. The Camana Veglia has a notably good chef, while the Bellavista wins many friends for its pizzas.

Après-ski

Tea del Vidal is a cheerful pit-stop on the Mottolino side. In town, the most popular watering holes are Foxi's Pub, famed for its burgers, and Marco's Bar, which offers ski videos. Both stay open until 3am. Noisy alternatives favoured by the British include The Underground and Galli's Pub in San Antonio. Il Cielo, which sometimes has live music, is rated as the smartest disco by the Italians, but the Kokodi is generally preferred by British visitors; both are quiet until after midnight but gather momentum towards closing time at 4am. Other attractions include a modern cinema showing up-to-date (but usually dubbed) American and British films and an ice-driving school. A sports centre financed by the local tax on duty-free goods is planned for the turn of the century.

Childcare

Skiing tuition is available at Livigno's four ski schools for children aged four years and over, but there is no formal childcare for toddlers.

Madonna di Campiglio

ALTITUDE 1520m (4,987ft)

Madonna di Campiglio is an attractive resort situated in a narrow valley in the Brenta Dolomites, 100km from Bolzano and within a three-hour drive of Verona. Madonna is officially rated as Italy's premier resort in terms of piste-grooming and lack of queues, and regularly hosts international winter-sports events, including World Cup ski races and snowboarding championships. The World Speedway On Ice motorcycle championships were recently held on the frozen lake. Ninety-five per cent of the resort's clientèle is Italian, and Madonna counts only Cortina d'Ampezzo and Sestriere as rivals in terms of social prestige. The better hotels are booked out for the season. Very few British visit and those who do share Italian tastes, especially for relaxed, unintimidating skiing.

■ **GOOD POINTS**

Beautiful scenery, extensive snow-making, congenial atmosphere, facilities for snowboarding, intensive piste-grooming, lack of queues, ideal for beginners and intermediates, excellent nursery slopes, attractive woodland cross-country trails

■ **BAD POINTS**

High prices (for Italy), peak-season traffic, limited advanced and off-piste terrain

The lift system dates from the 1950s and today counts out at a rather modest 29 lifts covering 90km of pistes in the Madonna core area, although an additional 25 lifts and 60km of pistes can be accessed with the Skirama lift pass, including the separate but linked resorts of **Folgarida** and **Marilleva**.

On the mountain
top 2505m (8,219ft) bottom 1520m (4,987ft)

Madonna is a resort with flattering skiing and excellent nursery slopes, as well as a good range of far-flung intermediate terrain. However, it has little to offer experts or off-piste skiers. Mountain access from the village itself is by cable car, chair-lift and gondola on the west side of town up to Pancugolo and Pradalago, and by gondola from the east side to Spinale. A chair-lift that begins a five-minute bus ride north of Madonna's centre, runs west up to Pradalago and the liaison with Folgarida and Marilleva. From the same point a gondola climbs west to Madonna's highest skiing on Grosté. The resort has accommodation for 25,000 visitors who can be carried uphill in less than an hour. Together with a clientèle in no rush for early-morning skiing, this means that queues appear only at peak holiday periods and only for the rather dated cable car.

When viewed from the village the mountain appears steep; above, it opens into a civilised network of wide trails. Only the Grosté sector is entirely above the tree-line and is not covered by the exhaustive system of around 500 snow-cannon. Madonna's late-season skiing can suffer from the generous Dolomite sun, but last season the resort had good skiing until the end of March on some of the best snow in the Alps. Skiers with a Skirama lift pass are somewhat redundantly issued with a separate ticket and piste-map as soon as they cross into the Folgarida or Marilleva zones.

Beginners

Novices joining the ski schools should not buy a ski pass, as they will be taken by bus to the private Campo Carlo Magno nursery area five minutes away. Beginners who are not enrolled at the ski school pay a small fee both for the shuttle bus and the use of the nursery lifts. This is a superb learning area, which is serviced by its own drag-lifts and snow-making. There is another private nursery area called Bambi, which is run by Des Alpes Ski School on the east side of Madonna.

All of Madonna's skiing is accessible to beginners; blue (easy) runs make up 26 of the 45 named slopes in the main Madonna area. The Zeledria blue continues for more than 3km all the way down to town from Pradalago, as does the Poza Vecia on the other side of the mountain; this run can be combined with the Boch blue to make a non-stop beginner cruise of 5km.

Intermediates

Intermediates will want to take advantage of the Skirama extended lift pass for the range of woodland skiing towards Folgarida and Marilleva, almost all of which is flatteringly easy. The two highest runs in the resort, reached by the Grosté chairs, are both intermediate and in the central Madonna ski area. At the top of the Boch chair you can ski Nube d'Oro, the resort's most challenging red (intermediate) piste that continues into the trees to meet Fortini.

Advanced

There is little challenge for advanced skiers in Madonna, where the piste-grooming is the best in Italy and bumps are taken as insult added to injury. However, the Canalone Miramonti is a short, steep shock. And the FIS 3-Tre racecourse on Pancugolo is a tiring and torturous 2.5km. Up on Grosté there is a dual slalom racecourse which is open to the public.

Off-piste

The ski schools seldom break away from the prepared pistes, although snowboarders do. There are tempting lines through the trees, but these do not always bring you back to the piste. Above Spinale and towards the Cima Brenta is a wide couloir, housing the summer Tuckett Refuge, which looks like a huge white canvas empty of tracks; it requires a guide and ski-touring equipment to access safely.

Ski schools and guiding

Confusingly, Madonna has six ski schools, all affiliated to the national Scuola Italiana Sci, each of which changes its uniform colour every season. English is indifferently spoken. Children's lessons are for three hours each morning in large classes of ten or more. Adult group lessons may have between 8 and 12 pupils and run for two hours in two shifts during the mornings. Nuova Campiglio and Nazionale receive good reports. The Scuola Alpinismo is recommended for ski-touring in the Dolomites.

Snowboarding

Madonna is rated one of the best snowboarding resorts in Italy, although the monster half-pipe used for the recent European World Championships has been dismantled, and the two pistes on Grosté set aside as a snowboard park are neither roped-off to skiers nor equipped with a dedicated lift. Although both the half-pipe and boardercross park are on Grosté, the former is not maintained and the latter is described as 'pathetic'. However, there should be improvements during preparations for the World Snowboard Championships in 1999. Professional Snowboarding is a hole-in-the-wall rental shop with English-speaking teachers, the sole snowboard-only refuge in Madonna.

Cross-country

There is a cross-country ski school and 30km of prepared track at Campo Carlo Magno, including a scenic valley itinerary up to Lago Malghette. Further wooded trails run through three separate parks between Madonna and Pinzolo.

Mountain restaurants

'All furs and no food', is how one reporter expecting a Zermatt and St Moritz truffles-and-caviar experience responded to the self-service inns, which are all you get in Madonna. The best of the *rifugi* here include Malga Montagnoli, which has great risotto with *porcini* mushrooms. Zeledria has the Italian version of pierrade steaks cooked on a hot stone. Boch has been refurbished in new pine and sometimes has a DJ from Zangola (see Après-ski). One reporter fell foul of the secret-recipe *grappa* ('wickedly potent') at Pichiorosso, a small bar near Refuge Agostini on Pradalago.

Off the mountain

The resort was the site of a mountain hospice dating back 800 years, and was developed as a summer holiday and skiing centre in the 1950s. Today it is compact and congenial with a mix of architectural styles (mostly modern) and an extremely high standard of accommodation. The village runs north-south and the slopes come right down into the town on either side. A park and a skating rink on a small lake in the village centre give a sense of space. Madonna is, if anything, more expensive than Cortina d'Ampezzo, although arguably less sophisticated. One reporter commented: 'The Italians in Madonna do wear furs to the floor, orange fluorescent moonboots and sunglasses at midnight, and they do parade their tiny rat-dogs outside the Bar Suisse. You will see them sunbathing with silver reflectors by the skating lake, hear them shouting on the slopes as they collide, and you wonder who still makes hand-painted ski suits that run in the rain.'

■ **OTHER SPORTS**

Parapente, swimming, skating, snow-shoeing

Traffic is a serious problem in high season when the one-way system goes into operation. By 1998 the resort promises to be car-free, thanks to an ambitious tunnel bypass project that is already half completed. The ski bus is not free, although it covers the region well. There are many elegant boutiques but no art galleries or museums. The cinema shows films in Italian only.

Accommodation

Most guests stay in the resort's 38 three- and four-star hotels, which are booked out for most of the season. Relais Club des Alpes carries the most cachet and is the most central. The Lorenzetti is also four-star, though more rustic in setting and décor, and has its own free shuttle bus. The Diana is friendly, close to the lifts and furnished to a high standard. Arnica is a conveniently central, modern bed-and-breakfast. Equally central is the old-style Villa Principe, which has some of the cheapest rooms in town. There are chalet-apartments and self-catering establishments like the Ambiez apartments, which boast a swimming-pool and fitness centre.

Eating in and out

A Madonna must is piling into heated snowcats and jolting up to the mountain restaurants of Malga Montagnoli, Cascina Zeledria or Malga Boch, where the service and food are better by night. In town, Artini is top for cuisine and price. Papagallo has a generous set menu on Wednesdays. Cliffhanger is new, serves fish platters and shows heli-skiing videos. The Golden River has the only non-Italian menu, a kind of Tex-Mex, but even here gorgonzola makes an appearance. La Sfizio is vegetarian, and Spaghetti Haus serves huge helpings. Le Roi has the best pizzas until 2am, and like Belvedere it also does take-aways. There are numerous supermarkets and speciality cheese-and-meat shops.

Après-ski

Madonna is often said to be lively, but in fact it is dead until 2am. It then goes wild until 4 or even 8am in what has been for 25 years one of the most famous discos in the Alps; the old cow barn, Zangola, features male strippers and dancing girls and is a legend across Italy. Des Alpes has techno music as well as an upstairs piano bar. The Stork Club's clientèle is seriously underage and closes when the school holidays end. Right after skiing, the furs gather at Bar Suisse or Josef's Stube to flutter eyelashes under dark glasses and make dates for later. Not to be confused with the bar of the same name, Cantina Suisse is a warm-up nightspot for Zangola. Extremely popular with Italian boys are the two garish video-game centres and the billiard bar.

Childcare

Most Italians leave the little ones at home or bring nanny or granny. There is informal childminding for guests only at Des Alpes and an outdoor playground by the skating rink. The ski schools accept children from five years of age for morning lessons only.

TOURIST OFFICE
Tel 39 465 42000
Fax 39 465 40404

The Milky Way

ALTITUDE Montgenèvre 1850m (6,068ft), Sauze d'Oulx 1500m (4,920ft), Sestriere 2035m (6,675ft)

The Milky Way is one of the most attractive and unsung of the giant ski circuits in Europe, its reputation unjustly marred by the infamy of Sauze d'Oulx as an alpine haunt of lager-louts on which the fun never sets. It straddles the Franco–Italian border and is reached more easily from Turin, than from Geneva. Snow cover is surprisingly sound for its southerly location. However, spring arrives a month earlier here than in the Haute Savoie, and this factor should be taken into account in choosing when to visit.

The three major centres all have markedly different characters. **Montgenèvre**, the only French resort on the circuit, is an old stone village perched on the pass into Italy. It has been developed for tourism in a pleasant enough manner and retains considerable charm despite the busy international arterial road that runs through its centre.

■ **GOOD POINTS**

Large ski area, easy runs, skiing convenience, extensive tree-line skiing, varied off-piste, value for money, lively après-ski (Sauze d'Oulx), reliable snow cover (Sestriere)

■ **BAD POINTS**

Lack of activities for non-skiers, shortage of mountain restaurants, few tough runs, lack of alpine charm, heavy traffic (Montgenèvre)

Sauze d'Oulx (pronounced Sow-zee Doo) has tried to clean up its act by heading upmarket, a feat at which it cannot succeed until more luxurious hotels are built to cater for a better class of clientèle. In contrast, Sestriere, just a few kilometres away as the mountain chough flies, ranks as one of the two smartest and most fashionable resorts in Italy (Cortina d'Ampezzo is the other).

The Milky Way (*Voie Lactée* or *Via Lattea*) is bounded by Montgenèvre at one end and by Sauze d'Oulx at the other. In between lie the villages of **Sestriere**, **Clavière**, **Cesana Torinese** and **Sansicario**, as well as a handful of small hamlets that are little more than ski-lift access points. The area is very spread out; it takes a long time to work one's way from one sector of the circuit to another, so a car is useful.

On the mountain
top 2820m (9,250ft) bottom 1350m (4,428ft)

Montgenèvre's slopes are on both sides of the pass. The south-facing side, Chalvet, is slightly higher with runs up to 2600m and is usually less crowded than the north-facing pistes, which create the main link with the Italian Milky Way resorts. Mountain access on the other side of the pass is by gondola from the **Briançon** end of the village, as well as by drag-lifts and a chair from the centre. These serve easy runs through woods, opening into wide nursery slopes above the road.

From the top of the gondola there is a choice of three small ski areas. The wide, sheltered bowl of Le Querelay/Les Anges has ruined fortress buildings around the crest with some red (intermediate) and black (difficult) runs beneath them, but no challenging skiing overall.

The Milky Way link from Montgenèvre starts with a poorly sign-posted traverse around the mountain, which is easy to miss in bad light. Otherwise, it is not difficult and leads to a long run, which starts as red and becomes blue (easy) past the Gimont drag-lifts and down to Clavière. The north-facing slopes of Monti della Luna above Clavière and Cesana Torinese offer plenty of challenge, including some vast trails through the woods and good off-piste.

■ **WHAT'S NEW**

Quad chair-lift at Clavière

Reporters are unanimous in their opinion that the best skiing in the Milky Way is above **Sestriere**. Lifts are being upgraded systematically in preparation for the 1997 Alpine World Championships, and the resort does not suffer from the lack of investment apparent elsewhere in the area. The bulk of the skiing around Sestriere is on mainly north- and west-facing slopes on two mountains, Sises and Banchetta, which are separated by a deep valley.

The **Sauze d'Oulx** slopes face west and north and the majority of them are below the tree-line. The lifts are positively old-fashioned in comparison with those of Sauze's smart neighbour, even though they are run by the same company. A quad-chair takes you up to the centre of the skiing at **Sportinia**, a sunny woodland clearing with a few hotels, a small busy nursery area and a variety of restaurants. Above it, there is some wide, open intermediate skiing served by several chairs and drags. Below Sportinia there are wide runs back through the woods, graded red and black; these are quite steep in places, although never really demanding. There are also blue and black runs down to Jouvenceaux.

Queues in **Montgenèvre** are bad only at weekends and when snow in the nearby resorts is poor. The main queue problems at the Italian end of the Milky Way are on the Sauze side of the mountain, which a reporter who was there during an Italian bank holiday describes as 'horrendous'. The local lift map has been improved, but it is still difficult at times to work out exactly where you are. A number of reporters describe trail-marking as virtually non-existent to the point of being dangerous, which adds to the problems of orientation.

Beginners

A dozen nursery slopes are scattered around the different resorts of the Milky Way on both sides of the border, and the area is good learner territory. The main nursery slope for Sauze is at Sportinia; it is open and sunny, but often very crowded. There are also nursery slopes at Belvedere on the Genevris side, as well as in the village when there is

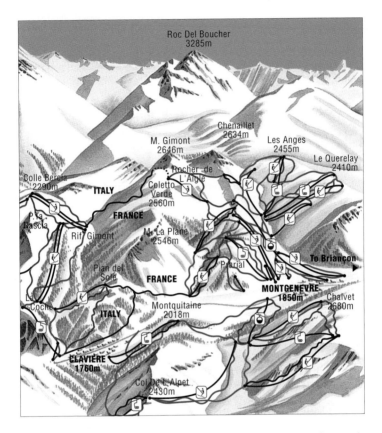

snow. Sauze d'Oulx and Montgenèvre in particular are geared towards international clients. The Montgenèvre end of the circuit has the best choice of blue runs for those who have graduated from the novice slopes.

Intermediates

The long red runs down to Sansicario from Monte Fraiteve are satisfyingly varied and some of the best on the circuit. Red run 29, back through the trees to Sauze, is the favourite of several reporters. Old hands to the area say that high-season crowds are a problem throughout the Milky Way, but particularly around Sestriere. The secret is to ski the remote Genevris/Moncrons/Bourget sector on Saturdays and Sundays ('a pleasure to ski and no queues at all').

Advanced

An assortment of difficult runs scattered throughout the Milky Way makes this an underrated playground for advanced skiers, who will find plenty of challenge. The Sauze sector quite wrongly has a novice label attached to it because of the predominance of beginner and early-inter-mediate skiers that it attracts. In fact, some of the reds here could easily be graded black in other resorts, and a few of the blacks (notably 33 and 21) are seriously challenging in difficult snow conditions. The best of the skiing is found above Sansicario and Sestriere, although this may not be apparent from the local map.

The steep Motta drag-lift and chair serve the highest and toughest of Sestriere's skiing and reach the top point of the Milky Way. Here the slopes beside the drag can have gradients of up to 30 degrees and are often mogulled.

Off-piste

Monte Fraiteve is an exposed crest with impressive views of the French mountains, where the ski areas of Sauze d'Oulx, Sestriere and Sansicario meet. It is also the start of the famous Rio Nero off-piste run, which is a long descent that follows a river gully down to the Oulx–Cesana road, 1600m below. An infrequent bus service takes you back to the lifts at Cesana.

The long dog-leg drag, La Crête, travels through magnificent rocky scenery to Rocher de l'Aigle and the start of an outstanding off-piste bowl and an alternative steep couloir. Anyone attempting the latter draws admiring glances from those on the piste below.

Ski schools and guiding

We have sound reports of the French Ski School (ESF) at Montgenèvre ('friendly and helpful instructors with good English') for all grades of skier and for private lessons. The Sauze d'Oulx Ski School has two rivals: Sauze Project and Sauze Sportinia. We have mixed reports of the Sauze d'Oulx ('too much follow-my-leader and the grading on the first day took an eternity, with 200 people lined up in knee-deep snow'). Sportinia has a high standard of teaching, but one reader complained that his instructor only had a few English phrases. Reports of the Sestriere Ski School are not enthusiastic: 'Huge classes and not much tuition'.

Snowboarding

Montgenèvre Ski School has group and private lessons, Sestriere Ski School offers private ones, and Sauze's three ski schools all provide tuition.

Mountain restaurants

'You can eat out in the mountain restaurant on the Italian side for the cost of a drink in Courchevel', enthused one reporter. Montgenèvre is seriously short of mountain restaurants, with just the Altitude 2000 and Gondrands. The excellent and inexpensive bars and restaurants above Clavière (particularly La Coche) help make up for this shortfall.

The five restaurants at Sportinia include the Capanna, which is said to be 'the busiest but not the best'. La Capannina, 100m away, is 'cosier

and with a more authentic feel to it'.

At Sansicario, Bar Soleil Boeuf is described as 'elegant and tradition-ally furnished'. Chalet Genevris at Genevris is renowned for its barbecue, with all you can eat or drink for around £10 ('very friendly with an excellent atmosphere of camaraderie at lunchtimes, which often stretched well into the afternoons').

Sestriere's Bar Chisonetto, halfway down Red 8 on Banchetta, is recommended for its hamburgers. Bar Conchinetto is a traditional wood and stone restaurant renowned for its polenta, and La Gargote has plenty of atmosphere but is more expensive. Alpette is praised for its Glühwein and pasta.

Off the mountain

The first impression of **Montgenèvre** is of a rather untidy and higgledy-piggledy collection of bars, restaurants, shops and hotels lining an extremely busy main road where skiers joust with pantechnicons. The real village is tucked away on the northern side and has plenty of atmosphere, despite the heavy traffic. Shopping facilities are limited, but the weekly open-air market adds considerable colour and the occasional bargain. Prices are markedly lower than in most other French resorts. Italy begins at the border post on the outskirts of town, and both currencies are in circulation here.

In its prime, the main street of **Sauze d'Oulx** was at its noisiest at 3am. Raucous revellers, still in their ski boots and awash with cheap lager and tequila slammers, staggered homewards from the infamous Andy Capp Bar to a dozen shabby two-star hotels for a few hours of further recreation before hitting the slopes once more. To the 2,000 young British skiers (50 per cent of the resort's customers) who flocked to this corner of Piedmont each winter in search of snow, sex and mind-shattering amounts of alcohol, it was known as 'Suzy does it'.

Suzy, it seems, has matured beyond the abandoned follies of her youth, and after a decade in the doldrums is enjoying a more classy comeback. If she still does it, she has at least drawn the curtains and turned down the lights. At the height of recession the number of weekly British visitors slumped into the hundreds, but the resort has climbed back gradually without the extreme yobbo element, which has moved on to fresh grazing elsewhere.

The local tourist board aims to transform Sauze into an upmarket family resort and in no uncertain terms has told tour operators to provide a better class of visitor. To achieve its aim, however, the resort needs to provide better accommodation. The old village retains its charm, but the more recent development that contains most of the accommodation and restaurants is an unappealing hotchpotch of mainly ugly, modern buildings.

Sestriere was Europe's original purpose-built ski resort. After years of negligence, it has now torn down its rusty cable cars and invested heavily in snow-cannon and new lifts, much of it in preparation for the 1997 Alpine World Championships. Its high altitude of 2035m makes Sestriere one of the more snow-sure resorts at this end of the Alps. Although it has the reputation of attracting rich Italians from Turin, it does not wear its mantle of affluence with any great show of style — this collection of unappealing modern edifices spread across a high, windy pass generates a rather soul-less atmosphere. As one reporter put it, 'there is no continuity, resulting in a confusion of styles, which seem to compete rather than harmonise'.

The landmarks are the tall, round towers of the old Duchi d'Aosta Hotel, now occupied by Club Med, and the Gothic turrets of the restored Principi de Piemonte Hotel. This is some way from the resort centre but has its own lift access to the Sises ski area. Buses run to and from **Borgata**, **Grangsises** and the end of the Rio Nero run (on the

Oulx–Cesana road).

The more shrewd Italians have now swapped Sestriere for nearby Sansicario, which is a smaller, more sophisticated and modern development with its own ski area. It is linked to Sestriere and Sauze on the one side and Cesana Torinese on the other.

Accommodation

Montgenèvre's accommodation is mostly in apartments scattered along the road, in the old village and on the lower south-facing slopes; there are also a few catered chalets. Access to the skiing is easy from most places, but the Italian end of the village is more convenient. The pick of Montgenèvre's half-a-dozen less than luxurious hotels are the Napoléon, which is convenient but basic, and the more attractive Valérie, near the church. Others include the Chalvet and the simple La Grange.

> **■ OTHER SPORTS**
>
> Parapente, snowmobiling, dog-sledding, ice-driving, skating, hang-gliding, skating, tobogganing, swimming, indoor tennis and squash

Accommodation in Sauze is mostly in cheap hotels, which reporters generally find adequate. The best location is around the bottom of Clotes, with the hotels in this area the Hermitage, Stella Alpina, and the Sauze ('clean and spacious'). The Gran Bàita is recommended as 'excellent — very clean, the staff are pleasant and the hotel is five minutes' walk from everything'. San Giorgio is far from luxurious and badly placed but friendly and inexpensive.

The Chaberton is a simple bed-and-breakfast, and the Savoia is close to the lifts. The Palace is the biggest and the most expensive hotel, although not particularly stylish. Il Capricorno at Clotes is expensive and attractive. You can be first on the nursery slopes by staying at the Monte Triplex or the Capanna at Sportinia. The Ciao Pais above Clotes offers cheap and simple accommodation.

Sestriere's accommodation is in hotels, modern apartments and at Club Med. Apart from the Principi, the most luxurious hotel is the modern, low-rise Hotel Sestriere. The Savoy Edelweiss is simple and central. The Grand Hotel is five minutes' walk from the lifts. The Miramonti is not well situated but is friendly, attractive and good value. The Biancaneve is just outside the town with its own mini-bus service to the slopes. Hotel du Col is 'warm, comfortable and clean'.

Eating in and out

In Montgenèvre, there are more than a dozen eating-places, including the Ca Del Sol for pizzas, Les Chalmettes, L'Estable, Pizzeria La Tourmente, the smart Le Jamy and Chez Pierrot for pizzas and grills.

In Sauze, La Griglia is strongly recommended. Del Falco is praised for its relaxed and friendly service ('food great and not expensive'). Albertino's is more of a café than a restaurant, with prices to match. Del Borgo has 'a pleasant buzz' and is famed for its *tiramisù*.

Eating-places in Sestriere range from pizzerias to smart, international restaurants. The Last Tango is for grills, and the Fraiteve in the Grand Hotel specialises in local Piedmont cuisine. Jolly Market is said to be the most reasonably priced of the five supermarkets.

Après-ski
After-skiing activity in Montgenèvre is extremely limited, but there is a good choice of inexpensive bar-restaurants; three have nightclubs attached. The Ca del Sol is a popular bar in the centre. The Blue Night and Play Boy are the two discos. There is little for non-skiers, although the village has a good skating rink.

In Sauze, the infamous Andy Capp and the New Scotch Bar near the bottom of the home run catch the early evening crowd and are awash with pints of Tartan long before dark. Later on, the action moves to the Cotton Club, Hotel Derby Bar and Moncrons. Max's Bar shows British sport on satellite TV. Osteria da Gigi and The Village Gossip both have live music. The Chicchirichi, Schuss, New Life, and Rimini Nord discos 'keep you dancing as long as you want'. One reporter notes that entry to all clubs is free, which is a pleasant contrast to France.

Sestriere's après-ski is fairly lively and stylish when the Italians are in residence at weekends and during holiday periods, although at other times it is quieter. The Black Sun and Tabata discos are popular at weekends. Besides ice-driving, there is little else for non-skiers here.

Childcare
Montgenèvre has a non-ski kindergarten, which takes children from 12 months to four years of age. The ESF takes three to five-year-olds in its ski kindergarten. Italy is not renowned for its childcare facilities, but the Milky Way is an important exception. Sauze's Pro Loco kindergarten takes infants from six months to six years of age, with ski tuition for the older ones; the ski schools take children from four years old. Sestriere has no public crèche, but Club Med looks after its smallest members from four years of age, as does the ski school.

Linked or nearby resorts

Bardonecchia
top 2750m (9,022ft) bottom 1312m (4,303ft)
This is a large and traditional market town set in a sunny valley and surrounded by beautiful scenery. Although it is not part of the Milky Way circuit, it lies close to both Montgenèvre and Sestriere. It is a popular place with Italians, who swarm in from Turin at weekends and on public holidays. The skiing is spread over three areas, linked by free ski bus, with a total of 140km of piste served by 24 lifts, and offers a surprising amount of challenge. The nightlife is strictly limited to a couple of rather dull bars and a disco.

Hotels include La Bettula, close to the shopping centre, the Tabor, near the ski bus stop, and the Larici, 250m from the heart of the resort.

Facilities for small children are non-existent.

TOURIST OFFICE
Tel 39 122 99032
Fax 39 122 980612

Borgata
top 2820m (9,250ft) bottom 1840m (6,035ft)

This is a small resort five minutes by road from Sestriere, with an infrequent bus service between the two. Hotel Hermitage is recommended ('nice rooms, but the food was not up to much'). Reporters who stayed in the Nube d'Argenta self-catering apartments praised them as 'clean, modern and convenient for the lifts'. There are complaints about the ski school ('very poor, with limited spoken English; little progress was offered in the lessons, but the teachers were pleasant enough'). Shopping is almost non-existent ('a poor selection of postcards and no stamps'). The après-ski is quiet ('a couple of sleepy bars with miserable staff and no, or few, customers'). As another reporter put it: 'When the sun goes down, it is time to eat and go to bed'.

TOURIST OFFICE
as Sestriere

Cesana Torinese
top 2820m (9,250ft) bottom 1350m (4,428ft)

This attractively shabby old village dates from the twelfth century and is set on a busy road junction at the foot of the Italian approach to the Montgenèvre Pass. It is rather confined and shaded, and accommodation is mainly in apartments and a few hotels. The chair-lifts up to the skiing above Clavière and Sansicario are a long walk from the centre, and the place can be safely recommended only to those with a car. The Chaberton is a three-star hotel, and there are half-a-dozen small one-stars. Restaurant La Selvaggia specialises in regional dishes, La Noblerot is for French cuisine, and the smart Fraiteve serves truffles; Brusachoeur is a popular pizzeria. Après-ski spots include the Pussy-Cat pub and the Cremeria Rinaldo e Luciana bar.

TOURIST OFFICE
Tel 39 122 89202
Fax 39 122 811315

Clavière
top 2820m (9,250ft) bottom 1760m (5,773ft)

Clavière is a small border town in the northern Valle di Susa, with a customs post in its centre. During the eighteenth century it was part of Montgenèvre. The village consists of a few hotels and a row of shops (including several good supermarkets) on the Italian side, specialising in food and cheap local alcohol, with prices in both francs and lire.

Reporters say the village has a pleasant, relaxed atmosphere; it is tightly enclosed by wooded slopes, and the nursery area is small and steep. Lifts give access to the skiing above Montgenèvre and Cesana, with easy runs back from both. Queuing is not usually a problem, although it does tend to become busier at weekends. Mountain eating-places close to the village are the Località Gimont and La Coche. There is a cross-country trail up to Montgenèvre and back. The ski school has some English-speaking instructors and, outside high season, mainly English-speaking pupils. At weekends there is heavy through-traffic.

There are eight hotels along the road; the two-star Hotel Roma, close to the main chair-lift, is recommended ('good value, plenty of food, and comfortable rooms'). Others include the Passero Pellegrino, Pian del Sole and the Savoia. The recommended restaurants are the Ski-Lodge, the Sandy and the Gran Bouc crêperie. Clavière is 'not a place for those interested in a hectic après-ski'. It has half-a-dozen bars including the Bar Caffé Torino and the Pub Kilt, plus disco La Scacchiera.

TOURIST OFFICE
Tel 39 122 878856
Fax 39 122 878888

Sansicario
top 2820m (9,250ft) 1710m (5,609ft)
The village is in a sunny position halfway up the west-facing mountain-side, and is well placed for exploring the Milky Way. It is purpose-built, consisting mainly of apartment buildings linked to a neat commercial precinct by shuttle-lift. Facilities for beginners, and especially children, are generally good. There is a ski- and non-ski kindergarten (the Junior Club), which provide daycare including lunch for 3- to 11-year-olds. Sansicario has its own ski school.

There is little variety among the après-ski facilities, with only a disco and a handful of restaurants and bars. Accommodation is of a generally high standard, mostly in apartments but with a few comfortable and expensive hotels. The most attractive of these is the Rio Envers, a short walk from the centre. Others include the four-star Monti della Luna and the simpler San Sicario.

TOURIST OFFICE
Tel 39 122 831596
Fax 39 122 831880

Skiing facts: **Montgenèvre**

TOURIST OFFICE
F-05100 Montgenèvre, Hautes-Alpes
Tel 33 4 92 21 90 22
Fax 33 4 92 21 92 45

THE RESORT
By road Calais 978km
By rail Briançon 10km
By air Turin 2 hrs, Grenoble 3 hrs
Visitor beds 8,000
Transport bus service throughout the resort
and to Briançon

THE SKIING
Linked or nearby resorts Bardonecchia
(n), Borgata (I), Clavière (I), Cesana
Torinese (I), Grangesises (I), Jouvenceaux
(I), Sansicario (I), Sauze d'Oulx (I), Sestriere
(I), Sportinia (I)
Longest run Le Chalvet, 2.5km (red)
Number of lifts 24 in Montgenèvre, 101 in
Milky Way
Total of trails/pistes 65km in Montgenèvre
(49% easy, 32% intermediate, 19%
difficult), 400km in Milky Way
Nursery slopes 1 free drag-lift
Summer skiing none
Snowmaking 15% of runs covered

LIFT PASSES
Area pass Montgenèvre 610FF for 6 days,
extension pass for Milky Way
Day pass Montgenèvre 120FF, Milky Way

180FF
Beginners Petit Réseau pass for beginners
(covers 7 lifts), 80FF a day for adults, 60FF
for children
Pensioners 60-69 yrs, 480FF for 6 days,
free for 70 yrs and over
Credit cards accepted yes

SKI SCHOOLS
Adults ESF, 745-770FF for 6 days (5 hrs
per day)
Private lessons ESF, 165FF per hr
Snowboarding ESF, prices and times as
regular ski school
Cross-country ESF, 485FF for 6 half-days.
Loipe 50km on either side of the pass and at
Les Alberts, 7km away
Other courses off-piste, moguls, slalom
Guiding companies through ski school

CHILDREN
Lift pass 5-12 yrs, 480FF for 6 days, free
for 4 yrs and under
Ski kindergarten Jardin d'Enfants, 3-5 yrs,
100FF per half-day
Ski school ESF, 3-5 yrs, 695FF for 6 days
Non-ski kindergarten Haute Garderie, 12
mths-4 yrs, 9am-5.30pm, 550FF for 6 days
not including lunch

FOOD AND DRINK PRICES
Coffee 6-7FF, glass of wine 9-12FF, small
beer 10-12FF, dish of the day 60-70FF

Skiing facts: **Sauze d'Oulx**

TOURIST OFFICE
Piazza Assietta 18, I-10050 Sauze d'Oulx,
Piedmont
Tel 39 122 858009
Fax 39 122 850497

THE RESORT
By road Calais 998km
By rail Oulx 5km, frequent buses to resort
By air Turin 2 hrs
Visitor beds 4,350
Transport free ski bus runs from 8.30am-
5.30pm daily

THE SKIING
Linked or nearby resorts Bardonecchia
(n), Borgata (l), Clavière (l), Cesana
Torinese (l), Grangesises (l), Jouvenceaux
(l), Montgenèvre (l), Sansicario (l), Sestriere
(l), Sportinia (l)
Longest run number 12, 12km (red)
Number of lifts 22 in Sauze d'Oulx, 101 in
Milky Way
Total of trails/pistes 120km in Sauze
d'Oulx (27% easy, 61% intermediate, 12%
difficult), 400km in Milky Way
Nursery slopes 3 lifts in Sauze d'Oulx
Summer skiing none
Snowmaking 5km in Sauze d'Oulx

LIFT PASSES
Area pass Milky Way (covers Sauze d'Oulx,
Sestriere, Sansicario, Cesana and Clavière),
L210,000-230,000 for 6 days

Day pass L44,000 (Milky Way)
Beginners points tickets
Pensioners 60 yrs and over,
L188,000-210,000 for 6 days
Credit cards accepted yes

SKI SCHOOLS
Adults Sauze d'Oulx, Sauze Project and
Sauze Sportinia, 10am-1pm, L160,000
for 6 days (3 hrs per day)
Private lessons all ski schools
L42,000-46,000 per hr
Snowboarding group and private lessons
through ski schools
Cross-country very limited. Loipe 3km
Other courses heli-skiing from Sestriere
Guiding companies through ski schools

CHILDREN
Lift pass 8-12 yrs, L188,000-210,000 for
6 days, free for 7 yrs and under
Ski kindergarten The Village Kindergarten,
6 mths and over, 9am-5pm, L280,000 for 6
days. Pro Loco, 4-6 yrs, 9am-5pm,
L250,000 for 6 days
Ski school all ski schools, 4-6 yrs,
10am-1pm, L172,000 for 6 days
Non-ski kindergarten Pro Loco,
18 mths-6 yrs, 9am-5pm, L250,000 for
6 days

FOOD AND DRINK PRICES
Coffee L1,400, glass of wine L1000, small
beer L3,000, dish of the day L25,000

Skiing facts: **Sestriere**

TOURIST OFFICE
Piazza Agnelli, I-10058 Sestriere,
Piedmont
Tel 39 122 755444
Fax 39 122 755171

THE RESORT
By road Calais 1020km
By rail Oulx 22km, buses to resort
By air Turin 2 hrs
Visitor beds 16,846
Transport ski bus L2,500 per day

THE SKIING
Linked or nearby resorts Bardonecchia
(n), Borgata (I), Clavière (I), Cesana
Torinese (I), Grangesises (I), Jouvenceaux
(I), Montgenèvre (I), Sansicario (I), Sauze
d'Oulx (I), Sportinia (I)
Longest run Rio Nero, 7km (black)
Number of lifts 19 in Sestriere, 101 in
Milky Way
Total of trails/pistes 120km in Sestriere
(39% easy, 42% intermediate, 19%
difficult), 400km in Milky Way
Nursery slopes several areas
Summer skiing none
Snowmaking 70km covered

LIFT PASSES
Area pass Milky Way (covers Sauze d'Oulx,
Sestriere, Sansicario, Cesana Torinese and
Clavière) L210,000-230,000 for 6 days

Day pass L44,000 (Milky Way)
Beginners L26,000 per day
Pensioners 60 yrs and over, L188,000-
210,000 for 6 days
Credit cards accepted no

SKI SCHOOLS
Adults Sestriere Ski School, 10am-1pm,
L45,000 per day, L180,000 for 6 days
Private lessons L47,000 per hr
Cross-country private lessons through
ski school, details on request.
Loipe 15km
Snowboarding private lessons through
ski school, details on request
Other courses heli-skiing
Guiding companies through ski school

CHILDREN
Lift pass 8-12 yrs, L188,000-210,000,
free for 7 yrs and under
Ski kindergarten Sestriere Ski School, 4
yrs and over, 10am-1pm, L45,000 per hr,
L180,000 for 6 days
Ski school as ski kindergarten
Non-ski kindergarten Mini Club of
Grangesises, 3-12 yrs, 9am-1pm and
3-7pm, L15,000 per day, extra L15,000
per day for lunch

FOOD AND DRINK PRICES
Coffee L1,400, glass of wine L1,000-1,500,
small beer L3,000, dish of the day L20,000

Monte Rosa

ALTITUDE Champoluc 1570m (5,150ft), Gressoney-la-Trinité 1640m (5,379ft)
Alagna 1188m (3,898ft)

As far as British skiers are concerned, the Monte Rosa area is a well-kept Italian secret, but this is changing fast with the rising demand for holidays in the only Alpine country that has a favourable exchange rate. The villages of **Champoluc**, **Gressoney-la-Trinité** and **Alagna** lie at the heads of parallel valleys on the southern side of the border with Switzerland. The Matterhorn is more pimple than peak from this perspective, but the Monte Rosa range, with its crags and glaciers, provides spectacular views. The valleys were settled by the Walser people in the Middle Ages and their geographical isolation has resulted in a distinctive culture and a strong Germanic dialect that persist today. Although the three villages are close as the crow flies and well-connected by the lift system (at least in the case of Champoluc and Gressoney), it takes two to three hours to drive between any two of them.

■ GOOD POINTS

Varied intermediate ski area, excellent off-piste, strong regional identity, rustic charm, high-quality local cuisine, no crowds or queues

■ BAD POINTS

Little advanced piste-skiing, shortage of non-skiing activities, poor rental equipment, limited nightlife

On the mountain
top 3370m (11,056ft) bottom 1188m (3,898ft)

In the Monte Rosa ski area, all pistes eventually lead to **Stafal**, a modern hamlet above Gressoney-la-Trinité that is the central link in the lift chain. Head up the two chair-lifts to the west and you reach the Colle Bettaforca, the departure point for the descents to Champoluc. Take the two-stage gondola to the east and you come to the Passo del Selati, the start of the Alagna connection. With slopes on both sides of the valley, Gressoney has the lion's share of the skiing, and the fastest lifts.

There are two points of departure from Champoluc, one on the outskirts of the village and the other up the hill in **Frachey**, which provides much quicker access to the main area. There are also three small satellite areas — **Antagnod**, **Brusson** and **Gressoney-St-Jean**, which are not connected to the central system. Alagna's facilities consist of a venerable three-stage cable car, which is almost empty except on Sundays, and is supplemented by four minor lifts. Although its impressive vertical drop and its extensive powder fields attract rugged skiers, its links with Gressoney are unpisted, which makes it unsuitable for anyone else.

Beginners

The best place to learn is the sunny nursery slope at Crest, at the top of the first stage of the Champoluc gondola. In Gressoney, beginners congregate around the Punta Jolanda lift, then progress via the Sitte chairlift to the wide plateau above Stafal on the Champoluc side.

Intermediates

Both Gressoney and Champoluc have plenty of interlinked intermediate cruising, rather more in fact than the piste-map suggests; it is so badly printed that most of the blue (easy) runs appear to be black (difficult).

Advanced

The best black piste in the area is the 7-km descent from the top of the Punta Indren in Alagna, but it would not be so severely rated in other resorts. The same could be said of the only mogul field, which is at Sarezza in Champoluc.

Off-piste

In the right conditions, all three resorts present challenges that are made all the more testing by bumpy terrain and narrow defiles between rock walls. The Mos and the Bertolina in Gressoney are excellent examples and they should not be attempted without a guide. The same is true of most of the skiing in Alagna, where the cable car provides rapid access to huge snowfields that inevitably in a predominantly south- and west-facing resort are prone to avalanche. The north-facing slopes in the Alta Valsesia National Park give a sense of extreme adventure, especially when accessed by the couloir at the top of the Malfatta. Alternatively, there is extensive heli-skiing, with glacier drops at over 4000m in the Monte Rosa range. Some of the routes take skiers down to Cervinia for the 25-km return to Champoluc.

Ski schools and guiding

English-speaking instruction can be hard to come by. In Gressoney, only 5 out of 30 instructors speak the language, so one of them should be requested when booking lessons. Qualified alpine guides are available through the respective tourist offices, but again the language can be a problem. In Alagna, the young mountain guide Roberto Valzer arranges exciting off-piste adventures, as well as accommodation and evening meals in restaurants that are more like private homes.

Snowboarding

As there are no soft boots to rent in Gressoney or Champoluc, the learning curve is unnecessarily painful. The beginner's slope at Crest has an awkward camber, but the slow-moving Fontenay chair that accesses it is exceptionally user-friendly for first-timers. Individual and group lessons are available in Gressoney and Champoluc, but riders are not allowed on the Jolanda nursery slope in Gressoney. A qualified alpine guide can be hired for off-piste and heli-boarding expeditions.

Cross-country

The Champoluc catchment area has 35km of trails, the best of them lower down the valley in Brusson. Likewise, the pick of Gressoney's 25-km network are to be found in neighbouring Gressoney-St-Jean.

Mountain restaurants

There are 28 mountain restaurants in the Monte Rosa area, so the choice is wide and if you look off the beaten track you are likely to find the most interesting eating places. The Lys Rifugio at Gabiet is recommended for its local meats and cheeses as well as its ambience. The Edelweiss at Crest serves a reasonably priced set lunch in the restaurant and quick snacks in the bar. In Alagna, the La Bàita Refuge has superb mushroom pasta and exceptionally friendly service.

Off the mountain

Champoluc, at the top of the Ayas Valley, is set around a traditional church and a fast-running mountain river. The old quarter was built in the fifteenth century, but the village has expanded in recent years to accommodate the requirements of a small ski resort. **Gressoney-la-Trinité** is on a similar scale, a network of cobbled streets and wooden chalets surrounded by contemporary buildings. **Gressoney-St-Jean**, 5km down the valley, is larger and more attractive, while the outpost of Stafal tries to make up in convenience for what it lacks in soul. Given its remote location, Alagna is built on a puzzlingly large scale, with decaying buildings surrounding a church where bell-ringing rules. This is a genuine oddball of a place, which has unique wooden houses with built-in hay frames, and a charm all of its own.

> **■ OTHER SPORTS**
>
> Squash, swimming, skating, winter walks

Accommodation

In Champoluc the best choice is the Farve, which is central, small, well-managed and friendly according to its extremely enthusiastic British clients. The Petit Prince in Antagnod also finds favour, but the welcome is less warm at the awkwardly located, though authentically rustic Villa Anna Maria. The four-star Monboso at Stafal is as ski-in ski-out as you can get, but the Scoiàttolo in Gressoney itself is equally comfortable with a better ambience. In Alagna the Bar Mirella, a bed-and-breakfast with rooms over a cake shop, is a must if you can get in. If not, try the Genzinella.

Eating in and out

Le Sapin in Champoluc looks unpromising, not least for its multi-lingual tourist menus, but the food is something of a revelation. Otherwise, the Farve is consistently good, with a bias towards gargantuan feasts of local game. Cuisine at the Villa Anna Maria is described as 'variable, but the restaurant has an honest wine list'. In Alagna the Servan is surprisingly sophisticated and should not be missed.

Après-ski

This is the kind of area where the nightlife is described by tour operators as 'informal and relaxed' — a euphemism for dead in the water. What there is takes place in the bars of family hotels, where locals and tourists drink and play cards without much overlap between the different cultures. The Champoluc disco scene is divided between the Gram Parsons in Frachey and La Boryula in Antagnod, while Gressoney-St-Jean offers the Futuro. Gamblers with their own transport can visit the casino in **St-Vincent** (25km from Champoluc, 70km from Gressoney).

Childcare

Childcare in the area is extremely limited, with no crèche or kindergarten facilities in Champoluc. The ski school takes children from five years of age. Hotel Monboso, above Gressoney, has a mini-club for children aged four to eight years (residents only). Those over six years can join adult classes at the ski school.

Passo Tonale

ALTITUDE 1884m (6,181ft)

Passo Tonale is a thin line of settlement running for 1700m east to west along both sides of a high mountain pass, with a steep glacier to the south and open, rolling snowfields to the north, which mark the border between Lombardy and Trentino. What was only a scattering of roadside lifts in the 1960s has grown into the Adamello Skipass network shared with **Pontedilegno**. Its 29 lifts carry 30,000 skiers per hour across 80km of pistes, which are a two-and-a-half hour drive from Bergamo Airport. The resort is becoming increasingly popular with British skiers and Eastern Europeans are also arriving in numbers. Pontedilegno is a charming village in its own right, 600m along the pass to the west of Passo Tonale.

■ GOOD POINTS

Excellent snow record, value for money, ideal for beginners, varied off-piste itineraries, lack of weekday queues

■ BAD POINTS

Through-village traffic, lack of alpine charm, budget and youth group ambience

On the mountain
top 3016m (9,895ft) bottom 1270m (4,167ft)

Passo Tonale is a resort with exceptional snow quality, ideal beginner and easy intermediate terrain, as well as extensive ski-touring off-piste. Mountain access is on either side of the main road, with most of the chair- and drag-lifts starting from the south-facing snowfields. The only cable car is a 1000-m walk from the village; at the top is a chair-lift, which leads to four drags on the Presena Glacier. The cable car is the only lift prone to queues, but they are rarely longer than 15 minutes, and then only on Sundays.

The skiing looks temptingly easy and open, which it is apart from the off-piste adventure routes. Pontedilegno is a separate sector, normally accessible on skis, or by bus, with a handful of lifts starting at the edge of the forest.

Beginners

Few resorts offer such reliable snow quality and wide scope of blue (easy) runs for beginners. Six lifts rise up the south-facing side of the valley to access easy blue pistes; Valbiolo, the longest, is nearly 3km. The blue run off the Tre Larici drag is fenced in on both sides of its carpet-like expanse, and is a run that frightens no one. Beginners who insist on going to the top should think twice before tackling the blue glacier runs, as they involve skiing some red (intermediate) sections to get back to the cable car.

Intermediates

The 3-km Bleis run takes you all the way back to town and is easy cruising terrain. The two glacier reds, accessed by drag-lifts, connect with the single red piste down to the cable-car station for the best snow in the resort. Adventurous intermediates might try the Alpino, a 4.5-km excursion around the back of Monte Serodine and out of sight of the pistes.

Advanced

The Sinistro black (difficult) run on the glacier sounds threatening, but is really a reclassified red. Its 300-m vertical drop in the space of one kilometre makes it steep enough to be a regular

> ■ WHAT'S NEW
>
> Additional chair-lift and piste extending above the Valbiolo area

training slope for the Italian ski team. The only run under the cable car is also marked as black, but skiers from Chamonix or Verbier would scarcely give it a red rating.

Off-piste

Italians adore ski-touring, and the best itineraries usually require some walking uphill. The 16-km Pisgana Glacier route runs from the drag-lift down the back of the Presena Glacier with an optional climb up Monte Adamello at 3554m. It follows on over open snowfields into the ravine of Valnarcanello and at least 1000m of flat skating into Pontedilegno.

Ski schools and guiding

Thanks to the state border, Passo Tonale has a choice of two ski schools: one from Lombardy and the other from Trentino. Instructors at both are described by one reporter as 'unspoilt, simple and sympathetic; they try just as hard with beginners, love a joke, and even if they aren't technically the best teachers, they put their hearts into it'.

Snowboarding

With no snowboard park, half-pipe or dedicated school, there are few boarders at this resort. Three of the four snowboard teachers at the Trentino Ski School speak English. Delpero, next to Hotel Redivalle, is the only shop that hires out soft snowboard boots. The terrain around Passo Tonale is too tame for freestylers looking for natural jumps and dips.

Cross-country

Down valley to the east towards Vermiglio, on the south side of Passo Tonale and at the bottom of Valnarcanello are some 30km of scenic prepared trails.

Mountain restaurants

The old hospice complex on Valbiolo, restored by the municipality and now called Hotel Mirandola, is warmly recommended ('the best food in the region'). Malga Valbiolo is a popular old chalet, while Negritella serves 'good junk food and *vin brûlé*'.

Off the mountain

For centuries the Mirandola hospice sheltered pilgrims crossing Passo Tonale, but tourism dates only from the 1960s. Prosperity has brought some new paint, three 12-storey tower blocks and rows of condominiums that resemble army barracks. Hotels hug the single roadway, but fortunately there is little through-traffic by night. You can walk across the village in ten minutes. The only bus runs seven times daily to Pontedilegno. British tour operators collaborate on a weekly coach trip to the ski slopes of **Folgarida** and **Marilleva**, touching on the **Madonna di Campiglio** area.

■ OTHER SPORTS

Snowmobiling, dog-sledding in Pontedilegno, skating

Accommodation

Passo Tonale's 3,000 beds include only one chalet and limited self-catering apartments. Hotel Redivalle is the oldest hotel and a landmark by which directions are given. Orchidea is the most recent and one of the most attractive hotels, along with the historic Mirandola Hospice, whose guests can rely on snowmobile transport til 2am.

Bianca Neve features bright orange décor in a 12-storey, white tower block, but has good food. Sporthotel Vittoria has a pub with live music and is often used by school parties.

Eating in and out

For fine dining the snowmobile ride up to the Mirandola Hospice is mandatory. Intimate decor and delicious gorgonzola *spätzle* are found at Il Focolare ('impressive, but not cheap'). La Torretta is praised for 'the best thin, crispy-base pizza'. Palla di Neve and the newly opened Antares are recommended for pasta. There are two fully stocked supermarkets with good selections of local meats and cheeses.

Après-ski

Bar Candy, Nico's and the UFO are popular bars. Monti and Cantuccio offer sports events on television. El Bait is quiet and cosy. Crazy Horse opens with a happy hour between 5 and 9pm, continues with a live band until 2am, then becomes a disco. The Embassy disco gives free entrance to British visitors. Antares features live music several nights a week.

Childcare

The kindergarten in the Hotel Miramonti takes children from four years of age.

TOURIST OFFICE
Tel 39 364 903838
Fax 39 364 903895

Sella Ronda

ALTITUDE Selva Gardena 1550m (5,084ft), Canazei 1440m (4,724ft)

The largest ski area in the world is set in the most dramatic and beautiful mountain range in Europe. For palates jaded by the stolid commercial realities of holidays in the French Alps and in Austria, this is a much-needed and refreshing sorbet on the menu of European skiing. It comprises an astonishing 464 lifts serving 1180km of largely intermediate skiing set against a backdrop of craggy peaks and dramatic granite cliffs, which turn a distinctive and glorious shade of rose pink in the light of the setting sun.

By no means are all of these runs linked, but nearly all are included in the Superski Dolomiti lift pass, which represents the best value in the Northern Hemisphere.

At the core of the Dolomites lies the Sella Ronda, a celebrated circuit of four valleys involving 90 minutes of lifts, 120 minutes of downhill skiing, and an always undetermined Joker factor of queuing-time. Miss the crucial lift home because of deteriorating weather or volume of people and you are in for an expensive taxi ride.

The best-known, but by no means the most important, of these valleys is Val Gardena, scene in 1981 of Britain's best ever World Cup Downhill result when Konrad Bartelski claimed second place, a feat so surprising that live television commentator David Vine at first thought the clock was wrong. **Selva Gardena**, or Wolkenstein as it is also known in this bilingual border area of Italy, is the actual name of the resort, barely more than a small village strung along the main valley road.

The second most popular resort is **Canazei**, in the Italian-speaking Val di Fassa. This large and bustling village acts as one of the main holiday bases for skiing the region and is the best for those in search of non-skiing activities and a good nightlife.

On the periphery of the Sella Ronda circuit lies a whole range of resorts, from established international ski towns like chic **Cortina d'Ampezzo**, to the sleepy and essentially Italian villages of **San Martino di Castrozza** and **Vigo di Fassa**. You cannot hope to ski it all in a week, or even a season.

Vastly improved services to the upgraded airports at Venice and Verona, coupled with two-and-a-half-hour motorway transfers to most

SELVA GARDENA
■ GOOD POINTS

Enormous intermediate ski area, outstanding scenery, variety of mountain restaurants, extensive ski-touring opportunities, many activities for non-skiers, comprehensive beginners' and children's facilities, excellent-value lift pass

■ BAD POINTS

Unreliable snow record, heavy traffic, lack of village centre

Dolomite resorts, have reopened this unspoilt corner of the European ski map.

As one veteran visitor to the area put it: 'What you find here is a lack of complacency in comparison to Italy's alpine neighbours. They don't turn on the snow-cannon at the start of the season, they turn them on a month earlier to ensure conditions will be perfect from the word go. Gone are the days of dangling your legs off ancient lifts, which closed at lunchtime while the operator went off for a plate of pasta and a bottle of wine; they have been replaced with modern gondolas and detachable quads. Combine this professionalism with excellent prices, good food and wine and the current popularity of everything Italian, and you have the formula for success'.

The layout of the Sella Ronda and the whole Superski Dolomiti region is not as confusing as it sounds and you will soon get your bearings, provided you invest in the Ordnance Survey-style map of the region, called Sellaronda e Valli Ladine Carta Sciistica, which costs about £3 from any newsagent. It shows all the lifts and the standard of each run. The local tourist board piste-maps raise more questions than they answer.

> **CANAZEI**
> **■ GOOD POINTS**
>
> Superb intermediate skiing, outstanding scenery, wide choice of shops, lively après-ski, variety of mountain restaurants, excellent-value lift pass
>
> **■ BAD POINTS**
>
> Large sprawling resort, heavy traffic, uncertain resort-level snow

On the mountain
top 2950m (9,676ft) bottom 1225m (4,018ft)

With its mainly blue (easy) and unproblematic red (intermediate) runs, the Sella Ronda is better for wonderful scenery than for really challenging skiing. Although the peaks of these mountains are high, virtually all the skiing takes place lower down; this is the main cause of the Dolomites' variable snow record, a handicap that has been offset by heavy investment in modern snowmaking techniques. Nevertheless, the south-facing slopes in particular become very worn and unpleasant. One reporter recounted having to remove her skis and walk certain sections of the circuit during a mild spell, and indeed short walks between lifts are not uncommon, even when conditions are good.

The Sella Ronda can be skied in either direction with all kinds of variations, but it is wise to stick to the basic circuit until you have worked out how long it takes to complete the homeward section.

Clockwise mountain access from Selva is via the Dantercëpies gondola to the start of a long and mainly red cruise through 730m vertical all the way to **Colfosco**. From here a chair-lift takes you to Corvara and a 12-person gondola brings you to Boè and the Crep de Munt for a short red run down to **Campolongo**. You can take a drag-lift up to the Rifugio Bec de Roces, which is the start of a pleasant red and blue run with dramatic backdrops down into **Arabba**. Queues here can be unacceptable

353

during busy weeks ('a 40-minute wait mid-morning for a four-minute uplift'). A chair-lift is the most direct, but not necessarily the quickest onward route. The cable car to Belvedere involves more skiing and a much more challenging piste, which allows you to rejoin the blue route before Pont de Vauz.

Two slow chairs, which can produce an unpleasant bottleneck, bring you to Sas Becè and the red run down to Lupo Bianco. Take a short red off the circuit into Canazei, or continue with two chairs up to Col Salei. From here, a short red and a long blue cruise through 700m vertical to return to Selva.

Beginners
The best of the novice skiing is found in the Alta Badia sector, bordered by **Armentarola** in the east, **Corvara** in the west and **La Villa** in the north. The gentle wooded meadows here are reminiscent of the Austrian Tyrol. At the other end of the circuit, try the long blue that starts above the Passo Sella at 2400m and takes you gently all the way down to Selva at 1570m.

Intermediates
The whole of the Sella Ronda is ideally suited to cruisers who really want to put some mileage beneath their skis each day in this outstanding setting. Where to base yourself is a matter of personal choice. The Selva–Canazei end of the circuit has some of the better long runs, though fans of Corvara and Colfosco would strongly disagree.

Advanced
Arabba is the Argentière of Italy and the place to base yourself for the toughest skiing in the area. Anyone who imagines that the Dolomites consists solely of scenic blue cruising runs is in for a wicked shock here. From the edge of the village a two-stage jumbo gondola and a cable car take you up nearly 900m over the granite cliffs off the Soura Sass to the start of what is, by any standard, some serious advanced skiing. The black (difficult) runs down the front face are testing in the extreme.

Alternatively, from the halfway stage of the gondola you can ski off the Sella Ronda on a wonderful 20-km journey down usually deserted pistes to the town of **Malga Ciapela**. From here you pay an approximate £10-supplement to your lift pass for the long cable car to the top of the 3269-m Marmolada, revered by mountaineers in the same breath as the Matterhorn, the Eiger and Mont Blanc; the lift only opens in February. After admiring the views from the top, a mighty 12-km red run takes you to within one drag-lift of the home run back down to Arabba. Powderhounds can also enjoy moderately priced heli-skiing on the Marmolada.

Off-piste
Passo Pordoi, between Arabba and Canazei, is the base-station of the Sas Pordoi cable car, which takes you up to the Rifugio Maria at 2958m.

Piste-grooming machines have never made it up here and all the skiing is as nature intended. The long run down the Val de Mesdi is one of the most taxing in the Dolomites and should not be attempted without a guide. The front face of Sas Pordoi is a shorter, difficult challenge, with a steep and usually icy entrance guaranteed to get anyone's adrenalin pumping; falling is not advised.

Ski schools and guiding
The Selva Gardena Ski School as usual generates excellent reports and tuition appears to be of a high standard ('good teaching and no silly end-of-week races'). The only drawback in Selva and indeed in all the Sella Ronda resorts is the instructors' often limited knowledge of English. The Canazei Marmolada Ski School offers group and private lessons. The other two ski schools in the Val Gardena area are at **Ortisei** and **Santa Cristina**, but we have no reports of them.

Snowboarding
The Selva Gardena Ski School offers private snowboarding tuition. Boards are available for hire through the ski school at Ortisei. The Canazei Marmolada Ski School also gives snowboarding lessons. Colfosco now has a half-pipe.

Cross-country
The Dolomiti Superski area claims a mighty 1033km of prepared loipe scattered throughout the region; some of the most scenic (98km) are situated in Val Gardena.

Mountain restaurants
The Dolomites abounds with mountain eateries, but standards between the Italian and German-speaking regions vary markedly, with the better food found in the former. Pizzeria El Table in Arabba is strongly recommended. Plan Boé above the village is popular for traditional Austro–Italian fare. Trapper's Bar, on the Passo Campolungo between Corvara and Arabba, has a sun-terrace and live music.

Rifugio Crep de Munt, above Corvara, also has a terrace and a warm welcome. Try Mesules — its position on the edge of the road and the piste between Selva and Colfosco means it can be reached by skiers and non-skiers alike.

Rifugio Scotoni is a welcome wayside warming-hut on the run down from **Lagazuoi** if you are unable to make it to the even cosier Alpina, 2 kilometres further on. Either way you may need some refreshment before the next lift, which is one of the quaintest in the region — a horse-drawn tow. A more gastronomic lunch can be found at the Hotel Grand Angel on the edge of the Armentarola cross-country track. Bàita del Gigio, on the nursery slopes above Malga Ciapela, is worth the long run down and is exceptionally good value.

Chez Anna, on the run from Secada to Ortisei, is said to be worth a visit for spectacular ham-and-eggs. Bàita Frederola, near Belvedere, is recommended for its pizzas. Way off the beaten track is the Ospizio di Santa Croce, reached by taking a ski bus from La Villa to **Pedraces** and two lifts up to the Abbey of the Holy Cross. Ristorante Lé, at the top of the chair, is renowned for the best *Gulaschsuppe* in the Sud Tirol.

Off the mountain

Selva is an unassuming village, which sprawls in suburban style up the Val Gardena. Traffic is heavy and weary skiers are more at risk crossing the road than they ever are on piste. For all that, the village maintains a quiet, unsophisticated charm, which makes it popular with families. Examples of the local woodcarving industry colourfully adorn houses and even lamp-posts.

Canazei is a large, attractive and lively village on a busy main road in the Italian-speaking Val di Fassa. It is the best place to stay for those in search of non-skiing activities and a good nightlife. The village itself is a tangle of narrow streets with a mixture of old farm buildings, new hotels and some delightful shops.

Such is the scramble for beds in the Val di Fassa that tour operators offer hotels in outlying villages as far away as **Pera**, **Pozza**, Vigo di Fassa, and even **Moena**. These little Italian communities have their own tiny ski areas, which suit only beginners and slalom specialists (Olympic champion Alberto Tomba stays at the extremely comfortable Parc Corona in Vigo). If you don't meet Tomba, you will at least see his equally beefy dog, which winters at the hotel. However, the valley ski bus is slow, irregular and enormously oversubscribed. If you want to ski Canazei and the Sella Ronda from here you need a car.

Accommodation

In Selva, Hotel Gran Bàita is the pick of the four-stars, together with the Aaritz and the Alpinroyal. Hotel Laurin is a favourite amongst visitors and is renowned for its good food. Accommodation is mainly in small hotels, most of which are very comfortable. We have good reports of the Hotel Solaia and, in particular, its buffet breakfast. The centrally situated Hotel Antares is so praised, as is the simple Stella. Inexpensive bed-and-breakfasts include the Eden and the Somont. The more comfortable Savoy also has a restaurant. Hotels Freina and Serena have been renovated for this season.

In Canazei, the Croce Bianca is the best hotel in town, with hand-painted pine furniture in abundance. The Dolomiti is built in Grand Hotel style, while the newly upgraded four-star Astoria has the friendliest atmosphere. Hotel Bellevue is well-placed for the skiing, which is inconvenient from many of the village hotels.

Eating in and out

In Selva, two of the best restaurants are the Salfeur Pizzeria and Pizzeria Rino. A wider selection of dishes can be found at Café Mozart and the restaurant of the Hotel Laurin. Other eating-places include Armin, Lo

Sciattolo, La Freina, the restaurant in the Hotel Gran Bàita, and in Santa Cristina, La Plaza and Dosses.

Canazei abounds with modestly priced restaurants. Try Al Vecchio Mulino for local Italian dishes. Rosticceria Melester also has a warm atmosphere.

Après-ski

At first sight, Selva does not appear to have much of a nightlife. Half-a-dozen cafés serve homemade cakes and pastries, but the resort is quiet in the evening, with few lights, seemingly little activity and none of the buzz of a serious party resort. In fact, behind the shutters there is a thriving après-ski scene and a good choice of nightspots, but light sleepers are unlikely to have their slumbers disturbed.

The De Luisl is the most popular haunt after skiing ('the only place with any real life between skiing and dinner'). Bar La Stua has twice-weekly folk-music evenings. Also recommended are the Hotel Laurin Bar, La Frainela, the Monica and Mozart bars. The Dali and Stella Club discos throb through the night. The Savoy nightclub has live music and is said to be 'very expensive'. In nearby Santa Cristina, Yeti's Ombrella Bar is popular, and other bars include Calés and I Tublà.

> ### ■ OTHER SPORTS
> Selva: skating, curling, indoor shooting range, sleigh-rides, helicopter rides, parapente, indoor tennis and squash, swimming, tobogganing
> Canazei: parapente, tobogganing winter walks, swimming

In Canazei, the Montanara Bar is the place to meet after skiing, as is the Frogs Pub a few kilometres up the valley road in **Alba**. Nightlife centres largely around the numerous bars, and the busy Gatto Negro and Veruschka discos in Canazei and Alba respectively.

Childcare

Selva is an excellent area for children of all ages to learn to ski. The nursery slopes are based below the Dantercëpies gondola at the northern edge of the village. There is a kindergarten at the bottom of the Biancaneve drag-lift, where toddlers and small children are taught the rudiments of skiing among cartoon characters. Instructors are plentiful and patient and there seems to be none of the 'here is an entire generation to be put off skiing' attitude that you encounter in some French resorts. The surrounding area is ideal for older children to learn or improve their skiing.

Linked or nearby resorts

Arabba
top 2516m (8,255ft) bottom 1600m (5,250ft)

This small, unspoilt village is tucked away in a fold of the landscape and is surrounded by the most challenging skiing in the area. The village itself is hopeless for non-skiers, and facilities for babies and toddlers are non-existent. The language here is Italian, although Arabba is only a couple of kilometres south of the Sud-Tirol border. The Sport is the smartest hotel, but the Porto Vescovo is more lively and houses the Stübe Bar which, along with Peter's Bar, just about sums up the nightlife. The Rue de Mans is an excellent restaurant just outside the village.

TOURIST OFFICE
Tel 39 437 940083
Fax 39 437 940073

Campitello
top 2395m (7,858ft) bottom 1440m (4,723ft)

A small collection of old buildings make up this quiet village set beside a stream, well back from the main road. The Col Rodella cable car (45-minute queues reported) goes up to the ski area; there is no piste back down again. The village is ideal for complete beginners as some of the area's best nursery slopes are right on its doorstep. Hotels include the Fedora, next to the lift station, and the Medil, a modern hotel built in traditional alpine style with its own fitness centre and bar with music. Hotel Sella Ronda is an alpine-style hotel owned by a priest. Hotel Rubino has a swimming-pool and piano bar among its many facilities.

TOURIST OFFICE
Tel 39 462 61137
Fax 39 462 62771

Colfosco
top 2010m (6,594ft) 1650m (5,412ft)

Colfosco has easy access to both Selva and Corvara's skiing, although the village also has a small ski area of its own with good nursery slopes. Recommended hotels are the Kolfuschgerhof and the Centrale. Speckstube Peter, Mesoles, Stria, Matthiaskeller and Tabladel are the most popular eating places. Black Hill Nevada is a pub serving food, and the Capella is the smartest eating place.

TOURIST OFFICE
Tel 39 471 846176
Fax 39 471 847277

Corvara
top 2193m (7,195ft) bottom 1550m (5,085ft)

This pleasant Sella Ronda resort fails to attract any British tour operators, but it is strategically placed for some of the best skiing in the region. Hotel Posta-Zirm, the old post house at the bottom of the Col Alto chair-

Skiing facts: **Selva Gardena**

TOURIST OFFICE
Str. Mëisules 213, I-39048 Selva Gardena
Tel 39 471 795122
Fax 39 471 794245

THE RESORT
By road Calais 1226km
By rail bus service from Bressanone 35km,
Bolzano 40km, Chuisa 27km
By air Munich 4 hrs, Verona 3 hrs, Milan
4 hrs, Innsbruck 1½ hrs
Visitor beds 16,800 in Val Gardena area
Transport free ski bus between Ortisei and
Selva Gardena

THE SKIING
Linked or nearby resorts Arabba (I),
Armentarola (I), Campitello (I), Canazei (I),
Colfosco (I), Cortina d'Ampezzo (I), Corvara
(I), La Villa (I), Ortisei (I), Pedraces (I), San
Cassiano (I), Santa Cristina (I)
Longest run Seceda–Ortisei, 9km (red)
Number of lifts 464 in region
Total of trails/pistes 175km in
Val Gardena/Alpe di Suisi, 1180km in region
(30% easy, 60% intermediate,
10% difficult)
Nursery slopes 10 runs
Summer skiing none
Snowmaking 80km covered in
Val Gardena-Alpe di Suisi

LIFT PASSES
Area pass Superski Dolomiti (covers
464 lifts), L243,000-279,000 for
6 days

Day pass Superski Dolomiti L49,000-
56,000
Beginners points tickets
Pensioners 20% discount for 60 yrs and
over
Credit cards accepted yes

SKI SCHOOLS
Adults Selva Gardena Ski School, L215,000
for 6 days (4 hrs per day)
Private lessons Selva Gardena Ski School,
L50,000 per hr
Snowboarding Selva Gardena Ski School,
private lessons L50,000 per hr
Cross-country Selva Gardena Ski School,
L51,000 per hr. Loipe 98km
Other courses freestyle, off-piste, race
training, slalom, heli-skiing
Guiding companies Mountain School
Catores Val Gardena, L190,000 for
3 days

CHILDREN
Lift pass 6-14 yrs, Superski Dolomiti
L170,000–195,000, free for 5 yrs
and under
Ski kindergarten none
Ski school Selva Gardena Ski School, 4-12
yrs, L385,000 for 6 days
Non-ski kindergarten Selva Gardena Ski
School, from 12 mths, L50,000 per day
including lunch

FOOD AND DRINK PRICES
Coffee L2,500, glass of wine L2,000, small
beer L3,500, dish of the day L20,000

Skiing facts: **Canazei**

TOURIST OFFICE
APT Val di Fassa, Via Costa, I-38030 Alba di Canazei
Tel 39 462 602466
Fax 39 462 602278

THE RESORT
By road Calais 1240km
By rail Bolzano 40km
By air Munich 4 hrs, Verona 3 hrs, Milan 4 hrs, Innsbruck 1½ hrs
Visitor beds 49,300 in Val di Fassa
Transport free ski bus

THE SKIING
Linked or nearby resorts Arabba (I), Armentarola (I), Campitello (I), Canazei (I), Colfosco (I), Cortina d'Ampezzo (I), Corvara (I), La Villa (I), Ortisei (I), Pedraces (I), San Cassiano (I), Santa Cristina (I), Selva Gardena (I)
Longest run Pista del Bosco, 6.5km (red)
Number of lifts 464 in region
Total of trails/pistes 1180km in region (30% easy, 60% intermediate, 10% difficult)
Nursery slopes 10 runs
Summer skiing none
Snowmaking 60km covered in Val di Fassa

LIFT PASSES
Area pass Superski Dolomiti (covers 464 lifts), L243,000-279,000 for 6 days
Day pass Superski Dolomiti L47,000-56,000
Beginners points tickets
Pensioners 20% discount for 60 yrs and over
Credit cards accepted yes

SKI SCHOOLS
Adults Canazei Marmolada, L155,000 for 5 days (3 hrs per day)
Private lessons Canazei Marmolada L42,000 per hr
Snowboarding as regular ski school
Cross-country Scuola Fondo Fassa-Canazei, details on request.
Loipe 25km
Other courses monoski, off-piste, competition, heli-skiing
Guiding companies Guide Alpine Val di Fassa

CHILDREN
Lift pass Superski Dolomiti, 6-14 yrs, , L170,000-195,000 for 6 days, free for 5 yrs and under
Ski kindergarten Canazei Ski School, 4 yrs and over, L65,000 per day, L290,000 for 6 days (2½ hrs per day)
Ski school as ski kindergarten
Non-ski kindergarten as ski kindergarten

FOOD AND DRINK PRICES
Coffee L2,500, glass of wine L3,000, small beer L5,000, dish of the day L25,000

lift, is the place to stay. The building dates from 1808 and has been carefully renovated; the hotel also keeps alive the tradition of the tea dance. The Pensione Ladina nearby is a less expensive alternative and is renowned for its homemade blueberry *grappa*. There is cross-country skiing and a skating rink in the village. The ski school has a kindergarten for children from three years of age, but English is not widely spoken.

TOURIST OFFICE
as Colfosco

San Cassiano
top 2000m (6,562ft) bottom 1537m (5,041ft)

A small, roadside village with mainly new Dolomite-style buildings, San Cassiano has some excellent skiing for beginners and early intermediates who want to avoid challenges. Long, easy runs go down to the village from Pralongia and Piz Sorega. Reporters mention the lack of English in a resort that attracts mainly wealthy Italians. The down side of this is being the sole English speaker in a ski school class where lessons become 'laborious, with everything spoken in German and Italian'.

The Rosa Alpina is a large and comfortable hotel in the village centre and is also the focal point for après-ski with a live band. The Ski Bar is recommended for good, cheap pizzas; the Capanna Alpina, Saré, and Tirol are all busy restaurants. La Siriola, Rosa Alpina, Fanes and the restaurant in Hotel Diamont are more expensive. There is bowling at the Daimant, but otherwise the village tends to be on the quiet side. Armentarola, with its own hotels and restaurants, is a kilometre away.

TOURIST OFFICE
as Colfosco

La Thuile/La Rosière

ALTITUDE La Thuile 1441m (4,726ft), La Rosière 1850m (6,068ft)

L a Thuile, an old mining town clawing its way back to tourist-led prosperity, and La Rosière, a third-generation purpose-built resort, form
an extensive linked ski area stretching in an uneasy *entente cordiale*
across the Italian-French border. La Thuile, a winding 10-km drive off
the Courmayeur-Aosta highway, is
resolutely progressive; La Rosière, in
the Tarentaise Valley above **Bourg-St-
Maurice**, is content to rely on the rustic charm of its 1970s chalet-style
architecture and the popularity of its
low prices with the organisers of
school group holidays. With power
divided between three local councils, it
is not surprising that development at
La Rosière on the French side over the
last six years has been restricted to a
single high-speed quad; this is a source
of much irritation to its go-ahead
Italian neighbour.

In summer, the resorts are joined
by road over the Petit-St-Bernard Pass
— in winter the car journey via the Mont Blanc Tunnel takes four hours.
It is widely held that Hannibal led his elephants over the Pass in the
course of his epic journey from Spain to Rome in 218 BC, during which
he lost half of his army. If legend is correct, the ghosts may linger on in
old La Thuile, a collection of distressed industrial and residential buildings that are only now being restored in the interests of tourism.
Ironically, new La Thuile, as represented by the modern Planibel complex on the other side of the river, is already looking a bit frayed about the
edges.

LA THUILE
■ GOOD POINTS

Excellent nursery slopes, lack of
crowds, variety of intermediate skiing,
off-piste opportunities, extensive
tree-level skiing, choice of
restaurants, lively on-mountain bars

■ BAD POINTS

Lack of atmosphere in the central
complex, limited nightlife, shortage
of challenging pistes, disappointing
mountain restaurants, lack of
childcare facilities

On the mountain
top 2642m (8,668ft) bottom 1150m (3,773ft)

Both La Thuile and La Rosière have wide open slopes well suited to
beginners and intermediates. In La Thuile these are supplemented by
much tougher runs through the steeply wooded area just above the
resort. In La Rosière, due to the greater height of the base, the slopes are
predominantly above the tree-line.

The highest point in the linked area is Belvedere. In the short term,
the replacement of the existing Belvedere chair by a quad-chair in 1997

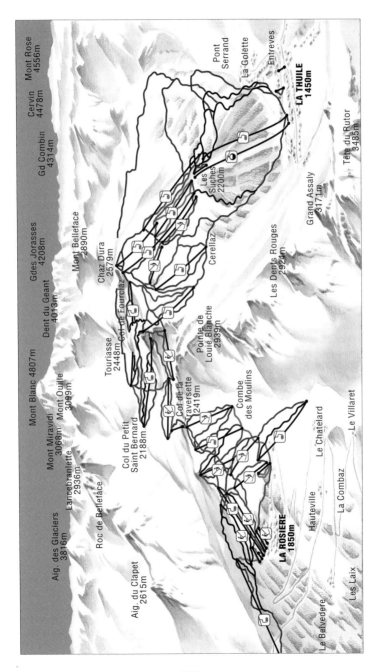

Mont Rose 4556m
Cervin 4478m
Gd Combin 4314m
Gdes Jorasses 4208m
Dent du Géant 4013m
Mont Blanc 4807m
Mont Miravidi 3068m
Mont Ouille 3099m
Lancebranlette 2936m
Aig. des Glaciers 3816m
Roc de Belleface
Aig. du Clapet 2615m
Col du Petit Saint Bernard 2188m
Touriasse 2448m
Col de Fourclaz
Chaz Dura 2579m
Mont Belleface 2890m
Col de la Traversette 2419m
Pointe de Louïe Blanche 2939m
Combe des Moulins
Les Dents Rouges 2924m
Cerellaz
Les Suches 2200m
Grand Assaly 3171m
Tête du Rutor 3485m
Pont Serrand
La Golette
Entrèves
LA THUILE 1450m

LA ROSIÈRE 1850m
Hauteville
La Combaz
Le Chatelard
Le Villaret
Le Belvedere
Les Laix

will speed up the existing connection. Between 1998 and 2002, the ski area will be extended to the top of Mont Valaisan (2891m), opening up the Bella Valetta Valley in the process. There are also plans to install lifts on Mont Miravidi (3068m) in the early years of the new century, further increasing the ski area by 50 per cent.

LA ROSIERE
■ GOOD POINTS
Ski-in ski-out convenience, pleasant village atmosphere, good childcare
■ BAD POINTS
Lack of advanced skiing, limited for non-skiers, sparse snow on south-facing slopes, poor nightlife

La Thuile's main slopes face east, with a steeper north-facing area going down to the Col du Petit-St-Bernard. By taking the long loopy alternative routes it is possible for novices to cover the whole area. Most of the skiing in La Rosière faces south; these slopes are generally easier, with gentle blue (easy) pistes above the resort giving way to red (intermediate) ones on the higher part of the Col de la Traversette. As a result of being on different sides of an Alpine divide, each resort has its own micro-climate; this often means that one is shrouded in cloud while the other is bathed in sunshine. By checking at the respective base-stations before deciding where to go, it may be possible to turn an unpromising day into a brilliant one.

Beginners

Although there is a small nursery slope at resort level, the steepness of the lower mountain at La Thuile means that beginners soon take Les Suches gondola to the green (beginner) pistes served by La Combe lift. In La Rosière, there are several short nursery slopes near the resort, with more at the altiport nearby. Adventurous learners will soon move up the mountain to Les Echuerts, La Poletta and Roches Noires lifts, which serve a network of blue runs.

Intermediates

The 135km of mainly red pistes on offer provide plenty of challenges for the average motorway cruiser. La Thuile offers a long run around the edges of the ski area from Chaz Dura and Belvedere, augmented by more aggressive terrain towards the Col du Petit-St-Bernard road, which usually holds the best snow. The main link with La Rosière has a tricky start, but the runs below the Col de la Traversette are mainly short reds with plenty of blue alternatives on the way down to lunch.

Advanced

The most testing black (difficult) runs are in the Touriasse sector from Belvedere or Chaz Dura to the Petit-St-Bernard Pass, between the San Bernardo and Fourclaz chair-lifts. In bad light, the Europa World Cup track through the woods from Les Suches to Golette is more user-friendly. The Ecureuil and Eterlou runs down to Les Ecudets below La Rosière do not deserve their black gradings, although their severity is frequently increased by indifferent snow conditions.

Off-piste

First-timers will be surprised by the variety and quality of La Thuile's off-piste possibilities. Wannabe powderhounds will find the regular pitch they need to gain confidence on the ungroomed sections under the chairs, while experts will enjoy the challenge of wooded, north-facing slopes between the pistes on the Touriasse. Better still is the heli-skiing, which begins on the Italian side as it is forbidden in France. The 20-km run from the Ruitor Glacier to La Rosière is suitable for intermediates and upwards, but the descent to La Thuile is a real adventure, complete with a short rope section across an ice gully and a long walk-out at the bottom. There are further extensive heli-skiing options in neighbouring **Valgrisenche**.

Ski schools and guiding

There is a simple choice between the Italian Ski School in La Thuile and the French Ski School (ESF) in La Rosière. Accounts are divided as to the standard of spoken English, especially on the Italian side. We have satisfactory reports of the Italian Ski School ('the instructor's English was excellent and the standard of tuition high').

Snowboarding

The centre of operations in La Thuile is La Combe, an encouragingly wide, flat area above Les Suches. The transition to blue runs is best made in the catchment area of the Chalet Express, a chair-lift that is particularly easy to get on and off. Board cred requires regular visits to the noisy La Clotze Bar at the bottom of it. Group snowboard lessons are also available in La Rosière, where the focus is on the green runs near the altiport area.

> ■ **WHAT'S NEW**
>
> Additional snowmaking at La Thuile

Cross-country

La Thuile caters for all levels of expertise, with six graded tracks between 1km and 10km looping up the valley floor between Thovex and Promise. La Rosière has 12km of well-designed scenic tracks near the altiport.

Mountain restaurants

La Thuile is the exception to the rule that skiers invariably eat well on Italian mountain tops. This is not so much a question of quality as of availability. Les Suches self-service is undeniably soulless ('a motorway-style cafeteria, but the food was not bad'), while Le Foyer, higher up on the same hill, offers substantial but unsophisticated fare; both restaurants are criticised by reporters for their 'hole-in-the-ground style loos; it is not easy to balance in ski boots'. There are two fashionable Blues bars — the Roxi at the bottom of the Forclaz chair and nautical Off Shore by the Belvedere chair. Both serve sandwiches and drinks to an aggressive backing track. The atmospheric restaurant at the bottom of the San Bernardo chair — the ski school's meeting-point for the weekly torchlight procession — serves a simple selection of Italian dishes at lunchtime. The only on-mountain option in La Rosière is Plan Repos, an adequate but crowded self-service with a large and sunny terrace.

Off the mountain

The heart of La Thuile is the Planibel, an integrated tourist unit with a hotel, apartments, a sports complex and a selection of shops and bars. There are two swimming-pools and facilities for bowling, squash and fitness training. The shops major on ski clothing and equipment, with no thought for the chic boutique factor that dominates in neighbouring **Courmayeur**. The efficient, but discouragingly clinical complex contrasts sharply with the rest of the resort, which sprawls haphazardly through the surrounding woods.

Over the 30 years of its existence, La Rosière has developed along the bends of the mountain road from Seez to the Petit-St-Bernard Pass. The result is an attractive neo-Savoyard tiered village with low-rise accommodation built out of wood and local, rough-hewn stone. In winter, the road runs out at the Relais du Petit-St-Bernard, a hotel and restaurant that supports a dynasty of the lovable rescue dogs. No matter what the weather, the brandy-bearers are ready and willing to pose for snaps in exchange for scraps.

■ OTHER SPORTS

La Thuile: Swimming, snow-shoeing, squash, indoor football
La Rosière: Parapente, tobogganing, winter walks, snow-shoeing, ski jumping

Accommodation

The four-star Planibel Hotel in La Thuile is the most convenient and luxurious place to stay, but reports suggest that the warmth of the reception can leave much to be desired. This is certainly not true of the Chalet Alpina, a 500-m walk away across a stream. Eddy Nico (South African-born but of Italian descent) and his British wife, Debbie, extend a warm welcome and provide a very extensive service on and off the slopes to clients who return year after year. In the two-star category, the Edelweiss above the village offers simple accommodation adjacent to the nursery slope, while the Entreves has a cheerful family atmosphere. The Château Blanc is recommended for bed-and-breakfast accommodation ('comfortable rooms and the owners are extremely welcoming'). The Planibel Apartments have the advantages of the hotel with none of the disadvantages. Early booking is recommended for the bargain, spacious two-, four-, and six-person units.

In La Rosière, the emphasis is on self-catering apartments, which can be reserved through one of four local agencies. Hotel accommodation is limited, but the Relais du Petit-St-Bernard, the Roc Noir, the Vanoise and the Plein Soleil offer simple facilities in central locations. The family-run Solaret in the hamlet of **Les Eucherts** (linked to La Rosière by a free bus service while the lifts are open) is also recommended.

Skiing facts: **La Thuile**

TOURIST OFFICE
I-11016 La Thuile, Aosta
Tel 39 165 884179
Fax 39 165 885196

THE RESORT
By road Calais 938km
By rail Pré-Saint-Didier 10km
By air Geneva 2½ hrs, Turin 3 hrs
Visitor beds 3,123
Transport free bus service in the village

THE SKIING
Linked or nearby resorts Pila (n), La Rosière (l), Courmayeur (n)
Longest run San Bernardo, 11km (red)
Number of lifts 15 in La Thuile, 33 in linked area (with La Rosière)
Total of trails/pistes 85km (48% easy, 31% intermediate, 21% difficult). 135km in linked area
Nursery slopes 3 lifts
Summer skiing none
Snowmaking 15km covered

LIFT PASSES
Area pass Aosta Valley (covers La Thuile, La Rosière, Pila and Courmayeur) L245,000 for 6 days.
La Thuile/La Rosière
L190,000-215,000 for 6 days
Day pass L46,000
Beginners 1 free baby lift
Pensioners no reductions
Credit cards accepted yes

SKI SCHOOLS
Adults La Thuile, 10am-12.30pm, L155,000 for 6 days
Private lessons La Thuile, L49,000 per hr
Snowboarding through ski school, prices and times as regular ski lessons
Cross-country through ski school. Loipe 16km
Other courses slalom, off-piste, racing, heli-skiing on the Ruitor Glacier
Guiding companies through ski school

CHILDREN
Lift pass 50% reduction for 5-10 yrs, free for 4 yrs and under (cable car only)
Ski kindergarten none
Ski school La Thuile, 5 yrs and over, 10am-12.30pm, L155,000 for 6 days
Non-ski kindergarten none

FOOD AND DRINK PRICES
Coffee L1,400, glass of wine L1,500, small beer L3,500, dish of the day L18,000

Eating in and out

Valdostana cuisine, with its emphasis on game, polenta and mushrooms, is well represented in La Thuile. The recently opened Le Rascard specialises in guinea-fowl stuffed with green peppers and spinach, while the long-running La Bricole, a converted barn, is known for its chamois, polenta and extensive wine list. Fish lovers can enjoy lake perch at La Fordze. The Lo Creton Pizzeria and the Fast Food Spaghetti House are sound budget choices. For ice-cream lovers the Cremeria in the Planibel complex is 'unmissable'. In the old village, La Grotta specialises in pizza.

Much of La Rosière's off-slope life focuses around two restaurants: that at the Relais du Petit-St-Bernard, which serves local specialities,

Skiing facts: **La Rosière**

TOURIST OFFICE
F-73700 La Rosière Montvalezan, Savoie
Tel 33 4 79 06 80 51
Fax 33 4 79 06 83 20

THE RESORT
By road Calais 940km
By rail Bourg-St-Maurice 23km
By air Chambéry 1½ hrs, Lyon 3 hrs,
Geneva 3 hrs
Visitor beds 7,119
Transport free ski bus runs every
15-30 mins, 8am-6pm

THE SKIING
Linked or nearby resorts Les Arcs (n), La
Thuile (I), Sainte-Foy (I)
Longest run Choucas, 4.1km (blue)
Number of lifts 18 in La Rosière, 33 in area
Total of trails/pistes 65km in La Rosière
(15% beginner, 36% easy, 34% intermedi-
ate, 15% difficult), 135km in area
Nursery slopes 2 free lifts
Summer skiing none
Snowmaking 2 hectares covered

LIFT PASSES
Area pass Domaine International
(covers La Rosière and La Thuile)
786FF for 6 days including 1 free day in Les
Arcs. La Rosière only 661FF for 6 days
Day pass La Rosière 125FF, Domaine
International 160FF
Beginners 2 free lifts
Pensioners 60 yrs and over: La Rosière

417FF, Domaine International 519FF, both
for 6 days
Credit cards accepted yes

SKI SCHOOLS
Adults ESF, 9.15-11.45am and
1.30-5pm, 620FF for 6 days
Private lessons ESF, 145FF per hr,
Nouvelles Traces, 150FF per hr
Snowboarding ESF, private lessons 142FF
per hr (group lessons also available)
Cross-country ESF, 145FF per hr.
Loipe 12km
Other courses monoski, telemark,
off-piste, heli-skiing on Ruitor Glacier
Guiding companies ESF and Nouvelles
Traces

CHILDREN
Lift pass 12 yrs and under, La Rosière
417FF for 6 days, Domaine International
519FF for 6 days
Ski kindergarten Le Village des Enfants,
12 mths-10 yrs, 9am-5.30pm,
170FF per day
(including 1-hr ski lesson)
Ski school ESF, 4 yrs and over,
times as adults, 590FF for 6 days
Non-ski kindergarten Le Village des
Enfants, 12 mths-10 yrs, 9am-5.30pm,
970FF for 6 days including lunch

FOOD AND DRINK PRICES
Coffee 7FF, glass of wine 10-12FF,
small beer 12FF, dish of the day 60-70FF

pizza and crêpes, and Toni's, the most popular bar in town. Favoured alternatives include La Pitchounette, L'Ancolie and Le Christophi. However, gourmets should make the 7-km trek to La Chaumière, a converted Savoyard farmhouse in the village of Montvalezan.

Après-ski

Given their attraction for families, it is hardly surprising that neither La Thuile nor La Rosière are known for riotous nightlife. Planibel's Rendezvous bar is 'decidedly laddish, especially late at night when the karaoke gets going'. La Bricole video disco has a genuine pub atmosphere that appeals to British visitors; at weekends it also features live music and dancing. Dedicated night-owls go to La Thuile's only disco, the Fantasia, where the average age is around 20. The piano bar in the Hotel Planibel attracts a more sedate crowd.

La Rosière's entertainment starts briskly at Toni's or the Yeti when the lifts close, but peters out later on as families return to their apartments. The Neige et Chocolat tea room is also popular.

Childcare

La Thuile has no kindergarten facilities and the ski school only accepts children aged five years and over. Residents of the Planibel hotel and apartments can use the Mini Club (for children aged three to ten), but the opening hours (10am-12.30pm and 3pm-5.30pm) are hardly skier-friendly.

In La Rosière, Le Village des Enfants takes care of children aged 12 months to 10 years old from 9am-5.30pm. The programme includes skiing as appropriate, plus organised games and lunch.

Round-up

RESORTS COVERED Macugnaga, Madesimo

Macugnaga
top 2984m (9,790ft) bottom 1327m (4,353ft)

The resort of Macugnaga is made up of the two adjoining and attractive villages of **Staffa** and **Pecetto**. Staffa forms the centre while Pecetto is the quieter end of town. They lie on the opposite side of the Monte Rosa to **Gressoney**, close to the Swiss border and three hours' drive from Turin. Macugnaga's proximity to the border has resulted in a style of architecture far more in keeping with Switzerland than Italy.

Staffa and Pecetto have their own small ski areas, which are linked by ski bus. They offer, as one reporter summed it up, 'A marvellous introduction to skiing'. Reporters praise the 'short queues, if any at all. Often you could finish your run and ski right back on to an empty chair-lift'. Staffa has the better skiing for beginners ('only ten people on the nursery slopes at the very busiest'), a cable car rising to the summit, and a number of longer runs. Scuola Sci Macugnaga receives mixed reports: 'A very relaxed manner of instruction. English not always clear'. Off-piste enthusiasts can hire a local mountain guide to ski over the back of Monte Moro to **Saas-Fee** in Switzerland.

Hotel du Four in Staffa's main square is 'clean and friendly, with food plentiful and delicious'. Hotel Zumstein is close to the resort centre and the cable car. There are various bars and restaurants in town, as well as a few small shops, but on the whole there is not much après-ski. Two small supermarkets sell basic provisions. Skating, floodlit skiing and cross-country are the other activities on offer.

TOURIST OFFICE
Tel/Fax 39 324 65119

Madesimo
top 2884m (9,459ft) bottom 1530m (5,018ft)

This small, attractive resort, centred around an old church, is a two-and-a-half hour drive north of Bergamo. Right on the Swiss border, it is close enough for a shopping spree in St Moritz. The old town has narrow streets with a few shops, and some old converted farm houses, as well as less pleasing concrete buildings. Madesimo's appeal is that it is cheaper than other, better-known resorts, and excellent value for money.

The skiing is mostly intermediate and is concentrated on the slopes of the 2984-m Piz Groppera, with long runs leading down into the neighbouring **Valle de Lei**. There are 19 lifts serving 45km of mostly red (intermediate) pistes with some challenging black (difficult) trails, including the famous Canalone run. The nursery slopes are pleasant. The lower slopes have snow-cannon and the ski school has a reputation for small classes.

Hotels include the centrally situated Emet, which is said to have 'beautiful décor', and the family-run Andossi has a fitness room and a lively bar. Hotel Cascata e Cristallo has excellent facilities including a swimming-pool, piano bar and a mini-club for 4- to 12-year-olds; you can ski back to the hotel.

TOURIST OFFICE
Tel 39 342 53015
Fax 39 342 53782

Switzerland

Modern skiing began in Switzerland and, while it may well be an exaggeration to suggest that British winter holidaymakers introduced the sport, they certainly helped to promote it in the Parsenn, the Bernese Oberland and the Engadine. In November 1883, the editor of a Davos newspaper wrote: 'As you probably know, skis are a kind of elongated snow-shoe with which you can travel very quickly in deep snow, both up and down mountains. Why should these "skis" not replace the ungainly snow-shoes, which are commonplace around here?'.

Six years later a certain Miss Katherine Symonds took to skis in the Parsenn, and in 1894 Sir Arthur Conan Doyle wrote passionately of a ski-tour to Arosa. It is, therefore, a great sadness that few of their countrymen can afford to visit Switzerland any longer. The combination of a prohibitive rate of exchange against sterling, the imposition of across-the-board 6.5 per cent VAT and rising prices through domestic inflation have forced even affluent tourists to seek fresh pastures. It is hoped that this situation is merely a bare patch on the piste of time, and that British skiers will once again return in numbers to what are some of the most colourful resorts and beautiful mountains in the world.

Ecological pressure to preserve the natural mountain environment has largely prevented the overdevelopment of Swiss ski villages. The 1960–70s concept of the giant linked ski area was never fully realised here; even the Portes du Soleil only brushes marginally into Switzerland via the Illiez Valley. As a result, most resorts remain traditional villages, still largely unspoilt by the demands of mass tourism. The downside of this has been lack of investment in uphill transport and lift systems in comparison to its more free-spending neighbours.

Despite or because of this, the skiing remains delightfully unhomogenised, with natural rather than man-made runs against outstanding alpine backdrops. Mountain restaurants, for those who enjoy and can afford the relaxed ski lunch, are among the best in Europe, and the standard of hotels and apartments is consistently high. Almost all Swiss resorts can be reached by train from Geneva and Zurich airports.

> Most Swiss telephone area codes are changing during 1996. The numbers given here are the new ones

Switzerland has two types of rail pass, which can be purchased in advance from the Swiss Tourist Board before leaving home. These vouchers allow either airport transfers to and from your resort, or 'rover' facilities for the duration of your stay.

As expected in Switzerland, trains run to the strictest of timetables and you are strongly advised to send your luggage in advance wherever possible. The Swiss rarely travel with more than hand luggage; trolleys are consequently scarce, with little provision for suitcases on trains.

Crans Montana

ALTITUDE 1500m (4,920ft)

Crans Montana is a classic Swiss resort, which has evolved from its early days as a health spa into an interlinked skiing complex above the three agglomerations of **Crans**, **Montana** and **Aminona**; the official umbrella name for the resort is Crans Montana.

Two hours from Geneva Airport, by motorway for the most part, Crans Montana sits on what is claimed to be the sunniest plateau in the Alps, dotted with larches and lakes.

Crans Montana is a destination that cultivates an elite clientèle (mostly middle-aged), half of whom are Swiss. Its shopping, in chic boutiques, is advertised as the finest in the Alps. The skiing is irretrievably intermediate.

Although the first hotel was built in 1893, a ski lift did not appear until 1936. The new 30-person Funitel gondola has three times the capacity of the queue-prone cable car, which used to run up to the glacier on Plaine-Morte at 3000m from Violettes. Most visitors are content with making a few casual runs in the sunshine each day on the 160km of groomed piste served by 40 lifts. Of these, two are modern high-speed quads, but more than half are antiquated drag-lifts.

■ **GOOD POINTS**

Well-linked intermediate skiing, exceptional sunshine record, high standard of hotels, ample non-skiing activities, superb mountain views, glacier skiing, good nursery slopes, facilities for children

■ **BAD POINTS**

Primarily low-altitude skiing, urban landscape, high prices, heavy traffic, inconvenient to get around on foot

On the mountain
top 3000m (9,840ft) bottom 1500m (4,920ft)

Mountain access is via five points spread from west to east across the base of the mountains from Crans to Montana, to the satellite of Aminona. Queuing is not a serious problem here.

A single gondola from Montana, and the Chetseron and Cry d'Err gondolas at Crans, lead up through the woods to Cry d'Err, where a cable car and chair-lift continue to the 2600-m summit of that sector. Between Montana and Aminona, the glacier skiing at 3000m on Plaine-Morte is reached by a new Funitel gondola continuing upwards from the Violettes gondolas, which start from the outskirts of Montana at **Barzettes**. Reporters say the new lift is fast and efficient but prone to delays and closure due to high winds.

The resort's longest run is the 1500 vertical metre drop from the glacier to town-level at Barzettes.

Beginners

Starting at the top, beginners have three short but easy runs on the Plaine-Morte Glacier, where good snow is guaranteed. The nursery slopes down by the golf course in Crans are even easier but susceptible to sun. Cry d'Err has the most beginner runs; a handful are accessible by no fewer than eight lifts which provide skiing all the way down into Crans or Montana.

Intermediates

Despite the generally superior standard of piste-grooming everywhere, passages between rock walls, such as on the long red (intermediate) run from Plaine-Morte, add a genuine thrill. The largest conflux of intermediate pistes is in the Violettes sector, with winding trails through the woods. The Toula chair- and drag-lifts lead to steeper reds. Most exciting are the Nationale World Cup piste and Chetseron, which are well groomed but have the occasional banked drop-off designed to make the stomach flip at high speed. One reporter describes the Nationale as 'an excellent run with some testing sections — a proper red run'. Two short sections in the middle of red pistes are more difficult; one is the women's downhill racecourse on Chetseron, the other is an innocuous link between the Violettes mid-station and the long red coming down from the glacier.

Advanced

The only officially graded black (difficult) run in the entire resort is a bumpy fall-line pitch on the ridge under the Toula chair-lift ('no more than a red really'), often groomed impeccably on the lower section. The Plaine-Morte run is said to be the most avalanche-prone in Switzerland. Although perfectly safe when officially open, its gunbarrel passages and changes in direction require a high level of commitment from even the most adept skier.

Off-piste

Crans Montana has no death-defying couloirs, but there are three unmarked itineraries which require guides. From the Plaine-Morte Glacier it is possible to ski across open slopes and through three bands of rock down to the lake at **Zeuzier**. Walking through tunnels (torches required) and skiing a summer roadway leads to the ski lifts in the neighbouring resort of **Anzère**. Another route from the glacier guarantees fresh tracks in powder straight down into the Vallon d'Ertenze. The only way out at the bottom is by helicopter.

Each weekend some 200 skiers attack the Faverges itinerary from Plaine-Morte down to Aminona, a route which is deserted on weekdays. It offers steep, scenic skiing with lots of alternative routes.

Ski schools and guiding

There are two branches of the Swiss Ski School (ESS), in Crans and in Montana, each of them separately operated. Teaching in Montana is said to be 'imaginative, with a lot of emphasis on technique. Most instructors speak very good English'. There is a separate mountain guiding bureau in the Hotel Intergolf, which offers heli-skiing and ski-tours, such as the long run down to **Lenk**.

Snowboarding

Crans Montana is an active snowboarding centre with parks in Aminona and **Merignou**, and a half-pipe at Cry d'Err. Aminona is equipped for snowboarding jumps. Surf Evasion, affiliated with the Montana Ski School, offers group snowboard lessons during holiday periods, private lessons at other times and heli-snowboarding. The Swiss Snowboard School in Crans, part of the ESS, is another learning centre. The Pacific Surf Shop and the Avalanche Pro Shop sell surf fashion and accessories. The local snowboard club, Vague Blanche, has frequent events.

Cross-country

Crans Montana has 50km of tracks including a 12-km loipe at an altitude of 3000m on the Plaine-Morte Glacier. A 15-km touring trail starts at Plans Mayens and winds across the pistes and through the woods all the way to Aminona.

Mountain restaurants

The Crans Montana clientèle apparently prefers to eat in town. The best cuisine on the slopes is down at the Chamois d'Or, set in the woods of the Hauts de Crans Hotel. Lift station eateries at Cry d'Err, Petit Bonvin ('we were revolted to find horse meat on the menu') and Plaine-Morte are adequate but not inspiring. The Cabane des Violettes is an authentic alpine club touring hut with simple meals. The Café de la Cure alongside the blue run down to Aminona has character, but the two best inns are Merbe for its tortellini, and Plumachit for its wild strawberry tart; both are old chalets with sunny terraces. The bar/restaurant at the Aminona lift station 'has the charm of a French café; the *Käseschnitte* — with a flagon of *fendant* — is wonderful'.

Off the mountain

The resort has 40,000 beds between its apartments and 55 hotels, which spread out across the three communities with few pretensions to charm. The tower-block Résidence Vermala, sticking out like a sore thumb on a hill above Montana, is arguably the greatest eyesore in the Alps. Sprawling as it is, the resort has ample underground parking in town and possibly the best parking facilities at lift bases anywhere in the Alps — all free. Aminona is a ten-minute bus ride from Montana. The main lift complexes are a five-minute walk uphill from their respective town centres.

Accommodation

Hotels in Montana are cheaper than in snooty Crans, where in the early years regulations denied entry to any guest suspected of the respiratory illnesses that were the resort's *raison d'être* in the first place. Hotel service is excellent, thanks to apprentice staff from the local hotel school. The five-star Crans-Ambassador and four-star Les Hauts-de-Crans hotels are in Montana. The Grand Hotel du Golf is the ultimate in Crans, but the three-star Mont Blanc, on a hill above the resort, has the biggest terrace and best views. Hotel de la Forêt is recommended and caters for vegetarians. The Hostellerie du Pas de L'Ours in Crans is 'sublimely luxurious' and the five-star Royal has been completely refurbished. Reporters have mixed views of their reception at the family-run Hotel National in Crans. Self-catered apartments are readily available.

Eating in and out

The most celebrated non-hotel gourmet dining is at the Cervin, the chic Rôtisserie de la Reine, and the Jeanne d'Arc. The Mont Blanc in the woods above Crans has a marmot zoo for children and serves delicious sea bass. The Crans Ambassador, Pas de l'Ours and St George have varied haute cuisine menus. Dun Huang is Cantonese Chinese, the Diligence serves Lebanese food and wine, and the Christina has Portuguese specialities. Steaks from America and Argentina are grilled at Le Ranch and are accompanied by Californian wines.

Après-ski

Floor shows and dancing girls liven up late-night Montana at the Mazot and Noctambule cabarets. Immediately after skiing the younger crowd gathers at Amadeus; Le Pub and Studio 7 in Crans are popular. Teenagers flock to the Number One Club, then on to the Number Two Bar for late drinking. The Absolut disco attracts the under 35s. The Pascha Club, also in Crans, is more for 'show-offs and snobs'. The Memphis in Crans is a comfortable piano bar for the older set.

Childcare

Infants from two months old can attend the Fleurs des Champs kindergarten, next to Hotel Eldorado in Montana. Bibiland, underneath the tourist office in Crans, takes children from two years old. Les Libellules, in Montana, is for two-year-olds and above. The Montana Ski School has its own Jardin des Neiges up on the Grand Signal mid-station. The Crans Ski School also accepts children at its kindergarten, which is by the golf course.

Davos/Klosters

ALTITUDE Davos 1560m (5,117ft), Klosters 1130m (3,706ft)

The transformation of Davos from a remote farming community into an international resort began when Dr Alexander Spengler sought political asylum in Switzerland from his native Germany. In 1860 he welcomed the first foreign patients to his tuberculosis clinic and by 1865 they were coming in such numbers that other rival clinics opened. Thirty years later, another foreigner, the Dutch entrepreneur, Jan Holsboer, founded the Rhätischebahn railway to provide easier access to the high Alpine valley. He also secured financial backing for further spas and boarding houses, making Davos the leading health resort in Switzerland, with 700,000 annual overnight bookings by the turn of the century.

By this time, tobogganing and skating were well established as extra-curricular activities but skiing only became part of the equation after the local saddler, Tobias Branger, visited the World Fair in Paris in 1878. There he saw his first 'Norwegian snow-shoes', 240-cm long elm planks which he subsequently ordered for his shop. When they arrived without bindings, he and his brother, Johannes, devised leather straps to attach them to their boots, then worked out techniques for using them under cover of darkness to avoid the ridicule of their fellow citizens. In 1893 they attempted the first ski-tour via the Maienfeld Furka Pass to **Arosa**, a journey they repeated the next year with Dr Arthur Conan Doyle, the creator of Sherlock Holmes. As Davos already had an English Quarter, with some 400 residents, the novelist's adventure set a fashion for the new sport that escalated after the vivid description of his experiences in *Strand* magazine.

In the early part of the twentieth century, both sanatoriums and ski-ing prospered mightily as Davos grew from large village to small town. The slopes of the Parsenn, which Davos shares with Klosters, its much more attractive neighbour, developed gradually with the introduction of the annual Parsenn Derby race in 1924, the opening of the funicular railway in 1931 and the installation of one of the earliest T-bars in Switzerland in 1934. With the decline of tuberculosis after the Second World War, many of the old clinics were converted into hotels to serve

DAVOS
■ GOOD POINTS

Some of the longest runs in Europe, huge linked intermediate area, good restaurants at all levels, great potential for off-piste tours, tree-level skiing, choice of cultural and other non-skiing activities, good-value lift pass

■ BAD POINTS

Congested town on main road, little alpine atmosphere, inconvenient mountain access, limited pistes for beginners and advanced skiers, uninspiring nightlife the tourists who now come in winter and summer. The opening of the Davos Congress Centre, since 1971 the venue for the annual meeting of the prestigious World Economic Forum, has allowed Davos to develop a lucrative parallel role as a conference town.

Meanwhile Klosters, which welcomed its first winter sports enthusiasts in 1904, has prospered from its connection with the British royal family, and especially Prince Charles. His liking for the sport and the resort has not been affected by the avalanche that killed his equerry, Major Hugh Lindsay, and threatened his own life in 1988.

KLOSTERS
■ GOOD POINTS

Village atmosphere, north-facing expert slopes, sunny intermediate motorways in large linked area, tree-level skiing, off-piste for all standards, high-quality shops and restaurants, good-value lift pass

■ BAD POINTS

Inconvenient for families, limited for beginners, dull nightlife, limited ski-in ski-out accommodation

On the mountain
top 2844m (9,328ft) bottom 813m (2,667ft)

The core of the Davos/Klosters ski area is the Parsenn, accessed most directly by funicular from Davos Dorf, but also connected to Davos Platz

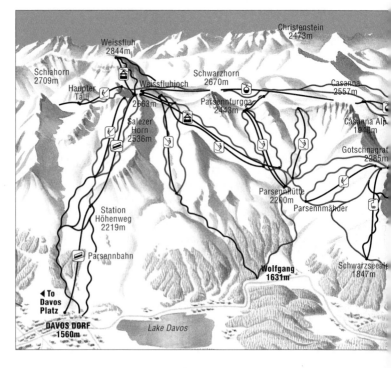

via the Schatzalp/Strela lift system, and to Klosters by the two-stage Gotschna cable car. It is dominated by the Weissfluh, the highest point on the piste-map, and it also includes the lowest — the marked run down to Küblis. The piste linking the two is a 12-km red (intermediate) descent. This is the terrain that made Davos famous, the wide sweeping runs that flatter more often than they deceive.

This skiing heartland is supplemented by four further lift systems, three of them on the other side of the Davos Valley and the fourth beyond Klosters. In the Davos catchment area, the three peaks are Pischa, Jakobshorn and Rinerhorn. They are accessed respectively by bus from Dorf, directly from Platz and by bus or train from Glaris (the next stop on the line down to Chur). In Klosters, the alternative is the Madrisa where the slopes stretch up to the Swiss/Austrian border.

When people talk queues in Davos/Klosters — and they frequently do — they are talking Parsenn. Whether you start from Dorf or Platz, you are faced with a slow journey in a funicular before you reach more modern forms of transport; even these may not be as modern as you would like, given that the T-bar, largely phased out in many parts of the Alps, still rules on the Parsenn. In 1996, the Schatzalp/Strela gondola — the back-door route to the main ski area — was replaced by a chair to the Strelapass drag-lift, but improvements of this kind are not happening as

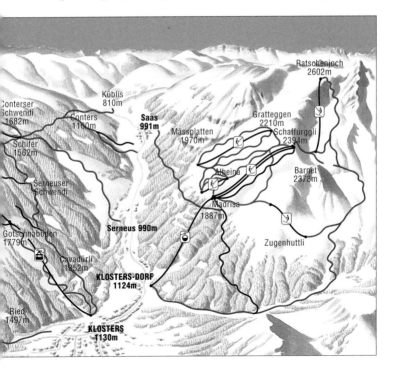

fast as effective crowd-management requires.

In Klosters, the doubling in size of the bottom section of the Gotschna cable car reduced what was once a notorious alpine black spot to a minor irritant on crowded weekends. By contrast, the quartet of outlying areas, with their lower profiles and more progressive lift systems, are enticingly empty. A word of praise is due for the Davos/Klosters 'no-hands' lift pass, an electronic card that allows passage through the barriers when tucked away in a pocket. There is a SF10 deposit, returnable at the end of your stay.

Beginners

Like many large non-purpose-built resorts, Davos is not the place to learn to ski from scratch. If you must, the wide Bolgen nursery slope at the bottom of the Jakobshorn, a short walk from Platz, is the best starting point. In Dorf, the equivalent is Bunda, a longer but steeper pitch. In Klosters, the sunny user-friendly nursery slopes are up the mountain on the Madrisa, which means buying a full lift pass and downloading by gondola at the end of the day. Once the basics are mastered, there is no shortage of blue (easy) runs to progress to, particularly on Pischa and Madrisa.

Intermediates

Those who profit most from the Davos/Klosters area are progressive intermediates with the energy to ski all the hours the lift company allows. Nearly all the marked runs are red or blue, most are invitingly wide and several are over 10km long. The ones from the top of the Weissfluh to the valley villages of **Küblis**, **Saas** and **Serneus** start high above the tree line, then track down through the woods to the railway line, providing a sense of adventure that is definitely not available in more tightly knit places. Another unmissable cruiser starts at the top of the Madrisa lift system and descends to Klosters Dorf via the Schlappin Valley. All five ski areas offer lots of easy terrain, so there is no excuse for not ranging far and wide. The result, in terms of variety at least, is a lift pass of remarkable value.

Advanced

As the mountains in the area become steeper near the bottom, the black (difficult) runs are mostly confined to the lower sections, which means that they can be icy in all but the most favourable snow conditions. The up side is that they are generally among trees and therefore the visibility is always good. The best conditions are usually on the north-facing Klosters side; the Gotschnawang, which is no longer marked as a piste and is in any case rarely open, and the Drostobel, provide serious challenges. Turn right from the Gotschnagrat and you come instead to a prime mogul-basher under the Schwarzeealp chair. There are further gruelling bump runs on the Standard Ersatz and the Unterer Standard immediately above Davos Dorf. The most highly recommended black run starts on the Meierhofer Tälli at the top of the Parsenn and goes on down to **Wolfgang**, a hamlet that makes a peaceful lunch stop.

Off-piste

Those who are prepared to put on skins and climb a bit can explore the huge potential for deep snow adventure in one of Switzerland's most extensive areas. The longest, but by no means the most exciting, of the runs are the 18-km descents to Fideris and Jenaz, each with short climbing sections along the way. The Madrisa provides excellent possibilities for learning powder technique and is also the starting point for the transborder loop to the hamlet of **Gargellen** at the head of the Montafon Valley. Although Prince Charles does the uphill section of this tour on a snowmobile, the majority must supplement the Gargellen lifts (covered by the area pass) with an hour-long climb. The best part of the tour is the section down to the attractive village of **St Antönien**.

Skiing to Arosa in the tracks of Conan Doyle is a more serious business, with a three- to four-hour climb to the Maienfeld Furka Pass above **Frauenkirch**, followed by a benevolent descent through woods to the bottom of the valley and, a bitter sting in the tail, a 40-minute plod up through the town to the railway station for the three-hour return to Davos. Those not seeking the true Conan Doyle experience can ski to Arosa from the Strelapass. Although Conan Doyle's second foray on skins on the Jakobshorn is now covered by the Brämabühl lift, there is an attractive alternative down the adjacent Dischmatal to Teufi. The Sertigtal, between the Jakobshorn and the Rinerhorn, also provides powderhounds with a high pay-off, as does the Mönchalptal from Pischa to **Laret**.

Ski schools and guiding

The Swiss Ski School (SSS) in both resorts has classes for adults and teenagers, either in groups or with private guides. There are half-day safety classes for off-piste debutantes (for a maximum of six) on the use of ABS-rucksacks and avalanche transceivers. Daily or weekly guided ski-tours can be arranged from January until Easter. Bruno Sprecher also runs the Saas Ski and Snowboard School in Klosters, which receives complimentary reports, and from February each year an exclusive off-piste guiding service.

Snowboarding

Throwing tradition out of the window Davos has, with admirable commercial acumen, embraced snowboarding with enthusiasm. There is even a piste-map symbol to suggest where it may best be done, but as it appears on all the mountains its value is debatable. In fact, it is the Jakobshorn that has acquired the status of area snowboard capital, partly because it hosted the World Snowboarding Championships in 1995 and partly because it has a dedicated snowboard hotel, the Bolgenschanze, conveniently close to the lift station. There are three snowboard schools: Top Secret in Platz, Snowboardschool Davos (part of the SSS) and the PaarSenn, both in Dorf.

Cross-country

Davos offers 75km of prepared langlauf trails on the valley floor and in the Sertigtal and Dischmatal areas. Evening expeditions can be made on the 2.5-km floodlit section, and dogs are allowed on some of the trails. The SSS has a cross-country division, which teaches both the classic and the skating methods in group classes or privately. The highlight of the cross-country year is the 20-km Volks Langlauf, held in early March. Klosters has some 50km of prepared trails and langlauf teaching in both disciplines.

Mountain restaurants

Go low is the main recommendation in an area where skiing to lunch should be an integral part of a long adventure run. Intelligent use of the piste-map makes it possible to locate the many small establishments in the woods on the way down to the outlying villages. The restaurant at the Teufi on the off-piste descent from the Jakobshorn is recommended, as is the Hotel Kulm (confusingly known as Jakob's) in Wolfgang. Another winner is the pizzeria at the end of the Schlappin run in Klosters Dorf but enterprise should yield gastronomic dividends. The Conterser Schwendi is recommended for its *Rösti* and other local specialities, as is the Serneuser Schwendi, 'popular, but a bit noisy and smoky'. The Strelapass Hut is also praised as is the Bahnhof Buffet in Küblis.

Off the mountain

Davos is a straggling, no-nonsense town built along a major road, with all the traffic problems that suggests. In recent years, these problems have been partially solved by a one-way system that at least keeps things moving. There is also a highly efficient bus service, which is included on the lift pass. It runs primarily between the two main centres, **Davos Dorf**, quiet and stately with handsome old hotels, and **Davos Platz**, the bustling commercial heart. Dorf has the most direct access to the Parsenn, but Platz has excellent facilities and the lion's share of the nightlife; therefore, the choice of where to stay depends on where your priorities lie. Davos attracts a wealthy, cosmopolitan crowd whose tastes are catered for by designer boutiques with names like Bogner and Blaser and exclusive shops specialising in furnishings, art and jewellery. Enthusiasts will enjoy the newly opened Wintersport Museum, which traces the development of equipment and clothing through the years.

Klosters is also divided into **Platz**, an extensive traditional village clustered around the railway station and the Gotschna cable car, and **Dorf**, a sleepy outpost at the bottom of the Madrisa lift system. Again, the two are connected by a regular bus service, but only those of a reclusive disposition should consider staying in Dorf. Platz is conveniently compact, with a range of hotels in each category and the kind of shops required by lovers of designer clothes, fine wines and Havana cigars.

Accommodation

Davos has two five-star hotels, the Steigenberger Belvédère, up on the hillside above Platz, and the Flüela, opposite the railway station in Dorf. Both offer old-fashioned comfort in the stolid Swiss manner, a style copied by many of their competitors in the four- and three-star brackets. In Platz, the Waldhotel Bellevue is rich in tradition, though rather far removed from the mainstream. The same can be said of the Berghotel Schatzalp, a converted sanatorium offering turn-of-the-century grandeur.

In Klosters, the smart choice is the Hotel Vereina, which has impressive public rooms and comprehensive facilities, including a swimming-pool and crèche. The Steinbock is less conveniently situated, but it offers a warm welcome and good food. Those on a British insider track cluster in the Wynegg, where the incorrigible Ruth Guler rules with a broad smile and an iron handshake. The overspill can find a quieter refuge in the Bundnerhof next door.

Eating in and out

As in all places with a huge choice of restaurants in every category, the main criterion must be price. In Davos, as elsewhere in contemporary Switzerland, those who stray outside half-board deals must be prepared to pay highly for the privilege unless they are prepared to eat in chains like Burger King or Charly's Bakery.

> **■ OTHER SPORTS**
>
> Davos curling, paragliding, hang-gliding, indoor tennis and squash, badminton, swimming, sleigh rides, skating, climbing wall, tobogganing Klosters paragliding, tobogganing, sleigh rides, curling, skating, squash, badminton, indoor tennis

Money should be well spent in the Davoserhof, Hubli's Landhaus, the Magic Mountain Restaurant in the Bellevue and the Stübli in the Flüela. The Montana Sporthotel, opposite the Flüela, served 'the best pizza I have ever eaten at a very reasonable price', according to one reporter. Try the Zauberberg restaurant in the Hotel Europe for Chinese, the Steinhof for Thai and the Cascada in the Hotel Seehof for Mexican cuisine. Localised dining at correspondingly lower prices can be found in the outlying villages of Frauenkirch, Wolfgang and Laret.

In Klosters, the Chesa Grischuna aspires to the kind of cuisine that has to be booked three days in advance, but tables at rival establishments require at least one day's notice. This is certainly true of the Wynegg, which profits from its royal connections to sell meals that are more rustic than gastronomic. The Walserhof is expensive but good and the Vereina's pizzeria is popular.

Après-ski

In the late afternoons, the high-lifers at Davos congregate in the Café Schneider in Platz and the Café Weber in Dorf, both specialists in

Skiing facts: **Davos**

TOURIST OFFICE
Promenade 67, CH-7270 Davos Platz
Tel 41 81 415 2121
Fax 41 81 415 2100

THE RESORT
By road Calais 1000km
By rail Davos Dorf and Davos Platz
stations in resort
By air Zurich 2½ hrs
Visitor beds 23,406
Transport free ski bus with lift pass, free
ski train with Rega Pass

THE SKIING
Linked or nearby resorts Arosa (n),
Klosters (l),Wolfgang (l), St Moritz (n),
Gargellen (n), Glaris (l), Kublis (l), Saas (l)
Longest run Weissfluhgipfel-Küblis,
12km (black/red)
Number of lifts 55 in area
Total of trails/pistes 315km in area
(30% easy, 40% intermediate,
30% difficult)
Nursery slopes 1 lift on Bunda
Summer skiing none
Snowmaking limited

LIFT PASSES
Area pass Rega Pass (covers all Davos
and Klosters lifts, buses and railway),
SF259 for 6 days
Day pass Jakobshorn SF46, Parsenn SF52,
Pischa SF38, Rinerhorn SF40, Schatzalp
SF25
Beginners no free lifts

Pensioners 20% reduction for women 62
yrs and over and men 65 yrs and over
Credit cards accepted yes

SKI SCHOOLS
Adults SSS, 10am-midday and 2-4pm,
SF220 for 5 days
Private lessons SF145 per half-day,
SF250 per day
Snowboarding Top Secret Snowboarding
School, PaarSenn, SSS, all SF160-215 for
5 half-days, private lessons SF130 per
half-day
Cross-country SSS, SF220 for 5 days,
times as regular ski school. Loipe 75km
Other courses off-piste, ski-touring,
telemark
Guiding companies Stefan Welz, SSS

CHILDCARE
Lift pass 6-16 yrs, Rega Pass SF155,
Gotschna/Strela/Parsenn SF134,
both for 6 days, free for 5 yrs
and under
Ski school SSS, 3-16 yrs, 8.30-11.30am
and 2-4.30pm, SF200 for 5 days including
lunch
Ski kindergarten Pinocchio Kindergarten
(3-5 yrs), and through SSS, details on
request
Non-ski kindergarten Pinocchio
Kindergarten , 3-5 yrs, details on request

FOOD AND DRINK PRICES
Coffee SF4, glass of wine SF6-8, small beer
SF4-5, dish of the day SF15-25

Skiing facts: **Klosters**

TOURIST OFFICE
CH-7250 Klosters, Graubunden
Tel 41 81 410 2020
Fax 41 81 410 2010

THE RESORT
By road Calais 1000km
By rail Klosters Dorf and Klosters Platz
stations in resort
By air Zurich $2\frac{1}{2}$ hrs
Visitor beds 8,800
Transport free ski bus with lift pass, free
ski train with Rega Pass

THE SKIING
Linked or nearby resorts Davos (l) Arosa
(n), Gargellen (n), Küblis (l), Saas (l),
Glaris (l), Wolfgang (l)
Longest run Weissfluhgipfel-Küblis,
12km (black/red)
Number of lifts 31 in Klosters,
Gotschna/Parsenn and Madrisa, 55 in area
Total of trails/pistes 315km in area (30%
easy, 40% intermediate, 30% difficult)
Nursery slopes 5 lifts
Summer skiing none
Snowmaking 4.3km (last part of
Schwendi–Klosters run) covered, plus 1
mobile snow-cannon in Madrisa area

LIFT PASSES
Area pass Rega Pass (covers all Davos
and Klosters lifts, buses and railway),
SF259 for 6 days
Day pass Parsenn SF52, Madrisa SF42
Beginners no free lifts
Pensioners 20% reduction for women 62
yrs and over and men 65 yrs and over
Credit cards accepted yes

SKI SCHOOLS
Adults SSS, 9.45am-midday and
1.45-4pm, SF200 for 5 days. Saas Ski
and Snowboard School, 10am-midday
and 1.30-3.30pm, SF295 for
6 days
Private lessons both ski schools, SF250
per day, SF60 per hr
Cross-country SSS, SF141 for 6
half-days, private lessons SF55 per hr.
Loipe 50km
Snowboarding SSS, SF175 for 3 days,
Saas Ski and Snowboard School, SF50 per
day, private lessons as ski prices
Other courses junior race camps, off-piste,
ski-touring, telemark
Guiding companies Bruno Sprecher, or
through ski schools

CHILDREN
Lift pass 6-16 yrs,
Gotschna/Parsenn/Madrisa SF134,
Madrisa SF113, Rega Pass SF155,
all for 6 days, free for 5 yrs and under
Ski kindergarten as ski school
Ski school SSS, 4-12 yrs, SF190 for
5 days, times as adults. Saas Ski
and Snowboard School, 4 yrs and over,
9.30am-3.30pm, SF315 for 6 days
including lunch
Non-ski kindergarten Hotel Vereina, 2 yrs
and over, 9am-4.30pm, prices on request.
Madrisa Kindergarten, 3 yrs and over,
10am-12.30pm and 1.30-4pm, SF6 per hr
or SF20 per day not including lunch

FOOD AND DRINK PRICES
Coffee SF4, glass of wine SF6-8,
small beer SF4-5, dish of the day SF15-25

temptation cakes. The most favoured bar is the rustic Chämi, which is full to bursting with revellers of all ages until closing time. In the pre-dinner hours, there are major league ice-hockey matches in the handsome Sports Centre, plus facilities for ice-skating (on the largest natural rink in Europe), indoor tennis, curling, squash and swimming. The Montana has a pool bar, with four good tables. The Cinema Arkadeu in Platz shows second-run films, but check whether they have been dubbed into German before you buy the ticket.

The area's pulsing nightlife can be found in Davos Platz, and especially in the Ex-Bar, which has developed the novel idea of shutting at 11pm in order to re-open from 2am to 7am. The laser show at the Cabanna Club disco attracts the very young, while the Postli in the Posthotel Morosani caters for an older crowd. The Cava Grischa has live folk music and there is a popular Piano Bar in the Hotel Europe. Graubunden's largest casino, also in the Hotel Europe, is now up and running despite gambling options that are limited to 150 slot machines and a boule table. The Scala restaurant in the same building now stays open until 3am.

After-skiing activities in Klosters start with tea and cakes at A Porta's. However, when it comes to nightlife, this resort, with its many chalets and few bars, is not a major player. The Hotel Vereina has two popular bars, the Brasserie and the Scotch, while the Steinbock Bar attracts locals as well as tourists. Alternative watering holes include the Verruckte Baustellen in the Hotel Kaiser, the piano bar in the Aldiana Club and the cellar bar in the Chesa Grischuna. For late nights try the Casa Antica, once Princess Diana's favourite disco, the Kir Royal in the Aldiana Club or Rufinis in Klosters Dorf.

Childcare

The Pinocchio Kindergarten in Davos takes care of children over three years of age throughout the day from Monday to Friday. Their programme includes playing in the snow and an introduction to skiing. More advanced group instruction is available to the over-fours during the week, with a race every Friday. There is also a special course at Bolgen on Sundays.

In Klosters, the Hotel Vereina offers good childcare facilities from infancy onwards, including a crèche and evening baby-listening service. Alternatively there is a kindergarten on the Madrisa for the over-threes, an inconvenient arrangement as parents have to take their children there for a 10am start, while they themselves would probably choose to ski in another area a bus-ride away.

Gstaad

ALTITUDE 1050m (3,444ft)

Skiing is only a decorative accessory to Gstaad's charm. Not everyone does it, and those who do don't do it all the time. The regulars do not hit the slopes until 11.30am as they are too busy preparing for nightfall and a fresh round of partying. The Palace Hotel, with its fairytale turrets, sits on a hill like some feudal castle, dominating Gstaad and its daily life. The bar of the Hotel Olden, a haunt of the rich and famous, has a collection of mugs inscribed with the names of regulars including Roger Moore and Julie Andrews. The resort is, however, more secluded than flashy and still manages to retain the atmosphere of a farming community.

The first impression of the village is of typical Swiss chalets and delightful scenery, but the main street pays homage to designer labels and their international collectors; Gucci, Cartier, Versace and others vye for the best position. 'Think expensive, then double it,' was one comment. Another reporter said: 'The woman in the dress shop peered suspiciously at my green American Express card as if she had never seen one that colour before.'

■ GOOD POINTS

Uncrowded ski area, attractive village, short airport transfer, extensive skiing in region, variety of activities for non-skiers

■ BAD POINTS

Limited expert skiing, unconnected ski areas, poor snow record, high prices

On the mountain
top 3000m (9,842ft) bottom 1000m (3,280ft)

To serious skiers the lure of Gstaad is a mystery: the village stands at 1050m and none of the local skiing is above 2200m, which means that even during a good winter, snow cover is unreliable. The redeeming factor is the presence of the nearby Glacier des Diablerets where the lifts go up to 3000m. Regulars argue that the sheer extent of the skiing included in the Gstaad Super Ski lift pass — 69 lifts covering 250km of pistes and 10 villages — makes up for the lack of challenge. The local skiing is rather inconveniently divided into three separate areas, but regular ski buses to the surrounding villages of **Rougemont**, **Saanenmöser** and **Schönried** give access to slopes offering considerably more scope. However, reporters say that buses to the glacier are both infrequent and oversubscribed. The other villages covered on the lift pass are **St Stephan**, **Zweisimmen**, **Lauenen**, **Gsteig**, **Saanen** and **Château d'Oex**. The weekly lift pass also includes a day's skiing in **Adelboden-Lenk** and the Vaudoise Alps (**Villars**, **Leysin**, **Gryon**, and **Les Mosses**).

Beginners

The nursery slopes nearest to the town centre are at the bottom of Wispile, but the snow is often unreliable. There are some easy slopes at the top of the same area, at Schönried and further afield at Saanenmöser. The best beginner slopes are at La Braye above Château d'Oex; they are covered by the lift pass and can be reached by train or bus.

Intermediates

The intermediate skiing in the Gstaad area is broken up into three segments: Eggli, Wispile and Wasserngrat. The Eggli area interconnects with Rougemont at the top of La Videmanette, and you can also ski from Eggli to Saanen on long, varied runs. The Hornberg area is a few kilometres away and is reached by bus or train; it has the most extensive lift network in the area, with 14 lifts reaching St Stephan at the far end of the valley.

Advanced

Advanced skiers should head to the Wasserngrat, which hosts the challenging Tiger Run piste. Les Diablerets Glacier is a long run with a fairly steep start, though it is not too difficult. There are few black (difficult) runs.

Off-piste

From Wispile there are a few off-piste runs from the top down to Feutersoey and to the Chlösterli restaurant. Heli-skiing is available on the Gstellihorn, Wallig, Stalden, Gummfluh and Les Diablerets Glacier.

Ski schools and guiding

The English-speaking ski school has a good reputation, with classes for children from four years of age. The ski school meets in several ski areas, including Gstaad, Schönried, Saanen, Saanenmöser and Rougemont. The two off-piste guiding companies are Experience Gstaad Saanenland and Mountain Guide Company Gstaad Saanenland.

Snowboarding

There are three snowboarding parks in Gstaad, including one on Les Diablerets Glacier, which is weather dependent. The others are at Hornberg above Saanenmöser and Rinderberg above Zweisimmen and include a half-pipe and other special facilities. Snowboarding is permitted everywhere in the ski area and the Snowboardschool Saanenland offers group and private lessons.

Cross-country

There are 100km of classic loipe and 40km of the freestyle variety spread around the valley and on the mountain.

Mountain restaurants

Members of the exclusive Eagle Ski Club at Wasserngrat lunch behind closed doors in their own private restaurant. Lesser mortals still have an extensive, albeit expensive, choice of mountain eating-places. The average price for the dish of the day in a mountain restaurant during the 1996 season was between £18 and £25; a small cup of coffee cost between £2.34 and £4.68 and a small beer between £2.10 and £5.26.

Chemistube above St Stephan is recommended, as is Cabane de La Sarouche at Château d'Oex. Ruble-Rougemont at the bottom of the Gouilles chair-lift is 'half the price of anywhere else' according to one report. Other choices include the Berghaus Wasserngrat ('excellent sun-terrace and a good place to spot the ludicrous ski outfits'), and the waiter-service Eggli, where the glitterati lie out on the terrace and work on their tans.

Off the mountain

The village of Gstaad is filled with top-quality hotels and a cluster of well-preserved wooden buildings bordering the often busy main road. 'Property prices here are higher than Mayfair or Manhattan and rival only Tokyo,' said a local estate agent. This largely explains the lack of lower-priced accommodation in a village that boasts 13 luxury hotels but only a couple of modest two-stars, where you can get a room for £40 a night.

Accommodation

In its time, the Palace Hotel used to attract so many celebrities at Christmas and in February that it was actually difficult to spot a guest who wasn't famous. The opulent Gstaad Hotel Park, downhill but not necessarily downmarket from the Palace, is picking up much of the new business.

> **■ OTHER SPORTS**
>
> Parapente, hang-gliding, winter walks, swimming, skating, curling, indoor tennis, squash and badminton, climbing wall, hot-air ballooning, tobogganing

Gstaad's four-stars include Grand Hotel Alpina, the Arc-en-Ciel and Hotel Bellevue Gstaad. The Bernerhof is conveniently close to the station, and the Christiania has individually designed bedrooms. The three-star Olden is family-run and cosy, as is the Posthotel Rössli, while Sporthotel Rutti is the cheapest and most basic but has good food and is said to be good value for money. Most of the cheaper hotels are in the surrounding villages of Schönried and Saanenmöser. The most favourable reports are of Rougemont ('a beautiful undiscovered village of traditional chalets') and Château d'Oex (best known for its celebrated balloon festival in January). We have good reports of the Hotel Viva in Rougemont and the Alpenrose in Schönried.

Eating in and out

The best restaurants are in the hotels, but these are also the most expensive. La Cave in the Hotel Olden is good and there is also cheaper food at the bar. The sixteenth-century Chlösterli is large but has a great atmosphere. The Bellevue Gstaad is famous for its Chez Fritz restaurant. The Alpenrose at Schönried serves light cuisine, The Bären at Gsteig offers traditional Swiss fare, and the smart Chesery receives top marks, as does The Rialto for its pasta.

Après-ski

After hot chocolate and cakes at Charly's Tea Room beside the skating rink, or at the Café Pernet, it is time for a drink and some star-gazing in the Hotel Olden. Then you can step out at the Greengo nightclub in the Palace Hotel, which has a glass dance floor over the daytime swimming-pool. As you might expect from its name, everything in it is green, from the walls to the doors. Entrance costs between £15 and £26 depending on the season, but it is free to hotel guests. The locals meet at Richi's. Other haunts include the Hotel Boo in Saanen, Club 95 at the Sporthotel Victoria and the Grotte in the Hotel Alpin Nova in Schönried. In Château d'Oexôcheck out Café du Cerf.

Childcare

There are non-ski kindergartens at Gstaad, Saanen, Schönried and Saanenmöser for a limited number of hours each day, and the children's ski school takes children from four years of age. Some hotels can arrange babysitting, and The Palace has a nursery.

TOURIST OFFICE
Tel 41 33 748 8181
Fax 41 33 748 8183

Jungfrau

ALTITUDE Wengen 1274m (4,180ft), Grindelwald 1034m (3,391ft),
Mürren 1650m (5,412ft)

The Jungfrau region, the Edwardian nursery of modern skiing, has an edge on quality, which it has somehow managed to maintain over the years. Trains are a crucial part of any holiday to its principal resorts of **Mürren**, **Wengen** and **Grindelwald**; Wengen's mountain railway, which dates back to the 1880s, is still the backbone of the lift system today, making both Wengen and Grindelwald ideal bases for non-skiers. Wengen and Mürren remain traffic-free and remarkably unspoilt by the passage of a century. The three resorts share a lift pass, which covers 49 lifts in the Jungfrau Top Ski region, offering 195km of wonderfully scenic skiing against the awesome backdrop of the Eiger, Mönch and Jungfrau mountains.

The Jungfrau region was one of the birthplaces of modern alpine skiing. Henry Lunn, a Methodist minister and one-time lawn tennis equipment salesman, is credited with introducing the first-ever ski package holidays here in the winter of 1910–11. To encourage the class-conscious British to come on his tours he founded the Public Schools Alpine Sports Club and somehow managed to persuade the Swiss to continue to operate their mountain railways during the winter. His more distinguished son, Sir Arnold, went on to found the Kandahar Ski Club in Mürren where slalom racing was first introduced in 1922.

Ski tourism started in Wengen with the Downhill Only Club, a pioneer band of British skiers formed in February 1925 to race against their Kandahar Club rivals in Mürren. The club's name developed from its members' customary train-ride up the mountain in order to ski down, a process considered distinctly unsporting by the standards of the time. Both British ski clubs are alive and functioning in the resorts today.

Wengen, Grindelwald and Mürren are all reached by rail from Interlaken. The track divides at Zweilutschinen, with the left-hand fork veering to Grindelwald. The right-hand fork goes to **Lauterbrunnen**, which is more of a railway halt than a resort, although it does have a number of hotels and some reporters consider it a convenient and much cheaper base from which to ski the area. From Lauterbrunnen, trains

■ GOOD POINTS

Beautiful scenery, variety of slopes, attractive traffic-free villages (Wengen and Mürren), convenient for family skiing, wide range of activities for non-skiers (Wengen and Grindelwald), excellent nursery slopes at Wengen

■ BAD POINTS

Poorly linked ski areas, limited number of challenging pistes, lower slopes can become icy or worn run steeply up to Mürren on one side of the valley and up to Wengen on the other. The railway climbs as high as the main ski area at Kleine Scheidegg, above Wengen, before descending into Grindelwald. Trains stop at wayside halts throughout the area. They run as accurately as a Swiss watch to a timetable printed on the back of the piste- map.

However, this form of transport is painfully slow and the trains can be as crowded as the London Underground at peak times, but the network has been augmented by conventional cableways and chairs. Although the Jungfrau Top Ski region is not as vast a ski area nor as well-knit as the classic French resorts, it nevertheless provides satisfyingly varied skiing amongst beautiful scenery for its faithful clientèle.

On the mountain
Wengen top 2320m (7,610ft) bottom 1274m (4,180ft)
Grindelwald top 2486m (8,154ft) bottom 943m (3,093ft)
Mürren top 2970m (9,724ft) bottom 796m (2,611ft)

To a great extent the runs are dictated by the contours of the mountains and the prevailing weather. The pistes are not cut out arbitrarily from forest, nor bulldozed down scarps but simply follow the best, easiest or most exciting ways down. Slight variations in both bearing and difficulty are influenced each season by the amount of snow and the direction in which the wind was blowing when it fell.

A circuit of lifts around the Lauberhorn and Tschuggen peaks links the ski areas of **Wengen** and **Grindelwald** through the Männlichen and Kleine Scheidegg. From the centre of Wengen a cable car rises to the Männlichen, while the train leads up to Kleine Scheidegg and Eigergletscher. Between Eigergletscher and Kleine Scheidegg there are high alps served by chairs and tows. On the long run down from Kleine Scheidegg to Wengen there is an interesting diversion off to **Innerwengen**.

From Grindelwald a gondola rises to the Männlichen while the train also carries on up to Kleine Scheidegg. On the other side of Grindelwald, the First area is easily accessible, even for Wengen-based skiers. The areas complement each other well, and one of the pleasures of visiting any of them is to spend days exploring the others.

Mürren, separated from the other two resorts by the Lauterbrunnen Valley, sits on an east-facing shelf. Its skiing is spread across three parallel ridges — the Schiltgrat, Allmendhubel and Maulerhubel — that run roughly north and south above the village. These slopes provide decent skiing conditions whatever the weather: powder on the north slopes, spring snow on the south, high bowls for fine weather, trees for shelter and visibility in blizzards.

Beginners
Wengen has an excellent nursery area in the middle of the village with two baby lifts and an unusual three-person drag-lift. There are also satisfyingly long blue (easy) runs on which even those with little technique

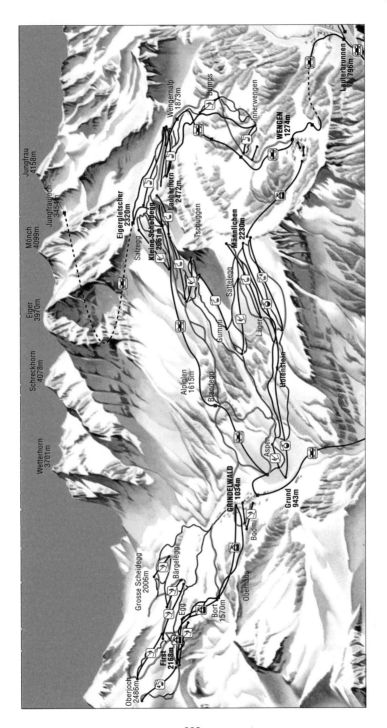

Jungfrau 4158m

Mönch 4099m

Jungfraujoch 3454m

Eiger 3970m

Schreckhorn 4078m

Wetterhorn 3701m

Lauterbrunnen 796m

Wengernalp 1873m

Brüggs

Innerwengen

WENGEN 1274m

Eigergletscher 2320m

Lauberhorn 2472m

Kleine-Scheidegg 2061m

Salzegg

Tschuggen

Männlichen 2230m

Sattelegg

Gumpi

Läger

Alpiglen 1615m

Brandegg

Honegg

Hollenstein

Aspen

GRINDELWALD 1034m

Grund 943m

Bodmi

Oberhaus

Grosse Scheidegg 2006m

Bärgelegg

Egg

Bort 1570m

First 2168m

Oberjoch 2486m

393

can stretch their legs. From Kleine Scheidegg, a broad tree-lined road down Schattwald leads to Brandegg. If, instead of the train, you take the Männlichen cable car from Wengen, you arrive at the top of a big sunny scarp, which is served by several lifts. The easiest route is down under the Männlichen chair.

Grindelwald also has nursery slopes right by the village and others up on the Hohwald and Bargelegg lifts, although beginners will want to return to base via the First gondola.

Mürren is not an ideal resort for beginners. The small nursery slope is on the upper road behind the Jungfrau Hotel; this is historic ground where the world's first modern slalom was set. Another small beginners' area lies at the top of the Allmendhubel lift, served by a small tow. The next stage is to move to the Allmendhubel area, which is not particularly easy.

Intermediates

Wengen and Grindelwald owe much of their popularity with families to their long, medium difficulty runs. You can take the Männlichen cable car and explore the route under the gondola right down to **Grund**. From there the train goes up to Kleine Scheidegg, which has a similarly well networked area improved recently by the installation of a detachable quad on the Lauberhorn. The famous World Cup racecourse, at two-and-a-half kilometres the longest in the world, forms a fairly testing descent. The nearby Standard run offers an easier way down.

From Grindelwald, the First gondola leads to the Stepfi, a satisfying red (intermediate) run from Oberlager down to the Hotel Wetterhorn. As you pass the hotel, you can see the old cable car cabin, which was built in 1908 to take summer climbers up to the Gleckstein hut on the Wetterhorn. The lift was closed in 1914 after being damaged by avalanche and the cabin was left as a relic. This is a convenient stop-off before returning by bus to Grindelwald.

At Mürren, some very attractive intermediate skiing can be reached by taking the Allmendhubel railway and then a small T-bar to the Hog's Back area; turn right towards the Maulerhubel T-bar, at the top of which there is a wide area of open slopes leading either back to the bottom of Maulerhubel or off to the halfway station on the main railway. You can return to the village from the bottom of the Maulerhubel on the wide Palace Run.

The Muttleren and Kandahar chair-lifts halfway up the Schilthorn give access to plenty of intermediate skiing in a snow-sure bowl. However, the only way out for those unwilling to face the often icy Kanonenrohr, is by a steep and uncomfortable T-bar. This is one of the very few places in the area where queues form.

Advanced

From Wengen, the train up to Eigergletscher leads to the black (difficult) runs of Blackrock and Oh God. In sunny weather these are best left until late morning, as they can be hard and icy before the sun reaches them. The Aspen run is the steepest way down from the Männlichen towards

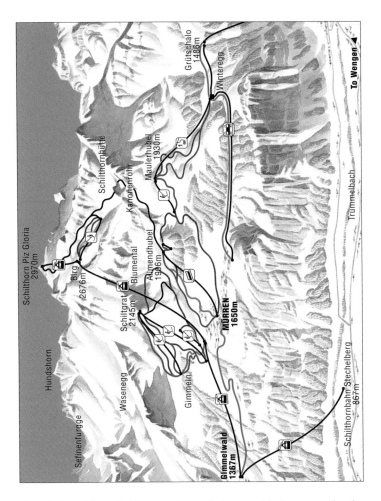

Grund. Grindelwald's First area has a challenging black piste under the gondola. At Mürren the extremely steep run from the top of the Schilthorn can be followed by another steep pitch alongside the new Muttleren, and then the Kanonenrohr, to give an almost continuous black run with plenty of challenge.

Off-piste

All three resorts have a great deal of easily accessible off-piste skiing between the beaten trails. In Mürren the Blumental is famous for its powder, Tschingelchrachen off the Schilthornbahn should be treated with care as it is very steep and often closed, and Hidden Valley from the summit of the Maulerhubel to Grutsch is a delight. The White Hare, which starts from the foot of the Eigerwand, is a dramatic and exciting powder run; it can be accessed from both Wengen and Grindelwald.

Local mountain guides are essential here and Grindelwald's Bergsteigerzentrum is one of the most famous guiding establishments in the world; both ski-touring and heli-skiing can be organised through the centre. Day tours over to the **Lötschental** and other separate areas can be arranged, weather permitting.

Ski schools and guiding

The Swiss Ski School (SSS) operates in each village and all three centres have good reputations. Lessons are given daily (excluding Sundays); most instructors speak English. However, the standard of service provided continues to vary alarmingly. One reader encountered a class of 14 in Grindelwald: 'Our instructor was just interested in skiing madly downhill; it took a sit-in at the ski school office to get the teacher we wanted.' Another praised the ski school in Wengen: 'A well-organised class of eight; I started as a slowish snowplougher and finished the week as a quicker parallel skier.' Another reporter in Mürren complained that his mountain guide 'didn't speak English, kept losing people and wouldn't say where he was going'.

■ OTHER SPORTS

Skating, tobogganing, ice hockey, parapente, hang-gliding, curling, swimming, indoor climbing wall, indoor tennis and squash

Snowboarding

Wengen has the best set-up for riders, with its Snowboard Valley Kleine Scheidegg located in the centre of the ski area. Its 1200 vertical metres are properly maintained and cover a range of difficulty, from snake jump to quarter-pipe. Novice snowboarders are well catered for by the SSS and by the Privat Ski Snowboard Schule. On the nursery slopes there is a three-person T-bar, which is particularly snowboard-friendly. Grindelwald has the SSS, Backside and Lupo snowboard schools, and the SSS at Mürren also offers tuition.

Cross-country

There are loipe in Grindelwald, Lauterbrunnen and at **Bonigen**, close to Interlaken. Mürren has a small trade in the main ski area.

Mountain restaurants

The area is littered with enjoyable eating places. The Hotel Jungfrau at Wengernalp is among our top ten mountain restaurants in the Alps, with beautiful views and a friendly atmosphere, not to mention the high standard of cooking. The Brandegg restaurant is famed for its 'quite extraordinarily delicious' apple fritters. The Kleine Scheidegg station buffet is much more interesting than it looks, and besides its variety of Swiss fare offers its own *Rostizza*, a cross between *Rösti* and pizza. The Männlichen restaurant has spectacular views and is 'very welcome on a bitterly cold day'. The Aspen above **Grund** has a loyal clientèle. Mary's Café on the home run to **Wengen** is recommended for its raclette. Café Oberland is an agreeable alternative and is right on the piste. The Hotel Victoria-Lauberhorn, near the skating rink, has a pizzeria/crêperie with quick service and is therefore ideal for families with children of ski school age, as there is only an hour between morning and afternoon lessons. The *Rösti* in the Stübli of the Eiger Hotel is also recommended.

The restaurant at Bort above **Grindelwald** is 'pleasant and reasonably priced, but the food is not exceptional'. The big self-service at First boasts 'a glorious hamburger'. The Hotel Wetterhorn on the way down to Grindelwald has a convivial atmosphere and delicious food.

Above **Mürren** the Birg restaurant is 'nothing to write home about'. The Gimmeln has 'tasty raclette and *Apfelküchen*'. We have a whole series of complimentary reports of the revolving Piz Gloria on the summit of the Schilthorn ('not expensive and good value'). One reporter had 'a very imaginative salad, and it took a full revolution to demolish it'. Another claimed it to be 'the best and the cheapest menu to be found in Switzerland — what a surprise!' The Schilthornhütte on the descent from here is a mountain refuge serving simple dishes, with a 'fun atmosphere and wonderful views'. Sonnenberg chalet in the valley between the Hog's Back area and the top of the Schiltgrat maintains a high standard. Winteregg, at the mid-station on the railway, is acclaimed for its *Rösti mit Speck*.

Off the mountain

A car is of little or no use in the area. **Wengen** is almost car-free, although a handful of four-wheel drive vehicles are allowed to operate as taxis. Otherwise, luggage is carried by electric buggy around this charming resort which, despite expansion, has lost none of its character and appears to have changed surprisingly little since the foundation of the Downhill Only Club. Many of its visitors are still British, the same families who return year after year to create their own entertainment. The presence of Club Med at the northern end of town seems incongruous in this otherwise neo-Edwardian setting.

The handful of old hotels have been refurbished and others built, but the village remains much as it was — a single pedestrian street of unremarkable shops and a cluster of chalets around one of the best nursery slopes in the Alps. There is also a magnificent skating rink. At the heart of it all on a sunny balcony above the Lauterbrunnen Valley is the railway station.

Grindelwald is the original of the three villages, a large and busy year-round resort spread along the valley floor between the soaring peaks of the Wetterhorn and the Eiger on the one side and the gentler wooded slopes of its First ski area on the other. There are few more cosmopolitan resorts to be found in the world, with every nationality imaginable listed among its guests, not least the Japanese who come here in numbers to visit the Eiger and the Jungfraujoch, which at 3454m is the highest station in Europe.

Mürren has few rivals as the prettiest and most unspoilt ski village in Switzerland. Old chalets and hotels line the paths between the railway station at one end and the cable car at the other. The car-free village is on a sunny shelf perched on top of a 500-m rock face above Lauterbrunnen. Again, the same British families, nearly all of them members of the Kandahar Club, have been returning here for generations and have forged firm links with the villagers.

Accommodation

In **Wengen** the accommodation is split between hotels, apartments and chalets. The attractive resort is quite spread out and distinctly steep. While location is of little importance for the skiing (if staying high up you can ski both down to the train and back to your hotel), a long uphill slog after midnight tends to deter many a holidaymaker from exploring what limited nightlife there is.

The Hotel Eiger is central and has long been a favourite among the British. The Falken is variously described as 'delightfully old-fashioned', 'ramshackle', and ' very comfortable'. The Hotel Regina is 'spacious, clean and comfortable', and is renowned for its English breakfast. Hotel Brunner, situated on the piste a ten-minute walk above the village centre, is: 'One of those alpine secrets that visitors – many of them with children – like to keep to themselves', Hotel Wengener Hof, five minutes' walk from the station, is 'very comfortable' and serves delicious food.

Hotel Silberhorn is 'excellent, with multi-national and very friendly staff, superb and substantial food'. Hotel Alpenrose is said to be of an exceptionally high standard ('we particularly liked the large lounge area with log fire'). Hotel Bernerhof and Hotel Bellevue are also both recommended. The three-star Hotel Belvédère is 'rather isolated at the end of town' but has a range of facilities. The four-star Hotel Sunstar has family 'maisonettes', a swimming-pool, and is one of the most conveniently placed hotels. Club Med here has a fine reputation, although the presence of large, noisy French-led classes on crowded pistes can lead to Agincourt-style confrontations with the more conservative British element.

Grindelwald has the five-star Grand Hotel Regina, which is partly decorated with eighteenth-century antiques and is famous for the ice sculptures in its grounds. A host of four-star hotels include the 'excellent' Hotel Spinne. Hotel Jungfrau is praised for 'good and plentiful food. We would have paid twice the price for the view from our window'. The Hotel Alpenhof, a few minutes' walk from the village, has a sound reputation. Hotel Derby and Hotel Hirschen are both recommended. Hotel Bodmi, situated on the nursery slopes, is convenient for families and Parkhotel Schonegg is warmly acclaimed.

In **Mürren**, the Hotel Eiger by the railway station has some luxurious suites as well as hotel rooms and apartments. The Palace Hotel is central but keeps changing hands. The Alpenruh at the Schilthornbahn end of the village has an excellent restaurant. The popular Edelweiss is 'convenient, clean, and friendly'; the Bellevue-Crystal and the Blumental are both recommended, together with the simpler Belmont. The supermar-

Skiing facts: **Wengen**

TOURIST OFFICE
CH-3823 Wengen, Bernese Oberland
Tel 41 33 855 1414
Fax 41 33 855 3060

THE RESORT
By road Calais 835km
By rail station in resort
By air Zurich 3½ hrs, Geneva 4 hrs
Visitor beds 5,170
Transport traffic-free resort

THE SKIING
Linked or nearby resorts Grindelwald (l),
Grund (l), Lauterbrunnen (n), Mürren (n)
Longest run Mettlen–Grund 8.5km (blue);
Männlichen, 8.5km (red)
Number of lifts 49 in Jungfrau Top Ski
Region
Total of trails/pistes 195km in Jungfrau
Top Ski region (28% easy, 57%
intermediate, 15% difficult)
Nursery slopes 3 lifts
Summer skiing 1 lift at Jungfraujoch
Snowmaking mobile snow-cannon on
nursery slopes

LIFT PASSES
Area pass Jungfrau pass (covers Wengen,
Grindelwald and Mürren), SF232 for 6 days
Day pass Kleine Scheidegg/Männlichen
SF52

Beginners points tickets
Pensioners no reduction
Credit cards accepted yes

SKI SCHOOLS
Adults SSS, SF240 for 6 days (4 hrs per
day)
Private lessons SSS, SF160 per half-day
Snowboarding Swiss Snowboard School,
SF218 for 6 half-days, private lessons as
regular ski lessons
Cross-country SSS, times and prices on
request. Loipe 17.5km in Lauterbrunnen
Valley
Other courses ski-touring, telemark,
skiing for partially sighted
Guiding companies through SSS

CHILDREN
Lift pass 6-16 yrs SF116,
17-21 yrs SF186, both for 6 days,
free for 5 yrs and under
Ski kindergarten SSS, as below
Ski school SSS, 4-12 yrs, 2 hrs am and pm,
SF330 for 6 days including lunch
Non-ski kindergarten at Sport Pavilion,
3-7 yrs, 8.45am-4.30pm, SF130 for 6 days
including lunch

FOOD AND DRINK PRICES
Coffee SF3.20, glass of wine SF3.20, small
beer SF3.20, dish of the day SF16

---

ket is said to be adequate and there is also a butcher's shop.

The village of **Lauterbrunnen** in the valley below is well placed for those who want less expensive accommodation and the chance to try a different area each day, but it does suffer from being hemmed in by sheer mountains on all sides.

Eating in and out

Most restaurants in Wengen are in hotels, but Da Mario near Club Med is strongly recommended for pizzas. Mary's Café offers cheese fondue accompanied by alp-horn blowing contests. Restaurant Wengen in the

Skiing facts: **Grindelwald**

TOURIST OFFICE
CH-3818 Grindelwald, Bernese Oberland
Tel 41 33 854 1212
Fax 41 33 854 1210

THE RESORT
By road Calais 835km
By rail station in resort
By air Zurich 3 hrs, Geneva 4 hrs
Visitor beds 11,700
Transport ski bus between Grund,
Grindelwald centre and First lift, free with
lift pass

THE SKIING
Linked or nearby resorts Wengen (l),
Mürren (n), Lauterbrunnen (n), Grund (n)
Longest run Lauberhorn–Grund,
13km (red)
Number of lifts 49 in Jungfrau Top Ski
region
Total of trails/pistes 195km in Jungfrau
Top Ski region (28% easy,
57% intermediate, 15% difficult)
Nursery slopes 2 lifts on Bodmi nursery
slopes
Summer skiing none
Snowmaking 20km covered in Grindelwald

LIFT PASSES
Area pass Jungfrau pass (covers
Grindelwald, Mürren and Wengen), SF232
for 6 days
Day pass Kleine Scheidegg/Männlichen
SF52, First and Mürren SF50

Beginners points tickets
Pensioners no reduction
Credit cards accepted yes

SKI SCHOOLS
Adults SSS, SF192 for 5 days
(4 hrs per day)
Private lessons SSS, SF288 per day
(5 hrs), SF170 per half-day (2½ hrs)
Snowboarding SSS, Backside or Lupo
snowboard schools, SF140 for 5 days
(2 hrs per day), private lessons
SF288 per day, SF170 per half-day
Cross-country SSS, SF122 for 5 half-days,
private lessons SF52 per hr. Loipe 30-35km
around the Grindelwald Valley
Other courses telemark, ski-touring,
heli-skiing, skiing for partially sighted,
race training, off-piste
Guiding companies Bergsteigerzentrum
Grindelwald

CHILDREN
Lift pass 6-16 yrs SF116, 17-21 yrs SF186,
both for 6 days, free for 5 yrs and under
Ski kindergarten SSS, as below
Ski school SSS, 3-14 yrs, times and prices
as adults
Non-ski kindergarten Children's Club
Bodmi, 3 yrs and over, 9.30am-4pm, SF42
per day including lunch

FOOD AND DRINK PRICES
Coffee SF3, glass of wine SF3.60, small
beer SF3.50, dish of the day SF14-19

Hotel Hirschen specialises in fondue *chinoise*. The Felsenkeller in the
Hotel Silberhorn is also praised. The Berghaus is known for its fresh fish
and the Bernerhof for fondue and raclette. The restaurant in the
Schonegg Hotel in Wengen is popular. On sunny days, the Hotel Eiger
has outdoor tables next to the railway station.

The à la carte Bahnhof restaurant is one of the best places to dine in
Grindelwald. Reporters also speak warmly of the Schweizerhof. One

Skiing facts: **Mürren**

TOURIST OFFICE
CH-3825 Mürren, Bernese Oberland
Tel 41 33 856 8686
Fax 41 33 856 8696

THE RESORT
By road Calais 940km
By rail station in resort
By air Zurich 3 hrs, Geneva 4 hrs
Visitor beds 2,160
Transport traffic-free resort

THE SKIING
Linked or nearby resorts Grindelwald (n), Grund (n), Lauterbrunnen (n), Wengen (n)
Longest run Schilthorn–Lauterbrunnen, 15.8km (black/red)
Number of lifts 49 in Jungfrau Top Ski region
Total of trails/pistes 195km in Jungfrau Top Ski region (28% easy, 57% intermediate, 15% difficult)
Nursery slopes 2 runs and 1 lift
Summer skiing none
Snowmaking limited

LIFT PASSES
Area pass Jungfrau pass (covers Mürren, Wengen and Grindelwald), SF232 for 6 days
Day pass Mürren SF50
Beginners points tickets
Pensioners no reduction

Credit cards accepted yes

SKI SCHOOLS
Adults SSS, 10am-midday, SF123 for 6 half-days
Private lessons SSS, SF110 per half-day
Snowboarding Swiss Snowboard School, SF49 per half-day, private lessons SF110 for 2 hrs
Cross-country lessons not available. Loipe 3km
Other courses heli-skiing, ski-touring
Guiding companies Bergführervermittlung Lauterbrunnen/Wengen/Mürren

CHILDREN
Lift pass 6-16 yrs SF116, 17-21 yrs SF186, both for 6 days, free for 5 yrs and under
Ski kindergarten none
Ski school SSS, 4 yrs and over, prices and times as adults
Non-ski kindergarten guest kindergarten at the sports centre, 3 yrs and over, SF32 per day or SF192 for 6 days, both including lunch. 2-3 yrs old, SF16 per half-day or SF192 for 6 half-days, not including lunch

FOOD AND DRINK PRICES
Coffee SF3, glass of wine SF3.60, small beer SF3.60, dish of the day SF15-18

reader recommends the pizza bar, Chinese and Mexican restaurants in the Hotel Spinne as all having 'great food and fantastic, authentic decor'. The Cava restaurant in the Hotel Derby has 'the best fondue and pasta in town'. The Alte Post by the First lift-station has a good reputation.

In Mürren the stübli in the Hotel Eiger has an excellent, if somewhat expensive menu. At the other end of the village, the Alpenruh has a fine reputation and the Belmont offers 'excellent value'.

Après-ski
Wengen's nightlife remains muted in comparison to other Alpine

resorts. The last ski trains are full of families with toboggans going up to Wengernalp for the four-kilometre descent back to the village. Crowds gather in Café Oberland and in Mary's Café on the home run and the ice-bar outside the Hotel Brunner is busy. In the village itself the twin skating rinks at times offer ice-hockey matches on one and curling on the other. In the afternoons it seems that there are almost as many people skating as there are skiing.

Reporters complain that Wengen has no real tea-and-cakes places, apart from Café Grubi, which is full of atmosphere but rather cramped. The Stübli, next to ski school, offers snacks. The stübli in the Hotel Eiger is packed out, as is the independent Eiger Bar in the main street. The Tanne, Sina's Pub, and the Crystal are the most popular bars, while Tiffany's is the disco. The Paradise in the Hotel Belvédère even sports topless go-go dancers.

For such a small village **Mürren** is surprisingly lively after skiing. It has an excellent sports centre with skating, curling, a swimming-pool, sauna and squash courts. The Ballon bar in the Palace Hotel, together with the Grübi in the Jungfrau and the Pub in the Belmont are all popular. The Tächi bar in the Hotel Eiger is one of the main meeting places. The Bliemlichäller disco in the Blumental and the Inferno disco in the Palace Hotel are packed at weekends and in season.

In **Grindelwald** the Expresso bar draws a young crowd after skiing, while the Gepsi attracts a slightly older clientèle. Later on the Chälli bar in the Hotel Kreuz and Post, the Cava in the Derby, and Herby's in the Regina are the most popular. The Plaza Club and the Spyder disco rock on into the small hours.

Childcare

We have pleasing reports of high standards of tuition in all three resorts. The SSS at Mürren has come in for considerable criticism for the attitude of its often elderly instructors and outdated methods; under the dynamic leadership of Angélique Feuz however, all that appears to be in the past. Her teachers apparently speak a high standard of English and the standard of instruction is said now to be on a par with the ski schools in both Wengen and Grindelwald. Mürren has little easy skiing and is not suitable for small children. One reporter with an eight-year-old child praised the ski school at Wengen: 'The teacher was Dutch and spoke perfect English. The lessons were such fun that my son couldn't wait to go back each day.' The non-ski kindergarten here is also praised.

Saas-Fee

ALTITUDE 1800m (5,904ft)

On the morning of 20 December 1849 Johann Imseng, the parish priest of **Saas-Fee**, was visiting the village inn when he heard that one of his parishioners in the valley hamlet of **Saas-Grund** was dying. Despite the heavy snowfall he set off immediately on his eight-kilometre journey downhill. He strapped a couple of barrel staves on his feet, so the story has it, and managed to reach the man in time, thereby fulfilling his pastoral duty and becoming the first skier in Switzerland. A bronze statue of Imseng today stands beside the modern church in the village square.

Saas-Fee remains a delightfully unspoilt and picturesque village set against one of the most dramatic glacial backdrops in the Alps. Its narrow streets are lined with 56 hotels interspersed with ancient barns and chalets of blackened wood. Designer ski shops stand beside working farmhouses where you can buy fresh milk by the pail.

Saas-Fee is a resort unspoilt by weekenders and is well suited to families. It is wonderfully traffic-free and has been so ever since it was linked by paved road from the valley in 1951. You leave your car on the outskirts of town and travel by electric taxi or trundle your luggage by handcart to where you are staying.

Saas-Fee has been a pioneer in the development of hi-tech ski lifts. Rejecting the Funitel system, the resort invested instead in a far more sophisticated cableway for the Alpin Express — the first stage alone cost £24 million. It also boasts the world's highest underground funicular system, the Metro Alpin. These have done much to reduce the long queues that used to dog the resort but the enclosed pistes still lead to some overcrowding in high season.

Apart from a mainly modern lift system (there are still some ancient T-bars), a certain level of complacency has been allowed to creep into other aspects of the resort, including the ski school.

On the mountain
top 3600m (11,811ft) bottom 1800m (5,904ft)

Saas-Fee has excellent nursery slopes, limited but challenging intermediate skiing and exceptional ski-touring possibilities. Mountain access to

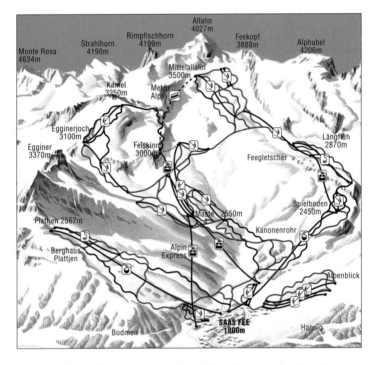

3500m is direct from the entry point of the village via the Alpin Express and Metro to Mittelallalin. From the south of the village the Plattjen gondola rises to the left, and to the right the Spielboden gondola connects with the Längfluh cable car.

Faced with the spectacular array of tumbling blue icefalls and wicked crevasses above, it is hard to concentrate on what is going on beneath your feet. The higher up the mountain you go, the more dramatic the scenery becomes, although constant glacier activity has severely limited the number of pistes and the resort has none of the cruising offered by the larger ski arenas. Each run is enclosed by roped markers and anyone who ventures beyond these without a local guide runs a serious risk of falling down a snow-covered crevasse.

A separate area, the Hannig, is served by gondola and is reserved for hiking, cross-country and tobogganing.

Beginners

Five drag-lifts at the bottom of the mountain make an excellent nursery complex flanked by a horseshoe of eight of the highest glaciers in Europe. The Stafelwald and Leeboden lifts are away from the path of fast skiers returning to the village. Ambitious beginners will want to try the Weisse Meile, a long blue (easy) run, which cuts across the Feegletscher from 3500m at Mittelallalin over to Längfluh, where the cable car must be taken back to the village. From the Mittaghorn drag, a long blue itinerary with some interesting twists winds right down to the nursery slopes.

Intermediates

There is no solid red (intermediate) run from the top to the bottom of Saas-Fee. Plattjen has only two short easy reds under the chair-lift. The Egginerjoch piste is more challenging. The Felskinn alongside the Egginer 2 drag-lift offers the most direct fall-line skiing. From 3500m the Metro piste leads to a series of reds, which leads all the way down to the base of the Kanonenrohr lift where a series of blues returns to Saas-Fee.

Advanced

Advanced skiing in the resort is severely constrained by crevasse danger. One reader commented 'there is not much room to ski here'. The longest sequence of fall-line skiing begins with a steep wall under the Mittelallalin revolving restaurant, following the Alpin, Surprise and Gletscherschuss black (difficult) trails down past the Kanonenrohr lift to the Bach off-piste trail and blue pistes into the village. The Hinterallalin drag-lift is between two steep but short blacks, Chessjen and Hinterallalin, which often present difficult ice bumps.

Off-piste

Reclassified as off-piste, the Weisse Perle, Bach and National ungroomed runs are now marked on the piste-map. More exciting is the climb up the Strahlhorn at 4190m to ski all the way down into **Zermatt**. It is also possible, without climbing, to cross over the Kamel ridge above the Hinterallalin drag-lift to ski down the Allalingletscher to the lake at Mattmark; a local guide is strongly recommended for this run.

Ski schools and guiding

The Swiss Ski School (SSS) in Saas-Fee is run both as a co-operative and a monopoly and suffers from poor organisation and overcrowding in group lessons during peak holiday weeks. Its co-operative status means that no instructor can be fired for incompetence, laziness, drunkenness, old age or any other of the ills that can befall individuals in any such group. It provides group lessons for just over three hours a day from 9.45am to 1pm. Amazingly, it fails to offer any lessons at all at weekends, forcing beginners to take private lessons (£64 for two hours) if they want to ski at all on their first day. The separate mountain guide association, Bergsteigerschule Saastal, has an excellent programme, ranging from two-and-a-half-hour tours to ski itineraries into **Zermatt**.

Snowboarding

Snowboarding is bigger business here than in almost any resort in Switzerland. While the SSS gives lessons, it suffers fierce and healthy competition from the refreshingly radical Paradise Snowboard School. Paradise offers a group lesson for beginners on Sundays in preparation for a five-day course. There are two half-pipes, one by the Mittelallalin 1 lift, the other near the Maste 4 lift. Powder Tools and Popcorn Snowboardpoint are specialist shops.

Mountain restaurants

The Hannig mountain inn offers fondue evenings on Tuesdays and Thursdays, including a toboggan run down wearing miners' headlamps. The Britanniahütte is a hike from the pistes but is a classic ski-touring cabin. The rustic Berghaus Plattjen describes its *Rösti* as 'world famous'. The Gletschergrotte has even better 'alpine macaroni'. The world's highest revolving restaurant at Mittelallalin has equally high prices. The views and food over at Längfluh are better. The Belmont and Waldrand both overlook the nursery slopes and are good places for parents to take their children after class.

Off the mountain

Roman coins have been found high above Saas-Fee, but the first hotels date from the mid-nineteenth century. Traditional chalets remain hemmed in by glaciers and steep walls, which do not allow much sun in mid-winter. The eight local families who preside over the village have admitted little outside influence, with the consequence that service is sometimes obdurate and inefficient. Most hotels have been modernised within recent years, giving them a functional look that subtracts from the otherwise cuckoo-clock ambience. There are no buses and electric taxis are not always available.

■ OTHER SPORTS

Skating, curling, ice hockey, indoor tennis and badminton, swimming, tobogganing, dog-sledding

The Ice Pavilion at Mittelallalin (entry SF7 for adults, SF3.50 for children) is well worth a visit, if only to see what a glacier looks like from the inside. Among the fascinating hands-on memorabilia are life-size wax models of climbers being rescued from crevasses as well as a *Pingu* igloo for children. Beware of the effects of altitude here — the long stairway up to the exhibition starts at 3500m and can leave one feeling dizzy and short of breath.

Ice-skating and curling are popular in Saas-Fee, with a large rink in the central nursery slope area, which is both well-maintained and free.

Accommodation

Where you stay is of some importance if you do not want to end up with a long trek to the skiing — it is a 2-km walk from the parking area to the ski lifts on the snowfield to the south. The leading hotel is the Walliserhof. The Burgener is a small, single-storey family hotel close to the lifts and the four-star Saaserhof is also conveniently situated. Up in the forest is the romantic Landgasthof Hohnegg.

Apartments in the Allalin, Atlantic and Tobias are bigger than their French counterparts, but are a good hike from the lifts. More central is the spacious, old, palace-style Glacier, now converted into apartments.

The Interhome apartments are recommended ('huge, with three bedrooms, living and dining areas').

Eating in and out
The Fletschorn Waldhotel is rated as one of Switzerland's better restaurants. The Hofsaal in the Schweizerhof is recommended for fish and the Cheminée for flambées. The Mandarain, which serves Thai food, and El Palatino with its Mexican food are the only escape from *Rösti*, fondue, raclette and grilled meats. The best of the latter is found at the Belmont, Käse Keller, Zur Mühle, Schäferstube and the Mistral, which is also recommended for its saffron risotto. Trattoria Mamma-mia and Boccalino have reasonable pizzas.

Après-ski
The Crazy Night is the hippest techno venue. John's Pub, in the Metropol Hotel, tries for an English ambience, and the VIP Bar (also in the Metropol) goes in for cocktails and higher prices. Rowdy drinking is frequent at Nesti's Ski Bar and the Go-Inn. The Sissy Bar and Pic-Pic are popular and comfortable. The Why-Not pub is loud and raucous.

Childcare
The ski school accepts children from five years old, although as with the adults there are no weekend or afternoon lessons. Pulvo ski courses are available for children of four to five years old for one-and-a-half hours each afternoon. The Bären-Klub in the Hotel Garni Berghof takes children from two-and-a-half years old and offers babysitting in the evening. The Alphubel and Schweizerhof hotels organise childminding for their guests, and the Hotel Dom has an unsupervised playroom.

Linked or nearby resorts
Saas-Grund, **Saas-Almagell** and **Saas-Balen** are nearby villages with another 12 lifts and 25km of pistes, but not worth the inconvenience of the bus journey for most skiers.

Saas-Grund
top 3100m (10,170ft) bottom 1559m (5,114ft)
Saas-Grund is strung out along the valley road towards Saas-Almagell. The skiing, which is mainly suited to intermediates and off-piste enthusiasts, is centred around Kreuzboden at 2400m and is reached by gondola. The SSS at Saas-Grund gives lessons in skiing and snowboarding and there are two mountain guiding companies, Bergsteigerschule Weissmies and Arthur Anthamatten. The PIPO Club kindergarten accepts children from four to six years old on weekday mornings. Most of the accommodation is in chalets, apartments and in 17 small hotels.

New additions last season were a freestyle park for snowboarders and an 11-km toboggan track.

Saas-Almagell's main claim to fame is its illustrious son, Olympic

Skiing facts: **Saas-Fee**

TOURIST OFFICE
CH-3906 Saas-Fee, Valais
Tel 41 27 957 1457
Fax 41 27 957 1860

THE RESORT
By road Calais 1072km
By rail Visp 27km, buses from station
By air Geneva or Zurich, $3\frac{1}{2}$ hrs
Visitor beds 7,500
Transport traffic-free village; ski bus
service SF25 for 6 days, children SF10 for
6 days

THE SKIING
Linked or nearby resorts Saas-Almagell
(n), Saas-Balen (n), Saas-Grund (n),
Riederalp (n), Zermatt (n),
Crans Montana (n)
Longest run Mittelallalin-Felskinn-
Saas-Fee, 14km (red)
Number of lifts 27 in Saas-Fee,
38 including Saas-Grund and
Saas-Almagell
Total of trails/pistes 100km (50% easy,
25% intermediate, 25% difficult)
Nursery slopes 6 runs and 5 lifts
Summer skiing 20km of runs and 3 lifts on
Feegletscher
Snowmaking 60,000m^2 covered by 7
snow-cannon

LIFT PASSES
Area pass (covers Saas-Almagell, Saas-
Balen, Saas-Fee and Saas-Grund) SF278
for 6 days

Day pass SF56
Beginners SF90 for 6 days, using 5 village
lifts only
Pensioners 10% reduction for 63 yrs and
over
Credit cards accepted yes

SKI SCHOOLS
Adults SSS, 9.45am-1pm (weekdays only),
SF163 for 5 days
Private lessons SF55 per hr
Snowboarding SSS, SF150 for 5 half-days,
private lessons SF55 per hr. Paradise
Snowboard School, 10am-1pm, SF156 for 5
days, private lessons SF50 per hr
Cross-country SSS, as regular ski lessons.
Loipe 26km in Saas Valley
Other courses telemark, ski-touring
Guiding companies Bergsteigerschule
Saastal

CHILDREN
Lift pass 6-15 yrs, SF168 for 6 days, free
for 5 yrs and under (accompanied by an
adult)
Ski kindergarten SSS Pulvo, 4-5 yrs, 1.30-
3pm, SF23 per day
Ski school SSS, 5 yrs and over, 9.45am-
1pm, SF163 for 5 days
Non-ski kindergarten Hotel Garni Berghof
Bären-Klub, $2\frac{1}{2}$-6 yrs, SF60 per day including lunch

FOOD AND DRINK PRICES
Coffee SF3.30 , glass of wine SF3.20,
small beer SF3.60, dish of the day SF26

gold medallist Pirmin Zurbriggen. The village is slightly higher than its
neighbour, Saas-Grund, at 1672m, and has its own skiing.

TOURIST OFFICE
Tel 41 27 957 2403
Fax 41 27 957 1143

St Moritz

ALTITUDE 1800m (5,904ft)

St Moritz is an urban resort on two levels, above and along the shores of a fir-lined lake in Switzerland's most scenic valley. Four hours from Zurich, St Moritz is where winter holidays were invented — by the British. Twice host to the Winter Olympics, the resort sets the world standard for luxury and indulgence. Polo, golf and a number of exotic horse-racing events take place throughout the winter on the frozen lake; the 'season' ends abruptly in February. The Cresta Run, still closed to women, has been the ultimate test of male machismo for more than a hundred years. The truly international clientèle is dominated by Germans.

St Moritz is not simply a ski area, but a winter-sports resort. Warmed by the Engadine sun and vitalised by the local 'champagne climate', the first visitors took to tobogganing in 1864. Ice-skating, curling, bob-sledding, golf and horse-riding on ice all had their European premiers in St Moritz.

■ **GOOD POINTS**

Exceptional climate, unparalleled choice of winter sports, wealth of grand hotels and fine dining, good snow record, extensive snowmaking

■ **BAD POINTS**

Lift queues, skiing sectors widely dispersed, expensive accommodation and dining, lack of architectural charm

Today, the Engadine regional ski pass covers 60 lifts and 350km of pistes from one end of the valley to the other. **Celerina** and **Pontresina** are outlying villages with ski lifts, as are **Silvaplana** and **Sils Maria**. **Dorf** is the name used for St Moritz proper, and **Bad** is down on the lake below.

On the mountain
top 3303m (10,834ft) bottom 1720m (5,642ft)

Few skiers in St Moritz are fanatics. However, despite its wide range of skiing this is not the ideal resort in which to learn. There are sunny nursery slopes, abundant red (intermediate) runs and adequate expert and off-piste routes scattered around the dozen lifts rising from the valley floor. The region divides into the sectors of Corviglia, Corvatsch and Diavolezza-Lagalb. From St Moritz itself, the home mountain is Corviglia, accessed by a funicular from the centre of town with skiing up to 3057m at Piz Nair. Celerina and Bad also access the mostly red runs of Corviglia. Corvatsch, on the other side of the valley, has more expert terrain, accessed from Sils Maria and **Surlej**. Diavolezza and Lagalb, both at nearly 3000m, are much further down the valley and are reached by train or bus. Skiing here is less crowded and more challenging.

Queues of over an hour at Corvatsch are made more bearable by a system of allocating reservations. A number of lifts, in particular at Piz Nair, have queues longer than half-an-hour. Snowmaking ensures skiing on six Corviglia pistes, to the bottom of Corvatsch at Surlej, and from top to bottom of Diavolezza.

Beginners

Crucial for ski-to-lunch addicts is the long, gentle blue (easy) run down from the Marmite restaurant on Corviglia, through the woods back into St Moritz or all the way across to the cable car at Bad. Every sector has some blue runs. The Furtschellas drag-lifts go up to blue runs at 2800m above Sils Maria, but beginners will have to ride the cable car down.

Intermediates

Corvatsch has the highest skiing and links with even more red runs on Furtschellas via the Curtinella drag-lift. South-facing Corviglia has a number of flattering reds. The run under the Piz Grisch chair always has excellent snow. However, the best intermediate skiing, with the least crowds, is out of St Moritz in the Lagalb sector at nearly 3000m. The Giandas red under the cable car is the longest and most direct fall-line skiing in the Engadine.

Advanced

The black (difficult) Hahnensee run, from the top of Corvatsch, winds over open snowfields and into the woods at the edge of Bad; it provides 8km of non-stop skiing for 1600 vertical metres. At Diavolezza, the Schwarzer Hang black piste drops through bands of rock for some excellent, steep skiing down on to the Bernina black run to the bottom.

Off-piste

The steep face of Piz Nair provides incredible thrills when there is enough powder snow to cover the sheer rock. One of the classic off-piste routes in the Alps is the long glacier itinerary from the top of Diavolezza, around and over crevasses to Morteratsch in the forest.

Ski schools and guiding

The St Moritz and Suvretta ski schools are both branches of the Swiss Ski School (SSS). Together they employ 185 instructors, many of whom seem to consider teaching a form of escort service, with paid lunch included. The Palace Hotel has its own school. Off-piste guiding is not widely in demand.

Snowboarding

At Corviglia (accessed by the Munt da San Murezzan chair-lift) there is a snowboard park with a half-pipe and obstacle course. Snowboard

Maloia
1809m

P.da la Margna
3159m

M.Disgrazia
3678m

P.Grisch

P.Mair 3057m

Sass
Corviglia
3057m

P.Ot 3246m

P.Jüter
3380m

P.Albana

Isola

Fex

Sils 1797m

P.Fora

Marguns
2279m

Paradis.

Corviglia
2488m

Val Fex

P.Corvatsch
3451m

2311m

Furtschellas

Silvaplana
1815m

Champfèr

Suvretta

Val Suttver

Chapütschin
3386m

Murtèl

Val
Fex

Signal

Chantarella

P.Glüschaint
3594m

Fex Suvel

Bad

ST.MORITZ
1800m

Celerina
1720m

La Sella
3584m

P.Rosatsch
3134m

Roseg

Punt
Muragl

P.Roseg
3937m

P.Tscherva
3546m

Pontresina
1800m

P.Bernina
4049m

P.Morteratsch
3751m

Muottas Muragl
2453m

P.Zuppò
3995m

Bellavista
3922m

Morteratsch

Alp Languard
2262m

Val Muragl

P.Palü
3905m

P.Albris
3166m

P.Cambrena
3603m

Diavolezza
2973m

P.Languard
3262m

P.Padret

Diavolezza

To Lagalb

School St Moritz offers lessons, as does The Wave Snowboard School, which is part of the SSS at Suvretta. The best shop is Boon Sport in Bad.

Cross-country

The frozen lakes of St Moritz make this one of the most interesting and beautiful cross-country areas in the Alps, with loipe of every standard. Ideally, serious Langlaufers should stay in Bad, as this is where the tracks are based. The 42-km Engadine Marathon is held here each season and attracts thousands of entrants.

Mountain restaurants

Renowned among skiers and gourmets alike, the Marmite on Corviglia has been radically rebuilt. Reservations are necessary for the midday and 2pm sittings. Reto Mathis, whose father, Hartly, was the first man to bring haute cuisine to the high mountains, counts caviar and truffles by the kilo. But his daily specials in the Brasserie or self-service sections of the restaurant are always budget-priced.

Also on the Corviglia mountain, the Skihütte Alpina is great for pasta and rustic charm. Cheese specialities are best at the Piz Nair.

Off the mountain

Since the beginning of tourism here in 1864, St Moritz has been a hotel town. No other resort has so many luxury hotels — 63 per cent are four- or five-star rated. The urban architecture is bland at best. St Moritz's beauty lies not in the views of the resort itself but in the views from it. The resort is small enough to walk around, although most hotels have shuttle vans, and buses and trains provide adequate public transport to all regions. Designer boutiques are as thick on the ground as furs, but the old-fashioned shops are still here.

■ OTHER SPORTS

Skating, curling, horse-racing, polo, cricket and golf on the frozen lake, swimming, parapente, Cresta Run, Olympic bob run, hot-air ballooning, hang-gliding, winter walks, climbing wall, indoor tennis and squash, tobogganing

Accommodation

The Palace Hotel, with its grotesque tower, is the most famous of the five-stars and has its own ski school. The pastel blocks of the Kulm are preferred by the Cresta crowd. Less central, the Suvretta House attracts older, European money. The Carlton has a country-house atmosphere. The four-star Schweizerhof and Steffani hotels, both with active après-ski, are downtown and affordable.

Eating in and out

Hanselmann's in the town centre has been around for more than 100 years and serves coffee, pastries and ice cream to die for. Lunch at the Chesa Veglia, an architectural museum-piece owned by the Palace Hotel, is not expensive compared with dinner. All the top hotel restaurants

Skiing facts: **St Moritz**

TOURIST OFFICE
CH-7500 St Moritz, Graubunden
Tel 41 81 837 3333
Fax 41 81 837 3377

THE RESORT
By road Calais 1047km
By rail station in resort
By air Zurich 4 hrs
Visitor beds 13,425
Transport bus service between Bad and
Dorf

THE SKIING
Linked or nearby resorts Celerina (l),
Champfèr (n), Pontresina (n), Samadan
(n), Sils Maria (l), Silvaplana (l), Surlej (l),
Zuos (n)
Longest run Hahnesee, 8km (black)
Number of lifts 23 in St Moritz, 60 in linked
area
Total of trails/pistes 80km in St Moritz
(10% easy, 70% intermediate, 20%
difficult), 350km in linked area
Nursery slopes 3 lifts in St Moritz
Summer skiing June-July on Diavolezza
Glacier
Snowmaking 11km covered

LIFT PASSES
Area pass Upper Engadine (covers St
Moritz, Celerina, Silvaplana, Pontresina,
Sils), SF258 for 6 days including a day's
skiing in Samnaun and Livigno
Day pass St Moritz/Celerina SF50, linked
area SF54
Beginners points tickets
Pensioners no reductions
Credit cards accepted yes

SKI SCHOOLS
Adults St Moritz Ski School, 10am-midday
or 1.30-3.30pm, SF220 for 5 days. Suvretta
Ski School, 10am-midday and 2-4pm,
SF220 for 5 out of 6 days, Palace Hotel Ski
School, details on request
Private lessons St Moritz SF280 per day,
Suvretta SF280 per day
Snowboarding St Moritz Snowboard
School, prices, times and private lessons as
regular ski school. The Wave Snowboard
School, SF220 for 5 days.
Cross-country St Moritz, SF125 for 5
half-days. Loipe 150km in area
Other courses off-piste, competition,
freestyle, slalom, delta, telemark
Guiding companies The St Moritz
Experience, All Activities Agency (AAA)

CHILDREN
Lift pass 50% reduction for 6-15 yrs, free
for 5 yrs and under
Ski kindergarten St Moritz Ski School, 4
yrs and over, 10am-3.30pm, SF40 per day,
extra SF25 per day for lunch
Ski school St Moritz Ski School, 6-12 yrs,
prices and times as adults. Suvretta Ski
School, 12 yrs and under, 10am-midday or
2-4pm, SF170 for 6 half-days. All Activities
Agency, details on request
Non-ski kindergarten Parkhotel Kurhaus
SF29 per day, Hotel Carlton, SF22 per day,
Hotel Schweizerhof, SF34 per day, all 3 yrs
and over, 9am-5pm, including lunch

FOOD AND DRINK PRICES
Coffee, SF3.40-4.50, glass of wine SF5-7,
small beer SF3.60-5.50, dish of the day
SF20-25

require jacket and tie. Out in Celerina, Peter Graber's beef marinated in hay and herbs, served at the Stuvetta Veglia, is a local legend.

Après-ski

At the Palace Hotel's Kings Club an orchestra plays until 4am (jacket and tie required). The Stübli at the Schweizerhof has late-night dancing on tables, but after 10pm it is so crowded that you could not possibly fall off. The Steffani Stübli across the street is less popular than the Vivai disco in the same hotel. Muli Bar has country-and-western music. Bobby's Bar is for the under 20s.

Childcare

The kindergartens in the Carlton, Schweizerhof and Parkhotel Kurhaus all accept children over three years old on a daily basis with lunch included. The Parkhotel Kurhaus is in Bad next to the cross-country track. The Suvretta and St Moritz SSS accept children over four years old. The St Moritz SSS collects children from their hotels in the morning.

Linked or nearby resorts

Celerina
top 3057m (10,030ft) bottom 1720m (5,643ft)

A village atmosphere, old, stone houses painted with the local graffito designs and ski access to Corviglia make Celerina a quiet alternative. Chesa Rosatsch is a 350-year-old inn now run by a British couple.

TOURIST OFFICE
Tel 41 82 833 3966
Fax 41 82 833 8666

Pontresina
top 2262m (7,421ft) bottom 1800m (5,904ft)

With no big lifts of its own, Pontresina is about midway between the outlying Diavolezza sector and Corviglia. It has good indoor-sports facilities and a loyal clientèle of Italian and German families. Kochendorfer's Albris is an inexpensive hotel with its own bakery and chocolate shop. The Steinbock and Engadinerhof are comfortable and traditional.

TOURIST OFFICE
Tel 41 81 842 6488
Fax 41 81 842 7996

Verbier

ALTITUDE 1500m (4,920ft)

Verbier is Switzerland's best resort for range and ruggedness of skiing. Only 90 minutes from Geneva, on a route consisting mostly of motorways, the resort caters primarily for Swiss visitors (52 per cent) who own holiday apartments or rent them for the winter season. The resort is set on a high plateau with an excellent sunshine record. Its chalets have sprawled unchecked by development restrictions, providing an abundance of self-catered and chalet-party accommodation. Most buildings are wood-clad and few blocks are taller than six storeys.

■ **GOOD POINTS**

Excellent sunshine record, extensive off-piste and snowboarding terrain, summer skiing on the glacier, numerous unspoilt satellites, beautiful scenery

■ **BAD POINTS**

Bottleneck queues, poor resort information, overcrowded pistes, lack of easy runs, inadequate parking, limited snowmaking

The resort has tried desperately to change its mass-market image by building a vertical golf course on the ski slopes, and dropping its 'smiling at the sun' slogan in favour of an unambiguous play for the Cartier crowd with 'Le Must des Vacances'. British visitors have declined from 18 per cent in 1987 to around 9 per cent and the most important foreign visitors are now the Germans.

Verbier was one of the last resorts in Switzerland to be developed. Since 1946 the area has linked with its neighbouring resorts of **Thyon**, **Veysonnaz** and **Nendaz** to form the Four Valleys network with an estimated 400km of piste and 100 lifts on the same ski pass.

In 1987 the 150-person Jumbo cable car was inaugurated by sometime resident Diana Ross. Two years ago Verbier opened the Funispace, a 30-person hi-tech gondola, which virtually eliminated queues at the Ruinettes mid-station. However, peak-period queues of one to two hours' duration persist at the Tortin 'black hole'. Aside from the satellite resorts in the Four Valleys, Verbier's lift pass extends to the small family areas of **Bruson** and **Champex-Lac**. **Vichères**, **Fouly** and even **Super-St-Bernard** on the Italian border can be included on payment of a small supplement. Although Verbier's weekly ski pass is the most expensive in Europe, prices for families with children under 16 are surprisingly moderate.

On the mountain
top 3330m (10,925ft) bottom 1500m (4,920ft)
Verbier's Four Valleys lift pass accesses a smorgasbord of slopes, some of which are so far-flung that getting back before closing time requires

careful planning. With guidance, skiers of every calibre will find suitable blue (easy), red (intermediate) and black (difficult) pistes. However, it takes an expert to appreciate the resort's vast off-piste potential.

From Verbier there are two areas to choose from. Savoleyres, towards the top of the village, is a dated four-person gondola, which carries intermediates up to a ridge at 2354m; from here there is skiing on sunny slopes back towards the south as well as over the top on better snow down to another gondola station in **Tzoumaz**.

The Medran lift complex, a five-minute walk from the central square, is the main entry point for the Four Valleys and the best skiing. A fast six-person gondola ends at the Ruinettes mid-station and there is a chair-lift, which runs only at peak periods.

Medran queues, once legendary, now seldom last more than half an hour. Skiers have the choice of various chair-lifts from the mid-station at Ruinettes. At Ruinettes itself they can board the essentially queue-free 30-person Funispace gondola to access Attelas; from here the sectors of Lac des Vaux and La Chaux are skiable. Further lifts are required to reach the Mont Gelé, Tortin, Gentianes and Mont-Fort sectors.

The multifold terrain of the Four Valleys continues to confuse skiers, despite improved signposting. Snow cover on the final approach to Medran has also been improved by mobile snow-cannon. However, Verbier has no overall snowmaking system, and La Chaux and the main route from Attelas to Medran suffer badly when nature is niggardly. The automated telephone information service in English is useless in determining which sectors are open early in the morning.

Beginners

Verbier has no true beginner runs, though the baby slope at Moulins and the blue at Esserts are easy training grounds for the most inexperienced skier. The Rouge, marked as a blue, is at least a red thanks to drop-offs bulldozed on to the formerly easy slope when it was made into a golf-course. Beginners with a taste for the big mountain can ski blues down to the Jumbo cable car and ride up to a flat blue piste on the glacier at Gentianes.

Intermediates

The main red route down from Attelas to Medran, some 700m of vertical, is densely populated. From the bottom of the Mayentzet chair the only way back to Medran is along a winding road. Pedestrians walking dogs, children on toboggans and homeward-bound racers all share this path. The Savoleyres sector offers intermediates more scope, but the easy road back from Savoleyres to Medran via Carrefour is frequently closed because of serious avalanche risk, and there is no pisted route back to the Savoleyres base-station.

La Chaux sector, home of the Jumbo gondola, is served by two chair-lifts and offers easy, undulating terrain. The spring snow skiing here is superb, although in the late afternoon the chairs are clogged with skiers returning from Mont-Fort.

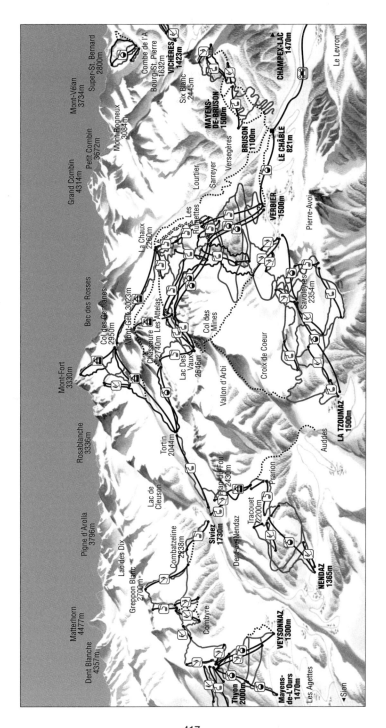

Matterhorn
4477m

Dent Blanche
4357m

Pigne d'Arolla
3796m

Rosablanche
3336m

Mont-Fort
3330m

Bec des Rosses

Col des Gentianes
2950m

Mont-Gelé 3023m

Chassoure
2740m

Les Attelas

Lac Des
Vaux
2546m

Col Des
Mines

La Chaux
2260m

Les
Ruinettes

VERBIER
1500m

Croix de Coeur

Savoleyres
2354m

Pierre-Avoi

LE CHÂBLE
821m

BRUSON
1100m

MAYENS-
DE-BRUSON
1500m

Six Blanc
2445m

Sarreyer

Versegères

Lourtier

CHAMPEX-LAC
1470m

Le Levron

VICHÈRES
1423m

Bourg-St. Pierre
1632m

Combe de l'A

Super-St. Bernard
2800m

Mont-Vélan
3734m

Grand Combin
4314m

Petit Combin
3672m

Mont Rogneux
3084m

Grand Combin

Pigne d'Arolla

Lac des Dix

Lac de
Cleuson

Greppon Blanc
2700m

Combatzeline
2938m

Siviez
1730m

Tortin
2044m

Vallon d'Arbi

Plan-du-Fou
2430m

Tracouet
2200m

Dent-de-Nendaz

Prarion

Audles

LA TZOUMAZ
1500m

NENDAZ
1365m

Combyre

VEYSONNAZ
1300m

Thyon
2000m

Mayens-
de-l'Ours
1470m

Les Agettes

▶Sion

Bruson and Champex are far less crowded and are ideally suited to intermediate skiers or a family day out. The Four Valley resorts contain a wealth of red runs, but it is impossible to reach the Siviez starting point without descending either Tortin or Gentianes, both graded beyond black as 'ski itineraries'.

Advanced

Verbier officially marks only a handful of runs as black. The most interesting is the steep bump-run down Mont-Fort. In icy conditions this can be lethal, but is usually merely irritating. Frightened skiers tend to go across rather than down, cutting the bumps into metre-deep trenches. The black trail from Attelas to Carrefour, once a racecourse, is arguably easier than the reds next to it; fewer skiers mean there is much less risk of collisions.

Off-piste

Verbier's off-piste is divided into itineraries marked on the piste-map, and unmapped areas such as Stairway to Heaven and Hidden Valley, which nonetheless are secrets known to thousands. Mapped itineraries are routinely bombed by avalanche-control teams; they may have cursory markings but they are not patrolled. Many of these routes, like Tortin and Gentianes, are really black pistes that have been reclassified. Unmapped off-piste routes like Cleuson are true *ski sauvage*, but are trafficked by scores of skiers per weekend.

Tortin is a notorious bump-run, which is glorious in powder. Over the top of Tortin is another bowl, Col de Mouche, which is less skied out. Gentianes is a heavily travelled bowl under the eponymous cable car, which is negotiable by most intermediates. The Vallon d'Arbi and Col des Mines are both reached by a traverse at the bottom of Lac des Vaux. Unless the warning rope is down, indicating that a bulldozer has made this traverse into a roadway with high walls, it can be a dangerously narrow ledge of ice. Arbi is an entire valley without pistes or lifts, which usually retains powder in the trees on the skier's left.

The front face of Mont Gelé, under the cable car, is awkward to access. However, after side-stepping over rocks the shaded powder in a choice of couloirs is worthwhile. The best and longest route in Verbier is the back of Mont-Fort, down to the Cleuson dam and through trees to Siviez; it would be unwise to explore here without a local guide. Verbier falsely advertises a skiing range from 3330-800m at Le Châble. In fact, this route is not usually advisable. Wire fences, stone terraces and water standpipes are only some of the hazards. One reporter skied into a fountain and another broke his skis. The snow rarely lasts all the way to the bottom.

Ski schools and guiding

The Swiss Ski School (ESS) is a lottery. Tuition skills and concern for the class vary erratically. More than half the school's 170 red jackets are worn by 'auxiliary' teachers. These are students or ski bums with no qualifications who work on a temporary basis. Private lessons are better.

The rival Ecole de Ski Fantastique specialises in off-piste teaching and guiding. Half of its 40 members are qualified mountain guides, who conduct all off-piste parties. Both schools offer heli-skiing and ski-touring. Fantastique also offers ice-waterfall climbing.

Snowboarding

Verbier is a boarder's dream, and shredders are often the first off-piste. Europe's first ever extreme snowboarding event was held in winter 1995 on Bec de Rosses. However, the snowboard park at La Chaux has lost its half-pipe and the jumps there are described as 'few and pathetic'. In summer there is a snowboard camp at Mont-Fort. X-treme offers the best range of boards for hire. No Bounds is another speciality shop, and is affiliated with the Swiss Snowboard School, the only place to go for lessons.

Cross-country

The largest cross-country area is at Le Châble/Val Bagnes, which has 30km of loipe. Verbier has 4km at resort level and 4km at altitude.

Mountain restaurants

Chez Dany is the favourite lounging and lunching spot. Cabin Mont-Fort, one of the Haute Route waystations, has a more limited menu but better views and higher ski-cred. The Marmotte, on Savoleyres, has its own rope-tow, but access back to Verbier is often closed because of avalanche risk.

The cafeteria at Ruinettes has Verbier's best pastries and a good wait-service restaurant upstairs. The two Attelas lift-station eateries only offer an advantageous locale. The worst place to eat is La Chaux, where orders are blared out incessantly over a loudspeaker. Reporters recommend Les Chottes, near the base of drag-lift 21, but warn that to avoid the after-lunch queues for the drag below the restaurant you need to ski across to drag 65. The Buvette Chez Simon, halfway down the slopes of Savoleyres, is said to be 'laughably inadequate'. The ramshackle wooden cafeteria at Gentianes does good sausage and *frites*. Watch out everywhere on Verbier's terraces for Swedish and other ski bums 'grazing' leftovers.

Off the mountain

Driving in Verbier is difficult and parking is impossible. The roundabout in the central square is highly hazardous, owing to a confusing right of way system. Parking at the main Medran lift station is £5 per day. The free buses are overcrowded and prone to delays. Skiers walking from the main square to Medran are forced on to the road, both by illegally parked cars and by the absence of any pavement.

Thanks to its hard-core clientèle, Verbier has the best ski shops in the Alps. British-owned Mountain Air is headquarters for off-piste, telemark and the latest boot fitting technology. Number One has the best ski tuning.

Accommodation

Visitors to Verbier stay mainly in chalets and self-catered apartments. There are only 1,500 hotel beds among 30,000 skiers in peak season. The majority of visitors (the Swiss) actually own apartments or rent them for the season. There is no five-star hotel here; the Rosalp is the poshest and has the only serious restaurant. The Vanessa is the brightest of the four-stars. The Hotel Verbier in the main square is spartan in style but popular with long-time visitors. The most appealing hotel is the Rois Mages, five floors of light pine tucked away down a residential side street not far from the church. Its elegant interior has the air of a Parisian drawing-room.

■ OTHER SPORTS

Swimming, squash, climbing wall, indoor tennis and golf, hang-gliding, ice-climbing, parapente, skating, winter walks, snow-shoeing

Eating in and out

Aside from the Rosalp, with its kitchens presided over by celebrity chef Roland Pierroz, Verbier's restaurants seem more interested in making a profit than dishing out decent food. The Vieux Valais by the Medran lifts is popular. The Caveau cheese den next to the tourist office receives mixed reports.

The Verluisant at Savoleyres has an honest bourgeois menu. The Relais de Neige at Medran is the best in Verbier for inexpensive eating. For pizzas the Borsalino beats Al Capone. If you want fast food, Harold's has the burgers. Verbier's 'in' place to meet at breakfast (English and served all day) is the Offshore, right next to the Medran lifts and decorated with surf boards and a pink VW Beetle.

Après-ski

The Farm Club, once frequented by Fergie, is still the most expensive and sophisticated nightclub in town. However, it is not as popular as in its heyday and now has serious competition. The Tara is more fashionable with the in-crowd and Marshall's attracts a younger clientèle. The younger still go to Big Ben while the older generation lounge contentedly in Jacky's Bar in the Grand Combin. Disco-goers on a budget flock to The Scotch.

At the Pub Mont-Fort, behind Medran, ski bums line up for a 'cement mixer', imbibing a shot of aquavit from the freezer before being issued with a helmet by the bartender and having their heads smashed against the wall. The Farinet features a live rock band immediately after skiing hours. The Fer à Cheval is a busy rendezvous spot at all hours.

Childcare

Chez Les Schtroumpfs non-ski kindergarten accepts youngsters between five months and seven years old for full- or half-days, lunch included. The Kids Club, run by the ESS, is in the Moulin nursery area. We have good reports of the the club, which takes children from 3 to 10 years and has its own lift. We have mixed reports of Tip Top, underneath the tourist office, which takes children from 2 to 5 years of age.

Linked or nearby resorts

Bruson
top 2445m (8,022ft) bottom 1080m (3,543ft)

Bruson has no accommodation, but it does have off-piste tree-level ski-ing, which can be as good as Canadian heli-skiing. Bruson is reached within 15 minutes by free buses departing hourly from Le Châble train station. Bruson rarely has even the shortest queue on its shaded north-facing steeps when Verbier is seething with weekending Genevans fight-ing for a thin line of powder. It provides adequate piste-skiing on reds and blues, but the challenges are limited.

Verbier's piste-map shows several proposed lifts in Bruson, including a gondola from the valley, but ecologists argue convincingly that none of these will ever be built.

TOURIST OFFICE
as Verbier

Champex-Lac
top 2188m (7,178ft) bottom 1470m (4,823ft)

Champex is a retreat from resort hassles and is the most scenic of Verbier's satellites. An hour's drive or an awkward train and bus journey from Le Châble, it is lushly forested and graced by a small frozen lake. A total of 10km of terrain make up the ski area. Two chair-lifts access very easy skiing along a forest road from the top, which is inexplicably marked as intermediate terrain. Experts will adore the steep face with powder and bumps, right down the open fall-line. Weeks after Verbier is tracked out, untouched powder remains at Champex. Nearby resorts include **La Fouly** and Super-Saint-Bernard; the latter has heli-skiing on the Swiss–Italian border.

The Belvédère restaurant, 100m to the right of the village entrance, offers much more in haute cuisine — at a third of the price — than any-where in Verbier. The Swiss Ski School at Champex offers lessons in alpine, cross-country and snowboarding; mountain guides are available through the Bureau des Guides La Fouly. The Garderie Les Petits Lupins takes children from three years of age.

TOURIST OFFICE
as Verbier

Nendaz
top 3330m (10,925ft) bottom 1365m (4,478ft)

This ugly and inconvenient resort is at a dead-end of the Four Valleys. Most skiers anxious to get to the Verbier sector opt to take the bus to Siviez (formerly Haute Nendaz) to connect with the region's only high-speed quad, and on through Tortin to Gentianes and Mont-Fort.

Skiing facts: **Verbier**

TOURIST OFFICE
CH-1936 Verbier, Valais
Tel 41 27 7716222
Fax 41 27 7713272

THE RESORT
By road Calais 998km
By rail Le Châble 15 mins
By air Geneva 2 hrs
Visitor beds 25,000
Transport free ski bus

THE SKIING
Linked or nearby resorts Bruson (n), Champex-Lac (n), La Fouly (n), Nendaz (l), Super-St-Bernard (n), La Tzoumaz (l), Thyon (l), Veysonnaz (l), Vichères (n)
Longest run Mont-Fort to Verbier, 13km (red/blue/black)
Number of lifts 100 in area
Total of trails/pistes 400km in area (39% easy, 43% intermediate, 18% difficult)
Nursery slopes 3 slopes with 3 lifts
Summer skiing 2 lifts, open from end of June to mid-August
Snowmaking 30km covered in area

LIFT PASSES
Area pass SF297 for 6 days (covers Four Valleys)
Day pass SF59
Beginners no free lifts
Pensioners 65 yrs and over, SF178

Credit cards accepted yes

SKI SCHOOLS
Adults ESS, 9.15-11.45am, SF112 for 6 half-days
Private lessons ESS, SF55 per hr, Ecole du Ski Fantastique, details on request
Snowboarding ESS, 10am-midday, SF32 per lesson, or SF88 for 4 days
Cross-country ESS and Ecole du Ski Fantastique, prices and times on request. Loipe 9km in Verbier, 43km in Four Valleys
Other courses off-piste, telemark, heli-skiing, ski safari, ski lessons for the blind
Guiding companies ESS and Ecole du Ski Fantastique

CHILDREN
Lift pass 5 yrs and under, SF89, 6-16 yrs SF178 for 6 days
Ski kindergarten ESS Kids Club, 3-10 yrs, 8.50am-4.30pm, SF225 for 5 days, extra SF23 per day for lunch
Ski school ESS Kids Club (see above)
Non-ski kindergarten Chez Les Schtroumpfs, 7 yrs and under, SF248 for 6 days (54 hrs). Tip Top, 2-5 yrs, SF300 for 6 days (51 hrs), both including lunch

FOOD AND DRINK PRICES
Coffee SF3, glass of wine, SF2.80, small beer, SF3.50-4, dish of the day SF15-20

TOURIST OFFICE
Tel 41 289 5589
Fax 41 289 5583

Siviez
top 3330m (10,925ft) bottom 1730m (5,676ft)

This sunny resort contains nothing more than a serviceable cluster of new concrete apartments, a complex of shops and a swimming-pool. Germans looking to cut down the cost of skiing in Verbier have made it home. Tactically, there is no faster way to the Four Valleys high spot, Mont-Fort, than the jump-start from Siviez's quad. However, after 11am, mind-numbing queues at Tortin caused by skiers coming from Verbier, eliminate any advantage.

TOURIST OFFICE
as Nendaz

Zermatt

ALTITUDE 1620m (5,314ft)

Zermatt's narrow lanes, lined with old wooden barns and world-class hotels, lie under the angular eminence of the Matterhorn at the top of a dead-end valley. This is Switzerland's southernmost skiing terrain, four-and-a-half hours from Geneva and five-and-a-half hours from Zurich by train. The resort was an isolated hamlet until it was adopted as a mountain base-camp by British climbers and, later, skiers. The canny burghers began milking the cash cow in earnest during the nineteenth century, committing communal funds to build the Gornergrat Railway and passing local legislation forcing every inhabitant of the village to labour on construction of the Zermatterhof Hotel. Surrounded by 30 summits over 4000m, Zermatt today inspires awe among its visitors and envy among its rivals. The older clientèle splits almost equally between Germans and Swiss, with most skiers in the higher income brackets.

■ GOOD POINTS

Superlative scenery, excellent mountain restaurants, high standard of accommodation, alpine charm, lively après-ski, plenty of activities for non-skiers, long runs, extensive ski area, car-free resort, glacier skiing

■ BAD POINTS

Inadequate ski school and nursery slopes, awkward access between ski areas and around town, high prices, long airport transfer

The lift system dates from construction of the Gornergrat cog railway in 1898. New express trains can now run twice as fast as the older carriages still in use. However, due to a single track, the express trip is only ten minutes shorter than the standard 40-minute trip, which stops at every station.

On the mountain
top 3899m (12,788ft) bottom 1620m (5,314ft)

Zermatt is a resort for the adept skier with deep pockets and a taste for good living. The resort's burghers believe that all good things come to those who wait — and walk. Getting around town and from one lift complex to another is expensive and inconvenient by taxi, sleigh or solar bus. No competent skier will find him or herself outclassed by any groomed slope in Zermatt, but queues for the Klein Matterhorn cable car and Gornergrat railway — not to mention packed crowds on narrow, icy trails coming down to the village at the end of the day — will keep even experts on the edge. One reporter notes that Zermatt suits 'bump lovers and people who like skiing on paths'.

An underground funicular begins by the mainline train station and

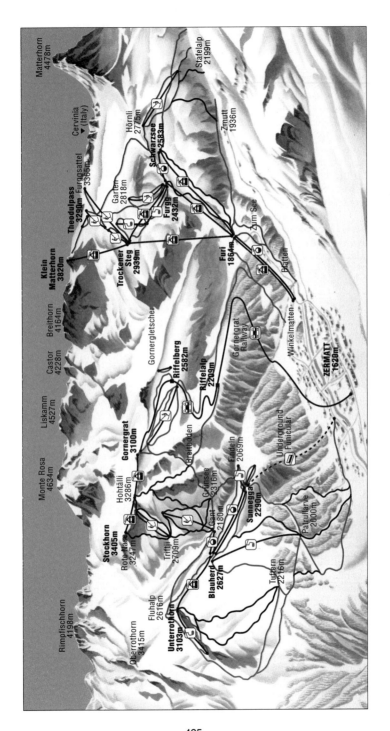

425

runs up to the Sunnegga sector, with sunny slopes continuing up to Blauherd and Rothorn, which are now connected by a new 150-person cable car. The Gornergrat mountain railway station, just across from the main railway terminus, is the start of a trip up past Riffelalp and Riffelberg to Gornergrat, from where cable cars go onwards to Hohtälli, Rote Nase and Stockhorn. At the Matterhorn edge of Zermatt a cable car and various gondolas head out to Furi. From there, lifts branch left for the Trockener Steg and Klein Matterhorn sectors and right for the Schwarzsee area, with Furgg straight up the middle. Among its impressive cable cars, Zermatt retains 18 antiquated drag-lifts.

It is possible, in theory, to ski all three Zermatt sectors in one day, and to ski from one to another in both directions, although not without some awkward sections and uphill walking. Surprisingly, the free lift inside the Klein Matterhorn station, which delivers sightseers to the summit view of a 360-degree panorama, is little visited.

Reporters complain of inconsistent piste-grading: 'some blue (easy) runs seemed more like red (intermediate) ones and yet the reds were very straightforward, especially on Trockener Steg'. After years of discussion by the town fathers and irritation for skiers, credit cards are now accepted as payment for lift passes.

Beginners

Zermatt's skiing cannot be recommended for beginners, but it offers a rare chance to ski at exceptionally high altitude. The ski school takes beginners to Blauherd, where the blue run, marked 2A on the piste-map, returns over flattering terrain to the Sunnegga lift station. But be careful not to turn right on to the National black (difficult) run. At Sunnegga, beginners have a short blue called Easy Run. Tuftern, although marked as a blue from Blauherd all the way down to Patrullarve, is actually quite tricky in parts. Gornergrat appears to offer more beginner terrain, but it is important to get off the train at Rotenboden, one stop earlier, to avoid a 'nasty bit' at the top. Guaranteed skiing on the glacier above 3000m is flat and easy on the blues alongside the Gandegg and Theodulpass drag-lifts, going over to Cervinia from Trockener Steg, as well as on the Plateau Rosa and Testa blues well above 3500m.

Intermediates

Zermatt's red runs often become more than ordinarily testing due to icy conditions and extreme overcrowding on narrow sections down to the village. The highest intermediate skiing, and the easiest, is up in the Klein Matterhorn and Trockener Steg sectors. From the Klein Matterhorn, the long KL red flows alongside blue-ice crevasses down past the Plateau Rosa T- bars to the Führer piste and over to the Testa T-bar.

Aggressive intermediates will be thrilled by the Kelle run from Gornergrat, passing over a 'scary' ridge to link up at Breitboden with the classic White Hare red, which begins with a narrow, challenging passage up at Hohtälli. Both reds proceed on terrain bordered by woods all the way to Furi, a good 30 minutes on skis without stopping.

Intermediate skiing on the Sunnegga-Blauherd sector is sunnier and smoother, resembling traditional 'ski to lunch' terrain. The Fluhalp red leads down to the Gant drag-lift, which gives access to the black runs back down from Rote Nase, but also links with the start of the red White Hare and the Furi sector.

Advanced

Triftji is one of the most famous black pistes in the Alps. Unfortunately, this and the other black runs down under the Hohtälli-Rote Nase sector require so much snow to make them skiable that they are often closed until mid-January. Together, the Stockhorn and Grieschumme blacks make an almost perfect fall-line descent from Rote

> ■ **WHAT'S NEW**
>
> 150-person cable car carrying 1,950 per hr replaces the old Blauherd to Rothorn cabin
> Direct Saturday trains from Paris to Brig
> Credit cards now accepted
> Children ski free until their 10th birthday; 10- to 15-year-olds half-price

Nase down to Gant, a bone-jarring bump bonanza only the most rubber-legged will achieve without stopping. Further afield, and invisible to spectators, is Zermatt's least crowded, best black-run skiing. Sloping sharply down from the Stafel-Hörnli drag-lift into the tree-line, Tiefbach and Momatt are steep runs, which dive towards Zmutt and the borders of the resort. Notorious as an accident black-spot as well as an expert run, the Furgg to Furi stretch is described by one reporter as being 'like the M25' in late afternoon, when it is the main homeward-bound route. But early in the morning, when Furgg-Furi has yet to be scraped clean of snow, it makes an excellent downhill course for the more advanced.

Off-piste

The Schwarzsee sector is cold and uncrowded. The Aroleid trail under the cable car is normally a bump run all the way to Furi. Less skied are the Garten gullies. From the top of the Furgg-Garten drag, and to the left of the Garten red run, the two Garten couloirs offer a choice of narrow chutes, very steep for the first 40m but less than life-threatening should you fall. At the bottom there is a favourite 'sky ramp' jump of about 20m, which has the attractions of a perfect landing and good views for spectators from the Garten lift. Down from Rothorn on the sunny side of the mountain, three itineraries (Chamois, Marmotte and Arbzug) become wide-open powder routes after a good storm.

Zermatt has been described as the biggest heli-skiing centre in the Alps. In fact, that honour goes to Lacadur Heliskiing in Valgrisenche in Italy, which has seven times the landing sites at one-third of the price of Air Zermatt's offering. That said, a day's excursion to **Monte Rosa** or Alphubeljoch above Zermatt is a popular way to escape the pistes.

Ski schools and guiding

Few ski schools have been so heavily criticised as the Swiss Ski School (SSS) here. Zermatt's 50-plus mountain guides also have a reputation, even among the Swiss, for aloof indifference. One explanation is that many guides and instructors work as a hobby, making their real living from local shops or hotels: 'Neither of the two instructors we experienced bothered to ask the names of the class members. Nor did many of the instructors show any respect for each other; on several occasions one ski class would cut straight through another.' Another reporter comments: 'The instructor seemed more concerned with getting a sun-tan than anything else'.

Ski classes are often overpopulated and somewhat chaotic, despite a pool of around 175 teachers: 'The instructor failed to make sufficient allowances for the weaker skiers, frequently skiing on far ahead and often going on again before the last members of the class had caught up', and 'The instructor started off on the first morning by heading down a steep powder-filled gully without any preliminary check on the standard of the class'. Another reporter notes: 'no, or very little, tuition is given'.

Snowboarding
The SSS has around 20 snowboard instructors. Julen Sports houses a Swiss Snowboard School called Stoked. There is a half-pipe in the Klein Matterhorn sector, but Zermatt is not overly adoring of the snowboard ethos.

Cross-country
The Furi-Schweigmatten trail is 7km long and a second 15-km loipe winds from Täsch to Randa. The ski school offers private lessons by the hour and three-day group courses.

Mountain restaurants
Lunching on a wooden terrace comes a close second to gazing at the Matterhorn as the main occupation in Zermatt. This is no place to pack a picnic. Not when old wooden barns like Chez Vrony provide crystal glasses, starched napkins, sofas on the terrace and intimate nooks and crannies for serious dining. The Findeln plateau also offers Chez Adler, which some reporters prefer to Vrony, perhaps because Max, the host, is so genial.

Enzian at Findeln is famous for its salmon dumplings, but should not be confused with the legendary Enzo's. In fact, Enzo has gone, the inn has been renamed the Findlerhof and is run by Heidy and Franz. 'It still has good food', was one laconic report.

The centuries-old hamlet of Zum See houses an inn of the same name, which has a rising reputation as Zermatt's best — try the curried noodles and king prawns here. Higher up in the Furi sector, Simi is the *Rösti* headquarters, but also serves delicious salads at reasonable prices. Tony's Grotta has delectable pasta. Fluhalp, at the top of Rothorn, has pancakes and the best panorama of the Matterhorn. The Gandeg Hütte is very popular: 'The restaurant was so full we ate outside in a blizzard, but they did provide rugs and the atmosphere was still amazing'.

Off the mountain

Zermatt was a settlement from the early Middle Ages, and inaugurated its first three tourist beds in 1838. Development has since been constrained by steep valley walls, leaving nothing between the Matterhorn and the village edge but open pasture dotted with wooden barns.

In Zermatt's much vaunted car-free lanes, sheep are still shorn outside centuries-old wooden mazots (ramshackle barns on stilts fitted with stone

> **■ OTHER SPORTS**
>
> Skating, curling, sleigh rides, swimming, tobogganing, winter walks

discs to keep rats at bay), but the conflux of electric taxis and horse-drawn carriages on the main thoroughfare is so frantic that radar traps have been installed.

There are a number of expensive jewellery and souvenir shops, but few of the chic boutiques one finds in Crans Montana or St Moritz. 'Expensive for food and wine, otherwise not too bad for ski gear, T-shirts and gifts', comments one reporter. Computers can be rented at Laser-Druck and software is obtainable at Easy-Hot, giving a measure of the type of clientèle in Zermatt.

Accommodation

Hotel-keepers rule in Zermatt (there are 113 of them), and chalet accommodation is minimal. It is important to choose a hotel close to where you want to ski and spend your evenings. For indulgent romantics nothing compares to the five-star experience of the venerable Zermatterhof, right in the village centre near the bronze sculpted marmots. The five-star Mont Cervin has fewer balconies, but has opened sumptuous apartments in a recently built annex. All have private saunas, whirlpools, fireplaces and large kitchens. The four-star Alex Schlosshotel Tenne is a mix of Byzantine and chalet-style architecture. The Monte Rosa, a favourite of Sir Winston Churchill and the base from which Edward Whymper, the Victorian mountaineer, set off to conquer the Matterhorn, exudes understated opulence. The chalet-style Malteserhaus has generously sized apartments.

Many reporters express satisfaction with the simple Bristol, which is renowned for its cuisine. Hotel Parnass, located close to the Sunnegga Express and with a bus-stop outside the door, is said to have 'a quiet and relaxed atmosphere — not wildly luxurious, but good value for money'. Hotel Bijou, two minutes' walk from the Klein Matterhorn lift, is praised as 'small and friendly with rooms even better than four-star; the food was a culinary delight each evening'.

Eating in and out

Zermatt's restaurants (there are more than 100) have a deservedly high reputation for quality and price. As elsewhere in the Alps, world-class cuisine is hard to find. Excepting menus at the Chinese restaurant next to the London Bar and the Fuji Japanese restaurant in the Hotel Albana, meat, cheese and potatoes prevail. Le Mazot is at the top of most lists for

Skiing facts: **Zermatt**

TOURIST OFFICE
Train Station Square (Bahnhofplatz), CH-3920 Zermatt, Valais
Tel 41 27 967 1181
Fax 41 27 967 1185

THE RESORT
By road Calais 1076km
By rail station in resort, or Visp 36km
By air Geneva 4 hrs, Zurich 5 hrs
Visitor beds 13,500
Transport ski bus SF2-3, also electric taxis and horse-drawn sleighs

THE SKIING
Linked or nearby resorts Cervinia (I), Grächen (n), Saas-Fee (n), Riederalp (n), Crans Montana (n)
Longest run Klein Matterhorn to Zermatt, 15km (red/black)
Number of lifts 73 with Cervinia
Total of trails/pistes Zermatt only 150km, 245km including Cervinia (5% beginner, 25% easy, 40% intermediate, 30% difficult)
Nursery slopes 3 nursery slopes
Summer skiing 25km of trails and 9 lifts on Klein Matterhorn Glacier
Snowmaking 19.5km covered

LIFT PASSES
Area pass SF292 for 6 days
Day pass SF60, or SF91 including Cervinia
Beginners no free lifts

Pensioners 25% reduction for men 65 yrs and over, and women 62 yrs and over
Credit cards accepted yes

SKI SCHOOLS
Adults SSS, SF215 for 6 days (4 hrs per day)
Private lessons SSS, SF270 per day (4 hrs)
Snowboarding SSS group lessons, SF125 for 3 half-days (2 hrs), private lessons, SF270 per day, Stoked Snowboard School, details on request
Cross-country SSS, details on request. Loipe 22km
Other courses off-piste, heli-skiing
Guiding companies Zermatt Mountain Guide Association

CHILDREN
Lift pass 50% reduction for 6-15 yrs, free for 5 yrs and under
Ski kindergarten SSS, 4-6 yrs, 1-3.15pm, SF150 for 6 afternoons
Ski school SSS, 6-12 yrs, SF255 for 6 days (4 hrs per day) including lunch
Non-ski kindergarten Kindergarten Hotel Nicoletta, 2-8 yrs, 9am-5pm, SF55 including lunch. Kinderclub Pumuckel at Hotel La Ginabelle, $2\frac{1}{2}$-6 yrs, 9am-5pm, SF90 per day including lunch

FOOD AND DRINK PRICES
Coffee SF3, glass of wine SF2.8, small beer SF3.50-4, dish of the day SF15-20

haute cuisine, although the Buffet Royal in the Zermatterhof Hotel is more sumptuous. American-style steaks are grilled at the Viktoria-Centre and Cheminée Steakhouse. Fish, even in fondue, is good at the Coquille Fischstube. Lamb, from the Julen's own flock (watch out for the sheepdog in the foyer) is excellent at the Schäferstübli. The Whymperstube in the Hotel Monte Rosa serves traditional fondue in a setting of Edwardian ambience.

Zermatt has around 15 grocery shops. Migros is the least expensive, followed by PAM; the Gastromatt has a good selection of food, as does La Source.

Après-ski

Elsie Bar, by the church, is expensive but irresistible for champagne and oysters after skiing or late at night. The Post Hotel complex caters for everybody: its Brown Cow snack bar boasts the best sandwiches in Europe, the Pink Elephant has a high standard of live jazz and Le Broken disco incites dancing on huge beer barrels until 3am. However, the Post's Boathouse wine bar, not to be confused with the Zermatt Yacht, Golf and Country Club, is a tiny haven of cocktail civilisation decorated like the inside of a sloop. For a whale of a time Moby Dick is open until late and has pool tables. The Alex Hotel's nightclub is sedate, but it is the only place where older folk and teens can dance to music that allows conversation. Grampi's Pub is a glass-fronted haunt with the cheapest beer in Zermatt. The North Wall is British-run, has excellent pizzas and shows ski videos: 'A worker's bar', says one patron. The Olympia Stübli, on the route down from Sunnegga, has live music into the early hours.

Childcare

The SSS takes children from four to six years old, but only in the afternoons as the school considers mornings too cold for teaching on Sunnegga. Often there are no more than two children per instructor, although up to six are accepted. Children aged six years and over can be enrolled in the ski school. At the Nicoletta Hotel, Seiler's Children's Paradise takes kids from two years old. Childminding, with optional ski lessons on a baby slope by the river, is available at the Kinderclub Pumuckel, at the Hotel La Ginabelle, for children from two years old.

Round-up

RESORTS COVERED Andermatt, Arosa, Flims, Lenzerheide-Valbella, Villars

Andermatt
top 2965m (9,725ft) bottom 1445m (4,740ft)

Andermatt is a retreat for a dedicated skiing minority. Its enormous off-piste opportunities and reputation for generous dumps of snow make it one of Switzerland's lesser-known little gems. It is situated at a major alpine crossroads on the route to the St Gotthard Pass into Italy and was once one of the busiest Swiss resorts. Now the high Urseren Valley, of which Andermatt is the main village, is underpassed by the Gotthard road and rail tunnels, making it a virtual dead-end in winter.

There are four ski areas along the sides of the Urseren Valley, between the Furka and Oberalp passes. The two main ones lie at either end of Andermatt; the two smaller and less popular areas lie to the south-west, above the villages of **Hospental** and **Realp**. Descents down the shaded face of Gemsstock, which has 800m of severe vertical and treacherous off-piste skiing in the bowl, should not be tackled without a guide; nor should some of the long off-piste alternatives in other direc-tions from the top-station.

Andermatt itself has cobbled streets and a traditional character, but is one of Switzerland's major centres for the training of alpine troops, and severe barrack buildings are a feature of the architecture. The heart of the old village receives little sun as it is hemmed in by mountains. There is not much traffic and no public transport. Accommodation is in a mix-ture of hotels and appealing old chalets.

TOURIST OFFICE
Tel 41 41 887 1454
Fax 41 41 887 0185

Arosa
top 2653m (8,702ft) bottom 1800m (5,904ft)

In 1883, ski-tourer Dr Otto Herwig-Hold stumbled across the tiny vil-lage of **Inner Arosa** high in the Swiss Graubunden. He climbed to the top of the 2512-m Hörnli, looked down at the village and its frozen lake and realised that it was the perfect site for his new tuberculosis sanato-rium. The hospital was built and, with its wide range of international patients, soon put Arosa on the alpine map. Today it remains one of the truly all-round ski resorts of the Alps.

Arosa's skiers are not here to bash the pistes from dawn until dusk. Instead, they are more in search of a rounded winter-sports experience.

The ski area consists of wide, sunny slopes mostly above the tree-line and covering the three peaks of Hörnli, Weisshorn and Bruggerhorn. It is well linked and although small with only 16 lifts, there is a total of 70km of piste. Much of this is made up of blue (easy) and red (intermediate) runs over hilly rather than mountainous terrain.

One of the only hazards of Arosa's skiing is the number of pedestrians and tobogganers on the piste. Non-skiers can buy hiking passes covering gondolas and some chair-lifts.

The lift system is modern and efficient, by Swiss standards. Main mountain access from **Obersee** is by chair- or drag-lift or two-stage cable car. Access from Inner Arosa is by gondola. This is not a resort for expert skiers, although it does have some off-piste; the top of the Hörnli is the starting point for a variety of tours involving skins and public transport to neighbouring resorts. The more difficult piste-skiing is reached from the top of the 2653-m Weisshorn, a treacherous black (difficult) run that brings you down to the Carmennahütte, which is the best of half-a-dozen mountain restaurants.

Access to the village is not easy, with 244 bends in the 32-km dramatic road from the busy medieval valley town of Chur. Taking the train through stunning scenery is a much better option. Once in the village, the toboggan is an essential form of transport.

TOURIST OFFICE
Tel 41 81 377 1621
Fax 41 81 377 3135

Flims
top 2980m (9,774ft) bottom 1080m (3,542ft)
This year-round destination lies on the road from Chur to Andermatt. Together with its neighbours, **Laax** and **Falera**, it serves the wide south-facing ski area known as the White Arena. Flims itself consists of bustling **Dorf** and tranquil, forested **Waldhaus**.

Dorf is the livelier and more convenient place to stay. The hotels in Waldhaus are not within easy walking distance of the lifts, but the larger ones have a courtesy mini-bus service to the Dorf base-station. The pleasant old village of Laax is 5km to the west, with a modern satellite base-station at **Murschetg** and low-cost, on-mountain accommodation at Crap Sogn Gion. The farming hamlet of Falera provides a rustic alternative.

Waldhaus has a nursery area, as well as gentle practice slopes near the base-stations and higher up the mountain. There is no shortage of confidence-building motorways and any competent intermediate has the run of the whole mountain. The longest black run is the FIS downhill from Crap Sogn Gion to Murschetg. The off-piste potential is unexpectedly high with tree-level runs above Laax.

In Flims, the choice of tuition is between the Swiss Ski School (SSS) and the Swissraft Ski School. The Swiss Snowboard School (a subsidiary of the SSS) and Swissraft give snowboarding lessons and there is a half-pipe at Crap Sogn Gion. Flims has extensive langlauf trails along the valley floor, including a 3-km loipe which is floodlit for night-skiing.

The best mountain restaurants in the area are at the lower levels to attract customers all year round. This means that they are not on the skiing trails, though the Runca hut below Startgels and the Tegia at Larnags are well worth the detour. Among the higher alternatives, the Segnes-Hütte is welcoming, the Foppa is an old wooden chalet with a sun-terrace, and Nagens has a huge choice of dishes. The Elephant restaurant at Crap Masegn has excellent food.

There is a wide choice of accommodation from the five-star Parkhotel Waldhaus, which offers opulent rooms in five buildings, to the well-run two-star Encarna in Falera. Hotel Adula is praised for its food and child facilities. The top choice in Laax is the Posta Veglia. Recommended restaurants include Pizzeria Pomodoro, the Barga in Hotel Adula, La Cena in the Waldhaus and the fish restaurant in the National.

The all-glass Iglu Bar opposite the Dorf base-station is the height of Flims chic for après-ski drinks. Later on the action focuses on the MacGeorge Pub in the Albana and the quieter Segnes Bar. In Flims Waldhaus, Rock Fabrik attracts teenage snowboarders.

The SSS has classes for children from four years of age and upwards, and we have excellent reports of the ski kindergarten. The Swissraft Ski School offers skiing in its Husky-Land centre. Both the Parkhotel Waldhaus and the Hotel Adula have crèches.

TOURIST OFFICE
Tel 41 81 920 9200
Fax 41 81 920 9201

Lenzerheide-Valbella
top 2865m (9,397ft) bottom 1500m (4,920ft)

These two resorts used to attract a fair number of British families but in recent years they have decreased in popularity. The area has considerable charm, including magnificent cross-country skiing, but alpine skiers may find the terrain limited with a distinct lack of variety.

The villages of **Lenzerheide** and **Valbella** lie at either end of a lake in a wide, wooded pass with high mountains on either side. 'Transport is based on a very efficient system of buses travelling clockwise and anti-clockwise', was one report. 'Jump on the bus going in the wrong direction and you still arrive at your destination' was another.

The main street of Lenzerheide has some attractive old buildings. Valbella has less identity; it is no more than a large community of hotels and concrete-box holiday homes crammed on to a hillside, but it is less of a roadside strip and gives direct access to the western ski area.

The skiing is in two separate areas, Rothorn and Danis/Stätzerhorn, on either side of the inconveniently wide pass. Both have about half woodland and half open-skiing terrain. There are no particularly difficult pistes, although the Rothorn cable car opens up some off-piste skiing.

TOURIST OFFICE
Tel 41 81 384 34 34
Fax 41 81 384 53 83

Villars/Les Diablerets
top 2979m (9,744ft) bottom 1128m (3,700ft)

Villars, situated on a sunny balcony above the Ollon Valley, is reached either by a winding road or a quaint Edwardian mountain railway. It has a strong international following as a quiet, family resort. Its impressive intermediate skiing is linked directly by a new quad-chair to the neighbouring glacial resort of Les Diablerets. Together, the two areas provide 200km of piste served by 45 lifts. The glacier provides high-altitude, snowsure skiing but can get crowded when conditions are poor in Villars and nearby Gstaad.

The quickest access to the hub of the skiing is via a gondola from the edge of town. A second gondola from the nearby village of Barboleusaz also feeds into the system. The nursery slope at Bretaye is gentle, and after a few days first-timers can graduate to a wide choice of blue runs. Les Diablerets' separate ski area, Isenau, has easy but limited skiing.

The Swiss Ski School (ESS) in Villars is well spoken of and has friendly instructors. The Modern Ski School uses the ski évolutif method of teaching beginners and also teaches snowboarding and parapente. Two snowboard fun-parks were opened last season.

The Villars ESS children's classes are praised by reporters and the Pré Fleurie ski kindergarten is said to be 'quite excellent'. Les Diablerets ESS runs Club Pinocchio at the Hotel des Sources for children from three years of age.

The Lac des Chavonnes, above Villars, is one of the great alpine restaurants, tucked away in a delightful lakeside setting, and the Buffet Col de Soud is an attractive chalet with superb views of Les Diablerets Glacier. The Refuge de la Rasse, also known as Chez Mic's, is a rustic mountain eating-place.

In the centre of Villars, Hotel Bristol has a comfortable and modern interior. Hotel du Cerf is family run with 'home-style cooking'. The three-star Hotel du Golf opposite the station is strongly recommended. The Eurotel, Le Chamois and the Mon Abri hotels are recommended.

Dining in Villars varies between a few fine restaurants and some informal Stüblis. Vieux Villars and Café Carnotzet specialise in fondue and raclette. Le Mazarin in the Grand Hotel du Parc is the smartest establishment in town. In Les Diablerets, the Auberge de la Poste and the Buvette du Pillon are praised. The nightlife in both resorts is quiet and centred around a few bars.

TOURIST OFFICES
Tel Villars 41 25 353232/Les Diablerets 41 25 531358
Fax Villars 41 25 352794/Les Diablerets 41 25 532348

North America

What started as a trickle has developed into a flood over the past five years. More and more Europeans are crossing the Atlantic to experience the slopes of North America. We are frequently told by readers how even the most famous Alpine resorts fail to measure up to the expectations they now have after skiing, the United States and Canada.

The invasion has been led by both price and service. The poor standing of sterling has pushed up the price of skiing in the main Alpine countries to an often unacceptable level. The cost of a holiday in Canada or the US no longer compares unfavourably. However, it is important to note that, with the exception of chalet holidays, most packages to North America are offered on a room-only basis, and the extra cost of food, plus a more expensive lift pass, must be taken into consideration.

The first point to strike the European visitor is the small size of the average North American ski area; a dozen lifts constitute a large resort. The second, with few exceptions, is that the infrastructure of each North American resort is owned and operated by a single company. The result is a co-ordinated policy of keeping customers happy.

The skiing (except for resorts like Jackson Hole) is blander in North America (some would say homogenised) and nearly always consists of man-made trails cut through wooded slopes, their exotic names belying the similarity of those graded the same colour. However, such is the structured layout of most ski areas that families or groups of different standards can ski together, with individuals choosing trails of varying gradients, all of which end at the same lift station.

It is important to note that Americans operate a different form of piste colour-coding: green is easy, blue is intermediate, black or black-diamond is difficult, and double-black-diamond is very difficult. The standard of piste-grooming and trail-marking, fuelled by the threat of skier litigation, is outstanding.

Off-piste, in the European sense, does not really exist. While a few major resorts permit vast tracts of mountainside to be left untouched by machine, leaving the designated ski area is absolutely forbidden, and if you do so you face forfeiting your lift pass — or even arrest. However, Canada has superb heli-skiing both in the region around recognized resorts and from purpose-built lodges in the Bugaboo, Cariboo and Monashee mountain ranges.

Accommodation in both hotels and condominiums bares no comparison with the Alps. Anyone who has ever experienced the confines of an Avoriaz apartment for six will be delighted to discover that the entire French unit would probably fit in the bedroom of its US or Canadian counterpart.

It is an indictment of European skiing that the overall packaging of a winter holiday in North America is considered by many to offer greater value for money as well as being, quite simply, more enjoyable.

Aspen

ALTITUDE 7,945ft (2422m)

Many factors helped shape North America's most famous and fashionable ski resort, but among the most important was the role played by European skiing enthusiasts and the influence of the 10th Mountain Division, Colorado's militiamen on skis. The input of both was combined with the original Aspen infrastructure that dated from the early silver-mining days. The brave and sometimes desperate miners, who defied vicious weather and marauding Ute Indians to set up a rickety camp in the Roaring Fork Valley in the late 1870s (Ute City), would have been staggered to see how their improvised hovels eventually gave way to America's smartest ski town.

The miners struck it rich. During the boom years, Aspen's population reached 12,000 and was served by two railroads, six newspapers, three schools, ten churches and a notorious red-light district. But by 1893 it was all over; the silver market collapsed, and the town virtually died. It did not start to recover for almost 50 years.

The forces of change were generated some 5,000 miles away in Europe. During the 1936 Winter Olympics at Garmisch-Partenkirchen, Theodore Ryan, a wealthy American, compared notes with the bobsleigh champion William Fiske III about the need for good ski resorts in America. The following summer they were approached by an Aspen mine-owner who was convinced that the snowfields of his home town would make an ideal setting for their plans. He was right. Fiske and Ryan encouraged other investors to help them develop the resort.

■ GOOD POINTS
Wide choice of skiing for all standards, excellent children's facilities, fascinating Victorian town with large choice of restaurants, ideal for non-skiers, eclectic nightlife

■ BAD POINTS
No link between four mountains, no nursery slopes on Aspen Mountain, expensive lift ticket

On the mountain
Aspen top 11,212ft (3418m) bottom 7,945ft (2422m)
Snowmass top 12,310ft (3750m) bottom 8,223ft (2507m)
Aspen Highlands top 11,675ft (3559m) bottom 8,040ft (2451m)
Buttermilk top 9,900ft (3018m) bottom 7,870ft (2399m)
Aspen has four completely separate mountains: **Aspen Mountain**, which is also known as Ajax, a name taken from an old mining claim; **Aspen Highlands**; **Buttermilk**; and **Snowmass**, 12 miles (19km) out of town. They are linked by a free bus service.

Aspen Mountain is strictly the reserve of good skiers and has no beginner slopes. Anyone less than a strong intermediate will struggle to cope with the home-run gradient here, although there are less demanding trails. Buttermilk is ideal beginner and child terrain with no hidden surprises but plenty of variety for novices. Snowmass, which has skiing for all levels, is the furthest of the separate ski areas from Aspen and is a resort in its own right under the same ownership. Aspen Highlands, the newest acquisition, has the toughest, most radical terrain and has greatly added to Aspen's appeal for expert skiers.

Beginners

Buttermilk is one of North America's best mountains for beginners, and Snowmass also has excellent novice slopes. The area below Buttermilk's West Summit is packed with green (easy) runs like Westward Ho and Homestead Road, and more advanced beginners will thrive on a large network of long blue (intermediate) runs with an impressive vertical drop of more than 1,800ft. The nursery slopes at Snowmass hug the lower slopes, and most are accessed by the Fanny Hill high-speed quad. At Aspen Highlands the main nursery slopes, such as Apple Strudel, Riverside Drive and Nugget, are concentrated mid-mountain and reached most quickly by the Exhibition quad-chair. The Skiwee lift at the base also serves a small beginner area.

Intermediates

Of Aspen's four mountains, Snowmass has the largest intermediate appeal. Almost every run mid-mountain and below provides good cruising, and the region below Elk Camp at the far perimeter of the ski area (with runs like Bull Run, Grey Wolf and Bear Bottom) is another popular intermediate haunt. Snowmass is famous for its Big Burn area, where a clutch of blue trails separated by a few trees provide almost unlimited scope for cruising.

There is plenty of intermediate skiing with top-to-bottom cruising on Ajax. Straying on to more difficult terrain by mistake is less likely here than at many resorts; most of the black (difficult) runs tend to be hidden away from the main slopes. The best area for middling skiers at Highlands is near the top of the mountain where the Cloud Nine lift accesses runs such as Scarlett's, Grand Prix and Gunbarrel. Golden Horn and Thunderbowl offer enjoyable cruising. All of Buttermilk is suitable for intermediates, but the lack of challenging runs means that stronger skiers will become bored quickly.

Advanced

Aspen Mountain is riddled with short, sharp and quite steep double-black-diamond (very difficult) chutes, including the famous 'dump runs' like Bear Paw, Short Snort and Zaugg Dump, which were created by miners throwing out spoil as they were tunnelling their way into Aspen Mountain. Walsh's is considered the most challenging. Bell Mountain, a peak that juts out from Ajax, looking as if it has been stuck on, provides excellent opportunities for mogul skiers with its variety of individual

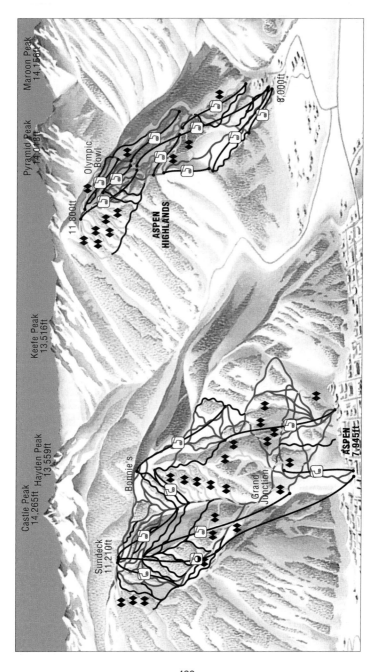

Maroon Peak 14,156ft

Pyramid Peak 14,018ft

Keefe Peak 13,516ft

Castle Peak 14,265ft

Hayden Peak 13,559ft

Olympic Bowl

11,800ft

8,000ft

ASPEN HIGHLANDS

Bonnie's

Sundeck 11,210ft

Grand Junction

ASPEN 7,945ft

faces, including Face of Bell, Shoulder of Bell and Back of Bell.

Much of the skiing at Aspen Highlands falls into the advanced category. There is a large and challenging gladed area to the left of the Exhibition quad-chair, including Bob's Glade, Upper Stein and Golden Horn Woods, which are all double-black-diamond trails. At Snowmass, real challenges are to be found in the largely gladed chutes in the Hanging Valley Wall and Hanging Valley Glades, and The Cirque has even steeper terrain mainly above the tree-line; access to these runs involves a short hike.

Off-piste

Aspen Highlands has some of the most exhilarating off-piste terrain in the valley, much of it accessed by the Lodge Peak quad-chair at the top of the ski area. The chair follows a ridge with steep terrain on both sides. As you ride up, a dramatic area known as Steeplechase opens up on your left; this comprises about half a dozen steep chutes. On your right there is even steeper terrain in Olympic Bowl, although the gradient is not always fully appreciable until you have progressed some way down the slopes. Deception, in particular, is aptly named; it starts off at a fairly moderate pitch, but the further down you ski, the steeper it becomes. There is some good snowcat skiing off the back of Aspen Mountain.

Ski schools and guiding

As well as traditional lessons, the Aspen Ski School offers Discover Aspen and Snowmass, and Master The Mountains courses, which are multi-day ski school weeks that include accommodation, lift tickets and lessons.

Aspen Highlands offers the gradulated-length method (GLM), which is similar to the French *ski évolutif* instruction, as well as race and telemark clinics and extreme terrain lessons. Snowmass Ski School offers special bumps, powder, telemark and racing programmes. At Buttermilk it is claimed: 'We guarantee you will be able to ski from the top to the bottom by the third day!'

Snowboarding

Snowboarding is not permitted at Aspen Mountain, but the other three mountains encourage it. First Time on Snowboard lessons are available at Aspen Highlands, and Snowmass has special snowboard clinics.

Cross-country

A 65-km track begins at the Snowmass Club Touring Center. The club organises rentals, lessons and tours. Daily group lessons start at 10.30am, and on Tuesdays and Thursdays at 1pm there is an introduction to skating.

Mountain restaurants

There is a large, busy restaurant at the Sundeck on top of Aspen Mountain, where non-skiers can join skiing friends. Bonnie's, a little way

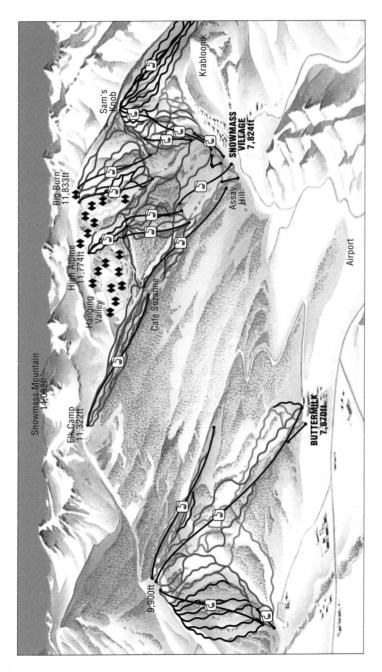

down the mountain just off to the side of the top section of Ruthie's, is smaller and more intimate and prides itself on its *Strudel* and hot apple dumplings. La Bàita, at the bottom of Ruthie's and Roch Run, is the old Ruthie's Restaurant, which has been considerably revamped to include a separate wait-service restaurant specialising in Italian food. At the base of the Silver Queen gondola is the Ajax Tavern (formerly Shlomo's), which serves Mediterranean food. At Snowmass, Up 4 Pizza (home-made) is at the top of the Big Burn lift, and Ullrhof (hearty skiers' break-fast, wood-burning stove and sun-deck) is at the bottom. Gwyn's/High Alpine at the top of the Alpine Springs quad is for skiers wanting some-thing more leisurely and sophisticated. The Café Suzanne, at the bottom of the Elk Camp lift, features a southern French menu, and Krabloonik, near the Campground parking lot, specialises in smoked meats and wild game. At Aspen Highlands, the Merry Go Round Restaurant at mid-mountain offers home-made soups, chilli and burgers.

There are three mountain restaurants at Buttermilk: the Café West near the bottom of Lift 3, which is designed in the style of a French café; Bump's, at the base, includes a rôtisserie and grill; the Cliffhouse, at the top of the Summit Express, has food indoors and outdoors along with some of the best scenery on the mountain.

Off the mountain

Skiers making their first visit to Aspen will have heard about the glitz and glamour of this celebrated resort and may be a little over-awed by the prospect: in reality, Aspen is a cheerful, friendly place with a variety of ski-ing, and is an attractive old town with plenty to do in the evenings. You might well bump into the odd celebrity, but Aspen is certainly not teem-ing with them as some tabloid newspapers like to suggest. And while it might be a little more expensive than the average Rocky Mountain resort, it is still possible to have a moderately priced ski holiday.

Accommodation

In Aspen, skiers who can afford to live like celebrities should try the Little Nell and the Ritz Carlton, although many people's favourite is the his-toric Hotel Jerome. For those on limited budgets there are numerous modestly priced lodges such as the Limelite, the Alpine and the Christiania. The Christmas Inn, the Snow Queen and the Innsbruck Inn are all recommended. The Aspen Bed and Breakfast is a little more expensive but is also praised.

Accommodation at **Snowmass** tends to be a little cheaper than in the town of Aspen. Many of the lodges are ski-in ski-out. Top-of-the-range accommodation includes the Silvertree, the Snowmass Lodge and Club, the Chamonix and Crestwood. More reasonably priced are the Mountain Chalet, the Stonebridge Inn and Shadowbrooks. For those counting their cents, the Pokolodi Lodge and the Snowmass Inn are both close to the slopes, as are the Aspenwood and Laurelwood condo-miniums.

Eating in and out

Aspen has a huge variety of restaurants, with almost every type of cuisine imaginable. Bentley's is a Victorian-style pub and restaurant at the Wheeler Opera House featuring American food and a selection of 35 beers from around the world. The Jerome provides excellent fare at its Century Room. The Chart House on East Durant is well known for steaks and seafood. Little Annie's (East Hyman Avenue) has an all-American menu and calls itself 'Aspen's neighbourhood restaurant'. Pinons, which achieved an 'Extraordinary to Perfection' rating in a recent US food

> ### ■ OTHER SPORTS
> Skating, curling, indoor tennis, squash, swimming, sleigh rides, tobogganing, rifle shooting, parapente, snow-shoeing

survey, is one of Aspen's most exclusive restaurants, with prices to match. *Entrées* (as they call the main course in America) include Colorado pheasant breast with *foie gras*.

Farfalla's, on East Main Street, is another fashionable restaurant, which specialises in Italian cuisine. Poppies Bistro Café has 'rustic Victorian charm', while the Red Onion on East Cooper, which is more than a century old, serves food at more modest prices. Aspen has four Japanese restaurants plus a Japanese take-away (Sushi Ya Go-Go). The Takah Sushi is highly recommended. The Hard Rock Café and Planet Hollywood chains both have restaurants here.

Après-ski

Aspen has wall-to-wall après-ski in dozens of nightspots. The Jerome Bar (better known as the J-Bar), where miners once congregated to celebrate when they struck silver, is always lively. The sun-deck at the Ajax Tavern attracts the crowds at the bottom of Ajax when the lifts close. Shooters is a country-and-western saloon with live bands. The Howling Wolf is a late-night coffee bar. Legends of Aspen is a bar featuring memorabilia from prominent local sportsmen and women. The Caribou Club is a smart members-only establishment.

Childcare

Aspen has an in-town nursery service and a nursery ski-school programme in each resort. At Snowmass, Snow Cubs caters for children between 18 months and 3 years. Older children can join the Big Burn Bears. Snowmass also runs a series of Kids Ski Weeks. The Powder Pandas Ski School is at Buttermilk. Parents register their children at Aspen Mountain, and the Max the Moose Express brings them to Buttermilk, where they can take part in The Brave Good Eagle Great Feather Chase and the Max the Moose Challenge race.

Skiing facts: **Aspen**

TOURIST OFFICE
425 Rio Grande Place, Aspen, CO 81611
Tel 1 970 925 1940
Fax 1 970 920 1173

THE RESORT
By air Eagle County 75 mins, Aspen 10 mins
Visitor beds 16,000 in area
Transport shuttle-bus between all 4
mountains (free in daytime, small charge
in evening)

THE SKIING
Linked or nearby resorts Snowmass (n)
Longest run Big Burn to Fanny Hill at
Snowmass, 4.1 miles (7km) - blue
Number of lifts 40 in area
Total of trails/pistes 4,225 acres (1709
hectares) - 12% easy, 46% intermediate,
21% difficult, 21% expert
Nursery slopes 3 slopes and 4 beginner
lifts
Summer skiing none
Snowmaking 483 acres (195 hectares)
covered

LIFT PASSES
Area pass (covers all 4 mountains) $228-
260 for 6 days. Aspen-Vail Premier
Passport gives 1 day's free skiing in Vail
Day pass $52
Beginners no reduction
Pensioners 65-69 yrs, $192 for 6 days,
free for 70 yrs and over
Credit cards accepted yes

SKI SCHOOLS
Adults ski schools at Aspen Mountain,
Aspen Highlands, Buttermilk and
Snowmass: Levels 1-4, 10.15am-3.15pm,

$55 per day; Levels 5-10, 9.30am-3.30pm,
$310 for 4 days. Semi-private
(groups limited to four) $135 per day
Private lessons $145 for 1½ hrs
Snowboarding as regular ski lessons
Cross-country Snowmass Club
Touring Center, 10.30am, $30 per day.
Private lessons $45 per hr.
Loipe 80km
Other courses Nastar racing, moguls,
off-piste, telemark, dynamic stunts,
ski-touring, women's seminars
Guiding companies Aspen Mountain
Powder Tours

CHILDREN
Lift pass 7-12 yrs, $162 for 6 days, free
for 6 yrs and under
Ski kindergarten Snow Puppies at
Highlands, 3½-6 yrs, 9.30am-3.30pm,
$330 for 5 days including lunch. Powder
Pandas at Buttermilk, 3-6 yrs, 8.30am-
4pm, $350 for 5 days including lunch. Big
Burn Bears at Snowmass, 4 yrs and over,
8.30am-4pm, $350 for 5 days including
lunch
Ski school Aspen Mountain, Highlands,
Snowmass and Buttermilk, 12 yrs and
under, Levels 1-4, 10.15am-3.15pm, $140
for 3 days. Semi-private (groups restricted
to 4), Levels 5-10, 10.15am-3.15pm, $345
for 3 days
Non-ski kindergarten Kid's Club at Aspen,
12 mths-3 yrs, $315 for 40 hrs, Snow Cubs
at Snowmass, 18 mths-3 yrs, 8.30am-4pm,
$350 for 5 days including lunch

FOOD AND DRINK PRICES
Coffee $2, glass of wine $4, small beer $2,
dish of the day $10-15

Banff/Lake Louise

ALTITUDE 5,350ft (1631m)

This is a singularly beautiful and wide-ranging ski area, which is made up of three resorts – **Banff/Lake Louise**, **Mount Norquay** and **Sunshine Village** – that have nothing much to do with each other except in the minds of marketing people. Lake Louise, by far the most important, is in fact 34 miles (58km) from Banff and its local resort of Mount Norquay. It is also 24 miles (39km) from the quite separate destination of **Sunshine Village**. A free and rather slow bus service links the resorts but a rental car is a highly useful extra.

Lake Louise could hardly be set in a more breathtaking location. The backdrop to the slopes is formed by some of the finest peaks in the Canadian Rockies. They also make up the cornerstone of Banff National Park, which has more than 4,000 square miles of mountains, lakes, rivers, canyons and forests.

■ **GOOD POINTS**

Spectacular scenery, good snow record, long skiing season, ideal for mixed-ability groups, extensive children's facilities

■ **BAD POINTS**

Strung-out resorts, low temperatures, lack of accommodation near the slopes

On the mountain
top 8,954ft (2730m) bottom 5,350ft (1631m)

Because of the distances involved, there is little point in attempting to ski more than one area in a day. Lake Louise itself is the furthest from Banff, but easily the most varied ski area. From the Mount Whitehorn base at Whiskeyjack Lodge, the choice of three chairs includes the Friendly Giant Express quad, which takes skiers to mid-mountain at Whitehorn Lodge. From here the Top of The World Express is another high-speed quad, providing the fastest way up and over to the Back Bowls or down to Mount Lipalian's Larch area. The four faces of Whitehorn and Lipalian share some 4,000 acres (1,619 hectares) of terrain, which genuinely caters for every grade of skier.

Sunshine Village is the highest of the three resorts and has predominantly medium-length, moderately steep, intermediate terrain above the tree-line. Despite its name, sunshine is not guaranteed and it can be a bleak and cold place on a grey day. Goat's Eye Mountain at Sunshine opened last year and has doubled the size of the ski area. Mount Norquay is four miles (6km) from Banff and used to offer both very easy and very steep skiing, with nothing in between. It includes Mystic Ridge, a primarily intermediate area opened in 1990 to give the resort a broader appeal.

Beginners

Because of Lake Louise's policy of ensuring an easy way down from each major lift, novices can share the pleasure of roaming almost at will among the intermediates. Although riding high-speed quads could seem daunting in other resorts, here you can board them confidently and meander down the green (easy) Saddleback and Pika trails to the Larch chair. This leads to runs like Marmot and Look-out before returning to the main base via Eagle Meadows. If this feels too adventurous, you can warm up on the Sunny T-bar and try skiing the long but gentle Wiwaxy trail.

Beginners at Norquay are recommended to ski the runs off the Cascade chair or the Sundance tow. Sunshine has an easy run from the top of Lookout Mountain. There is also some gentle skiing around the Strawberry triple-chair and the new quad-chair, which recently replaced the Assiniboine T-bar.

Intermediates

At Lake Louise, intermediates can clock up huge mileage over all the terrain, with the possible exception of some of the steeper bowls. Meadowlark, one of the longest runs on the mountain, is an excellent blue (intermediate) cruising trail. Stronger skiers will want to sample the black-diamond (difficult) Ridge Run and Whitehorn One on the Back Bowls side. Most of the runs at Sunshine are within the grasp of intermediates. Nearly all of the 12 new runs at Mystic Ridge were specifically created for recreational skiers of medium experience.

Advanced

At Lake Louise, the Front Face has good men's and women's downhill runs. Other tough black-diamond runs including Outer Limits, Sunset and Flight Chutes, start higher up. Ptarmigan and Raven are testing glade runs on the Back Bowls side, and Exhibition has the additional challenge of exposing skiers to the gaze of people riding the Ptarmigan chair. Lynx is the one advanced trail (the others are off-piste) in the Larch area. Lone Pine, which is fiercely steep and mogulled, is the big challenge at Norquay. At Sunshine, runs like Little Angel, Ecstasy and Big Angel offer steep chute skiing from the top of Lookout Mountain. Goat's Eye Mountain at Sunshine offers additional glade-skiing.

Off-piste

Large areas of the Back Bowls at Lake Louise are permanently closed because of avalanche danger. These are well marked, but sometimes bowls that are normally skiable can be closed too. Paradise Bowl and East Bowl provide challenging off-piste skiing. Serious powder skiers who do not mind a hike claim Purple Bowl provides the best fresh tracks on the

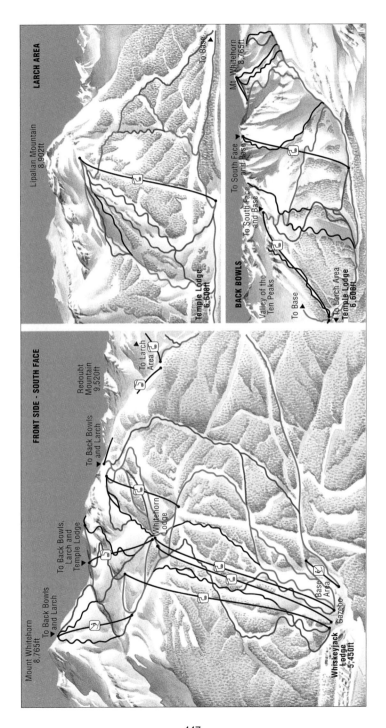

LARCH AREA

Lipalian Mountain
8,902ft

Mt. Whitehorn
8,765ft

Temple Lodge
6,608ft

To Base

BACK BOWLS

To South Face
and Base

To South Face
and Base

Valley of the
Ten Peaks

To Base

To Larch Area
Temple Lodge
6,608ft

FRONT SIDE - SOUTH FACE

Mount Whitehorn
8,765ft

To Back Bowls
and Larch

To Back Bowls,
Larch and
Temple Lodge

To Back Bowls
and Larch

Redoubt
Mountain
9,520ft

To Larch
Area

Whitehorn
Lodge

Base
Area

Gazebo

Whiskeyjack
Lodge
5,450ft

mountain. Some of the most rewarding tree-level skiing can be found between the upper parts of the Larch chair and the Bobcat run below.

Ski schools and guiding

Lake Louise offers a special package for beginners, which includes equipment rental, a beginner area lift ticket and a half-price ticket valid for all areas for the following day, as well as a ski lesson. Instruction at Sunshine is said to be 'friendly and positive'. The Club Ski Program enables skiers to stay with one instructor for four hours a day, visiting all three areas. All the resorts offer a free piste-guiding service and Yamnuska Mountain Ski School organises guided off-piste skiing.

Snowboarding

There are virtually no limits to where snowboarders can go, except at Mount Norquay. Although Norquay hosted the North American Snowboarding Championships in 1988, boarders are not allowed to use the North American chair.

Mountain restaurants

Whiskeyjack at the main base is the location for the Northface Restaurant, a popular après-ski haunt. One reader recommends taking the free bus down to Chateau Lake Louise ('a longer lunch break but the deli is great value'). Other eating-places include the Sitzmark ('an excellent watering-hole'), and Sawyer's Nook at the Temple Lodge.

Norquay's Cascade Lodge has three restaurants, including the Lone Pine, and a cafeteria. The Eagle's Nest at Sunshine Inn, Trapper Bill's and the Day Lodge Cafeteria are all recommended.

Off the mountain

Banff is a small, attractive community with a frontier-town atmosphere, just 10 miles (16km) inside Banff National Park. Apart from the breathtaking scenery, the town is famous for its railway history and the wildlife. It is quite common to see elk grazing on vegetation protruding through the snow or even rummaging through dustbins. Bighorn sheep can also be spotted. For humans, there is a wide variety of shopping and dining opportunities.

After Canadian Pacific Railways started bringing tourists here to marvel at the scenery after the park opened in 1885, two neo-Gothic railway hotels were established. The first, the Banff Springs, was completed in 1888. Two years later the magnificent Chateau Lake Louise opened its doors, and today remains the country's most celebrated hotel. This towering fairytale castle is almost cut off from the rest of the world by a magical lake and glaciers on one side, and lush pine forests on the other.

Accommodation

Unfortunately, not everyone has the budget to stay at the two Canadian Pacific hotels. However, there is plenty of choice elsewhere, with almost

40 hotels and lodges in Banff itself, and four more at Lake Louise Village. In Banff, the Mount Royal is conveniently located in the right part of Banff Avenue ('very important not to have to walk far with a temperature of -27°C'). Charlton's Cedar Court is 'brilliant, but a 20- to 25-minute walk from the town centre'. Caribou Lodge is also recommended, along with the Inns of Banff. Bed-and-breakfast establishments and back-country lodges make up the rest of the accommodation. Norquay has no lodging of its own and the only on-mountain accommodation at Sunshine is the Sunshine Inn.

Eating in and out

Banff has a surprisingly wide range of restaurants serving cuisine from at least a dozen countries. 'If you haven't been to Bumper's, you haven't been to Banff' is the motto of Bumper's Beef House. Joe Btfsplk's Diner looks like a misprint but serves 'meals like Mom used to make', including apple-pie. There are five Japanese restaurants, as well as Cantonese and Korean establishments. El Toro is a Greek restaurant despite its Spanish-sounding name; similarly, the Magpie and Stump is not an English pub but a Mexican cantina. Guido's Spaghetti Factory is long-established and 'has good-value Italian food at reasonable prices, so don't be put off by the tatty entrance'. The Barbary Coast has 'plenty of atmosphere and a wide range of dishes including vegetarian options'. Melissa's serves fish steaks and 'potent home-brewed ale'.

At Lake Louise Station you dine in vintage railway carriages. Frankie's Pizza and Pasta provides a 'cheap and cheerful alternative'.

Après-ski

One reader described Banff's nightlife as 'refreshingly unsophisticated, plenty of cowboy bars and line dancing'. You can dine and dance at the Rob Roy Room at the Banff Springs Hotel, or at the Edelweiss or Victoria Dining Room at Chateau Lake Louise. Alternatively, let your hair down at various establishments with live music on Banff Avenue: there is rock 'n' roll at Eddy's Back Alley, country-rock at Wild Bill's, blues at The Barbary Coast, live entertainment at Bumper's, and live bands at the Silver City Beverage Co. The Caboose Restaurant at the Railway Depot has karaoke. The Rose and Crown is one of Banff's most popular bars.

> **■ OTHER SPORTS**
>
> Snowmobiling, swimming, dog-sledding, sleigh rides, skating, broomball, snow volleyball, ice-fishing

At Chateau Lake Louise there is dancing until 1am in the Glacier Saloon, and in Charlie II's Pub in the Lake Louise Inn until 2am.

Childcare

At Lake Louise, Chocolate Moose Park organises ski and play programmes for children up to 12 years of age. The Kinderski programme is geared for three- to six-year-olds. There is also a Kids Ski programme where children are guided round the mountain with instruction along the

Skiing facts: **Banff/Lake Louise**

TOURIST OFFICE
Ski Banff/Lake Louise
PO Box 1085, Banff, Alberta
Tel 1 403 762 4561
Fax 1 403 762 8185

THE RESORT
By rail none
By air Calgary Airport $1\frac{1}{2}$ hrs
Visitor beds Banff 9,920,
Lake Louise 2,400
Transport ski buses from hotels to all
3 ski areas

THE SKIING
Linked or nearby resorts Sunshine Village
(n), Mount Norquay (n)
Longest run Lake Louise, 5 miles
(8km) - blue
Number of lifts 11 in Lake Louise, 12 in
Sunshine Village, 5 in Mount Norquay
Total of trails/pistes 62 miles (100km) in
Lake Louise, 43 miles (70km) in Sunshine
Village, 10.2 miles (16.4km) at Mount
Norquay (area: 25% easy, 45% intermedi-
ate, 30% difficult)
Nursery slopes 1 tow-rope at Lake Louise
Summer skiing none
Snowmaking 1,400 acres (567 hectares)
at Lake Louise

LIFT PASSES
Area pass CDN$279 for 6 days
Day pass Lake Louise CDN$42, Sunshine
Village CDN$42, Mount Norquay CDN$33
Beginners tow-passes available
Pensioners Lake Louise and Sunshine, 65
yrs and over, CDN$35 per day.
Mystic Ridge, 55 yrs and over,
CDN$28 per day
Credit cards accepted yes

SKI SCHOOLS
Adults CDN$134 for 3 days, times vary
between areas
Private lessons CDN$40 per hr
Snowboarding group lessons only
available with Club Ski Program, CDN$25
for 2 hrs, private lessons, CDN$39 per hr
Cross-country CDN$20 for $1\frac{1}{4}$ hrs, group
lessons not available. Loipe 56km
Other courses heli-skiing, telemark,
off-piste, night skiing, moguls, Club Ski
Program in all areas includes instruction,
slalom, lift priority and NASTAR racing
Guiding companies Yamnuska Mountain
School

CHILDREN
Lift pass 6-12 yrs, CDN$102 for 6 days,
reductions for 13-17 yrs, free for 5 yrs and
under
Ski kindergarten Lake Louise, 3-6 yrs,
9am-4pm, CDN$31 per day
Ski school Lake Louise, 7-12 yrs,
CDN$39 per day including lunch, Club Ski
Program in all areas, 6-12 yrs, details on
request, teen ski, 13-19 yrs, CDN$39
per day
Non-ski kindergarten Lake Louise,
newborn-18 mths, 8am-4.30pm, CDN$21
per day, Lake Louise, 19 mths-6 yrs, 8am-
4.30pm, CDN$3.75 per hr

FOOD AND DRINK PRICES
Coffee CDN$1.25, glass of wine CDN$2.50,
small beer CDN$2.50, dish of the day
CDN$6.75

way. Mystic Ridge has a 'mini-mountain' exclusively for children.
Sunshine has a Kids Kampus Day Care Center for children between 19
months and 6 years of age.

Jackson Hole

ALTITUDE 6,311ft (1924m)

The average American visitor has to fly 1,400 miles to reach the remote resort of Jackson Hole, Wyoming. What they find at the end of their pilgrimage is dramatic scenery, some of the most exciting skiing on the continent, and the wildest ski mountain of them all — Rendezvous Mountain. While other North American resorts make do with three colour codings for the degree of difficulty of their ski trails, Jackson needs five. It has a worldwide dedicated band of followers, mainly expert skiers who delight in the rugged, awesome terrain which has escaped the homogenisation of so many American resorts. However, times are changing. For understandable commercial reasons the new owners of Jackson Hole are seeking to increase its appeal to less advanced skiers. Their master plan includes the

■ **GOOD POINTS**

Real cowboy-town atmosphere, tough skiing, lively après-ski, ideal for non-skiers, beautiful scenery, attractive town, well-organised kindergarten

■ **BAD POINTS**

Distance from Jackson to Teton Village, queues at cable car, short ski season, lack of easy skiing, resort access

'taming' of some existing trails, and the development of more intermediate terrain. Seven new lifts are to be constructed, most of the existing ones will be upgraded and extensive snowmaking on the lower slopes should prolong the season. Three new restaurants, new hotels, condominiums and car parks in Teton Village are all part of the plan.

Until now, the resort's position on the edge of an elk reserve 60 miles (97km) from Yellowstone National Park has meant that environmental considerations have taken precedence. However, should only the outdated lift system of old double-chairs and an ancient cable car remain, Jackson will surely die. On the other hand, if it loses its appeal as a Nirvana for disciples of the steep and deep, it may become just another overly bland American resort with no international following. The owners are well aware of how thin is the ice on which they tread.

The ski area and resort of Jackson Hole is situated beside Teton Village, 12 miles (19km) from the town of Jackson, which also has its own resort of **Snow King**. The town was named by a nineteenth-century trapper, Davey Jackson, who hunted in this rugged corner of Wyoming. The Hole is a 50-mile (80-km) section of the Snake River, famous for its fishing, which twists its way between the Teton and Gros Ventre mountain ranges. Skiers either choose the convenience of Teton Village or make the 20-minute commute from Jackson by ski bus or car.

Jackson is a genuine Wild West town, complete with boardwalks, wooden Victorian shop fronts and tough bars, straight off the set of a western. The locals derive their living not just from skiers, but also from the summer tourists who stop here en route to Yellowstone National Park. Working ranches still surround the town and the horse is the secondary means of transport behind the four-wheel drive.

One criticism of Jackson Hole is that for a resort of such international fame the ski area is quite small and there is little other skiing within driving distance. Snow King, overlooking the town of Jackson, is smaller still. **Grand Targhee**, 47 miles (76km) away, is well worth a day's excursion.

On the mountain
top 10,450ft (3186m) bottom 6,311ft (1924m)

Despite claims from Big Sky in Montana, Jackson Hole offers the longest continual vertical drop in the US. The main ski area is on the extremely challenging Rendezvous Mountain. It has mostly black (difficult) runs, steep chutes and unlimited off-piste, which is a rarity in the US. Intermediate skiers will find that even some of the blue (intermediate) runs are left ungroomed. Easier runs are to be found in the Casper Bowl and on neighbouring Apres Vous Mountain.

A veteran 63-person cable-car tram is the main means of uphill transport and the only way up to the peak of Rendezvous Mountain. Despite a refit, it is in urgent need of replacement, which has been promised by the resort's new owners as part of development over the next few seasons. The tram carries a lift pass supplement and queues at peak times can result in an hour's journey to reach the summit.

> **■ WHAT'S NEW**
>
> First high-speed quad-chair to replace the Teewinot Ski School lift

Beginners

All the beginner slopes are concentrated at the base of Teton Village, where both the Kids' Ranch and ski school meet. The nursery slopes are serviced by two short chair-lifts, one of which is a new high-speed quad; this allows beginners to start on the easiest slopes and then graduate to steeper gradients. Advanced beginners will find easier blue runs down Apres Vous Mountain, and should tackle these before venturing into Casper Bowl.

Intermediates

Like St Anton and Chamonix, the colour-grading here is radical. For most skiers 'intermediate' means 'difficult', and 'difficult' means 'extreme'. While much of the terrain provides varied skiing for good intermediates, gradients can change suddenly and in certain conditions runs that are unpisted can be unpredictable and difficult. The friendliest intermediate skiing can be found on Apres Vous Mountain; Casper Bowl, serviced by a triple-chair, has good, wide pistes. The runs are well-marked, but you must pay attention as several blues turn into black runs on the lower part of the mountain. Only the truly confident should stray

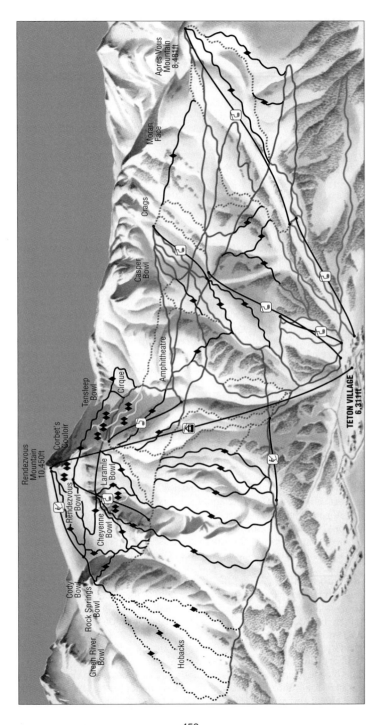

Rendezvous Mountain 10,450ft

Corbet's Couloir

Tensleep Bowl

Cirque

Casper Bowl

Crags

Moran Face

Apres Vous Mountain 8,481ft

Amphitheatre

Rendezvous Bowl

Laramie Bowl

Cheyenne Bowl

Cody Bowl

Rock Springs Bowl

Green River Bowl

Hobacks

TETON VILLAGE 6,311ft

453

up the tram. Plenty of mid-skill skiing can be found here in most conditions, but you have to negotiate a harsh black to find any of it.

Advanced
Most of the advanced skiing is in steep chutes and couloirs, and on tree-lined runs. The skiing initially reached from the tram is all graded black. The simplest way down is to take Rendezvous Trail, which is the longest run. Here you can get into the Hobacks or into Laramie Bowl by taking the Upper Sublette Ridge quad-chair. You can also enter the steep Alta chutes from here. Upper Teewinot, under the chair on Apres Vous Mountain, is excellent in fresh powder.

Off-piste
Jackson Hole is one of the few US resorts that has limitless off-piste skiing. The Hobacks on the lower section of Rendezvous Mountain are marked as black runs but are, in fact, one large steep snowfield, which is best skied in the morning and is completely ungroomed. Many steep chutes such as the Expert Chutes, Alta Chutes and Tower Three Chutes, cut through the trees, as well as steep bowls such as Cody, Cheyenne, Rendezvous and Tensleep.

For those with plenty of nerve, there is Corbet's Couloir off the top of Rendezvous Mountain. This is a chute so steep it seems inconceivable that anyone could ski it and survive. It is entered by a 20-ft (6-m) jump off a cornice; if you manage to control your skis, you land on a ribbon of snow dropping away at 50 degrees, where you must either turn or fall.

A short climb accompanied by a local mountain guide who knows the area well opens up vast tracts of powder on Headwall and Green River, especially in spring.

Ski schools and guiding
The ski school, under the direction of former Olympic medallist Pepi Stiegler, emphasises having fun and being able to tackle simple slopes in a short time. Group, private and three-day courses are offered in alpine and nordic skiing. Individual and some group lessons include video evaluations. The many special clinics include race camps, steep skiing, women's clinics, mountain experience classes, deep powder instruction, and a guiding service. All classes meet at Teton Village.

Snowboarding
Individual and group lessons are available at the ski school. Complete courses and packages for an hour or half-day all include equipment rental. There are two rental shops at the base of Teton Village. Women-only snowboarding camps are also offered.

Cross-country
The Nordic Center teaches telemark and cross-country skiing. Cross-country tours into the wilderness provide the opportunity for viewing moose, elk and other wildlife.

Mountain restaurants

Eating on the mountain is limited, so many skiers head to Teton Village for the oyster bar downstairs at the Mangy Moose or the Alpenhof, a Tyrolean-style restaurant. On the mountain, Casper Restaurant serves both hot food and salads and there are two small snack-bars — one at the base of the Thunder chair-lift and the other at the top of the tram. There is a basic cafeteria at the bottom of the home run.

Off the mountain

Jackson is one of the few Western frontier towns turned ski resort where the past does not clash with the present. Stetsons are as common on the slopes as in the bars. In the summer, it is the gateway to Yellowstone National Park, and three million visitors pass through in their trailers on their way to see the wildlife and Old Faithful, the world's largest geyser. In winter the resort returns to its natural state, a small market-town with surprisingly adventurous shops, restaurants and vast country bars. Here, cowboys who may not be cowboys at all but renegade dentists from Omaha, gulp shots of Wild Turkey, shoot pool and dance to a Wild Frontier rhythm called the Western Swing.

The charismatic town of Jackson is largely made up of single- or double-storey buildings, many of which are renovated saloon-type structures. The central square has gates fashioned from elk horns. At night their former owners are quite likely to be ambling across the road or foraging in a dustbin.

Teton Village, 20 minutes away by car, is a cluster of hotels and condominiums centred around a picturesque clock tower and the tram. There is a regular bus service between Teton and Jackson. Fervent skiers will stay in Teton Village and avoid the daily commute, but will miss out on the overall experience that helps to make Jackson Hole such a unique all-round resort.

Accommodation

If you are looking for a traditional half-board hotel, then the Wort Hotel in Jackson is the one that comes closest to it; it is right in the centre of town, by all the shops and nightlife. Other hotels include the Forty Niner, Rusty Parrot Lodge and the Days Inn. The Lodge at Jackson on the outskirts of town is decorated with wooden bears scaling the upper storeys. Motels include the Parkway Inn, which has a swimming-pool but no restaurant.

The Inn at Jackson Hole is, in fact, at Teton Village, and is well positioned at the base of the slopes. Self-caterers need to go to Jackson for the supermarkets. Spring Creek Resort, the smartest and most unusual place to stay in the area, is out of town so a car is essential.

Eating in and out

Breakfast is a serious business in cowboy country. The real McCoy of 'eggs-over-easy', stacks of pancakes, hash browns and grits are on offer at the Mangy Moose in Teton Village. In the evening, the art-deco-style Cadillac Grille in Jackson is a good place for hamburgers, seafood and fresh pasta; it is also fun for children. J.J.'s Silver Dollar Bar and Grill in the Wort Hotel has the ubiquitous ribs in various forms. The Blue Lion is a costlier option, and Stiegler's serves Austrian cuisine. The best pasta is at Nani's. For a more expensive treat try the Snake River Grill.

Après-ski

Unless you can prove you are 21 or over, you are not going to enjoy yourself outside skiing hours here. So strict are Wyoming's licensing laws that anyone who could be taken for under 40 should carry identification at all times. The Million Dollar Cowboy Bar, the Silver Dollar Bar, and the Rancher in Jackson are where the action is. You can dance in all three to live music for most of the season. The Cowboy Bar has the most atmosphere, with real leather saddles as bar stools and a full-sized, stuffed grizzly bear silently directing proceedings.

Teton Village has the Mangy Moose, one of the finest après-ski bars in The Rockies. It has live music in the evenings and a video room for those under age. The Wingback Lounge at the Inn is a quieter option and the Stockman's Lounge at the Sojourner usually has ski videos and free appetizers. If you have hired a car you can drive to Wilson on the road towards the Teton Pass for an evening at the Stagecoach Inn with live music, cowgirls in flounced dresses, and good-value food. It is the kind of place where you eat with your hat on and go easy on the eye contact with strangers.

■ OTHER SPORTS
Snowmobiling, snow-shoeing, parapente, swimming, heli-skiing, skating, snowcat skiing at Grand Targhee, indoor tennis, climbing wall, dog-sledding

Other après-ski activities include night-skiing at the Snow King resort in Jackson, sleigh-rides through the elk compound, and snowmobiling tours of Yellowstone National Park. Shopping is another important pastime; the Polo Ralph Lauren Factory Store sells end-of-line designer clothes at a fraction of the normal prices.

Childcare

The Kinderschule, which has changed its name to 'Kids Ranch' and is at the base of Teton Village, is one of the better ski kindergarten in the US. Children are taught the 'Edgie Wedgie' technique where ski tips are clipped together with brightly coloured, bendy strips of plastic. This stops the skis from crossing and encourages children to make a wedge or snowplough. Children are taken to and from the nursery slopes in a snow-mobile trailer.

The non-ski kindergarten is for infants from two months to five years of age. 'My four-year-old son had his first lessons here, and we could not have hoped for a better or more enthusiastic introduction to skiing. We just wish the French Ski School would come here and watch how it is done', commented one reporter.

Skiing facts: **Jackson Hole**

TOURIST OFFICE
PO Box 290, Teton Village, WY 83025
Tel 1 307 733 2292
Fax 1 307 733 2660

THE RESORT
By air Jackson Airport 15 mins from
Jackson and 20 mins from Teton Village
(reasonably priced airport shuttle-
bus to resort)
Visitor beds 12,000
Transport bus service operates day and
night between Jackson and Teton Village
($2 each way)

THE SKIING
Linked or nearby resorts Snow King (n),
Grand Targhee (n)
Longest run Rendezvous Trail, 7.2 miles
(11.5km) - blue
Number of lifts 9 in Jackson Hole
Total of trails/pistes 2,500 acres (1011
hectares) - 10% easy, 40% intermediate,
50% difficult)
Nursery slopes 10% of total slopes
Summer skiing none
Snowmaking 80 acres (32 hectares)
covered

LIFT PASSES
Area pass $234 for 6 days ($252
 including tram)
Day pass $46 including tram
Beginners no free lifts
Pensioners 65 yrs and over, $25 per day
Credit cards accepted yes

SKI SCHOOLS
Adults Jackson Hole Ski School,
$45 per day (4 hrs), or $80 for 3 days
(2 hrs each morning)
Private lessons $115 per morning (2 hrs),
afternoon extension $90 (1¾ hrs), full day
$260 (6 hrs), half-day $170
Snowboarding Jackson Hole Ski School,
prices as ski lessons
Cross-country Jackson Hole Nordic Center,
$32 per day including lesson, equipment
hire and trail pass. Loipe 17km at base of
resort
Other courses moguls, disabled skiing,
mountain experience (off-piste), race
camps, women's ski clinics
Guiding companies Jackson Hole Alpine
Guides

CHILDREN
Lift pass 14 yrs and under, $117 for 6 days,
$135 including tram. Free for 5 yrs and
under on Eagle's Rest
Ski kindergarten Rough Riders at the Kids
Ranch, 3-5 yrs, $60 per day including day-
care, lunch and 2-hr lesson
Ski school Jackson Hole Ski School
Skiwee, 6-13 yrs, $210 for 5 days (4 hrs
per day) including lunch. Rough Riders for
older, more experienced children,
$60 per day including lessons, snacks
and lift ticket. (Upper mountain skiers
need to purchase a $17 lift ticket in
addition)
Non-ski kindergarten Tenderfoots Infant
Care (2-18 mths), or Wrangler Childcare
(18 mths-5 yrs), both 8am-5pm, $52 per
day including lunch

FOOD AND DRINK PRICES
Coffee $1.25, glass of wine $2.75-3.50,
small beer $2.75, dish of the day
$6.50-8.50

Linked or nearby resorts

Grand Targhee
top 10,230ft (3118m) bottom 8,000ft (2438m)

The small resort is 47 miles (76km) north-west of Jackson and just inside the Wyoming border. It is blessed with an excellent snow record, which is why the main attraction is snowcat skiing in the virgin powder. This is by previous arrangement only, as the cat takes a maximum of ten passengers, plus the guide and a patrolman. If you can't get a booking for snowcat skiing, the resort's own 3,000 skiable acres (1214 hectares) are varied as well as exciting and are often left ungroomed in fresh snow. The resort has a small shopping centre but limited restaurant choice. Accommodation includes the Teewinot Lodge.

TOURIST OFFICE
Tel 1 307 353 2304
Fax 1 307 353 8148

Lake Tahoe

ALTITUDE Heavenly 6,500ft (1982m) Squaw Valley 6,200ft (1890m)

California is a world unto itself, so it is not surprising that its ski resorts are also unique. **Heavenly** (on the Nevada–California state-line) and **Squaw Valley** could not be more different. From the top of the Sky Express chair-lift at Heavenly you can turn left to ski in Nevada with views of the arid vastness of the Nevada Desert, or turn right to the California side overlooking the lush beauty of Lake Tahoe. This stretch of cobalt blue water lives up to its reputation as the second largest and most magnificent alpine lake in the world after Lake Titicaca in Peru.

> ### ■ GOOD POINTS
> Beautiful scenery, large number of resorts on one lift pass, extensive facilities for children, excellent snow-making at Heavenly, variety of expert skiing at Squaw Valley and intermediate skiing at Heavenly, separate cross-country resorts, plenty of tree-line skiing, lively après-ski at South Lake Tahoe
>
> ### ■ BAD POINTS
> No resort centre at Heavenly, lack of non-skiing activities, limited accommodation at Squaw Valley

Across the waters, Squaw Valley, which hosted the 1960 Winter Olympics, provides the steeper and altogether more demanding terrain in a corner of the Sierra Nevada that has a long skiing tradition. As far back as 1856 John 'Snowshoe' Thompson, a Norwegian immigrant, used to carry the mail on skis between the mining camps in these mountains. Until the railroad was built in 1872, he was the miners' only winter link with the outside world.

These two are the largest and best known of the 14 alpine and 7 cross-country resorts set above the shores of Lake Tahoe. **Granlibakken** ski area, with its two lifts, is the oldest, and Squaw has the toughest skiing, but it is Heavenly that stands out from the pack because of its exquisite scenery and unusual nightlife.

Off the slopes, serenity switches to frenzy amid the green baize of the tables and the clunk of one-arm bandits in the 24-hour casinos. Gambling is legal in **South Lake Tahoe** on the Nevada side of the state-line.

Interchangeable lift tickets can be used at Heavenly, Squaw Valley, **Kirkwood**, **Northstar**, **Alpine Meadows**, and **Sierra-at-Tahoe**.

On the mountain
Heavenly top 10,100ft (3079m) bottom 7,200ft (2195m)
Squaw Valley top 9,050ft (2759m) bottom 6,200ft (1890m)

Heavenly is one of America's largest ski areas, and almost all of it is below the tree-line. It also has one of America's most extensive snowmaking programmes, with 37 miles (59km) of terrain covered by snow-cannon — a total of 66 per cent of the resort's pistes. The skiing is divided between the Nevada and the Californian sides of the mountain. The Nevada face consists mainly of blue (intermediate) runs; the expert skiing is in the Mott Canyon area, a north-facing wall with a selection of chutes through the trees and Killebrew Canyon, which has steep unpisted chutes. The green (easy) trails are mostly on the lower and middle slopes. The upper Californian side is mainly fast, blue cruising terrain. The most difficult skiing on the Californian side is just above the Base Lodge and on the bowl runs. Higher up the mountain there are some black-diamond (difficult) runs off Skyline Trail.

■ **WHAT'S NEW**

Exhibition & Searchlight lift replaced by detachable quad (Squaw)

The skiing at Squaw Valley takes place on six peaks: Granite Chief, Red Dog, KT-22, Squaw, Emigrant and Broken Arrow. The area is divided into three sectors, but the lifts rather than the runs are colour-graded. All the main lifts on Red Dog, KT-22 and Granite Chief are black, and Squaw and Emigrant's are blue. Intermediates will find a huge amount of skiing, with the highlight a 3-mile (5km) trail from the High Camp area down to the mountain base.

Beginners

There are three beginner areas at Heavenly. The Enchanted Forest at the California base is a secluded area with lifts and simple runs. Another beginners' centre is at Boulder Base Lodge. Midway up the mountain on the California side are a number of green (beginner) runs, including a gentle but long slope called Mombo Meadows. Squaw's nursery slopes are in the centre of the ski area up on the mountain.

Intermediates

Intermediates will find they can ski virtually every run on the mountain at Heavenly. The skiing here is 45 per cent intermediate; much of it is long cruising runs bordered by banks of pine trees, and there is always a stunning view of the lake. Take the Sky Express chair and try Liz's or Betty's, then head to Nevada for the Big Dipper, Sand Dunes, Perimeter and Galaxy runs. You need to make your way back to the state in which you started by 3.30pm.

Squaw Valley has three main intermediate areas: the runs off the Squaw Creek and Red Dog lifts, which are best tackled later in the day; the area off Squaw One Express; and the bowls on Emigrant Mountain and Shirley Lakes. The runs are groomed but not named on the trail-map, which only shows the lifts.

Advanced

Heavenly's Milky Way Bowl provides challenging skiing, but the most advanced skiing is in Mott Canyon and Killebrew Canyon. Steep chutes are cut through the trees, with runs such as Snake Pit. There are huge areas of tree-level skiing and the odd black run such as Ellie's from the Sky Express and The Face near the California base-lodge. Gunbarrel is a challenging mogul slope.

Squaw is a paradise for the advanced skier, with its couloirs, steep gullies and overall fairly steep territory (many Ski Extreme videos have been filmed here). The most adventurous skiers will find endless terrain; some of the most radical is off the KT-22 lift and Olympic Lady.

Off-piste

There is almost unlimited off-piste skiing at Heavenly. Many of the trees are packed tightly together, and there are some vast untracked areas to discover. The Milky Way, Mott Canyon and Killebrew Canyon are large expanses of off-piste; you need to arrive early on powder days as they are quickly skied-out. Black-diamond runs cut through huge areas of forest, where you can always find untouched snow.

At Squaw Valley, the further away from the lifts you travel the more likely you are to find good powder snow. The locals ski by the cliffs behind the tram (cable car), but you need to be accompanied by a local guide in this tricky area. Many skiers opt for Headwall and KT-22, but there is also some excellent skiing off Granite Chief and Silverado.

Ski schools and guiding

The ski school at Heavenly offers private and group lessons. Special courses include three-hour lessons for first-timers and improvers, Mountain Adventure (off-piste) courses and women's ski seminars. The Squaw Valley Ski School has programmes for all ages and abilities, including Ski Your Pro, which aims to get beginners to intermediate level. Advanced lessons and mogul clinics are also available.

Snowboarding

Heavenly has the Airport Snowboard Park on the Nevada side of the mountain. The 'Shred Ready' Snowboard School gives lessons at both Boulder Lodge and California Lodge. The Boardinghouse is a specialist snowboard shop on Highway 50 next to Long's drugstore. The Squaw Valley Ski School offers group and private snowboard lessons. At Children's World in Squaw Valley, young people between the ages of 7 and 12 can try snowboarding.

Cross-country

At Heavenly, Spooner Lake cross-country ski area has 21 prepared trails and 100km of loipe. At Squaw, the prepared cross-country circuit is from Squaw Creek Resort to the base area.

Mountain restaurants

The Monument Peak restaurant, cocktail lounge and cafeteria is at the top of the tram at Heavenly and has an outdoor deck. Sky Meadows has an outdoor barbecue and snack shop. The California Lodge has a cafeteria and a bar. Boulder Lodge has a bar, cafeteria and sun-deck.

Stagecoach Lodge has a cafeteria. East Peak Lodge is the place to go to soak up the sun; it has a barbecue, delicatessen, pizzeria, bar and cafeteria. You can also order a picnic in a secluded off-piste area for what is billed as 'a fun, personalised, private dining experience on the mountain'. The Sushi Bar at the California Base Lodge is recommended along with the Slice of Heaven Pizza Pub at the Stagecoach Base Lodge.

At Squaw Valley the highly recommended Resort at Squaw Creek has a daily barbecue. At the base there are several lunch places serving pizza and sandwiches. Gold Coast at the top of the Super Gondola has restaurants and bars on three levels, with a large, sunny deck. High Camp has five different restaurants and bars, and the main dining-room is open at night.

Off the mountain

The blatant flashing lights, huge neon signs and monstrous casino complexes are such a contrast from the lake front and its simple, single-storey homes that it takes a while to digest South Lake Tahoe. 'Interesting sightseeing,' said one reporter about the casinos, 'but if you don't know the rules, the gambling seems pretty daunting.' Après-ski includes taking in a show — some excellent cabaret acts and pop concerts are staged here and often feature top artists. There is dancing at Nero's casino, where the disco may temporarily be stopped for 'The Best Buns' contest, or you can have a flutter at the tables.

Alternatively, you can ignore the tacky glitter and find a small restaurant for an intimate dinner. This is easier in Tahoe City, a 15-minute drive from Squaw Valley, where several of the fine restaurants are on the lakeside. The drive to Squaw Valley along the lake is spectacular, with a castle on a small inlet, known as Emerald Lake.

Accommodation

The ski area of Heavenly and the town of South Lake Tahoe are separate, although Tahoe Seasons Resort hotel complex is close to the lifts at the California base. Harrah's and the Horizon Casino Resort in South Lake Tahoe are two of the bigger casino-hotels; others include Caesar's Tahoe, and Harvey's Resort (all have good health spas). Much of the accommodation is in condominiums. On the quieter Californian side, motels are stacked side by side, with little to choose between them. The Station House Inn and the Timber Cover Lodge are singled out by reporters. There are also condominiums at the Nevada base.

The Resort at Squaw Creek is a large ski-in ski-out complex near the base of Squaw Valley and has its own restaurants, bars, fitness centre and skating rink. Squaw Valley Lodge is also close to the base lifts, and the Olympic Village Inn is nearby. The Squaw Valley Inn is opposite the tram. There are also lodges in and around Tahoe City, which is the liveliest place to stay.

Eating in and out

The big casino resorts have numerous restaurants, and some of them are excellent. Caesar's has Planet Hollywood, complete with movie paraphernalia. Try the Mexican restaurant at Harvey's or Carlos Murphy's, an Irish/Mexican restaurant. Zachery's and Dixie's specialise in Cajun cooking. The Station House Inn serves reasonably priced meals, and The Chart House is more expensive but has great views. The Cal-Neva Lodge in Crystal Bay has two restaurants and an oyster bar, and The Dory's Oar has good seafood.

At Squaw Valley, the Resort at Squaw Creek has excellent food, Glissandi is a high-priced Italian, but Graham's, midway between the Resort and the Squaw Valley base, is cosier. The restaurants in Tahoe City and a

> **■ OTHER SPORTS**
>
> Skating, snowmobiling, night-skiing (Squaw), rifle shooting, parapente, snow-shoeing

couple in Truckee, half-an-hour away, are more fun. In Tahoe City, Za's is a cheap and basic Italian, while Christy Hill's is upmarket and overlooks the lake. A couple of boathouse complexes have medium-priced restaurants serving seafood and wholesome American fare.

Après-ski
There is no après-ski at the resort of Heavenly except for the California Bar at the base. All the after-skiing activities take place in South Lake Tahoe, with bars in all the hotels and most of the motels. Try McP's, which is a lively Irish pub. Turtle's has dancing, and the Christiania Inn, close to the ski area, has a good atmosphere.

The gaming tables attract money, and money attracts the top names in showbusiness. The Tahoe region is renowned for its Vegas-style celebrity shows, although some of the US television names will mean little to Europeans.

Squaw has the Plaza Bar and Salsa, and there is dancing at Bar One in the Squaw Valley Mall, Humpty's in Tahoe City, and at the Olympic Village Inn at weekends.

Childcare
Heavenly has a number of programmes for children, including Ski Explorers for 4- to 12-year-olds and first-timer lessons. There is also a mini-clinic and junior ski school. Children's Ski World is at the base of the mountain, where there are a few simple runs for youngsters.

At Squaw, the Children's World at Papoose is convenient for families. Parents can deliver their offspring before buying their lift tickets and proceeding up the mountain on the Red Dog lift. Ten Little Indians is a kindergarten that takes two- to three-year-olds for snow play and arts and crafts. The Children's World Ski School is for children aged 4 to 12 years of age.

TOURIST OFFICE
Tel Heavenly: 1 702 586 7000 Squaw: 1 916 583 6985
Fax Heavenly: 1 702 588 5517 Squaw: 1 916 581 7106

Mammoth Mountain

ALTITUDE 7,953ft (2425m)

Ask how Mammoth got its name and there will be several answers. Some say it was named after the dinosaur bones found in the meadow, others that the mountain owes its name to the Spanish, who dubbed this extinct volcano the 'big mountain'. It is not because the mountain is huge, nor because it is shaped like a prehistoric elephant. The real reason stems from mining days when gold was discovered in 1878. The main mining company called itself the Mammoth Mining Company because it was so big, and gradually local geographical features including the mountain were named Mammoth.

■ **GOOD POINTS**

Variety of skiing for all standards, long ski season, large ski area, extensive snowmaking, many activities for non-skiers

■ **BAD POINTS**

Long airport transfer, limited après-ski, lack of mountain restaurants, weekend lift queues

Mammoth Mountain is one of the few top American resorts that is run by its founder instead of an anonymous corporation. Dave McCoy set up a portable rope-tow in 1941 and bought the resort in 1953. Today, he still runs the mountain with his family. Most days he can be seen out on the slopes skiing or checking lift tickets. Mammoth has expanded since those early days and now has 150 named runs and 31 lifts, most of them chairs.

Mammoth Lakes, the closest town, is four miles (7km) away. It is a sprawling place with not much nightlife, which is supported by a year-round tourist business. Thirty minutes away is **June Mountain**. The McCoys opened this area in the 1980s and today it has one large, state-of-the-art gondola, two detachable quads and five double-chairs. The Mammoth lift ticket covers both ski areas, but if you buy your pass at June Mountain (which costs less) there is a nominal extra daily charge to ski at Mammoth.

Mammoth and June are popular with southern Californians who head for the Sierra Nevada Mountains on sunny weekends. The ski resorts lie 300 miles (480km) to the north of Los Angeles, necessitating a spectacular six-hour drive through the Mojave Desert, followed by a climb into the mountains. Richard Branson rates Mammoth as one of his favourite destinations for skiing families, which may in part explain why Virgin flies into Los Angeles.

While a car is useful, an efficient shuttle-bus service plies between Mammoth Lakes and the ski area during the main season. Taxis (about $10) are also available. Plans to build a gondola between the two are on the drawing-board but have yet to materialise.

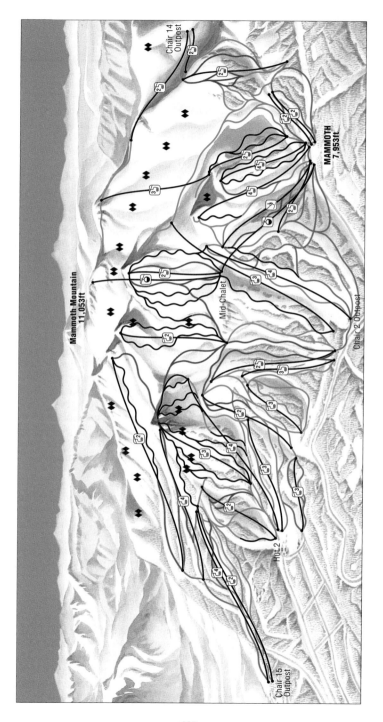

On the mountain
top 11,053ft (3370m) bottom 7,953ft (2425m)

Mammoth has an impressive average annual snowfall of over 27ft (8m), and a tree-line going up to 9,000ft (2743m). Higher up, open bowl-skiing provides a variety of steep black-diamond (difficult) runs as well as wide blue (intermediate) trails. Above the trees there are five small peaks accessed by chairs. The rim of an old volcano runs right across the skyline.

The six-seater Gondola 2 takes you up to the highest point, while a little further to the right as you look up the mountain the three-person Grizzly chair takes you up to the next highest point. Between the two lifts there are three double-black-diamond (very difficult) trails — Climax, Hangman's Hollow and Drop Out. For those of a more cautious nature, a black-diamond trail takes you down a less forbidding gradient into Cornice Bowl.

Even though Mammoth is known for its sunny days and mild temperatures, the mountain does not receive its fantastic snowfalls without its share of white-outs and storms. Be prepared to spend days on end in limited visibility during the main winter months.

There are four easy mountain-access points, each served by one or other of the shuttles. Mountain 'hosts' help you find your way around.

No one should miss the more gentle skiing at June Mountain; the summits of Rainbow and June are just over 10,000ft (3049m), with trees right up to the top. There are magnificent views to the more jagged peaks in the Sierras. This 500-acre (200-hectare) ski area is a great place to ski at weekends while the Los Angelinos swarm to Mammoth. A few lean years led Mammoth to expand its snowmaking facilities, which now cover 200 acres (80 hectares) and 22 runs, and can ensure skiing into July.

> **■ WHAT'S NEW**
>
> Increased snowmaking providing an additional 100 acres of skiing

Beginners
All the novice slopes are below the tree-line with most runs concentrated on the Main Lodge, which is also where the ski school meets. Most of the runs are green (easy) and can be reached by two chairs. Another novice area is at Warming Hut II. There are a few beginner runs at Chair 15, but these are longer and less accessible. In both easy skiing areas there is a choice of blue runs.

Intermediates
Every area of the mountain has varied intermediate skiing, except for the peak, which has some steep black (difficult) runs. The top of chairs 14 and 18 above the tree-line and the gondola offers good open bowl-skiing. The runs through the trees have been designed to give some tight tree-skiing as well as some wide pistes. The longer runs are accessed from Chair 16 and Chair 10 and from the Mid-Chalet. To benefit from good light all day, start at Chair 15 and gradually follow the sun towards Warming Hut II and the Main Lodge, ending up at chairs 13 and 14. At

3 miles (4.8km), Road Runner is the longest run. It starts as a blue and then turns into a green before ending at the Main Lodge.

Advanced

One look at the map, scrawled with double-black-diamond runs, will fire up any advanced skier. There are steep chutes, good tree-level skiing, bowl-skiing and off-piste. On fresh powder days, of which there are many, exhaustion will hit you long before you have explored the whole mountain. When the snow cover is good, the black runs at the top of the mountain are steep but wide. Off Chair 22, the trees between Stump Alley and Patrolmen's, and Stump Alley and Mambo, provide challenging runs. Around the ridge underneath Chairs 13 and 14, where the area is shaded, the snow stays firm late in the day and offers some excellent tree-level skiing.

Off-piste

The large bowls above the tree-line provide endless off-piste, and it is also easy to find your own route through the trees. If there is fresh powder you should be able to ski it all day, although this is more of a challenge at weekends. The pisteurs start work early in the morning from the Main Lodge and the Warming Hut II; to get to the good snow before they do you need to head high to Chairs 3, 5, 13 and 14, then 9, 15 and 24. Some of the best first runs of the day include Powder Bowl, Fascination, Stump Alley, Broadway, Mambo and St Anton.

Ski schools and guiding

Mammoth Mountain Ski School has packages that include group lessons, learn-to-ski specials and two-day weekend courses. Specialist day camps include a women's ski seminar and senior ski clinics. Special courses include bump lessons and steep skiing clinics. 'Good-quality instruction, thoroughly worthwhile', said one reporter.

Snowboarding

The ski school offers learn-to-snowboard packages as well as individual and group lessons. Snowboard camps are available for adults and children. Six shops hire out boards. Riders should try Dragon's Back chute and Hemlock Ridge, which are challenging steep runs. Upper Dry Creek has numerous walls and drop-offs, and you can follow the run into the trees to arrive at Lower Dry Creek, which is a natural half-pipe. For off-piste boarding, hike up to Hole-in-the-Wall or Sherwin Ridge. For the less advanced, there is Meadows Plateau, a 500-acre (200-hectare) area, which is excellent for snowboarding. At June Mountain there is a snowboarding fun park with a half-pipe.

Mountain restaurants

Mammoth has only one large restaurant on the mountain, at the Mid-Chalet. Chair 14 Outpost and Chair 15 Outpost are both for snacks. June Mountain has one on-hill snack bar. The four base areas all have cafeterias and prices are reasonable. The best restaurant is in The Yodler, a Swiss chalet at the base area that was brought over from Europe and reconstructed plank by plank. The Mammoth Mountain Inn is also recommended, as is the Mountainside Grill.

Off the mountain

Keen skiers should stay at the Mammoth Mountain Inn at the base. The complex contains a bar and restaurant and a separate building with sports facilities and a whirlpool. The town of Mammoth Lakes has no real centre and, while there are a number of bars and restaurants, there is no community feeling. The single main street has excellent shopping with numerous sports shops where you can buy equipment and clothing for considerably less than in the UK. There are six brand-name factory stores including Polo Ralph Lauren and Van Heusen, and good ski-wear shops including The North Face and Patagonia.

Accommodation

There is a large number of hotels, guest houses, apartments and rooms in Mammoth Lakes, many of them with whirlpools and spas. The Alpenhof ('well above average') is a cheerful place that looks as Tyrolean as its name suggests. Jägerhof Lodge is another recommended hotel, just out of town on the ski-shuttle route. The Austrian influence on the early days of American skiing is reflected in some other, more economical, establishments such as Holiday Haus and the Kitzbühel Lodge. The newest additions are Sierra Lodge (a no-smoking hotel), Shilo Inn, and the Quality Inn bed-and-breakfast. The luxury Silver Bear condominiums are within walking distance of the lifts. Mammoth Mountain Inn, the 1849 and Bridges condominiums are located at the ski resort base.

■ **OTHER SPORTS**

Snowmobiling, bob-sleigh, tobogganing, snow-shoeing, sleigh rides, dog-sledding, hot-air ballooning, indoor tennis

Eating in and out

Mammoth Lakes comes into its own in this category, with well over 40 restaurants, delicatessen, ice-cream parlours and pizzerias. There are six steak and seafood establishments, three Mexican restaurants, four Italian, one Chinese and one Japanese. The Lakefront (nouvelle cuisine in a historic lodge), Natalie's and The Mogul (serving high-quality steaks) are among the more expensive eating-places, while Goats Bar, La Sierras and the Swiss Café are three of the least costly. Slocum's Italian and American Grill is a good place for dining out. The Shogun is the resort's sushi bar, Roberto's offers some of the best Mexican cuisine in town, and The Good Life Café has healthy, wholesome food. Angel's has creative cooking in a cosy atmosphere. Self-caterers can shop at Von's supermarket, which has a large variety of goods, Pioneer Market (a smaller alternative), or the Gourmet Grocer.

Skiing facts: **Mammoth Mountain**

TOURIST OFFICE
1 Minaret Road, Mammoth Lakes,
CA 93546
Tel 1 619 934 2571
Fax 1 619 934 0603

THE RESORT
By air Mammoth/June Lake
40 mins, Los Angeles 6 hrs
Visitor beds 8,200
Transport Mammoth area shuttle-bus
provides free transport around the town and
to the Main Lodge, Warming Hut II and Chair
15 areas

THE SKIING
Linked or nearby resorts June
Mountain (n)
Longest run Road Runner, 3 miles (4.8km)
- blue/green
Number of lifts 31
Total of trails/pistes over 3,500 acres
(1,400 hectares) - 30% easy, 40%
intermediate, 30% difficult
Nursery slopes 30% of ski area
Summer skiing none
Snowmaking 300 acres (120 hectares)
covered

LIFT PASSES
Area pass (covers Mammoth and June
Mountain) $187 for 5 days
Day pass $45
Beginners free for those taking ski
lessons
Pensioners 65 yrs and over, $23 per day
or $94 for 5 days
Credit cards accepted yes

SKI SCHOOLS
Adults Mammoth Ski School, 10am-midday
and 1.30-3.30pm, $190 for 5 days
Private lessons adults and children, $60
per hr, $180 per half-day, $360 per full day
Snowboarding Snowboard Learn to Ski
package, $68 per day including board and
lifts. Group lessons $38 per day. Private
lessons $60 per hr, $180 per half-day,
$360 per full day
Cross-country Tamarack Cross-country
Ski Center or Mammoth Ski School (private
or group lessons on demand), prices on
request. Loipe 35km around the lakes
Other courses powder skiing, moguls, race
training, slalom, extreme skiing, women's
ski seminars
Guiding companies through ski school

CHILDREN
Lift pass 7-12 yrs, $94 for 5 days, 13-18
yrs, $144 for 5 days, free for 6 yrs and under
Ski kindergarten Woollywood Ski
Academy, 4-12 yrs, 10am-3.30pm, $65 per
day including lunch. Small World Day
Center, 4-12 yrs, 8am-5pm, $70 per day
including ski lesson, supervision and lunch
Ski school Woollywood Ski Academy, as ski
kindergarten. Mammoth Teens Program,
13-18 yrs, 10am-midday and 1.30-3.30pm,
$41 per day
Non-ski kindergarten Small World Day
Center: 0-23 mths $54 per day, 2-12 yrs
$44 per day, both 8am-5pm, including lunch

FOOD and DRINK PRICES
Coffee $1, glass of wine $3, small beer
$2.75, dish of the day $8.95

Après-ski

Directly after skiing, the Yodler offers great cocktails, and the Austria Hof at the base of Warming Hut II has spiced wine and a variety of après-ski drinks. When it comes to late-night entertainment, the scene is limited. It is worth looking in on Grumpy's, Annie Rose's, Slocums or Gringo's, but mid-week they can be quite subdued. The Clocktower is where the locals go. Whiskey Creek offers live entertainment,while Rafters, Ocean Harvest, Kegs and Cue's (for pool) are the other main nightspots. The pace hots up at weekends when the Los Angelinos hit town.

Childcare

There are special learn-to-ski packages with prices that include lifts, lessons and equipment rental. The expanded Woollywood Ski Academy takes children from four to twelve years old. Mammoth Teens Program is for intermediate and advanced skiers. Children six years and under ski free. The Mountain Inn's Small World Day Center takes newborn to 12-year-old children.

Park City

ALTITUDE 6,900ft (2104m)

Park City consists of three distinctive resorts in one town — **Park City**, **Deer Valley** and **Wolf Mountain** (formerly known as Park West). Together they make up the largest ski area in Utah, which was, no doubt, a contributory factor in its successful bid to win the right to host the Winter Olympics in 2002. By Utah's strict Mormon standards, Park City is sin city. This means that a degree of polite rowdiness that would be frowned upon in **Snowbird** is tolerated on Main Street. As the crow flies, it is barely 6 miles (10km) from Snowbird to Park City, yet Utah's two leading resorts could hardly be more different. Where Snowbird is confined in its canyon and trapped in purpose-built glitz, Park City sprawls along a much wider valley with little regard for convenience and none at all for land conservation.

Since mining began here in the mid-nineteenth century, silver to the value of $400 million has been extracted from the hills surrounding Park City. George Hearst, father of William Randolph Hearst, made his fortune in the 1880s (the era of maximum prosperity). Today, Park City has a reputation for being rather more than a ski resort. Its cultural aspirations have been enhanced by the emergence of the Sundance Film Festival. This event, which takes place over the last ten days in January under the patronage of Robert Redford's Sundance Institute, is now recognised as the premier show-case for independent American films.

■ GOOD POINTS

Varied skiing for all standards, wide choice of restaurants and shops, ideal base for visiting other Utah resorts, plenty of activities for non-skiers, tree-level skiing, extensive snowmaking

■ BAD POINTS

Inconvenient resort layout, uninspiring scenery, restrictive licensing laws

On the mountain
top 10,000ft (3049m) bottom 6,900ft (2104m)

As the year 2002 approaches, we can expect to see major on-mountain improvements to all three ski areas. The main Park City skiing lies on rolling, wooded terrain on the slopes of Jupiter Peak. Although the United States Ski Team has used the resort as its headquarters since 1973, the skiing is much less challenging than at Snowbird. This is because the slopes are not steep and the lower altitude makes for a greater percentage of glade-skiing on trails cut from the forest. Access to the top of the main ski area is by the Silver Queen gondola, which takes 20 minutes from the Resort Center (a moderately well-designed complex on three levels, with shops and cafés set around an open-air skating rink) to the Summit House Restaurant. The highest point is Jupiter Bowl, which is reached by the two-seater Jupiter chair and is for experts only.

Skiers of all standards will find suitable runs from the summit to the bottom of the Prospector high-speed quad. The easiest is Claimjumper, a broad green (easy) boulevard curving round the mountain towards the Snow Hut restaurant. Park City has night-skiing on PayDay and First Time.

Beginners

There are two beginner areas, one at the base of the resort with two lifts and another at the top of the gondola, where runs are concentrated around the Silverlode chair. Beginners can profit from a $3\frac{1}{2}$-mile (5.5-km) green descent from the Summit House to the Resort Center, via the top of Claimjumper, Bonanza and Sidewinder. This is broad, flat territory, which is perfect for discovering the pleasures of the beautifully groomed snow. The less experienced should avoid it late in the afternoon when it becomes a race-track back to base as the lifts close.

Intermediates

The 89 trails covering 2,200 acres (890 hectares) of terrain are 48 per cent intermediate and cover every area of the mountain except Jupiter Bowl. Confident intermediates will not find themselves unduly tested by Hidden Splendour, Mel's Alley, Powder Keg and Assessment. However, Prospector, Single Jack, Sunnyside and Parley's Park take rather more direct routes down the mountain. Park City has 650 acres (263 hectares) of open bowls: 'Overall we found the bowl-skiing excellent', was one report. Another reporter found the grading of blue (intermediate) runs unpredictable: 'The variation in the blues is quite alarming for lower intermediates'. Favourite runs include Blue Slip Bowl and 10th Mountain.

Advanced

Advanced skiers have a choice of moderate black (difficult) runs, including The Host, Thaynes, Double Jack, Ford Country and Glory Hole, which all lead into the Thaynes Canyon, a blue cruiser that marks the eastern boundary of the ski area. Halfway down, they can take the Motherlode chair-lift back to the Summit House or continue down to the King Consolidated chair-lift, the access point for ten short blue runs leading into Broadway and Hot Spot.

Off-piste

Those in search of adventure should take the Jupiter Access trail from the Summit House to the Jupiter chair-lift. This goes up to the top of the

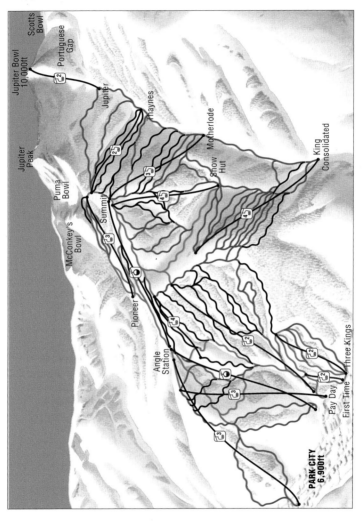

resort, a wind-blown ridge with a variety of ungroomed options. Shadow Ridge and Fortune Teller go straight down under the chair through sparsely wooded snowfields, but a ten-minute walk along the ridge to the east brings skiers to the top of Scott's Bowl. Further along, Portuguese Gap is a narrow, often heavily mogulled, field between the trees. A 20-minute walk along the ridge to the west leads to Jupiter Peak. Here there is a choice between the steep descent into Puma Bowl via the East Face or back to the chair-lift via the West Face. All these runs are well worth the walk, but expert skiing in Park City is dependent on the Jupiter chair-lift being open.

When the wind gets up (as it frequently does) or the cloud closes in, the options are drastically reduced. The black alternatives to the west of the resort are six parallel descents through aspen trees and are also prone to closure because of poor snow conditions. A guided programme called Ski Utah Interconnect is a full-day off-piste adventure that covers five ski areas.

Ski schools and guiding

The Park City Ski School uses the American teaching system as prescribed by the Professional Ski Instructors of America (PSIA). There are full-day and half-day adult group lessons for visitors aged 14 years and over.

The Mountain Experience programme takes good intermediate to advanced skiers into the high bowls on Jupiter Peak. Private lessons are also available. The Utah Winter Sports Park is one of the few places in the world offering recreational ski-jumping on three days each week during the mid-winter months.

Beginners and low intermediate 'wedge turners' meet at the bottom of the mountain, and intermediate to advanced at the Summit Ski School area at the top of the Silverlode high-speed quad. Special courses include moguls, freestyle, slalom, off-piste, race clinics and women's ski performance workshops.

Snowboarding

Park City is opening its entire mountain to snowboarding for the 1996–7 season. Until now, the sport has not been permitted in either Park City or Deer Valley, although it has long been embraced at Wolf Mountain, Utah's snowboarding headquarters. The area has five half-pipes as well as a floodlit snowboard park. Jans Mountain Outfitter at Wolf Mountain's base-area has a wide range of boards for hire.

Cross-country

The White Pine Touring Center has 18km of prepared loipe, which are suited to all standards, on the Park City golf course. The Homestead Resort has a further 12km. Both have ski schools.

Mountain restaurants

The Mid-Mountain restaurant, a low, wooden cabin, which was built to serve the miners in 1898, moved to its present site in 1987. It offers high-quality fast food ('simply heaven on a sunny day — at weekends they even have a live band'), but is only open at lunchtime. Its rivals, the Summit House at the top of the gondola, and the Snow Hut at the bottom of the Silverlode high-speed quad, serve breakfast as well. Steeps, a cavernous ski-in ski-out bar at the bottom of the main run back to the Resort Center, has table service at lunchtime. It is also an essential après-ski stop, with live music, happy-hour prices and a party atmosphere.

Off the mountain

Park City, like many of its Colorado rivals, has artfully converted a mining past into a colourful touristic present. Its focus is Main Street, home to the Wasatch Brewery, the Egyptian Theater, and a host of art galleries and boutiques. Between them there are numerous bars, coffee shops and restaurants.

A less cosmopolitan area is Prospector Square, where you can find Albertsons the supermarket, a video shop and one of Park City's two liquor stores (the other is on Main Street), which are the only places besides the bars where you can buy alcohol. Main Street is also the shopping area where specialities include pottery and native American artifacts. The Factory Stores at Wolf Mountain,

> ### ■ OTHER SPORTS
>
> Ice-driving, snowmobiling, snow-shoeing, parapente, aeroclub, hang-gliding, swimming, helicopter rides, skating, curling, indoor tennis and racket-ball, climbing wall, hot-air ballooning, sleigh rides, snowcat skiing, ski-jumping, nature treks, night-skiing

4 miles (6km) away, is a large shopping centre selling end-of-the-line designer clothing.

A car is useful for exploring the area and the nearby resorts of Snowbird, **Alta**, **Solitude**, **Brighton**, **Wolf Mountain**, **Sundance** and Deer Valley. All of them are less than 45 minutes' drive from Park City.

Accommodation

Much of the accommodation is in condominiums, many of which are on the ski slopes. One of the most convenient places to stay is the Silver King Aparthotel, a complex offering 85 units, ranging from studios to penthouses. Most of the hotels are a few miles from Park City on the free bus route, including The Radisson Inn and Yarrow Hotel. The Chamonix Lodge is at the foot of the slopes, and The Prospector Square Hotel, which is about 15 minutes away by free shuttle bus, resembles a collection of Nissen huts and is priced accordingly. It also has a superb athletics club with an Olympic-sized indoor swimming-pool, four racket-ball courts and an impressively mechanised gym. The Best Western Landmark Inn at Wolf Mountain is good value and has its own sports complex.

Eating in and out

An evening on Main Street could have no more traditional start than dinner at The Claimjumper, an all-American establishment serving portions of 'surf-and-turf' and buffalo so huge that a 'wolfie bag' is the only way to clear your plate. Finer dining is available at Alex's, another popular Main Street haunt, where the menu includes decidedly non-American ingredients such as frogs' legs and sweetbreads. They tend to be over-sauced to conceal what many clients might see as their dubious origins, but a request for sauce on the side reveals that both the raw material and the cooking are good. The Ichiban Sushi and Japanese Cuisine, newly located opposite the Claimjumper, has a wide selection of fresh fish.

Après-ski

Main Street, which looks deceptively full of knick-knack shops and empty restaurants during the day, comes to life at night. There is a variety of bars to suit all tastes, with the Alamo bar serving as headquarters for the Park City Rugby Club. Its memorabilia shares the walls with stuffed moose and elk heads, omnipresent symbols of the great American West.

The Alamo has pool, table football, darts and occasional live music. Although it is a private club (often a prerequisite in the state of Utah because of the tough drinking laws), it has a relaxed approach towards sponsorship. This means that strangers ask the barman if he can find them a sponsor and he turns to the nearest drinker and asks him to oblige; he nods, you buy him a drink and you and your party are members for the evening.

Cisero's Club, further up Main Street on the opposite side, is owned by a pair of musicians who use their expertise to maintain high standards for their nightly live music sessions. It, too, is a private club, so again sponsors must be found. Exceptions to this rule include Park City Billiards, a pool hall near the Resort Center, The Shaft and the Wasatch Brew Pub at the top of Main Street. By 1.30am, Main Street is as quiet as London's Bond Street on Christmas Day.

Childcare

The Park City Ski School divides its tuition into Youth (7 to 12 years) and Kinderschule (3 to 6 years) programmes. The Kinderschule package also includes lunch and indoor supervision. The Kinderschule Mountain Adventure is for children aged three to six who are capable of snow-plough turns.

TOURIST OFFICE
Tel 1 801 649 8111
Fax 1 801 647 5374

Linked or nearby resorts

Deer Valley
top 9,400ft (2865m) bottom 7,200ft (2195m)

Unashamedly luxurious, Deer Valley is 3 miles (5km) north-east of Park City, up a winding mountain road lined with multi-million-dollar homes. It is a place where grooming counts, both on the meticulously pisted slopes ('the best grooming I have ever seen'), and with the clientèle, who are a walking advertisement for designer clothing. 'It is worth a visit for two or three days,' says one reporter, 'if only to observe the outfits'.

The skiing is on three different mountains served by 14 lifts and is constantly being expanded. A further 640 acres of Empire Canyon off the back of Flagstaff Mountain, which is served by a new chair-lift, will be opened during the 1996–7 season. Snowmaking has also been improved on all three mountains.

The Deer Valley Ski School offers group and private lessons, and special ski courses including black-diamond workshops, parallel break-through, style clinics, ladies-only clinics, mountain extreme and teen equipe (for 13- to 18-year-olds). Snowboarding is not allowed at Deer Valley. Children aged 2 months to 12 years are looked after by Deer Valley Child Care, and Deer Valley Children's Ski School takes children from 4½ to 12 years of age.

The resort is a short, free bus ride from Park City. There is no town as such, but there are several large condominiums and a few small hotels, including the Stein Eriksen Lodge. Restaurants include The Mariposa, and The Lounge is a popular bar.

TOURIST OFFICE
Tel 1 801 649 1000
Fax 1 801 649 1910

Wolf Mountain
top 9,600ft (2926m) bottom 6,800ft (2073m)
The resort is reached by a short, free shuttle-bus ride from Park City and offers a wide variety of terrain on three mountains served by seven chairs. All the lifts and trails are named after endangered animal species. Kids Central takes children from 18 months of age all day with or with-out ski or snowboard lessons. Its Skiers in Diapers programme offers private lessons for toddlers aged three years and under.

TOURIST OFFICE
Tel 1 801 649 5400
Fax 1 801 649 7374

Ski the Summit

ALTITUDE 9,300ft (2835m)–9,594ft (2925m)

Ski the Summit refers to four jointly marketed resorts incorporating a total of ten mountains within a 30-mile radius in Summit County, Colorado. The area, and in particular **Breckenridge**, attracts more European skiers than any other in the United States. Since **Keystone**, which already owned **Arapahoe Basin** five miles up the road, bought Breckenridge from its Japanese owners in 1993, **Copper Mountain** has become the odd resort out and is not included on the regular joint lift pass. There is all-round family skiing with no frills, and ample scope for stronger skiers on some mountains.

Only the old mining town of Breckenridge has a historic centre and any ambience. Arapahoe Basin, or A-Basin as it is known locally, is an older ski area without a developed base area. Keystone and Copper Mountain are both purpose-built, with Keystone having the most extensive night-skiing operation in the USA. The Summit County resorts are all close to each other and are reached easily by free shuttle bus or car.

> ### ■ GOOD POINTS
> Choice of ten mountains, ideal for family skiing and mixed-ability groups, excellent night-skiing, extensive snowmaking
>
> ### ■ BAD POINTS
> Extremely high altitude can cause health problems, busy at weekends, lift queues during high season

On the mountain
top 13,050ft (3978m) bottom 9,300ft (2835m)

Breckenridge has four linked mountains, part of the Ten Mile Range, the peaks of which are prosaically given numbers rather than names. The town sits at the foot of Peaks 7, 8, 9 and 10, and the skiing takes place on mainly north-east facing slopes. Peak 7 has a T-bar, which is its only lift. The summit can be reached only on foot, and there is no grooming. Each of the other mountains has at least one high-speed quad-chair. Peak 8 provides the most varied skiing and Peak 9 is gentler, with only about 10 per cent of the runs in the advanced category. Peak 10 is the toughest: two-thirds of the trails are difficult, and most of the others are intermediate. Any reasonably strong intermediate should be able to attack Breckenridge's skiing with gusto. One repeated criticism from European skiers is that the runs are annoyingly short.

Keystone, often the first North American resort to open each season, once had a reputation for bland skiing. Despite its long cruising trails, advanced skiers tended to ski at Keystone's funky old satellite of A-Basin. Then came North Peak, with its predominantly intermediate and

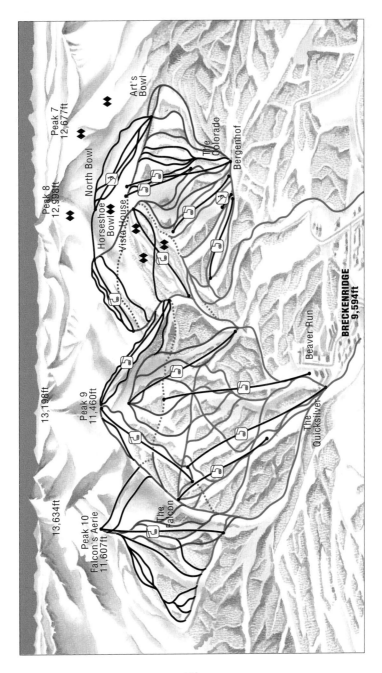

Peak 7
12,677ft

Art's Bowl

Peak 8
12,998ft

North Bowl

The Colorado

Bergenhof

Horseshoe Bowl

Vista House

13,198ft

Peak 9
11,460ft

BRECKENRIDGE
9,594ft

Beaver Run

The Quicksilver

13,634ft

Peak 10
Falcon's Aerie
11,607ft

The Falcon

advanced terrain. Hardly had these new runs opened when a third mountain, the Outback, was on the drawing board. This joined the lift system five years ago with a mix of open bowls, chutes and tree-line skiing.

Copper Mountain likes to describe its ski area as one of the best-designed in the North America. There is a natural tendency for the tree-lined trails to become more difficult as you move east (left on the piste-map). Thus experts tend to stick to the main face of Copper Peak, and beginners will find little beyond their capabilities on Union Peak. In between, the terrain is mainly intermediate. Last season, the opening up of 600 acres of Copper Bowl (over the back of Copper Peak) and a further 300 acres at Western Union greatly enhanced the resort.

Beginners

About a third of the runs on Breckenridge's Peak 9 are green (easy). Sawmill runs gently down the gulch, separating Peaks 8 and 9, to the Peak 9 base. Much of Peak 9's face is a network of green trails, notably Silverthorne, Lower American and Sundown. On Peak 8, the nursery slopes such as Freeway, Powerline and Park Lane are confined mainly to a wooded ridge close to the base. Beginners will find little for them on Peak 10. Similarly, there is little point in beginners at Keystone attempting to venture beyond Keystone Mountain, where a third of the trails are in the 'easiest' category. For complete beginners, Energiser and Bunny Slope are right at the base and have their own drag-lift. For adventurous novices, a long green trail called Schoolmarm runs from the top of the Skyway gondola all the way to the base, linking with other easy runs.

At A-Basin, Dercum's Gulch accesses the only long beginner trails of Wrangler, Sundance and Chisholm, however, there is also a small nursery area at the base. The substantial network of novice skiing can be summed up by one run, Easy Feelin', below Union Peak at Copper Mountain. Those who have logged a few days of skiing can ride the long high-speed American Flyer quad-chair to the top.

Intermediates

Intermediates will have a field-day working their way around the trails spread across the Ski the Summit slopes. They will have no trouble with the terrain on Peaks 8 and 9 at Breckenridge, except for a few short, sharp, black-diamond (difficult) chutes. On Keystone Mountain you can wander at will. From the top of the Lenawee and Norway lifts at A-Basin, almost every run down the middle is intermediate or beginner terrain. In spite of Copper Mountain's notion that the skiing is packaged into easily separated advanced, intermediate and beginner terrain, there is little here on the groomed trails that could intimidate a parallel skier.

Advanced

The principal lift-served advanced terrain at Breckenridge is a string of chutes between Peaks 8 and 9, with emotive names like Psychopath, Adios and Lobo. The extreme flank of Peak 10 also includes some harsh runs like Black Hawk, Dark Rider and Mustang. Some of the mogulled chutes on the otherwise benign Peak 9, such as Mineshaft and Devil's Crotch, are fierce and challenging.

Keystone's North Peak has black-diamond trails like Ambush, Black Hawk and Cat Dancer, plus the Black Forest runs of Timberwolf, Bushwacker, Badger, or the Grizz in The Outback.

A-Basin has the highest lift-served skiing, and Palivacinni is one of the longest bump runs in North America.

Off-piste

Peak 7 Bowl and Art's Bowle off Peak 7 are the areas that off-piste skiers will want to try at Breckenridge, along with the other bowls off neighbouring Peak 8: Imperial, Horseshoe, Contest and Cucumber. Horseshoe Bowl is accessed by a T-bar, which is a rarity in America. The Burn area of Peak 10 provides some fun tree-line skiing.

The bowls at Keystone's Outback are challenging but short. A-Basin has exciting ungroomed terrain in the Alleys and off the East Wall.

Copper Mountain now has substantial off-piste in Copper Bowl, served by the Extreme Access double-chair, as well as snowcat tours. There is also excellent ungroomed terrain on the flanks of Copper Peak, off both sides of the Storm King lift, in Spaulding Bowl and Enchanted Forest, which link with Hallelujah Bowl, Looking Glass and Cache Glades.

Ski schools and guiding

The highly rated Breckenridge Ski School offers special courses and ski clinics, including mogul tuition. One reporter echoed the thoughts of many others: 'Organisation from beginning to end was superb. The tuition was professional, friendly, and effective. Would that anyone could match this in Europe'. Keystone's ski school has small classes of up to eight pupils. Copper Mountain Ski School offers group and private lessons, as well as bumps and powder workshops and beginner packages.

Snowboarding

Breckenridge has a snowboard park and half-pipe and permits the sport on all four mountains; two-day Catch The Wave Snowboarding clinics are available. It is not permitted at Keystone, where riders are advised to go to nearby A-Basin. Copper Mountain has an annual snowboard race series, and boarding is allowed everywhere on the mountain. There is also a half-pipe.

Mountain restaurants

In Breckenridge, the Bergenhof Restaurant is at the base of Peak 8, while the Vista House with its homemade specialities is at the top of the Colorado Super Chair. Peak 9 has the Copper Top and Maggie at its base, as well as the uninspiringly named Peak 9 Restaurant on the slopes. Falcon's Aerie at the top of the Falcon Super Chair on Peak 10 is recommended for snacks. Peak 8 is generally quieter than Peak 9, but one reporter comments that such is the demand for seats that lunch after 1pm can result in a cold hot-dog.

The Alpenglow Stube is the ultimate US version of a European mountain restaurant. Perched at 11,444ft (3490m) at the Outpost on top of North Peak, the attractive restaurant offers four-or-more-course gourmet lunches. These are enhanced by magnificent scenery and a splendid crackling fire; unbooted feet relax in the moccasins that are provided. Quicker, cheaper fare at the Outpost can be found at the Timber Ridge Cafeteria ('beautifully situated with marvellous views'). At the top of the main mountain is Taco's On, a separate cafeteria, and a barbecue in fine weather. At the base area, Gassy's is a popular lunch spot, while the Mountain House Cafeteria is ideal for a quick pit-stop. Ernie's Pizzeria is also recommended.

A-Basin has a cafeteria and bar at the base and a barbecue mid-mountain. At the top of the American Flyer quad-chair in Copper, Flyers features 'gourmet sandwiches' and 'patio-dining at its best'. Solitude Station, at the summit of the American Eagle quad-chair, has an outdoor grill. At the base is O'Shea's and the Copper Commons Day Lodge. In the Mountain Plaza building at the base, Pesce Fresco offers excellent fresh fish and homemade pasta. The Clubhouse and the Union Creek Day Lodge both have barbecues.

Off the mountain

All visitors arriving from sea-level should take serious heed of the high altitude, which takes several days of acclimatisation. The top-station is the best part of two miles above sea-level, and at 9,596ft (2925m) Breckenridge is 2,051ft (625m) higher than Val Thorens in France. Alcohol intake should be reduced at the start of your holiday, and you should drink plenty of water. If you ski at all on the first day, take it very easy indeed.

■ **OTHER SPORTS**

Swimming, snowmobiling, racket-ball, skating, sleigh rides, snow-shoeing, indoor tennis, climbing wall

Breckenridge has seen it all: the old mining town went from boom to bust, and then found new life and prosperity as one of America's most famous ski resorts. Because of surveying errors, Breckenridge was accidentally left off the map of America until 1936. Today, the formula of four linked mountains, plus an old but cleverly spruced-up main street awash with Victorian buildings, has proved successful. A horse-drawn sleigh driven not by an Austrian in Tyrolean jacket, but by a cowboy in stetson and floor-length duster, incongruously plies for hire in streets heavy with traffic.

Keystone started life as an old railhead. It was not until the 1960s that a group of developers created this lakeside mountain resort. A 15-year, $400-million development plan to transform the base area into an 'old' town with real character is now under way with the construction of The Village at River Run at the foot of the Skyway Gondola. Expect to see enormous changes here as the new town of Keystone takes shape.

Copper Mountain, purpose-built on the site of an old lumber and mining town (Wheeler Junction), is rather drab; copper-brown is the dominant colour. More recent development has broken away from this, providing a brighter and more cheerful ambience.

Accommodation

Breckenridge rather preciously describes itself as 'the motherlode' of lodging, boasting more slope-side accommodation than any other Colorado ski resort. There is certainly a wide range of hotels (including a Hilton), lodges, condominiums and bed-and-breakfast accommodation. The Village At Breckenridge Resort has its own sports centre as well as 40 shops and restaurants. The Beaver Run Resort is handy for the slopes. Breckenridge Mountain Lodge ('outdoor hot tubs, comfortable rooms, good breakfasts') offers comfortable but cheap accommodation near the town centre, and the Powderhorn Apartments, Pine Ridge, and the Liftside Condominiums are also recommended. The Lodge at Breckenridge is a spa outside the resort with its own shuttle bus. Williams House is a restored gold-miner's home offering bed-and-breakfast with en-suite bedrooms, which are furnished with antiques ('excellent and highly recommended.')

Keystone and Copper have predominantly condos, and A-Basin has no lodging at all. Keystone's accommodation includes the lakeside Keystone Lodge, which has a swimming-pool, restaurant and fitness centre, and the luxurious slopeside Chateaux d'Mont condos. Just outside the main village there is accommodation at the delightful Ski Tip Lodge, which was a stagecoach inn during the 1860s. The Inn at Keystone is another pleasant country lodge.

Eating in and out

Breckenridge has a wide range of restaurants, but we have consistent complaints of unacceptable queues for tables between 6.30 and 8pm, caused by failure to accept advance bookings. Reporters spoke of estimated 45-minute waits lasting twice as long. However, 'it is cheaper to eat out in Breckenridge than in Sheffield', said one reporter. Le Bon Fondue is singled out for consistently good crêpes and pasta ('served with Austrian beer') along with Pierre's Terrace for 'fine French fare'. Fa-Heatas Bar and Grill offers Mexican food. Mi-Casa, another long-established Mexican restaurant, received mixed comments. Blue River Bistro 'serves consistently excellent Italian fare'. The Breckenridge Brewery offers good-value food and 'brilliant beer'. The Whale's Tail is singled out for its 'excellent food and service'. The Hearthstone is highly rated for its 'unbelievably good Jalepeño prawns'. Fatty's and Downstairs at Eric's are both recommended for pizzas. The Snow Goose serves 'an astounding breakfast'. The resort is adequately served with food shops, and one supermarket, a mile out of town.

The restored Keystone Ranch serves six-course dinners, The Bighorn Steak House in the Keystone Lodge is known for fresh seafood, and the Ski Tip Lodge serves candle-lit four-course dinners in an intimate, wood-beamed dining-room. The Alpenglow Stube stays open for late-night diners using the resort's gondolas, and Der Fondue Chessel opens for Swiss-style fondue and raclette. You can also try the 'progressive dinner', which involves taking each course in a different restaurant, with a stagecoach for transport.

At Copper Mountain, the Racquet and Athletic Club offers above-average dining, and Farley's, in the Snowflake building, is also popular. The B-Lift pub is another favourite. The Imperial Palace offers Chinese food in the Village Square, where other restaurants include That Soup Place. The Corner Grocery provides a reasonable choice for self-caterers.

The Chateaux d'Mont at Keystone provides guests with a welcome pack of groceries. Grocery shopping is not easy at the Keystone Condominiums as you have to cross the main road to get to the shops.

Après-ski

At Breckenridge, the Gold Pan Saloon has a smoky, olde-worlde atmosphere and dancing. An equally lively evening can be spent sampling the local brew at the Breckenridge Brewery and Pub. Jake T Pounder has cowboy music. Other popular night haunts include the Whale's Tail and Shamus O'Toole's Roadhouse Saloon. Downstairs At Eric's and Joshua's at the bottom of Peak 9 both provide loud music. Tiffany's in the Beaver Run Resort has live music as the lifts close ('lots of audience participation'). Tiger Run Tours offers guided snowmobiling into the backwoods then on to an abandoned mining camp for dinner; it is alcohol-free because you have to drive back again.

At Keystone, Bandito's has live entertainment and pool tables. The Snake River Saloon in Dillon is a lively spot, and Montezuma's in Keystone village has a large dance floor.

The Copper Mountain Racquet and Athletic Club has excellent facilities, including a swimming-pool, indoor tennis and racket-ball courts. Visiting international ski-racers make use of the gymnasium. Skating on West Lake is free from midday until 10pm. In Copper Mountain the liveliest haunts include the B-Lift Pub, Farley's and O'Shea's.

Childcare

As the Ski the Summit resorts are particularly high, children, especially, can suffer from dehydration caused by the altitude. In Breckenridge, Kid's Castle at the base of Peak 8 incorporates a Children's Center. The equivalent at the base of Peak 9 takes children from three years old for skiing or play. The Cuddly Bear Toddlers' Center at the Hilton looks after one- to three-year-olds.

The Children's Center at Keystone Mountain Base accepts infants as young as two months, and the nursery at A-Basin from 18 months of age. Keystone Nursery is a non-ski kindergarten for infants and upwards. Mini-Minors is a ski kindergarten for three- to four-year-olds,

Skiing facts: **Breckenridge**

TOURIST OFFICE
PO Box 1058, Breckenridge, CO 80424
Tel 1 970 453 5000
Fax 1 970 453 3202

THE RESORT
By air Denver International Airport 2 hrs
Visitor beds 26,000
Transport free bus and trolley system runs
throughout resort

THE SKIING
Linked or nearby resorts Arapahoe Basin
(n), Copper Mountain (n), Keystone (n)
Longest run Four O' Clock, $3\frac{1}{2}$ miles
(5.6km) - blue/green
Number of lifts 17
Total of trails/pistes 2,023 acres (818
hectares) (14% easy, 26% intermediate,
60% difficult)
Nursery slopes 3 children's areas with
lifts: the Village Center, Beaver Run and
Peak 8 Children's Center
Summer skiing none
Snowmaking 369 acres (149 hectares)
covered

LIFT PASSES
Area pass Ski the Summit (covers
Breckenridge, Keystone and A-Basin), $198
for 6 days
Day pass $44 (all three areas)
Beginners no free lifts
Pensioners 60-69 yrs $23 per day, free for
70 yrs and over

Credit cards accepted yes

SKI SCHOOLS
Adults Breckenridge Ski School (Peak
8/Peak 9/Village), 9.45am-4pm, $240 for
6 days
Private lessons $70 per hr
Snowboarding as regular ski lessons
Cross-country Breckenridge Nordic Center,
details on request. Loipe 38km
Other courses moguls, race training,
women's seminars
Guiding companies none

CHILDREN
Lift pass 6-14 yrs, $20 per day
Ski kindergarten Peak 8 and Peak 9
Children's Centers: 6-12 yrs, 8.30am-
4.30pm, $52 per day including lunch;
4-5 yrs, 8.30am-4.30pm, $60 per day
including lunch, or $265 for 5 days
Ski school Breckenridge Ski School,
6-12 yrs, 9.45am-4pm, $150 for 6 days
including lunch
Non-ski kindergarten Snow Play at Peak 8
(2-5 yrs) and Peak 9 (3-5 yrs),
8.30am-4.30pm, $55 per day including
lunch. Infant and toddler care at Peak 8
Children's Center, 2 mths-5 yrs,
8.30am-4.30pm, $55 per day

FOOD AND DRINK PRICES
Coffee $1, glass of wine $4,
small beer $2.50,
dish of the day $10-15

and Minor's Camp is for children from five years of age.

At Copper, the Belly Button Babies accepts children from two months to two years old, and its stable-mate the Belly Button Bakery caters for children over two and skiers over three years of age. Copper Mountain has Junior and Senior Ranch ski programmes for children.

Snowbird

ALTITUDE 8,100ft (2468m)

In the state of Utah, which proclaims it has the greatest snow on earth, Snowbird is generally considered a prime example of where this fortunate phenomenon can be experienced. Like Alta, its near neighbour up the road in the steep-sided Little Cottonwood Canyon, Snowbird receives some of the deepest and driest snow in North America. The skiing terrain is prettier than in many Utah resorts, but the architecture is uglier. The resort, situated less than 30 miles (48km) from Salt Lake City International Airport, is dominated by the Cliff Lodge, a huge 11-storey building of concrete and glass.

On the mountain
top 11,000 ft (3352m) bottom 8,100ft (2468m)

Snowbird has one of America's few cable cars, or 'aerial trams' as they are called in the US. This whisks 125 skiers almost 3,000ft (914m) to the top of Hidden Peak in eight minutes. There is only one easy run down: Chips, a 3-mile (5-km) trail back to the base area. Elsewhere, the higher skiing is dominated by bowls, chutes and gullies — an exciting arena for advanced skiers who enjoy powering through steep, ungroomed snow. There is a shortage of real novice skiing, but intermediates are well catered for.

Beginners
The new Baby Thunder lift opens up a network of green (easy) runs and the slightly more demanding blue (intermediate) trail, Thunder Alley, which all end up below the village. Novice skiers should stay away from the top of Hidden Peak unless they really feel they can cope with Chips Run, which is a very long blue. If you have the stamina only for part of Chips, the Peruvian lift goes almost halfway. Complete beginners might want to ski off the Chickadee lift down by the Cliff Lodge. Otherwise, the Mid Gad Lift (with a midway unloading station) and the Wilbere lift serve some of Snowbird's least intimidating terrain. This includes Big Emma, which is one of the widest green slopes in the Rockies.

Intermediates
The area offers a number of well-groomed runs best suited to confident parallel skiers. Bassackwards, Election, Bananas and Lunch Run are all

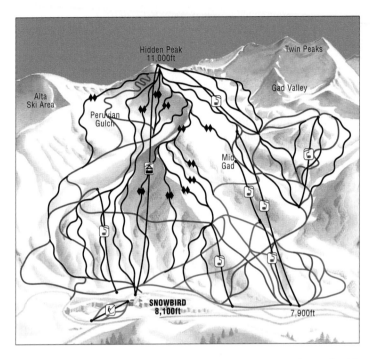

straightforward cruising trails. However, the ski area is littered with black-diamond (difficult) slopes and intimidating double-black-diamond (very difficult) runs; considerable care should be taken to avoid embarking on a slope that may be too testing.

Advanced

Strong skiers are spoilt for choice, with everything from fairly easy, open-bowl skiing to very difficult bump chutes. With the exception of Chips, all the runs off Hidden Peak are classified as either single- or double-black-diamond. There are also challenging black (difficult) runs through spruce and lodgepole pine, such as Gadzooks and Tiger Tail, which are reached from the Gad 2 lift. The Road To Provo traverse from Hidden Peak (also reached by the Little Cloud lift) leads to other challenging runs like Black Forest and Organ Grinder.

> **■ WHAT'S NEW**
>
> Gad 2 chair-lift now open to snowboarders

Off-piste

Snowbird's off-piste terrain is superb, and the key to it is the Cirque Traverse from Hidden Peak. From this narrow ridge skiers can drop off both sides into a large selection of chutes and gullies. Some are sandwiched between pines, which have been twisted and stunted by blizzards; others are guarded by imposing outcrops of granite. Plunges into Silver Fox, Great Scott and Upper Cirque on one side and Wilbere Chute, Wilbere Bowl, Barry Barry Steep and Gad on the other can be exhilarating in fresh, deep snow and quite frightening in difficult conditions. There is also some challenging back-country skiing below Twin Peaks in Gad Valley.

Ski schools and guiding
As well as normal lessons, the ski school operates speciality workshops for style, bumps-and-diamonds and racing. There is also a Mountain Experience clinic as well as free guided tours.

Snowboarding
Snowboarders are now allowed on the whole of the mountain. Speciality snowboard workshops are available.

Mountain restaurants
The only real restaurant on the mountain is at Mid Gad. The Snowbird trail-map describes it as a 'fuel stop', which is exactly what it is. The Peak Express warming hut on Hidden Peak serves coffee and light snacks.

Off the mountain
Snowbird is no beauty. When Dick Bass, a fast-talking Texan oilman, built Snowbird almost 30 years ago he had apparently fallen under the spell of the latest concrete additions in the Alps. Officially, the heart of the resort is Snowbird Center, the departure point for the aerial tram, but it is the mirrored walls of the Cliff Lodge with its 11-storey atrium that dominate the long, narrow sprawl of contemporary buildings and car-parking facilities.

The Center consists of the Plaza Deck and open space surrounded by limited shops on three levels. Outlying buildings house condominiums, and the overall impression is of a single-function resort with few alternatives for non-skiers.

Accommodation
Most people stay either at the Cliff Lodge or one of the three other condominium lodges nearby: The Lodge at Snowbird, The Inn and the Iron Blosam Lodge.

Eating in and out
The choice of 12 restaurants includes the Aerie at the top of the Cliff Lodge, which is enclosed by glass and offers continental cuisine and a sushi bar, and the Keyhole Junction (also in the Cliff Lodge), which serves South-western food. Pier 49 at Snowbird Center serves gourmet pizzas, and the Steakpit offers a choice that includes king crab. The Wildflower Ristorante at the Iron Blosam Lodge specialises in Italian

food. Several reporters commented on the lack of anywhere suitable to take children to eat.

Après-ski

Due to Utah's licensing laws, all of Snowbird's bars are designated as private clubs, and those who wish to drink in them must buy a resort membership card ($5 for two weeks). Each member may be accompanied by four friends. This is more a bureaucratic nonsense than a deterrent, but Snowbird's bars are few in number and formal enough to deter all but the most enthusiastic nightlifers. Immediately after the lifts close, skiers gravitate to the Forklift, just across the plaza from the tram (cable car) and the Wildflower Lodge. Later on, the Aerie often has a pianist, but sitting here until closing time at 1am is not particularly exciting. If the roads are clear and no storms are imminent you could try a night out in Salt Lake City, 25 miles (40km) away.

Childcare

Daycare for children of two months and upwards is available at the Camp Snowbird Children's Center at the Cliff Lodge. The ski school offers programmes combining ski instruction with daycare.

Linked or nearby resorts

Alta
top 10,595ft (3229m) bottom 8,550ft (2606m)

This is an old-fashioned, unpretentious resort revered by powder skiers, ski bums and skiers in search of a cheap lift ticket and powder that can sometimes better Snowbird's. Alta, just a mile up the hill from Snowbird, was here some 30 years before Snowbird and likes to remind you of that fact. It has rather more beginner/lower intermediate terrain but has

> ■ **OTHER SPORTS**
>
> Climbing wall, indoor tennis, squash and racket-ball

phenomenal chutes and secret powder caches reached only by back-country hiking. Devotees refuse to accept that Snowbird is in the same class, and realists count their blessings that two outstanding powder resorts are so close together. Many believe that eventually the two will be linked; they already form the most challenging section of the back-country Interconnect circuit, which includes **Park City**, **Solitude** and **Brighton**, in an attempt to reproduce the alpine concept of skiing from one resort to another.

TOURIST OFFICE
Tel 1 801 742 3333
Fax 1 801 742 3333 411

Steamboat

ALTITUDE 6,900ft (2104m)

The resort lies at the foot of Rabbit Ears Pass in north-west Colorado, a three-and-a-half hour drive from downtown Denver. Legend has it that Steamboat Springs came into being in 1865 when three French trappers mistook a chugging noise on the River Yampa for a paddle-steamer, only to discover that it came from bubbling mineral springs. With Gallic logic they duly conjured up Steamboat Springs. Over the next few decades, the broad Yampa Valley was permanently settled for the first time, mostly by homesteaders raising cattle. In 1912, Norwegian, Carl Howelsen, introduced ski-jumping lessons, followed two years later by the first Winter Carnival, with jumping competitions as the main attraction.

■ GOOD POINTS

Ski-in ski-out convenience, easily accessible nursery slopes, excellent snow record, easy tree-level skiing, large choice of quality restaurants, wide range of activities for non-skiers

■ BAD POINTS

Limited ski area, restricted challenge for advanced skiers, lack of resort atmosphere (Steamboat), town not within walking distance of lifts

Skiing took off in the 1960s, triggered by the opening of the first double chair-lift on Storm Mountain in 1963 and the silver medal won by local boy, Billy Kidd, in the Innsbruck Olympics the following year. When Kidd retired, he was appointed Steamboat's Director of Skiing. In this capacity, he joined forces with world champion cowboy, Larry Mahan, to found the Cowboy Downhill, a unique slalom with roping and saddling elements, which is held each January for more than 100 professional rodeo riders in full costume.

Steamboat trades heavily on this cowboy motif in its marketing strategy, but the reality is that it has much less Western atmosphere than some of its Colorado rivals. As is often the case in the Rockies, what you actually get is a two-tier resort connected by a shuttle bus. Steamboat, at the base of the mountain, is all ski-in ski-out convenience, but the real action is in **Steamboat Springs**, 4 miles (6km) away in the valley.

On the mountain
top 10,385ft (3165m) bottom 6,900ft (2103m)

The skiing covers three interlinked mountains: Sunshine Peak, Storm Peak and Mount Werner (formerly Storm Mountain). Although the area is served by a modern lift system backed up by extensive snowmaking, the terrain is of even pitch, which limits the variety of the challenge. The efficient Silver Bullet gondola takes skiers up to the Thunderhead

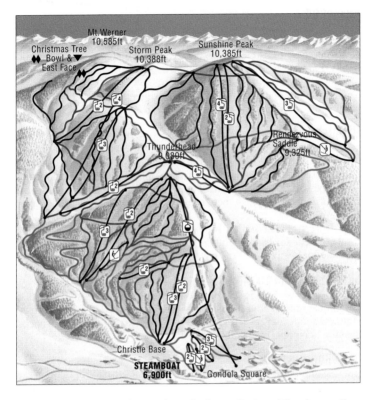

mid-station and two high-speed quads, Storm Peak and Sundown, allow them to fan out rapidly over the upper slopes.

Beginners

The wide, flat area at the base of the gondola within two minutes' walk of Ski Time Square is an ideal place to learn to ski or snowboard. It is served by six learner lifts, several of them chairs, which are readily slowed down on request for easy access. Phase two is from the Christie Chairs, which rise out of the base area to give access to friendly green (easy) runs with silly names like Yoo Hoo and Giggle Gulch. By the third day, competent beginners should be able to ride the Silver Queen lift and return to base easily via Why Not and Right-O-Way.

Intermediates

As Steamboat has a relatively low altitude by Colorado standards, there are trees all the way up the mountain, which means that almost all the skiing is in glades cut out of the forest. Most of the trails are extremely wide and all are impeccably prepared, giving plenty of cruising on all three mountains. The visibility is always excellent.

Advanced

The only 'real' black (difficult) runs are the chutes on Mount Werner, on the extreme edge of the ski area. As you hike along the access ridge, you come to Chutes One, Two and Three, Christmas Tree Bowl and finally East Face, short shots which become progressively steeper. Otherwise, the toughest skiing is on Three o'Clock, Two o'Clock and Twilight; these parallel glades on Sunshine Peak quickly become mogulled.

Off-piste

Whenever new snow falls, Steamboat's great glory is the easy tree-skiing within the resort boundaries. At the top of Sunshine Peak, the forest is quite dense but it soon opens out to allow uninhibited action among the aspens between Closet and Shadows trails. Another excellent area is off the Storm Peak Express, between Cyclone, Typhoon, Tornado and Nelson's Run.

The irrepressible Jupiter Jones, owner of Steamboat Powder Cats, runs excellent day trips to Buffalo Pass in the Routt National Park, a few miles out of town.

Ski schools and guiding

The Steamboat Ski School in Gondola Square offers a Beginner's Guarantee scheme for complete novices, plus group lessons for adults, children and teenagers. The Billy Kidd Center provides more advanced training in bumps, racing and other disciplines.

Snowboarding

Snowboarders are made extremely welcome in this resort, with easily accessible nursery slopes and a specialist board-park at Sunnyside, near the Elkhead lift. Last season, riders bought an estimated one-in-three lift tickets and the Steamboat Snowboard School employed ten more instructors to meet the extra demand for lessons.

Cross-country

The Steamboat Ski Touring Center at the base of Mount Werner has 30km of groomed trails. One-hour group lessons can be arranged at the day lodge and half- and full-day back-country tours on Rabbit Ears Pass are also available.

Mountain restaurants

In tune with the current trend in the Rockies, Steamboat provides gourmet lunches as a supplement to the customary cafeteria fare. The most sophisticated option is Hazie's at the Thunderhead mid-station, but the printed caveat against drinking alcohol in the course of a skiing day may not suit some European visitors. The alternative sit-down choice, Ragnar's at Rendezvous Saddle, specialises in Scandinavian dishes. Both the Thunderhead and Rendezvous self-services have sun-deck barbecues.

Off the mountain

Steamboat's commercial heart is Gondola Square, the focal point of the whole ski area, but the dominant element is the concrete and glass bulk of the Sheraton Hotel crouched on the hilltop above it. This is surrounded by malls and condominiums, which become progressively more attractive the further you fan out from the centre. The Steamboat Springs Old Town consists almost entirely of Lincoln Avenue, a broad street that has not been prettified to the same degree as rivals like Breckenridge. Lincoln Avenue boasts a first-run multi-screen cinema, shops that go far beyond the normal range of ski-related goods and most of the best restaurants.

> **■ OTHER SPORTS**
>
> Ice-driving, dog-sledding, swimming, sleigh rides, winter fly-fishing, bungee jumping, hot-air ballooning, snowmobiling

Accommodation

The Sheraton is convenient, but once you are inside, you could just as well be in Los Angeles or Houston. Those who need to be within a stone's throw of the lifts might prefer the Ptarmigan Inn, which also has an outdoor pool and hot tub, plus a more cheerful bar. Steamboat Springs offers a choice between renovated old-style and simple new, represented most centrally by the Harbor Hotel and the Alpiner Lodge on opposite sides of Lincoln Avenue.

Eating in and out

For a resort of this size, the range and quality of the restaurants is impressive. Remingtons at the Sheraton represents hotel-chain grandeur and expense, but there is finer dining at L'Apogee, Antares, Cipriani's and the Steamboat Yacht Club. Riggio's has a cheaper line in Italian fare and the Chart House has the best salad bar in town. There is Chinese cuisine at the Panda Garden and the Canton, excellent sushi at Yama Chan's and Mexican at La Montana. Alternatively, you can ride the Silver Queen by night and dine on the mountain at Hazie's, or plunder the eat-as-much-as-you-can buffet at the BK Corral. Another on-mountain option is the snowcat ride to Ragner's. Condo dwellers will appreciate the chain supermarkets, but they are inconveniently sited halfway between Steamboat and Steamboat Springs.

Après-ski

When the lifts close, beer lovers gather at Steamboat's Heavenly Daze Brewery in Ski Time Square and the Steamboat Brewery and Tavern on Lincoln Avenue at Steamboat Springs. Lively watering holes include the Inferno (live country and western music), the Tugboat and Dos Amigos, which are all near the base of the mountain. In the downtown area, BW-3 (live music) and the Old Town Pub, which first opened its saloon doors in 1904, have happy hours and pool tables. More active après-ski takes place on Howelsen Hill, a floodlit area overlooking Steamboat Springs with facilities for night-skiing and skating. It also has a one-mile, four-man bobsled track and two ski jumps. The natural springs at Strawberry Park Hot Springs, located a few miles out of town, provide a less stressful alternative. Murphy's Exchange Pub is lively until late, as is Harwigs. Those who are prepared to brave the locals should try ZZ but be prepared for regulars to say, 'this is my chair, so get out of it'.

Childcare

Kiddie Corral Child Care has programmes for infants and pre-school children. The Buckaroos is for two- to three-and-a-half year olds, while the Sundance Kids and Mavericks is for children over three-and-a-half. Evening care is available from Tuesday to Saturday at the Kids Adventure Club, an indoor camp with supervised games, snacks, videos and rest for children aged two-and-a-half to twelve years.

TOURIST OFFICE
Tel 1 970 879 6111
Fax 1 970 879 7844

Vail/Beaver Creek

ALTITUDE Vail: 8,200ft (2500m) Beaver Creek: 8,100ft (2470m)

Vail is consistently voted top resort in the US and it is easy to see why. This picturesque, pedestrianised village, modelled on those in the Tyrol, is one of the biggest ski areas in North America. It has perfectly groomed slopes, serviced by an efficient lift system, which provide good skiing for all standards. Colorado boasts 300 days of sunshine a year, and while the Rockies may not provide the dramatic peaks, couloirs and glaciers of the Alps, guaranteed sun and consistent light powder weigh heavily in its favour.

By European standards, Vail's 26 lifts seem a small number, especially when compared to the Trois Vallées, which have over 200. However, the eager visitor can get as much skiing in Vail as in Europe by consistently riding the high-speed quads. Nearby **Beaver Creek** is now linked to **Arrowhead**; together these two resorts provide a further 13 lifts and 78 trails.

■ GOOD POINTS

Favourable snow record, terrain to suit all standards, separate children's ski area, recommended ski school, good introduction to off-piste skiing, wide choice of restaurants and après-ski

■ BAD POINTS

Limited steep skiing, few activities for non-skiers, lack of characterful mountain restaurants, high-priced accommodation and restaurants

Unlike some of the Wild West resorts historically linked with mining, Vail is a new town. The mountain was developed by Pete Siebert, a 10th Mountain Division ski trooper, who, together with local resident Earl Eaton, opened the slopes on 15 December 1962 with three lifts and eight instructors. Today, Vail, Beaver Creek and Arrowhead together have one of the largest ski schools in the world, with 1,100 instructors and more than two million pupils a season.

Whereas Aspen attracts the Hollywood crowd, Vail tends to play host to Wall Street bankers. As a result, the restaurants and shops are largely upmarket. However, there are nooks and crannies where you can buy a *cappuccino* for under $3 and a reasonably priced lunch.

The outward growth of Vail has been limited by the ever present I-70 freeway, which borders the 7-mile (4-km) stretch of conurbation from **East Vail** to **Cascade Village**. East Vail, a free bus ride away from the slopes, is where much of the chalet accommodation is located. **Lionshead** is at the west base of the Vail ski area. The only advantage of Vail's motorway location is that it is possible to ski other resorts such as **Copper Mountain, Breckenridge, Aspen** and **Steamboat** for the day and be back in Vail for the evening.

The resort's successful bid to host the 1999 World Alpine

Championships means that the next few years will see substantial capital expediture on new lifts, restaurants, snowmaking and trail development.

Ten miles west of Vail lies Beaver Creek, one of the most luxurious ski resorts in America, which is included on the Vail lift pass. Many visitors to Vail ski Beaver Creek for a day out of curiosity, and then wish they had more time to ski it again. Its long winding trails, lack of crowds, and family-oriented facilities are fast helping to develop its reputation as a rival to Vail. On powder days, when the hounds head to the Back Bowls, the locals hit Beaver Creek's Grouse Mountain. The base area that is now steeped in exclusive condominiums and five-star hotels was once a mining village. In 1880 two miners who were prospecting in the waterfalls at Eagle River struck gold. The two miners named the nearby stream Beaver Creek, and the name has proved to be more durable than the mine. Beaver Creek is the first ski area to be designed by a computer programme, and plans have had to satisfy a growing hardcore of Colorado environmentalists.

■ **WHAT'S NEW**

Bachelor Gulf Express lift allows village-to-village skiing between Beaver Creek and Arrowhead.

$27-milllion redevelopment of Golden Peak base

Chair 6 upgraded to quad and realigned

In 1994, Vail Associates bought neighbouring Arrowhead Mountain, which is now linked into the ski area by the Bachelor Gulch Express quad, giving access to a further 180 acres of trails and creating a rare North American example of village-to-village skiing.

On the mountain

Vail: top 11,450ft (3491m) bottom 8,200ft (2500m)
Beaver Creek/Arrowhead: top 11,440ft (3488m) bottom 7,400ft (2255m)

The limited ski-in ski-out access to Vail is compensated for by the free bus system, which drops off skiers five minutes from the main high-speed chair-lift, the Vista Bahn. This is often congested at morning peak-times, but there are three other access points: Golden Peak, near the beginner slopes on the east side of the mountain; Lionshead, with its gondola and high-speed quad; and Cascade Village, outside the Westin Resort on the west side. The Lionshead gondola has been rebuilt for this season with capacity increased from 800 to 3,000 skiers per hour.

The three main areas on the front face of the mountain have mostly pisted runs on north-facing slopes. On the back side are the Back Bowls, which are not pisted except for the occasional blue (intermediate) run.

For skiers who have battled against icy conditions, breakable crust and poor snow-cover in Europe, typical Colorado conditions will come as a great delight. The light, fluffy snow is easy to ski and described as velvet or corduroy — so named because of the stripes left from the piste-bashers. State-of-the-art snowmaking, which ensures cover from late November throughout the season, means the mountain is always in good condition; ice is unusual in the Rockies. In a country where the

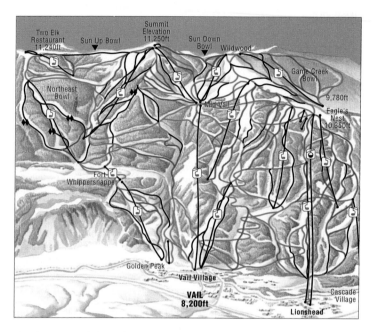

development of skiing has been dictated by costly lawsuits, the result is immaculate and consistent piste-grooming, excellent signposting, and diligent patrolling. The courtesy of the local people is much commented on: 'Being helped on to chair-lifts makes a pleasant change from Europe — in fact, everyone seems to try harder to make things work.'

The 4,112 acres (1664 hectares) of skiing includes 121 trails. The variety of pistes ranges from challenging mogul runs to long, easy cruises. The tree-line goes up to 11,000ft (3353m) and there are many areas to explore that are not marked on the map. Getting around the mountain is easy enough to enable beginners and experts, parents and children to meet at one of the mountain restaurants or base areas for lunch.

However, readers experienced high-season queues of up to 30 minutes on the Orient Express lift, which serves 15 runs, though 'the signboards at the top of the mountain indicating whether a lift was clear or had a wait of at least 20 minutes were very useful, usually making it possible to find some skiing without too long a delay'.

The skiing at Beaver Creek covers four areas: Spruce Saddle, Grouse Mountain, Strawberry Park and Arrowhead. Most of it is intermediate, with several double-black-diamond (very difficult) runs on Grouse Mountain. There are 78 runs covering 1,371 acres (554 hectares) and 13 lifts. The longest run, Piece of Cake, is 3½ miles (5.6km).

Free mountain tours, which take three hours for intermediate skiers, depart daily at 9am from the Guest Information Centers in Vail Village and Lionshead. There is a similar tour at Beaver Creek.

Beginners

Most of the beginner slopes are located at Golden Peak, where there are a variety of runs and short lifts to suit most standards. The base area here is currently the target for a $27-million reconstruction programme, and Chair 6 is being uprgraded to a quad and realigned so that skiers can access the Back Bowls by two swift lifts. The children's ski area is reached via the Golden Peak lift, where there is an enclosed area called Fort Whippersnapper, which is a model of an old frontier fort. Ski school beginner classes meet here or at Lionshead, which has the other main beginner area. Golden Peak is a quieter area off the beaten track from the main pistes, whereas Lionshead is a major thoroughfare, especially at lunchtime and at the end of the day. For second-week skiers there are many runs on all parts of the mountain. The beginner slopes (green on the piste-map) are wide and flat with no sudden steep pitches, and are always groomed. There are novice slopes off all the main lifts and from all the mountain restaurants.

At Beaver Creek, the beginner area is at the base of the Centennial Express lift, and there is a park for children at Spruce Saddle. There are a number of green (easy) runs suitable for confident beginners off the top of Stump Park lift.

Intermediates

It takes about two runs for intermediate skiers to become instant con-verts to American skiing. Those who have never skied powder or bump runs will find Vail Mountain the perfect training ground. Others who want to clock up vertical feet may feel they need new legs at the end of the day. The main skiing area is reached by taking the Vista Bahn to Mid-Vail, where many of the runs funnel into an area served by two high-speed quads. The Mountaintop Express lift goes to the summit from where you can access the Back Bowls, take long winding runs back to Mid-Vail or ski blue or black (difficult) runs to the Northwoods chair.

Game Creek Bowl can be accessed by challenging black runs, includ-ing Ouzo and Faro, that lead through the trees (keep an eye out for por-cupines), or by the medium-gradient runs such as The Woods and Dealer's Choice, which usually have some bumps. Do not be put off by the Back Bowls; while recommended for advanced skiers, they are not steep. Test out the terrain in China Bowl; you can always bale out on to the Poppyseeds blue run.

At Beaver Creek, intermediates can enjoy limitless runs on usually uncrowded slopes in beautiful surroundings. Some runs from the Centennial Express lift, such as Latigo and Centennial, start as blacks (mostly because there are a few moguls) and then turn into long blues. From the Strawberry Express lift, runs such as Bitteroot, Stacker and Pitchfork will soon help to clock up a few miles.

Advanced

Most good skiers head to the Back Bowls area, which on powder days is Utopia. Both the Sun Bowls and China Bowl are skied-out quickly.

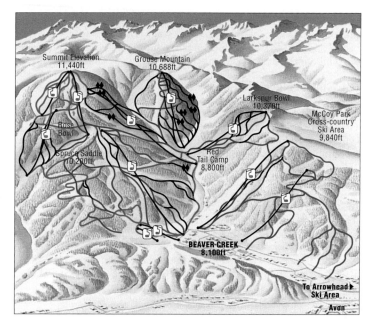

However, it is possible to ski powder all day by heading over to the Mongolia Bowls, accessed by a short drag-lift, and also as far as you can go along Game Creek Bowl. The bowls are south-facing, so head over in the morning. Do not miss the Underwear Tree as you ride up the High Noon Lift. This unusual sight is a constantly growing rack of men's and women's garments, which skiers add to throughout the season.

The front side of the mountain has equally challenging skiing, and often better snow. For steep skiing there is a cliff area off the Mountaintop Express lift; recommended entry points are marked on the map, but you can also take your own line down with caution. Immediately off the Northwoods there are some steep drops along the north and south rim; the steepest skiing is almost directly under the chair-lift. For moguls head to Highline, Roger's Run and Blue Ox. Vail has excellent tree-skiing and it is easy to find untracked powder. Try Ouzo Woods, just past Ouzo Glade, which has evenly spaced trees. Kangaroo Cornice and Look Ma are good, steep tree-line runs.

Grouse Mountain at Beaver Creek is an expert's mountain with plenty of double-black-diamonds and some mogul runs such as Bald Eagle and Falcon Park. There are some difficult runs off the Centennial Express lift, but the basic black classification here often means that only one or two short pitches are truly testing.

Off-piste

Most of the ungroomed skiing is in the Back Bowls. If conditions are good, the Minturn Mile is a long run off the back side of the mountain that ends in the town of the same name; you will need a guide for this. For back-country (off-piste) skiing there is a hut system, but this involves a day's hike and overnight stay to access the seemingly limitless terrain.

Ski schools and guiding

The Vail/Beaver Creek Ski School has a justified worldwide reputation for excellence. In Vail the adult ski school has three base locations: Golden Peak, Lionshead and Vail Village. It also has three on-mountain offices at Two Elk, Mid-Vail and Eagle's Nest. Several readers comment favourably on the private lessons. The Beaver Creek locations are at Village Hall and on the mountain at Spruce Saddle. Arrowhead also has its own ski school.

Snowboarding

This growing sport is well catered for, with an increasing number of exclusive snowboarding shops offering rental equipment. A half-pipe on Golden Peak draws crowds of spectators, as well as participators. The ski school offers private and group lessons at Golden Peak, Lionshead, Beaver Creek and Arrowhead. Beaver Creek has Stickline Snowboard Park and a dedicated learning area. Also available at Beaver Creek are the Delaney snowboard camps run by Brian Delaney, the US and Australia snowboarding champion.

Cross-country

Vail has two cross-country centres: one at Golden Peak and the other at the Nordic Center on the golf course. The Beaver Creek Cross-Country Center is at Strawberry Park, at the base of Chair 12. McCoy Park, at the top of Chair 12, has 20 miles (32km) of track.

Mountain restaurants

Size rather than intimacy seems to be the priority at most mountain restaurants. Beautifully designed but overpoweringly large is the all-wood Elk Two Restaurant (referred to as 'Too Elkspensive' by locals). This luxurious cafeteria serves pasta, grills, pizzas, and salads. At mid-Vail the Cook Shack has two cafeterias and wait-service. The Wine Stube at the top of Lionshead has self-service and wait-service. Eagle's Nest has a cafeteria. Buffalo's, at Chair 4, is an outdoor establishment, and Wok 'n Roll at the bottom of the Orient Express lift has *teriyaki*-style sandwiches. The members-only Game Creek Club, off the Ouzo ski trail, opens this year.

At Beaver Creek, Beano's cabin in Larkspur Bowl is as close to an alpine Stube as you will get (although substantially larger). It is a private members' club at lunchtime and open to the public at night. At Spruce Saddle there is a cafeteria and wait-service at Rafters. Red Tail Camp has an open-air barbecue. McCoy's Bar and Restaurant is cafeteria-style. Tater's is a new, small ski-and-snack venue, due to open for the 1996–7 season, at the top of the Strawberry Park Express lift.

Off the mountain

The Vail Valley is deceptively large, and while most skiers will find themselves limited to areas covered by the free bus route between East Vail,
Vail Village, Lionshead and **West Vail**, there is far more to the area than
meets the eye. However, unless you have a car it is unlikely you will visit
more than Vail and Beaver Creek. Between the two lies the small town of
Minturn, which has a few good
restaurants including the Saloon, the
unofficial end of the Minturn Mile off-
piste itinerary. It is decorated with
autographed photos of celebrities,
including John Wayne, who has his
own memorial booth. In the valley
town of Avon, try Cassidy's Hole in
the Wall Saloon, a bar and restaurant

■ OTHER SPORTS
Snowmobiling, snow-shoeing, bob-sleigh, hot-air ballooning, ice-hockey, dog-sledding, skating, sleigh rides, snowcat tours, indoor squash and tennis, climbing wall

with live music, which is decorated with moose heads. In Edwards, the
next town along, go to the Gashouse for cheap succulent steaks or
Fietas' Café and Cantina for Mexican cuisine. For unsurpassed luxury
try lunch or visit the spa at Cordillera, 25 minutes from Vail. This stunning 28-room lodge has one of the most spectacular views in the valley.
The shopping is reasonable, ranging from 'the more utilitarian to the
definitely glamorous; nothing was very cheap, but most of it was good
quality'. Readers of *Snow Country* magazine voted Kenny's Double
Diamond in Vail one of the top-six ski shops in the Rockies.

Accommodation

Vail, Beaver Creek, Arrowhead and Avon have a total of 41,305 beds,
mostly in condominiums and hotels. The smartest hotels in **Vail Village**
are the Sonnenalp Hotel and The Lodge at Vail, which is owned by
Orient Express Hotels. Also centrally located, but cheaper, are the Vail
Village Inn and Holiday Inn's Chateau Vail. The Marriott has two hotels,
one in Lionshead and one in West Vail. Best Western has the Vailglo
Lodge in Lionshead. Most of the budget chalets are in East Vail and these
tend to be of a far higher quality than equivalents in Europe. En-suite bedrooms, modern décor and outdoor whirlpools are standard here.

Luxury knows no bounds in Beaver Creek: from the exclusive
Saddleridge Hotel to suites at the St James or the Hyatt Regency
Hotels, or the remoteness of Trappers Cabin up the mountain. The
Poste Montane is a small, more intimate hotel. Beaver Creek Lodge
only has suite accommodation. Christie Lodge, in Avon, is good value.

Eating in and out

Whatever your mood, you will be able to choose somewhere to suit you
from the endless list of eating-places, although most are expensive. La
Tour, the Left Bank, Wildflower in The Lodge at Vail and Mirabelle in
Beaver Creek, have the best French cuisine. Sweet Basil and Terra Bistro
in the Vail Athletics Club are Californian-style, the Swiss Chalet in the

Skiing facts: **Vail**

TOURIST OFFICE
PO Box 7, Vail, CO 81658
Tel 1 970 476 5601
Fax 1 970 845 5728

THE RESORT
By air Eagle Country 45 mins, Denver 2½ hrs
Visitor beds 41,305
Transport free bus between Vail and Beaver Creek

THE SKIING
Linked or nearby resorts Arrowhead (n), Beaver Creek (n)
Longest run Flapjack/Riva, 4½ miles (7km) - green/blue
Number of lifts 26 in Vail, 11 in Beaver Creek, 2 in Arrowhead
Total of trails/pistes 4,112 acres (1664 hectares) in Vail (32% easy, 36% interme-diate, 32% difficult), 1,371 acres (554 hectares) in Beaver Creek/Arrowhead
Nursery slopes 2 areas at Golden Peak and top of Eagle's Nest
Summer skiing none
Snowmaking 347 acres (140 hectares) covered in Vail

LIFT PASSES
Area pass (covers Vail, Beaver Creek and Arrowhead) $264-270 for 6 days. Aspen-Vail Premier Passport gives 1 day's free skiing at Aspen
Day pass $48
Beginners no free lifts
Pensioners free for 70 yrs and over

Credit cards accepted yes

SKI SCHOOLS
Adults Vail/Beaver Creek Ski School (at Golden Peak, Vail Village, Lionshead, Beaver Creek and Arrowhead)
$60 per day
Private lessons $98 per hr, $395 per day
Snowboarding as regular ski lessons
Cross-country $55 per day at Golden Peak and Beaver Creek. Loipe 32km in McCoy Park and at Strawberry Park Nordic Skiing Center
Other courses telemark, women's ski courses
Guiding companies Paragon Guides or through ski school

CHILDREN
Lift pass 12 yrs and under, $186-192 for 6 days
Ski kindergarten Vail/Beaver Creek Ski School (Golden Peak, Lionshead and Beaver Creek), 3-6 yrs, $438 for 6 days including lunch, lessons and lift pass
Ski school Vail/Beaver Creek Ski School (Golden Peak, Lionshead and Beaver Creek), 6-13 yrs, $438 for 6 days including lessons and lift
Non-ski kindergarten Small World Nursery, 2 mths-6 yrs, 8.30am-4.30pm, $55 per day at Golden Peak, Lionshead and Beaver Creek

FOOD AND DRINK PRICES
Coffee $2, glass of wine $4, small beer $2.75, dish of the day $10-15

Sonnenalp has cheese fondue and other Swiss specialities. The Siamese Orchid serves Thai food, and Nozawa in the West Vail Lodge is Japanese. Up the Creek is 'quite pleasant with good food'. The Holiday Inn's Fondue Stube 'provided a memorable meal, with caramel and chocolate fondue'. For elk and venison try the Tyrolean Inn; for pasta and medium-priced food go to Vendetta's, Blu's or the Bully Ranch in the Sonnenalp. Montauk in Lionshead is good for seafood. Pazzo's Pizzeria in Vail is low-priced and strongly recommended.

There are two supermarkets: Safeway in West Vail and City Market in Avon. Alfalpha's in Vail Village is an upmarket healthfood shop and delicatessen with many speciality foods. For take-away pizza try Domino's or Chicago Pizza.

Après-ski

There is no shortage of bars, but most of them look the same and it is hard to find somewhere with real atmosphere. In Vail check out the sun-set with a Margarita at Los Amigos, which has been completely rebuilt. The Red Lion and Hong Kong Café are always full, the Ore House has $1.50-Margaritas during happy-hour, and the Hub is a small brewery. Gartons has live music and country-and-western dancing. Try Pepi's with its *dirndl*-clad waitresses. For a quiet drink head for Mickey's Piano Bar in The Lodge at Vail or the sofas around the fire in the Sonnenalp.

In Lionshead, Trail End and Bart & Yeti's are popular. Garfinkels has a huge fish-tank on the bar, and the Sundance Saloon is good for pool. In West Vail try the Dancing Bear or Jackalopes for live music. The Westin Resort also has live music, and Booco's Station in Minturn has jazz or blues bands. For late-night dancing Nick's has rock 'n' roll, The Club is popular, and the revamped Sheika attracts the snow-boarding crowd. DJ McCadams in Lionshead stays open all night except on Mondays.

Beaver Creek's nightlife is limited, but après-ski begins at the Coyote Café, Beaver Trap Tavern or in the Hyatt, where bartenders are trained to entertain à la Tom Cruise in the film *Cocktail*.

Childcare

The Vail/Beaver Creek Ski School has learn-to-ski programmes for three- to six-year-olds and six- to thirteen-year-olds. Small World Nursery at Golden Creek, Lionshead and Beaver Creek is a non-ski nursery for children from 2 mths to to 6 years of age. Ski Break is super-vised time for tired child skiers at Eagle's Nest and Spruce Saddle from 1.30-3.30pm. Arrowhead has learn-to-ski programmes for children from 4 to 16 years. Children and Family programmes include Kid's Night Out Goes Western and The Buckaroo Bonanza Bunch, with Western characters who ski with the children and tell stories of the old Wild West. Children's ski school centres are at Lionshead and Golden Peak in Vail and at the Village Hall in Beaver Creek.

Whistler/Blackcomb

ALTITUDE 2,214ft (675m)

Whistler/Blackcomb has the longest vertical and the biggest growth of any resort in North America. These neighbouring resorts with peaks of the same name in British Columbia's coastal range, 75 miles (121km) north of Vancouver, are jointly marketed and have captured the imagination of North American skiers and others to the east and west. The base areas are now being transformed by Intrawest, the largest resort developer in the world, to cater for global interest in Canada's supreme ski area.

The resort is extremely popular with Japanese skiers, and during Tokyo holiday periods they can account for up to 50 per cent of the clientèle. The sight of so many smiling Orientals clad in Samurai-style ski clothing comes as a culture shock to other overseas visitors. Add in European and US imports as well as Australians, New Zealanders and others who have put their ski tips over the Pacific Rim, and at times you will be hard pressed to find a genuine Canadian here.

■ **GOOD POINTS**

Highest vertical drop in North America, spectacular scenery, wide choice of runs for all standards, modern lift system, long ski season, extensive off-piste skiing

■ **BAD POINTS**

Unfriendly maritime climate, short skiing days, weekend queues

Rarely does a ski resort rise to such international fame so soon after becoming a twin-mountain resort (1980). Whistler continues to hold Vail in second place as North America's most popular ski area.

With some 7,000 acres (2,833 hectares) of skiable terrain, the slopes are extensive and test the most finely tuned abilities. What is surprising is Whistler Village's modest altitude of only 2,214ft (675m), which is 280ft (85m) lower than Kitzbühel and would be worrying were Whistler not situated at such a northern latitude.

The low altitude and maritime climate are the downside of this otherwise perfect North American resort, since much of the almost continuous mid-winter precipitation falls as rain in the village and only as powder snow higher up. Sunshine days are statistically scarce in comparison to its US Rocky Mountain cousins. Changes in temperature between village and summit can be frostbitingly dramatic.

On the mountain
top 7,492ft (2284m) bottom 2,214ft (675m)

The two mountains of Whistler and Blackcomb stand side by side and share a lift pass, but they are divided by Fitzsimmons Creek and only

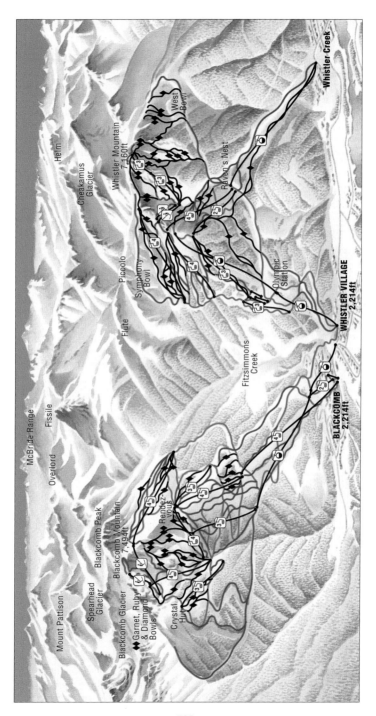

Whistler Creek

West Bowl

Whistler Mountain
7,160ft

Raven's West

Picolo

Symphony Bowl

Flute

Olympic Station

Helm

Cheakamus Glacier

WHISTLER VILLAGE
2,214ft

McBride Range

Fissile

Overlord

Fitzsimmons Creek

BLACKCOMB
2,214ft

Blackcomb Peak

Rendez Vous

Mount Pattison

Spearhead Glacier

Blackcomb Mountain
7,494ft

Blackcomb Glacier

◆ Garnet, Ruby
& Diamond
Bowls

Crystal Hut

linked at the foot. The eight-person Excalibur gondola up Blackcomb from the Whistler base has dramatically improved communications between the two.

Superficially, the two mountains are not dissimilar: each claims more than a hundred runs and each has long cruising trails. But whereas Whistler is known for its bowls, Blackcomb prides itself on its two glaciers and its couloirs. Together the mountains share one of the most modern lift systems in the world.

Beginners

Both areas have easy trails high on the mountain, meaning novices can enjoy the wide-open spaces and a vertical drop usually associated with intermediate ambitions. At Whistler, you can ride all the way up to the Roundhouse on the gondola, and also access ski trails such as Upper Whiskeyjack and Pony Trail (where packhorses once helped transport lift equipment). Papoose, Bear Cub and Expressway are other options lower down.

■ **WHAT'S NEW**

Creekside gondola replaces Quicksilver chair on Whistler Mountain

Opening of Town Plaza residential area between Whistler Village and Village North

At Blackcomb, take the Wizard Express quad-chair and switch to the Solar Coaster Express, which takes you to the easy Expressway link with the Seventh Heaven Express quad and Xhiggy's Meadow — a black-diamond (difficult) run but also the top of the easy Green Line trail. From here novices can also ski from the top of Crystal Traverse, which leads to the Jersey Cream and Glacier Express quads, both of which access some easy beginner trails. There are also nursery slopes around Whistler gondola's Olympic Station and at the Blackcomb base area.

Intermediates

Whistler and Blackcomb both offer exhilarating top-to-bottom skiing, much of it below the tree-line. Half of the runs on both mountains are graded intermediate. Both the Blackcomb and Horstman Glaciers have some excellent skiing.

The Peak Chair leads to the bowls and has a mid-station which provides access to the blue (intermediate) Last Chance run down to two T-bars. These take skiers to a predominantly intermediate area, where the Ridge Run (just above Pika's and the Roundhouse) links with long blue trails such as Ego Bowl, Jolly Green Giant and Ratfink. The Green Express quad-chair is the fastest way back up to the Roundhouse area. Franz's run offers cruising all the way from mid-mountain to Whistler Creek.

At Blackcomb, the Seventh Heaven Express quad and Showcase T-bar to the Blackcomb Glacier serve mainly intermediate terrain at the top of the mountain. The mid-mountain area beneath the Solar Coaster Express quad-chair is dominated by a large number of intermediate runs, including the long Springboard trail. Zig Zag and Cruiser are also popular pistes.

Advanced

At Whistler, much depends on whether the Peak chair or Harmony Express quad are open. If not, there is some good expert terrain around Chunky's Choice and GS. Lower down, Seppo's and Raven off the Black chair provide black-diamond skiing and the Orange chair accesses the long Dave Murray Downhill and two expert cut-offs: Bear Paw and Tokum.

Some of Blackcomb's best expert runs are among the trees in a broad triangle between the lower sections of the Glacier Express and Crystal chair, which means you can inspect them before you ski. Trapline, Straight Shot, Rock'n Roll and Overbite are Crystal chair's featured runs, and The Bite, Staircase and Blowdown are on your right as you board the Glacier Express.

Off-piste

Blackcomb's couloirs and Whistler's bowls are the main areas of interest for off-piste skiers. Saudain Couloir, now renamed Couloir Extreme, separates the advanced skier from the expert. It is the unlikely location for an annual extreme ski-race in which more than a hundred competitors, both professional and amateur, compete in a contest described as '2,500ft of thigh-burning hell'.

Pakalolo is another couloir that attracts experienced skiers. It has a fearsome reputation but is not quite in the same league as Couloir Extreme. The Blackcomb and Horstman glaciers usually provide excellent intermediate off-piste conditions. Whistler's five bowls — Symphony, Glacier, Whistler, Harmony and West Bowls — offer a wide spectrum of off-piste challenges. Two local companies run daily heli-skiing excursions, which should not be compared to the dramatic experiences offered by heli-skiing in the Bugaboo, Monashee or Cariboo mountain ranges in Canada.

Ski schools and guiding

Each resort runs its own large ski school, and Ski Esprit covers both. We have mixed reports of the Blackcomb School ('I came here to get away from language problems and was given a French-speaking instructor with heavily accented English that was difficult to understand'). Ski Esprit courses are consistently praised: 'I got lost and missed most of one lesson, but was given another free of charge without asking.'

Whistler's free guiding programme is strongly recommended: 'Grade yourself into Nice and Easy, Cruise The Blues, or Steep and Deep — great fun.' The ski-patrol's Avalanche Awareness Course is described as 'a must for all advanced skiers, but you don't need to be an expert to do it'.

Snowboarding

The terrain on both mountains is exceptionally suited to riders.

Blackcomb has a snowboard park where regular boardercross races are held. The resort has two half-pipes and some ski-patrol members use boards rather than skis to make riders feel they have equal status on the mountain. The best freeriding and off-piste is accessed by the Peak chair-lift. Blackcomb Ski and Snowboard School offers a comprehensive range of courses. The Snowboard Shop is a celebrated hanging-out spot; the Westbeach Shop provides healthy competition. Heli-boarding is offered by Tyax Heli-skiing.

There is also a summer training camp for snowboarders run by Craig Kelley, five-times World Champion. The resort estimates that 50,000 snowboarders visit Whistler every year.

Cross-country
Whistler has 28km of loipe around the scenic Lost Lake and across its three golf courses. Rental equipment and trail-maps are available at the Whistler Activity and Information Centre.

Mountain restaurants
At Whistler, the Roundhouse and Pika's offer a selection of meals from vegetarian to outdoor barbecues. The Raven's Nest at the top of the new Creekside gondola specialises in pasta. Dusty's is a popular lunch location.

At Blackcomb, Christine's Restaurant in the Rendezvous Lodge serves a leisurely 'linen and silverware' lunch, while the Rendezvous offers more casual, faster service. The River Rock Grill, upstairs at the Glacier Creek, is praised for 'a cosmopolitan choice of cuisine with wonderful glacier views'. Béla's in the Excalibur Base II Daylodge serves all-day breakfasts. Essentially Blackcomb at Excalibur Village Station has an outdoor barbecue.

Off the mountain
Whistler was originally known as Alta Lake, a wild and beautiful area north of Vancouver accessible only by train or on horseback. The first trails in the valley were cut by Indian hunting parties and during the gold-mining era the peaks were a landmark on the Cariboo Gold Rush Trail. The first commercial ski trails appeared when Whistler — renamed after the cry of the marmot — opened in 1966. Earlier in the 1960s there had been some weekend skiing with the help of petrol-driven drag-lifts.

■ OTHER SPORTS
Snow-shoeing, swimming, sleigh rides, indoor tennis, skating, parapente, snowmobiling

Whistler Village, built in the late 1970s, provides a good example of how a purpose-built resort can be made attractive. It is a mixture of chalet-style apartments, inns, lodges and condominiums with wood more in evidence than concrete. There are few huge buildings and the largest hotel, the Chateau Whistler Resort, is modelled on the neo-gothic style of other Canadian Pacific hotels. The centre of Whistler is car-free and getting from the village square to the base of the two gondolas involves a short walk.

Whistler Village and the much smaller Upper Village (Blackcomb Base) and Village North are also only a five-minute walk apart.

Accommodation
The 13-storey Chateau Whistler Resort dominates the skyline and was previously the most popular hotel ('top marks for friendliness, helpfulness and general efficiency'). However, a hike in prices for this season has resulted in tour operators diversifying. We also have good reports of the Delta Mountain Inn ('next to the mountain and very convenient'). Timberline Lodge is 'comfortable, well-situated and friendly'. The Crystal Lodge and the Listel Whistler Hotel are both popular. Condominiums at the Blackcomb Lodge and Mountainside Lodge are both recommended. Carney's Cottage is 'the best bed-and-breakfast in, or rather on the edge of town'.

Eating in and out
The resorts have more than 30 restaurants. Umberto Menghi, an Italian chef who has a TV show in Canada and restaurants in Vancouver, runs Trattoria di Umberto ('good fun') and Il Caminetto di Umberto. Recently, Umberto's manager in Whistler, Mario Enero, opened his own Blackcomb restaurant, La Rua, which is described as being 'delightful and delicious'. The Wildflower Restaurant in the Chateau Whistler Resort is strongly recommended for 'smart dining, not too expensive, and very worthwhile'. Peter's Underground and the Mad Café are good value. Zeuski's Taverna at the gondola base is said to have 'soundly priced and tasty meals'. Sushi Village ('excellent and expensive') is one of the eight Asian restaurants. The Rim Rock Café has a strong local following for its fish and steaks. Local supermarkets are expensive but Nester's, a ten-minute walk away, is said to be cheaper.

Après-ski
The Longhorn Saloon at the foot of the slopes catches skiers as they come off the mountain but is much quieter in the evening. Tapley's Pub is 'friendly, cheap and used by the locals'. Garfinkel's, Tommy Africa's and the Savage Beagle are all extremely popular.

Childcare
Blackcomb runs a range of courses in its Kids Kamp: Wee Wizzards caters for children between 18 months and 3 years; Wee Wizzards Plus includes a daily one-hour private ski lesson; Mini Merlins combines three hours of lessons with play; Super Kids is for children aged 5 to 12 years of all standards. Whistler Ski School runs a programme for children aged 2 to 12 years.

Skiing facts: **Whistler/Blackcomb**

TOURIST OFFICE
4010 Whistler Way, Whistler, BC VON 1B4
Tel 1 604 932 3928
Fax 1 604 932 7231

THE RESORT
By air Vancouver 2 hrs, frequent coach
service to resort
Visitor beds 16,800
Transport free shuttle bus within the
village loop

THE SKIING
Linked or nearby resorts Whistler
Creek (l)
Longest run Whistler: Burnt Stew,
Sidewinder, Olympic, 7 miles (11km) -
blue/green. Blackcomb: The Green Line, 7
miles (11km) - green
Number of lifts 30
Total of trails/pistes 6,996 acres (1,480
hectares) - 20% easy, 55% intermediate,
25% difficult
Nursery slopes 6 baby lifts
Summer skiing mid-June to mid-August on
Horstman Glacier at Blackcomb Mountain
Snowmaking 19 snow-cannon at Whistler
covering 1,500 vertical ft (457m) of trails,
48 snow-cannon at Blackcomb covering
4,000 vertical ft (1219m) of trails

LIFT PASSES
Area pass Dual Mountain Pass, CDN$276
for 6 out of 7 days
Day pass one mountain only CDN$49,
Dual Mountain Pass CDN$51
Beginners no free lifts

Pensioners reduction for 65 yrs and over
Credit cards accepted yes

SKI SCHOOLS
Adults Whistler Mountain Ski School,
Blackcomb Mountain Ski School, Ski Esprit,
all CDN$199 for 4 days
Private lessons Whistler CDN$65 per hr,
Blackcomb CDN$70 per hr
Snowboarding Whistler 2-day Oxygen
Camp CDN$140, private lessons CDN$68
per hr. Blackcomb 2-day Arc Camp
CDN$160, 10-day Team Divo (13-16 yrs),
CDN$325. Private lessons CDN$70 per hr
Cross-country through ski schools. Loipe
28km around Lost Lake and golf courses
Other courses Dave Murray Ski Camps,
moguls, women's clinics, slalom, off-piste,
men's mountain masters, heli-skiing
Guiding companies Whistler Alpine Guides
Bureau, Tyax Heli-skiing

CHILDREN
Lift pass Dual Mountain Pass, CDN$42 for
13-18 yrs, CDN$22.50 for 7-12 yrs, free for
6 yrs and under
Ski kindergarten Ski Scamps at Whistler,
3-12 yrs, CDN$195 for 5 days. Kids Kamp
at Blackcomb, 5-12 yrs, CDN$195 for 5
days (5 hrs per day)
Ski school as ski kindergarten
Non-ski kindergarten childminding at
Blackcomb, 18 mths-3 yrs, CDN$60 per day

FOOD AND DRINK PRICES
Coffee 75c, glass of wine CDN$4.50, small
beer CDN$3.50, dish of the day CDN$5-15

Round-up

RESORTS COVERED Alberta: Jasper. Colorado: Crested Butte, Telluride, Winter Park. Idaho: Sun Valley. Montana: Big Sky. New Mexico: Taos. Vermont: Killington, Smuggler's Notch, Stowe

ALBERTA

Jasper
top 8,533ft (2601m) bottom 5,640ft (1719m)

The friendly old frontier town of Jasper is three-and-a-half hours from Edmonton, to the north-west of Banff and Lake Louise. The unspoilt resort is a half-hour drive from the Marmot Basin ski area in the heart of the Jasper National Park. A thousand acres (405 hectares) of terrain and 52 trails make up a ski area that is best suited to intermediates. However, advanced skiers are also catered for, with bump runs, steep chutes and some excellent tree-skiing. Almost all the lifts give access to easy slopes, and the ski school has a fine reputation. Snowboarding is recommended in the Marmot Basin, and there is terrain for all standards. Other sports available in Jasper include ice-climbing, heli-skiing, ski-touring and cross-country.

The resort has a wide choice of hotels including the luxurious Jasper Park Lodge on the outskirts of town, which has accommodation in a mixture of log cabins and newer cedar-wood chalets along the shore of Lake Beauvert. The Tonquin Inn and Chateau Jasper are both recommended, and Whistlers Inn is a friendly place. Jasper's nightlife is varied and some bars feature live music. The Jasper Park Lodge is a mini resort in itself, containing four restaurants, a nightclub, several bars and an indoor shopping mall.

Children between the ages of 19 months and five years of age are looked after in the Little Rascals nursery at the foot of the ski area.

TOURIST OFFICE
Tel 1 403 852 3816
Fax 1 403 852 8533

COLORADO

Crested Butte
top 11,400ft (3476m) bottom 9,100ft (2774m)

This small, historic town is one of the most attractive ski resorts in Colorado. In the old town's Main Street, 40 of the original nineteenth-century buildings, with their colourful wooden façades, have been converted into shops and restaurants, and give the place a Wild West atmosphere. The town is overlooked by the 'butte' (pronounced as in 'beauty'), a mountain that stands alone. Hotels and guesthouses scattered around the town include the Nordic Inn, a family-run ski lodge that is firmly recommended. The other option is to stay at The Grand Butte Hotel, 3 miles (5km) away at the base of the ski slopes.

Crested Butte is renowned for its steep skiing and each year hosts ski extreme championships; it also has some of the easiest skiing in Colorado. The resort's 12 lifts serve 82 trails spread over 1,150 acres (460 hectares) of ski terrain. A high 58 per cent of the runs are classed as difficult, 29 per cent intermediate and 13 per cent easy. The Extreme Limits area comprises some 260 acres (104 hectares) of ungroomed extreme skiing, which locals claim is some of the most challenging in Colorado.

Irwin Lodge, 12 miles (19km) away at 10,700ft (3262m), offers snowcat skiing among 2,400 acres (960 hectares) of ungroomed terrain. The lodge has 23 rooms set on a gallery around a central fireplace, and can only be reached by snowcat or snowmobile.

TOURIST OFFICE
Tel (freephone) 0800 894085
Fax 1 719 349 2250

Telluride
top 12,247ft (3625m) bottom 8,725ft (2660m)
This quirky Wild West town has a history of mining, but also seems like a throw-back to the 1960s; what other resort has a Mushroom Festival followed by a Nothing Festival in the summer? Locals complain that now it has been discovered, vast amounts of acres have been bought by famous residents, including Tom Cruise, Oprah Winfrey and Christie Brinkley, forcing up the price of land.

Butch Cassidy robbed his first bank here, and the town's name is said to be an abbreviation of 'To Hell You Ride', although a more likely explanation is that it derives from the mineral tellurium. The town is at the end of a remote and beautiful closed canyon, it has fine restaurants and bars and operates at a laid-back pace.

The San Juan Mountains are the most visually rewarding in Colorado; their awesome jagged peaks are quite different from the rounded, tree-covered 'hills' of the state's northern resorts.

The skiing is steep and deep and a favourite location for shooting ski extreme videos. The area is not huge, with just 10 lifts and 1,050 acres (405 hectares) of piste, of which 47 per cent is graded intermediate. Mountain access is via two lifts from the town of Telluride, with another access point at Telluride Mountain Village Resort. The plan to link the two centres by three-stage gondola (which was on hold for several years for technical as well as legal reasons) is now going ahead. Chair 1 is also being replaced by a 'chondola' — a cross between a gondola and a chair-lift. The main skiing is divided between Gorrono Basin and Telluride Face; The Face is dominated by double-black-diamond (very difficult) runs, such as the Plunge, Spiral and Power Line, but there are also slightly easier ways down. The easiest terrain is off Chair 10.

TOURIST OFFICE
Tel 1 970 728 6900
Fax 1 970 728 6475

Winter Park
top 12,057ft (3676m) bottom 8,973ft (2735m)
As it is the closest resort to Denver, only 67 miles (108km) away, Winter Park has a high number of weekend skiers and with its limited accommodation and nightlife would probably disappoint those used to international resorts. But the skiing here is excellent, with long, wide runs, challenging mogul fields, few mid-week queues, efficient lifts and perfectly manicured slopes. The skiing is divided into two main areas — Winter Park, which is mostly intermediate, and Mary Jane, which has hard bump-skiing as well as tree-level runs and long blues from the Parsenn Bowl. There are 20 chairs covering 1,358 acres (550 hectares). On powder days the Parsenn Bowl has excellent off-piste. The children's area has a 'magic carpet' and a good ski school. There are no mountain restaurants, but there is a choice of cafeteria and wait-service at both the Mary Jane and Winter Park base areas. Other après-ski is in Winter Park Resort, a few miles from the ski area.

TOURIST OFFICE
Tel 1 970 726 5514
Fax 1 970 892 5823

IDAHO

Sun Valley
top 9,150ft (2789m) bottom 5,750ft (1753m)
Sun Valley is the oldest ski resort in America and has a history of glamour and style. It was first discovered in 1935 by a dashing Austrian, Count Felix Schaffgotsch, who was sent by Averell Harriman of the Union Pacific Railroad to find the best place to start a ski resort. It has long been a favourite of Hollywood stars, and photographs of Greta Garbo, Marilyn Monroe and Clark Gable line the walls of the Sun Valley Lodge.

This corner of Idaho is gloriously sunny and, by following the mountain from east to west, you can ski in the sun all day. The skiing is on two mountains; Bald Mountain has 13 of the 17 lifts and most of the runs, while Dollar is for beginners. Together they offer 73 runs, 2,067 acres

(837 hectares) of skiing and 600 acres (243 hectares) of snowmaking. Most of the skiing is intermediate, with many wide cruising runs. Its mogul slopes, such as Exhibition, are legendary.

A lot of money has recently been pumped into Sun Valley, which now has some of the best mountain restaurants in America. The stylish yet cosy Sun Valley Lodge and Sun Valley Inn were built in the mid 1930s. Last year the River Run Day Lodge opened as a sister establishment to the luxurious Warm Spring Lodge. Sun Valley and **Ketchum**, the base area for the main skiing, have over 60 restaurants, including the Pioneer, which is Clint Eastwood's favourite.

TOURIST OFFICE
Tel 1 208 724 3423
Fax 1 208 726 4533

MONTANA

Big Sky
top 11,150ft (3399m) bottom 9,700ft (2957m)
Big Sky claims that its aerial tram to the top of Lone Mountain now gives it the longest vertical drop in the US, a fact which needs to be taken with a pinch of snow. At 4,180ft (1,274m) the longest it may be, but it is not the longest continuous vertical (you have to take a lift during the descent) – that honour still belongs to Jackson Hole.

Montana is in the heart of real cowboy country. Custer's last stand was in Bighorn, two hours' drive away, and many of the pioneer routes crossed this state. The scenery is dramatic, with wide gurgling rivers and an abundance of wildlife and unspoilt countryside. It is here that *A River Runs Through It* (directed by Robert Redford) was filmed.

Big Sky has not yet been 'discovered' by the mass market. You can hire a snowmobile without a guide (not permitted in more developed US resorts) and go to Yellowstone National Park. However, while the area's appeal lies in its rustic charm, après-ski is a new concept here. There are few restaurants and, though the Corral is a real cowboy bar, with the skins of grizzlies pinned to the wall, it is 8 miles (14km) away from the base area. The ski area has no resort as such and the nearest large super-market is in **Bozeman**, a 45-minute drive away.

The skiing is suitable for all levels and spread over two mountains with 65 miles (110km) of skiing on more than 60 trails. The longest, Morning Star and Mr K, are both 3 miles (5km). Beginners can ski on rolling slopes, intermediates can find good cruising pistes, and advanced skiers have a choice of steep chutes, mogul fields and extensive bowl-skiing in the dry, light, 'cold smoke' powder that Big Sky is famous for.

TOURIST OFFICE
Tel 1 406 995 5000
Fax 1 406 995 5001

NEW MEXICO

Taos
top 11,819ft (3603m) bottom 9,207ft (2807m)

This corner of New Mexico shows a number of different historical influences. It was inhabited first by Native Americans and then by the Spanish. Small wonder that the Taos Ski Valley is a curious mixture of chalet and cacti, set in arid desert. The ski resort, with its alpine architecture, is situated in the Carson National Forest, 20 miles (32km) above the town of Taos, which, with its eclectic collection of authentic sun-dried brick houses, concrete low-rises and neon signs, provides the only break in the desert scenery.

The fact that it was two Europeans who discovered the area near the old mining town of Twinings may explain this dichotomy. Ernie Blake, a German-born Swiss, created a ski resort here in 1955. A year later, Jean Mayer, a French racer, set up the ski school and the Hotel St Bernard. What they created was an alpine-style village on a mountain-top above the deserts of New Mexico. The après-ski here is lively and usually begins with a Margarita.

Taos has a reputation for extremely challenging skiing. Al's Run, the steep mogul field beneath the main chair, is not encouraging on first sight. A sign at the bottom of the lift reads: 'Don't panic! You are looking at $\frac{1}{80}$th of Taos Ski Valley. We have many easy runs too.' Indeed, Taos does have slopes for lower levels, although the terrain is rated 51 per cent advanced. All the skiing is at tree-level, with most of the runs carved through the woods. From the main ridge there are green routes back to base, and the groomed blue runs give access to some tougher options. Several black-diamond (difficult) trails are left unpisted, enabling experts to tackle everything from moguls to powder. Toughest of all are the chutes off the High Traverse. Snowmaking has been expanded to cover 95 per cent of the beginner and intermediate terrain. A new quad-chair has greatly improved transport to the top of the mountain.

TOURIST OFFICE
Tel 1 505 776 2291
Fax 1 505 776 8591

VERMONT

Killington
top 4,220ft (1287m) bottom 1,045ft (319m)

As a ski resort, Killington had modest beginnings. Avid skier Preston Smith recognised the mountain's potential and spent three years raising enough money to buy it. When the resort opened in December 1958 the original ticket booth was a converted chicken coop. Today Killington is the biggest ski resort in Vermont. Combined with neighbouring **Pico**, a ten-minute drive away, the area offers 8 mountains served by 29 lifts.

The major disadvantage is that there is no resort centre; hotels, condominiums, the odd bar, restaurant and shopping centre straggle along the 5-mile (8-km) road off the highway. Killington has one of the world's largest snowmaking operations, which covers 44 miles (70km) of runs that are dependent on low temperatures. Indeed, temperatures can be so low here that skiing is extremely unpleasant.

This harsh environment is reflected in the quality of the snow, which is well groomed but often difficult to ski. Ice is common and the rock-hard pistes mean you need a high standard of skiing technique in order to cope with them. Killington has the only heated gondola in any ski resort.

There are wide, gentle green (easy) and blue (intermediate) runs at Ram's Head, while the tougher skiing is on Snowdon, Killington and Skye. Bear Mountain has the awesome Outer Limits mogul run.

TOURIST OFFICE
Tel 1 802 422 3333
Fax 1 802 422 4391

Smuggler's Notch
top 3,640ft (1109m) bottom 1,030ft (314m)

The resort's name originates from when the pass was used for the illicit passage of goods to and from Canada before the War of Independence. Years later in the 1930s it became a ski resort. Today it is known as one of the top family skiing centres in North America; indeed, in recent years the resort's childcare and teen programmes have been rated the best in the US. It also has a reputation as a snow-catcher and averages 250 inches a year. The skiing, which is mainly for beginners and intermediates, is on three interconnected mountains: Madonna, Morse and Sterling. From Sterling you can ski over the back to Stowe. The village has a compact centre, comprising condominium buildings and some hotels.

TOURIST OFFICE
Tel (freephone) 0800 897159
Fax 1 802 644 2713

Stowe
top 3,650ft (1113m) bottom 1,300ft (396m)

Stowe is the epitome of a New England resort. Covered bridges, red barns and small shops selling maple syrup and hand-made quilts make up this 200-year-old village, which is overlooked by a white, steepled church. Skiers began to come here from Manhattan and Boston in the late 1930s and the first lift opened in 1937. Today Stowe has 11 lifts and 45 trails cut through the woods, covering more than 480 acres (194 hectares). The ski area is 7 miles (11km) away from the town and although there are regular shuttle buses, a car is a distinct advantage here. Boston is three-and-a-half hours away by road.

Stowe is home to Vermont's highest mountain, Mount Mansfield, which is reached by gondola and suffers from queues at weekends. It has been said that if you can ski the Front Four at Stowe, you can ski anywhere — Goat, National, Starr and Liftline are the double-black-diamond (very difficult) runs equal to the steepest in the top resorts of the Alps. Skiers have to learn to cope in numbingly low temperatures with the additional problem of what they call 'frozen granular patches' and we call ice. Apart from the big four trails, the ski terrain comprises mainly intermediate cruising.

TOURIST OFFICE
Tel 1 802 253 3000
Fax 1 802 253 3406

Andorra

RESORTS COVERED Pas de la Casa/Grau Roig,
Soldeu-El Tarter, Arinsal, Pal, Arcalis

Andorra has a reputation for 'supermarket skiing', a low-cost, duty-free way for the rowdier end of the British market to don their anoraks, reverse their baseball caps, give snowploughing a try and party long into the night. However, while the price of a ski trip to Andorra is comparable with one to Eastern Europe, the quality of equipment and facilities is years ahead.

Andorra is bordered by Catalonia in Spain and Les Pyrénées Orientales in France. The closest airports are Barcelona in Spain, Carcassone, Perpignan and Toulouse in France. The country's population of 55,000 inhabitants lives within an architecturally dreary area of just 464 square kilometres, and Catalan is the official language.

Much of the country's income is still derived from the summer season when visitors come from all over Europe to take advantage of Andorra's tax-free status. Even this is misleading because, while alcohol, perfumes and tobacco are cheap, other prices are similar to those in Britain. However, bargains can certainly be found, especially in skiwear and equipment, but are the exception rather than the rule.

Andorra is an ideal starting point for those new to skiing. Its five ski resorts are cheap, friendly, and generally offer a decent standard of ski instruction and equipment hire. The food in all resorts can be surprisingly good, with a choice of French or Catalan dishes. Andorra is not quaint, nor does it provide any testing skiing for experts. However, with a careful choice of resort and an expectation level to match your purse, anyone from a competent intermediate downwards (particularly those under 25) can have an enjoyable and rewarding trip.

Pas de la Casa/Grau Roig
top 2580m (8,465ft) bottom 2095m (6,872ft)
This is the first resort you reach after crossing the French border. The fundamental impression is of a brash city of giant advertising hoardings, scores of tacky shops, crowds of shoppers and choking traffic fumes. The architecture is both higgledy-piggledy and ugly. The town feels like a resort that owes its existence to dime stores, not skiing. Supermarket

shelves are piled high with cut-price alcohol, much of it produced locally.

The skiing in the Pas de la Casa and linked Grau Roig area takes place mainly within two main bowls on either side of the 2600-m pass, making it the highest resort in Andorra. The 27 lifts serve 42 pistes, which are well-covered by snow-cannon.

Main access to the pass is via an efficient but usually oversubscribed quad chair-lift. From the top you can return to the resort via a choice of different coloured runs, which can be crowded and very icy. Alternatively, you can ski on down the gentler but more rewarding pistes to Grau Roig, which is little more than a car park and a hotel on the floor of the adjoining valley.

The Del Cubil chair gives access to a handful of red (intermediate) and blue (easy) runs; all are fairly short and the snow tends to disappear quickly here. The better alternative is to catch the drag up to Mont Malus, where two short but very enjoyable reds or, snow

> **■ WHAT'S NEW**
>
> Additional snowmaking at Pas de la Casa and Arinsal
> Half-pipe and competition stadium at Pas de la Casa
> Surf park and new black slope at Soldeu
> High-speed quad-chair and three new slopes at Arcalis

permitting, the black (difficult) Granota (several reporters voted this one of their favourite runs) take you back to Grau Roig.

One major complaint is that beginners in Pas de la Casa are forced to buy a full area lift pass just to use the two short drag-lifts on the nursery slopes. One reporter gripes: 'During February half-term the resort was overcrowded, the ski school overloaded and the lift queues enormous'.

TOURIST OFFICE
Tel 376 820 399
Fax 376 823 036

Soldeu-El Tarter
top 2560m (8,399ft) bottom 1800m (5,904ft)

Readers are unanimous in their praise of Soldeu and its neighbour, El Tarter: 'I would recommend Soldeu to anyone. It is especially great for beginners and the ski school is excellent for all levels. The nightlife is cheap and suitable for anyone of any age who wants to let their hair down and who knows how to have a good time. I am hoping to go to Andorra twice next season.'

For many years there has been talk of linking Soldeu and El Tarter with Pas de la Casa, just 15 minutes over the pass, but as yet this has not happened. Soldeu and El Tarter provide a marked contrast to their neighbour, consisting of little more than a ribbon of stone-and-wood buildings along the main road. Environmentally sympathetic building regulations mean that even the recent constructions are much more attractive than those in Pas de la Casa.

From Soldeu the ski area is reached by a single-span bridge ('difficult and tiring in ski boots') that would make Indiana Jones think twice. The

Edelweiss restaurant is situated between the resort and the bridge for those in need of duty-free Dutch courage along the way. Once that has been negotiated, mountain access is via the old Espiolets lift, which takes you slowly up to Pla dels Espiolets and the main skiing area. A chair-lift provides alternative mountain access from El Tarter, 2km down the road, and is an altogether faster and easier way into the lift system that is optimistically described on the piste map as 'the most advanced ski lift system in Europe'.

The ski area of Soldeu and El Tarter is made up of mainly long cruising runs, with open terrain going up to the top of the area and forest from the mid-mountain downwards. The 22 lifts serve some 60km of varied skiing, which is mainly suitable for intermediates.

TOURIST OFFICE
Tel 379 851 151
Fax 379 851 337

Arinsal
top 2573m (8,442ft) bottom 1550m (5,084ft)
Arinsal does not look like a ski resort at all, with its small row of shops and bars, and apartment buildings scattered along the road. When snow is scarce in the resort itself, the only sign that this is a winter sports centre is the old double chair-lift, which follows the path of a bubbling stream. This takes you to the start of the main skiing at 1950m, in a bleak and treeless region enclosed between two ridges, which offers the least variety of all Andorra's skiing. Easier access to the main ski area is by road. The two main pistes, the black La Devesa and the blue Les Marrades 1, run from the top of the main Arinsal lift down to the resort, and are sometimes closed owing to lack of snow. This limits the remainder of the terrain to pistes suitable for beginners and lower-intermediates. As all the runs are channelled into a V shape that ends on the nursery slopes, even beginners will feel the pressure of the limited runs.

TOURIST OFFICE
Tel 376 835 822
Fax 376 836 242

Pal
top 2358m (7,736ft) bottom 1780m (5,840ft)
Pal is a small village down the road from Arinsal, with a separate ski area further up a winding road that can be reached by bus. The 13 lifts and 30km of piste are accessed from four different points and share a lift pass with Arinsal. Pal has the smaller, but more interestingly laid-out ski area of the two resorts. Of its 24 runs, half are graded red and 80 per cent of the skiing terrain is covered by artificial snow.

The skiing at Pal goes up to its highest point at the Pic del Cubil, where you can either come straight down to Coll de la Botella via two red runs or ski over towards Refugi Pla de la Cot at the centre of the ski area on a choice of four red runs. Further to the left of the area is Edifici La Caubella, where most of the shorter and easier runs are situated.

TOURIST OFFICE
Tel 376 836 236
Fax 376 836 904

Arcalis
top 2600m (8,530ft) bottom 1940m (6,363ft)
Arcalis is one of Andorra's higher resorts, with skiing on wide runs above the tree-line. The village of Ordino is 25 minutes from Arcalis and neighbouring La Massana and has delightful scenery. The 11 lifts serve 20km of pistes, which suit all standards of skier. Arcalis has the highest percentage of difficult skiing in Andorra, which includes a special slalom piste. Reporters are lavish in their praise: 'The sheer variety of the skiing makes it a great place. No lift queues, one of the best smaller resorts we have been to'.

TOURIST OFFICE
Tel 376 836 320
Fax 376 837 300

Ski schools and guiding
Andorra attracts a much higher than average percentage of beginners to its slopes and this is reflected in the excellent quality of tuition at the ski school in most resorts. Classes are kept to a maximum of 12 pupils and the standard of English spoken is praised by several reporters, possibly due to the large amount of BASI-qualified English and Antipodean instructors. Pas de la Casa, however, appears to be the exception: 'We counted 30 people in one class', said a couple of reporters.

In past editions of the Guide, the ski school in Soldeu has been lavishly praised. It has more than 100 downhill instructors who also teach cross-country, telemark, off-piste and competition. Four of the instructors specialise in teaching children. The instruction still appears to be reliable but congestion on the learner slopes is a growing dilemma: 'There is a real problem with overcrowding on the nursery slopes, especially early in the week. There were 100 beginners (British) at each session plus snowboarding classes and various members of other nationalities. This problem did ease by the middle of the week, although it then transferred to the green runs where groups of beginners, intermediates and better often became entangled — literally.' Arinsal's ski school has 65 instructors who are mainly BASI-trained; special courses include Golden Ski for mature skiers.

Snowboarding
All the resorts welcome snowboarders, and both group and private lessons can be arranged in all resorts. Budget-conscious riders can find some spectacular equipment bargains. Pas de la Casa has a new half-

pipe at La Coma III in the Grau Roig area, and Soldeu has a surf park with bumps and a powder snow zone.

Cross-country

Andorra offers only limited cross-country opportunities and lacks the scenic beauty of the Alps. However, all resorts except Arinsal have loipe and instruction on request. Soldeu has the best facilities, with two loipe of 5km and 7km, as well as a new itinerary.

Mountain restaurants

The five mountain eating-places in the Pas de la Casa/Grau Roig ski area are mainly cheap and functional, and are little more than snack bars. The Bar El Piolet at the bottom of the Del Clot drag-lift is said to have 'the best baguettes I have ever tasted — especially the hot bacon ones'. However, one reporter comments: 'All the mountain restaurants are rubbish except the Refugi de Pessons, which has a log fire, pleasant food and service.'

The Esqui Calbo restaurant in Soldeu, across the bridge from the base ski-lift, is recommended for its service and value for money. Xalet Sol I Neu, at the bottom of the mountain at Soldeu, serves 'very tasty chicken curry made with better cuts of chicken breast than I have ever experienced in an English curry house'.

Mountain restaurants in Arinsal are, on the whole, 'shabby and over-priced', say reporters, although there are one or two exceptions. At the bottom of the Arinsal chair-lift, Asteric's serves local dishes ('a warm and friendly place with delicious food, especially the Catalan sausages'), as does it sister establishment, Obelic's, which has been renovated. For such a small place, Arinsal is well supplied with good off-slope restaurants and bars. Pick of the resort is the Red Rock bar, which has a vibrant ambience after the bleakness of the skiing. Thrifty reporters noted that they were able to buy an entire packed lunch in Andorra's 'extremely cheap' supermarkets for under £1 each day.

Accommodation

While Pas de la Casa cannot in any way be called attractive, it does have a large variety of accommodation, ranging from the comfortable to the very basic. Two of the more expensive hotels, which receive favourable comment from reporters, are the Sporting and the Central, both at the lower end of the resort. The budget hotel Llac Negre has a varied local menu and friendly staff.

Much of the resort accommodation is in apartments. One reporter comments: 'Many of the younger people choose the apartments close to the slopes, while families and those seeking a quieter life choose the hotels.' Of the many self-catering apartments Paradis Blanc, next to the slopes, is certainly no paradise, with its limited space, lack of cupboards and paper-thin walls. Reporters do not recommend it for families: 'Drunken parties in the corridors kept our children awake into the early hours'. The Lake Placid apartments also seem to have few admirers;

reporters complain about their small size and lack of sound-proofing.

The roadside resort of Soldeu has a few well-run hotels, including El Duc, a comfortable chalet-style hotel in the village centre opposite the ski slopes. Beside it is the traditional Sport Hotel with its own fitness centre boasting a sauna, gym and even a physiotherapist. Aparthotel Edelweiss and the Cabo apartments both share the Sport Hotel's facilities. The Naudi is a small, family-run hotel on the main through-road: ('A pleasant hotel with friendly staff, but we were glad not to be at the front of the hotel as there was

> **■ OTHER SPORTS**
>
> Skating, swimming, ice-driving, winter walks, night-skiing (Pas de la Casa), heli-skiing, snowmobiling, tobogganing, indoor tennis and squash

considerable traffic noise until the early hours of the morning'). Readers also complain about the poor quality of the food: 'Soggy, lukewarm chips, overcooked, cold, tinned vegetables, meat of variable taste and texture. It reminded me of British café food of the 1950s and 60s'. At the foot of the slopes in El Tarter is the conveniently placed Hotel Llop Gris, which has satellite television in every room. The hotel also boasts a swimming-pool and sauna. Further down the road is the congenial Parador Canaro.

Reporters who stayed in **Encamp**, 20 minutes from Soldeu, do not recommend it. Although it is an even cheaper alternative to the main resorts, it has no skiing and there is nothing else to do here ('it would have been worth the extra £30 to £70 to stay in Soldeu simply to avoid the hassle of travelling'). Hotel La Mola is said to be 'a vegetarian's nightmare. Everything contained meat, usually in great big chunks'.

Arinsal goes in for cheap but basic accommodation, with the Poblado apartments securing particular praise and Hotel Rossell receiving criticism for its basic food. Attitude and service at the Hotel Font is not singled out either, and we have mixed views of the Hotel Erts. The Hotel Daina, 15 minutes from the centre, is a newer addition, while Hotel Janet is a small, family-run place on the outskirts. The large, modern Hotel St Gothard is also one of the village's main nightspots. The Hotel Solana is said to have the resort's best facilities, with an indoor swimming-pool, steam room and sauna. Hotel Coma Pedrosa has 'a friendly atmosphere, a reasonable four-course meal and good value in the bar; however, we were woken up every night by people shouting and coming home drunk. A cooked breakfast was served twice a week but unfortunately it was cold.'

Eating in and out

The restaurants in Pas de la Casa are cheap and cheerful. The food is mainly Spanish, with fresh seafood and the ubiquitous paella, although some concessions have been made to the French. By browsing with care, your can eat well at a reasonable price.

La Braza, Rapid' Pasta and La Gratinada in Pas de la Casa are all praised by reporters for their friendly atmosphere: 'The restaurants welcomed my small, noisy children in the evenings and let them draw on the paper tablecloths with crayons. There was always suitable food for children, such as pizzas, pasta and ice cream.' Les Delicies is recommended as being good value.

The Esquirol and the Hard Rock Café in Soldeu are reporters' favourites, and the Hotel Bruxelles is commended for its food. The El Pi is said to be excellent value for money. Cisco's in Arinsal is for Mexican food, while Asteric's was 'dead by 8pm and you had to walk back to the hotel because the ski buses finish early'.

Caldea, the thermal-spring centre at Escaldes in the heart of Andorra, has two restaurants: the informal Oasis, with an all-day buffet, and the Aquarius, which is smarter with higher prices. The complex also contains a bar.

Après-ski

Most of the bars in Pas de la Casa are cheap, and even the ones with dancing seem to have resisted the urge to charge for entry. Most have fluorescent lighting and deafening music, although the Marseilles bar ('it was often crowded by 5pm when the slopes closed') is somewhere you can drink and talk at the same time.

The Discoteca Bilboard is popular and is split into two with 'general nightclub music played in one half and house/garage music in the other. There is no entry fee and you are able to roam between the two halves'. Another favourite nightspot is Milwaukee's. Le Pub has a happy-hour each evening and holds weekly theme nights. Most of the British tour operators organise weekly pub crawls.

Soldeu's nightlife ('great for such a small resort') centres around the Pussycat, Aspen and El Duc discos. The Piccadilly Pub has 'something going on every night, including an Irish night and karaoke'. The Sport Hotel has a friendly bar.

The Caldea thermal-spa centre has an enormous swimming-pool, man-made rock pools to soak in, a gym, shopping mall, and a variety of health treatments to help you relax. It is open between 10am and 11pm each day and is certainly worth a day trip if the weather is bad.

Skydance at the Hotel St Gothard in Arinsal is a popular disco, the Red Rock bar has live music and is recommended for its food, and the Solana disco-pub has plenty of atmosphere. Cisco's bar stays open until 5am. Asteric's has live guitar music in the evenings.

Childcare

The fact that all the runs in Pas de la Casa end in one area is a big advantage for meeting children after lessons. There are two crèches, one in town and the other on the piste. The Jardi di Neu kindergarten is set in a small wooden hut with its own fenced-off ski and play area; it has a button-lift and is close to a diesel-driven drag-lift and the busy car park.

We have good reports of the nursery slopes in Soldeu, which are 'well prepared and fenced off from the rest of the pistes'. The ski school is also well spoken of, with children's instruction from English staff, and there are two crèches. Arinsal, Pal and Arcalis have a crèche each.

Eastern Europe

RESORTS COVERED Bulgaria: Bansko, Borovets, Pamporovo
Romania: Poiana Brasov, Sinaia
Slovenia: Bled, Bohinj, Kranjska Gora

The mountains of the Czech Republic, Slovakia and Slovenia, Poland, Bulgaria and Romania all lend themselves to skiing. Development has been slow, but as the twenty-first century approaches, the mountains of Eastern Europe could still represent one of the great future areas for skiers.

While these countries have a struggling domestic ski market, the single biggest advantage for international skiers is the low cost. Skiers on a budget tend to look to Bulgaria, Romania and Slovenia. Not yet well-known to tourists are Slovakia and Poland, which to date only attract the more adventurous skiers from abroad, including former East Germans.

In comparison with the standards expected of Alpine resorts, accommo-

> ■ **GOOD POINTS**
> Low prices, excellent beginner skiing, excursions for non-skiers, fascinating cultural experience
>
> ■ **BAD POINTS**
> Poor-quality food, limited challenging skiing, lack of alpine charm, few consumer goods

dation, food, slope preparation and tuition are inferior, but a holiday in Eastern Europe will be cut-price, and the lack of sophistication is compensated for by the generosity, enthusiasm and honesty of the people.

The slopes in the resorts close to large towns can be crowded at weekends, so this is the ideal time to hang up your skis and explore further afield. These countries provide a fascinating cultural experience that can easily be combined with skiing. For example, in the Romanian resort of Poiana Brasov, you can ski in the morning and visit Dracula's Castle in the afternoon. The local people are trying hard to adjust to the rapid changes and in particular to a market economy. The gradual recovery from years of Communist rule means that things do not always run smoothly. There are still shortages, electricity cuts, delays, slow service and sometimes only basic facilities. However, the majority of reporters have been exceptionally impressed by the friendliness and eager-to-please attitude of Eastern Europeans.

We have not given the telephone numbers of the local tourist offices. We recommend that you travel through a bonded tour operator or via a country's own state tourist office (*see Skiing by Numbers*).

BULGARIA

More so than other Eastern European destinations, Bulgaria's hotel accommodation, food and internal travel have been steadily improving:

'On my most recent visit to Borovets I noticed a clear overall improvement in the standard of the holiday, without any dramatic difference in price'. Reporters also agree that the skiing experience here bears scant resemblance to skiing in the mainstream alpine countries. The verdict seems to be that you should enjoy it for what it is: a budget-priced cultural picnic with some skiing thrown in; anyone planning a holiday in Bulgaria should not set off wearing rose-tinted goggles.

A harsh crack-down on the black market has led to fairly uniform exchange rates, but this can still fluctuate during a two-week stay. The rate of inflation is high, and most hotels and bars do not accept credit cards. Reports on the quality of food are varied, even from the same hotels. A general rule of thumb seemed to be to avoid miscellaneous soups and stick to simple foods such as roast meat, chicken and vegetables. Food for vegetarians is limited more by availability than cooking skills.

Ski lifts are old-fashioned, and the standard of piste maintenance, or rather lack of it, comes in for continued criticism: 'The gondola broke down on two busy mornings — power failure caused delays of about one hour'. Similarly, those unfortunate enough to require medical treatment are shocked by the basic hospitals and the lack of facilities. On the other hand, mountain rescue seems to be efficient, with minor injuries treated speedily and effectively by first-aiders on the slopes. Simple medications such as aspirin are not readily available. Lavatory paper on the mountain and in cheaper hotels is scarce.

The quality of hire equipment, once a major problem throughout Eastern Europe, has improved in Bulgaria in that a wider choice is now available. However, one reporter comments: 'The ski equipment provided by the ski school was very poorly maintained — the instructor was clearly embarrassed by the standard. The ski shop was happy to re-edge the skis but they didn't seem to care that the ski bases were gouged to death'. Visitors are also advised to check the release setting on their bindings for themselves before taking the first lift. Reporters mention a shortage of snowboards for hire.

Bansko
top 2000m (8,202ft) bottom 936m (3,079ft)

The newest addition to the ski atlas is Bansko, a two-and-a-half-hour drive from Sofia. Mount Vihren, Bulgaria's second highest mountain, is half an hour by free ski bus from the old medieval town of Bansko, with its attractive townhouses. The 1950s-style ski centre has 10 lifts and 22km of piste with mainly easy to intermediate terrain. The Bansko MST Ski School offers tuition in alpine and cross-country skiing and snowboarding; guides can be hired to find some surprisingly good tree-skiing. There are four nursery slopes but no kindergarten.

Accommodation includes the two-star Pension Sema, which is small, wooden and homely. Hotels Velyan and Todork are both rated three-star. Sharkova Hashta restaurant is in one of the old houses and has an excellent-value menu and interesting local wines. Cheaper still is Pizzeria

Alex where pizzas cost under £1 each. Other activities include snowmobiling, parapente and a visit to the Sunday market in the old town.

Borovets
top 2540m (8,333ft) bottom 1323m (4,339ft)

The skiing at Borovets compares favourably with that of many smaller
alpine resorts. Spectacularly situated among pine forests high in the Rila
Mountains, the resort is more a spread-out collection of hotels than a village. The skiing is divided into three areas: a variety of wooded runs on
the mountain directly above the resort; more wooded intermediate runs
reached by gondola to the right; and open skiing above the gondola top-
station served by a series of rather untrustworthy parallel drag-lifts,
which 'seemed to open and close for no apparent reason'.

There is a small nursery area at the foot of the main mountain and
some long, meandering trails, including one of 6km from the top of the
ancient single-chair ('well past its sell-by date'). The skiing, with its 8
lifts and 40 runs, is generally more suited to intermediates who have the
choice of some fairly testing red (intermediate) and black (difficult)
slopes. There is little in the way of challenging skiing.

Mountain restaurants are few and basic. There is an old café on the
6-km blue (easy) run, which is well worth a visit. The gondola is the only
means of mountain access to the higher slopes and is prone to serious
queuing: 'arrangements for queuing were very frustrating as rude
Bulgarians and Germans shoved past the more patient British'. The
quality of piste-grooming is poor, and runs are unmarked ('the lack of
signposts would have been a problem had we not been accompanied by
an instructor'). Piste-maps are hard to come by and may only be found
in brochures.

The Borosport Ski School receives mixed reports ('variable standard
of instruction'), snowboarding classes are praised by reporters, and the
kindergarten has a favourable reputation. Off-piste guiding is available
through Peter Popangelov's Ski School.

Most of the hotels are within a five-minute walk of the slopes. Horse-
or donkey-drawn carts circuit the main hotels and are remarkably cheap.
The Rila is a huge, rather impersonal hotel, which has its own studios
('very cramped and the hot water usually ran out around 6pm'). Hotel
Samakov has a swimming-pool, better food by Bulgarian standards, and
is comfortable but again large and impersonal. The smaller twin hotels of
the Ela and Mura offer satisfactory accommodation. The pizzeria opposite the Rila is good value, but the Hemingway restaurant is heavily criticised: 'the food was very sparse indeed and the wine unpalatable'.

Après-ski takes place in the local bars, where there are discos and
floor-shows, with the Rila and Samakov acting as principal entertainment centres. Karaoke and Russian strip-shows are much in evidence.
BJ's and Bonkers are popular bars ('beer and wine were cheaper than in
the hotel bar'). The Breza bar is recommended, as is Peter's, which is
opposite the gondola. Various excursions are available, including trips to
the old town of Plovdiv.

Pamporovo
top 1925m (6,316ft) bottom 1450m (4,757ft)

South-west of Borovets is Pamporovo, a large resort well-suited to first-time skiers. Pamporovo is the southernmost mountain resort in Eastern Europe, and snow conditions can be unreliable in the latter part of the season.

The total nine lifts serve 25km of mainly easy pistes on the Snezhanka Mountain. There are several nursery areas and a number of confidence-building pistes through the trees, including one from the top to the bottom of the mountain. There are two more difficult runs, including the Wall, which is not as steep as it sounds but is used as a slalom race-course. Advanced skiers would find little to maintain their interest here.

We have favourable reports of the Pamporovo Ski School: the instructors take an obvious pride in their English and instruction is technically sound ('tuition was outstanding in terms of enjoyment and friendliness'). Snowboarding classes are offered, and there is ski tuition for children from four years of age.

The snack bars on the mountain are numerous but of poor quality. The Pizza Caravan near Stoudnets receives a strong recommendation. The resort itself is a five-minute free bus ride from the slopes and consists of a handful of unattractive modern hotels that offer a surprisingly high standard of accommodation. The Perelik is adequate but slightly faded; reporters note that its food is 'not great, but buffets are excellent and the Cabernet Sauvignon is fantastic value'. The hotel has a vast swimming-pool.

Après-ski is limited to a few folksy restaurants and hotel discos, although there are nightclubs at the Perelik and at the Somolyan (a 45-minute bus ride away). The Molina Bar and the White Hart are reputed to have good food. Also recommended are the traditional local evenings laid on for tourists: barbecues at the Cheverme restaurant and 'game' evenings where local fare is sampled.

ROMANIA

Prices in Romania are even lower than in Bulgaria. Hire equipment has improved, with the main resorts getting the previous year's equipment from European resorts. English is spoken everywhere. The lifts are old-fashioned, in serious need of upgrading and prone to delays, but the standard of ski tuition is generally high.

Poiana Brasov
top 1775m (5,823ft) bottom 1021m (3,350ft)

This is the best-known resort in Romania, located three hours' drive north of Bucharest in the attractive Carpathian Mountains. It is an unusual, purpose-built resort, founded by the Ceauşescu administration in the 1950s to promote tourism, and resembles more of an enormous holiday camp than a village. A few hotels, restaurants and a large sports centre are set back from the base of the ski area; the furthest hotels are about 2km away, far enough to need a bus, which is free but infrequent.

The 14-km ski area is reached either by gondola (an antiquated open-air bucket where you are provided with blankets) or by two cable cars (do not expect them both to be running at the same time) up to the summit. The nursery slopes are at the bottom of the mountain, but when there is a lack of snow, beginners are taken to a gentle slope at the top of the gondola. Most of the skiing is intermediate, with runs roughly following the line of the lifts from top to bottom. There are two black runs, one of which circumnavigates the mountain and ends at the base. Although the slopes are north-facing, snowmaking has not yet come to Romania, and in bad conditions you could easily come to a bare patch halfway down a run.

The ski school is unanimously recommended: 'Exceptionally good value and the teachers are of an excellent standard'. There is no shortage of ski-school instructors who speak fluent English and are keen to show you a good time, 'even if it means buying them all their drinks in the bar at night and then coping with their hangovers the next day at class'.

There are a couple of simple mountain restaurants. The best is a wooden chalet at the top of the gondola. The food is cheap and basic and there is a balcony for sitting in the sun.

Reporters speak of the resort's dated feeling; one warned he found it 'full of British yobbos on cheap drunken sprees', but at the same time described his holiday as 'a culturally fascinating experience'. Of the hotels, the Alpin is the best, but even this is likely to have threadbare curtains and peeling wallpaper, and the Teleferic and Sport are adequate.

Non-skiing activities are limited; other sports include skating, bowling and swimming. The après-ski takes place in the hotels, nearly all of which have discos or floorshows. The most popular disco is in the Sport Hotel. Dinner at The Outlaws Hut is a lively evening out that starts with musicians playing around a log fire ('lively, cheap and full of atmosphere'). Alternatively, you can take part in a wine-tasting and folklore dinner at the Carpathian Stag in Brasov. The Dacia restaurant specialises in wild boar. There are excursions to Dracula's Castle and cheap buses and taxis that can take you into the town of Brasov for limited shopping. It is worth spending a day in Bucharest.

Sinaia
top 2219m (7,280ft) bottom 855m (2,805ft)

Sinaia is where the Romanian Royal Family used to spend their summers. Each monarch built a summer residence and, while some of these are now run down, the beautiful Peles Palace should not be missed. The old Royal Palace is now a hotel and is a short walk from the cable car.

Sinaia's role as a ski resort is relatively minor. A two-stage cable car from the town, its top section duplicated by a chair-lift, serves long intermediate runs down the front of the mountain. These are poorly marked and are consequently quite challenging in poor visibility. The main area is on exposed, treeless slopes behind the mountain and on subsidiary peaks beyond. It consists of short intermediate runs with some variety, and plenty of scope for skiing off-piste. Snowboarding is not encouraged in the resort. Hotel Palace is a traditional place overlooking a park and is a short walk from the lifts. The town is quiet with just a few bars and restaurants.

SLOVENIA

While Slovenia is an independent state, it is still unfairly associated with the tragic upheavals in other parts of former Yugoslavia. Slovenia, in the extreme north-west, has some good skiing, and those few tour operators who stuck with it protest correctly that their resorts are a long way from the fighting. However, the proximity has been enough to seriously damage the tourist industry.

Like other Eastern European countries, Slovenia is reasonably priced. Food, drink and internal travel are about one-third of British prices. Reports of the ski schools are generally favourable, with English widely spoken and the video analysis helpful.

Bled
top 1275m (4,183ft) bottom 880m (2,657ft)

The attractive, old spa town of Bled looks on to a seventeenth-century church on an island in the middle of a lake. Its main, simple ski area is 8km away at **Zatrnik**, where a total of five lifts serve 18km of easy wooded slopes in a bowl, which are ideal for beginners in good snow conditions but provide little challenge for intermediates. Another even smaller area is **Straza**, which has just two lifts; both areas have artificial snowmaking. The Golf, a quiet hotel set slightly away from the main centre, is recommended, while the Lovec is an older, wood-panelled hotel.

Bohinj
top 1800m (5,906ft) bottom 569m (1,867ft)

Bohinj is a lakeside village in the Triglav Alpine National Park with skiing above it at Mount Vogel. A cable car takes you to a plateau where nine lifts conveniently connect a handful of easy and intermediate runs among the trees and a small nursery area. If conditions are fine you can ski the 8.5-km run all the way down to the lake.

There is accommodation at the base of Mount Vogel in the Zlatorog Hotel near the Vogel cable-car station. It is recommended for skiing convenience, although it is rather isolated in the evenings as it is not really part of the village. The Ski Hotel Vogel, at the top of the cable car, is an ideal place to stay as are the hotels Jezero and Kompass, both situated above beautiful Lake Bohinj.

The other skiing area is Mount Kobla, 5km away, which consists of a mixture of easy and intermediate runs entirely below the tree-line served by six lifts. Together the two ski areas give a total of 48km of piste.

Bohinj has a few pizzerias and discos with extremely reasonable prices, and other activities include skating and curling on the frozen lake.

Kranjska Gora
top 1630m (5,348ft) bottom 810m (2,667ft)

Set in an attractive valley, this is one of the best-known resorts in the region. It is close to the Italian and Austrian borders and is Tyrolean in ambience, even down to its domed church, although its modest hotels are not comparable to cosy Austrian gasthofs, and its chalets are slightly more severe than their Tyrolean equivalents. The setting, in a flat-bottomed valley between craggy wooded mountains, is a pretty one.

The four nursery runs are fairly short, wide and gentle, set right on the edge of the village, and the transition to real pistes is rather abrupt, with the mountains rising quite steeply from the valley floor. A total of 30km of pistes, the majority of which are blue, are covered by the lift pass. The longest run, Vitranc, is reached by chair-lift to the top of the ski area and is graded red. The other lifts only go halfway up the small mountain, which means limited skiing and a danger of poor snow cover.

The Alpine Ski Club offers both group and private lessons, but only private snowboarding and cross-country lessons are available. Children are catered for in the ski school but there is no kindergarten.

There are swimming-pools and saunas in several of the slightly institutional hotels, as well as some discos and bars. The Kompass is one of the resort's best hotels and boasts a swimming-pool and disco. The equally modern Hotel Larix is recommended for its location and facilities. The Prisank has a friendly atmosphere.

Norway

RESORTS COVERED Geilo, Hemsedal, Lillehammer, Oppdal, Trysil, Voss

Thanks mainly to the Olympic torch which burnt through the 1994 Winter Games in Lillehammer, the flames of British skiers' love affair with Norway are being re-kindled after almost three decades. That, at least, is what the Norwegians would like to believe, and a continued increase in the number of overseas visitors has given some support to it. However, it must be stated clearly that while the experience of downhill skiing here may be less pressurised and at least as enjoyable, it bears no genuine comparison to the Alps.

■ **GOOD POINTS**

Extensive beginner/intermediate slopes, good family skiing, few queues, good-value equipment rental and lift tickets, English widely spoken

■ **BAD POINTS**

Low mountains, lack of challenging skiing, few long runs, expensive alcohol

British skiers have of course remained loyal to Norway, but many began to desert the country's slopes with the advent of regular packages by air to the Alps in the 1960s. By the 1970s only the staunchest of supporters remained. But what will the others find should they return today?

First, Norway will seem cheaper than they remember. This is because prices in the Alps have risen faster in the interim period than in Scandinavia. Ski rental and lift tickets are now about one-third of the price of their alpine counterparts. On the other hand, food and drink, especially alcohol, are still expensive.

Second, some of the old lifts have been upgraded. Although the T-bar is still prominent, the high-speed quad-chair has found its way to some resorts, notably Hemsedal.

Third and most important, Norway's snow record is not subject to the peaks and troughs experienced in more southerly latitudes.

Traditionally, British skiers travelling to Norway tend to be beginners, intermediates and cross-country enthusiasts. It is fair to say that Norway is not the best destination for experienced skiers, even though there is some good off-piste. Although the country has almost 200 locations where skiing is possible, including scores of cross-country centres and some very small ski hills, Norway's mountains are not huge, with vertical drops of 300 to 750m. Only about a dozen ski areas can truly be called resorts.

Night-skiing is popular, English is widely spoken and the Norwegians are well-disposed towards British skiers. There is little serious queuing. Some resorts offer a Winterlandet card, which allows you to ski more than one resort. For example **Gol**, **Geilo**, **Hallingskarvet**, **Hemsedal**, **Uvdal** and **Al** are on the same lift pass, offering a total of 74 runs and 45 lifts.

Geilo
top 1178m (3,864ft) bottom 800m (2,624ft)

This is a traditional favourite with British skiers, especially for cross-country. The downhill skiing, which comprises 32 pistes served by 18 lifts, is excellent for beginners and intermediates. Although there are seven notional 'black' (difficult) runs and some fun tree-level skiing, advanced skiers will quickly run out of steam in Geilo. However, several novice and intermediate reporters described the terrain as 'perfect'.

The skiing is divided into two areas on opposite sides of town. The only way to get from one to the other is by snow-taxi; these offer a special, cheaper rate for skiers. However, many people resent the payment, and the resort is looking at ways to remove the charge — possibly by laying on a free ski-bus service.

The Vestlia area, with a vertical drop of around 244m, has the easiest skiing, but is well worth a visit. The highlight is Bjornloypa, a popular long green (beginner) run. The main area has a much wider selection of pistes, including some quite steep terrain and a vertical drop of 378m. Four new chair-lifts were added to the area during the 1995–6 season. There is also night-skiing.

TOURIST OFFICE
Tel 47 320 86300
Fax 47 320 86850

Hemsedal
top 1450m (4,756ft) bottom 650m (2,132ft)

Although only an hour's drive from Geilo, in the heart of Norway's Winterland region between Oslo and Bergen, Hemsedal's peaks look a lot more mountainous than Geilo's rounded ski hills; psychologically this helps create the feeling of being in a serious ski resort. In addition, despite the fact that Hemsedal has fewer runs than Geilo, and Oppdal has a larger ski area and more off-piste, the resort has some of the best skiing in Norway, with a healthy vertical drop of 800m and a long season stretching from mid-November to May.

In a country where ski resorts are dominated by the T-bar, Hemsedal also has the most modern lift system, with three quads and three more planned additions to its current total of 16 lifts serving 30 runs. The resort has a couple of genuinely steep black runs and some entertaining tree-line skiing.

One snag is that the village is about 3km from the ski area, and the free ski-bus service is infrequent (two go from the village in the morning and two return in the afternoon). This means, for example, that guests staying at the Skogstad Hotel who wish to take advantage of the much advertised night-skiing, run the risk of missing dinner, which is served between 6 and 8pm. One of the planned new lifts will go straight from the village to the ski area.

Hemsedal has some good tree-level skiing, which is known as 'taxi skiing'; this is because it is necessary to organise transport to return to the slopes or to your base. The resort also has a severe off-piste run called Reidarskaret, which starts with a steep, narrow couloir, and is, more often than not, too dangerous to attempt unless snow conditions are perfect.

TOURIST OFFICE
Tel 47 320 60156
Fax 47 320 60537

Lillehammer
top 1050m (3,444ft) bottom 180m (590ft)

Lillehammer resembles an American frontier town with its clapboard houses and single main street. The nearest skiing is based 15km away at **Hafjell**, which has 23km of prepared pistes, 7 lifts and 9 runs. The best are from Hafjelltoppen (1050m) down either the Kringelas or Hafjell runs; both are graded black and formed part of the 1994 Winter Olympic slalom courses. Night-skiing is also available once a week.

Kvitfjell, 50km from Lillehammer, was created specifically for the Winter Olympics and is virtually a downhill course and nothing else; its 4km of pistes are closed to everyone but competitors and officials on race days.

TOURIST OFFICE
Tel 47 612 66443
Fax 47 612 56585

Oppdal
top 1300m (4,265ft) bottom 545m (1,788ft)

Oppdal lies 120km south of Trondheim and is one of Norway's most northerly downhill resorts; technically it is also the biggest. Although it has only 28 runs (fewer than Hemsedal and Geilo) and a vertical drop a little lower than Hemsedal, it has extensive areas of off-piste terrain spread between its four ski areas. It offers 78km of piste served by 16 lifts. The most challenging marked trails — Bjorndalsloypa, Hovdenloypa and Bjerkeloypa — were enjoyed by Italian gold medallist Tomba when he was here for a World Cup race and are on the front face of Hovden, the central ski area.

The Vangslia area also offers a mixture of terrain, while Stolen at the other end of the resort is made entirely of slopes best suited to beginners and intermediates. The fourth area, Adalen, is set in a huge bowl behind Hovden and is dominated by long, mainly blue (easy) cruising runs. Snowcats will take up to 50 skiers at a time to the top of the mountain at Blaoret for sightseeing and an additional 240 vertical metres of off-piste skiing.

TOURIST OFFICE
Tel 47 72 42 17 60
Fax 47 72 42 08 88

Trysil
top 1132m (3,714ft) bottom 600m (1,969ft)

This is an expanding resort three hours' drive from Oslo. Its 85km of piste served by 23 lifts are spread across the wooded slopes of Trysilfjellet at 1132m. It is said to have the most reliable snow cover anywhere in the country. In common with many Norwegian resorts, the lifts are several kilometres from the resort centre. The

■ **WHAT'S NEW**
6-seater chair at Trysil

skiing varies from easy beginner trails to some more challenging red (intermediate) runs, but is often criticised for having too many green runs, which are described as 'cross-country tracks in disguise'.

TOURIST OFFICE
Tel 47 624 50511
Fax 47 624 51165

Voss
top 945m (3,100ft) bottom 57m (187ft)

In spite of its low altitude, Voss has a reasonable ski area for beginners and lower intermediates. The 40km of prepared piste include three black runs, two of which are reasonably challenging, and some off-piste. The nine lifts (almost one for each run) include a cable car, and the longest descent is 3km.

TOURIST OFFICE
Tel 47 565 10051
Fax 47 565 11715

Ski schools and guiding
The Norwegians are justly proud of their ski schools, which are well-organised with English-speaking instructors. There is a keen emphasis on safety, and Norwegians actively encourage the use of ski helmets for children. Voss and Trysil even provide free lift passes for children up to eight years old who are wearing helmets. Hemsedal lends out free helmets with its children's lift passes. Children's ski areas are often roped off with netting to stop fast adult skiers hurtling into them at the end of a downhill run.

Oppdal has a specialist guiding service called Opplev Oppdal; guides escort skiers around the area and carry a full kit of safety equipment, including avalanche transceivers (rarely used in Norway), shovels and avalanche probes. Apart from its three ski schools, Geilo also has Aktivitets Guiding for off-piste skiing.

Snowboarding
Snowboarding is still in its infancy in Norway, while telemarking is making a big comeback in its country of origin. However, at Oppdal 'night boarding' with special floodlit courses — complete with rental equip-

ment and a buffet — is held on Wednesday evenings at the Sletvold Park slope. Hemsedal also has a snowboard park offering floodlit boarding and a self-timing course. There are snowboarding classes on offer at Geilo and Voss.

Cross-country

Norway is famous as the home of cross-country skiing and nowhere more so than Geilo, which is the traditional cross-country resort with 175km of loipe on both the valley floor and up on the Hardangevidda Plateau at 1312m. The resort also has floodlit cross-country skiing. Oppdal also has 150km of trails covering a variety of terrain; five of its tracks are floodlit. Enthusiasts of the sport will certainly not be disappointed with Voss and its 63km of prepared trails.

Mountain restaurants

Geilo has six restaurants scattered around its two ski areas. The fast-food restaurant at the top of the main area at Geilohovda is popular, but the splendid Dr Holms Hotel is at the bottom of the slopes and many skiers choose to congregate here for lunch. Hemsedal's two mountain restaurants are near the top of the Hollvinheisen triple-chair. The third, Skistua, is at the base area and has the option of self- or wait-service.

Oppdal has six mountain restaurants: one at the bottom of each base area, and two more at the top of the Hovden and Stolen lift complexes. Only the Vangslia lifts are without a mid-mountain restaurant. The semi-circular restaurant at the top of Hovden was originally part of a water-storage structure. The restaurant at the bottom of Stolen, where most of the easiest family skiing takes place, is usually the busiest.

Accommodation

Apart from hotels, Norwegian resorts have an abundance of usually expensive cabins and apartments. The sprawling and stately Dr Holms Hotel in Geilo is famous throughout Norway and has a fascinating history. During the Second World War German U-boat officers took it over and entertained girls from the Moulin Rouge in Paris in one of the hotel wings. The slopes are only a minute away, and the nearest lift is 100m away. You can ski to the three-star Solli Sportell Hotel, and the Highland Hotel is also recommended.

■ OTHER SPORTS

Squash, sleigh-rides, parapente, dog-sledding, skating, ice-fishing, snowrafting, waterfall-climbing, Up-ski, telemark, swimming, snow-shoeing

In Oppdal the recently refurbished Hotel Nor is a sound choice, and guests at the 75-room Hotel Oppdal, right by the (not busy) railway station describe it as cosy and quaint, despite its size.

Accommodation in Trysil is mainly hotel- and apartment-based, although mountain cabins, notably the Trysilfjellet, make a pleasant change for hardy self-caterers. Hotel Soria Moria, 2km from the lifts, is favoured by reporters.

Eating in and out

Visitors to Norway are pleasantly surprised by the range and quality of dishes on offer. Fish lovers are in for a treat, with endless permutations of lax (salmon), sardines and herrings ranging from smoked or fried to marinated or poached, plus seemingly endless supplies of shrimps. Reindeer is often on the menu. In Geilo the buffet at the Highland Hotel is strongly recommended. For traditional Norwegian food the Hallingstuene is excellent.

The Skogstad Hotel at Hemsedal offers a good menu at its bistro and has a good brunch on Sundays. However, some guests eating in the normal dining-room commented on the limited choice and poor quality of the food for what is claimed to be a four-star hotel. In Oppdal it is worth trying the so-called 'Viking evening' (a misnomer) in a timbered roundhouse in the woods, where local stews, patés and sausage are served in front of a roaring fire with accordion accompaniment.

Après-ski

If you like packed, noisy bars, try some of Hemsedal's 'in' places during a busy weekend. You will be lucky if you can get near the Garasjen (the old bus garage), where it can become so crowded that skiers overflow on to the street and those left inside have to come to a tacit agreement as to the moment when snatching a quick sip of beer in unison is possible. The Skogstad Piano Bar and Hemsedal Café are almost as crowded. You may have more room to breathe at the Kro Bar in the Fanitullen apartment block.

In Geilo, the new ski-bar at the Dr Holms Hotel is proving to be extremely popular. Other well-patronised bars include the Hos Josn and the Laven at the Vestlia Hotel. Although Oppdal is a fair-sized town the nightlife — apart from a few bars and restaurants — is slightly limited.

Buying wine in Norway can be a major problem. One British guest in Geilo expressed alarm that the nearest place he could buy a bottle — at an outrageous price — was 50km away.

Childcare

For children of three months and over the resorts have Trollia (Troll Club) kindergartens for skiing and play, which are usually open seven days a week. English is almost invariably spoken. At Hemsedal the excellent — and free — slope-side babysitting service operates a simple but effective way of telling anxious parents that their toddlers are sleeping soundly in their cots at afternoon nap time: if the curtain closest to their infant is closed, all is well, if drawn open, the child would appreciate prompt return of parents.

Scotland

RESOURCES COVERED Cairngorm (Aviemore), Glencoe, Glenshee,
The Lecht, Nevis Range (Aonach Mor)

The success of Scotland's ski areas is entirely reliant on the weather and on the type of snow that falls. On the one hand, a sudden temperature rise can bring a rapid thaw or rain, and gale-force winds can make life on the mountain extremely unpleasant as well as closing vital access lifts. On the other hand you can experience beautiful sunshine and no wind, with temperatures low enough to keep the snow crisp. When this happens, however, swarms of enthusiastic Scottish skiers clog up the car parks, rental shops and ticket counters as foreplay to creating horrific lift queues and overcrowded slopes.

■ GOOD POINTS

Friendly atmosphere, wide range of non-ski activities, late-season skiing, British Association of Ski Instructors (BASI) tuition

■ BAD POINTS

Unpredictable weather conditions, lift queues at peak periods, limited skiing

Because of the weather it is a constant battle for the resort operators to groom the slopes effectively, and they have to put up chestnut paling fences everywhere to try to catch and contain drifting snow. Rapid temperature fluctuations make the manufacture of artificial snow difficult. The positive side of all this is summed up in one reader's comments on Cairngorm: 'Although the weather and snow conditions can be disappointing, to me they just make an otherwise limited mountain more challenging.'

The five ski centres in the Scottish Highlands are often marketed together. The newest is **Nevis Range** on the west coast, 33 miles (55km) from **Glencoe**. **Aviemore** is in the Spey Valley, in the Central Highlands, and **The Lecht** and **Glenshee** lie to the east.

The achievements of the resort operators and their staff cannot be overstated. Managing to maintain and build their operations against this background of meteorological unpredictability, while persuading public and private institutions to invest the capital needed to expand and improve the centres, shows a dedication that is the reality of Scottish skiing. While many moan about Britain's standing in competitive world skiing, it is Scotland that provides most of the national team members.

It is unrealistic to expect to have the same sort of skiing holiday in Scotland as you would in the Alps, but it is possible to have an excellent time simply by keeping an open mind and being flexible. The Highlands are so used to uncertain weather that the range of alternative outdoor pursuits available puts even the world's top ski resorts to shame.

There is friendly and healthy rivalry between the ski areas, notably between the Cairngorm (Aviemore) and Nevis Range, which opened in

1989. The fortunes of both the major ski areas are often seen as key to the overall economic picture of the larger communities around them.

In reality, Cairngorm's infrastructural shortcomings were highlighted by the new lifts at Nevis Range, where the gondola generates more tourist income in the summer than in the winter. There are plans for a funicular lift on the Cairngorm slopes, which would overcome the problem encountered by Nevis Range of wind forcing the gondola (the only access to the slopes) to cease operating. So far these plans have been thwarted by protests from conservationists. The Nevis Range slopes are 7 miles (11km) from Fort William, which is closer than Cairngorm's are to Aviemore.

The changeable snow and weather conditions mean that it makes sense to be based where you have access to more than one centre, and not invest in a week's lift ticket for just one resort. Ski Hotline (0891) 654654 provides up-to-date news of conditions.

Aviemore
top 3,608ft (1100m) bottom 1,804ft (550m)
Aviemore is located about 120 miles (192km) north of Edinburgh and Glasgow on the A9 and is the nearest town to the **Cairngorm** ski area, which lies ten miles to the east. It is served by rail direct from Inverness, and there are daily flights from Heathrow.

As a ski resort, the town suffered in the 1980s by having its facilities based around a large, 20-year-old concrete development, the Aviemore Centre, which resembled the ugly French resort of Les Menuires on a bad day and has been in a serious state of decay for the last ten years. While planners have optimistically renamed the area Aviemore Mountain Resort and hope to invest £15 million over the next few years. The Centre itself has been left behind by developments on Aviemore's main street and on the outskirts of the town ('a modern sprawl with large hotels'), where high-quality accommodation and leisure attractions have emerged, helping to make Aviemore and the Spey Valley more of an appealing outdoor holiday destination.

Parts of the medium-sized ski area are often closed due to poor weather conditions or snow shortage: 'When the top chair-lifts are closed due to winds it can be infuriating, especially if the snow conditions are good on the runs that are affected.' The 17 lifts serve 2 distinct sectors, which are accessed from separate bases at Coire Na Ciste and Coire Cas, meeting below the 4,084ft (1245m) Cairngorm peak. Head Wall offers challenging skiing, and White Lady has some excellent moguls. West Wall and Ciste Gully are recommended 'first thing in the morning before most skiers are on the hill'.

Trail-marking is not one of the region's strong points, and you need to keep an eye out for half-buried snow fences. Some of the old queues can now be avoided by using the M1 drag-lift, which last season was extended to reach the top-station at Ptarmigan, taking pressure off both the Coire Cas and the White Lady T-bars. However, reporters found 'prices expensive considering the skiing on offer'.

Off-piste routes include the East Wall gullies and Coire Laogh Mor; these are reached by a long traverse, which often has wind-broken snow, and a guide is necessary for both.

There are four snack bars, two at the base lodges, Shieling at the mid-station and the fourth at the panoramic Ptarmigan, which is popular for drinks and short breaks. Shieling is one of the only restaurants in Scotland that allows skiers to eat packed lunches at the table.

TOURIST OFFICE
Tel (01479) 810363
Fax (01479) 811063

Glencoe
top 3,637ft (1109m) bottom 2,001ft (610m)

The White Corries ski area at Glencoe has attracted a dedicated following for four decades (Britain's first chair-lift opened here in 1961) and the past few seasons have seen considerable investment in infrastructure as the centre is packaged with Nevis Range as 'Ski Lochaber'. There are 6 miles (10km) of piste and 15 runs. A museum of Scottish skiing and mountaineering contains mementos from home and abroad, including Chris Bonnington's ice axe from the 1985 Everest exhibition. The centre is the closest to Glasgow, which is 85 miles (136km) to the south.

TOURIST OFFICE
Tel (01855) 851226
Fax (01855) 851233

Glenshee
top 3,502ft (1068m) bottom 2,001ft (610m)

Marketed as 'Britain's largest network of ski lifts and tows', and even more optimistically as 'the UK's Three Valleys', Glenshee's vital statistics are impressive, with a total of 26 lifts and 25 miles (40km) of trails. The centre is on a rather desolate pass on the A93, with the lifts located on both sides of the road. There is a run-of-the-mill café at the base and a better high-altitude restaurant, the Cairnwell.

TOURIST OFFICE
Tel (01250) 875509
Fax (01250) 875733

The Lecht
top 2,600ft (793m) bottom 2,109ft (643m)

The Lecht ski area is made up of a series of lifts along both sides of the A939, 40 miles (25km) from Cairngorm and 35 miles (22km) from

Glenshee. Eleven lifts give access to 20 runs, the longest of which is 900m. Although this is a small ski area with no sizeable town nearby, The Lecht does have a reputation for friendliness and quality piste-grooming. The centre also has a 200-m artificial ski slope. The nearest accommodation is 3 miles (5km) away at Corgarff.

TOURIST OFFICE
Tel (01975) 651440
Fax (01975) 651426

Nevis Range
top 4,006ft (1221m) bottom 2,148ft (655m)

With its new access road and modern six-seater Doppelmayr gondola, Nevis Range looks on arrival like an alpine resort. Previously skiers had to join a large queue on a slow beginner's drag-lift or slog uphill to reach the bottom of the quad-chair. However, the addition of two new lifts last season opened up several new trails and made access to the Back Coire easier. The 10 lifts and 35 trails are well integrated, albeit poorly marked.

> **■ WHAT'S NEW**
> Combined lift pass for Glencoe and Glenshee
> Additional T-bar and chair-lift at Nevis Range
> Double-chair at Nevis Range planned for 1996–7 season

Queues for the gondola back down the mountain can be huge when the weather is good. These develop at about 4pm when the Snowgoose restaurant has standing room only.

Nevis Range opened for the 1989–90 season and was formerly known as Aonach Mor, until it was realised that few non-Scots could pronounce it. Locals continue to call the resort by its former name, finding the new name to be 'scarcely sensible, since Ben Nevis is two miles away and separated by a deep rift'. Most of the accommodation is in Fort William, which has a leisure centre and good shopping facilities.

TOURIST OFFICE
Tel (01397) 705825
Fax (01397) 705854

Ski schools and guiding

Scotland boasts an exceptional number of ski schools, many of them based at Cairngorm and in the Spey Valley. Most offer a high standard of tuition under the auspices of the British Association of Ski Instructors (BASI), whose excellent teaching method is internationally accepted. The Nevis Range Ski School runs various courses, including 'over the back' guided trips, clinics for steep skiing and bumps, over 50s, and women's workshops.

Snowboarding

British interest in snowboarding was pioneered in Scotland in the late 1980s and riders are now a common sight at all the centres. Most of the local ski schools offer tuition and the rental shops have boards for hire. Cairngorm has a fun park with a ramp and an on-slope shop where you can hire equipment and book tuition. A Ride Guide, a map written in snowboarding lingo, is available in addition to the ordinary piste-map. Nevis Range has several specialist snowboard shops including Mach, where lessons can also be booked.

Cross-country

Besides its five centres for alpine skiing, Scotland offers plenty of opportunities for cross-country skiing. However, due to the cold winds, clothing needs to be extra protective. Most of Scotland's cross-country skiing is along forest trails, which hold the snow better than the more open terrain. The season runs from early January to mid-March on the lower, wooded trails, and until early May higher up the mountain. The most challenging routes are on the rounded mountains of the Central and Eastern Highlands. The Cross-country Hot Line on (0891) 654659 is updated daily, giving conditions at the main areas and details of where you can hire equipment, arrange accommodation and book tuition.

Accommodation

The area surrounding the Scottish ski centres offers an excellent array of accommodation, from the cheap and cheerful to the luxury of the Inverlochy Castle Hotel, which is frequented by Hollywood stars and the occasional US president, and is one of the closest properties to the Nevis Range slopes. It is possible to base yourself in the Spey Valley close to Aviemore and still remain within an hour of the other four resorts. Alternatively, you can stay in Inverness, which is 45 minutes by road from both Cairngorm and Nevis Range. Fort William is the base for Nevis Range and Glencoe; staying near Balmoral places you within 30 minutes' drive of Glenshee and The Lecht.

■ OTHER SPORTS

Canoeing, climbing, fishing, gliding, golf, gorge walking, hang-gliding, skating, off-road vehicles, hiking, shooting, go-karting, squash, swimming, tennis, trekking, water-skiing

Between Aviemore and the Cairngorm slopes is the Stakis Coylumbridge Resort, which has plenty of facilities including a swimming-pool and a wide range of children's activities. In nearby Carrbridge, the An Airidh Ski Lodge recreates the cosy 'open-house' atmosphere of an alpine ski chalet, and in Aviemore itself the Mercury offers good-value accommodation.

Eating in and out

Scotland is still saddled with an unfair reputation for poor dining opportunities. Littlejohns restaurant in Aviemore has a friendly atmosphere, with 1930s paraphernalia and copious quantities of American and Mexican food. The Gallery is at Inverdruie, a mile outside Aviemore; readers praise its food and recommend booking in advance as it has few tables. The Taverna French Bistro has reasonable prices. In Fort William, the pink loch-side Crannog restaurant has a good reputation for seafood.

Après-ski

Scottish après-ski is largely hotel-based. Aviemore used to have a reputation for its rowdy and sleazy nightlife, but most of the bars have been refurbished and there is now less of the tough, hard-drinking Scottish pub atmosphere. Crofters is one of the most popular of Aviemore's clubs, and the bar at the Highland Hotel is also recommended. Activities include a theatre, cinema, swimming and skating. Reporters generally found the nightlife 'disappointing', with the disco stopping at 11pm. Prices for drinks are 'at the usual pub rates but somewhat inflated in the more expensive hotels'.

Fort William is an old loch-side town beneath Ben Nevis and has a strong tourist appeal, with a wide variety of hotels, bars and restaurants to suit all tastes. There is also a cinema and a leisure centre with bowling, a swimming-pool and a crèche.

Childcare

Nevis Range, Glenshee and The Lecht operate non-ski crèche facilities, which should be booked in advance. The Nevis Range crèche accepts children from three years old. The Mercury Hotel in the Aviemore Centre has a crèche for children aged two to eight years of age, and the ski schools arrange children's tuition on demand (in good weather, according to the local tourist board). Glencoe has no childminding facilities, but the ski school can arrange lessons.

Spain

RESORTS COVERED Baqueira-Beret, Sierra Nevada

Spain is the only country in Europe where the number of skiers is increasing significantly as the sport undergoes a major surge in popularity. In the main French Tarentaise resorts the Spanish are now considered to be an important section of the tourist trade, and it is hard to spend a day in the Trois Vallées or L'Espace Killy without hearing the language spoken.

■ **GOOD POINTS**

Efficient lift systems, typically Spanish après-ski, low prices

■ **BAD POINTS**

Lack of resort charm, generally limited ski areas, short runs

This increase has also been apparent in Spain, fuelled by the World Alpine Championships in Sierra Nevada, which was postponed for a year due to lack of snow. The rate of exchange of the peseta against the pound, although not as good as it was, still makes Spanish skiing some of the more affordable in Europe.

Spain does not have a historical connection with skiing and, indeed, it seems surprising that a country so associated with beaches and summer sunshine should have any skiing at all. It does, in fact, have two quite separate mountain ranges — the Pyrenees and the Sierra Nevada — which both normally receive adequate winter snowfalls, regardless of what is happening in the main alpine countries.

The high and usually snow-sure resort of **Sierra Nevada** lies in the far south of the country in the mountains of the same name. After a lack of snow in February 1995, the entire winter sports programme had to be put on hold for a year — and even then snow was scarce.

The resultant publicity has seriously and unfairly damaged the overseas perception of Spanish skiing. Most of it takes place hundreds of kilometres to the north-east in the Pyrenees, which had superlative cover again last season for the third consecutive year.

Baqueira-Beret remains the most important of the Pyrenean resorts, a small but smart development much loved by King Juan Carlos, which attracts wealthy skiers from Madrid and Barcelona.

Baqueira-Beret
top 2510m (8,235ft) bottom 1500m (4,920ft)

Baqueira-Beret is Spain's answer to Gstaad: a smart and fashionable resort where not all the designer ski suits you see parading down the main street ever make it on to the snow. It lies at the head of the beautiful Val d'Aran, near **Viella** on the northern side of the Pyrenees; access from France is easy, and the drive from Toulouse Airport takes less than two hours.

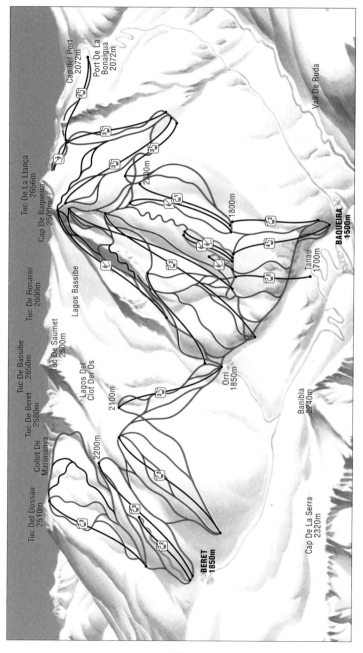

The skiing takes place on four wide, well-linked mountains with a vertical drop of about 1000m over varied, often exciting terrain, which is mostly suited to intermediates. However, one icy couloir, evocatively called Where Goats Tumble, is a real challenge. The opening up of the Bonaigua area has greatly enhanced the resort's appeal to good skiers.

Plans to expand the already extensive skiing into the next valley and increase this impressive area by 40 per cent are in the final stages of discussion. At present it has 24 lifts covering 47km, with the main mountain access by quad-chair from the top of the village. The lower slopes are extensively covered by snow-cannon, and a further 74 at **Beret** have been introduced for the 1996–7 season.

Baqueira is still largely unknown outside Spain, mainly because of the small number of rental beds available. However, it is no newcomer to winter sports — in December 1994 it celebrated its 30th birthday and, at a time when even big-name resorts are struggling financially, Baqueira as a ski resort is operating efficiently at a handsome profit.

What makes Baqueira unique in Europe is that the resort has just one owner. The Cerra family from Barcelona are passionate about skiing and they also have a controlling interest in one of Spain's largest insurance companies. Cerra Occidente owns the land, the lifts, the mountain restaurants and the ski school. Until recently it even owned all of the real estate in the village, although it has now relinquished a prime building lot in return for a further lift development permit from the regional government.

If all this sounds familiar to transatlantic skiers, it should. Vail Associates, the hugely successful owner of Vail in Colorado, acted as development consultant to Baqueira. Americans have long since discovered that a single corporate identity in a ski resort is the sure way to create customer satisfaction and profitability. In concept, Baqueira is a little slice of the USA — in the Pyrenees.

The terrain, right down to the scrubby Engelmann spruce which grow here at the lower altitudes, is strongly reminiscent of Squaw Valley in California. But here the resemblance ends. Baqueira is purpose-built in an aesthetically adequate style and is as Spanish as the siesta, which is an essential part of ski survival here. The village lies beside the road that leads up to the very high Bonaigua Pass, which is often, but not always, closed in winter. Recent sympathetic development has increased its appeal as a base, with some good shops, hotels, restaurants and a leisure centre. The atmosphere is relaxed and friendly. Beret is the second base area rather than a separate resort and consists of little more than a car park and a cafeteria.

Veteran Olympic skier José Moga, who taught King Juan Carlos to ski and who also runs the main ski shop in town, describes it as 'the best-value skiing in a less pretentious atmosphere than you can find anywhere in Europe'.

TOURIST OFFICE
Tel 34 73 64 44 55
Fax 34 73 64 44 88

Sierra Nevada
top 3470m (11,385ft) bottom 2100m (6,888ft)

Sierra Nevada lies in Andalusia, 32km from the ancient Moorish city of Granada, and offers mainland Europe's most southerly skiing. Unlike the other Spanish ski resorts, which are nearly all in the Pyrenees in the north-east of Spain, Sierra Nevada is a stark contrast to the surrounding area and nearby resorts of Marbella and Malaga with their yacht clubs and golf courses. The resort used to be marketed under the name of Sol y Nieve (Sun and Snow), and the purpose-built village in which most skiers stay (at 2100m) is known as **Pradollano**.

The ski area is extremely vulnerable to bad weather, and the mountain range as a whole is exposed to Atlantic gales. When the weather here is bad, everything stops, but when conditions are good the skiing can be excellent and the views striking; on a clear day you can even see Morocco. However, because of its proximity to Granada and the Costa del Sol, the resort suffers from extreme crowds at weekends and on public holidays.

Some £60 million was invested in the resort in preparation for the disastrous Alpine World Championships, and it now has 19 lifts serving 34 mainly intermediate pistes totalling 61km. Access to the main skiing area is by a choice of three lifts (including a gondola) from the edge of the village.

Most of Pradollano's buildings date from the 1960s and 1970s. It is not an attractive place ('just like Torremolinos with snow and litter'), but the atmosphere is 'quiet, with quite a Spanish feel to the resort'.

TOURIST OFFICE
Tel 34 58 24 91 00
Fax 34 58 24 91 31

Ski schools and guiding

We have generally unhappy reports about Spanish ski schools, largely because a proportionately low number of instructors speak English in comparison with those at alpine schools, and few British speak Spanish. Reporters in Baqueira complained that the instruction was mainly of the 'follow-my-leader' type.

Sierra Nevada attracts a more international clientèle and accordingly caters better, with a choice of three schools.

Snowboarding

Spanish youth has endorsed the board with typical noisy enthusiasm, and shredders account for around 10 per cent of lift tickets sold in all the main Spanish resorts.

Mountain restaurants

Baqueira's mountain eating-places serve good food at reasonable prices but lack atmosphere. However, one exception is Restaurant 1800 ('wonderful paella for eight, but you must order a day in advance'). A new restaurant at 2200m is to be opened for the 1996–7 season. The restaurant at Bonaigua 'resembles a gothic castle and is cheaper and better than anywhere else'. Sierra Nevada is rather better served by its wide choice of eateries in the main bowl.

Accommodation

Baqueira has 12,000 beds, many of which are owned or rented for the season by Spaniards who make the journey here every weekend from Barcelona and other cities. The four-star Hotel Montarto is widely praised, as is the less expensive Hotel Tuc Blanc. Many regular visitors prefer to stay in the more traditional hotels further down the valley. There are good *paradors* (inns) in nearby Viella.

In Sierra Nevada the accommodation is mainly in hotels. The Melia Sol y Nieve and the four-star Melia Sierra Nevada, both near the main square, are convenient and pleasant. The Melia Sol y Nieve has a mini-club for children between 5 and 11 years old. Melia Sierra Nevada has a swimming-pool, disco and its own shops. The Kenia Nevada is recommended by a reporter: 'a quiet hotel, most guests were Spanish but the service was generally friendly and attentive and the bedrooms comfortable and clean'. The chalet-style Parador, set on its own above Pradollano (accessible by chair-lift and piste), is fairly functional but has exceptional views. The Albergue Universitani is said to be excellent value and clean.

Eating in and out

The menus in Baqueira are truly international and they come in three versions: Spanish, Catalan, and Aranes (a language peculiar to this corner of the Pyrenees). Fortunately, Baqueira's proximity to the border means that French is also widely understood, if not spoken. This is not a place for vegetarians or the culinary squeamish; Borda Lobato is a lavishly converted cow shed and is considered to be the best restaurant in town ('barbecued rabbit was followed on my second evening by a choice of roast suckling pig or whole baby lamb carved with garden shears'). Other recommended restaurants include La Perdiu Blanca, La Ticolet for pierrade, and Tamarro's for tapas.

Prices are among the lowest in any significant ski resort in the northern hemisphere. In Sierra Nevada there is a small range of restaurants serving local, French, Turkish or Italian cuisine. The Borreguiles is one of the most popular eating-places.

Après-ski

In Spain, partying is an even more serious business than skiing. Wise Anglo-Saxons who stray into this completely alien ski-resort environment either adopt local hours or suffer from what quickly develops into a severe Latin mutation of jetlag. Local skiers hit the slopes at a leisurely 10am and ski furiously until lunch at 2pm. They grab a final hour on the piste before the lifts close at 5pm and then head for the tapas bars before an evening snooze. The length of the 7pm ski siesta is largely dependent on ski energy expended, the size of the paella you ate for lunch and your intake of *calamares* and Rioja at tea-time. Nobody (not even families with young children) sits down to dinner before 9pm, and restaurants begin to get busy at 11pm. Dancing does not begin before 1pm and can carry on into daylight hours.

In Baqueira, Tiffany's is the busiest nightclub. Sierra Nevada's late nightspot is Sierra Nevada 53. Early action is centred on a choice of crowded bars. Excursions can be made to Granada, which is famous for the spectacular Alhambra Palace and beautiful Renaissance and baroque buildings.

Childcare

Baqueira has three good non-ski and ski kindergarten, which cater for children from three months to eight years old. The Sierra Nevada kindergarten is for children aged three months to four years.

Offbeat resorts

RESORTS COVERED Australia: Thredbo, Perisher Blue, Mount Buller
New Zealand: Coronet Peak/The Remarkables,
Treble Cone, Whakapapa, Craigieburn, Mount Hutt
Chile: Portillo, La Parva/Valle Nevado, El Colorado, Termas de Chillán
Argentina: Gran Catedral (Bariloche), Las Leñas
Japan: Happo One, Shiga Kogen, Naeba

Every true ski enthusiast will have a dream list of exotic resorts which he or she hopes to ski if the opportunity arises. The principal attraction of such resorts lies in their far-away location rather than in what they have to offer in terms of skiing, as few resorts in the Southern Hemisphere begin to compare with their classic Alpine and North American counterparts. However, the chance to ski during the European summer months is hard to resist.

Australia's mountains would probably attract fewer skiers than France's Jura range if they were transported without their flora and fauna to Europe. However, in their rightful place in New South Wales and Victoria, with the ubiquitous eucalyptus trees and abundant semitropical bird life, they have a definite charm of their own. Given reasonably good snow, skiing in Australia is not to be sneered at.

The skiing in **New Zealand** is of a higher quality, with some moderately impressive resorts in the Southern Alps, together with numerous 'club fields' (these are less sophisticated than ski resorts, with rope-tows, no grooming, but cheap lift-tickets) and some formidable slopes at Whakapapa on the North Island. Prepare yourself for some hair-raising mountain roads which, in the absence of on-mountain accommodation, must be negotiated twice a day. However, unless you need or want to visit this beautiful country during the British summer for reasons other than skiing, it is hardly worth the long journey.

The South American Andes are considerably more accessible, with excellent skiing to be found in both **Chile** and **Argentina**. The mountains are mystically beautiful and the skiing unusually varied. Unfortunately, the most breathtaking scenery and the best slopes do not always go together; the further south down the Cordillera you travel, the more intriguing the scenery becomes, but the less challenging and extensive the skiing tends to be.

The ski season in **Japan** corresponds to that of the Alps and North America. Although the country has hundreds of ski areas, they are mainly of insignificant size. Among the notable exceptions are the resorts in the Hakuba Valley where the 1998 Nagano Winter Olympics downhill will be held at Happo One.

We have not given the telephone numbers of the local tourist offices.

We recommend that you contact the country's own tourist office (*see Skiing by numbers*).

AUSTRALIA

Thredbo
top 2037m (6,683ft) bottom 1365m (4,478ft)

This New South Wales resort 450km from Sydney, has arguably the best skiing in the country, plus extensive and sophisticated snowmaking and an attractive alpine-style village. A significant number of Austrians came here to work on the Snowy Mountain hydro-electric scheme in the 1950s and stayed on to take an active part in the skiing business. The 40 runs are served by 12 lifts.

Perisher Blue
top 1980m (6,496ft) bottom 1680m (5,512ft)

What originally were the three separate resorts of **Perisher/Smiggins**, **Blue Cow** and **Guthega** in New South Wales have combined to form the largest ski area in Australia (1250 hectares). Perisher alone has 20 lifts and altogether there are 50. The only way to reach the main complex is by train or lift; the modern Ski Tube takes skiers through 10km of tunnels on a 20-minute journey to Perisher and Blue Cow from Bullocks Flat. The name Smiggins refers to the 'smiggin holes' formed by cattle gouging the soil for salt licks. Blue Cow prides itself on its testing terrain and the high proportion of black-diamond (difficult) runs, including one named Kamikaze.

Mount Buller
top 1790m (5,873ft) bottom 1600m (5,249ft)

The principal area for Melbourne-based skiers has the largest lift capacity in Australia. Among the 26 lifts are 8 quads, including the recently installed Wombat. The resort is a three-hour (240-km) drive from the state capital through Ned Kelly country, and has some of the most impressive scenery in the Victorian Alps, with extensive views across the gum forests. There is substantial snowmaking and 80km of trails, including one that is 2.5km long.

NEW ZEALAND

Queenstown (Coronet Peak/The Remarkables)
Coronet Peak: top 1620m (5,315ft) bottom 1200m (3,937ft)
The Remarkables: top 1957m (6,421ft) bottom 1620m(5,315ft)

New Zealand's best known ski centre — an effervescent and picturesque lakeside town — offers two separate resorts, the old and the new, with interchangeable lift passes. Situated in the south-west of the South Island, the traditional resort at **Coronet Peak**, with a vertical drop of

434m, has been modernised and enlarged and now provides a wide variety of good all-round skiing and a much improved lift system. **The Remarkables**, which opened for skiing in 1985, is visually exciting, but has fewer options than Coronet Peak. From Queenstown the range seems impossibly steep, with the peaks resembling a range of sharp, pearly-white teeth, which dominate the shoreline of Lake Wakatipu. Fortunately the skiing area is on the other side, where gentle bowls belie the severity of the mountains.

Although The Remarkables provides predominantly intermediate terrain, some short, sharp couloirs, including Escalator and Elevator, add challenge. There are steep off-piste sections for skiers who are prepared to walk up, including the Homeward Runs, which finish at the road below the resort from where a truck takes skiers back up to the base-area.

Treble Cone
top 1860m (6,102ft) bottom 1200m (3,937ft)

Lake Wanaka is as tranquil as Lake Wakatipu is vibrant, and is the idyllic gateway to Treble Cone. Although it ranks as one of the country's top three resorts, Treble Cone is not well known outside New Zealand. It once had a reputation for favouring expert skiers, but in recent years some good beginner terrain has been developed. Advanced skiers can hike for 20 minutes to the 2100m summit to enjoy some of the best off-piste in the area. Challenging heli-skiing can be found nearby. The resort now has a six-seater chair-lift.

Whakapapa
top 2300m (7,546ft) bottom 1625m (5,331ft)

The country's largest resort has a vertical drop of 615m, a wide selection of cruising runs, exciting off-piste in its Black Magic area, and some severe terrain below the magnificent, snow-encrusted Pinnacles, which resemble a scaled-down version of the jagged Teton Mountains of Jackson Hole in Wyoming. The area is wonderful but frustrating, due to unpredictable weather. However, in good conditions it has some of the best skiing in the Southern Hemisphere.

The resort is built on the flanks of the Mount Ruapehu volcano, which attracts some of the more inclement weather on the North Island, with storms moving in fast and furiously. Until 1995, when a series of spectacular volcanic eruptions brought the ski season to a premature close, it was possible to make the three-hour climb to the Ruapehu crater lake and then ski down. One reporter who skied here on the final afternoon said: 'We spent most of the time looking over our shoulders at the fireworks, rather than concentrating on the slopes in front of us.'

The neighbouring resort of **Turoa** offers even more vertical metres than Whakapapa.

Craigieburn
top 1811m (5,942ft) bottom 1570m (5,151ft)

New Zealand's club fields offer cheap, but not necessarily cheerful skiing. Try battling to get up the slopes on a primitive 'nutcracker' rope-tow, then battling to get down them in crusty, ungroomed snow. Unlike almost all commercial resorts, club fields usually have on-mountain accommodation, albeit fairly basic hostel bunk-beds in lodges. Craigieburn deserves special mention because of its unusually challenging and spectacular terrain and, by hiking up, its 725-m vertical drop — one of the longest in Australasia. However, because of its primitive facilities it attracts only hard-core skiers.

Mount Hutt
top 2075m (6,808ft) bottom 1585m (5,200ft)
The most famous of New Zealand's resorts is often patronised by Northern Hemisphere race teams for training out of season. Mount Hutt is on the South Island and has magnificent views across the Canterbury Plains. It is a 35-minute drive from Methven and 70 minutes from Christchurch. It is also renowned for its access route: 12km of unsurfaced road at the mercy of strong winds, with somewhat alarming drops. The skiing can be excellent, although unpredictable weather has given the resort the rather unfair sobriquet 'Mount Shut'; a more flattering one is 'Ski field in the sky'. It does, however, have one of the most extensive snowmaking systems in the Southern Hemisphere. The 655m vertical drop is helped by the South Face runs that end up below the base-area. Heli-skiing is also available here.

CHILE

Portillo
top 3348m (10,984ft) bottom 2512m (8,241ft)
This picturesque but slightly quirky ski area is situated in a steep-sided valley next to the breathtakingly beautiful Laguna (lake) del Inca. It is in the heart of the Southern Andes close to the Argentine border and just under 160km north of Santiago. Access is via the awe-inspiring Uspallata Pass, one of only two passes between Chile and Argentina accessible during the winter. Engineers on the old Trans-Andean railway were the first to ski here. Most visitors to Portillo stay at the bright yellow Hotel Portillo, which dominates the resort. A delightful 1950s atmosphere still pervades, with the red-and-white-jacketed waiters scurrying around the vast lakeside dining-room.

The resort is run by a veteran American, Henry Purcell, and therefore the grooming and signposting on the 23 runs, served by 11 lifts, is as efficient as you would expect to find in any North American resort. Portillo also has the only serious snowmaking programme in Chile. The strong North American influence includes a large number of US ski instructors and a resort manager from Heavenly in California.

Portillo has two bizarre but exhilarating *va et vient* lifts specially designed for accessing the steep chutes in avalanche-prone areas. It is are a combination of a conventional cableway and a towerless cable tow.

Should an avalanche hit the lift, the cable drops and is buried until it can be located again. It can then be repaired or replaced, and reinstalled. The largest, Roca Jack, hauls five skiers at a time on linked platters at considerable speed to the top of the chute before suddenly coming to a halt; skiers must disengage backwards. *Va et vient* lifts are unique to Portillo, and were designed by the Pomagalski lift company, also responsible for the invention of the 'poma' lift.

La Parva/Valle Nevado/El Colorado
Valle Nevado: top 3670m (12,040ft) bottom 2880m (9,450 ft)
El Colorado: top 3333m (10,935ft) bottom 2430m (7,972ft)
La Parva: top 3630m (11,909 ft) bottom 2670m (8,760ft)

These three more-or-less linked resorts comprise the best conventional skiing in Chile, as well as being the closest major slopes to any capital city in the world (less than 64km north of Santiago): so close that Santiago's pollution causes magnificent sunsets on the slopes. The ski areas offer excellent off-piste as well as some 37 lifts.

Valle Nevado, purpose-built by the French a decade ago, looks like a smaller version of Whistler in Canada. It is the only true destination resort of the three and attracts an international clientèle. **El Colorado** tends to serve skiers from Santiago and is therefore busy at weekends, but quiet during the week. **La Parva**, which has the most varied skiing, has no real hotels for the time being and remains a second- or third-home resort for affluent Chileans.

Termas de Chillán
top 2500m (8,200ft) bottom 1800m (5,900ft)

For skiers in search of the more offbeat face of the Chilean Andes without sacrificing quality skiing, this is the resort that best combines the two. But beware, the more exotic the location, the more treacherous the access road is likely to be. Do not attempt to reach Termas de Chillán without a four-wheel drive vehicle or at least chains; the final 29km of the journey is on an icy, rocky and potholed road. The resort itself is 407km south of Santiago. The Don Otto chair-lift is reputedly the longest on the continent, and the excellent off-piste includes the 14-km Shangri-La run with its volcanic scenery, and Pirigallo, one of the resort's most celebrated itineraries, which comes complete with fumaroles belching sulphur fumes. There is also good cross-country touring to the west of the ski area and below the tree-line.

ARGENTINA

Gran Catedral (Bariloche)
top 2050m (6,725ft) bottom 1050m (3,445ft)

Gran Catedral is the newer name given to the ski resort on Catedral Mountain, which used to be called **Bariloche**. Confusingly, like many resorts that change their name, it is still also known as Bariloche. This is

Argentina's most celebrated ski area, which was also the first in the country to instal mechanised lifts during the late 1930s. It is a large, attractive and vigorous area in the south-west of this vast country, near the Chilean border, on the northern end of a range that extends from Lake Nahuel Huapi to Lake Mascardi in the south.

However, it has two serious flaws: its snow record is unpredictable and, because of its history of fragmented ownership, it lacks organisation and direction. One typical shortcoming is inadequate trail-marking — often it is difficult to tell whether the sticks at the side of a slope are to give warning of rocks or to mark the piste. The resort is perched above beautiful Lake Nahuel Huapi and attracts considerable precipitation, much of it falling as rain.

Fortunately, Bariloche has good beginner slopes at the top of the mountain as well as at the bottom, so in the event of heavy rain at the base, beginners can be taken higher. Only when the rain is accompanied by strong winds do the vital lifts to the higher nursery slopes close, leaving beginners with nowhere to ski. However, with 32 lifts and 50 runs, Bariloche can still justify its claim to be South America's biggest ski area.

Las Leñas
top 3340m (10,959ft) bottom 2240m (7,349ft)

Ski purists would almost certainly place the terrain at Argentina's most recent resort above that of its oldest, Bariloche. Las Leñas, constructed almost entirely from a chocolate-brown, wood-lookalike material, was built in 1983 with the French resort of Les Arcs acting as consultant. Most hotels and lifts are named after planets and signs of the zodiac; Pisces is the best hotel in town.

Although it is not the easiest of resorts to get to (1127km west of Buenos Aires), the powder is some of the best on the entire continent. The Marte (Mars) chair-lift feeds what amounts to a separate ski area that includes 40 challenging chutes, but when the lift is closed by the frequent high winds, only the more mundane main ski area of ten lifts is accessible.

JAPAN

Happo One/Hakuba Valley
top 1831m (6,007ft) bottom 760m (2,493ft)

Happo One will be the site for the men's downhill and Super G at the Nagano Winter Olympics in 1998. Nagano is 200km west of Tokyo. As well as offering splendid mountain scenery, some challenging terrain and longer-than-average runs for Japan, Happo One is one of the prettiest ski villages in the country. Another advantage is the quick access to other ski areas in the same valley, including **Hakuba 47**, **Iwatake**, **Goryu-Toomi** and **Sunalpina Sanosaka**. All are about four hours from Tokyo's Ueno railway station.

Among the endless tannoy announcements and musical refrains

broadcast over the resort are quaint messages in English, such as: 'Please avoid paging your friends very often over the public address system.'

Shiga Kogen
top 2305m (7,562ft) bottom 1228m (4,028ft)

Nagano's largest resort, Shiga Kogen, is where the bulk of the 1998 Winter Olympic events will take place. It is an extraordinary patchwork of around 24 different 'resorts' served by more than 80 lifts dotting six inter-linked mountains. None is big or particularly difficult; in alpine terms the whole area would make up just two or three linked resorts of reasonable size. A competent skier could cover all the terrain in a couple of days. Apart from skiing, another major tourist attraction is the hot sulphur baths into which monkeys sometimes leap from the surrounding trees.

Naeba
top 1800m (5,905ft) bottom 900m (2,953ft)

This bustling ski area in Niigata Prefecture is one of the most frenetic resorts in the Northern Japan Alps. It is dominated by the Naeba Prince, said to be the largest ski hotel in the world with more than 40 restaurants, including one that stays open all night. This enables skiers anxious to pack in as many hours on the slopes as possible to take breakfast at 3.30am and ski under floodlights between 4 and 4.30am. There is no need to stop skiing until 11pm, which means that die-hard skiers can keep going for 18 hours. At weekends, when packed bullet trains and buses bring their human cargo, an almost absurd number of skiers flood the slopes — the record stands at 40,000 skiers in one weekend — so at least at 4.30am there is some chance of finding a little space.

Snowboarding

Snowboarding has come of age. What started as a fad, yet another interpretation of *la nouvelle glisse*, is now a permanent fixture in the Alps and North America. Not only is it not going to go away, as the more short-sighted skiers have hoped, it may even be instrumental in the future survival of winter sports.

Rivalry, not to mention animosity, between skiers and snowboarders has been nurtured on youth, cultural differences and wholly erroneous misinformation that snowboarders account for a high proportion of collision accidents.

Talk to any sports shop owner and you will discover that in the 1995-6 season sales of boards equalled or outstripped sales of skis. Already there are a couple of million riders out there and manufacturers predict that this will rise to three million over the next five years. Major resorts are selling 15 to 20 per cent of their lift passes to snowboarders and there is no indication that the storm is abating. However, whether we will ever see the day when there are more riders than skiers on the slopes of the Trois Vallées or Val d'Isère remains a matter for conjecture.

A handful of resorts like Keystone in Colorado and Alpine Meadows in Nevada stubbornly maintain a no-board policy, but it remains to be seen for how long these resorts can afford to marginalise themselves. Both sets of enthusiasts have an equal right to enjoy themselves on the mountain.

The essential key to the snowboard revolution is youth — the largest participant age group of the sport is 17- to 24-year-olds — and it appeals to a great number of people who have never tried skiing but are attracted from surfing or skateboarding backgrounds. The strong snowboard fashion, culture and attitude, which project a rebellious image, particularly to the more traditionalist skiers, attest to its youth popularity.

The sport requires greater physical dexterity than skiing and demands a considerable amount of body contact with the mountain. Despite this, an increasing number of more mature riders are taking it up, and it is not uncommon to see a 50-year-old gingerly falling down the nursery slopes or even executing graceful turns in the powder.

However, what happens when riders become even more mature is still uncertain. As Franz Klammer says: 'If you learn to ski and later take up snowboarding then you can always return to skiing in your old age, but the reverse is not true'. Learning to ski at an advanced age is difficult, but if you have perfected your ski technique it is possible to continue late into the twilight years. Toni Seelos, who is credited with the invention of the parallel turn, is still to be seen at the venerable age of 85 whizzing down the mountain above his native Seefeld. It is hard to imagine a snowboarder of this age having the physical strength and mobility, but only time will tell.

Climbing on board
by Lloyd Rogers, British Snowboard Champion

Once you have tried snowboarding it is easy to understand why it is one of the fastest growing sports in the world. Combining the best of snow skiing, ocean surfing and skateboarding, snowboarding provides an unrivalled sense of freedom, particularly off-piste.

The great news about snowboarding, for those who have never tried it, is that it is relatively easy to learn in comparison to skiing. The first few days, which must be spent with a qualified instructor, will almost certainly result in a bruise or two. However, persevere and the rewards come quickly. Progression from the tremendous feeling of linking your first few turns to enjoying deep powder snow comes to most within only two weeks. Multiply that by at least ten for skiing.

If you are thinking of trying snowboarding on your next ski holiday, the following is a useful guide to the main factors to consider:

Freestyle, freeride or alpine?

The distinction between the three types of snowboarding is not particularly important for your first day on a snowboard, but understanding the difference between them may help you make your choice later.

Freestyle snowboarding is like skateboarding on snow and is the most popular variety. The boards are short, wide and flexible.

Freeriding is a combination of both freestyle and alpine, and will no doubt become the most important style of riding when snowboarding fully comes of age. Soft boots are preferable for this style but hard boots remain an option. Boards are of a similar overall length to alpine ones, but have a raised tail and nose to allow both carving and freestyle performance; these are the true all-round boards and are the eventual choice of all off-piste fanatics.

Alpine snowboarding is at the other end of the spectrum. Hard boots and relatively stiff and narrow boards with much longer edge contact lengths (the amount of edge in contact with the snow when laid flat) are necessary. This style of snowboarding is the closest to skiing and is often the skier's first choice when switching camps. Pursuit of the graceful carved turn replaces 'big air' as the *fait accompli*.

Board and boots: try or buy?

My advice to the aspiring snowboarder considering whether or not to buy equipment is to try it first. The multitude of board types available makes it very difficult to choose the one that will be right for you, and at around £400 each, a mistake is expensive. Many snowboard and ski shops in Britain offer reasonably priced hire packages with up-to-date equipment. If you like the board you try, the hire cost can often be deducted should you decide to buy it upon your return. The obvious disadvantage of hiring at home is that if you don't like the board, or experience problems with it during your holiday, you may have to hire a second board in the resort. If you are certain of finding the equipment you need in the resort, then it may be better to hire when you get there.

The choice of board for a beginner, whether hiring or buying, is best left to the snowboard expert in the shop. Your main decision will then be whether you wish to use soft or hard boots. Both are equally good for learning, with hard boots slightly superior on hard snow and soft boots better in soft and fresh conditions. In general, experienced 'crossover' skiers will be used to hard boots, whereas young newcomers to snow sports will feel more comfortable with 'softs'. In Britain soft boots account for around 90 per cent of the market.

What to wear

Clothing can include your existing ski gear. However, specific snowboard clothing is a good investment. Snowboard clothes are currently worn much looser than skiwear to allow for the greater physical mobility required, as well as for reasons of fashion. For its longevity and your comfort, clothing should incorporate waterproof reinforcement at the knees, bottom and elbows. These are the impact areas, and also the ones that come into contact with the snow when you are resting in the sitting or kneeling positions common to all snowboarders.

Snowboard gloves are probably the wisest investment of all. Snow is extremely abrasive and even the most expensive ski gloves will wear out very quickly if used for snowboarding. Look for waterproof, seam-free gloves with reinforced palms; your hands are now your ski poles and outriggers.

Choosing a resort

Snowboarding is now very big business, and most ski resorts have finally realised this. Almost all are open to snowboarders, with some even offering special snowboard-only pistes or fun parks.

To help further in your choice of resort we have included snowboard reports for each of the main resorts covered in this year's Guide. These contain information on specialist facilities such as snowboard parks, and many list the best sources of snowboard hire and instruction.

Size of resort

If you do not know which resort to choose, then big is often best. Larger resorts generally have more riders so there is more chance of finding specific snowboard areas, instruction, shops and 'snowboard friendliness'. However, be aware that the pisted areas of larger resorts are generally closely geared to the requirements of the skiers they have grown up with, and not the quite different needs of snowboarders. Any information you can get from other snowboarders, rather than skiers, on the resort you are considering will be invaluable.

Types of runs

The ideal terrain for snowboarding is quite specific and different from that for skiing. Also, the actual number of runs is of much less importance to snowboarders than to the majority of skiers. Once snowboarders have found a couple of good runs they tend to stick to them.

Reasonably wide blue (easy) and red (intermediate) runs are the snowboarding favourites, especially those with varied terrain and a few potential jumps to the sides for the younger or more expert members of your party. Not at all popular with snowboarders are narrow runs, runs with long flat sections and runs that traverse around the mountain. When snowboarding you do not have the snow-plough option on narrow paths, nor do you have ski poles to push you along the flat. Long traverses are simply very uncomfortable.

However, for beginners a large and flat nursery slope at the bottom of the resort is as ideal for snowboarding as it is for skiing. For experts, steeper resorts with good off piste areas (small number of lifts relative to size of ski area) and pistes that follow the fall-line quite closely are best. Try to get hold of the lift maps of a selection of resorts and have a close look at the nature and predominance of the runs in each before you make your decision.

Snowboard parks and dedicated snowboarding areas

A growing number of resorts now offer areas exclusive to snowboarders. These vary from a snowboard-only piste in some resorts to whole areas of a mountain in others. Most popular with the younger freestyle-oriented rider is the snowboard park. These usually come with their own lifts and contain such snowboarding delights as fun-boxes, table-top and gap jumps, a boardercross course, a quarter-pipe and/or half-pipe. In some of the larger resorts, the snowboard park may also cater for the hard-booted alpine rider, with a parallel slalom or banked slalom course to test the racing technique.

Types of lift

Drag-lifts (buttons and T-bars) are never an enjoyable exercise on a snowboard, so look for plenty of of chair-lifts and cable cars, particularly on the red and blue runs within a given resort.

Finding instruction

Instruction is now very easy to find, and most countries have their own national snowboard associations, which produce snowboard instructors. There is a huge advantage to being taught by a qualified snowboard instructor, rather than by a ski instructor who teaches snowboarding during quiet periods and may have no separate qualification for what is a very separate sport.

As well as learning on snow, it is also possible to employ the services of a British Snowboard Association (BSA) instructor at all good dry ski slopes in Britain. Although the 'plastic snow' is less forgiving to fall on than real snow, a short lesson before you go on holiday will certainly help. This can be followed up later with more advanced tuition on your return.

If you would like further information on snowboarding and where to find instruction in Britain, contact Steve Davis of the BSA at 5 Cressex Road, High Wycombe, Bucks HP12 4PG. Tel (01494) 462225.

By car or train

A set of overall ski market statistics produced last spring by Crystal Holidays suggested that the number of skiers who travel independently to the Alps has increased by 15 per cent in the past two seasons. The ferry companies, competing with Le Shuttle and Eurostar, claim twice the figure. The real number of DIY skiers is almost impossible to calculate because independent air, train and car travellers do not necessarily state the purpose of their visit to airline, railway or ferry companies.

However, if the true answer lies somewhere between the two, more than 25 per cent of Britain's estimated 800,000 skiers arrange their own travel and accommodation. Most of them travel across or beneath the Channel to the Alps by car or train, taking advantage of cut-price winter rates. Anyone who has ever suffered a Saturday at Gatwick Airport in high season will understand why these options are growing rapidly in popularity.

The result has been the emergence of a new genre of tour operator — the ski-drive specialist — offering holidays inclusive of ferry or tunnel, plus accommodation. More adventurous skiers dial the tourist office number of their chosen resort and make their own arrangements.

Route planning

The continued upgrading of the European motorway network allows easy travel to within often only a few miles of both major and minor ski resorts, and journey times have not only been greatly reduced but, weather conditions permitting, can be accurately forecast. Both the AA and the RAC offer a personalised route-planning service, which is strongly recommended by reporters; you specify your destination, and for a basic fee they supply a computer print-out of your exact route. It is important to note that the hidden extras (petrol, tolls, car wear-and-tear, meals and accommodation en route) add greatly to the cost, although the convenience may well outweigh the additional outlay. Driving to the Alps is only really a viable economic option for a full car-load of four or more people.

Service and insurance

Drivers should obtain a Green Card from their insurance company to guarantee adequate cover in the event of an accident. Breakdown insurance is also advisable. It is essential to have your car fully serviced before encountering what may be seriously cold conditions in the Alps. Have the battery checked by a garage before leaving home and replace it if you are in any doubt as to its efficiency. The level of anti-freeze should be topped up to the manufacturer's handbook recommendation for temperatures down to -30°C. You will also need a stronger solution of winter screen-wash. Take with you a torch, a shovel, an old pair of gloves and a tow-rope.

Snow chains

Whatever the month of your holiday you are advised to buy snow chains; if renting a car abroad, ensure that the chains supplied match the tyres before you set off. If a vehicle is fitted with winter tyres, it will only be necessary to attach chains in the most extreme conditions; however, most British cars are equipped with normal summer tyres so you must be prepared to fix on chains. It is illegal in all the main Alpine countries not to carry chains when driving in the mountains.

Chains cost between £20 and £150. Basically, the more you pay the easier they are to fit. Make sure you know whether your car is front- or rear-wheel drive and attach the chains to the drive wheels.

Technological advances, so swift in other areas of the car industry, have clanked slowly in the traction department, but last winter automatic chains were introduced, revolutionising the whole fastening operation. Anyone can put on the Centrax Steg in 20 seconds per wheel without getting their hands dirty. The chains have hardened metal spikes for ice and provide even greater traction.

Rud Chains Ltd of Whitstable (01227 276611) manufactures the new Centrax Steg. The AA hires out less sophisticated chains at £36.50 for 10 days and £1.60 per extra day.

Motorway tolls

You can calculate the exact cost of French motorway tolls to and from your destination in advance by contacting any of the motoring organisations. Switzerland charges a flat fee of around £20 for a windscreen sticker that allows usage of all motorways for a year. Cars are often frowned upon in ski resorts, and you are liable to incur heavy parking costs (as high as £80 a week for a covered space) in the most popular resorts.

Trains

The Snowtrain to the French Alps rattles on slowly in the face of all the hype surrounding high-tech improvements to the European rail system. It is inconvenient, uncomfortable, crowded and surprisingly praised by almost every reporter who has tried it, mainly because, against the charter flight, it allows you almost eight instead of six days' skiing in a conventional 'one week' holiday. The disadvantage lies in having to carry luggage on and off ferries, transfer buses, and the train itself; storage space on the train is limited, the couchettes are cramped and washing conditions are primitive.

Motorail services run between Calais and Moutiers on Friday evenings, returning on Saturday nights. This cuts out the tedium of the long drive and provides the flexibility of having your own transport in the Alps; however, the cost is high. Eurostar from Waterloo International, followed by the TGV from Paris to Moutiers, is at present a comfortable but slow alternative because of inconvenient connections in the French capital. However, it can only be a question of time before express train services direct to the Alps are in operation from London, providing the best possible way of reaching the snow.

Safety on the slopes

The mountains are like the sea: they give enormous pleasure but they can also be dangerous and should be treated with the utmost respect at all times. Only when you find yourself in an awkward and potentially dangerous situation, or witness an accident at first hand do you fully appreciate what the risks can be. All the information below applies to skiers and snowboarders.

Weather and exposure

Mountain weather can change at a moment's notice and vary dramatically at different altitudes. Always dress with this in mind and be prepared for all conditions. Several layers of clothing are best, and never set off without sunglasses or goggles, a hat or headband; it is always preferable to be too hot than too cold. More heat escapes through the head than any other part of the body. In the event of an accident a 'space blanket' (it folds to handkerchief size and can be bought from any reputable ski or mountaineering shop) can save a life.

All young children should wear safety helmets, preferably with chin guards. They can be worn on their own or over a thin balaclava or hat on extremely cold days. Unfortunately, helmets are not yet compulsory. However, in the United States, more adults are now wearing helmets for recreational skiing and we applaud this trend.

Never ski with a baby or small child in a backpack; anyone, however competent, can catch an edge, or someone could crash into you.

Exposure to bad weather can result in frostbite or hypothermia. Frostbite is the excessive cooling of small areas of the body, usually of the fingers, toes, nose, cheeks or ears. The affected tissue first turns white and numb. This is called first-degree frostbite and can be dealt with by immediate, gentle re-warming. In cold conditions, watch out for signs of frostbite in each other. Hypothermia results from a drop in the body's temperature. It is difficult to diagnose; some of the more obvious symptoms are physical or mental lethargy, slurring of speech, spurts of energy and abnormal vision.

Rules of the slopes

The FIS (International Ski Federation) has established rules of conduct for skiers and snowboarders. In short, they are:

Respect Do not endanger others.

Control Adapt the manner and speed of your skiing to your ability and to the general conditions on the mountain.

Choice of route The skier in front has priority — leave enough space.

Overtaking Leave plenty of space when overtaking a slower skier.

Entering and starting Look up and down the mountain each time before starting or entering a marked run.

Stopping Only stop at the edge of a piste or where you can be seen easily.

Climbing When climbing up or down, always keep to the side of the piste.

Signs Obey all signs and markings — they are provided for your safety.

Assistance In case of accidents, provide help or alert the rescue service.

Identification All those involved in an accident, including witnesses, should exchange names and addresses.

All the above rules may be binding in law and apply to both skiers and snowboarders. You could be in serious trouble if you cause an accident while in breach of these rules.

Important guidelines for skiers and snowboarders

- You ski at your own risk.
- Pay attention to all signs and markers.
- Ski on marked runs — these are protected from unexpected alpine dangers.
- Watch out for piste machines.
- Respect nature — take care not to ski in areas where young trees or wildlife will be disturbed and do not drop litter.
- Consider fitness sessions and taking lessons on a dry slope before going on holiday.

Special rules for snowboarders

- The front leg must be tethered firmly to the board by a safety strap.
- It is essential to look carefully to the right and left when changing direction, especially when starting a turn heelside — look backwards.
- The ability to ski does not automatically mean you have the ability to snowboard.
- Do not attempt the sport without instruction.

Off-piste

Outside the marked pistes and itineraries are areas which are NOT protected from alpine dangers.

Signs and flags around the ski area may warn you when avalanche danger is present, but do not rely on these alone. Take local professional advice. Even when there is no warning of avalanches there could be localised snow slides.

Only venture off-piste with a fully qualified guide. This rule applies particularly to glacial terrain where the risk of crevasse is added to that of avalanches. Always wear a recognised avalanche bleeper and take the time to learn how to use it, and carry out a grid search before you set off. The chances of survival after an avalanche deteriorate rapidly after the first five minutes beneath the surface of the snow.

Listen to your guide, learn basic snowcraft and how to read a slope. However, it is important to remember that your guide is fallible and that you alone must take overall responsibility for decisions concerning your safety. In the event of an avalanche, try to ski to the side. If you fall, try to get rid of your skis, poles and backpack. Swim and fight to stay on the surface.

Tips to remember when skiing off-piste

- Always ski in a group, never alone.
- Always ski in control behind the guide.
- Always stop behind the guide (there may be cliffs or other hazards ahead).
- Carry a map of the area and a compass. Know how to use both.
- Be wary of slopes where the run-out is not clearly obvious from the start. Following other skiers' tracks does not necessarily mean the route is safe.

Accident procedure

Speed is essential when an accident has occurred:

- Secure the accident area

Protect with crossed skis planted in the snow above the casualty. If necessary post someone above the accident site to give warning to other skiers.

- First aid

Assess the general condition of the casualty:

Airway — check it is clear. Make sure nothing is obstructing the mouth or throat.

Breathing — if the casualty is not breathing, administer artificial respiration (mouth-to-mouth resuscitation). If the casualty is breathing but unconscious, turn him/her on to his/her side to minimise the risk of choking. Protect any fractured limb from movement. Do not remove the ski boot if there is injury to the lower leg as it acts as a splint.

Circulation — check for pulse. Cover any wound with a clean handkerchief or scarf and apply direct pressure to the bleeding.

Provide warmth — keep the casualty warm, comfortable and as cheerful as possible. Give nothing to eat or drink, especially alcohol. If the accident victim appears to be in shock, by going pale, cold and faint, he/she should be encouraged to lie with his/her head lower than the feet.

- Alert the rescue service

Contact ski patroller, ski teacher or lift attendant. Give place of accident (piste name and nearest piste-marker), number of people injured, types of injury.

- Establish the facts of the accident

Take names and addresses of people involved and of witnesses. Note place, time and circumstances of the accident, terrain, snow conditions, visibility, markings and signs. Report to the police as soon as possible.

Which tour operator?

Below is a list of bonded ski operators who offer inclusive package holidays from Britain

AA SKI-DRIVEAWAY
AA Motoring Holidays, PO Box 128,
Copenhagen Court, Basingstoke,
Hants RG21 7DT
Tel (01256) 814433
Fax (01256) 493875
Ski-drive holidays

ABT SKI
Shepperton Marina,
Felix Lane, Shepperton,
Middlesex TW17 8NJ
Tel (01932) 252025
Fax (01932) 246140
Small chalet operator to St-Martin-de-Belleville

ACCESSIBLE ISOLATION
44 Downing Street, Farnham,
Surrey GU9 7PH
Tel (01252) 718808
Fax (01252) 718818
Tailor-made holidays to Canada

AIRTRACK SNOWBOARDING
16–17 Windsor Street, Uxbridge,
Middlesex UB8 1AB
Tel (01895) 810810
Fax (01895) 254088
Snowboarding in Serre Chevalier

ALL CANADA SKI
90 High Street, Lowestoft,
Suffolk NR32 1XN
Tel (01502) 585825
Fax (01502) 500681
Ski holidays in Canada

ALPINE ACTION
10 Kings Road, Lancing,
West Sussex BN15 8EA
Tel (01903) 761986
Fax (01903) 766007
Small operator to Trois Vallées

ALPINE TOURS
54 Northgate, Canterbury, Kent CT1 1BE
Tel (01227) 454777
Fax (01227) 451177
Schools and groups

ALTOURS
41a Church Street, Stavely,
Chesterfield S43 3TL
Tel (01246) 471234
Fax (01246) 471999
Group operator

AMERICAN CONNECTIONS
10 York Way, Lancaster Road, High
Wycombe, Buckinghamshire HP12 3PY
Tel (01494) 473173
Fax (01494) 473588
A la carte skiing in North America

BALKAN HOLIDAYS
Sofia House, 19 Conduit Street,
London W1R 9TD
Tel 0171-493 8612
Fax 0171-491 7068
Holidays to Bulgaria and Romania

BALKAN TOURS
61 Ann Street, Belfast BT1 4EE
Tel (01232) 246795
Fax (01232) 234581
Holidays to Bulgaria and Romania

BLADON LINES
56/58 Putney High Street,
London SW15 1SF
Tel 0181-780 8800
Fax 0181-789 2592
Major chalet and hotel operator

BORDERLINE
Les Sorbiers, F-65120 Barèges, France
Tel (01963) 250117
Fax (01963) 250508
Holidays to French Pyrenees

CHALET SNOWBOARD
31 Aldworth Avenue, Wantage,
Oxon OX12 7EJ

Tel/fax (01235) 767182
Snowboard holidays to France

CHALET WORLD
PO Box 260, Shrewsbury,
Shropshire SY1 1WX
Tel (01952) 840462
Fax (01952) 840463
Chalet holidays in the Alps

CHINOOK-IT
30 Sansom Street,
London SE5 7RE
Tel/fax 0171-252 5438
Skiing and snowboarding in North America

CLUB EUROPE
Fairway House, 53 Dartmouth Road,
London SE23 3HN
Tel 0181-699 7788
Fax 0181-699 7770
FreeCall (0500) 026 366
School and group holidays

CLUB MED
106 Brompton Road, London SW3 1JJ
Tel 0171-581 1161
Fax 0171-581 4769
Upmarket holiday villages with crèche and own ski school

COLLINEIGE SKI
30–32 High Street, Frimley,
Surrey GU16 5JD
Tel (01276) 24262
Fax (01276) 27282
Small, flexible chalet operator to Chamonix and Argentière

CONTIKI
Wells House, 15 Elmfield Road, Bromley,
Kent BR1 1LS
Tel 0181-290 6422
Fax 0181-290 6569
Holidays for 18–35s in Hopfgarten, Austria

CRYSTAL
Crystal House, The Courtyard,
Arlington Road, Surbiton,
Surrey KT6 6BW
Tel 0181-399 5144
Fax 0181-390 6378
Major operator to more than 100 resorts in 11 countries

EQUITY TOTAL SKI
Dukes Lane House, 47 Middle House,
Brighton, East Sussex BN1 1AL
Tel (01273) 203202
Fax (01273) 203212
Specialists to Italy with all-in prices

ERNA LOW CONSULTANTS
9 Reece Mews, London SW7 3HE
Tel 0171-584 2841
Fax 0171-589 9531
UK representative for La Plagne, Les Arcs and Flaine

FANTISKI
The Oast, Warmlake Estate, Maidstone
Road, Sutton Valence, Kent ME17 3LR
Tel (01622) 842555
Fax (01622) 842458
Small operator to France and the US

FINLAYS SKIING
The Barn, The Square, Ancrum, Borders
TD8 6XH
Tel (01835) 830562
Fax (01835) 830550
Small specialist operator to Val d'Isère and Courchevel

FIRST CHOICE SKI
First Choice House, Peel Cross Road,
Salford, Manchester M5 2AN
Tel 0161-745 7000
Fax 0161-745 4622
Major operator to over 60 resorts in 9 countries

FLEXISKI
Crogen Stables, Corwen, Clwyd LL21 0SY
Tel 0171-352 0044
Fax (01490) 440446
Small specialist operator with weekend and 10-day breaks

LA FRANCE DES VILLAGES SKI
Model Farm, Rattlesden, Bury St
Edmunds, Suffolk IP30 0SY
Tel (01499) 737664
Fax (01499) 737850
Self-drive and self-catering to Champagny-en-Vanoise

FREEDOM HOLIDAYS
30 Brackenbury Road, London W6 0BA

Tel 0181-741 4471
Fax 0181-741 9332
Holidays to Châtel

FRENCH IMPRESSIONS
Image House, Station Road,
London N17 9LR
Tel 0181-324 4040
Fax 0181-324 4030
Ski-drive holidays to 24 resorts in France

FRESH TRACKS
Argyll House, All Saints Passage,
London SW18 1EP
Tel 0181-875 9818
Fax 0181-874 8827
Specialist in off-piste and weekends.
Heli-skiing in Canada

FRONTIER SKI
Winge Travel Ltd, 3rd Floor, Broadmead
House, 21 Panton Street,
London SW1Y 4DR
Tel 0171-839 1627
Fax 0171-839 5761
Holidays to Canada

HEADWATER HOLIDAYS
146 London Road, Northwich,
Cheshire CW9 5HH
Tel (01606) 48699
Fax (01606) 48761
Cross-country and alpine skiing in unspoilt
locations

HUSKI CHALET HOLIDAYS
63a Kensington Church Street,
London W8 4BA
Tel 0171-938 4844
Fax 0171-938 2312
Specialist operator to Chamonix

INGHAMS
10–18 Putney Hill, London SW15 6AX
Tel (Europe) 0181-780 4444
(Canada & US) 0181-780 6600
Fax 0181-780 4405
Major operator to over 80 resorts

INNTRAVEL
Hovingham, York YO6 4JZ
Tel (01653) 628811
Fax (01653) 628741
Specialist cross-country operator

INTERSKI
95 Outram Street, Sutton-in-Ashfield,
Nottinghamshire NG17 4BG
Tel (01623) 551024
Fax (01623) 558941
Group, family and individual holidays to
Italy. Own British ski school

KINGS SKI CLUB
Castle Mill, Lower Kings Road,
Berkhamsted, Hertfordshire HP4 2AP
Tel (01442) 876642
Fax (01442) 879968
Group specialist to France, Austria and Italy

KUONI
Kuoni House, Dorking, Surrey RH5 4AZ
Tel (01306) 742500
Fax (01306) 744222
Operator to 20 Swiss resorts

LAGRANGE HOLIDAYS
168 Shepherds Bush Road,
London W8 7PB
Tel 0171-371 6111
Fax 0171-371 2990
UK branch of French self-catering operator
to 88 resorts

LE SHUTTLE HOLIDAYS
PO Box 300, Cheriton Parc, Folkestone,
Kent CT19 4QD
Tel (0990) 353535
Fax (01303) 288784
Ski-drive holidays to the Alps

LE SKI
25 Holly Terrace, Huddersfield,
West Yorkshire HD1 6JW
Tel (01484) 548996
Fax (01484) 451909
Chalet specialist to Courchevel and
Val d'Isère

LOTUS SUPERTRAVEL
Sandpiper House, 39 Queen Elizabeth
Street, London SE1 2BT
Tel 0171-962 9933
Fax 0171-962 9965
Holidays to France, US and Canada

MADE TO MEASURE HOLIDAYS
43 East Street, Chichester,
West Sussex PO19 1HX

Tel (01243) 533333
Fax (01243) 778431
Tailor-made hoidays to 113 resorts

MARK WARNER
20 Kensington Church Street,
London W8 4EP
Tel 0171-393 3131
Fax 0171-393 0093
Chalet-hotel holidays with crèches

MASTERSKI
Thames House, 63–67 Kingston Road,
New Malden, Surrey KT3 3PB
Tel 0181-942 9442
Fax 0181-949 4396
Christian holidays

MERISKI
The Old School, Great Barrington,
Burford, Oxfordshire OX18 4UR
Tel (01451) 844788
Fax (01451) 844799
Chalet operator to Méribel with crèche

MOSWIN TOURS
Moswin House, 21 Church Street, Oadby,
Leicester LE2 5DB
Tel (0116) 2719922
Fax (0116) 2716016
Ski holidays to Germany

MOTOURS
Motours House, Old Government
Buildings, Forest Road, Tunbridge Wells,
Kent TN2 5JE
Tel (01892) 518555
Fax (01892) 518666
Ski-drive holidays to French Alps

**MOUNTAIN AND WILDLIFE
VENTURES**
Compston Road, Ambleside,
Cumbria LA22 9DJ
Tel (015394) 33285
Fax (015394) 34065
Nordic wilderness skiing holidays

NEILSON
29–31 Elmfield Road, Bromley,
Kent BR1 1LT
Tel (0113) 2394555
Fax (0113) 2393275
Major operator to 57 resorts

NSR TRAVEL
Norway House, 21/24 Cockspur Street,
London SW1Y 5DA
Tel 0171-930 6666
Fax 0171-321 0624
Holidays to Scandinavia

PANORAMA SKI
29 Queens Road, Brighton,
East Sussex BN1 3YN
Tel (01273) 206531
Fax (01273) 205338
*Budget holidays to Andorra, Italy and North
America*

PASSAGE TO SOUTH AMERICA
113 Shepherds Bush Road,
London W6 7LP
Tel 0171-602 9889
Fax 0171-602 4251
Specialists to South America

PGL SKI EUROPE
Alton Court, Penyard Lane, Ross-on-Wye,
Herefordshire HR9 5NR
Tel (01989) 768168
Fax (01989) 563162
Schools and groups

PLUS TRAVEL
9 Eccleston Street, London SW1W 9LX
Tel 0171-259 0199
Fax 0171-259 0190
Specialists to Swiss resorts

POLES APART HOLIDAYS
75 Compton Avenue, Plymouth,
Devon PL3 5DD
Tel (01752) 257752
Fax (01752) 229190
Ski and snowboard holidays to France

POWDER BYRNE
4 Alice Court, 116 Putney Bridge Road,
London SW15 2NQ
Tel 0181-871 3300
Fax 0181-871 3322
*Upmarket operator to Switzerland, France,
Italy and Canada*

RAMBLERS
Box 43, Welwyn Garden City,
Hertfordshire AL8 6PQ
Tel (01707) 331133

Fax (01707) 333276
Group cross-country holidays

SILVER SKI HOLIDAYS
Conifers House, Grove Green Lane,
Maidstone, Kent ME14 5JW
Tel (01622) 735544
Fax (01622) 738550
Catered chalets in France

SIMON BUTLER SKIING
5 Woodbine Cottages, Shalford Common,
Guildford, Surrey GU4 8JF
Tel (01483) 502897
Fax (01483) 452001
Small operator to Megève with ski instruction

SIMPLY SKI
Chiswick Gate,
598–608 Chiswick High Road,
London W4 5RT
Tel 0181-742 2541
Fax 0181-995 5346
Catered chalets with crèches

SKI ACTIVITY
Lawmuir House, Methven,
Perthshire PH1 3SZ
Tel (01738) 840888
Fax (01738) 840354
Operator to North America and France

SKI AIRTOURS
Wavell House, Holcombe Road,
Helmshore, Rossendale,
Lancashire BB4 4NB
Tel (01706) 260000
Fax (01706) 232824
Major operator to 40 resorts

SKI THE AMERICAN DREAM
1/7 Station Chambers, High Street North,
London E6 1JE
Tel 0181-552 1201
Fax 0181-552 7726
Specialist operator to the US and Canada

SKI AMIS
Alanda, Hornash Lane,
Shadoxhurst, nr Ashford,
Kent TN26 1HT
Tel (01233) 732187
Fax (01233) 732769
Chalet holidays to France

SKI BARRETT-BOYCE
14 Hawthorn Road, Wallington,
Surrey SM6 0SX
Tel 0181-647 6934
Fax 0181-647 8620
Small operator to France with ski instruction

SKI BEACH VILLAS
55 Sidney Street, Cambridge CB2 3QR
Tel (01223) 371371
Fax (01223) 68626
Specialist operator to the Dolomites

SKI BEAT
Metro House, Northgate, Chichester,
W. Sussex PO19 1BE
Tel (01243) 780405
Fax (01243) 533748
Chalets in France

SKIBOUND
Olivier House, 18 Marine Parade,
Brighton, East Sussex BN2 1TL
Tel (01273) 677777
Fax (01273) 600999
Specialist schools operator

SKI C&C
Penwood Lodge, Penwood, Burghclere,
nr Newbury RG15 9EX
Tel (01635) 255551
Fax (01635) 255553
Holidays to Canada

SKI CHAMOIS
18 Lawn Road, Doncaster DN1 2JF
Tel (01302) 369006
Fax (01302) 326640
Chalet in Morzine

SKI CHOICE
27 High Street, Benson, Wallingford,
Oxfordshire OX10 6RP
Tel (01491) 837607
Fax (01491) 833836
*Tailor-made holidays to Austria, France
and Switzerland*

SKI CLUB OF GREAT BRITAIN
118 Eaton Square, London SW1W 9AF
Tel 0171-245 1033
Fax 0171-245 1258
*Specialist holidays and courses for all
standards*

THE SKI COMPANY
Sloane Square House, Holbein Place,
London SW1W 8NS
Tel 0171-730 9600
Fax 0171-730 9376
*Luxury chalets in France, Switzerland
and US*

SKI EQUIPE
27 Bramhall Lane South, Bramhall,
Stockport, Cheshire SK7 2DN
Tel 0161-440 0010
Fax 0161-440 0080
*Chalets and apartments in the Alps and
North America*

SKI ESPRIT
Oaklands, Reading Road North, Fleet,
Hampshire GU13 8AA
Tel (01252) 616789
Fax (01252) 811243
*Chalet holidays to France and Switzerland
with crèches and ski tuition*

SKI EXPERIENCE
26 College Road, Clifton, Bristol BS8 3JF
Tel (0117) 9745351
Fax (0117) 9731179
Self-drive holidays to Méribel

SKI FAMILLE
Unit 9, Chesterton Mill, French's Road,
Cambridge CB4 3NP
Tel (01223) 363777/366220
Fax (01223) 361508
Family hoidays with crèches in France

SKI FRANCE
Acorn House, 60 Bromley Common,
Bromley, Kent BR2 9PF
Tel 0181-313 0690
Flexible travel to France

SKI GOWER
2 High Street, Studley,
Warwickshire B80 7HJ
Tel (01527) 854822
Fax (01527) 857236
*Tailor-made holidays for schools and
groups*

SKI HILLWOOD
2 Field End Road, Pinner,
Middlesex HA5 2QL

Tel 0181-866 9993
Fax 0181-868 0258
*Family holidays with crèches and junior
clubs*

SKI INDEPENDENCE
Broughton Market, Edinburgh Market,
Edinburgh EH3 6NU
Tel 0131-557 8555
Fax 0131-557 1676
Specialist operator to North America

SKI LEOGANG
150 Buckingham Palace Road,
London SW1W 9TR
Tel 0171-730 7234
Fax 0171-730 1180
*Operator to Leogang and Saalbach-
Hinterglemm in Austria*

SKI LES ALPES
20 Lansdowne Gardens,
London SW8 2EG
Tel 0171-720 7127
Fax 0171-720 7134
Flexible operator specialising in hotels

SKI MIQUEL
33 High Street, Uppermill,
nr Oldham OL3 6HS
Tel (01457) 820200
Fax (01457) 872715
Long-established operator to Alps and Spain

SKI MOOSE
23a High Street, Wealdstone,
Middlesex HA3 5BY
Tel 0181-427 4474/5
Fax 0181-861 4459
Small chalet operator to France

SKI MORGINS
The Sett, Badger, Burnhill Green,
Wolverhampton WV6 7JS
Tel/Fax (01746) 783005
Small specialist operator to Morgins

SKI NORWEST
8 Foxholes Cottages,
Foxholes Road, Horwich,
Bolton BL6 6AL
Tel (01204) 668468
Fax (01204) 668568
Ski weekends and coach trips to Scotland

SKI OLYMPIC
Pine Lodge, Barnsley Road, Doncaster,
South Yorkshire DN5 8RB
Tel (01302) 390120
Fax (01302) 390787
Chalet and hotel holidays in France

SKI PARTNERS
Friary House, Colston Street,
Bristol BS1 5AP
Tel (0117) 9253545
Fax (0117) 9293697
Schools operator

SKI PEAK
The Old Bakery, Dockenfield, Farnham,
Surrey GU10 4HX
Tel (01252) 794941
Fax (01252) 794942
Specialist operator to Vaujany with crèche

SKISAFE TRAVEL
Unit 4, Braehead Estate, Old Govan Road,
Renfrew, Scotland PA8 0XJ
Tel 0141-812 0925
Fax 0141-812 1544
*Ski holidays in Scotland, Flaine and
Andorra*

SKI SAVOIE
362–364 Sutton Common Road, Sutton,
Surrey SM3 9PL
Tel 0181-715 1122
Fax 0181-644 3068
*Specialist operator to Courchevel with
crèche*

SKI SCOTT DUNN
Fovant Mews, 12 Noyna Road,
London SW17 7PH
Tel 0181-767 0202
Fax 0181-767 2026
*Upmarket chalet and hotel operator with
crèches. Heli-skiing in Canada*

SKI SOLUTIONS
84 Pembroke Road, London W8 6NX
Tel 0171-602 9900
Fax 0171-602 2882
A la carte hotels and luxury apartments

SKI THOMSON
Greater London House, Hampstead Road,
London NW1 7SD

Tel (0990) 329329
Fax 0121-236 7030
*Major operator to Europe and North
America*

SKI TOTAL
10 Hill Street, Richmond,
Surrey TW19 1TN
Tel 0181-948 6922
Fax 0181-332 1268
Chalet operator to Alps and Canada

SKI VACATION CANADA
Cambridge House, Tours Dept,
Third Floor, 8 Cambridge Street,
Glasgow G2 3DZ
Tel 0141-332 1511/(0345) 090905
Fax 0141-353 0135
Holidays to Canadian Rockies and Quebec

SKI VAL
39a North End Road, London W14 8SZ
Tel 0171-371 4900
Fax 0171-371 4904
*Catered chalets and chalet hotels in France,
Austria and the US*

SKI WEEKEND
2 The Old Barn, Wicklesham Lodge Farm,
Faringdon, Oxon SN7 7PN
Tel (01367) 241636
Fax (01367) 243833
Weekend breaks with off-piste

SKIWORLD
41 North End Road, London W14 8SZ
Tel 0171-602 4826
Fax 0171-371 1463
*Holidays to France, Italy, Switzerland and
North America*

SLOPING OFF
High Street, Handley, Salisbury,
Wiltshire SP5 5NR
Tel (01725) 552247
Fax (01725) 552489
*Coach holidays for schools, groups and
families*

SNOWBIZZ VACANCES
69 High Street, Maxey,
Cambridgeshire PE6 9EE
Tel (01778) 341455
Fax (01778) 347422

Specialist to Puy-St-Vincent, crèche and children's ski school

SNOWLINE HOLIDAYS
Collingbourne House, Spencer Court,
140–142 High Street, London SW18 4JJ
Tel 0181-870 4807
Fax 0181-875 9236
Small operator to France and Switzerland with crèche

SNOW STORM SKIING
Courtlands Centre, Kingsbridge,
South Devon TQ7 4BN
Tel (01548) 550227
Fax (01548) 550675
Small, quality chalet operator to Megève and Chamonix

SNOWTIME
96 Belsize Lane, London NW3 5BE
Tel 0171-433 3336
Fax 0171-433 1883
Méribel specialist with chalets and crèche

STANFORD HOLIDAYS
213 Sandcross Lane, Reigate,
Surrey RH2 8LL
Tel (01737) 242074
Fax (01737) 242003
Small specialist operator to France

STENA LINE HOLIDAYS
Charter House, Park Street, Ashford,
Kent TN24 8EX
Tel (01233) 647022
Fax (01233) 202371
Ski-drive holidays

SUNQUEST BULGARIA
23 Princes Street, London W1R 7RG
Tel 0171-499 9991
Fax 0171-499 9995
Specialist operator to Bulgaria

SUSIE WARD COMPANY
54 Vicarage Road, St Agnes,
Cornwall TR5 0TQ
Tel (01872) 553055
Fax (01872) 553050
Chalet holidays to France and Switzerland

SWISS TRAVEL SERVICE
Bridge House, 55–59 High Road,

Broxbourne, Hertfordshire EN10 7DT
Tel (01922) 456123
Fax (01922) 448855
Quality holidays to 16 Swiss resorts

TOP DECK SKI
131–135 Earls Court Road,
London SW5 9RH
Tel 0171-370 4555
Fax 0171-373 6201
Holidays to the Alps and Pyrenees

TRAIL ALPINE
68 Mostyn Street, Llandudno,
Gwynedd LL30 2SB
Tel (01492) 871770
Fax (01492) 872437
Ski holidays to France and Canada

TRAVELSCENE SKI DRIVE
11–15 St Ann's Road, Harrow,
Middlesex HA1 1AS
Tel 0181-427 8800
Fax 0181-861 4154
Ski-drive apartment holidays in France

TT SKI
Tagney Tours, Pilgrim House,
Station Court, Borough Green,
Kent TN15 8AF
Tel (01732) 886666
Fax (01732) 886885
Specialist operator to Barèges and Cauterets

UCPA/ACTION VACANCES
30 Brackley Road, Stockport,
Cheshire SK4 2RE
Tel/Fax 0161-442 6130
18–40s budget ski and snowboard packages, and schools programme

VIP
Collingbourne House, Spencer Court,
140–142 Wandsworth High Street,
London SW18 4JJ
Tel 0181-875 1957
Fax 0181-875 9236
Exclusively Val d'Isère

VIRGIN SKI
Galleria, Station Road, Crawley,
West Sussex RH10 1WW
Tel (01293) 617181
Fax (02293) 536957

Operator to California, Utah and New England

WAYMARK
44 Windsor Road, Slough,
Berkshire SL1 2EJ
Tel (01753) 516477
Fax (01753) 517016
Cross-country specialist

WHITE ROC SKI
69 Westbourne Grove, London W2 4UJ
Tel/Fax 0171-792 1956
Weekend and tailor-made ski and snowboard holidays

WINTERSKI
31 Old Steine, Brighton,
East Sussex BN1 1EL
Tel (01273) 626242
Fax (01273) 620222
Schools and groups to Italy and North America

YSE
The Business Village,
Broomhill Road, London
W18 4JQ
Tel 0181-871 5117
Fax 0181-871 5229
Specialist chalet operator to Val d'Isère

Who goes where?

ANDORRA

Arcalis Snowcoach
Arinsal Crystal, First Choice, Neilson, Panorama, Ski Safe Travel, Ski Partners, Ski Thomson
Encamp First Choice, Top Deck
Pal Crystal, Panorama Ski, Ski Safe Travel, Snowcoach
Pas de la Casa First Choice, Lagrange, Neilson, Panorama, Ski Airtours, Ski Partners, Ski Thomson, Top Deck
Soldeu-El Tarter Crystal, First Choice, Neilson, Panorama, Ski Airtours, SkiSafe Travel, Ski Thomson, Top Deck

AUSTRALIA

No current tour operator

AUSTRIA

Alpbach First Choice, Inghams, Sloping Off
Altenmarkt Alpine Tours, Made to Measure
Axamer Lizum Ski Partners
Badgastein Crystal, First Choice, Inghams, SkiBound, Ski Miquel, Ski Partners
Bad Hofgastein Crystal, Inghams
Bad Kleinkirchheim Alpine Tours, Crystal
Ehrwald Crystal
Ellmau Crystal, First Choice, Inghams, Ski Airtours, SkiBound, Ski Thomson
Fieberbrunn Ski Partners
Filzmoos Inghams
Finkenberg Crystal
Flachau Club Europe, Made to Measure
Fulpmes Alpine Tours, Crystal
Galtür Crystal, Ski Thomson
Gargellen Alpine Tours, Made to Measure
Hochpillberg Crystal
Hopfgarten Contiki, Top Deck
Igls Inghams, Lagrange
Ischgl Crystal, Inghams, Ski Thomson
Itter Club Europe
Kaprun Crystal, Inghams, Neilson, Ski Airtours
Kirchberg Crystal, Neilson, Top Deck
Kirchdorf Crystal

Kitzbühel Bladon Lines, Crystal, First Choice, Inghams, Kings Ski Club, Lagrange, Neilson, PGL Ski Europe, Ski Airtours, SkiBound, Ski Partners, Ski Thomson, Stena Line
Kleinarl Club Europe, Made to Measure
Kolsass Weer Ski Airtours
Kühtai Alpine Tours, Inghams
Lech Inghams, Ski Choice, Ski Les Alpes, Ski Total
Leogang Ski Leogang
Lermoos Crystal, Made to Measure
Maria Alm PGL Ski Europe, Ski Partners
Mayrhofen Crystal, Equity Total Ski, First Choice, Inghams, Neilson, Ski Thomson, Snowcoach, Stena Line
Neustift Alpine Tours, Crystal, Inghams
Niederau/Oberau Alpine Tours, Club Europe, First Choice, Inghams, Lagrange, Neilson, PGL Ski Europe, Ski Thomson
Obergurgl/Hochgurgl Crystal, First Choice, Inghams, Neilson, Ski Thomson
Obertauern Club Europe, Crystal, Inghams, Ski Thomson
Pettneu Crystal
Saalbach-Hinterglemm Club Europe, Crystal, First Choice, Inghams, Kings Ski Club, Neilson, PGL Ski Europe, Ski Airtours, SkiBound, Ski Leogang, Ski Partners, Ski Thomson, Sloping Off
Scheffau Crystal, First Choice, Ski Thomson
Schladming Club Europe, Crystal, Equity Total Ski, Made to Measure, Neilson, PGL Ski Europe, SkiBound, Ski Partners
Schüttdorf Ski Airtours
Seefeld Crystal, First Choice, Inghams, Ski Thomson
Serfaus Alpine Tours, Made to Measure
Sölden/Hochsölden Crystal
Söll Crystal, First Choice, Inghams, Neilson, Ski Airtours, SkiBound, Ski Hillwood, Ski Thomson
St Anton Bladon Lines, Chalet World, Crystal, First Choice, Inghams, Mark Warner, Ski Equipe, Ski Les Alpes, Ski Thomson, Ski Total, Ski Val
St Johann-in-Tirol Club Europe, Crystal,

SkiBound, Ski Partners, Ski Thomson
St Michael Alpine Tours, Ski Partners
St Wolfgang Crystal, Inghams, Neilson,
Ski Airtours
Waidring Lagrange, Ski Thomson
Wagrain Club Europe, PGL Ski Europe
Westendorf Crystal, First Choice, Inghams,
Neilson, SkiBound, Ski Thomson
Zauchensee Made to Measure
Zell am See Altours, Bladon Lines, Crystal,
First Choice, Inghams, Lagrange, Neilson,
PGL Ski Europe, Ski Airtours, Ski
Partners, Ski Thomson
Zell am Ziller SkiBound, Ski Partners,
Stena Line
Zürs Made to Measure

BULGARIA

Borovets Balkan Holidays, Balkan Tours,
Crystal, First Choice, Inghams, Neilson
Pamporovo Balkan Holidays, Balkan
Tours, Crystal, First Choice, Neilson, Ski
Partners
Vitosha Balkan Holidays

FRANCE

Alpe d'Huez AA Ski-Driveaway, Altours,
Club Med, Crystal, First Choice, French
Impressions, Fresh Tracks, Inghams,
Lagrange, Motours, Neilson, PGL Ski
Europe, Ski Activity, Ski Airtours, Ski
Miquel, Ski Partners, Ski Thomson,
Skiworld, Stena Line, Travelscene Ski
Drive
Les Arcs AA Ski-Driveaway, Club Med,
Crystal, Erna Low, French Impressions,
Inghams, Lagrange, Made to Measure,
Motours, PGL Ski Europe, Ski Activity,
SkiBound, Ski Thomson, Skiworld, Stena
Line, Travelscene Ski Drive
Argentière Collineige, Crystal, Lagrange,
Poles Apart, Ski Esprit, Snowline, Stanford
Holidays, Susie Ward, White Roc
Auris-en-Oisans Lagrange
Avoriaz AA Ski-Driveaway, Chalet
Snowboard, Club Med, Crystal, First
Choice, French Impressions, Inghams,
Lagrange, Motours, Neilson, Ski Airtours,
Skibound, Ski Thomson, Stena Line,
Travelscene Ski Drive
Barèges Borderline, Ski Thomson, TT Ski
Brides-les-Bains French Impressions,
Kings Ski Club, Lagrange, Motours,

Neilson, Stena Line, Top Deck
Les Carroz Erna Low, Lagrange, Ski
Choice
Cauterets Lagrange, TT Ski
Chamonix AA Ski-Driveaway, Chinook-It,
Club Med, Collineige, Crystal, Erna Low,
First Choice, French Impressions, Fresh
Tracks, HuSki, Inghams, Lagrange,
Motours, Neilson, Powder Byrne, Ski
Airtours, Ski Choice, The Ski Company,
Ski Esprit, Ski Les Alpes, Ski Thomson,
Ski Weekend, Skiworld, Snow Storm
Skiing, Stanford Holidays, Stena Line,
Susie Ward, Travelscene Ski Drive, White
Roc
Champagny-en-Vanoise Erna Low, La
France des Villages Ski, French
Impressions, Lagrange, Stena Line
Châtel First Choice, Freedom Holidays,
French Impressions, Lagrange, Made to
Measure, Ski Partners, Susie Ward,
Travelscene Ski Drive
La Clusaz Erna Low, First Choice, French
Impressions, Lagrange, Silver Ski, Ski
Amis, Ski Weekend, Stena Line
Les Coches AA Ski-Driveaway, Erna Low,
French Impressions, Lagrange, Motours,
Ski Olympic, Travelscene Ski Drive
Les Contamines-Montjoie Ski Activity, Ski
Total, Skiworld
Le Corbier Lagrange, Motours
Courchevel AA Ski-Driveaway, Alpine
Action, Bladon Lines, Chalet World,
Crystal, Erna Low, Finlays, First Choice,
Flexiski, French Impressions, Inghams,
Lagrange, Le Ski, Lotus Supertravel, Mark
Warner, Motours, Neilson, PGL Ski
Europe, Powder Byrne, Silver Ski, Simply
Ski, Ski Airtours, Ski Amis, Ski Equipe, Ski
Esprit, Ski France, Ski Les Alpes, Ski
Olympic, Ski Savoie, Ski Scott Dunn, Ski
Thomson, Ski Val, Skiworld, Stena Line,
Travelscene Ski Drive, White Roc
Les Deux Alpes Chalet Snowboard,
Crystal, First Choice, French Impressions,
Inghams, Lagrange, Motours, Neilson, Ski
Activity, Ski Airtours, SkiBound, Ski
Partners, Ski Thomson, Skiworld,
Travelscene Ski Drive
Flaine AA Ski-Driveaway, Crystal, Erna
Low, First Choice, French Impressions,
Fresh Tracks, Inghams, Lagrange,
Motours, Neilson, Ski Airtours, Ski
Choice, Ski Les Alpes, Ski Safe Travel, Ski

Thomson, Stanford Holidays, Stena Line, Travelscene Ski Drive

Font-Romeu Lagrange

Les Gets Fantiski, Ski Famille, Ski Hillwood, Ski Les Alpes, Ski Total, Snowline

Le Grand-Bornand Headwater, Lagrange, Stena Line

La Grave Fresh Tracks, Ski Weekend

Les Houches Lagrange, Motours

Isola 2000 Made to Measure

Megève Lagrange, PGL Ski Europe, Simon Butler Skiing, Ski Barrett-Boyce, Ski Choice, Ski Les Alpes, Snowcoach, Snow Storm Skiing, Stanford Holidays

Les Menuires AA Ski-Driveaway, Club Europe, Club Med, Crystal, Erna Low, First Choice, Inghams, Lagrange, Made to Measure, Motours, Travelscene Ski Drive

Méribel AA Ski-Driveaway, Alpine Action, Bladon Lines, Chalet World, Club Med, Equity Total Ski, Erna Low, First Choice, French Impressions, Inghams, Lagrange, Lotus Supertravel, Mark Warner, Meriski, Motours, Neilson, PGL Ski Europe, Powder Byrne, Silver Ski, Simply Ski, Ski Airtours, The Ski Company, Ski Experience, Ski France, Ski Les Alpes, Ski Scott Dunn, Ski Thomson, Skiworld, Snowcoach, Snowtime, Stena Line, Travelscene Ski Drive, White Roc

La Mongie Lagrange

Montalbert Erna Low

Montchavin Erna Low, Lagrange

Montgenèvre Crystal, Equity Total Ski, First Choice, Lagrange, Made to Measure, Ski Airtours, Ski Thomson

Morillon Erna Low, Lagrange

Morzine Chalet Snowboard, Crystal, First Choice, Lagrange, SkiBound, Ski Chamois, The Ski Company, Ski Esprit, Ski Les Alpes, Ski Moose, Ski Thomson, Ski Weekend, Snowline, Trail Alpine, White Roc

La Plagne AA Ski-Driveaway, Altours, Chalet World, Club Med, Crystal, Erna Low, First Choice, French Impressions, Inghams, Lagrange, Mark Warner, Motours, Neilson, PGL Ski Europe, Silver Ski, Simply Ski, Ski Activity, Ski Airtours, Ski Amis, Ski Beat, Ski Esprit, Ski France, Ski Les Alpes, Ski Thomson, Skiworld, Travelscene Ski Drive, UCPA

Pra Loup Club Europe, Kings Ski Club,

Lagrange, PGL Ski Europe, Ski Airtours, Snowcoach

Puy-St-Vincent Club Europe, Snowbizz

Risoul/Vars Altours, Crystal, First Choice, Inghams, Lagrange, Neilson, Ski Airtours, Ski Thomson, Travelscene Ski Drive

La Rosière Erna Low, Ski Olympic

Samoëns Erna Low, Lagrange, Stena Line

Serre Chevalier/Briançon Airtrack Snowboarding, Altours, Club Europe, Crystal, First Choice, Inghams, Motours, Neilson, Ski Les Alpes, Ski Miquel, Ski Thomson, Sloping Off, Stena Line, Travelscene Ski Drive

Sixt Erna Low

St-Gervais Lagrange, Masterski, PGL Ski Europe, Ski Barrett-Boyce, Snowcoach

St-Lary Lagrange

St-Martin-de-Belleville ABT Ski, Poles Apart, Stena Line

Superbagnères Club Med

La Tania Crystal, Inghams, Lagrange, Silver Ski, Stena Line, Motours, Neilson, Ski Thomson

Tignes AA Ski-Driveaway, Bladon Lines, Club Med, Crystal, Erna Low, Fantiski, First Choice, French Impressions, Inghams, Lagrange, Masterski, Motours, Neilson, Ski Activity, Ski Beat, Ski Choice, Ski France, Ski Olympic, Ski Thomson, Skiworld, Stena Line, Travelscene Ski Drive, UCPA

Val d'Isère AA Ski-Driveaway, Altours, Bladon Lines, Chalet World, Club Med, Crystal, Finlays, First Choice, French Impressions, Inghams, Lagrange, Le Ski, Lotus Supertravel, Mark Warner, Motours, Neilson, Powder Byrne, Silver Ski, Simply Ski, Ski Activity, The Ski Company, Ski Equipe, Ski France, Ski Les Alpes, Ski Scott Dunn, Ski Thomson, Ski Val, Ski Weekend, Skiworld, Sloping Off, Stena Line, Travelscene Ski Drive, UCPA, VIP, White Roc, YSE

Valfréjus Lagrange, Motours

Valloire/Valmeinier First Choice, Lagrange, Snowcoach

Valmorel/St-François-Longchamp AA Ski-Driveaway, Altours, Crystal, Equity Total Ski, Erna Low, French Impressions, Inghams, Lagrange, Motours, Neilson, Simply Ski, SkiBound, Ski Thomson, Stena Line

Val Thorens AA Ski-Driveaway, Bladon

Lines, Club Europe, Crystal, Erna Low, Equity Total Ski, First Choice, French Impressions, Inghams, Lagrange, Motours, Neilson, Ski Airtours, Ski Choice, Ski France, Ski Les Alpes, Ski Thomson, Skiworld, Stena Line, Travelscene Ski Drive, UCPA
Vaujany Ski Peak

ITALY

Alagna Altours, Winterski
Alba Crystal
Andalo Equity Total Ski, PGL Ski Europe, Ski Partners, Winterski
Aprica Altours, Equity Total Ski, PGL Ski Europe
Arabba Neilson, Ski Beach Villas
Bardonecchia Crystal, Equity Total Ski, First Choice, Neilson, Ski Airtours, Sloping Off, Stena Line
Bormio Altours, Crystal, Equity Total Ski, First Choice, Inghams, Ski Airtours, Ski Thomson
Campitello First Choice, Inghams
Canazei First Choice, Inghams, Neilson
Cavalese Alpine Tours, First Choice
Cervinia Crystal, First Choice, Inghams, Ski Airtours, Ski Thomson, Stena Line
Cesana Torinese First Choice, PGL Ski Europe
Champoluc Crystal
Chiesa First Choice
Clavière Crystal, Equity Total Ski, First Choice, Neilson
Cortina d'Ampezzo Crystal, Powder Byrne, Ski Equipe
Courmayeur Bladon Lines, Crystal, Equity Total Ski, First Choice, Inghams, Interski, Mark Warner, Neilson, Ski Airtours, Ski Les Alpes, Ski Thomson, Skiworld, Stena Line, White Roc
Folgarida Alpine Tours, Altours, Crystal, Equity Total Ski, Ski Thomson, Winterski
Foppolo Altours, Crystal, First Choice, Ski Partners, Winterski
Grangesises Stena Line
Gressoney Crystal
Limone Neilson
Livigno Crystal, First Choice, Inghams, Panorama Ski, Ski Airtours, Ski Thomson
Macugnaga Crystal, Neilson, Ski Partners, Ski Thomson
Madesimo Altours, Crystal, Inghams, Ski

Airtours, Ski Thomson, Winterski
Madonna di Campiglio Alpine Tours, Altours, Crystal, Inghams, Ski Thomson, Winterski
Marilleva Alpine Tours, Equity Total Ski, Winterski
Passo Tonale Altours, Club Europe, Crystal, Equity Total Ski, First Choice, PGL Ski Europe, Ski Airtours, Ski Partners, Ski Thomson, Winterski
Pila Crystal, Interski
Pinzolo Equity Total Ski
Pozza di Fassa Crystal
San Cassiano First Choice
Sansicario Equity Total Ski, Stena Line
Santa Caterina Crystal, Equity Total Ski, First Choice, Ski Airtours, Ski Thomson
Sauze d'Oulx Crystal, First Choice, Inghams, Neilson, Panorama, Ski Airtours, Ski Thomson
Selva Gardena Bladon Lines, Crystal, First Choice, Inghams
Sestriere Club Med, Crystal, Neilson, Stena Line
La Thuile Bladon Lines, Crystal, First Choice, Interski, Interworld Ski Tours, Neilson, Ski Thomson
Vigo di Fassa Crystal
La Villa Ski Beach Villas

JAPAN
Sahoro Club Med

NEW ZEALAND
No current tour operator

NORTH AMERICA
Aleyska Crystal
Alpine Meadows Virgin Ski
Apex Frontier Ski
Aspen/Snowmass American Connections, Crystal, Lotus Supertravel, Ski the American Dream, Ski Independence, Skiworld
Banff/Lake Louise Accessible Isolation, All Canada Ski, American Connections, Chinook-It, Crystal, First Choice, Frontier Ski, Inghams, Lotus Supertravel, Neilson, Ramblers, Ski Airtours, Ski Canada, Ski Equipe, Ski Independence, Ski Thomson, Skiworld
Beaver Creek American Connections, Crystal, Inghams, Lotus Supertravel, Ski

the American Dream, Ski Equipe, Ski Independence

Big Sky Ski the American Dream

Big White All Canada Ski, Frontier Ski

Blue Mountain All Canada Ski

Breckenridge American Connections, Crystal, Equity Total Ski, First Choice, Inghams, Neilson, Ski Airtours, Ski the American Dream, Ski Independence, Ski Thomson, Ski Val, Skiworld

Bretton Woods Virgin Ski

Cannon Virgin Ski

Canmore Crystal

Copper Mountain Club Med

Crested Butte Altours, Fresh Tracks, Neilson, Ski the American Dream, Ski Equipe, Ski Independence

Deer Valley Made to Measure, Virgin Ski

Heavenly Altours, American Connections, Inghams, Ski the American Dream, Skiworld, Virgin Ski

Jackson Hole American Connections, Crystal, Lotus Supertravel, Ski the American Dream, Ski Independence, Ski Scott Dunn, Skiworld

Jasper All Canada Ski, American Connections, Crystal, Frontier Ski, Inghams, Neilson, Ramblers, Ski Activity, Ski Canada, Ski Independence, Ski Thomson, Skiworld

June Mountain Virgin Ski

Kananaskis All Canada Ski, Crystal, Made to Measure

Keystone American Connections, Crystal, Ski the American Dream, Ski Independence

Killington Crystal, Fantiski, Inghams, Panorama Ski, Ski the American Dream, Ski Independence, Virgin Ski

Kirkwood Virgin Ski

Mammoth Mountain American Connections, Crystal, Inghams, Ski Airtours, Ski the American Dream, Ski Independence, Skiworld, Virgin Ski

Mont Tremblant All Canada Ski, American Connections, Crystal, Inghams, Neilson, Ski Canada

Mont Sainte Anne American Connections, Ski Partners

Mount Mansfield Virgin Ski

Mount Snow Crystal

Northstar Virgin Ski

Okemo Altours

Panorama Frontier Ski

Park City American Connections, Crystal,

Ski the American Dream, Ski Independence, Skiworld, Virgin Ski

Pico Virgin Ski

Red Mountain Frontier Ski

Silver Star All Canada Ski, Crystal, Frontier Ski, Made to Measure

Smuggler's Notch Ski the American Dream

Snowbird Crystal, Ski the American Dream, Virgin Ski

Snowmass Crystal, Lotus Supertravel

Solitude Ski the American Dream

Spruce Peak Virgin Ski

Squaw Valley American Connections, Ski the American Dream, Virgin Ski

Steamboat Crystal, First Choice, Lotus Supertravel, Neilson, Ski the American Dream, Ski Independence, Skiworld

Stoneham Ski Partners

Stowe American Connections, Crystal, Ski the American Dream, Ski Independence, Ski Partners

Stratton Winterski

Sugarbush Crystal, Virgin Ski

Sunday River Crystal, Ski Partners

Sun Peaks Frontier Ski

Sun Valley Ski the American Dream

Taos American Connections, Ski the American Dream, Ski Independence

Telluride Made to Measure, Ski the American Dream, Ski Independence

Vail American Connections, Crystal, First Choice, Inghams, Lotus Supertravel, Neilson, Ski Airtours, Ski the American Dream, The Ski Company, Ski Independence, Ski Thomson, Ski Val, Skiworld

Whistler/Blackcomb Accessible Isolation, Altours, American Connections, Chinook-It, Crystal, First Choice, Frontier Ski, Inghams, Lotus Supertravel, Neilson, Powder Byrne, Ski Airtours, Ski the American Dream, Ski Canada, Ski Equipe, Ski Independence, Ski Miquel, Ski Thomson, Ski Total, Ski Weekend, Skiworld

White Fish Chinook-It,

Winter Park American Connections, Crystal, First Choice, Neilson, Ski the American Dream, Ski Independence, Ski Thomson

NORWAY

Geilo Crystal, NSR, Waymark

Hemsedal Crystal, NSR, Waymark

Lillehammer NSR
Voss NSR

POLAND
Zakopane Ski Gower

ROMANIA
Poiana Brasov Balkan Holidays, Balkan Tours, Crystal, First Choice, Inghams, Neilson
Sinaia Crystal

SCOTLAND
Aviemore Ski Norwest, Skisafe Travel
Glenshee Ski Norwest, Skisafe Travel
Nevis Range Ski Norwest, Skisafe Travel

SLOVENIA
Bled Alpine Tours
Bohinj Alpine Tours
Kransjska Gora Alpine Tours, Inghams

SPAIN
Baqueira-Beret Ski Miquel, Ski Thomson
Sierra Nevada First Choice, Neilson, Ski Thomson

SOUTH AMERICA
Bariloche Passage to South America
Las Leñas Passage to South America
La Parva Passage to South America
Valle Nevado Passage to South America

SWEDEN
Åre Crystal
Salens Crystal

SWITZERLAND
Adelboden Inghams, Kuoni, Plus Travel, Swiss Travel Service
Andermatt Made to Measure
Anzère Lagrange, Made to Measure
Arosa Inghams, Kuoni, Plus Travel, Ski Choice, Ski Gower, Swiss Travel Service
Celerina Made to Measure
Champéry Kuoni, Made to Measure, Ski Les Alpes, White Roc
Champoussin Snowline
Château d'Oex Kuoni
Crans Montana Inghams, Kuoni, Lagrange, Plus Travel, Ski Les Alpes
Les Diablerets Lagrange, Sloping Off
Davos Inghams, Kuoni, Plus Travel, Ski Choice, Ski Gower, Ski Les Alpes, Swiss Travel Service, White Roc
Engelberg Kuoni, Made to Measure, Plus Travel, Ski Gower
Flims/Laax Plus Travel, Powder Byrne, Ski Choice, Swiss Travel Service, White Roc
Grindelwald Inghams, Kuoni, Plus Travel, Powder Byrne, Ski Gower, Ski Thomson, Swiss Travel Service
Gstaad Made to Measure, Ski Gower
Interlaken Kuoni, Ski Gower, Swiss Travel Service
Kandersteg Kuoni, Made to Measure
Klosters Kuoni, Powder Byrne, The Ski Company, Ski Gower, Ski Les Alpes, White Roc
Lauterbrunnen Ski Miquel
Lenk Made to Measure, Swiss Travel Service
Lenzerheide/Valbella Club Med, Inghams, Kuoni, Ski Choice
Leysin Lagrange, Plus Travel
Morgins Ski Morgins, Snowline
Mürren Inghams, Kuoni, Made to Measure, Plus Travel, Ski Gower, Swiss Travel Service
Pontresina Club Med, Made to Measure, Swiss Travel Service
Saas-Fee Crystal, Inghams, Kuoni, Lagrange, Plus Travel, Ski Choice, Ski Gower, Swiss Travel Service
Saas-Grund Lagrange, Ski Gower
Samedan Kuoni
Surlej Made to Measure
St Moritz Club Med, Inghams, Kuoni, Plus Travel, Ski Gower, Swiss Travel Service
Verbier Bladon Lines, Chalet World, Crystal, Flexiski, Fresh Tracks, Inghams, Mark Warner, Neilson, Plus Travel, Simply Ski, Ski Equipe, Ski Esprit, Ski Les Alpes, Ski Thomson, Susie Ward, Swiss Travel Service
Visp Ski Gower
Villars Club Med, Kuoni, Made to Measure, Swiss Travel Service
Wengen Club Med, Crystal, Inghams, Kuoni, Plus Travel, Ski Gower, Ski Thomson, Swiss Travel Service
Zermatt Bladon Lines, Inghams, Kuoni, Plus Travel, Powder Byrne, Ski Choice, Ski Gower, Ski Les Alpes, Ski Scott Dunn, Ski Thomson, Ski Total, Swiss Travel Service
Zinal Club Med

Skiing by numbers

Travel to ski

NATIONAL TOURIST OFFICES
The tourist offices listed below are for countries with recognised ski resorts.

Andorran Delegation
63 Westover Road, London SW18 2RF
Tel 0181-874 4806 (no fax)

Argentinian Embassy
5th Floor, 100 Brompton Road,
London SW3 1ER
Tel 0171-589 3104

Australian Tourist Commission
Gemini House, 10–18 Putney Hill,
London SW15 6AA
Tel 0181-780 2229 **Fax** 0181-780 1496

Austrian National Tourist Office
30 St George Street, London W1R 0AL
Tel 0171-629 0461 **Fax** 0171-499 6038

Balkan Holidays (for Bulgaria)
Sofia House, 19 Conduit Street,
London W1R 9TD
Tel 0171-491 4499 **Fax** 0171-491 7068
Snowline (0839) 400 409

Cedok Travel Ltd (Czech Republic and
Slovakia)
53–54 Haymarket, London SW1 4PP
Tel 0171-839 4414 **Fax** 0171-839 0204

Embassy of Chile
Commercial Department, 12 Devonshire
Street, London W1N 2DS
Tel 0171-580 6392 **Fax** 0171-255 1848

French Government Tourist Office
178 Piccadilly, London W1V OAL
Tel (0891) 244123 (no fax)

Italian State Tourist Office
1 Princes Street, London W1R 8AY
Tel 0171-408 1254 **Fax** 0171-493 6695

Japanese National Tourist Organisation
Heathcoat House, 20 Saville Row,
London W1X 1AE
Tel 0171-734 9638 **Fax** 0171-734 4290

New Zealand Tourism Board
New Zealand House, Haymarket,
London SW1Y 4TQ
Tel (0839) 300900 **Fax** 0171-839 8929

Norwegian Tourist Board
Charles House, 5–11 Lower Regent Street,
London SW1Y 4LR
Tel 0171-839 6255 **Fax** 0171-839 6014

Romanian National Tourist Office
83a Marylebone High Street,
London W1M 3DE
Tel/Fax 0171-224 3692

Scottish Tourist Board
23 Ravelston Terrace, Edinburgh,
Lothian EH4 3EU
Tel 0131-332 2433 **Fax** 0131-343 1513

Slovenian Tourist Office
2 Canfield Place, London NW6 3BT
Tel 0171-372 3767 **Fax** 0171-372 3763

Spanish Tourist Office
57 St James's Street, London SW1A 1LD
Tel 0171-499 0901 **Fax** 0171-629 4257

Swedish Tourist Board
11 Montague Place, London W1H 2AL
Tel 0171-724 5868 **Fax** 0171-724 5872

Switzerland Tourism
Swiss Centre, Swiss Court,
London W1V 8EE
Tel 0171-734 1921 **Fax** 0171-437 4577

Tourism Canada
The Visit Canada Centre, 62–65 Trafalgar
Square, London WC2N 5DY
Tel (0891) 715000 **Fax** 0171-389 1149

Visit USA Association
Tel (0891) 600530 (recorded message)

SKI TRAVEL AGENTS AND CONSULTANTS

Alpine Answers
The Business Village, 3–9 Broomhill Road,
London SW18 4JQ
Tel 0181-871 4656 **Fax** 0181-871 9676

Erna Low Consultants
9 Reece Mews, London SW7 3HE
Tel 0171-584 2841/7820 **Fax** 0171-589
9531

Ski Solutions
84 Pembroke Road, London W8 6NX
Tel 0171-602 9900 **Fax** 0171-602 2882

Ski and Surf
37 Priory Field Drive, Edgware, Middlesex
HA8 9PT
Tel 0181-958 2418 **Fax** 0181-905 4146

Ski Travel Centre
1100 Pollokshaws Road, Shawlands,
Glasgow, Strathclyde G41 3NJ
Tel 0141-649 9696 **Fax** 0141-649 2273

Skiers Travel Bureau
Marco Polo Travel, 79 Street Lane,
Roundhay, Leeds LS8 1AP
Tel (0113) 2666876 **Fax** (0113) 2693305

Snowline
1 Angel Court, High Street, Market
Harborough, Leicestershire LE16 7NL
Tel (01858) 433633 **Fax** (01858) 433266

Susie Ward Company
54 Vicarage Road, St Agnes, Cornwall TR5
0TQ
Tel (01872) 553055 **Fax** (01872) 553050

HELI-SKI COMPANIES

ITALY
ETI 2000
Quart, Aosta
Tel 39 165 765417
Fax 39 165 765418
Courmayeur, Valgrisenche and Cervinia

Lacadur Heli-Ski
38 Ch du Rocher Nay, Le Tour, F-74400
Chamonix, France
Tel 33 4 50 54 08 40
Fax 33 4 50 54 18 45

Three-day packages in Aosta Valley

SWITZERLAND
Air Glaciers Trans-Heli SA
Box 236, CH-1868 Colombey
Tel 41 25 712626 **Fax** 41 25 719453

Bohag
3814 Gsteigwiler
Tel 41 33 828 9000 **Fax** 41 36 220972
Bernese Oberland

CANADA
Canadian Mountain Holidays (UK agent)
61 Doneraile Street, London SW6 6EW
Tel 0171-736 8191 **Fax** 0171-384 2592
Nine locations in British Columbia

Mike Wiegele Helicopter Skiing
Box 159, Blue River, British Columbia,
Canada
Tel 1 604 673 8381 **Fax** 1 604 673 8464
Blue River in British Columbia

Fresh Tracks (UK agents for Mike
Wiegele)
Argyll House, All Saints Passage, London
SW18 1EP
Tel 0181-875 9818 **Fax** 0181-874 8827

Ski Scott Dunn (UK agents for Mike
Wiegele)
Fovant Mews, 12 Noyna Road, London
SW17 7PH
Tel 0181-767 0202 **Fax** 0181-767 2026

GUIDED SKI COURSES

The names listed below specialise in ski
clinic holidays and do not appear in the
tour operators list. Note, several of the tour
operators in the main list also offer ski
clinic-type courses.

Ali Ross
Ski Solutions, 84 Pembroke Road, London
W8 6NX
Tel 0171-602 9900 **Fax** 0171-602 2882
*Specialist intermediate and advanced
courses in Tignes*

Alpine McAnnix
Suite 13, Hurlingham Studios, 1 Ranelagh
Gardens, London SW6 3PA

Tel 0171-731 2232 **Fax** 0171-736 0811
*Andi McCann's personal performance
courses in Soldeu, Crested Butte and Vail*

BEST
Tel (01803) 859075
*British European Ski Teachers is a co-oper-
ative of BASI-qualified instructors based
and licensed to teach worldwide*

British Alpine Ski School
*British instructors, licensed to teach skiing
and snowboarding in France, who have set
up their own ski school*

(Avoriaz)
7 Orleigh Court, Buckland Brewer,
Bideford, Devon EX39 5EH
Tel/Fax (01237) 451099

**(Morzine/Les Gets, Les Arcs and La
Plagne)**
4 Chilvers Place, Heacham,
Norfolk PE31 7JT
Tel (01485) 572596

Fred Foxon
The Old Vicarage, Merton,
Bicester OX6 ONF
Tel/Fax (01865) 331621
Personal performance weeks in Val d'Isère

Fun Ski
43 East Street, Chichester,
West Sussex PO19 1HX
Tel (01243) 533333 **Fax** (01243) 778431
*Personalised ski development courses in
Altenmarkt, Austria*

International Masterclass
Adjewhella Cottage, Penponds, Camborne,
Cornwall TR14 0QW
Tel (01209) 718297/33 4 76 80 42 77
BASI instructors based in Alpe d'Huez

McGarry The Ski System
5 Barnhill Road, Dalkey, Co Dublin,
Ireland
Tel (353) 1 285 9139 **Fax** (353) 1 284 9932
*Specialist clinics in Châtel including
women, junior racing and extreme skiing*

Mountain Experience
Pike View Barn, Whitehough Head,

Chinley, Stockport, Cheshire SK12 6BX
Tel/Fax (01663) 750160
*Guiding and ski-touring in Chamonix, Gran
Paradiso, La Grave, Haute Route and
Bernese Oberland*

Optimum Ski Courses
Chalet Tarentaise, Le Pré, Villaroger,
F-73640 Sainte-Foy, France
Tel 33 4 79 06 91 26/(01992) 561085
*Ski clinics in Les Arcs and Tignes with BASI
instructors*

Ski Club of Great Britain
118 Eaton Square, London SW1W 9AF
Tel 0171-245 1033 **Fax** 0171-245 1258
*Ski courses for all standards, off-piste and
ski safaris*

Ski Masterclass
Birchview, Railway Terrace, Aviemore,
Scotland PH22 1SA
Tel (01479) 810814/33 4 79 08 22 00
Fax (01479) 811659/33 4 79 08 39 91
*English-speaking classes with BASI
instructors in Courchevel*

Ski Principles
19 Church Street, Brixham,
Devon TQ5 8HG
Tel (01803) 852185/33 4 79 00 52 71
Personal performance courses in Méribel

The Ski Company
13 Squires Close, Bishop's Park, Bishop's
Stortford, Hertfordshire CM23 4DB
Tel (01279) 653746 **Fax** (01279) 654705
*Special ski weeks in Tignes, Courchevel and
Canada*

Roland Stieger
Route de Taconnaz, F-74310 Les
Houches, France
Tel 33 4 50 54 43 53 **Fax** 33 4 50 54 46 26
*Chamonix-based courses and mountain
guiding*

Top Ski
Galerie des Cimes, BP 41, F-73150
Val d'Isère, France
Tel 33 4 79 06 14 80
Fax 33 4 79 06 28 42
*Leading alternative ski school. Off-piste,
heli-skiing, piste clinics, early and late skiing*

SKI INSURANCE COMPANIES

American Express
Sussex House, Civic Way, Burgess Hill,
West Sussex RH15 9AQ
Tel (01444) 239900 Fax (01444) 235257

Douglas Cox Tyrie Ltd
Central House, High Street,
London E15 2PF
Tel 0181-534 9595 **Fax** 0181-519 8780

Endsleigh Insurance Services Ltd
97–107 Southampton Row, London
WC1B 4AG
Tel 0171-436 4451 **Fax** 0171-637 3132

Europ Assistance
Sussex House, Perrymount Road,
Haywards Heath, West Sussex RH16 1DN
Tel (01444) 442211 **Fax** (01444) 459292

Fogg Travel Insurance Ltd
Fullerton Lodge, Crow Hill Drive,
Mansfield, Nottinghamshire NG19 7AE
Tel (01623) 631331/645308 **Fax** (01623)
420450

Hamilton Barr
Bridge Mews, Bridge Street, Godalming,
Surrey GU7 1HZ
Tel (01483) 426600 **Fax** (01483) 426382

SKIING ORGANISATIONS

Artificial Ski Slope Instructors (ASSI)
The English Ski Council, The Area Library
Building, Queensway Mall, The Cornbow,
Halesowen, West Midlands B63 4AJ
Tel 0121-501 2314 **Fax** 0121-585 6448

**British Association of Ski Instructors
(BASI)**
Glenmore, Aviemore, Scotland PH22 1QU
Tel (01479) 861717 **Fax** (01479) 861718

British Ski Federation
258 Main Street, East Calder, West
Lothian, Scotland EH53 0EE
Tel (01506) 884343 **Fax** (01506) 882952

British Snowboarding Association
c/o Steve Davis, 5 Cressex Road, High
Wycombe, Buckinghamshire HP12 4PG
Tel (01494) 462225

SKI COUNCILS

These bodies govern the sport as a whole,
taking responsibility for promoting and
developing skiing and skiers' interests with
the aid of grants from the Sports Council.

English Ski Council
Area Library Building, Queensway Mall,
The Cornbow, Halesowen,
West Midlands B63 4AJ
Tel 0121-501 2314 **Fax** 0121-585 6448

Scottish National Ski Council
Caledonia House, South Gyle,
Edinburgh EH12 9DQ
Tel 0131-317 7280 **Fax** 0131-339 8602

Ski Council of Wales
240 Whitchurch Road, Cardiff CF4 3ND
Tel (01222) 619637 **Fax** (01222) 522178

SKI CLUBS

Alpbach Visitors Ski Club
Barhaus, A-6236 Alpbach,
Tyrol, Austria
Tel 43 5336 5282
*Based in Alpbach. Accommodation and ski
courses arranged*

British Ski Club for the Disabled
Springmount, Berwick St John,
Shaftesbury, Dorset SP7 0HQ
Tel (01747) 828515
*Helps would-be skiers who are physically or
mentally challenged*

Downhill Only Club
c/o Jenny Alban Davies, Troutbeck,
Otford, Sevenoaks, Kent TN14 5PH
Tel (01959) 525439
*Based in Wengen, Switzerland. Junior race
training also offered*

Kandahar Ski Club
c/o Mrs J Holmes, Woodside, Benenden,
Cranbrook, Kent TN17 4EZ
Tel (01580) 240606 **Fax** (01580) 241684
*Based in Mürren, Switzerland, offering
junior race training*

Ladies Ski Club
c/o J Glasson, 40 Aynhoe Road,
London W14 0QD

Tel 0171-603 7464
Supporters of women's ski racing

Mardens
c/o S Ingram, Southridge House,
Streatley, nr Reading, Berkshire RG8 9SJ
Tel (01491) 872710
Based in Klosters, Switzerland

Scottish Ski Club
11 Frogston Terrace, Edinburgh EH10
7AE
Tel 0131-477 1055

The Uphill Ski Club of Great Britain
12 Park Crescent, London W1N 4EQ
Tel 0171-636 1989 **Fax** 0171-436 2601
Organisation for disabled skiers

Ski Club of Great Britain
118 Eaton Square, London SW1W 9AF
Tel 0171-245 1033 **Fax** 0171-245 1258

Still the dominant club for British skiers, the SCGB was formed in 1903 by a group of 11 pioneers of downhill skiing 'to encourage the sport of skiing, assist novices, give information to members and bring together persons interested in the sport'. In the Club's early days, the organisation of ski racing formed a significant part of its activities (the first World Championships in downhill and slalom racing were organised by the Club at Mürren in 1931). Although the Club retains its original aims, it concentrates these days on recreational skiing and offers its members an impressive range of services and benefits to help them get the most out of their skiing holidays.

The aspect of the Club best known to non-members is its gathering of information about skiing conditions: its snow reports are widely published during the skiing season. These reports come from the Club's representatives who are present in over 30 major resorts (listed below) throughout the season to help visiting members. The reps organise weekly programmes, as part of which they lead groups of different standards

around the slopes, on- and off-piste. Members who like the idea of skiing for the whole of their holiday in a compatible group led by a qualified person, perhaps with the intention of improving a particular aspect of their skiing, are catered for by the Club's programme of organised skiing holidays. The Club also administers the British Ski Tests, designed to provide skiers with a measure of their skiing competence. It also runs an Information Department staffed by experienced skiers with access to extensive files of detailed information on resorts and other aspects of skiing including, for example, equipment stockists.

The Club has a network of regional and local representatives and links with many dry ski slopes. As well as an annual Members' Handbook, members receive *Ski Survey*, Britain's original skiing magazine. Among other benefits for members are discounts on the cost of ski holidays and equipment from a wide range of suppliers in the Alps as well as Britain.

Resorts expected to have SCGB representatives in the 1996–7 season include:

Andorra
Soldeu

Austria
Igls ● Kitzbühel ● Mayrhofen ● Obergurgl ● St Anton ● Söll

France
Alpe d'Huez ● Avoriaz ● Chamonix/Argentière ● Courchevel ● Flaine ● La Plagne ● La Tania ● Megève ● Méribel ● Serre Chevalier ● Tignes ● Val d'Isère ● Val Thorens

Italy
Cervinia ● Cortina d'Ampezzo ● Livigno

Switzerland
Crans Montana ● Gstaad ● Klosters ● Mürren ● Saas Fee ● St Moritz ● Verbier ● Villars ● Wengen ● Zermatt

GETTING THERE

GOING BY AIR
Main airlines in the UK

Those listed below offer international scheduled flights to airports close to the ski areas.
American Airlines
Tel 0181-572 5555
Austrian Airlines
Tel 0171-434 7300
Air Canada
Tel (0990) 247226
Air France
Tel 0181-742 6600
Alitalia
Tel 0171-602 7111
British Airways
Tel 0181-897 4000
Continental Airlines
Tel (01293) 776464
Delta Airlines
Tel (0800) 414767
Lauda Air
Tel 0171-630 5924
Northwest Airlines
Tel (01293) 561000
Swissair
Tel 0171-434 7300
United Airlines
Tel (0800) 888 555
Virgin Atlantic Airways
Tel (01293) 747747

GOING BY RAIL
Going to the Alps by rail is becoming more popular. It is often financially easier for families, with the added bonus of an extra day's skiing. A group of tour operators offer the Snow Train option, leaving Calais on Friday evenings and arriving in time for skiing the following morning.

Below are a few useful telephone numbers if travelling by rail.

British Rail International
Tel 0171-834 2345
French Railways
Tel (0990) 300003
Swiss Rail
Tel 0171-734 1921

GOING BY CAR
Travelling to the Alps by car has become an increasingly popular option. For further information on driving see page 561.

Brittany Ferries (Portsmouth–Caen)
Tel (0990) 360360
Hoverspeed (Dover–Calais, Folkestone–Boulogne)
Tel (01304) 240241
Le Shuttle
Tel (0990) 353535
North Sea Ferries (Hull–Zeebrugge, Hull–Rotterdam)
Tel (01482) 377177
P & O European Ferries (Portsmouth–Le Havre, Dover–Calais, Portsmouth–Cherbourg)
Tel (01304) 203388
Sally Lines (Ramsgate–Dunkerque, Ramsgate–Ostend)
Tel (01843) 595522
Stena Sealink Line (Dover–Calais, Harwich–Hook, Newhaven–Dieppe, Southampton–Cherbourg)
Tel (01233) 647047

BREAKDOWN INSURANCE
AA Five Star Services
Tel (0345) 555577
Autohome Ltd
Tel (01604) 232334
Europ Assistance
Tel (01444) 442211
Green Flag National Breakdown
Tel (0800) 800600
Mondial Assistance
Tel 0181-681 2525
RAC Travel Services
Tel (0800) 550055

CAR RENTAL COMPANIES
Alamo Rent-A-Car
Tel (01895) 443355
Avis
Tel 0181-848 8733
Budget Rent-a-Car
Tel (0800) 181181
Europcar Inter Rent
Tel (0113) 2422233
Hertz
Tel 0181-679 1799
Holiday Autos
Tel (0990) 300400

Reporting on the resorts

Writers of the most informative resort reports win a free copy of the next edition of the Guide. Reporters should use the structure set out below and send their reports to: Dept CD, Consumers' Association, FREEPOST, 2 Marylebone Road, London NW1 4DF. No stamp is needed. Please write, or preferably type, your reports clearly. A separate sheet must be used for different resorts, however short the report.

Please keep sending us your reports, they are an invaluable contribution to the essence of the book. You can now contact us via electronic mail.

E-mail address: guidereports@which.co.uk

Resort report checklist:

BASICS
Your name and address
Your skiing background (experience, competence)
Resort name/country
Date of visit
Tour operator you went with
Hotel/chalet/apartment block stayed in

VERDICTS
Your reaction to our 'good points' and 'bad points' verdicts on the resort

OPERATION OF LIFTS
New lifts, upgraded lifts, lift queues, lift passes (and where they cover) and other payment systems

OPERATION OF RUNS
Remarks on piste-marking, piste-grooming, piste closure, artificial snow, accuracy of resort piste-map. Name any favourite runs and interesting off-piste descents

MOUNTAIN RESTAURANTS
General comments, specific named recommendations, prices

SKI SCHOOLS
Remarks on organisation, tuition, language, use of time, allocation of pupils to classes, group size etc. Cover private lessons, guiding, and special courses if you tried them. It is absolutely essential to specify the name of the ski school on which you are commenting

CHILDREN'S FACILITIES
Remarks on skiing and/or non-skiing kindergartens: facilities, staff competence and attitude, instructors' knowledge of English, approach to ski tuition, meals, hours, and cost. Specify which kindergarten or ski school

LOCAL TRANSPORT
Transport within the resort, where you can get to and where you cannot, frequency, reliability, convenience, cost, crowding, value of having a car

ACCIDENT/MEDICAL FACILITIES
Your experience of any mountain rescue and hospital treatment

SHOPPING
Range of everyday (food/supermarket) shops, including quality, service and prices. Range of other (clothing/jewellery/gift) shopping

NON-SKIING FACILITIES
Range, quality, convenience, price of sports and other non-skiing facilities in the resort; excursion possibilities

EATING OUT
Range and type of restaurant, general comments (specific recommendations essential)

APRES-SKI
Range and style of bars, restaurants, discos, clubs; what happens in the resort after skiing, from tea-time until the small hours (specific recommendations essential)

ACCESS
Remarks on airport transfer to your resort, car parking, rail connections if you used them

ACCOMMODATION
Remarks on particular hotels, chalets or apartments (must be named). Advice on choice of location within the resort

PRICES
General observations on the cost of meals and drinks (village and mountain), entry fee to discos and clubs and prices of drinks. Please give examples whenever possible, such as the price of a beer, soft drink, glass of house wine, cup of coffee, dish of the day

SUMMARY
What did you particularly like and dislike about the resort? What aspect of the resort came as a surprise (pleasant or otherwise)? Who does the resort suit? And who does it not suit? On the whole, do you regret choosing this resort or would you go back there? If so, why?

Resort index

St Christophe 201	Taos 515	Vars 251
St-François 285	Telluride 512	Vaujany 163
St-Gervais 219	Termas de Chillán 554	Venosc 196
St Jakob 139	Teton Village 451	Vent 92
St Jean-d'Aulps 243	Thierbach 90	Verbier 415
St Johann im Pongau 151	Thovex 365	Veysonnaz 415
St Johann-in-Tirol 153	Thredbo 551	Vichères 415
St-Lary 179	La Thuile 362	Vigo di Fassa 381
St-Marcel 268	Thumersbach 144	La Villa 360
St Martin-de-Belleville 270	Thyon 415	Villandry 172
St Michel-de-Maurienne 262	Tignes 275	Villard-Reculas 165
St Moritz 409	Torgon 246	Villaroger 166
St Nicolas-de-Véroce 212	Le Tour 182	Villars 435
St Oswald 150	Treble Cone 552	Villeneuve 252
St Stephan 387	Les Trois Vallées 258	La Villette 163
Staffa 370	Trysil 535	Vorderlanesbach 83
Stafal 344	Turoa 552	Voss 535
Steamboat 490	Tuxer Glacier 83	Wagrain 151
Steinplatte 154	La Tzoumaz 422	Waidring 154
Stelvio 295	Untergurgl 94	Wengen 391
Stowe 516	Untertauern 102	Westendorf 131
Stubai 46	Uvdal 532	Whakapapa 552
Stuben 140	Vail 495	Whistler 504
Sun Valley 513	Val d'Isère 275	Winter Park 513
Sunalpina Sanosaka 555	Val Thorens 258	Wirl 59
Sundance 475	Valbella 434	Wolf Mountain 477
Sunshine Village 445	Valberg 291	Wolfgang 381
Super-St-Bernard 415	Valdidentro 294	Zauchensee 151
Super Châtel 230	Valdisotto 324	Zell am See 142
Superbagnères 180	Valgrisenche 365	Zell am Ziller 85
Surlej 409	Vallandry 172	Zermatt 424
La Tania 270	Valle Nevado 554	Zug 70
	Valloire 292	Zuos 413
	Vallorcine 182	Zürs 70
	Valmeinier 292	Zweisimmen 387
	Valmorel 285	Zwieselstein 124
	Valtournenche 300	